Creative Resources for the Early Childhood Classroom

RELATED TITLES IN THE DELMAR EARLY EDUCATION SERIES

Rosalind Charlesworth and Karen K. Lind, *Math and Science for Young Children*, 1995

Carol Gestwicki, *Developmentally Appropriate Practice*, 1995

Mary Mayesky, *Creative Activities for Young Children*, 5th edition, 1995

Rae Pica, *Experiences in Movement with Music, Activities, and Theory*, 1995

LaVisa Cam Wilson, Michael Watson, and Linda Douville-Watson, *Infants & Toddlers: Curriculum and Teaching*, 3rd edition, 1995

K. Eileen Allen and Lynn R. Marotz, *Developmental Profiles: Prebirth to Eight*, 2nd edition, 1994

Kathleen Dolinar, Candace Boser, and Eleanor Holm, *Learning Through Play: Curriculum and Activities for the Inclusive Classroom*, 1994

Robert Schirrmacher, *Art and Creative Development for Young Children*, 2nd edition, 1993

CREATIVE RESOURCES
FOR THE
EARLY CHILDHOOD CLASSROOM
Second Edition

Judy Herr
Yvonne Libby

Delmar Publishers Inc.™
I(T)P™ An International Thomson Publishing Company

New York • London • Bonn • Boston • Detroit • Madrid • Melbourne • Mexico City • Paris
Singapore • Tokyo • Toronto • Washington • Albany NY • Belmont CA • Cincinnati OH

NOTICE TO THE READER

Cover Design: Kristina Almquist Design
Insert Design: Spiral Design Studio
Insert Photography: Douglas Hyldelund

Delmar Staff
Acquisitions Editor: Jay S. Whitney
Developmental Editor: Christopher Anzalone
Project Editor: Theresa M. Bobear

Insert Photography Locations:
Greenberg Child Care Center at Skidmore College
  Saratoga Springs, NY
Capital District Beginnings Day Care Center
  Albany, NY

Production Coordinator: John Mickelbank
Art & Design Coordinator: Douglas Hyldelund

COPYRIGHT © 1995
By Delmar Publishers Inc.
an International Thomson Publishing Company

I(T)P™ The ITP logo is a trademark under license

Printed in the United States of America

For more information, contact:

Delmar Publishers Inc.
3 Columbia Circle Drive, Box 15015
Albany, New York 12212-5015

International Thomson Publishing
Berkshire House
168-173 High Holborn
London, WC1V7AA
England

International Thomson Publishing GmbH
Konigswinterer Str. 418
53227 Bonn
Germany

Thomas Nelson Australia
102 Dodds Street
South Melbourne 3205
Victoria, Australia

International Thomson Publishing Asia
221 Henderson Bldg. #05-10
Singapore 0315

Nelson Canada
1120 Birchmont Road
Scarborough, Ontario
M1K 5G4, Canada

International Thomson Publishing Japan
Kyowa Building, 3F
2-2-1 Hirakawa-cho
Chiyoda-ku, Tokyo 102
Japan

    3 4 5 6 7 8 9 10 XXX 01 00 99 98 97 96 95

Library of Congress Cataloging-in-Publication Data

Herr, Judith.
    Creative resources for the early childhood classroom / Judy Herr,
  Yvonne Libby.
        p.   cm.
    Includes bibliographical references and index.
    ISBN 0-8273-5871-7
    1. Education, Preschool—Curricula. 2. Unit method of teaching.
  I. Libby, Yvonne. II. Title.
  LB1140.4.H47 1995
  372.19—dc20

                                                    94-19870
                                                      CIP

CONTENTS

Table of Contents by Subjects

xiv

PREFACE

While reviewing early childhood curriculum resources, it becomes apparent that few books are available using a thematic or unit approach for teaching young children. As a result, our university students, colleagues, and alumni convinced us of the importance of such a book. Likewise, they convinced us of the contribution the book could make to early childhood teachers and, subsequently, the lives of young children.

Before preparing the manuscript, we surveyed hundreds of child care, preschool, and kindergarten teachers. Specifically, we wanted them to share their curriculum problems and concerns. Our response has been to design and write a reference book tailored to their teaching needs using a thematic approach. Each theme or unit contains a flowchart, theme goals, concepts for the children to learn, theme-related vocabulary words, music, fingerplays, science, dramatic play, creative art experiences, sensory, mathematics, cooking experiences, and resources. Additionally, creative ideas for designing child-involvement bulletin boards and parent letters have been included. These resources were identified, by the teachers included in our survey, as being critical components that have been lacking in other curriculum guides.

In addition to the themes included in this book, others can and should be developed for teaching young children. The authors, however, wish to caution the readers that it is the teacher's responsibility to select, plan, and introduce developmentally appropriate themes and learning experiences for his group of children. Specifically, the teacher must tailor the curriculum to meet the individual needs of the children. Consequently, we encourage all teachers to carefully select, adapt, or change any of the activities in this book to meet the needs, abilities, and interests of their group of children to ensure developmental appropriateness. The inside covers of this book should be used as handy references for checking developmental norms.

As you use this guide, you will note that some themes readily lend themselves to particular curriculum areas. As a result, the number of activities listed under each curriculum area will vary from theme to theme.

The detailed introduction is designed to help teachers use the book most effectively. It includes:

1. a discussion on how to develop the curriculum using a thematic approach;
2. a list of possible themes;
3. suggestions for writing parent letters;
4. methods for constructing and evaluating creative involvement bulletin boards; and
5. criteria for selecting children's books.

What's New in the Second Edition!

1. PRESENTING BRIGHT IDEAS FOR CHILD DEVELOPMENT FROM POLAROID

Offering creative new approaches to teaching and communicating that children find magical are the fifteen new photo activities found in the full-color insert. They are full of imaginative ideas for educational exploration.

Develop New Ways To Inspire Learning. Children love watching Polaroid instant photographs develop before their eyes. Even more than interactive fun, they're effective teaching tools. Teachers can use them to reinforce verbal skills with storytelling, introduce mathematical concepts like graphing, counting, and grouping, foster creative thinking with visual games, and strengthen social skills with activities that explore emotions, expressions, and interaction. Included are a variety of activities that have been tried and found truly motivational by other early childhood educators. They're sure to stimulate even more ideas of your own.

Give Parents A Clear Picture of Growth. The vocabularies of small children often fall short of their accomplishments. A picture is all it takes to say, "Look what I did," "Here's my new friend," "I was good today," or "See what I learned." Photos also speak volumes to parents. A series of photographs can capture the spirit of a program and cover the activities that take place in a way that words alone can't express. Enhancing their understanding of what their children do all day brings families peace of mind all year long.

Offer Every Child Instant Recognition. Taking a picture of a parent to keep handy can be a real comfort to a child who's away from home for the first time (not to mention establishing safe pickup procedures at your school). Instant photos can also help children find their cubbies when they can't read their names, label projects, or identify other belongings. They're a wonderful way to honor special achievements, too, building self-esteem and confidence. You'll like what develops, especially when it's the imagination and potential of a child.

2. NEW THEMES AND ACTIVITIES

More than 200 New Activities enrich this second edition. These new activities are spread through the book and cover the six new themes: Breads, Bubbles, Dairy Products, Fish, Mice, and Trees. Every thematic unit begins with a webbing of the curriculum. Webbing, in this context, informs teachers of additional areas of activities across the curriculum for each theme. Ideally, the teacher will expand on these webs to take the young children to other unique and exciting related themes.

3. NEW REFERENCE MATERIAL

Resources are listed in the updated Books and the new Multimedia sections which appear at the end of the themes throughout the book. Recognizing the value and growth of technology in today's classroom and society, we've added developmentally appropriate educational software and videos.

This book would not have been possible without the constant encouragement provided by our families, the laboratory teachers in the Child and Family Study Center, and the faculty, students, and alumni of the University of Wisconsin-Stout. Our thanks to all of these people and especially to Carla Ahmann, Susan Babler, Mary Babula, Terry Bloomberg, Margaret Braun, Renee Bruce, Anne Budde, Michelle Case, Jill Church, Bruce Cunningham, Jeanette Daines, Carol Davenport, Jill Davis, Mary DeJardin, Linda DeMoe, Rita Devery, Donna Dixon, Esther Fahm, Lisa Fuerst, Shirley Gebhart, Judy Gifford, Nancy Graese, Barbara Grundleger, Betty Herman, Patti Herman, John Herr, Mark Herr, Joan Herwig, Carol Hillmer, Priscilla Huffman, Margy Ingram, Paula Iverson, Angela Kaiser, Elizabeth (Betz) Kaster, Trudy King, Leslie Koepke, Beth Libby, Janet Maffet, Marian Marion, Janet Massa, Nancy McCarthy, Julie Meyers, Betty Misselt, Teresa Mitchell, Kathy Mueller, LaVonne Mueller, Robin Muza, Paula Noll, Sue Paulson, Mary Pugmire, Kelli Railton, Lori Register, Peg Saienga, Kathy Schaeffer, Mary Selkey, Cheryl Smith, Sue Smith, Amy Sprengler, Karen Stephens, Barbara Suihkonen, Judy Teske, Penny Warner, Connie Weber, Ed Wenzell, Mary Eileen Zenk, and Karen Zimmerman. We are also grateful to our reviewers: Gerri A. Carey, McLennan Community College, Waco, TX; Billie Coffman, PA College of Technology, Williamsport, PA; Ione Garcia, IL State University, Normal, IL; Ned Sauls, Wayne Community College, Goldsboro, NC; and Becky Wyatt, Murray State College, Tishomingo, OK. Finally, our special thanks to two individuals whose assistance made this book possible. Jay Whitney, our editor from Delmar, provided continous encouragement, support, and creative suggestions. Also, special thanks to Robin Muza, our typist and research assistant.

INTRODUCTION

The purpose of this introduction is to explain the process involved in curriculum planning for young children using the thematic, or unit approach. To support each theme, planning and construction ideas are included for bulletin boards, parent letters, and a wide variety of classroom learning experiences.

Curriculum Planning

As you use this guide, remember that children learn best when they can control and act upon their environment. Many opportunities should be available for seeing, touching, tasting, learning, and self-expression. Children need hands-on activities and choices. To construct knowledge, children need to actively manipulate their environment. To provide these opportunities, the teacher's primary role is to set the stage by offering many experiences that stimulate the children's senses and curiosity; children learn by doing and play is their work. As a result, it is the authors' intention that this book will be used as a resource. Specifically, the ideas in this book should help you to enrich, organize, and structure the children's environment, providing them an opportunity to make choices among a wide variety of activities that stimulate their natural curiosity. Knowledge of child development and curriculum must be interwoven. To illustrate, play in the classroom should be child-centered and self-initiated. To provide an environment that promotes these types of play, it is the teacher's role to provide unstructured time, space, and materials. Using a theme approach to plan curriculum is one way to ensure that a wide variety of classroom experiences are provided. Successful early childhood programs provide interesting, challenging and engaging environments. Children need to learn to think, reason, and become decision makers.

It is important that all curricula be adapted to match the developmental needs of children at a particular age or stage of development. An activity that is appropriate for one group of children may be inappropriate for another. To develop an appropriate curriculum, knowledge of the typical development of children is needed. For this reason, the inside covers of this book contain such information. Review these developmental norms before selecting a theme or specific activities.

Theme Planning

A developmentally appropriate curriculum for young children integrates the children's needs, interests, and abilities and focuses on the whole child. Cognitive, social, emotional, and physical development are all included. Before planning curriculum, observe the children's development. Record notes of what you see. At the same time, note the children's interests and listen carefully. Children's conversations provide clues; this information is vital in theme selection. After this, review your observations by discussing them with other staff members. An appropriate curriculum for young children cannot be planned without understanding their development and interests.

There are many methods for planning a curriculum other than using themes. In fact, you may prefer not to use a theme during parts of the year. If this is your choice, you may wish to use the book as a source of ideas, integrating activities and experiences from a variety of the themes outlined in the book.

Planning a curriculum using a theme approach involves several steps. The first step involves selecting a theme that is appropriate for the developmental level and interests of your group of children. Themes based on the children's interests provide intrinsic motivation for exploration and learning. Meaningful experiences are more easily comprehended and remembered. Moreover, curiosity, enjoyment of participation, and self-direction are heightened. After selecting a theme, the next step is developing a flowchart. From the flowchart, goals, conceptual understandings, and vocabulary words can easily be extracted. The final step in curriculum planning is selecting activities based upon the children's stages of development and available resources. While doing this, the covers of this book should be used as a reference to review development characteristics for children of different ages.

To help you understand the theme approach to curriculum development, each step of the process will be discussed. Included are assessing the children's needs, and developing flowcharts, theme goals, concepts, vocabulary, and activities. In addition, suggestions are given for writing parent letters, designing bulletin boards, and selecting children's books.

Assessment

Assessment is important for planning curriculum, identifying special needs children, and communicating a child's progress to parents. Assessment needs to be a continuous process. It involves a process of observing children during activities throughout the day, recording their behaviors, and documenting their work. Assessment involves records and descriptions of what you observe while the behavior is occurring. Logs and journals can be developed. The developmental norms on the inside cover of this text can be used as a checklist of behavior. You can create a profile of the children's individualized progress in developing skills. Your observations should tell what the children like, don't like, have discovered, know, and want to learn.

Samples of the children's work in an individual portfolio collection should be maintained. A portfolio documents the children's progress, achievements, and efforts. Included should be samples of the children's paintings, drawings, storytelling experiences, oral and written language. Thus, the portfolio will include products and evidence of the children's accomplishments.

By reviewing the assessment materials you can deduce the children's developmental needs and interests. This information will be important in selecting a theme that interests the children and selecting developmentally appropriate learning experiences.

Flowcharts/Webbings. The flowchart is a simple way to record all possible subconcepts that relate to the major concept or theme. To illustrate, plan a theme on apples. In the center of a piece of paper, write the word "apple." Then using an encyclopedia as a resource, record the subconcepts that are related. Include origin, parts, colors, tastes,

sizes, textures, food preparation, and nutrition. The following flowchart (See Figure I–1) includes these concepts. In addition, under each subconcept list content that could be included. For example, apples may be colored green, yellow, or red. By teaching using a thematic approach, we teach children the way environments and humans interconnect. This process helps children make sense out of the human experience.

Theme goals. Once you have prepared a flowchart webbing, abstracting the theme goals is a simple process. Begin by reviewing the chart. Notice the subheadings listed. For the unit on apples, the subheadings include: foods, parts, forms, and colors. Writing each of these subheadings as a goal is the next step of the process.

Since there were four subheadings, each of these can be included as a goal. In some cases, subheadings may be combined. For example, note the fourth goal listed. It combines several subheadings.

Through participation in the experiences provided by using apples as a curriculum theme, the children may learn:

1. Parts of an apple.
2. Preparation of apples for eating.
3. Apple tastes.
4. Textures, sizes, and colors of apples.
5. The origin of an apple.

Concepts. The concepts must be related to the goal; however, they are more specific. To write the concepts, study the goals. Then prepare sentences that are written in a simple form that children can understand. Examples of concepts for a unit on apples may include:

1. An apple is a fruit.
2. An apple has five parts: seed, core, meat, skin, and stem.
3. Apples grow on trees.
4. A group of apple trees is called an orchard.
5. Bread, pies, puddings, applesauce, dumplings, butter, and jellies can be prepared from apples.
6. Some apples are sweet; others are sour.
7. Apples can be colored green, yellow, or red.
8. Apples can be large or small.
9. Apples may be hard or soft.
10. Apples can be eaten raw.
11. Seeds from an apple can grow into a tree.

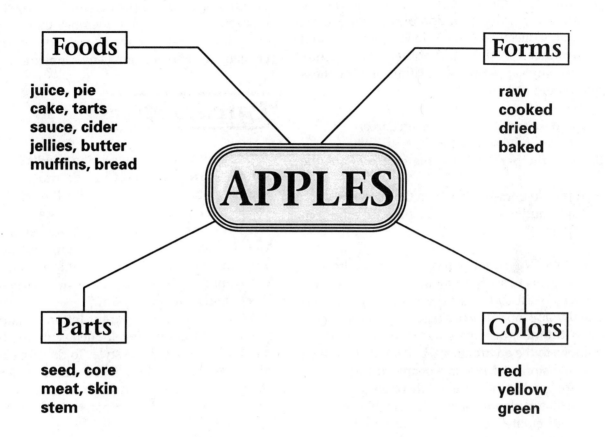

Foods

juice, pie
cake, tarts
sauce, cider
jellies, butter
muffins, bread

Forms

raw
cooked
dried
baked

APPLES

Parts

seed, core
meat, skin
stem

Colors

red
yellow
green

Vocabulary. The vocabulary should include new words that you want to informally introduce to the children. Vocabulary words need to be tailored to meet the specific needs of your group of children. The number of vocabulary words will vary, depending upon the theme and the developmental level of the children. For example, it might be assumed that the children know the word sweet, but not tart. So, the definition of the word tart is included. Collectively, the following words could be introduced in this unit: apple, texture, core, blossom, and apple butter. Definitions for these words could include:

1. apple—a fruit that is grown on a tree.
2. texture—how something feels.
3. core—the part of the apple that contains the seeds.
4. apple blossom—a flower on the apple tree.
5. apple butter—a spread for bread made from apples.

Activities. Now that you have learned how to develop goals related to a theme using a flowchart, you will need to learn how to select developmentally appropriate activities. You will find that many theme goals can be accomplished by additions to the environment, bulletin boards, field trips, and stories or resource people at large group time. Your major role as an adult, or teacher, is that of a facilitator, planning and preparing the environment to stimulate the child's natural curiosity.

To begin this process, review each goal and determine how it can be introduced in the classroom. For example, if you were going to develop a theme on apples, review the goals. A bulletin board or game could introduce the three colors of apples. The children could also learn these colors through cooking experiences. The third vehicle for teaching the colors of apples would be placing the three colors of apples on a science table.

The five parts of an apple could also be introduced through participation in a tasting or cooking experience, bulletin board, or even discussion on a field trip or at the snack table. Always remember that children need to observe and manipulate the concrete object while engaged in child-initiated or child-directed play that is teacher supported. For that reason, fresh apples could be cut horizontally and placed on the science table with a magnifying glass. Likewise, simultaneously, apple seeds and paper could be available on the art table to construct a collage. Always remember that the best activities for young children are hands-on and open-ended. That is: focus on the process, rather than the product. Children need to learn to think, reason, and become problem solvers. As a teacher, you should take the ideas in this book and use and adapt them for planning and preparing the environment. Always remember that successful early childhood programs provide interesting, challenging, and engaging environments.

Parent Letters

Communication between the child's home and school is important. It builds mutual understanding and cooperation. With the efficiency of modern technology, parent letters are a form of written communication that can be shared on a weekly basis. The most interesting parent letters are written in the active voice. It states the subject did something. To illustrate, "Mark played with blocks and read books today."

When writing the parent letter, consider the parent's educational level. Then write the letter in a clear, friendly, concise style. To do this, eliminate all words that are not needed. Limit the length of the letter to a page or two. To assist you with the process, an example of a parent letter is included for each theme.

Parent letters can be divided into three sections. Included should be a general introduction, school activities, and home activities. One way to begin the letter is by introducing new children or staff, or sharing something that happened the previous week. After this, introduce the theme for the coming week by explaining why it was chosen.

The second section of the parent letter could include some of the goals and special activities for the theme. Share with the parents all of the interesting things you will be doing at school throughout the week. By having this information, parents can initiate verbal interaction with their child.

The third section of the parent letter should be related to home activities. Suggest developmentally appropriate activities that the parents can provide in the home. These activities may or may not relate to the theme. Include the words of new songs and fingerplays. This section can also be used to provide parenting information such as the developmental value of specific activities for young children.

Bulletin Boards

Bulletin boards add color, decoration, and interest to the classroom. They also communicate what is happening in the classroom to parents and other visitors. The most effective bulletin boards involve the child. That is, the child will manipulate some pieces of the board. As a result, they are called involvement bulletin boards. Through the concrete experience of interacting with the bulletin board materials, children learn a variety of concepts and skills. Included may be size, shape, color, visual discrimination, eye-hand coordination, etc.

Carefully study the bulletin boards included for each theme in this book. They are simple, containing a replica of objects from the child's immediate environment. Each bulletin board has a purpose. It teaches a skill or concept.

As you prepare the bulletin boards provided in this book, you will become more creative. Gradually, you will combine ideas from several bulletin boards as you develop new themes for curriculum.

An opaque projector is a useful tool for individuals who feel uncomfortable with their drawing skills. Using the opaque projector, you can enlarge images from storybooks, coloring books, greeting cards, wrapping paper, etc. To do this, simply place the image to be copied in the projector. Then tape paper or tagboard on the wall. Turn on the projector. Using a pencil, color marker or crayon, trace the outline of the image onto the paper or tagboard.

Another useful tool for preparing bulletin boards is the overhead projector. Place a clear sheet of acetate on the picture desired for enlargement. This may include figures from a coloring or storybook. Trace around the image using a washable marker designed for tranparencies. Project the image onto a wall and follow the same procedures as with the opaque projector.

To make your bulletin board pieces more durable, laminate them. If your center does not have a laminating machine, use clear contact paper. This process works just as well, but it can be more expensive.

Finally, the materials you choose to use on a bulletin board should be safe and durable. Careful attention should be given when selecting attachments. For two-, three- and four-year-old children, adhesive velcro and staples are preferred attachments. Push pins may be used with older children under careful supervision.

Selecting Books

Books for young children need to be selected with care. Before selecting books, once again, refer to the covers and review the typical development for your group of young children. This information can provide a framework for selecting appropriate books.

There are some general guidelines for selecting books. First, children enjoy books that relate to their experiences. They also enjoy action. The words written in the book should be simple, descriptive, and within the child's understanding. The pictures should be large, colorful, and closely represent the actions.

A book that is good for one group of children may be inappropriate for another. You must know the child or group of children for whom the story is being selected. Consider their interests, attention span, and developmental level.

Developmental considerations are important. Two-year-olds enjoy stories about the things they do, know, and enjoy. Commonplace adventure is a preference for three-year-olds. They like to listen to things that could happen to them, including stories about community helpers. Four-year-old children are not as self-centered. These children do not have to be part of every situation that they hear about. Many are ready for short and simple fantasy stories. Five-year-olds like stories that add to their knowledge. That is, books that contain new information.

Curriculum Planning Guide

We hope you find this book to be a valuable guide in planning curriculum. The ideas should help you build curriculum based upon the children's natural interests. The book should also give you ideas so that your program will provide a wide variety of choices for children.

In planning a developmentally valid curriculum, consult the table of contents by subject. It has been prepared to allow you easy selection from all the themes. So pick and choose and make it your own! The contents are arranged as follows:

—Art
—Cooking
—Dramatic Play
—Features (by Theme)
—Field Trips/Resource People
—Fingerplays
—Group Time
—Large Muscle
—Math
—Rain Day
—Science
—Sensory
—Songs

Other Sources

Early childhood educators should refer to other Delmar publications when developing appropriate curriculum, including:

1. Ramirez, Gonzalo, Jr. & Ramirez, Jan Lee. *Multiethnic Children's Literature: A Comprehensive Resource Guide.*
2. Dolinar, Kathleen, Boser, Candace, & Holm, Eleanor. *Learning through Play: Curriculum and Activities for the Inclusive Classroom.*
3. Allen, K. Eileen & Marotz, Lynn. *Developmental Profiles: Prebirth to Eight* (2nd ed.).
4. Berns, Roberta M. *Topical Child Development.*
5. Mayesky, Mary. *Creative Activities for Young Children* (5th ed.).
6. Gestwicki, Carol. *Home, School, and Community Relations: A Guide to Working with Parents* (2nd ed.).
7. Essa, Eva L. *A Practical Guide to Solving Preschool Behavior Problems* (3rd ed.).
8. Sawyer, Walter E. & Jean C. *Integrated Language Arts for Emerging Literacy.*
9. Charlesworth, Rosalind & Lind, Karen K. *Math and Science for Young Children* (2nd ed.).
10. Bentzen, Warren R. *Seeing Young Children: A Guide to Observing and Recording Behavior* (2nd ed.).
11. Davidson, Jane. *Children's Emerging Literacy through Dramatic Play.*
12. Pica, Rae. *Experiences in Movement with Music, Activities, and Theory.*
13. Gestwicki, Carol. *Developmentally Appropriate Practice: Curriculum & Development in Early Education.*
14. Schirrmacher, Robert. *Art and Creative Development for Young Children* (2nd ed.).
15. Click, Phyllis. *Caring for School Age Children.*
16. Essa, Eva & Rogers, Penelope Royce. *Early Childhood Curriculum: From Developmental Model to Application.*

—— T H E M E **1** ——

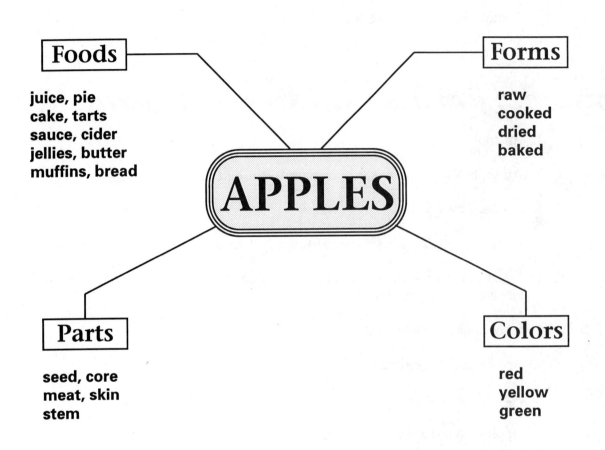

Foods

juice, pie
cake, tarts
sauce, cider
jellies, butter
muffins, bread

Forms

raw
cooked
dried
baked

APPLES

Parts

seed, core
meat, skin
stem

Colors

red
yellow
green

Here's an exciting new way to turn instant photography into an effective teaching tool. Refer to the full-color insert for the activity entitled Grouping.

Theme Goals:

Through participating in the experiences provided by this theme, the children may learn:

1. Parts of an apple.

2. Preparation of apples for eating.

3. Apple tastes.

4. Textures, sizes, and colors of apples.

5. The origin of an apple.

Concepts for the Children to Learn:

1. An apple is a fruit.

2. An apple has five parts: seed, core, meat, skin, and stem.

3. Apples grow on trees.

4. A group of apple trees is an orchard.

5. Bread, butter, cakes, pies, pudding, applesauce, dumplings, butter, and jelly can be prepared from apples.

6. Some apples are sweet; others are sour.

7. Apples can be green, yellow, or red.

8. Apples can be large or small.

9. Apples can be hard or soft.

10. Seeds from an apple can grow into a tree.

Vocabulary:

1. **apple**—a fruit that is grown on a tree.

2. **texture**—how something feels.

3. **core**—the part of the apple that contains seeds.

4. **apple blossom**—a flower on the apple tree.

5. **apple butter**—a spread for bread made from apples.

2

Bulletin Board

The purpose of this bulletin board is to develop the mathematical skill of sets, as well as to identify written numerals. Construct red apples. The number will depend upon the developmental level of the children. Laminate the apples. Collect containers for baskets, such as large cottage cheese or pint berry containers. Cover the containers with paper if necessary. Affix numerals on baskets, beginning with the numeral 1. Staple the baskets to the bulletin board. The object is for the children to place the appropriate number of apples in each basket.

Parent Letter

Dear Parents,

Is it true that "an apple a day keeps the doctor away?" I'm not sure, but the children will make many discoveries as we begin a new unit on apples at school. Through active exploration and interaction, they will become more aware of the different flavors of apples, colors of apples, and ways apples can be prepared and eaten.

At School

Some classroom activities for this unit include:
- preparing applesauce for Thursday's snack.
- drying apples in the sun.
- creating apple-shaped sponge prints in the art area.
- visiting the apple orchard! Arrangements have been made for a tour of the apple orchard on Wednesday morning. We will be leaving the center at 10:00 a.m. Feel free to join us.

At Home

Apples are a tasty and nutritious food—and most children enjoy eating them. Try a variety of apples for meals or snacks. You might also enjoy preparing caramel apples with your child. A recipe is as follows:

1 pound of vanilla caramels
2 tablespoons of water
dash of salt
6 crisp apples
6 wooden skewers or popsicle sticks

Melt the caramels with water in a microwave oven or double boiler, stirring frequently until smooth. Stir in the salt and stick a wooden skewer or popsicle stick in each apple. Dip the apple into the syrup, turning until the surface of the apple is completely covered.

Cooking is a great way to learn by experience because it involves the whole child—physically, emotionally, socially, and intellectually. It also builds vocabulary and involves amounts, measuring, and fractions, which are mathematical concepts. When a recipe is used, your child will also learn to follow a sequence. Enjoy cooking with your child.

Enjoy an apple with your child today!

Music:

1. **"If I Had an Apple"**
   (Sing to the tune of "If I Had a Hammer")

   If I had an apple
   I'd eat it in the morning,
   I'd eat it in the evening,
   All over this land.
   I'd eat it for breakfast,
   I'd eat it for supper,
   I'd eat it with all my friends and sisters and brothers
   All, all over this land.

   Source: Chenfield, Mimi Brodsky. *Creative Activities for Young Children.*

2. **"Little Apples"**
   (Sing to the tune of "Ten Little Indians")

   One little, two little, three little apples,
   Four little, five little, six little apples,
   Seven little, eight little, nine little apples,
   All fell to the ground.

   A variation for older children would be to give each child a number card (with a numeral from 1 through 9). When that number is sung, that child stands up. At the end of the fingerplay all the children fall down.

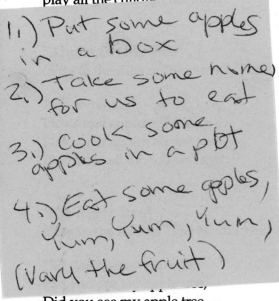

   1.) Put some apples in a box
   2.) Take some home for us to eat
   3.) Cook some apples in a pot
   4.) Eat some apples, Yum, Yum, Yum,
   (Vary the fruit)

   Did you see my apple tree,
   Full of apples red?

Fingerplays:

APPLE TREE

Way up high in the apple tree
  (stretch arm up high)
Two little apples smiled at me.
  (hold up 2 fingers)
I shook that tree as hard as I could
  (make shaking motion)
Down came the apples.
  (make downward motions)
Mmmm—they were good.
  (smile and rub stomach)

PICKING APPLES

Here's a little apple tree.
  (left arm up, fingers spread)
I look up and I can see
  (look at fingers)
Big red apples, ripe and sweet,
  (cup hands to hold apple)
Big red apples, good to eat!
  (raise hands to mouth)
Shake the little apple tree.
  (shake tree with hands)
See the apples fall on me.
  (raise cupped hands and let fall)
Here's a basket, big and round.
  (make circle with arms)
Pick the apples from the ground.
  (pick and put in basket)
Here's an apple I can see.
  (look up to the tree)
I'll reach up. It's ripe and sweet.
  (reach up to upper hand)
That's the apple I will eat!
  (hands to mouth)

AN APPLE

An apple is what I'd like to be.
My shape would be round.
  (fingers in circular shape)
My color would be green.
  (point to something green)
Children could eat me each and every day.
I'm good in tarts and pies and cakes.
  (make these foodshapes)
An apple is good to eat or to bake.
  (make stirring motion)

FIGURE 1 Help children discover all the wonderful foods prepared from apples.

THE APPLE

Within its polished universe
The apple holds a star.
   (draw design of star with index finger)
A secret constellation
To scatter near and far.
   (point near and far)
Let a knife discover
Where the five points hide.
Split the shiny ruby
And find the star inside.

After introducing the fingerplay the teacher
can cut an apple crosswise to find a star.

APPLE TREE

This is the tree
With leaves so green.
   (make leaves with fingers outstretched)

Here are the apples
That hang in between.
   (make fist)
When the wind blows
   (blow)
The apples will fall.
   (falling motion with hand)
Here is the basket to gather them all.
   (use arms to form basket)

Sensory:

1. Cut different varieties of apples for a tasting party. This activity can easily be extended. On another day provide the children applesauce, apple pie, apple juice, or apple cider to taste during snack or lunch.
2. Place several different kinds of seeds on the sensory table. In addition, to create interest provide scoops, bowls, and bottles to fill.

Math:

1. Cut apple shapes of various sizes from construction paper. Let the children sequence the shapes from smallest to largest.
2. Place a scale and various-sized apples on the math table. The children can experiment by weighing the apples.

Science:

1. **Solar Baked Apple Slices**

   Materials: 4 styrofoam cups
                    black paper
                    scissors
                    masking tape
                    apple
                    knife
                    plastic wrap
                    rubber bands
                    white paper
                    foil
                    newspaper

   Line 2 cups with black paper. Place 2 equal-sized slices of apple inside each cup. Cover with plastic wrap held by rubber band. With paper and tape make a cone. Place one apple cup into it. Cover the inside of another paper cone with aluminum foil and place second apple cup into it. Place both in a sunny window facing the sun on crumpled newspaper. Which one cooks faster? The apple baked in the aluminum foil.

Source: Sisson, Edith A. *Nature With Children of All Ages.*

2. **Dried Apples**

Peel, core, and cut apples into slices or rings about 1/8 inch thick. Prepare a salt water solution by mixing a tablespoon of salt in a gallon of water. Place the apples in this solution for several minutes. Remove from the solution. Place the apples in 180-degree oven for 3 to 4 hours or until dry. Turn the apples occasionally.

3. **Oxidation of an Apple**

Cut and core an apple into sections. Dip half the apple into lemon juice and place it on a plate. Place the remaining sections of apple on another plate. What happens to each plate of apples? Discuss the effects of the lemon juice coating which keeps oxygen from the apples. As a result, they do not discolor as rapidly.

4. **Explore an Apple**

Discuss the color, size, and shape of an apple. Then discuss the parts of an apple. Include the skin, stem, core, meat, etc. Feel the apple. Then cut the apple in half. Observe the core and seeds. An apple is a fruit because it contains seeds.

Dramatic Play:

Set Up an Apple Stand

Prepare an apple stand by providing the children with bags, plastic apples, cash register, money, stand, and bushels. Encourage buying, selling, and packaging.

Arts and Crafts:

1. **Apple Printing**

Cut apple shapes from sponges. Have available individual shallow pans of red, yellow, and green tempera paint. Provide paper. The apple can be used as a painting tool. To illustrate, the children can place an apple half in the paint. After removing the excess paint, the apple can be placed on paper to create a print.

2. **Seed Pictures**

Collect: apple seeds along with other seeds
paper
colors
glue

Each child who chooses to participate should be provided a small number of seeds. As they are distributed, discuss the seeds' similarities and differences. Provide uninterrupted time for the children to glue seeds onto paper and create pictures.

3. **Shakers**

Collect: appleseeds
paper plates (2 per child)
glue or stapler
color crayons or felt-tip markers

The children can decorate the paper plates with color crayons or felt-tip markers. After this, the seeds can be placed between the two plates. To create the shakers, staple or glue the two plates together by securing the outer edges of the plates. The children can use the shakers as a means of self expression during music or self-directed play.

Field Trips:

1. **Visit an Apple Orchard**

Observe the workers picking, sorting, and/or selling the apples. Call attention to the colors and types of apples.

2. **Visit a Grocery Store**

Observe all the forms of apples sold in a grocery store. Also, in the produce department, observe the different colors and sizes of apples. To show children differences in weight, take a large apple and place on a scale. Note the weight. Then take a small apple and repeat the process.

Group Time (games, language):

1. **What Is It?**

Collect a variety of fruits such as an apple, banana, and orange. Begin by placing one fruit in a bag. Choose a child to touch the fruit, describe it, and name it. Repeat with each fruit, discussing the characteristics. During the activity each child should have an opportunity to participate.

2. **Transition Activity**

The children should stand in a circle. As a record is played, the children pass an apple. When the record stops, the child holding the apple can get up to get a snack, put on outdoor clothes, clean up, etc. Continue until all children have a turn. For older children, more than one apple may be successfully passed at a time.

Cooking:

1. **Caramel Apple Slices**

Prepare the following recipe, which should serve 12 to 14 children.

1 pound caramels
2 tablespoons water
dash of salt
6 crisp apples

Melt caramels with water in the microwave oven or double boiler, stirring frequently until melted. Stir in the salt. Pour the melted caramel over the sliced apples and cool before serving.

2. **Applesauce**

30 large apples
2 1/2 cups water
1 1/2 cups sugar
1 tablespoon red hots

1. Clean apples by peeling, coring, and cutting into small pieces.
2. Place the apples in a large kettle containing water.
3. Simmer the apples on low heat, stirring occasionally until soft.
4. Add the remaining ingredients.
5. Stir and simmer a few minutes.
6. Cool prior to eating.

3. **Persian Apple Dessert**

3 medium apples, cut up
2 to 3 tablespoons sugar
2 tablespoons lemon juice
dash of salt

Place half the apples and the remaining ingredients in a blender. Cover and blend until coarsely chopped, about 20 to 30 seconds. Add remaining apples and repeat. Makes 3 servings.

4. **Charoses**

6 medium apples
1/2 cup raisins
1/2 teaspoon cinnamon
1/2 cup chopped nuts
1/4 cup white grape juice

Chop the peeled or unpeeled apples. Add the remaining ingredients. Mix well and serve.

5. **Fruit Leather**

2 cups applesauce
vegetable shortening or oil

Preheat oven to 400 degrees. Pour applesauce onto greased shallow pan. Spread to 1/8 inch in thickness. Place pan in oven and lower temperature to 180 degrees. Cook for approximately 3 hours until the leather can be peeled from the pan. Cut with scissors to serve.

6. Dried Apples

5 or 6 apples
2 tablespoons salt
water

Peel, core, and cut apples into slices or rings 1/8 inch thick. Place apple slices in salt-water solution (2 tablespoons per 1 gallon water) for several minutes. Remove from the water. Place in 180-degree oven for 3 to 4 hours until dry. Turn apples occasionally.

Books:

The following books can be used to complement this theme:

1. Rockwell, Anne. (1989). *Apples and Pumpkins*. New York: Macmillan.
2. Gibbons, Gail. (1984). *The Seasons of Arnold's Appletree*. San Diego, CA: Harcourt Brace Jovanovich.
3. *Apple Tree! Apple Tree! Big Book*. (1990). Emeryville, CA: Children's Press.
4. Genet, Barbara. (1985). *To-Poo-Ach Means Apple*. ARE Publishers.
5. *Who Took Apple Frapple's Cookbook?* (1992). Mentor, OH: Glue Books.
6. Maestro, Betsy. (1992). *How Do Apples Grow?* New York: Harper Collins.

T H E M E 2

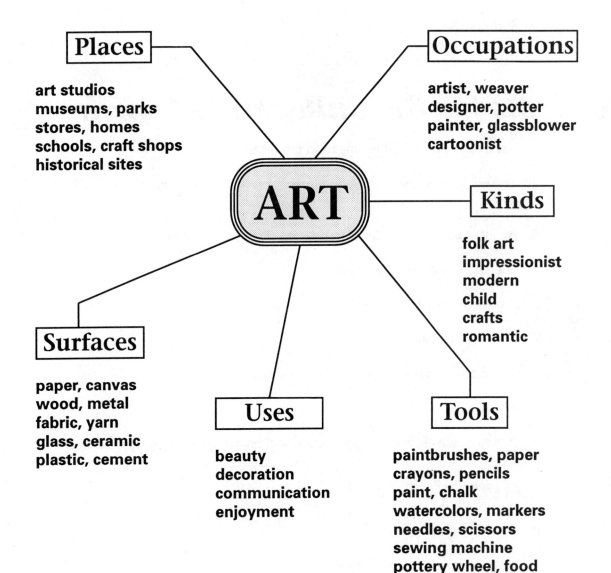

Places

art studios
museums, parks
stores, homes
schools, craft shops
historical sites

Occupations

artist, weaver
designer, potter
painter, glassblower
cartoonist

ART

Kinds

folk art
impressionist
modern
child
crafts
romantic

Surfaces

paper, canvas
wood, metal
fabric, yarn
glass, ceramic
plastic, cement

Uses

beauty
decoration
communication
enjoyment

Tools

paintbrushes, paper
crayons, pencils
paint, chalk
watercolors, markers
needles, scissors
sewing machine
pottery wheel, food

Here's an exciting new way to turn instant photography into an effective teaching tool. Refer to the full-color insert for the activity entitled *Photo Lotto*.

Theme Goals:

Through participating in the experiences provided by this theme, the children may learn:

1. The uses of art.

2. Places where works of art can be found.

3. Art tools.

4. Surfaces used for art.

5. Occupations associated with art.

Concepts for the Children to Learn:

1. Art is an expression of feelings and thoughts.

2. Brushes, paints, pencils, felt-tip markers, crayons, chalk, and paper are all art tools.

3. An artist uses art tools to make designs, pictures, or sculptures.

4. Art is a form of communication.

5. A museum has art objects.

6. An art gallery sells art objects.

7. Paper, canvas, and wood can all be painted.

8. We are all artists.

9. Artists create for many reasons—personal enjoyment, gift giving, and career.

Vocabulary:

1. **art**—a form of beauty.

2. **crayon**—an art tool made of wax.

3. **paint**—a colored liquid used for decoration.

4. **paintbrush**—a tool for applying paint.

5. **chalk**—a soft stone used for writing or drawing.

6. **artist**—a person who creates art.

7. **gallery**—a place to display works of art.

Bulletin Board

The purpose of this bulletin board is to reinforce color matching skills. Construct a crayon match bulletin board by drawing 16 crayons on white tagboard. Divide the crayons into pairs. Color each pair of crayons a different color. Include the colors pink, red, blue, yellow, purple, orange, brown, and green. Hang one from each pair on the top of the bulletin board and attach a corresponding colored string from the crayons. Hang the second set of crayons on the lower end of the bulletin board. A push pin can be added to the bottom set of crayons and the children can match the top crayons to their corresponding match on the bottom of the bulletin board.

Adjust the bulletin board to match the developmental needs and level of the children. For younger children, use fewer color choices. Let the children use the bulletin board during self-directed and self-initiated play periods. Repetition of this activity is important for assimilation providing it is child-initiated.

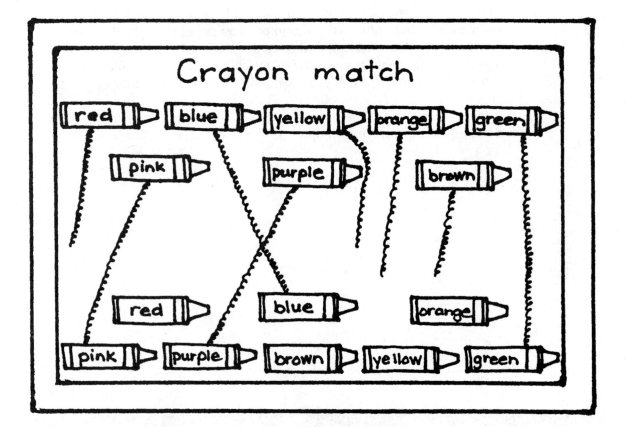

Parent Letter

Dear Parents,

Art is an expressive and aesthetic activity. It is also a curriculum theme that children always enjoy. During our focus on art, the children will be exploring many different types of art tools and supplies. They will also learn where works of art can be found. Moreover, the art work that they create will be displayed in an outdoor art gallery. You are invited to browse when you pick your child up from the center.

At School

Some of the artistic experiences planned include:

- creating chalk murals on the sidewalk.
- staging an art gallery in the dramatic play area.
- visiting on Tuesday with Bob Jones, a tour guide at the city museum. Mr. Jones will be sharing several art objects with us in our classroom.
- sorting art tools.
- participating in a wide variety of art activities.

At Home:

You can introduce the concepts of this unit into your home by collecting art tools and exploring them together. A fun art idea is to paint on paper using kitchen tools as applicators. Forks, potato mashers, and slotted spoons all work well for this activity. Through this and other art activities your child will discover interesting and creative ways to use materials. Art also provides opportunities to experiment with color.

Have fun looking at art with your child!

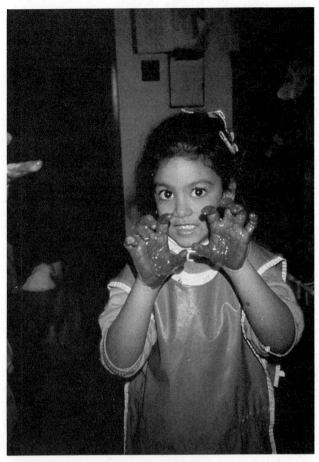

FIGURE 2 Through art, children can experience new outlets for self-expression.

Music:

"Let's Pretend"
(Sing to the tune of "Here We Are Together")

Let's pretend that we are artists,
are artists, are artists.
Let's pretend that we are artists
How happy we'll be.
We'll paint with our brushes,
and draw with our crayons.
Let's pretend that we are artists
How happy we'll be.

Fingerplays:

CLAY

I stretch it.
   (pulling motion)

I pound it.
   (pounding motion)
I make it firm.
   (pushing motion)
I roll it.
   (rolling motion)
I pinch it.
   (pinching motion)
I make a worm.
   (wiggling motion)

PAINTING

Hands are blue.
   (look at outstretched hands)
Hands are green.
Fingers are red,
In between.
   (wiggle fingers)
Paint on my face.
   (touch face)
Paint on my smock.
   (touch smock)
Paint on my shoes.
   (touch shoes)
Paint on my socks.
   (touch socks)

Social Studies:

The Feel of Color

This activity can be introduced at large group time. Begin by collecting colored construction paper. Individually hold each color up and ask the children how that particular color makes them feel. Adjectives that may be used include: hot, cold, cheerful, warm, sad, tired, happy, clean.

Group Time (games, language):

Toward the end of the unit, collect all art projects and display them in an art gallery at your center. The children can help hang their own projects and decide where to have the gallery. If weather permits, the art gallery can be set up on the playground using low clothes-lines and easels to display the art. If weather does not permit, a gallery can be set up in the classroom or center lobby, using walls and tables to display the art.

Cooking:

GRAHAM CRACKER TREAT

Give each child a graham cracker, honey, and a brush to spread the honey. Top with grated cheese, raisins, or coconut.

COOKIE DECORATING

Sugar cookies can be purchased commercially or baked and decorated. Recipes for the cookies and frosting are as follows:

1. **Drop Sugar Cookies**

   2 eggs
   2/3 cup vegetable oil
   2 teaspoons vanilla
   3/4 cup sugar
   2 cups flour
   2 teaspoons baking powder
   1/2 teaspoon salt

   Beat eggs with fork. Stir in oil and vanilla. Blend in sugar until mixture thickens. Add flour, baking powder, and salt. Mix well. Drop dough by teaspoons about 2 inches apart on an ungreased baking sheet. Flatten with the bottom of a plastic glass dipped in sugar. Bake 8 to 10 minutes or until delicate brown. Remove from baking sheet immediately. Makes about 4 dozen cookies that are 2 1/2 inches in diameter.

2. **Favorite Icing**

   1 cup sifted confectioner's sugar
   1/4 teaspoon salt
   1/2 teaspoon vanilla
   1 tablespoon water
   food coloring

   Blend salt, sugar, and vanilla. Add enough water to make frosting easy to spread. Tint with food coloring. Allow children to spread on cookie with spatula or paintbrush.

Science:

1. **Art Tools**

   A variety of art tools can be placed on the science table. Included may be brushes, pencils, felt-tip markers, crayons, and chalk. The children can observe, smell, and feel the difference in the tools.

2. **Charcoal**

   Place charcoal pieces and magnifying glasses on the science table.

3. **Rock Writing**

   Provide the children with a variety of soft rocks. The children can experiment drawing on the sidewalks with them.

Dramatic Play:

1. **Artist**

   Smocks, easels, and paint tables can be placed in the dramatic play area. The children can use the materials to pretend they are artists.

2. **Art Gallery**

   Mount pictures from magazines on sheets of tagboard. Let the children hang the pictures around the classroom. A cash register and play money for buying and selling the paintings can extend the play.

Arts and Crafts:

1. **Frames**

   During the course of this unit, the children can frame, with your assistance, their works of art by mounting them on sheets of colored tagboard and trimming it to a frame-like border. Older children may be able to do this unassisted. Display the works of art in the lobby, classroom—or outdoors, if weather permits.

2. Experimenting

In a unit on art, many kinds of art media need to be explored. Include the following art experiences:

- markers (both jumbo and skinny)
- chalk (both wet and dry)
- charcoal
- pencils (both colored and lead)
- crayons (jumbo, regular-sized, and shavings)
- paint (watercolors, tempera, fingerpaint)
- paper (colored construction, white, typing, tissue, newsprint, fingerpaint, tagboard)
- other (tin foil, cotton, glitter, glue and paste, lace, scraps, crepe paper, bags, waxed paper, yarn, and string)
- tools for painting (marbles, string, fingers, brushes of all sizes, straws, sponges)
- playdough and clay
- printing tools (stamps and ink pads, kitchen tools, sponges, potatoes, apples, and carrot ends)
- seeds

Sensory:

Additions to the Sensory Table

1. Goop

Mix together food coloring, 1 cup cornstarch, and 1 cup water in the sensory table. If a larger quantity is desired, double or triple the recipe.

2. Silly Putty

Mix food coloring, 1 cup liquid starch, and 2 cups of glue together. Stir constantly until the ingredients are well mixed. Add more starch as needed.

3. Wet Sand and Sand Mold Containers

Large Muscle:

1. Sidewalk Chalk

Washable colored chalk can be provided for the children to use outside on the sidewalk. After the activity the designs can be removed with a hose. The children may even enjoy using scrub brushes to remove the design.

2. Painting

Provide large paintbrushes and buckets of water for the children to paint the sidewalks, walls, and fences surrounding your center or school.

3. Foot Art

Prepare a thick tempera paint and pour a small amount in a shallow pan. Roll out long sheets of paper. The children can take off their shoes and socks, step into the tempera paint, and walk or dance across the sheets of paper. Provide buckets with soapy water and towels at the end of the paper for the children to wash their feet. Dry the foot paintings and send them home with the children.

Field Trips/Resource People:

1. Museum

Take a field trip to a museum, if one is available. Observe art objects. Point out and discuss color and form.

2. Art Store

Take a walk to a nearby art store. Observe the many kinds of pencils, markers, crayons, paints, and other art supplies that are available.

3. Resource People

Invite the following people to show the children their artwork.

- painter
- potter
- weaver
- glass blower
- sculptor

Math:

1. Counting Cans

Counting cans for this unit can be made from empty soup cans with filed edges. On each can write a numeral. The number prepared will depend upon the developmental needs of the children. Then provide an equal number of the following objects: pencils, pens, markers, paintbrushes, crayons, chalk sticks, sponges, etc. The object is for the children to relate the number of objects to numerals on the can.

2. **Measuring Art Tools**

Art tools come in all different lengths. Provide a variety of art tools and rulers, or a tape measure that has been taped to the table. The children can measure the objects to find which one is the longest. Make a chart showing the longest tool and continuing to the shortest.

3. **Sorting Art Supplies**

A large ice cream pail can be used to hold pencils, pens, markers, crayons, glue bottles, etc. that can be sorted into shoeboxes.

PAINTING SURFACES

There are many types of interesting surfaces that children can successfully use for painting. The list of possibilities are only limited by one's imagination. Included are:

construction paper	shelf paper	mirror
newsprint (plain/printed)	paper table cloths	plexiglass
tissue paper	paper place mats	paper bags
tracing paper	waxed paper	cookie sheets
tin foil	boxes	meat trays—plastic,
clear/colored acetate	leather scrap	cardboard, styrofoam
wood	sand paper	table surfaces
cardboard	paper toweling	

Multimedia:

The following resources can be found in educational catalogs:

1. Tsuroka, Linda, & Pliskin, Jacqueline. *Color a Song* [record].

2. Jenkins, Ella. *I Know the Colors in the Rainbow* [record].

3. *There's Music in the Colors* [record]. Kimbo Records.

4. *Fisher Price Picture Dictionary* [IBM software, PK–1]. Gametek.

Books:

The following books can be used to complement this theme:

1. Chevalier, Christa. (1982). *Spence Makes Circles*. Niles, IL: Albert Whitman and Co.

2. Williams, Vera B. (1986). *Cherries and Cherry Pits*. New York: Scholastic.

3. Tripp, Valerie. (1987). *The Penguin's Paint*. Chicago: Children's Press.

4. Kellogg, S. (1982). *Mystery of Stolen Blue Paint*. New York: Dial.

5. Moon, Marjorie (Ed.). (1988). *A Is For Art*. Milwaukee, WI: Author.

6. Reese, Bob. (1992). *Art*. Chicago: Children's Press.

7. Locker, Thomas. (1989). *The Young Artist*. New York: Dial Books for Young Readers.

8. Mayhew, James. (1989). *Katie's Picture Show*. New York: Bantam Books.

9. Carle, Eric. (1992). *The Art of Eric Carle*. Saxonville, MA: Picture Book Studio.

10. Venezia, Mike. (1988). *Van Gogh*. Chicago: Children's Press.

11. Venezia, Mike. (1991). *Michelangelo*. Chicago: Children's Press.

12. Turner, Robyn M. (1991). *Georgia O'Keefe*. New York: Little, Brown & Co.

13. dePaola, Tomie. (1988). *The Legend of the Indian Paintbrush*. New York: Putnam.

14. dePaola, Tomie. (1989). *The Art Lesson*. New York: Putnam.

15. Winter, Jeanette. (1991). *Diego*. New York: Knopf.

16. Alcorn, Johnny. (1991). *Rembrandt's Beret or the Painter's Crown*. New York: Tambourine Books.

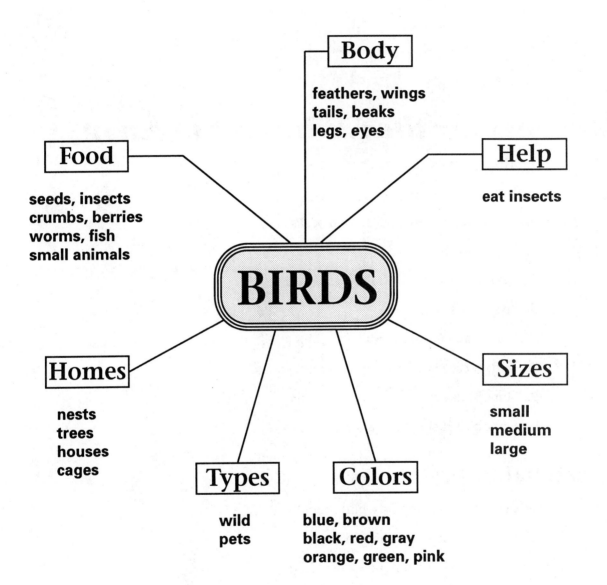

Body

feathers, wings
tails, beaks
legs, eyes

Food

seeds, insects
crumbs, berries
worms, fish
small animals

Help

eat insects

BIRDS

Homes

nests
trees
houses
cages

Sizes

small
medium
large

Types

wild
pets

Colors

blue, brown
black, red, gray
orange, green, pink

Here's an exciting new way to turn instant photography into an effective teaching tool. Refer to the full-color insert for the activity entitled Photo Peek-A-Boo.

Theme Goals:

Through participating in the experiences provided by this theme, the children may learn:

1. The bird's body parts.
2. Types of birds.
3. Bird homes.
4. Foods that birds eat.
5. Ways birds help.
6. Sizes of birds.
7. Colors of birds.

Concepts for the Children to Learn:

1. There are many kinds of birds.
2. Birds hatch from eggs.
3. Birds have feathers, wings, and beaks.
4. Most birds fly.
5. Birds live in nests, trees, houses, and cages.
6. Some birds are pets.
7. Many birds make sounds.
8. Birds eat seeds, insects, crumbs, and worms.
9. Some birds eat fish and small animals.
10. Some birds help us by eating insects.

Vocabulary:

1. **beak**—the part around a bird's mouth.
2. **bird watching**—watching birds.
3. **bird feeder**—a container for bird food.
4. **feathers**—covers skin of a bird.
5. **hatch**—to come from an egg.
6. **nest**—bed or home prepared by a bird.
7. **perch**—a pole for a bird to stand on.
8. **wing**—movable body part that helps most birds fly.

Bulletin Board

The purpose of this bulletin board is to develop skills in matching a set to its corresponding numeral. To construct the board, cut ten bird nests out of brown-colored tagboard. Draw a set of dots, beginning with one on each bird nest. Tack the nest on the bulletin board. Next, construct the same number of birds out of tagboard. On each bird, write a numeral beginning with one. By matching the numeral on each bird to the number of dots on the nests, the children can help each bird find a home. The number of birds and nests on this bulletin board should match the children's developmental needs.

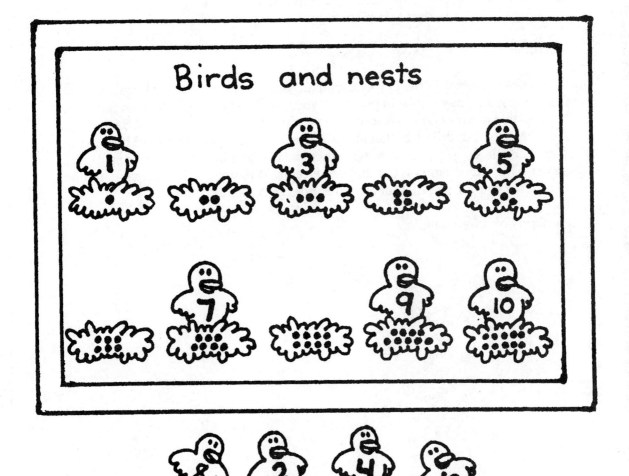

Parent Letter

Dear Parents,

Our class will be discussing our "feathered friends"—birds, which is the focus of our next unit. The children will be introduced to birds kept as pets and birds in the wild. In addition, they will discover the unique body parts of birds and the homes in which they live. The children will learn that birds are more similar than they are dissimilar.

At School

Some of the activities planned for the unit on birds include:

- observing different types of bird nests with a magnifying glass at the science table.
- visiting with Jodi's pet canary on Wednesday.
- creating collages using birdseed and glue in the art area.
- making bird feeders to hang outdoors in our play yard.

At Home

Whether you live in the city or country, chances are there are birds nearby. The following game may be fun to play with your child. Set an egg or kitchen timer for three to five minutes. Then look out the window and see how many birds you can see. For each bird, drop a button in a jar. When the timer goes off, count how many buttons are in the jar. This game will strengthen your child's observation skills and increase his understanding of number concepts. Variations of this game would be to observe for cars, squirrels, or any other object that can be counted.

Happy bird watching!

FIGURE 3 Children enjoy exploring bird habitats.

Music:

1. **"Birds"**
(Sing to the tune of "Here We Go Round the Mulberry Bush")
The first verse remains the same, with the children walking around in a circle holding hands.

This is the way we scratch for worms.
   (children move foot in a scratching motion like a chicken)
This is the way we peck our food.
   (children peck)
This is the way we sit on our eggs.
   (children squat down)
This is the way we flap our wings.
   (bend arms at elbows, and put thumbs under armpits, flap)
This is the way we fly away.
   (children can "fly" anywhere they want, but return to the circle at the end of the verse)

2. **"Pretty Birds"**
(Sing to the tune of "Ten Little Indians")

One pretty, two pretty
Three pretty birdies.
Four pretty, five pretty,
Six pretty birdies.
Seven pretty, eight pretty,
Nine pretty birdies,
All sitting in a tree.

Fingerplays:

THE DUCK

I waddle when I walk.
   (hold arms and elbows high and twist trunk side to side or squat down)
I quack when I walk
   (place palms together and open and close)
And I have webbed toes on my feet.
   (spread fingers wide)
Rain coming down, makes me smile, not frown
   (smile)
And I dive for something to eat.
   (put hands together and make diving motion)

Source: Hillert, Margaret. (1982). *Action Verse for Early Childhood*. Minneapolis: T.S. Denison and Co. Inc.

THE OWL

There's a wide-eyed owl
   (encircle each eye with thumb and forefinger)
With a pointed nose.
   (direct forefingers to a point downside of nose)
And two pointed ears
   (extend forefingers up from top of head)
And claws for toes.
   (curve fingers like claws)
He lives high in a tree.
   (point overhead)
When he looks at you
   (point to another child)
He flaps his wings
   (bend elbows and flap arms like wings)
And says "whoo, whoo, whoo."

Source: Hillert, Margaret. (1982). *Action Verse for Early Childhood*. Minneapolis: T.S. Denison and Co. Inc.

HOUSES

Here is a nest for a robin.
  (cup both hands)
Here is a hive for a bee.
  (fists together)
Here is a hole for the bunny;
  (finger and thumb make circle)
And here is a house for me!
  (fingertips together to make roof)

TWO LITTLE BLACKBIRDS

Two little blackbirds sitting on a hill,
  (close fists, extend index fingers)
One named Jack. One named Jill.
  (talk to one finger; talk to other finger)
Fly away Jack. Fly away Jill.
  (toss index fingers over shoulder separately)
Come back, Jack. Come back Jill.
  (bring back hands separately with index
  fingers extended)

BIRD FEEDER

Here is the bird feeder. Here are seeds and
crumbs.
  (left hand out flat, right hand cupped)
Sprinkle them on and see what comes.
  (sprinkling motion with right hand over left
  hand)
One cardinal, one chickadee, one junco, one
jay,
  (join fingers of right hand and peck at the
  bird feeder once for each bird)
Four of my bird friends are eating today.
  (hold up four fingers of left hand)

IF I WERE A BIRD

If I were a bird, I'd sing a song
And fly about the whole day long.
  (twine thumbs together and move hands
  like wings)
And when the night comes, go to rest,
  (tilt head and close eyes)
Up in my cozy little nest.
  (cup hands together to form nest)

TAP TAP TAP

Tap, tap, tap goes the woodpecker
  (tap with right pointer finger on inside of
  left wrist)
As he pecks a hole in a tree.
  (make hole with pointer finger and thumb)
He is making a house with a window
To peep at you and me.
  (hold circle made with finger and thumb in
  front of eye)

STRETCH, STRETCH

Stretch, stretch away up high:
On your tiptoes, reach the sky.
See the bluebirds flying high.
  (wave hands)
Now bend down and touch your toes.
Now sway as the North Wind blows.
Waddle as the gander goes!

Science:

1. **Bird Feeders**

   Make bird feeders. Suet can be purchased from a butcher shop or meat department of a supermarket. For each feeder, purchase 1/2 pound of suet, a 12" x 12" piece of netting, and birdseed. Begin by rolling the suet in birdseed. Place the seeded suet in the netting. Tie the four corners of the netting together and hang in tree or set outside on window ledge for children to observe.

2. **Grapefruit Cup Feeders**

   Place seeds in an empty grapefruit half. If possible, place the feeder in an observable location for the children. Some children may wish to take their feeders home.

3. **Science Table**

   On the science table, provide magnifying glasses and the following items:

   - feathers
   - eggs
   - nests

26

4. **Observing a Bird**

Arrange for a caged parakeet to visit the classroom. A parent may volunteer or a pet store may lend a bird for a week. Encourage the children to note the structure of the cage, the beauty of the bird, food eaten, and the behavior of the bird.

Dramatic Play:

1. **Birdhouse**

Construct a large birdhouse out of cardboard. Place in the dramatic play area, allowing the children to imitate birds. Unless adequate room is available, this may be more appropriate for an outdoor activity. Bird accessories such as teacher-made beaks and wings may be supplied to stimulate interest.

2. **Bird Nest**

Place several hay bales in the corner of a play yard, confining the materials to one area. Let the child rearrange the straw to simulate a bird nest.

3. **Hatching**

Here is a general idea of what you can say to create the hatching experience with young children. Say, "Close your eyes. Curl up very small; as small as you can. Lie on your side. Think of how dark it is inside your egg. Yes, you're in an egg! You're tiny and curled up and quiet. It's very dark. Very warm. But now, try to wiggle a little—just a little! Remember, your eggshell is all around you. You can wiggle your wingtips a little, and maybe your toes. You can shake your head just a little. Hey! Your beak is touching something. I think your beak is touching the eggshell. Tap the shell gently with your beak. Hear that? Yes, that's you making that noise. Keep tapping. A little harder. Something is happening. The shell has cracked—oh, close your eyes. It's bright out there. Now you can wiggle a little more. The shell is falling away. You can stretch out, stretch to be as long as you can make yourself.

Stretch your feet. Stretch your wings. Doesn't that feel good, after being in that little egg? Stretch! You're brand new—can you stand up, slowly? Can you see other new baby birds?"

Arts and Crafts:

1. **Feather Painting**

On the art table, place feathers, thin paper, and paint. Let the children experiment with different paint consistencies and types of feathers.

2. **Birdseed Collages**

Birdseed, paper, and white glue are needed for this activity. Apply glue to paper and sprinkle birdseed over the glue. For a variation, use additional types of seeds such as corn and sunflower seeds.

3. **Eggshell Collage**

Save eggshells and dye them. Crush the dyed shells into small pieces. Using glue, apply the eggshells to paper.

4. **Robin Eggs**

Cut easel paper into the shape of an egg. Provide light blue paint with sand for speckles.

5. **Dying Eggs**

Boil an egg for each child. Then let the children paint the eggs with easel brushes. The eggs can be eaten at snack time or taken home.

Sensory:

Additions to the Sensory Table

- feathers and sand
- eggshells
- sticks and twigs for nests
- worms and soil
- water, ducks, and other water toys
- birdseed and measuring tools

Field Trips/Resource People:

1. **Pet Store**

   Take a field trip to a pet store. Arrange to have the manager show the children birds and bird cages. Ask the manager how to care for birds.

2. **Bird Sanctuary**

   Take a field trip to a bird sanctuary, nature area, pond, or park. Observe where birds live.

3. **Museum**

   Arrange to visit a nature museum or taxidermy studio to look at stuffed birds. Extend the activity by providing magnifying glasses.

4. **Zoo**

   Visit the bird house. Observe the colors and sizes of birds.

5. **Resource People**

   Invite resource people to visit the classroom. Suggestions include:

   - wildlife management people
   - ornithologists
   - veterinarians
   - bird owners
   - bird watchers
   - pet store owners

Math:

1. **Feather Sorting**

   During the self-directed activity period, place a variety of feathers on a table. Encourage the children to sort them according to attributes such as color, size, and/or texture. This activity can be followed with other sorting activities including egg shapes and pictures of birds.

2. **Cracked Eggs**

   Cut tagboard egg shapes. Using scissors, cut the eggs in half making a jagged line. Record a numeral on one side of the egg and corresponding dots on the other side. The number of eggs prepared should reflect the children's developmental level.

Social Studies:

1. **Caring for Birds**

   Arrange for a pet canary to visit the classroom. The children can take turns feeding and caring for the bird. Responsibilities include cleaning the cage, providing water and birdseed. Also, a cuttlebone should be inserted in the bars of the cage within reach of the bird's bill. This bone will help keep the bird's bill sharp and clean, providing the bird uses it.

2. **Bird Feeders**

   Purchase birdseed and small paper cups. The children can fill a cup with a small amount of seed. After this, the teacher can attach a small string to the cup for use as a handle. The bird feeders can then be hung in bushes outdoors. If bushes are not available, they can be placed on window sills.

Group Time (games, language):

1. **Little Birds**

   This is a movement game that allows for activity. To add interest, the teacher may use a tambourine for rhythm. One child can be the mother bird and the remainder of the children can act out the story.

   All the little birds are asleep in their nest.
   All the little birds are taking a rest.
   They do not even twitter, they do not even tweet.
   Everything is quiet up and down the street.
   Then came the mother bird and tapped them on the head.

They opened up one little eye and this is what was said,
"Come little birdies, it's time to learn to fly,
Come little birdies, fly way up in the sky."
Fly fly, oh fly away, fly, fly, fly
Fly fly, oh fly away, fly away so high.
Fly fly, oh, fly away, birds, can fly the best.
Fly fly, oh, fly away, now fly back to your nest.

2. **Who Is Inside?**

The purpose of this game is to encourage the child to develop listening skills. To prepare for the activity, find a piece of large muscle equipment such as a jungle gym to serve as the bird house. Cover it with a large blanket. To play the game one child looks away from the group or covers his eyes. A second child should go into the bird house. The first child says, "Who is inside?" The second child replies, "I am inside the bird house." Then the first child tries to guess who is in the bird house by recognizing the voice. Other clues may be asked for, if voice alone does not work.

3. **Little Red Hen**

Tell the story of the Little Red Hen. After listening to the story, let the children help make bread.

Cooking:

1. **Egg Salad Sandwiches**

eggs
bread
mayonnaise
dry mustard (just a pinch)
salt
pepper

Boil, shell, and mash the eggs, adding enough mayonnaise to provide a consistent texture. Add salt, pepper, and dry mustard to flavor. Spread on the bread.

2. **French Bread Recipe**

1/2 cup water
2 packages rapid rise yeast
1 tablespoon salt
2 cups lukewarm water
7 to 7 1/2 cups all-purpose flour

Soften the yeast in 1/2 cup lukewarm water. Be careful that the water isn't too warm or the activity of the yeast will be destroyed. Add salt to 2 cups of lukewarm warm water in a large bowl. Gradually, add 2 cups of flour and beat well. Add the softened yeast and gradually add the remaining flour, beating well after each addition. Turn the soft dough out on a lightly floured surface and knead until elastic. Lightly grease a bowl and place the dough into it, turning once to grease surface. Let rise until double. Divide into 2 portions. Bake in a 375-degree oven until light brown, about 35 minutes.

3. **Bird's Nest Salad**

1 grated carrot
1/2 cup canned Chinese noodles
mayonnaise to moisten
peas or grapes

Have the children grate a carrot. Next have them mix the carrot with 1/2 cup canned Chinese noodles and mayonnaise to moisten. Put a mound of this salad on a plate and push in the middle with a spoon to form a nest. Peas or grapes can be added to the nest to represent bird eggs. The nest could also be set on top of a lettuce leaf. Makes 2 salads.

Source: Warren, Jean. (1982). *Super Snacks.* Alderwood Manor, WA: Warren Publishing.

4. **Egg Foo Young**

12 eggs
1/2 cup finely chopped onion
1/3 cup chopped green pepper
3/4 teaspoon salt
dash of pepper
2 16-ounce cans bean sprouts, drained

Sauce:
2 tablespoons cornstarch
2 teaspoons sugar
2 cubes or 2 teaspoons chicken bouillon
dash of ginger
2 cups of water
3 tablespoons soy sauce

Heat oven to 300 degrees. Beat eggs in a large bowl. Add remaining ingredients, except sauce ingredients; mix well. Heat 2 tablespoons of oil in a large skillet. Drop egg mixture by tablespoons into skillet and fry until golden. Turn and brown other side. Drain on a paper towel. Continue to cook the remaining egg mixture, adding oil to skillet if necessary. Keep warm in 300-degree oven while preparing sauce. Combine the first four sauce ingredients in a saucepan. Add water and soy sauce. Cook until mixture boils and thickens, stirring constantly.

Multimedia:

The following resources can be found in educational catalogs:

1. *The Animal Fair* [record]. January Productions.

   - Six Little Ducks
   - Three Crows
   - Bird's Courting Song
   - I Bought Me a Rooster
   - Cluck Old Hen
   - The Old Grey Hen
   - Listen to the Mockingbird
   - Animal Fair

2. Palmer, Hap. *Folk Song Carnival* [record]. Activity Records.

   - Going to the Zoo
   - Blue Bird
   - Hush Little Baby

3. Mills, Alan. *Fourteen Numbers, Letters and Animal Songs* [record]. Folkways Records.

   - Animal Alphabet
   - Six Little Ducks

Books:

The following books may be used to complement this theme:

1. Oppenheim, Joanne. (1986). *Have You Seen Birds?* New York: Scholastic Books.

2. Van Laan, Nancy. (1989). *Rainbow Crow*. New York: Alfred A. Knopf.

3. Gibbons, Gail. (1991). *The Puffins Are Back*. New York: Harper Collins.

4. Carey, Valerie Scho. (1990). *Quail Song*. New York: Putnam.

5. Knutson, Barbara. (1990). *How the Guinea Fowl Got Her Spots*. Minneapolis: Carolrhoda Books.

6. Lester, Helen. (1988). *Tacky the Penguin*. Boston: Houghton Mifflin.

7. Maddox, Tony. (1989). *Spike: The Sparrow Who Couldn't Sing*. New York: Barron's.

8. Pomerantz, Charlotte. (1989). *Flap Your Wings and Try*. New York: Greenwillow.

9. Prelutsky, Jack. (1986). *Ride a Purple Pelican*. New York: Greenwillow.

10. Yolen, Jane. (1990). *Cardinal*. New York: Philomel.

11. Lawson, Amy. (1987). *The Talking Bird and the Story Pouch*. New York: Harper Collins.

12. Yolen, Jane. (1987). *Owl Moon*. New York: Philomel.

13. Busch, Laura C. (1990). *Canary Books*. Little Readers.

14. Rockwell, Anne. (1992). *Our Yard Is Full of Birds*. New York: Harper Collins Children's Books.

15. Packard, Mary. (1992). *I Wonder How Parrots Can Talk and Other Neat Facts About Birds*. Racine, WI: Western Publishing Co.

16. National Wildlife Federation. (1991). *Birds Birds Birds*. Vienna, VA: Author.

17. Hirschi, Ron. (1987). *What Is a Bird?* New York: Walker and Co.

18. Hirschi, Ron. (1987). *Where Do Birds Live?* New York: Walker and Co.

19. Ehlert, Lois. (1990). *Feathers for Lunch*. San Diego: Harcourt Brace Jovanovich.

20. Stewart, Frances T., & Stewart, Charles P. (1988). *Birds and Their Environments*. New York: Harper Collins Children's Books, Inc.

21. Livingston, P. (1992). *Gullible the Seagull*. Sound Publishers.

22. Lyon, David. (1987). *The Runaway Duck*. New York: Morrow.

23. McLerran, Alice. (1991). *The Mountain That Loved a Bird*. Saxonville, MA: Picture Book Studio.

24. Pirotta, Saviour. (1992). *Little Bird*. New York: Tambourine Books.

25. Ross, Michael E. (1992). *Become a Bird & Fly*. Brookfield, CT: Millbrook Press.

26. Wolff, Ashley. (1985). *A Year of Birds*. New York: Puffin Books.

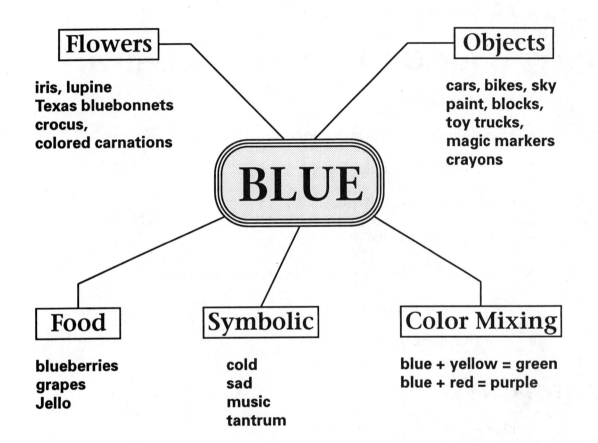

Flowers

iris, lupine
Texas bluebonnets
crocus,
colored carnations

Objects

cars, bikes, sky
paint, blocks,
toy trucks,
magic markers
crayons

BLUE

Food

blueberries
grapes
Jello

Symbolic

cold
sad
music
tantrum

Color Mixing

blue + yellow = green
blue + red = purple

Here's an exciting new way to turn instant photography into an effective teaching tool. Refer to the full-color insert for the activity entitled Photo Face.

Theme Goals:

Through participating in the experiences provided by this theme, the children may learn:

1. Blue is the color of many objects.

2. A type of berry is colored blue.

3. Some flowers are colored blue.

4. Blue can be mixed with other colors.

Concepts for the Children to Learn:

1. Blue is the name of a color.

2. Mixing blue with yellow makes green.

3. Blue mixed with red makes purple.

4. Some cars and bikes are a blue color.

5. On sunny, clear days the sky is a blue color.

6. Blueberries and grapes are examples of a blue-colored food.

7. There are many shades of blue.

8. An iris can be colored blue.

Vocabulary:

1. **blue**—a primary color.

2. **primary colors**—red, yellow, and blue.

3. **tints**—are created by adding white to a color.

4. **hue**—created by adding black to a color.

Bulletin Board

The purpose of this bulletin board is to develop visual discrimination skills. A blue bulletin board can be constructed by focusing on familiar objects. Draw pictures of many familiar objects on tagboard. Color them various shades of blue. Cut the objects out and laminate. Next, trace the pictures, allowing ¼-inch borders, on black construction paper. Cut out shadow pieces and hang on the bulletin board. Add a magnet piece to each shadow and picture. The children can match each picture to its corresponding shadow.

Parent Letter

Dear Parents,

Colors! Colors! Colors! We will be now focusing our activities on the color blue. The children will learn that blue can be mixed with red to make purple. Yellow mixed with blue makes green. The children will also become aware that many familiar objects are blue in color. Blue, moreover, represents many different things—sadness, cold, music, etc.

At School

Some of the learning experiences planned for this unit include:

- singing a song called "Two Little Bluejays."
- looking out our blue windows in the classroom.
- playing in a paint store in the dramatic play area.
- fingerpainting with blue paint.
- eating blueberries for snack.

At Home

You can make almost any meal entertaining by occasionally adding a small amount of food coloring to one of your food items. Children often find this amusing. The food coloring adds interest to your food and meal times become fun! Try adding a drop or two to milk, vanilla pudding, mashed potatoes, scrambled eggs, or cottage cheese. Does the color of a food affect its taste? (Try drinking green milk!) You be the judge! To further develop an awareness of color, identify foods that are red, blue, yellow, etc. This improves memory, classification, and expressive language skills.

Have a great time helping your child discover the color blue!

FIGURE 4 Constructing a bulletin board with items that are blue is one way to learn about colors.

Music:

1. **"Two Little Bluejays"**
   (Sing to the tune of "Two Little Blackbirds")

   Two little bluejays
   sitting on a hill
   One named Sue
   One named Bill.

   Fly away Sue
   Fly away Bill.
   Come back Sue
   Come back Bill.

   Two little bluejays
   sitting on a hill
   One named Sue
   One named Bill.

   To add interest, you can substitute names after the song has been sung several times. The children will enjoy hearing their names.

2. **"Finding Colors"**
   (Sing to the tune of "The Muffin Man")

   Oh, can you find the color blue,
   The color blue, the color blue?
   Oh, can you find the color blue,
   Somewhere in this room?

Science:

1. **Just One Drop**

   Each child will need a smock for this activity. Also, provide a glass of water and blue food coloring. Encourage the children to add a drop of blue food coloring to the water. Watch as the water becomes a light blue. Add a few more drops of food coloring, observing as the blue water turns a darker shade.

2. **Blue Color Paddles**

   Construct blue color paddles out of stiff tagboard and blue overhead transparency sheets. Make a form for the paddle out of tagboard, leaving the inside empty. Put the sheet of blue transparency paper on the back, glue, and trim. The children can hold the paddle up to their eyes and see how the colors have changed.

3. **Blue Windows**

   Place blue-colored cellophane or acetate sheets over some of the windows in the classroom. It is fun to look out the windows and see the blue world.

4. Dying Carnations

Place the stem of a white carnation in a bottle of water with blue food coloring added on the science table. Observe the change of the petal colors.

Dramatic Play:

Paint Store

Provide paintbrushes, buckets, and paint sample books. The addition of a cash register, play money, and pads of paper will extend the children's play.

Arts and Crafts:

1. Arm Dancing

Provide each child with two blue crayons and a large sheet of paper. Play music encouraging the children to color, using both arms. Because of the structure of this activity, it should be limited to older children.

2. Sponge Painting

Collect sponge pieces, thick blue tempera paint, and sheets of light blue paper. If desired, clothespins can be clipped on the sponges and used as handles. To use as a tool, dip the sponge into blue paint and print on light blue paper.

3. Easel Ideas

- Feature different shades of blue paint at the easel.
- Use blue paint on aluminum foil.
- Add whipped soap flakes to blue paint.
- Add a container of yellow paint to the easel. Allow the children to mix the yellow and blue paints at the easel. This activity can be extended by providing red and blue tempera paint.

4. Fingerpainting

Blue fingerpaint and large sheets of paper should be placed in the art area.

5. Melted Crayon Design

Grate broken blue crayons. Place the shreddings on one square of waxed paper 6 inches x 6 inches. On top of the shreddings, place another 6-inch x 6-inch piece of waxed paper. Cover with a dishtowel or old cloth. Apply heat with a warm iron for about 30 seconds. Let the sheets cool, and the child can trim them with scissors. These melted crayon designs can be used as nice sun catchers on the windows. (This activity needs to be closely supervised. Only the teacher should handle the hot iron.)

Sensory:

Additions to the Sensory Table

1. Water With Blue Food Coloring

2. Blue Goop

Mix together blue food coloring, 1 cup cornstarch, and 1 cup of water.

Large Muscle:

1. Painting

Provide a bucket of blue-colored water and large paintbrushes. Encourage the children to paint the sidewalks, building, fence, sandbox, etc.

2. Blue Ribbon Dance

Make blue streamer ribbons by attaching blue crepe paper to unsharpened pencils. Play lively music and encourage the children to move to the music.

Field Trips:

1. "Blue" Watching

Walk around your center's neighborhood and observe blue items. Things to look for include cars, bikes, birds, houses, flowers, etc. When you return, have the children dictate a list. Record their responses.

2. Paint Store

Visit a local paint store. Observe all the different shades of blue paint. Look carefully to see if they look similar. Ask the store manager for discarded sample cards. These cards can be added to the materials to use in the art area.

Social Studies:

Eye Color

Prepare an eye color chart with the children. Colors on the chart should include blue, brown, and green. Under each category, record the children's names who have that particular eye color. Extend the activity by adding the number of children with each color.

Group Time (games, language):

1. Bluebird, Bluebird

The children should join hands and stand in a circle. Construct one bluebird necklace out of yarn and construction paper. Choose one child to be the first bluebird. This bluebird weaves in and out of the children's arms while the remainder of the children chant:

"Bluebird, bluebird through my window
Bluebird, bluebird through my window
Bluebird, bluebird through my window
Who will be the next bluebird?"

At this time the child takes off the necklace and hands it to a child he would like to be the next bluebird.

2. I Spy

The teacher says, "I spy something blue that is sitting on the piano bench," or other such statements. The children will look around and try to figure out what the teacher has spied. Older children may enjoy taking turns repeating, "I spy something on the _____."

Cooking:

1. Blueberries

Wash and prepare fresh or frozen blueberries for snack. Blueberry muffins are also appropriate for this theme.

2. Blueberry Muffins

2 tablespoons sugar
1 3/4 cups flour
2 1/2 teaspoons baking powder
3/4 teaspoon salt
1 egg
1/2 cup milk
1/3 cup salad oil

Mix all of the ingredients together. Add 2 tablespoons of sugar to 1 cup frozen or fresh blueberries. Mix slightly and gently add to the batter. Bake at 400 degrees for approximately 25 minutes.

3. Cream Cheese and Crackers

Tint cream cheese blue with food coloring and spread on crackers.

4. Cupcakes

Add blue food coloring to a white cake mix. Fill paper cupcake holders with the batter and bake as directed.

- colors of clothing/types of clothing/patterns of fabrics (stripes, polka dots, plaid)
- shoes (boots, shoes with buckles, shoes with ties, shoes with velcro, slip-on shoes, jelly shoes) Also, number of eyelets on shoes, number of buckles
- ages in years
- number of brothers/ sisters
- hair/eye color
- birthdays in certain months
- name cards
- first letter of names
- last names
- rhyming names
- animal or word that starts with same sound as your name (Tiger-Tom)
- give each child a turn at something while putting rugs away (blowing a bubble, strumming a guitar, hugging puppet)
- play "I Spy" by saying, "I spy someone wearing blue pants and a Mickey Mouse sweatshirt."
- play a quick game of "Simon Says" and then have Simon tell where the children are to go next.

- "Two Little Blackbirds"
Two little blackbirds sitting on a hill
One named Jack, one named Jill
Fly away Jack, fly away Jill,
Come back Jack, come back Jill.
Two little blackbirds sitting on a hill,
One named Jack, one named Jill.

- "I Have a Very Special Friend"
(Sing to the Tune of "Bingo")
I have a very special friend,
Can you guess his name-o?
J-A-R-E-D, J-A-R-E-D, J-A-R-E-D,
And Jared is his name-o.

- "I'm Looking For Someone"
I'm looking for someone named Kristen,
I'm looking for someone named Kristen,
If there is someone named Kristen here now,
Stand up and take a bow. (Or, Stand up and go to lunch.)

- "Where, Oh, Where Is My Friend"
Where, oh, where is my friend Travis?
Where, oh, where is my friend Travis?
Where, oh, where is my friend Travis?
Please come to the door.

- "How Did You Come to School Today?"
How did you come to school today,
How did you come on Monday? (Child responds)
He came in a blue car,
Came in a blue car on Monday.
- "One Elephant Went Out to Play"
One elephant went out to play
Upon a spider's web one day.
He had such enormous fun
That he called for another elephant to come.

Group Dismissal

- hop like a bunny
- walk as quiet as a mouse
- tiptoe
- walk backwards
- count steps as you walk
- have footsteps for group to walk on or a winding trail to follow

- "This Train" (Tune: "This Train is Bound for Glory")
This train is bound for the lunchroom,
This train is bound for the lunchroom,
This train is bound for the lunchroom,
Katie, get on board.
Matthew, get on board.
Zachary, get on board.
Afton, get on board.
- Change lunchroom to fit situation.

Fillers

- "One Potato"
One potato, two potato, three potato, four
Five potato, six potato, seven potato, more.

- "And One and Two"
And one and two and three and four,
And five and six and seven and eight.
(Repeat faster)

- "Colors Here and There"
Colors here and there,
Colors everywhere.
What's the name of this color here?

- "This is What I Can Do"
This is what I can do,
Everybody do it, too.
This is what I can do,
Now I pass it on to you.

- "A Peanut Sat on a Railroad Track"
A peanut sat on a railroad track,
Its heart was all a-flutter.
Engine Nine came down the track,
Toot! Toot! Peanut butter!

  - apple-applesauce
  - banana-banana split
  - orange-orange juice

- "Lickety Lick"
Lickety lick, lickety lick,
The batter is getting all thickety thick.
What shall we bake?
What shall we bake?
A great, big beautiful carrot cake.

Change "carrot" to any kind of cake

- "I Clap My Hands"
I clap my hands. (Echo)
I stamp my feet. (Echo)
I turn around. (Echo)
And it's really neat. (Echo)
I touch my shoulders. (Echo)
I touch my nose. (Echo)
I touch my knees. (Echo)
And that's how it goes. (Echo)

Multimedia:

The following resources can be found in educational catalogs:

1. *Color Me a Rainbow* [record]. Melody House.

2. *There's Music in the Colors* [record]. Kimbo Records.

3. Palmer, Hap. "Colors" on *Learning Basic Skills Through Music* [record].

4. *Colors* [30-minute video]. Edu-vid.

5. *Pink Pete's ABCs* [Mac software, PK–2]. Orange Cherry.

Books:

The following books can be used to complement this theme:

1. Prelutsky, Jack (1990). *Beneath the Blue Umbrella*. New York: Greenwillow.

2. dePaola, Tomie. (1983). *The Legend of the Bluebonnet: An Old Tale of Texas*. New York: Putnam.

3. Pryor, Ainslie. (1988). *The Baby Blue Cat Who Said No*. New York: Viking.

4. Kaler, Rebecca. (1993). *Blueberry Bear*. Bloomington, IN: Inquiring Voices Press.

5. Dubar, Joyce. (1991). *I Want a Blue Banana*. Boston: Houghton Mifflin.

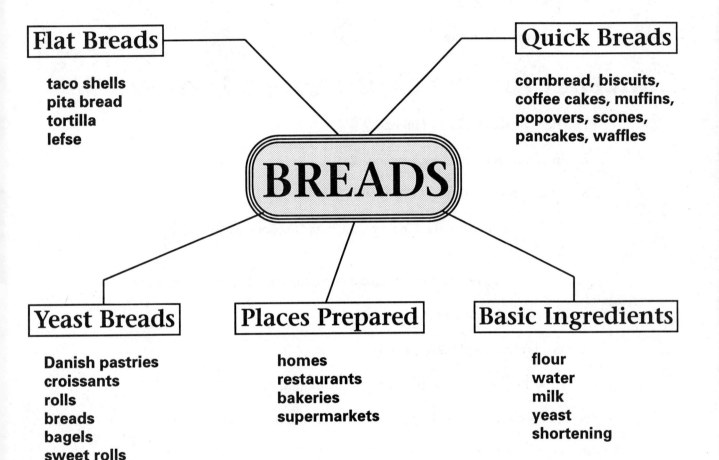

Flat Breads

taco shells
pita bread
tortilla
lefse

Quick Breads

cornbread, biscuits,
coffee cakes, muffins,
popovers, scones,
pancakes, waffles

BREADS

Yeast Breads

Danish pastries
croissants
rolls
breads
bagels
sweet rolls

Places Prepared

homes
restaurants
bakeries
supermarkets

Basic Ingredients

flour
water
milk
yeast
shortening

Here's an exciting new way to turn instant photography
into an effective teaching tool. Refer to the full-color
insert for the activity entitled Photo Open House.

Theme Goals:

Through participating in the experiences provided by this theme, the children may learn:

1. The basic ingredients of bread.

2. Places bread is prepared.

3. Types of yeast bread.

4. Types of flat bread.

5. Types of quick bread.

Concepts for the Children to Learn:

1. There are many kinds of breads.

2. Breads are important for good health.

3. Bread is the most widely eaten food.

4. The basic ingredients used in preparing bread are flour, water and/or milk, and shortening.

5. Bread can be prepared in homes, bakeries, supermarkets, and restaurants.

6. Breads can be large or small in size.

7. Breads can have different flavors.

8. Some breads contain a fruit filling and are called sweet rolls.

9. Breads can be shaped into different forms: round, twisted, and oblong.

10. Breads can be hard or soft.

11. Breads can be part of a meal or snack.

Vocabulary:

1. **bread**—a food prepared by mixing flour or grain meal with water or milk and shortening.

2. **crust**—the outside part of the bread.

3. **leaven**—a food that makes the bread dough rise.

4. **flour**—wheat that has been ground to a soft powder.

Bulletin Board

The purpose of this bulletin board is to promote visual discrimination skills and call attention to various types of baked goods. Create this bulletin board by drawing baked goods on a piece of tagboard as illustrated. Pictures from magazines could also be used. If drawn, color the bakery items with markers, cut out, and laminate. Trace these pieces onto black construction paper. Count out the pieces and attach to the bulletin board. Use map tacks or adhesive magnet pieces for children to match the corresponding baked good to its shadow.

Parent Letter

Dear Parents,

Did you know that bread is the most widely eaten food? It is often called the "staff of life" and it provides a large share of people's energy and protein. Our next curriculum will focus on a theme related to breads. Activities will help your child learn the different types of bread and the ingredients of bread, including the purpose of yeast. Your child will also participate in making bread. Special breads are also used in different cultural ceremonies.

At School

Some of the curriculum activities related to the theme will include:

- Tasting may kinds of breads.
- Sorting and then eating pretzels of various sizes and shapes.
- Baking bread on Thursday and observing the action of yeast.
- Making and selling baked goods in the Bakery Shop located in the dramatic play area.

At Home

We encourage you to participate in our celebration of bread. The next time you and your child are in the grocery store, find the bakery or bread department. Point out the different types and sizes of breads. Ask questions to help your child recognize similarities and differences.

Bake breads with your child and create warm family memories. Here is a simple recipe that you may want to try:

Zucchini Bread

1 1/2 cups all-purpose flour	1/4 cup cooking oil
3/4 cup sugar	1/4 teaspoon nutmeg
1 teaspoon ground cinnamon	1 beaten egg
1/2 teaspoon baking soda	1/4 teaspoon finely shredded lemon peel
1/4 teaspoon salt	1 cup shredded zucchini
1/4 teaspoon baking powder	1/2 cup chopped walnuts

Grease an 8x4x2-inch loaf pan. In a medium bowl mix together flour, sugar, cinnamon, baking powder, and nutmeg. Make well in the center of the dry mixture and add the zucchini. Stir only until mixture is folded in. Add the chopped walnuts.

Pour batter into the prepared loaf pan. Bake in a preheated oven set at 350 degrees for 55 to 60 minutes. Remove from the oven and cool on a wire rack for 10–12 minutes. Remove the bread from the pan and continue cooling on the wire rack. Wrap when cooled and let sit overnight before slicing.

A variation of this recipe would be to substitute shredded apples for the zucchini.

Enjoy a slice of bread with your child today!

FIGURE 5 It's tasty trying different kinds of bread and pastries.

Music:

1. **"If I had a Bagel"**
   (Sing to the tune "If I Had a Hammer")

   If I had a bagel.
   I'd eat it in the morning,
   I'd eat it in the evening,
   All over this land.
   I'd eat it for breakfast,
   I'd eat it for supper,
   I'd eat it with all my friends and sisters
   and brothers,
   All, all over this land.

2. **"Little Donuts"**
   (Sing to the tune of "Ten Little Indians")

   One little, two little, three little donuts
   Four little, five little, six little donuts
   Seven little, eight little, nine little donuts
   Ten donuts in the bakery shop.

3. **"Let's Pretend"**
   (Sing to the tune of "Here We Are Together")

   Let's pretend that we are bakers,
   Are bakers, are bakers
   Let's pretend that we are bakers,

As busy as can be.
We'll knead all the dough out
And bake loaves of bread.
Let's pretend that we are bakers
As busy as can be.

Fingerplay:

FIVE LITTLE DONUTS

Down around the corner, at the bakery shop
There were five little donuts with sugar on top.
   (hold up five fingers)
Along came _____ (child's name), all alone.
And she/he took the biggest one home.

Continue the verses until all the donuts are
gone.

Science:

1. **Bread Grains**

   On the science table set out containers of
   grains used to make bread for the children to
   examine. Examples include wheat, corn, oats,
   and rye. Provide magnifying glasses for
   children to explore the grains.

2. **Weighing Bread Grains**

The property of mass can be explored by providing a balance scale and bread grains at the science table. Scoops and spoons could be available to assist the children.

3. **Baking Bread**

The process of bread baking is definitely a science activity. The children can observe changes in substances and make predictions about the final outcome. Choose a bread recipe listed under the cooking section of this theme. Prepare a recipe chart for classroom use. Stress cooking safety with the children.

Dramatic Play:

1. **Bakery**

Prepare the housekeeping area to resemble a bakery where the children can pretend to make breads and bake goods to sell to their classmates as customers. Provide the following items: aprons, baker's hats, bowls, mixing spoons, pans, rolling pins, muffin tins, measuring cups, egg cartons, empty bread/roll mix boxes, oven mitts or hot pads, a cash register, and poster/pictures depicting baked goods.

2. **Restaurant**

Prepare the housekeeping area as a restaurant. Provide props such as a table cloth, dishes, cooking utensils, and a cash register with play money. Create menus by cutting pictures from magazines and gluing onto construction paper. Include pictures of different baked goods.

Arts and Crafts:

1. **Bread Collage**

Provide magazines for the children to find and cut out pictures of different types of breads. These pictures can be glued or pasted to a piece of construction paper or a paper plate, creating a bread collage.

2. **Play Dough**

The children can assist in preparing play dough. If the mixture is left uncolored, it will resemble bread dough and have a similar consistency. Place three cups of flour and one cup of salt in a mixing bowl. Add 3/4 cup of water and stir. Keep adding small amounts of water and mix until the dough is workable, but not sticky.

3. **Muffin Tin Paint Trays**

Fill muffin tins with various colors of paint in the art area for the children to use. Pastry brushes could be used as paint applicators.

4. **Biscuit Cutter Prints**

Place biscuit cutters and a shallow pan of paint out at the art table. The children can dip the biscuit cutter into the paint. After this, the biscuit cutter can be placed on a piece of construction paper. The children can repeat the process as desired.

5. **Bread Sponge Painting**

Cut sponges into different shapes and types of bread. Place the sponges and shallow trays of tempera paint on the art table. The children can dip a sponge into the paint and then press it onto a piece of paper to create a bread-shaped print.

Sensory:

1. Different types of grains can be placed in the sensory table. Examples include corn, rice, wheat, barley, and oats. Provide pails, scoops, measuring cups, flour sifters, and spoons to encourage active exploration.
2. Place play dough in the sensory table with rolling pins, measuring cups, muffin tins, and plastic knives.
3. Cooking utensils used for preparing baked goods can be placed in the sensory table with soapy water and dish cloths. The children can "wash" the items.

Large Muscle:

1. **Tricycles**

   During outdoor play, encourage children to use the tricycles for making bakery deliveries.

2. **Bread Trail**

   Set up a bread trail in the classroom. Tape pictures of the bread creating a trail on the floor. Have the children follow the trail by walking or hopping.

Field Trips:

1. **Bakery**

   Arrange a visit to a local bakery. Observe the process of bread and baked goods production. Discuss a baker's job and uniform.

2. **Farm**

   Take a trip to a farm where grains are grown. Notice the equipment and machinery used to plant and harvest the crops.

3. **Grocery Store**

   Tour a grocery store and find the bakery department. The children can look at the many types of breads and ways they are packaged.

Math:

1. **Favorite Bread Graph**

   After tasting various types of breads, the children can assist in making a class graph of their favorite types of breads. Across the top of a piece of tagboard, print the caption "Our Favorite Breads." Draw or paste pictures of different types or flavors of breads along the left-hand side of the tagboard.

   On the chart, place each child's name or picture next to the picture of his/her favorite bread. The results of the graph can be shared with the children using math vocabulary words such as most, more, fewer, least, etc. Display the graph for future reference.

2. **Muffin Tin Math**

   Muffin tins can be used for counting and sorting activities based upon the children's developmental level. For example, numerals can be printed in each cup, and the children can place the corresponding set of corn or toy pieces in each cup. Likewise, colored circles can be cut out of construction paper and glued to the bottom of the muffin cups. The children then can place objects of matching colors in the corresponding muffin cups.

3. **Pretzel Sort and Count**

   Provide each child with a cup containing various sizes and shapes of pretzels. Encourage the children to empty the cup onto a clean napkin or plate and sort the pretzels by size or shape. If appropriate, the children can count how many pretzels they have of each shape. Upon completion of the activity, the pretzels can be eaten by the children.

4. **Breadstick Seriation**

   Provide breadsticks or pictures of breadsticks of varying lengths. The children can place the breadsticks in order from shortest to longest.

Social Studies:

1. **Baker**

   The occupation of baker can be examined through books and discussion.

2. **Sharing Breads**

   Bake breads or muffins to give to a home for the elderly, the homeless, or some other organization. If possible, take a walk and have the children deliver them.

3. **Visitor**

   Invite people from various cultural backgrounds to bake or share breads originating from their native countries. As a follow-up activity, assist the children in writing thank-you notes.

Group Time (games, language):

1. Bread-Tasting Party

Bake or purchase various types and flavors of breads. Cut the bread into small pieces and place these samples on paper plates for the children to taste. Discuss the types of breads, textures, flavors, and scents.

2. Yeast Experiment

To demonstrate the effects of yeast, try this experiment. Pour one package of dry yeast, 1/2 cup of sugar, and one cup of warm water into an empty soda bottle. Cover the bottle opening with a balloon and watch it expand.

3. The Little Red Hen

Read the story of *The Little Red Hen* by Paul Galdone. After reading the story several times so that the children are familiar with the content, it can be acted out. Simple props can be provided to assist the children in creative dramatics and recreating the story.

4. Bread Basket Upset

This game is played in a circle formation on chairs or carpet squares. One child is asked to sit in the middle of the circle as the baker. Hand a picture of various breads—breads, rolls, muffins, etc.—to each of the other children. To play the game, the baker calls out the name of a bread. The children holding that particular bread exchange places. The game continues. When the baker calls out, "Bread Basket Upset," all of the children must exchange places, including the baker. The child who is unable to find a place is the new baker.

Cooking:

1. Bag Bread

Collect the following ingredients:

3 cups of bread flour
2 packages of fast-rising yeast
1/4 cup sugar
1 1/2 teaspoon salt
1 1/2 cup warm water (125 to 130 degrees)
4 teaspoons vegetable oil

In a gallon-sized heavy plastic zip-lock freezer bag place 1 1/2 cup flour, dry yeast, and salt. Close. Let the children mix the ingredients by shaking and working the bag with their fingers to blend the ingredients.

Add the oil and warm water to the ingredients in the bag. Reseal the bag and demonstrate to the children how to mix the ingredients. Gradually add the remaining flour until the mixture forms a stiff ball.

Grease your hands with a solid vegetable oil. Remove the dough from the bag and place on a lightly floured surface. Knead about five minutes. Small air pockets that appear as bubbles will form under the surface of the dough when it has been sufficiently kneaded. When they appear, let the children observe them.

Let the dough rest for 5–10 minutes. Grease two bread pans. Divide the dough in half. Shape into two loaves. Place each loaf in a greased bread pan. Cover with a kitchen towel. Let rise for an hour. Bake at 375 degrees for 25–30 minutes.

2. Pretzels

Collect the following ingredients:

1 teaspoon salt
2 1/2 teaspoons sugar
1 package of fast-rising yeast
1 cup warm water (125 to 130 degrees).
1 tablespoon vegetable oil
1 egg yolk, beaten with 1 tablespoon water
3–3 1/2 cups flour

Combine 1 1/2 cups of flour, the dry yeast, sugar, and salt in a large bowl. Add the warm water and vegetable oil and mix at low speed with an electric mixer for three minutes. Add an additional 1/2 cup flour and beat at high speed for two to three minutes. WHILE USING THE ELECTRIC MIXER THIS ACTIVITY NEEDS TO BE CAREFULLY SUPERVISED. Stir in the remaining flour to form a soft dough.

Lightly flour a surface. Place the soft dough on the floured surface and knead for approximately 10 minutes. Grease a bowl with vegetable oil and place the dough in to rise. Cover with a dish towel for 30-45 minutes.

Punch the air out of the dough and divide into 20 equal pieces. Demonstrate to the children how to roll a piece into a rope 12–14 inches long. Form the rope into a pretzel. Place on a greased baking sheet. Cover again and let rise in a warm place for about 25 minutes.

Brush each of the pretzels with the egg yolk mixture. Preheat the oven to 375 degrees. Bake for 15 minutes and remove from pan. Place on a wire rack to cool.

3. **Chappatis**

This recipe, which comes from India, serves 6; consequently, it will need to be adjusted to accommodate the number of children who need to be served.

1 1/2 cups of whole wheat flour
1/2 teaspoon salt
2/3 cup warm water
a small amount of cooking oil

Mix the flour and salt together in a bowl. Stir in water a small amount at a time until the mixture forms a ball.

On a floured surface, knead dough for 5–10 minutes, until it is a smooth, sticky ball. Let rise in a covered bowl for 30 minutes.

Cut the dough into six pieces. Roll each piece out into a circle that is about eight inches in diameter.

Lightly oil a frying pan with oil and heat until it smokes. THIS PORTION OF THE ACTIVITY NEEDS TO BE CAREFULLY SUPERVISED TO PROMOTE A SAFE ENVIRONMENT. Cook each circle of dough until it is brown and puffy on both sides. The chappatis is more flavorful when eaten warm.

4. **Cheesy Puff Bread**

3 3/4 cups of bread flour
1 package rapid-rise dry yeast
1 teaspoon salt
1/2 cup milk
2 tablespoons margarine
2 eggs
1 cup grated cheddar cheese
1/2 cup warm water
3 tablespoons sugar

Combine the dry yeast, sugar, salt, and 1 1/2 cups of flour in a large mixing bowl. Heat the milk, water, and margarine on the stove or in the microwave oven until warm to the touch. Add the dry ingredients. Then beat at low speed with an electric mixer. Add 1/2 cup of flour and the eggs. Beat at high speed for 2–3 minutes. Stir in the cheese and enough flour to make a soft dough.

On a lightly floured surface, knead the dough until it is elastic and smooth. Typically this will take 6–10 minutes. Place the dough in a greased bowl and let rise for 15–30 minutes.

Grease the entire inner surface of two l-lb. coffee cans. Divide the dough into two equal pieces. Place each piece in a can. Cover the top of the can with a piece of aluminum foil. Let the dough rise for 35 minutes.

Bake for 30 minutes in a 375-degree oven. Remove from cans and cool on a wire rack.

Multimedia:

The following resources can be found in educational catalogs:

1. Raffi. "Biscuits in the Ocean" on *Baby Beluga* [record].

2. Greg & Steve. "Muffin Man" on *We All Live Together—Volume Z* [record].

3. Sharon, Lois, & Bram. *Elephant Show Record* [record].

4. Sharon, Lois, & Bram. "Five Brown Buns" on *Books and Stories* [record].

Books:

The following books can be used to complement this theme:

1. Morris, Ann. (1989). *Bread, Bread, Bread*. New York: Lothrop.

2. Robbins, Ken. (1992). *Make Me a Peanut Butter Sandwich and a Glass of Milk*. New York: Scholastic, Inc.

3. Mancure, Jane. (1985). *What Was It Before It Was Bread?* Mankato, MN: Child's World, Inc.

4. Ziegler, Sandra. (1987). *A Visit to the Bakery*. Chicago: Children's Press.

5. Spohn, Kate. (1990). *Ruth's Bake Shop*. New York: Orchard Books.

6. dePaola, Tomie. (1989). *Tony's Bread*. New York: Putnam Publishing.

7. Galdone, Paul. (1975). *The Little Red Hen*. Boston: Houghton Mifflin Co.

8. Asch, Frank. (1992). *Bread and Honey*. New York: Putnam Publishing.

9. Lord, John V., & Burroway. (1990). *Giant Jam Sandwich*. Boston: Houghton Mifflin Co.

10. Lillegard, Dee. (1986). *I Can Be A Baker*. Chicago: Children's Press.

11. Kingston, Arlene. (1988). *The Bagels Are Coming*. West Bloomfield, MI.: Child Time Publishers.

12. McLean, Bill. (1990). *The Best Peanut Butter Sandwich in the Whole World*. Buffalo, NY: Firefly Books.

13. Dragonwagon, Crescent. (1989). *This Is the Bread I Baked for Ned*. New York: Macmillan.

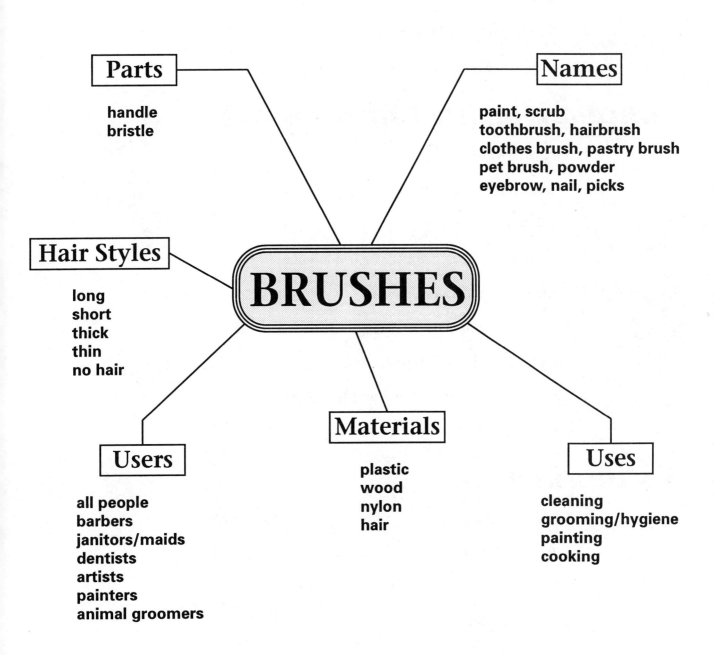

Parts

handle
bristle

Names

paint, scrub
toothbrush, hairbrush
clothes brush, pastry brush
pet brush, powder
eyebrow, nail, picks

Hair Styles

long
short
thick
thin
no hair

BRUSHES

Users

all people
barbers
janitors/maids
dentists
artists
painters
animal groomers

Materials

plastic
wood
nylon
hair

Uses

cleaning
grooming/hygiene
painting
cooking

Polaroid Education Program

Here's an exciting new way to turn instant photography into an effective teaching tool. Refer to the full-color insert for the activity entitled People and Uniforms.

Theme Goals:

Through participating in the experiences provided by this theme, the children may learn:

1. Parts of a brush.

2. Kinds of brushes.

3. Uses of brushes.

4. Materials used to make brushes.

5. Community helpers who need brushes for their work.

Concepts for the Children to Learn:

1. A brush is a tool.

2. Brushes come in many sizes.

3. Brushes have handles.

4. Some brushes are used in cleaning in our home.

5. Toothbrushes help clean our teeth.

6. Hairbrushes are used for grooming.

7. A pastry brush is used for cooking.

8. Brushes can be made of plastic, wood, or nylon.

9. Some people use brushes while working.

Vocabulary:

1. **brush**—a tool made of bristles or wires attached to a handle.

2. **bristle**—a short, stiff hair or thread-like object.

3. **handle**—the part of a brush that is held.

4. **groom**—to clean.

5. **powder brush**—a brush that is used to apply facial powder.

6. **toothbrush**—a small brush used to clean teeth.

7. **vegetable brush**—a stiff brush used to clean vegetables.

8. **dog brush**—a brush used to clean a dog's hair.

Bulletin Board

The purpose of this bulletin board is to promote the development of color identification and matching skills. Construct and paint pallets and brushes out of tagboard. Use a different colored marker to draw paint spots on each pallet and to "paint" the bristles of each brush. Laminate all the pieces. Attach the pallets to the bulletin board. Map tacks, putty, or velcro may be used to place the brushes next to the corresponding color of paint pallet.

Parent Letter

Dear Parents,

Did you ever stop to think about the number and types of brushes we use in a day? Brushes will be the next subject that we will explore. Each one has a different function and helps us do a different job. Through the activities related to the theme, the children will become aware of the many types and uses of brushes. In addition, they will be exposed to materials used in constructing brushes.

At School

Some of the learning experiences this week will include:
- setting up a hair stylist shop in the dramatic play area (and discussing different hair styles and colors).
- "painting" outside with buckets of water and brushes.
- observing teeth being cleaned with electric and hand-held brushes as we visit Dr. Smith's dental office on Thursday morning.
- painting with a variety of brushes at the easel each day.

At Home

With your child, go through your home and locate brushes. Examples include: toothbrushes, hairbrushes, paintbrushes, fingernail polish brushes, pastry brushes, and makeup brushes. Compare and sort the various brushes. This will help your child discriminate among weights, colors, sizes, textures, and shapes. The brushes can also be counted to determine which room contains the most and which the least number of brushes, which will promote the understanding of number concepts.

Paint a picture with your child today!

FIGURE 6 Painting with water-soluble paints on pavement is a creative activity.

Music:

"Using Brushes"
(Sing to the tune of "Mulberry Bush")

This is the way we brush our teeth,
brush our teeth, brush our teeth.
This is the way we brush our teeth
So early in the morning.

Variations:
- This is the way we brush our hair....
- This is the way we polish our nails....
- This is the way we paint the house....

Act out each verse, and allow the children to
make up more verses.

Fingerplays:

BRUSHES IN MY HOME

These brushes in my home
Are simply everywhere.
I use them for my teeth each day,
   (brushing teeth motion)
And also for my hair.
   (hair brushing motion)

We use them in the kitchen sink
   (scrubbing motion)
And in the toilet bowls
   (scrubbing motion)
For putting polish on my shoes
   (touch shoes and rub)
And to waterproof the soles.

Brushes are used to polish the floors
   (polishing motions)
And also paint the wall,
   (painting motion)
To clean the charcoal barbecue,
   (brushing motion)
It's hard to name them all.

MY TOOTHBRUSH

I have a little toothbrush.
   (use pointer for toothbrush)
I hold it very tightly.
   (make tight fist)
I brush my teeth each morning
   (pretend to brush teeth)
And then again at night.

SHINY SHOES

First I loosen mud and dirt,
My shoes I then rub clean.
For shoes in such a dreadful sight,
Never should be seen.

I spread the polish on the shoes.
And then I let it dry.
I brush the shoes until they shine.
And sparkle in my eye.

Science:

1. **Identifying Brushes**

   Inside the feely box, place various small brushes. The children can reach into the box, feel the object, and try to identify it by name.

2. **Exploring Bristles**

   Add to the science table a variety of brushes and magnifying glasses. Allow the children to observe the bristles up close, noting similarities and differences.

Dramatic Play:

1. **Hair Stylist**

   Collect hairspray bottles, brushes, empty shampoo bottles, chairs, mirrors, hair dryers, curling irons, and place in the dramatic play area. Cut the cords off the electrical appliances.

2. **Water Painting**

   Outdoors provide children with buckets of water and house paintbrushes. They can pretend to "paint" the building, sidewalks, equipment, and fence.

3. **Shining Shoes**

   In the dramatic play area place clear shoe polish, shoes, brushes, and shining cloths for the children to use to polish.

Arts and Crafts:

1. **Brush Painting**

   Place various brushes such as hair, makeup, toothbrushes, and clothes brushes on a table in the art area. In addition, thin tempera paint and paper should be provided. Let the children explore the painting process with a variety of brushes.

2. **Easel Ideas**

   Each day change the type of brushes the children can use while painting at the easel.

Variations may include: sponge brushes, discarded toothbrushes, nail polish brushes, vegetable brushes, and makeup brushes.

3. **Box House Painting**

   Place a large cardboard box outside. To decorate it provide smocks, house painting brushes, and tempera paint for the children.

Large Muscle:

Sidewalk Brushing

   Place buckets of water and paintbrushes for use outdoors on sidewalks, fences, and buildings.

Field Trips/Resource People:

1. **The Street Sweeper**

   Contact the city maintenance department. Invite them to clean the street in front of the center or school for the children to observe.

2. **Artist's Studio**

   Visit a local artist's studio. Observe the various brushes used.

3. **Dentist's Office**

   Visit a dentist's office. Ask the dentist to demonstrate and explain the use of various brushes.

4. **Animal Groomer**

   Invite an animal groomer to school. Ask the groomer to show the equipment, emphasizing the importance of brushes.

Math:

1. **Sequencing**

   Collect various-sized paintbrushes. Encourage the children to sequence them by height and width.

2. **Weighing Brushes**

Place a balance scale and several brushes in the math area. Encourage the children to weigh and balance the brushes.

3. **Toothbrush Counting**

Collect toothbrushes and cans. Label each can with a numeral. The children can place the corresponding number of brushes into each labeled can. If desired, the toothbrushes can be constructed out of tagboard.

Social Studies:

1. **Brushes Chart**

Design a "Brushes in our Classroom" chart. Encourage the children to find all that are used in the classroom.

2. **Helper Chart**

Design a helper chart. Include tasks such as sweeping floors, cleaning paintbrushes, putting brushes, and brooms away. This chart can encourage the children to use brushes every day in the classroom.

Group Time (games, language):

1. **Brush Hunt**

Hide several brushes in the classroom. Have one child search for the brushes. When he gets close to them, clap loudly. When he is further away, clap quietly.

2. **Brush of the Day**

At group time each day introduce a new brush. Discuss the shape, color, materials, and uses. Then allow the children to use the brush in the classroom during self-selected play period.

Cooking:

1. **Cleaning Vegetables**

Place several washtubs filled with water in the cooking area. Then provide children with fresh carrots and brushes. Encourage the children to clean the carrots using a vegetable brush. The carrots can be used to make carrot cake, muffins, or can be added to soup.

2. **Pretzels**

1 1/2 cups warm water
1 envelope yeast
4 cups flour
1 teaspoon salt
1 tablespoon sugar
1 egg
coarse salt (optional)

Mix water, yeast, sugar. Let stand for 5 minutes. Place salt and flour in a bowl. Add the yeast and stir to prepare dough mixture. Shape the dough. Beat egg and apply the egg glaze with a pastry brush. Sprinkle with salt if desired. Bake at 425 degrees for approximately 12 minutes.

PAINT APPLICATORS

There are many ways to apply paint. The size and shape of the following applicators produce unique results. While some are recycleable, others are disposable.

Recycleable Examples

paintbrushes, varying sizes and widths
whisk brooms
fingers and hands
tongue depressors or popsicle sticks
potato mashers
forks and spoons
toothbrushes
aerosol can lids
cookie cutters

spray bottles
string/yarn
roll-on deodorant bottles
squeeze bottles (plastic ketchup containers)
marbles and beads
styrofoam shapes
sponges
feet
spools
rollers

Disposable Applicators to Use with Paint

twigs and sticks
string/yarn
feathers
pinecones
rocks
cloth
cardboard tubes
straws
leaves
cotton balls
cotton swabs

Books:

The following books can be used to complement the theme:

1. Lillegard, Dee. (1987). *I Can Be a Beautician*. Chicago: Children's Press.

2. Tripp, Valerie. (1987). *The Penguins Paint*. Chicago: Children's Press.

3. dePaola, Tomie. (1988). *The Legend of the Indian Paintbrush*. New York: G. P. Putnam.

4. Hoban, Tara. (1987). *Dots, Spots, Speckles, & Stripes*. New York: Greenwillow.

5. Small, David. (1985). *Imogene's Antlers*. New York: Crown.

6. Testa, Fulvio. (1986). *If You Take a Paintbrush: A Book of Colors*. New York: Dial Books.

7. Quinlan, Patricia. (1992). *Brush Them Bright*. New York: Walt Disney Publishing.

THEME 7

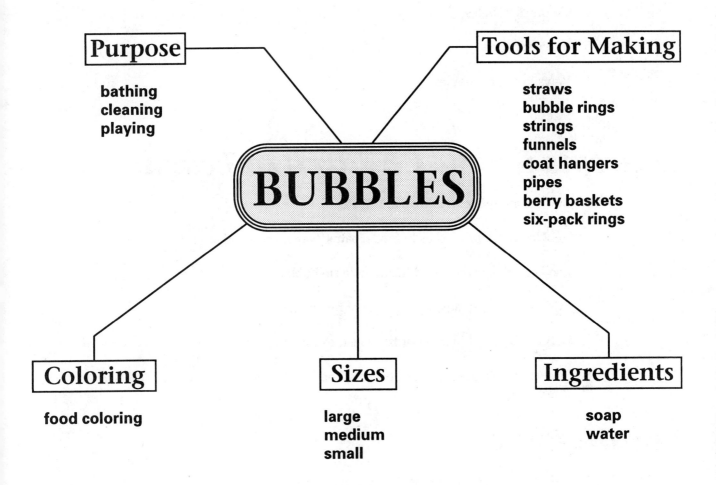

Purpose

bathing
cleaning
playing

Tools for Making

straws
bubble rings
strings
funnels
coat hangers
pipes
berry baskets
six-pack rings

BUBBLES

Coloring

food coloring

Sizes

large
medium
small

Ingredients

soap
water

Polaroid
Education
Program

Here's an exciting new way to turn instant photography into an effective teaching tool. Refer to the full-color insert for the activity entitled Photo Lotto.

Theme Goals:

Through participating in the experiences provided by this theme, the children may learn:

1. Purposes of bubbles.

2. Bubble ingredients.

3. Tools for making bubbles.

4. Colors of bubbles.

5. Bubble shapes.

6. Ways to create bubbles.

7. Sizes of bubbles.

Concepts for the Children to Learn:

1. Bubbles are made with soap and water.

2. Bubbles are all around us in foods, baths, water, and drinks.

3. Food coloring can be used to add color to bubbles.

4. Bubbles can be created by blowing or by waving a tool.

5. Bubbles have a skin that holds air inside of them.

6. Straws, bubble rings, strings, funnels, and coat hangers can be used as tools to make bubbles.

Vocabulary:

1. **bubble**—a round circle that has a skin and contains air.

2. **bubble skin**—the outside of the bubble that holds the air.

3. **bubble solution**—a mixture of water and liquid soap.

4. **bubble wand**—a tool used to make bubbles.

Bulletin Board

The purpose of this bulletin board is to promote the active exploration of household items that can be used to make bubbles. Collect items such as pipe cleaners, funnels, spools, six-pack rings, berry baskets, and scissors. Construct and label boxes and/or pockets to hold items on the bulletin board. Containers of bubble solution should be placed near the bulletin board for the children to experiment making bubbles with the household items. Provide towels in the area to encourage the children to assist in wiping up spills.

Parent Letter

Dear Parents:

What do you get when you mix water and soap? Bubbles! The children will make many fascinating discoveries as we focus on a Bubbles theme. Through experiences provided, the children will learn the ingredients used in making bubbles, size of bubbles, and tools for making bubbles.

At School

Some of the learning experiences planned to highlight bubble concepts are:

- Washing dolls and dishes in the sensory table.
- Testing many bubble solution recipes.
- Making bubbles with common household items such as plastic berry baskets, funnels, straws, pipe cleaners, spools, and scissors.
- Creating prints of bubbles in the art area.

At Home

Try the following activities with your child to reinforce bubble concepts at home:

- Allow your child to assist in washing dishes after a meal. This experience will give your child a sense of responsibility and promote self-esteem, as well as heighten his/her awareness of the purpose of bubbles for cleaning.
- Prepare the following bubble solution with your child, then blow some bubbles! You need one cup of water, two tablespoons of liquid dish soap, and one tablespoon of glycerine (optional). Enjoy!

Have a good time with your child!

FIGURE 7 Catching bubbles outdoors is a good science experience.

Music:

1. **"Pop! Goes the Bubble"**
    (Sing to the tune of "Pop! Goes the Weasel")

    Soap and water can be mixed.
    To make a bubble solution.
    Carefully blow,
    Now, watch it go!
    Pop! Goes the bubble!

2. **"Can you Blow a Big Bubble?"**
    (Sing to the tune of "The Muffin Man")

    Can you blow a big bubble?
    A big bubble, a big bubble?
    Can you blow a big bubble,
    With your bubble gum?

3. **"I'm a Little Bubble"**
    (Sing to the tune of "I'm a Little Teapot")

    I'm a little bubble, shiny and round.
    I gently float down to the ground.
    The wind lifts me up and then I drop.
    Down to the dry ground where I pop.

4. **"Ten Little Bubbles"**
    (Sing to the tune of "Ten Little Indians")

    One little, two little, three little bubbles.
    Four little, five little, six little bubbles.
    Seven little, eight little, nine little bubbles.
    Ten bubbles floating to the ground.

5. **"Here's a Bubble"**
    Here's a bubble, here's a bubble.
    Big and round; big and round.
    See it floating gently,
    See it floating gently,
    To the ground; to the ground.

Fingerplays:

HERE IS A BUBBLE

Here is a bubble
   (make a circle with thumb and index finger)
And here's a bubble
   (make a bigger circle with two thumbs and
   index finger)
And here is a great big bubble I see.
   (make a large circle with arms)

Let's count the bubbles we've made.
One, two, three.
    (repeat prior actions)

DRAW A BUBBLE

Draw a bubble, draw a bubble.
Make it very round.
    (make a shape in the air with index finger)
Draw a bubble, draw a bubble.
No corners can be found.
    (repeat actions)

Science:

1. **Bubble Solutions**

   Encourage the children to assist in preparing the following bubble solutions. (Note: The use of glycerine in preparing the bubble solution is optional. It helps to provide a stronger skin on the bubble, but the solutions can be prepared without this ingredient.)

   Recipe #1

   1/4 cup liquid dish soap
   1/2 cup water
   1 teaspoon sugar

   Recipe #2: Outdoor Use

   3 cups water
   2 cups liquid dish soap (Joy detergent)
   1/2 cup light corn syrup

   Recipe #3

   2/3 liquid dish soap
   1 gallon of water
   1 tablespoon glycerine

2. **Bubble Gadgets**

   Prepare a bubble solution and make some bubbles! Try and use of the following to make great bubbles.

   - plastic berry baskets
   - pipe cleaners or thin electrical wire shaped into wands
   - six-pack holders
   - egg poacher trays
   - funnels
   - scissors—hold the blades and dip the finger holders into the bubble solution
   - tin cans—open at both ends
   - paper cups—poke a hole in the bottom of a paper cup. Dip the rim into a bubble solution and blow through the hole.
   - plastic straws—use a single straw or tape several together in a bundle.
   - straws and string—thread three feet of thin thread through two plastic straws. Tie the string together. Hold the straws and pull them to form a rectangle with the string. Dip into a bubble solution and pull upward. As you move the frame, a bubble will form. Bring the two straws together to close off the bubble. This technique requires practice.
   - Hula Hoop—fill a small wading pool with two inches of bubble solution. The Hula Hoop can be used as a giant wand by dipping the hoop in a solution and lifting it up carefully.

3. **Wet/Dry**

   While blowing bubbles with the children try touching a bubble with a dry finger. Repeat using a wet finger. What happens? You will observe that bubbles break when they touch an object that is dry.

4. **Bubble Jar**

   Fill a small plastic bottle half-full of water. Add a few drops of food coloring, if desired. Add baby oil or mineral oil to completely fill the jar. Secure the bottle tightly. Then slowly tilt the bottle from side to side. When this occurs, the liquid in the jar resembles waves. Bubbles can be created by shaking the bottle. Encourage the children to observe these reactions.

5. **Air Bubbles in Food**

   Examine the air bubbles in pieces of bread, Swiss cheese, and carbonated drinks.

6. **Bubbling Raisins**

   Place two or three raisins in a small bottle of sparkling mineral water. Secure the cap and watch the bubbles form as the raisins sink and float.

Dramatic Play:

1. **Housekeeping**

   Fill the sink in the dramatic play area with soapy water. Provide dishes, dish cloth, towels, and a dish rack for the children to wash the dishes.

2. **Hair Stylist**

   Set up a hair stylist studio in the dramatic play area. Include props such as a cash register, empty shampoo and hair spray containers, mirrors, brushes, combs, barrettes, curlers, discarded hair dryer and curling irons, towels and smocks. Display pictures of hairstyles and hair products. (Caution: Cut the electric cords off the hair dryers and curling irons to prevent possible injuries.)

Arts and Crafts:

1. **Bubble Prints**

   For each bubble print color desired, mix one part liquid tempera paint with two parts liquid dish soap in a small container. Place a straw in the solution and blow until the bubbles rise above the rim of the container. Remove the straw and place a piece of paper over the bubbles. As the bubbles break, they will leave a print on the paper. (Each child will need a straw for this activity. A pin may be used to poke holes near the top of the straws to prevent the children from accidentally sucking in the paint mixture.)

   Variation: Small bubble wands can be dipped into the paint bubble solution and blown so the bubbles will land on a piece of paper, either at the easel or on the ground outdoors.

2. **Bubble Gum Wrapper Collages**

   Collect wrappers from bubble gum to be placed on the art with paper and glue. The children can use these materials to create collages.

3. **Bubble Paint Containers**

   Collect containers that hold commercially prepared bubble solutions. Recycle the containers by using them to hold various colors of paints at the easel or art table.

Sensory:

1. **Wash Dolls**

   Fill the sensory table with warm water and add a few tablespoons of dish soap. Provide plastic dolls, washcloths, and towels.

2. **Dish Washing**

   Place plastic dishes and dishcloths in the sensory table filled with warm soapy water. A dish drying rack could be set up nearby or towels provided to dry the dishes.

3. **Bubble Bath**

   Purchase or make bubble bath soap to put in the sensory table with scoops, measuring cups, and pails.

4. **Bubble Solution**

   The sensory table can be used to hold a bubble solution and bubble-making tools.

5. **Pumps and Water**

   Fill the sensory table with water. Add water pumps, turkey basters, and siphons to create air bubbles in the water.

Field Trips/Resource People:

1. **Hair Stylist**

   Visit a hair stylist to watch a customer receive a shampoo.

2. **Pet Groomer**

   Invite a pet groomer to demonstrate giving a dog a bath.

Math:

1. Bubble Count

If appropriate, encourage the children to blow a set of bubbles that you specify. For example, if you say the number "three," the children would try to blow three bubbles.

2. Bubble Wand Sort

Collect small commercially manufactured bubble wands and place them in a small basket. These wands can be sorted by size or color. They could also be counted or placed in order by size.

3. Geometric Bubble Shapes

Attach the ends of two straws together with duct tape or paper clips, creating the desired shapes. Six straws will be needed to make a pyramid and 12 to make a cube. The frames can be dipped into bubble solutions and observed.

Group Times (games, language):

1. What's Missing?—Game

Place several items to prepare bubbles on a tray. At group time, show and discuss the items. To play the game, cover the tray with a towel and carefully remove one item. Children then identify the missing item. The game can be made more challenging by adding more items to the tray, or by removing more than one item at a time.

2. Bubbles—Creative Dramatics

Guide the children through a creative dramatics activity as they pretend to be bubbles. They can act out being:

- a tiny bubble
- a giant bubble
- a bubble floating on a windy day
- a bubble landing on the grass
- a bubble floating high in the air
- a bubble in a sink
- a bubble in a piece of bread

3. Favorite Bubble Gum Chart

At the top of a piece of tagboard, print the caption "Our Favorite Bubble Gum." Along the left-hand side, glue bubble gum wrappers representing different brands or flavors. Present the chart at group time and ask each child to choose one as his/her favorite. Record the children's names or place their pictures next to the response. If appropriate, count the number of "votes" each brand received and print in on the chart. Display the chart in the classroom and refer to it throughout the unit.

Cooking:

1. Bubbly Beverage

6-oz. can frozen orange juice
6-oz. can frozen lemonade
6-oz. can frozen limeade
6-oz. can frozen pineapple juice (optional)
1 liter lemon-lime soda, chilled
1 liter club soda, chilled

Combine ingredients in a punch or large bowl. Stir to blend the ingredients. Serve over ice, if desired.

2. Root Beer

5 gallons cold water
5 lbs. white sugar
3-oz. bottle root beer extract
5 lbs. dry ice

In a large stone crock or plastic container (do not use metal) mix sugar with 1 gallon of water. Add the remainder of the water and root beer extract. Stir. Carefully add the dry ice. After the ice melts, the root beer can be transferred into other containers to store for 2–3 days.

Books:

The following books can be used to complement this theme:

1. Gaban, Jesus. (1992). *Tub Time for Harry*. Milwaukee, WI: Gareth Stevens.

2. Kudrna, C. Imbior. (1986). *To Bathe a Boa*. Minneapolis, MN: Carolrhoda Books.

3. Noble, Kate. (1992). *Bubble Gum*. Silver Seahorse.

4. Stevens, Kathleen. (1987). *The Beast in the Bathtub*. New York: Harper Collins.

5. Wood, Audrey. (1991). *King Bidgood's in the Bathtub*. San Diego: Harcourt Brace.

6. Mayer, Mercer. (1992). *Bubble Bubble*. Roxbury, CT: Rain Birds Production.

7. Simon, Seymour. (1985). *Soap Bubble Magic*. New York: Lothrop, Lee and Shepard Books.

8. Pluckrose, Henry. (1990). *Clean It!* New York: Franklin Watts, Inc.

9. Winer, Yvonne, & McLean-Carr, Carol Aitkin. (1987). *Never Snap at a Bubble*. Dominguez Hills, CA: Educational Insights.

10. Schubert, Ingrid, & Schubert, Dieter. (1985). *Magic Bubble Trip*. Brooklyn, NY: Kane-Miller.

11. Bridell, Norman. (1992). *Clifford Counts Bubbles*. New York: Scholastic Inc.

THEME 8

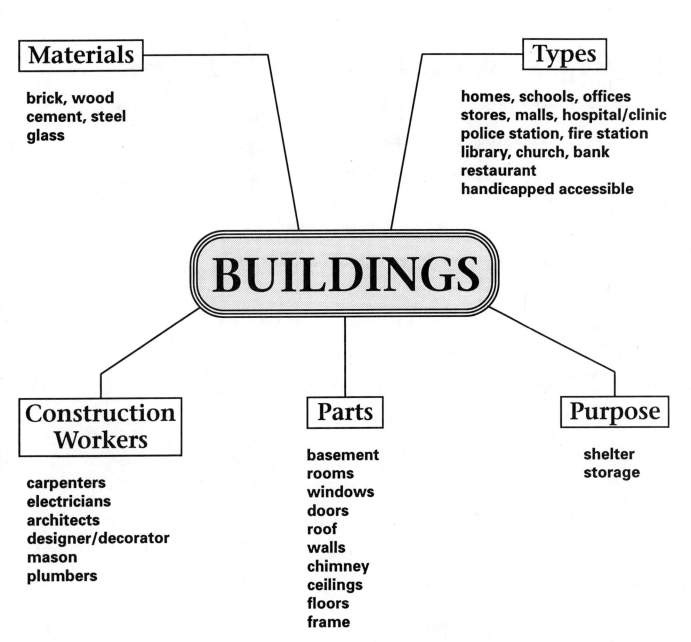

Materials

brick, wood
cement, steel
glass

Types

homes, schools, offices
stores, malls, hospital/clinic
police station, fire station
library, church, bank
restaurant
handicapped accessible

BUILDINGS

Construction Workers

carpenters
electricians
architects
designer/decorator
mason
plumbers

Parts

basement
rooms
windows
doors
roof
walls
chimney
ceilings
floors
frame

Purpose

shelter
storage

Polaroid
Education
Program

Here's an exciting new way to turn instant photography
into an effective teaching tool. Refer to the full-color
insert for the activity entitled Concentration Game.

Theme Goals:

Through participating in the experiences provided by this theme, the children may learn:

1. Types of buildings.

2. Purposes of buildings.

3. Materials used to make buildings.

4. Parts of a building.

Concepts for the Children to Learn:

1. There are many types of buildings: homes, offices, stores, hospitals, malls, etc.

2. Buildings can be made of brick, wood, cement, steel, and glass.

3. Many workers help construct buildings: architects, carpenters, electricians, plumbers, and masons.

4. Buildings can be used for shelter and storage.

5. Most buildings have a roof, walls, windows, and a floor.

Vocabulary:

1. **building**—a structure.

2. **mall**—a building containing many stores.

3. **skyscraper**—a very tall building.

4. **carpenter**—a person who builds.

5. **electrician**—a person who wires a building for light, heat, and cooking.

6. **architect**—a person who designs a building.

7. **room**—a part of a building set off by walls.

8. **ceiling**—the top "wall" of a room.

9. **roof**—the top covering of a building.

Bulletin Board

The purpose of this bulletin board is to develop awareness of size as well as visual discrimination skills. Construct house shapes out of tagboard ranging in size from small to large. Color the shapes and laminate. Punch a hole in the top of each house. Trace each house shape on black construction paper and cut out. Hang the shadow pieces on the bulletin board with a push pin inserted in the top of each. During self-directed and self-initiated play, the children match each colored house to the corresponding shadow piece by hanging it on the push pin.

Parent Letter

Dear Parents,

Your home, the library, our school...these are all buildings with which your child is familiar. Buildings will be our next theme. Discoveries will be made regarding different kinds and parts of buildings, materials used to make buildings, and the people who construct buildings.

At School

A sampling of the learning experiences include:

- building with various materials—such as boxes and milk cartons.
- working at the woodworking bench to practice hammering, drilling, and sawing.
- weighing and balancing bricks.
- taking a walk to a construction site.

At Home

You can reinforce building concepts on your way to and from school by pointing out any buildings of interest, such as the fire station, police station, hospital, library, shopping mall, and restaurants. Your children are naturally curious about why and how things happen. If you pass any construction sites, point out the materials and equipment used, as well as the jobs of the workers on the sites. This will help your child develop vocabulary and language skills. Concepts of time can also be fostered if you are able to visit the construction site over an extended period of time. You and your child will be able to keep track of progress in the development of the building.

Enjoy your child as you reinforce concepts related to buildings.

FIGURE 8 Together we will build a big house.

Music:

"Go In and Out the Window"

Form a circle with the children and hold
hands. While holding hands have the children
raise their arms up to form windows. Let each
child have a turn weaving in and out the
windows. Use the following chant as you play.

_____ goes in and out the windows,
In and out the windows,
In and out the windows.
_____ goes in and out the windows,
As we did before.

Fill in child's name in the _____.

Fingerplays:

THE CARPENTER'S TOOLS

The carpenter's hammer goes rap, rap, rap
(make hammering motion with fist)
And his saw goes see, saw, see.
(make sawing motion with arm and hand)
He planes and hammers and saws
(make motions for each)
While he builds a building for me.
(point to yourself)

CARPENTER

This is the way he saws the wood
(make sawing motion)
Sawing, sawing, sawing.

This is the way he nails a nail
(make hammering motion)
Nailing, nailing, nailing.

This is the way he paints a building
(make brushing motion)
Painting, painting, painting.

MY HOUSE

I'm going to build a little house.
(draw house with fingers by outlining in the
air)
With windows big and bright,
(spread out arms)
With chimney tall and curling smoke
(show tall chimney with hands)
Drifting out of sight.
(shade eyes with hands to look)
In winter when the snowflakes fall
(use fingers to make the motion of snow
falling downward)
Or when I hear a storm,
(place hand to ear)
I'll go sit in my little house
(draw house again)
Where I'll be snug and warm.
(hug self)

Science:

1. **Building Materials**

   Collect materials such as wood, brick, cement, metal, and magnifying glasses and place on the science table. Encourage the children to observe the various materials up close.

2. **Mixing Cement**

   Make cement using a small amount of cement and water. Mix materials together in a large plastic ice cream bucket. Allow the children to help. The children can also observe and feel the wet cement.

3. **Building Tools**

   Collect and place various tools such as a hammer, level, wedge, and screwdriver on the science table for the children to examine. Discuss each tool and demonstrate how it is used. Then place the tools in the woodworking area. Provide wood and styrofoam so that the children are encouraged to use the tools as a self-selected activity with close adult supervision.

Dramatic Play:

1. **Library**

   Rearrange the dramatic play area to resemble a library. Include books, library cards, book markers, tables, and chairs for the children's use.

2. **Buildings**

   Collect large cardboard boxes from an appliance dealer. The children can construct their own buildings and paint them with tempera paint.

3. **Construction Site**

   Place cardboard boxes, blocks, plastic pipes, wheelbarrows, hard hats, paper, and pencils in the dramatic play area to represent a construction site.

Arts and Crafts:

1. **Our Home**

   Provide paper, crayons, and markers for each child to draw his home. Collect all of the drawings and place them in mural fashion on a large piece of paper to create a town. To extend this activity, have the children also draw buildings in the town to extend the mural. (This activity may be limited to kindergarten children or children who have reached the representational stage of art development.)

2. **Blueprints**

   Blueprint paper, pencils, and markers should be placed in the art area. The children will enjoy marking on it. Older children may also enjoy using rulers and straight edges.

3. **Building Shapes**

   Cut out building shapes from easel paper. Place at the easel, allowing children to paint their buildings.

4. **Building Collages**

   Collect magazines with pictures of houses. Encourage children to cut or tear out pictures of buildings. The pictures can be glued on paper to create a mural.

5. **Creating Structures**

   Save half-pint milk cartons. Rinse well and allow the children to paint, color, and decorate the cartons to look like buildings.

Sensory:

1. **Wet Sand**

   Fill the sensory table with sand and add water. Provide cups, square plastic containers, bowls, etc., for children to create molds with the sand.

2. **Wood Shavings**

   Place wood shavings in the sensory table.

3. **Scented Playdough**

Prepare scented playdough and place in the sensory table.

Large Muscle:

Workbench

Call attention during group time to the wood-working bench explaining the activities that can occur there. Try to encourage the children to practice pounding nails, sawing, drilling, etc., during self-initiated play.

Field Trips/Resource People:

1. **Building Site**

Visit a local building site if available. Observe and discuss the people who are working, how buildings look, and safety. Take pictures. When the pictures are developed, post them in the classroom.

2. **Neighborhood Walk**

Take a walk around the neighborhood. Observe the various kinds of buildings. Talk about the different sizes and colors of the buildings.

3. **Library**

Visit a library. Observe how books are stored. Read the children a story while there. If possible, allow the children to check out books.

4. **Browsing at the Mall**

Visit the shopping mall. Talk about the mall being a large building that houses a variety of stores. Visit a few of the stores that may be of special interest to the children. Included may be a toy store, pet store, and a sporting goods store.

5. **Resource People**

Invite people to visit the classroom, such as:

- construction worker
- carpenter
- electrician
- architect
- decorator/designer
- plumber

Math:

1. **Weighing Bricks**

Set out balance scale and small bricks. The children can weigh and balance the bricks.

2. **Wipe-off Windows**

Cut out and laminate a variety of buildings with varying numbers of windows. Provide children with grease markers or watercolor markers. Encourage the children to count the number of windows of each building and print the corresponding numeral on the building. The numerals can be wiped off with a damp cloth. (This activity would be most appropriate for kindergarten children.)

3. **Blocks**

Set out blocks of various shapes including triangles, rectangles, and squares for the children to build with.

Social Studies:

1. **Buildings in Our Town**

Make a chart with the children's names listed vertically on the right-hand side. Across the top of the chart draw buildings or glue pictures of buildings that the children have visited. Suggestions include a theater, super-market, clinic, museum, post office, fire station, etc. At group time, ask the children what buildings they have visited. Mark the sites for each child.

2. **Unusual Buildings**

Show pictures of unusual buildings cut from various magazines, travel guides, etc. Allow the children to use their creative thinking by asking them the use of each building. All answers and possibilities should be acknowledged.

3. Occupation Match

Cut out pictures of buildings and the people who work in them. Examples would include: hospital—nurse, fire station—fire fighter. Glue these pictures to tagboard and laminate. The children should be encouraged to match each worker to the appropriate building.

Group Time (games, language):

1. Identifying Buildings

Collect several pictures of buildings that are easily identified such as school, fire station, hospital, home. Talk about each picture. Ask, "How do you know this is a school?" Discuss the function of each building. To help the children, pictures of buildings in their community can be used.

2. Exploring our Center

Explore your center. Walk around the outside and observe walls, windows, roof, etc. Explore the inside also. Check out the rooms, floor, walls, ceiling, stairs... Colors, materials and size are some things you can discuss with each. Allow the children to help make an, "Our Center Has...." chart.

Cooking:

Sugar Cookies

1 1/2 cups powdered sugar
1 cup margarine or butter
1 egg
1 teaspoon vanilla
2 1/2 cups all-purpose flour
1 teaspoon baking soda
1 teaspoon cream of tartar
granulated sugar

Mix the powdered sugar, margarine, egg, and vanilla together. Stir in the flour, baking soda, and cream of tartar. Chill, to prevent sticking while rolling the dough out. Heat the oven to 375 degrees. Roll out the dough. Cut into squares, triangles, diamonds, rectangles, circles. Sprinkle with sugar. Place on a lightly greased cookie sheet. Bake until lightly brown, about 7 to 8 minutes. Give each child 3 to 5 cookies. Allow them to make buildings with their shapes before eating.

Multimedia:

The following resources can be found in educational catalogs:

1. Jenkins, Ella. *My Street Begins At My House* [record]. Kaplan.

2. *Millie's Math House*. [IBM/Mac software, PK–1]. Edmark.

Books:

The following books can be used to complement the theme:

1. Royston, Angela, & Thompson, Graham. (1990). *Monster Building Machines*. Hauppauge, NY: Barron's Educational Series.

2. Moak, Alan. (1989). *Big City ABC*. Plattsburgh, NY: Tundra.

3. Oxenbury, H. (1991). *Shopping Trip*. New York: Dial Books for Young Readers.

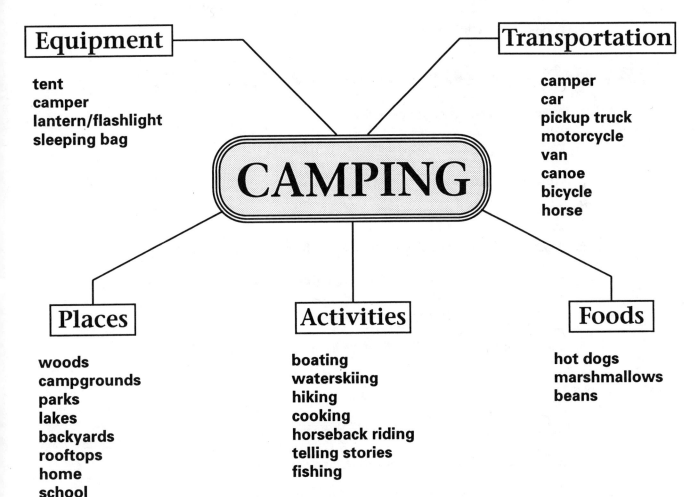

Equipment

tent
camper
lantern/flashlight
sleeping bag

Transportation

camper
car
pickup truck
motorcycle
van
canoe
bicycle
horse

CAMPING

Places

woods
campgrounds
parks
lakes
backyards
rooftops
home
school

Activities

boating
waterskiing
hiking
cooking
horseback riding
telling stories
fishing

Foods

hot dogs
marshmallows
beans

Polaroid
Education
Program

Here's an exciting new way to turn instant photography into an effective teaching tool. Refer to the full-color insert for the activity entitled *Photo Bingo*.

Theme Goals:

Through participating in the experiences provided by this theme, the children may learn:

1. Places where people camp.

2. Equipment used for camping.

3. Camping transportation.

4. Camping activities.

5. Foods we eat while camping.

Concepts for the Children to Learn:

1. A tent is a shelter used for camping.

2. We can camp in the woods or at a campground.

3. We can also camp in a park, at a lake, or in our backyard.

4. Hot dogs, marshmallows, and beans are all camping foods.

5. A camper can be driven or attached to the back of a car or pickup truck.

6. Lanterns and flashlights are sources of light used for camping.

7. A sleeping bag is a blanket used for camping.

8. Some people camp by a lake to water ski and go boating and fishing.

Vocabulary:

1. **backpack**—a zippered bag worn on one's back to carry objects.

2. **recreational vehicle**—a living and sleeping area on wheels.

3. **campfire**—a controlled fire that is made at a campground.

4. **campsite**—a place for tents and campers to park.

5. **camping**—living outdoors in sleeping bags, tents, cabins, or campers.

6. **woods**—an area with many trees.

7. **hiking**—taking a long walk.

8. **sleeping bag**—a zippered blanket.

9. **tent**—a movable shelter made out of material.

10. **lantern**—a covered light used for camping.

80

Bulletin Board

The purpose of this bulletin board is to develop recognition of colors and color words. Construct several tents out of tagboard. Make an identical set out of white tagboard. Color the first set of tents using the primary colors. Print the color names using corresponding colored markers onto the second set of tents. Laminate the materials. Staple the tents with color names to bulletin board. Punch holes in colored tents. Children can attach the tent to a push pin on the corresponding color word tent.

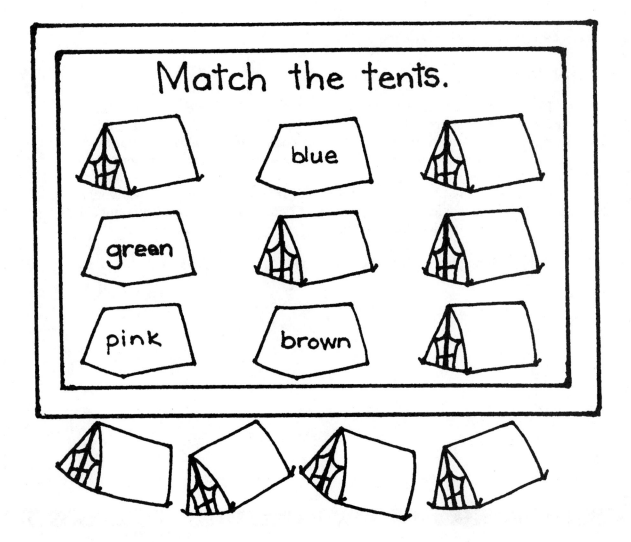

Parent Letter

Dear Parents,

With summer approaching, we will begin focusing on a fun family activity—camping! The children will become aware of items and equipment that are commonly used while camping. From listening to the children's conversations, it sounds as if many have already been camping with their family. It should be fun to hear the camping stories they will share!

At School

Some of the learning experiences planned include:

- setting up the dramatic play area with a tent, sleeping bags, and other camping items.
- singing songs around a pretend campfire.
- going on a "bear hunt" (a rhythmic chant).
- preparing foods that are eaten while camping.
- cleaning up after camping.

At Home

Help your child create a tent by draping a sheet over a table. Provide a flashlight and a blanket or sleeping bag and your child will be prepared for hours of indoor camping fun! Through dramatic play experiences children relive and clarify situations and roles. They act out how they see the world and how they view relationships among people.

If you have any photographs or slides of family camping trips, we would be delighted if you would share them with us. Contact me and we can work out a time that would be convenient for you. Thanks!

Plan a camping trip with your child today!

FIGURE 9 Having a picnic is one of the best things about camping.

Music:

1. **"A Camping We Will Go"**
(Sing to the tune of "The Farmer and the Dell")

    A camping we will go.
    A camping we will go.
    Hi ho we're off to the woods.
    A camping we will go.

    Sue will bring the tent.
    Oh Sue will bring the tent.
    Hi ho we're off to the woods.
    A camping we will go.

    Tom will bring the food.
    Oh Tom will bring the food.
    Hi ho we're off to the woods.
    A camping we will go.

    The names in the song can be changed to children's names.

2. **"Two Little Black Bears"**
(Sing to the tune of "Two Little Blackbirds")

    Two little black bears sitting on a hill
    One named Jack, one named Jill
    Run away Jack
    Run away Jill

    Come back Jack
    Come back Jill.
    Two little black bears sitting on a hill
    One named Jack, one named Jill.

3. **Campfire Songs**

    Pretend that you are sitting around a campfire. Explain to the children that often people sing their favorite songs around a campfire. Encourage the children to name their favorite songs, and then sing some of them.

Fingerplays:

BY THE CAMPFIRE

We sat around the campfire
On a chilly night
    (hug self)
Telling spooky stories
In the pale moonlight
    (look up to the sky)

Then we added some more logs,
To make the fire bright,
And sang some favorite camp songs
Together with all our might.
    (extend arms outward)
And when the fire flickered

and embers began to form.
We snuggled in our sleeping bags
all cozy, tired, and warm.
   (lie on ground, hug self)

Source: Wilmes, Liz & Dick. *Everyday Circle Times*. Building Block Publications.

FIVE LITTLE BEAR CUBS

Five little bear cubs
Eating an apple core.
One had a sore tummy
And then there were four.

Four little bear cubs
Climbing in a tree.
One fell out
And then there were three.

Three little bear cubs
Playing peek-a-boo.
One was afraid
And then there were two.

Two little bear cubs
Sitting in the sun.
One ran away
And then there was one.

One little bear cub
Sitting all alone.
He saw his mommy
And then he ran home.

Science:

1. **Scavenger Hunt**

   While outside, have the children find plants growing, insects crawling, insects flying, a plant growing on a tree, a vine, a flower, bird feathers, a root, a seed, etc.

2. **Sink/Float**

   Collect various pieces of camping equipment. Fill the water table with water and let the children test which objects sink or float. If desired make a chart.

3. **Magnifying Glasses**

   Provide magnifying glasses for looking at objects seen on a camping trip.

Dramatic Play:

1. **Camping**

   Collect various types of clothing and camping equipment and place in the dramatic play area or outdoors. Include items such as hiking boots, sweatshirts, raincoats, sleeping bags, backpacks, cooking tools, and a tent.

2. **Puppets**

   Develop a puppet corner in the dramatic play area including various animal puppets that would be seen while camping.

3. **Going Fishing**

   Set up a rocking boat or a large box in the classroom or outdoors. Prepare paper fish with paper clips attached to them. Include a fishing pole made from a wooden dowel and a long string with a magnet attached to the end.

4. **Going to the Beach**

   In the dramatic play area, set up lawn chairs, beach towels, buckets, shovels, sunglasses, etc. Weather permitting, these items could also be placed outdoors.

Arts and Crafts:

1. **Easel Ideas**

   - paint with leaves, sticks, flowers, and rocks.
   - paint with colors seen in the forest such as brown, green, yellow, and orange.
   - cut easel paper into the following shapes: tent, rabbits, chipmunks, and fish.

2. **Camping Collage**

   Collect leaves, pebbles, twigs, pine cones, etc. Provide glue and sturdy tagboard. Encourage the children to create a collage on the tagboard using the materials found while camping.

3. **Tackle Box**

   Make two holes approximately three inches apart in the center of the lid of an egg carton. To form the handle, thread a cord through the holes and tie. Paint the box. In the box, place paper clips for hooks and S-shaped styrofoam pieces for worms.

Sensory:

Sensory Table Additions

- leaves
- rocks
- pebbles
- mud and sand
- twigs
- evergreen needles and branches
- water

Large Muscle:

1. **Caves**

   Using large packing boxes or barrels placed horizontally on the playground, allow the children to pretend to be wild animals in caves.

2. **"Bear Hunt"**

   This is a chant. Prepare the children by asking them to listen and watch carefully so that they can echo back each phrase and imitate the motions as they accompany the story. Begin by patting your hands on your thighs to make foot-step sounds.

   Let's go on a bear hunt…(echo)
   We're going to find a bear…(echo)
   I've got my camera…(echo)
   Open the door, squeak…(echo)
   Walk down the walk…(echo)
   Open the gate, creak…(echo)
   Walk down the road…(echo)
   Coming to a wheat field…(echo)
   Can't go under it…(echo)
   Can't go over it…(echo)
   Have to walk through it…(echo)
       (stop patting your thighs and rub your
       hands together to make a swishing sound)
   Got through the wheat field…(echo)
   Coming to a bridge…(echo)
   Can't go under it…(echo)
   Can't go around it…(echo)

   Have to walk over it…(echo)
       (stop patting your thighs and pound your
       fists on your chest)
   Over the bridge…(echo)
   Coming to a tree…(echo)
   Can't go under it…(echo)
   Can't go around it…(echo)
   We'll have to climb it…(echo)
       (stop patting your thighs and place one fist
       on top of the other in a climbing motion)
   All the way to the top…(echo)
       (look from one side to the other)
   Do you see a bear…? (echo)
   No (shaking head)…(echo)
   We'll have to climb down…(echo)
       (place fist under fist to climb down)
   Coming to a river…(echo)
   We can't go under it…(echo)
   We can't fly over it…(echo)
   Can't go around it…(echo)
   We'll have to cross it…(echo)
   Let's get in the boat…(echo)
   And row, row, row…
       (all sing "Row, Row, Row Your Boat"
       accompanied with rowing motions)
   We got across the river…(echo)
   We're coming to a cave…(echo)
   We can't go under it…(echo)
   We can't go over it…(echo)
   Can't go around it…(echo)
   We'll have to go in it…(echo)
   Let's tip-toe
       (use fingertips to pat thighs)
       (whisper)
   It's dark inside…(echo)
   It's very dark inside…(echo)
   I can see two eyes…(echo)
   And a big furry body…(echo)
   And I feel a wet nose…(echo)
       (Yell)
   It's a BEAR….RUN….(echo)
       (patting hands very quickly)
   Run back to the river,
   Row the boat across the river,
       (rowing motion)
   Run to the tree
   Climb up and climb down
       (do climbing motion)
   Run to the bridge and cross it
       (pat chest)
   Run through the wheat field
       (swish hands together)
   Run up the road

Open the gate…it creaks,
 (open gate)
Run up the walk,
Open the door...it squeaks,
 (open door)
SLAM IT!
 (clap hands together)

Source: Wirth, Marion, Stassevitch, Verna, Shotwell, Rita, & Stemmler, Patricia. *Musical Games, Fingerplays and Rhythmic Activities for Early Childhood.* Parker Publishing Co. Inc.

Field Trips:

1. **Department Store**

   Visit a department store or a sporting goods store where camping tents and other equipment are displayed.

2. **Picnic**

   Pack a picnic lunch or snack and take it to an area campground.

3. **Camper Salesperson**

   Visit a recreational vehicle dealer and tour a large mobile home.

Math:

Camping Scavenger Hunt

Before the children go outdoors, instruct them to find things on your playground that you would see while camping. Sort them and count them when they bring them into the classroom (five twigs, three rocks, etc.).

Social Studies:

1. **Pictures**

   Collect pictures of different campsites. Share them by displaying them in the classroom at the children's eye level.

2. **Camping Experiences**

   At group time ask if any of the children have been camping. Let them tell the rest of the children what they did while they were camping. Ask where they slept, what they ate, where the bathroom was, etc.

Group Time (games, language):

1. **What's Missing**

   Have different pieces of camping equipment available to show the children. Include a canteen, portable stove, sleeping bag, cooking tools, lantern, etc. Discuss each item, and then have the children close their eyes. Take one of the objects away and then have the children guess which object is missing.

2. **Camping Safety**

   Discuss camping safety. Include these points:

   - always put out fires before going to sleep.
   - swim in safe areas and with a partner.
   - when walking, or hiking away from your campsite, always have an adult with you.
   - always wear a life jacket in the boat.

3. **Pack the Backpack**

   Bring into the classroom a large backpack. Also have many camping items available such as sweatshirts, flashlights, lanterns, foods, raincoats, etc. The teacher gives the children instructions that they are going to pretend to go on a hike to the beach. What is one thing they will need to bring along? Why? Continue until all of the children have had a chance to contribute.

Cooking:

1. **S'Mores**

   Place a large marshmallow on a square graham cracker. Next place a square of sweet chocolate on top of the marshmallow. After this, place the graham cracker on a baking sheet into a 250-degree oven for about 5 minutes or until the chocolate starts to melt. Remove the s'more and press a second graham cracker square on top of the chocolate. Let cool for a few minutes, and serve while still slightly warm.

2. **Venezuela Breakfast Cocoa**

   1/4 cup water
   3 tablespoons cocoa
   2 tablespoons sugar
   2 cups milk
   1 teaspoon vanilla

   1. Bring the water to a boil in a saucepan.

   2. Stir in the cocoa and sugar until they are blended. Turn the heat very low.
   3. Slowly pour the milk into the saucepan with the cocoa mixture. Stir steadily to keep the mixture from burning. Continue cooking the mixture over low heat for about 2 minutes. Do not let it boil or skin will form on the top.
   4. When the cocoa is hot, remove it from the stove and stir in the vanilla.
   5. Carefully pour the cocoa into the cups. Serve warm.

   Source: Touff, Terry, & Ratner, Marilyn. (1974). *Many Hands Cooking*. New York: Thomas Y. Crowell Company.

Multimedia:

The following resources can be found in educational catalogs:

1. Wood, Lucille. *Camping in the Mountains* [record].

2. *Sounds Around* [30-minute video]. Bo Beep Production.

3. *The Backyard* [Mac software, PK–2]. Broderbund.

Books:

The following books can be used to complement the theme:

1. Henkes, Kevin. (1989). *Bailey Goes Camping*. New York: Puffin Books.

2. Rey, Margaret, & Shalleck, Alan J. (1985). *Curious George Goes Hiking*. Boston: Houghton Mifflin Company.

3. Cooke, Tom (Illus.). (1990). *Hide and Seek Camping Trip: A Sesame Street Book*. New York: Random House Books for Young Readers.

4. Allen, Julia. (1987). *My First Camping Trip*. Provo, UT: ARO Publishing Co.

5. Eeebs, Aunt. (1991). *The Happy Campers*. Houston, TX: Rivercrest Industries.

6. Hoban, Lillian. (1993). *Arthur's Campout*. New York: Harper Collins Children's Books.

7. Roche, P.K. (1991). *Webster and Arnold Go Camping*. New York: Puffin Books

8. Singer, Marilyn. (1992). *In My Tent*. New York: Macmillian Children's Book Group.

9. Ziefert, Harriet. (1990). *Harry Goes to Day Camp*. New York: Viking Children's Books.

10. Hayward, Linda. (1990). *Elmo Goes to Day Camp*. New York: Random House.

11. Hort, Lenny. (1991). *How Many Stars in the Sky?* New York: Tambourine Books.

12. Fife, Dale H. (1991). *The Empty Lot*. Boston, MA: Little Brown & Company and Sierra Club Books.

13. Jeffers, Susan. (1990). *Brother Eagle, Sister Sky*. New York: Dial.

14. Ryder, Joanne. (1991). *When the Woods Hum*. New York: Morrow Junior Books.

15. Brett, Jan. (1987). *Goldilocks and the Three Bears*. New York: G. P. Putnam.

16. Rylant, Cynthia. (1986). *Night in the Country*. New York: Bradbury Press.

17. Oughton, Jerrie. (1992). *How the Stars Fell into the Sky*. Boston, MA: Houghton Mifflin.

18. Taylor, Jane. (1992). *Twinkle, Twinkle, Little Star*. New York: Morrow.

19. Skidmore, Steve. (1991). *What a Load of Trash*. Brookfield, CA: The Millbrook Press.

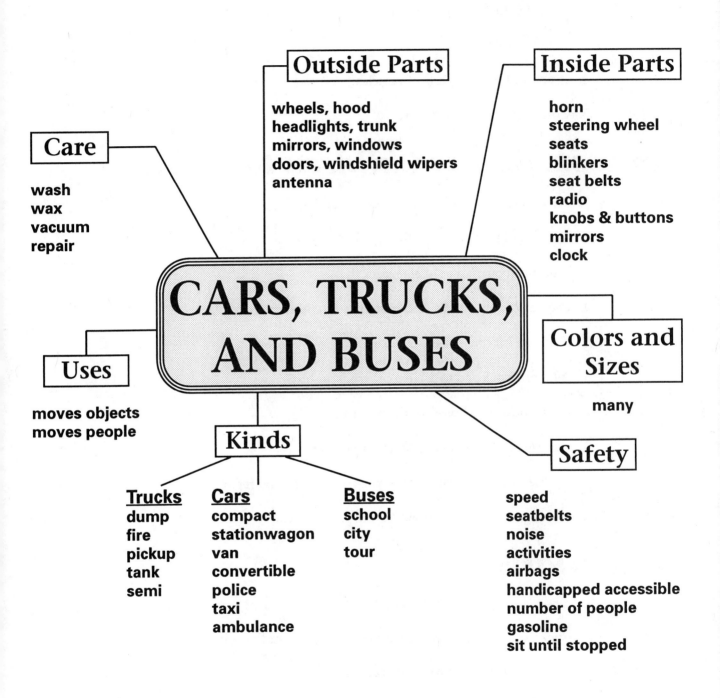

Outside Parts

wheels, hood
headlights, trunk
mirrors, windows
doors, windshield wipers
antenna

Inside Parts

horn
steering wheel
seats
blinkers
seat belts
radio
knobs & buttons
mirrors
clock

Care

wash
wax
vacuum
repair

CARS, TRUCKS, AND BUSES

Colors and Sizes

many

Uses

moves objects
moves people

Kinds

Safety

Trucks	**Cars**	**Buses**	speed
dump	compact	school	seatbelts
fire	stationwagon	city	noise
pickup	van	tour	activities
tank	convertible		airbags
semi	police		handicapped accessible
	taxi		number of people
	ambulance		gasoline
			sit until stopped

Here's an exciting new way to turn instant photography
into an effective teaching tool. Refer to the full-color
insert for the activity entitled Photo Peek-A-Boo.

Theme Goals:

Through participating in the experiences provided by this theme, the children may learn:

1. Kinds of cars, trucks, and buses.

2. Care of vehicles.

3. Uses of vehicles.

4. Inside and outside parts of vehicles.

5. Colors and sizes of vehicles.

Concepts for the Children to Learn:

1. There are many kinds of cars, trucks, and buses.

2. Trucks and buses are usually bigger than cars.

3. Trucks can be used to haul objects.

4. People use cars, trucks, and buses to move from place to place.

5. Compact cars are small.

6. A license is needed to drive a car, truck, or bus.

7. Cars, trucks, and buses need gas to run.

8. Gas can be obtained at a filling station.

9. Vehicles need to be vacuumed, washed, waxed, and repaired.

10. Headlights, mirrors, and wheels are parts of a car.

Vocabulary:

1. **car**—vehicle used for moving people.

2. **truck**—a wheeled vehicle used to move people and big objects.

3. **bus**—a vehicle that carries many people.

4. **driver**—operates the vehicle.

5. **passenger**—the rider.

6. **fuel**—gas, diesel, etc., used to produce power.

7. **gas**—produces power to move a vehicle.

Bulletin Board

The purpose of the bulletin board is to reinforce color recognition and matching skills, as well as develop one-to-one correspondence concepts. Construct garage shapes out of tagboard. Color each garage a different color and hang on the bulletin board. Hang a push pin in the center of each garage. Next, construct the same number of cars as garages from tagboard. Color each car a different color to correspond with the colors of the garages. Use a paper punch to make a hole in each car. The children can park each car in its corresponding colored garage.

Parent Letter

Dear Parents,

Cars, trucks, and buses—these are all transportation vehicles that your child sees on a regular basis. We are beginning a unit on "Cars, Trucks and Buses." Through participating in the planned experiences, the children will learn that there are many colors, sizes, and kinds of cars, trucks and buses. They will also become aware of the occupations associated with the vehicles including taxi drivers, bus drivers, and mechanics.

At School

Some of the activities planned for this unit include:

- painting with small cars at the art table.
- looking at many books about trucks, buses, and cars.
- setting up a gas station in the dramatic play area.
- a visit with Officer Lewis from the police department, who will show the children his squad car at 10:30 on Thursday.

At Home

You can foster the concepts of this unit at home by taking your child with you the next time you need to buy gas for your car. There are many different types of trucks and cars to observe at the filling station. Also, provide soapy water and a sponge and let your child help you wash the family car. Children enjoy taking part in grown-up activities and this helps to build a sense of responsibility and self-esteem.

Enjoy your child as you explore concepts related to cars, trucks, and buses.

FIGURE 10 Time to race cars.

Fingerplays:

OUR FAMILY CAR

This is our family car
   (make fists as if holding a steering wheel)
The engine purrs like new.
Four wheels and a body,
   (hold up four fingers)
It is painted blue.

Dad and Mom use it for business
   (hold fists as if holding a steering wheel)
Or to drive us to the store.
We take it on vacation
You couldn't ask for more.
   (shake head "no")

In the winter weather
If we should miss the bus,
   (make sad face)
We can still get to our school,
In the family car we trust.
   (hold fists as if holding a steering wheel)

Source: Wilmes, Liz & Dick. (1983). *Everyday
Circle Times*. Building Block Publishers, Illinois.

WINDSHIELD WIPER

I'm a windshield wiper
   (bend arm at elbow with fingers pointing up)

This is how I go
   (move arm to left and right, pivoting at
   elbow)
Back and forth, back and forth
   (continue back and forth motion)
In the rain and snow.
   (continue back and forth motion)

HERE IS A CAR

Here is a car, shiny and bright.
   (cup one hand and place on other palm)
This is the windshield that lets in the light.
   (hands open, fingertips touching)
Here are wheels that go round and round.
   (two fists)
I sit in the back seat and make not a sound.
   (sit quietly with hands in lap)

THE CAR RIDE

(Left arm, held out bent, is road; right fist is
car.)

"Vroom!" says the engine
   (place car on left shoulder)
As the driver starts the car.
   (shake car)

"Mmmm," say the windows
As the driver takes it far.
   (travel over upper arm)

"Errr," say the tires
As it rounds the final bend,
    (turn at elbow, proceed over forearm)

"Ahhh," says the driver
As his trip comes to an end.
    (stop car on left flattened palm)

SCHOOL BUS

I go to the bus stop each day
    (walk one hand across table)
Where the bus comes to take us away.
    (stop, have other hand wait also)
We stand single file
    (one behind the other)
And walk down the aisle
    (step up imaginary steps onto bus)
When the bus driver talks, we obey.

Science:

1. **License Plates**

   Collect license plates from different states and different vehicles and place them on a table for the children to explore.

2. **Feely Box**

   Put transportation toys in a feely box. Include cars, trucks, and buses. Individually let the children feel inside the box and identify the type of toy.

Dramatic Play:

1. **Filling Station**

   Provide cardboard boxes for cars and hoses for the gas pumps. Also, make available play money and steering wheels.

2. **Bus**

   Set up a bus situation by lining up chairs in one or two long rows. Provide a steering wheel for the driver. A money bucket and play money can also be provided. If a steering wheel is unavailable, heavy round pizza cardboards can be used to improvise.

3. **Taxi**

   Set up two rows of chairs side by side to represent a taxi. Use a pizza cardboard, or other round object, as the steering wheel. Provide a telephone, dress-up clothes for the passengers, and a hat for the driver. A "TAXI" sign can also be placed by the chairs to invite play.

4. **Fire Truck**

   Contact the local fire chief and ask to use old hoses, fire hats, and fire fighter clothing.

Arts and Crafts:

1. **License Plate Rubbings**

   Place paper on top of a license plate. Using the side of a large crayon, rub across the top of the license plate.

2. **Car Painting**

   Provide several small plastic cars, trucks, and large sheets of white paper. Also, have available low, flat pans of thin tempera paint. Encourage the children to take the cars and trucks and roll the wheels in the paint. They can then transfer the car to their own paper and make car or truck tracks on the paper.

3. **Designing Cars**

   Provide the children with large appliance-sized cardboard boxes. To protect the floor surface, place a large sheet of plastic underneath. Provide the children with paint, markers, and collage materials to decorate the boxes as cars. When the cars dry, they can be moved into the block building, dramatic play areas, or outdoor area.

4. **Scrapbooks or Collages**

   Provide magazines for children to cut or tear out pictures of cars and trucks to make a collage or small scrapbook.

Sensory:

Sensory Table Additions

- cars and trucks with wet sand
- baby oil and water

Large Muscle:

1. **"Fill 'er Up"**

   The trikes, wagons, and scooters can be used outside on the playground. A gas pump can be constructed out of an old cardboard box with an attached hose.

2. **Car, Car, Truck**

   Play this simple variation of "Duck, Duck, Goose" by substituting the words, "Car, Car, Truck."

3. **Wash a Car**

   If possible, wash a compact-size car. Provide a hose, sponges, brushes, a bucket, and soapy water. If an actual car is not available, children can wash tricycles, bicycles, scooters, and wagons.

Field Trips/Resource People:

1. **City Bus**

   Take the children for a ride around town on a city bus. When boarding, allow each child to place his own money in the meter. Observe the length of the bus. While inside, watch how the bus driver operates the bus. Also, have a school bus driver visit and tell about the job and the importance of safety on a bus.

2. **Taxi Driver**

   Invite a taxi driver to visit and show the features of the taxi.

3. **Patrol Car**

   Invite a police officer to bring a squad car to the center. The radio, siren, and flashing lights can be demonstrated. Let the children sit in the car.

4. **Fire Truck**

   Invite a local fire fighter to bring a fire truck to the center. Let the children climb in the truck and observe the parts.

5. **Semi-truck Driver**

   Invite a semi driver to bring the truck to school. Observe the size, number of wheels, and parts of the cab. Let the children sit in the cab.

6. **Ambulance**

   Invite an ambulance driver to bring the vehicle to school. Let the children inspect the contents.

Math:

1. **Cars and Garages**

   Car garages can be constructed out of empty half-pint milk cartons. Collect and carefully wash the milk cartons. Cut out one side and write a numeral starting with one on each carton. Next, collect a corresponding number of small matchbox cars. Attach a strip of paper with a numeral from one to the appropriate number on each car's top. The children can drive each car into the garage with the corresponding numeral.

2. **License Plate Match**

   Construct two sets of identical license plates. Print a pattern of letters or numerals on each set. Mix them up. Children can try to match the pairs.

3. **Car, Truck, or Bus Sequencing**

   Cut out various-sized cars, trucks, or buses and laminate. Children can sequence them from largest to smallest and vice versa.

4. **Sorting**

Construct cars, trucks, and buses of different colors and laminate. Children can sort according to color.

Social Studies:

Discussion on Safety

Have a group discussion on safety when riding in a car. Allow children to come up with suggestions. Write them down on a chart and display in classroom during the unit. The addition of pictures or drawings would be helpful for younger children.

Group Time (games, language):

1. **Thank-You Note**

Write a thank-you note to a resource person. Allow children to dictate and sign it.

2. **Red Light, Green Light**

Select one child to pretend to be a traffic light. The traffic light places his back to children lined up at the other end of the room. When the traffic light says, "Green Light," or holds up green paper, the other children attempt to creep up on the traffic light. At any time the traffic light can say, "Red Light," or hold up a red paper and quickly turn around. Creeping children must freeze. Any child caught moving is sent back to the starting line. Play continues until one child reaches the traffic light. This child becomes the new traffic light.

Multimedia:

The following resource can be found in educational catalogs:

Car Songs [record]. Kimbo Records.

Cooking:

1. **Cracker Wheels**

For this recipe each child will need:

4 round crackers
1/2 hot dog
1/2 a slice of 4" x 4" cheese

Slice hot dogs and place on a cracker. Place cheese over the top. Place in oven at 350 degrees for 3 to 5 minutes or microwave for 30 seconds. Let cool and eat.

2. **Greek Honey Twists**

3 eggs, beaten
2 tablespoons vegetable oil
1/2 teaspoon baking powder
1/4 teaspoon salt
1 3/4 to 2 cups all-purpose flour
vegetable oil
1/4 cup honey
1 tablespoon water
ground cinnamon to taste

Mix eggs, 2 tablespoons oil, baking powder, and salt in a large bowl. Gradually stir in enough flour to make a very stiff dough. Knead 5 minutes. Roll half the dough at a time as thin as possible on well-floured surface with a stockinet-covered rolling pin. Cut into wheel shapes. Cover with damp towel to prevent drying.

Heat 2 to 3 inches of oil to 375 degrees. Fry 3 to 5 twists at a time until golden brown, turning once, about 45 seconds on each side. Drain on paper towels. Heat honey and water to boiling; boil 1 minute. Cool slightly. Drizzle over twists; sprinkle with cinnamon. Makes 32 twists.

Source: *Betty Crocker's International Cookbook.* (1980). New York: Random House.

Books:

The following books can be used to complement the theme:

1. Rockwell, Anne. (1986). *Things That Go*. New York: E. P. Dutton, Inc.

2. *Fill It Up! All About Service Stations*. (1985). New York: Thomas Y. Crowell.

3. Kunhardt, Edith T. (1985). *The Taxi Book*. New York: Golden Books.

4. Geis, Darlen. (1987). *Rattle-Rattle Dump Truck*. Los Angeles: Price/Stern/Sloan.

5. Petrie, Catherine. (1987). *Joshua James Likes Trucks*. Chicago: Children's Press.

6. Royston, Angela. (1991). *Cars*. New York: Macmillan Children's Book Group.

7. Barrett, Norman. (1990). *Custom Cars*. New York: Franklin Watts, Inc.

8. Aldog, Kurt. (1992). *Some Things Never Change*. New York: Macmillan Children's Books.

9. Greenblat, Rodney A. (1990). *Uncle Wizzmo's New Used Car*. New York: Harper Collins Children's Books.

10. Owen, Annie. (1991). *Bumper to Bumper*. New York: Alfred A. Knopf, Books for Young Readers.

11. Ross, K. K. (1990). *The Little Red Car*. New York: Random House for Young Readers.

12. Stamper, Judith. (1990). *What's It Like to Be a Bus Driver*. Mahwah, NJ: Troll Associates.

13. Grosset and Dunlop Staff. (1991). *Wheels on the Bus*. New York: Putnam Publishing Group.

14. Zelinsky, Paul O. (1990). *Wheels on the Bus: With Pictures that Move*. New York: Dutton Children's Books.

15. Herman, Gail. (1990). *Make Way for Trucks: Big Machines on Wheels*. New York: Random Books for Young Readers.

16. Strickland, Paul. (1990). *All About Trucks*. Milwaukee: Gareth Stevens, Inc.

17. Wolf, Sallie. (1992). *Peter's Trucks*. Morton Grove, IL: Albert Whitman and Co.

18. Howard, Elizabeth Fitzgerald. (1988). *The Train to Lulu's*. New York: Bradbury Press.

19. Siebert, Diane. (1990). *Train Song*. New York: Thomas Y. Crowell.

20. Robbins, Sandra. (1990). *Big Annie*. New York: Berrent Publishers.

21. Cole, Joanna. (1986). *The Magic School Bus at the Waterworks*. New York: Scholastic, Inc.

22. Schubert, Ingrid, & Schubert, Dieter. (1985). *The Magic Bubble Trip*. Brooklyn, NY: Kane/Miller.

23. Crews, Donald. (1987). *Flying*. New York: Greenwillow.

24. Pomerantz, Charlotte. (1987). *How Many Trucks Can a Tow Truck Tow?* New York: Random House.

25. Powers, Mary Ellen. (1986). *Our Teacher's in a Wheelchair*. Niles, IL: Albert Whitman.

26. Crews, Donald. (1992). *Freight Train*. New York: Morrow.

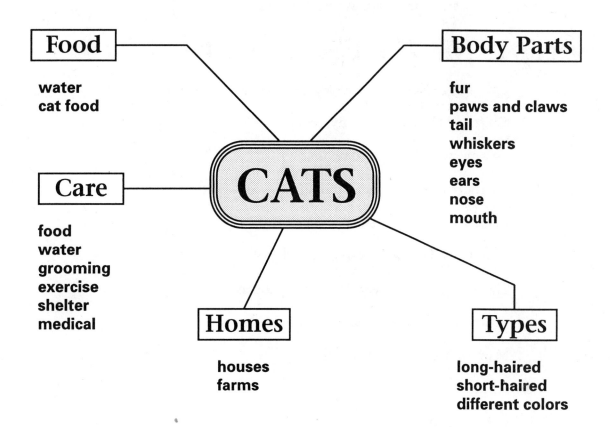

Food

water
cat food

Body Parts

fur
paws and claws
tail
whiskers
eyes
ears
nose
mouth

Care

food
water
grooming
exercise
shelter
medical

CATS

Homes

houses
farms

Types

long-haired
short-haired
different colors

Polaroid
Education
Program

Here's an exciting new way to turn instant photography into an effective teaching tool. Refer to the full-color insert for the activity entitled *Photo Expectations*.

Theme Goals:

Through participating in the experiences provided by this theme, the children may learn:

1. Types of cats.

2. Body parts of a cat.

3. Cats need special care.

4. What cats eat, drink, and where they live.

Concepts for the Children to Learn:

1. Cats can be black, brown, white, grey, yellow, or calico.

2. Cats use their claws for many things.

3. Cats meow and purr to communicate.

4. Cats have legs, eyes, ears, a mouth, nose, and a tail.

5. Cats have fur on their skin.

6. Cats should be handled carefully and gently.

7. There are many different sizes and types of cats.

8. Cats need food, water, and exercise everyday.

9. Many different people help cats.

10. A kitten is a baby cat.

11. Cats like to play.

Vocabulary:

1. **kitten**—a baby cat.

2. **pet**—an animal kept for pleasure.

3. **paw**—the cat's foot.

4. **veterinarian**—an animal doctor.

5. **leash**—a rope, chain, or cord that attaches to a collar.

6. **collar**—a band worn around the cat's neck.

7. **whiskers**—stiff hair growing around the cat's nose, mouth, and eyes.

8. **coat**—hair covering the skin.

Bulletin Board

The purpose of this bulletin board is to promote visual discrimination and pattern matching skills. Construct cats' bodies and heads out of tagboard, coloring each a different color and fur pattern. Laminate all pieces. Attach cat bodies to the bulletin board. Children then match the heads to the corresponding body.

Parent Letter

Dear Parents,

We have many exciting activities planned at school as we begin our study on cats. We will be learning about a cat's body structure, how to care and feed our cats, and different types of cats.

At School

Some of the learning experiences planned include:

- taking a field trip to the veterinarian's office.
- making a chart of different types of cats.
- setting up a cat grooming area in dramatic play.

At Home

We will be learning the fingerplay "Two Little Kittens." You may want to try it with your child at home:

Two little kittens found a ball of yarn
   (hold up 2 fingers…cup hands together to form a ball)
As they were playing near a barn.
   (bring hands together pointed upward for barn)
One little kitten jumped in the hay,
   (hold up 1 finger…make jumping then wiggling motion)
The other little kitten ran away.
   (make running motion with other hand)

Fingerplays and rhymes help children develop language vocabulary and sequencing skills. The actions that often accompany fingerplays develop fine motor development.

Have fun with your child!

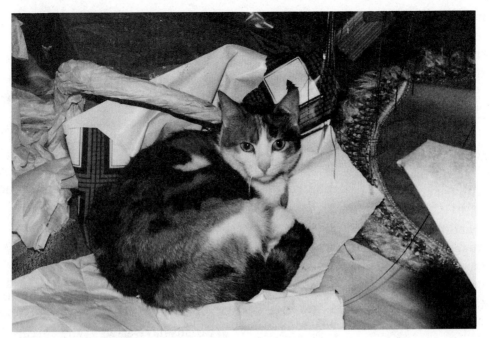

FIGURE 11 What is your favorite breed of cat?

Music:

1. **"Two Little Kittens"**
   (Sing to the tune of "Two Little Blackbirds")

   Two little kittens sitting on a hill
   One named Jack, one named Jill
   Run away Jack, run away Jill
   Come back Jack, come back Jill
   Two little kittens sitting on a hill
   One named Jack, one named Jill.

2. **"Kitty"**
   (Sing to the tune of "Bingo")

   I have a cat. She's very shy.
   But she comes when I call K-I-T-T-Y
   K-I-T-T-Y
   K-I-T-T-Y
   K-I-T-T-Y
   and Kitty is her name-o.

   Variation: Let children think of other names.

Fingerplays:

MRS. KITTY'S DINNER

   Mrs. Kitty, sleek and fat,
      (put thumb up with fingers folded on right hand)

With her kittens four.
   (hold up four fingers on right hand)
Went to sleep upon the mat
   (make a fist)
By the kitchen door.

Mrs. Kitty heard a noise.
Up she jumped in glee.
   (thumb up on right hand)
"Kittens, maybe that's a mouse?
   (all 5 fingers on right hand up)
Let's go and see!"

Creeping, creeping, creeping on.
   (slowly sneaking with 5 fingers on floor)
Silently they stole.
But the little mouse had gone
   (mouse is thumb on left hand)
Back into his hole.

A KITTEN

A kitten is fast asleep under the chair.
   (thumb under hands)
And Donald can't find her.
He's looked everywhere.
   (fingers circling eyes to look)
Under the table
   (peek under one hand)
And under the bed
   (peek under other hand)

He looked in the corner, and then Donald said,
"Come Kitty, come Kitty, this milk is for you."
    (curve hands for dish)
And out came Kitty calling "mew, mew, mew."

THREE CATS

One little cat and two little cats
went out for a romp one day.
    (hold up 1 finger and then 2 fingers with
    other hand)
One little cat and two little cats
make how many cats at play?
    (ask how many that makes)
Three little cats had lots of fun
till growing tired away ran _____?
    (take 1 finger away and ask how many ran
    away)
I really think that he was most unkind
to the _____ little cats that were left behind.
    (ask how many are left)

KITTEN IS HIDING

A kitten is hiding under a chair,
    (hide one thumb in other hand)
I looked and looked for her everywhere.
    (peer about with hand on forehead)
Under the table and under the bed,
    (pretend to look)
I looked in the corner and then I said,
"Come Kitty, come Kitty, I have milk for you."
    (cup hands to make dish and extend)
Kitty came running and calling, "Mew, mew."
    (run fingers up arm)

TWO LITTLE KITTENS

Two little kittens found a ball of yarn
    (hold up 2 fingers…cup hands together to
    form a ball)
As they were playing near a barn.
    (bring hands together pointed upward for
    barn)
One little kitten jumped in the hay,
    (hold up one finger…make jumping, then
    wiggling motion)
The other little kitten ran away.
    (make running motion with other hand)

Science:

1. Provide a scale and different cat items (such as cat toys, collar, food dish, etc.) to weigh.

2. During the social studies activity, "Share Your Cat," arrange for a cat and a kitten to be in the classroom at the same time. With the help of parents, weigh the cats or kittens and discuss with the children the differences.

3. Set out a magnifying glass to observe different kinds of dry cat food.

4. Talk about a cat who has claws and one that is declawed. Ask various questions such as: Why do cats have claws? Why are cats declawed? Where do cats go to be declawed? etc.

5. Discuss the various parts of a cat's body and how they can protect the cat. (Examples: fur, whiskers, etc.)

6. Discuss what a cat's body does when it feels danger.

Dramatic Play:

1. **Cat Grooming**

    Provide the children with empty shampoo and conditioner bottles, brushes, combs, ribbons, collars, plastic bathtub, towels, and stuffed animal cats.

2. **Veterinarian's Office**

    Provide various medical supplies such as a stethoscope, bandages, and thermometers along with stuffed cats.

3. **Cats!**

    Let children pretend they are cats by using cat masks or costumes. Also, you may want to try using yarn balls, boxes to curl up in, and empty cat food boxes. Allow the children to act out the story, "The Three Little Kitttens" or other cat stories.

4. **Circus or Zoo**

Lions, cheetas, panthers, leopards, and tigers are also cats. Use large boxes for cages.

Arts and Crafts:

1. **Kitty Collage**

Let children find and cut or tear out pictures of cats from greeting cards and magazines. Children can then paste their cats on pieces of construction paper.

2. **Pom Pom Painting**

Set out several different colors of tempera paint. Using pom-pom balls, let children create their own designs on construction paper.

3. **Cat Mask**

Using paper plates or paper bags along with paper scraps, yarn, crayons, scissors, and paint, let the children design cat masks.

4. **Paw Prints**

Let children pretend they are cats using their hands and paint to make prints.

Large Muscle:

1. **Bean Bag Toss**

Make a cat shape on plywood with holes of different sizes cut out. The children can try from varying distances to throw bean bags through the holes.

2. **Yarn Balls**

Set up baskets at varying distances from a masking tape line on the floor. Toss yarn balls into the baskets.

3. **Cat Pounce**

Children pretend to be cats and pounce from one line to another.

4. **Climbing Cats**

Bring into the classroom or outside a wooden climber. The children can pretend to be cats and climb on the climber.

5. **Cat Movements**

Write down all the words that describe how cats move. Allow the children to demonstrate the movements. Also, use music in the background.

Field Trips/Resource People:

1. **Pet Store**

Take a field trip to a pet store. Ask the manager how to care for cats. Observe the different types of cats, cages, collars, leashes, and food.

2. **Veterinarian's Office**

Take a field trip to a veterinarian's office or animal hospital. Compare the similarities and differences to a doctor's office.

3. **Variety Store**

Visit a variety store and observe pet accessories.

4. **Resource People**

Invite resource people. Suggestions include:

- cat groomer
- humane society representative
- pet store owner
- veterinarian
- parents to bring in pet cats

Math:

1. **Matching Game**

Have the children match the number of cats on a card to the correct numeral. (Cat stickers work well.)

2. How Many Paper Clips

Make several different sizes of cats out of tag-board. Children measure each cat with the paper clips.

3. Whisker Count

Make several cat faces with one numeral on each face. Children attach the correct number of whiskers (pipe cleaners, felt, paper strips, etc.) according to the numeral on the cat.

Social Studies:

1. Chart

Make a chart with the children of different types of cats.

2. Displays

Display different pictures of cats around the room.

3. Share Your Cat

Invite the children and the parents to bring in a pet cat on specified days. (Have your camera ready! Take pictures and display them on a bulletin board.) Encourage the children to talk about their cat's colors, likes, body, etc.

4. Cat Safety

Discuss cat safety with the class. Items that may be discussed include why cats use their claws, what to do if you find a stray cat, the uses of collars and leashes.

Group Time (games, language):

1. Copy Cats

Have one child be the cat and clap a rhythm for the group. The other children listen and then be the copy cats. They clap the same rhythm as the cat did. Another child now becomes the cat and creates a rhythm for the copy cats to imitate.

2. Nice Kitty

One child is chosen to be the kitty. The rest of the children sit in a circle. As the kitty goes to each child in the circle he pets the kitty and says, "nice kitty," but the kitty makes no reply. Finally, the kitty meows in response to one child. That child must run around the outside of the circle as the kitty chases him. If the child returns to his original place before the kitty can catch him, the child becomes the new kitty. This activity is appropriate for four-, five-, and six-year-old children.

3. Listen Carefully

The children should sit in a circle. One child is selected to be the mother cat. After mother cat has left the room, choose several other children to be kittens. All of the children cover their mouths with both hands and the kittens start saying, "meow, meow, meow." When the mother cat returns she should listen carefully to find all of her kittens. When she has found them all, another child should be chosen mother cat and the game can continue.

4. Farmer in the Dell

The children can play "Farmer in the Dell."

Cooking:

1. Cheese Cat

English muffins
cheese slices

Allow the children to cut out a cat face on their own slice of cheese. Put the cheese on top of the English muffin and bake long enough to melt the cheese.

2. Cat Face

1/2 peach (head)
almonds (ears)
red hots (eyes)
raisin (nose)
stick pretzels (whiskers)

Create a cat face using the ideas above or a variety of other items.

Multimedia:

The following resources can be found in educational catalogs:

1. Crume, Marion. *I Like Cats* [record].

2. Carr, Rachel. "Stretch Like a Cat" on *Be a Frog, a Bird or a Tree* [record].

3. Sharon, Lois, & Bram. "The Cat Came Back" on *Singing, Swinging* [record].

4. Seeger, Pete. "My Little Kitty" on *Birds, Beasts, Bugs and Little Fishes* [record].

5. *Kittens, Kids and a Frog* [Apple/IBM software (Ages: 6–7)]. Hartley.

6. *Sugar and Snails and Kitty-Cat Tails* [Mac/Apple software, PK–2]. Entrex.

Books:

The following books can be used to complement the theme:

1. Brown, Ruth. (1986). *Our Cat Flossie*. New York: E. P. Dutton.

2. Kunhardt, Edith. (1987). *Kittens, Kittens, Kittens*. New York: Golden Books.

3. Matthias, Catherine. (1987). *I Love Cats*. Chicago: Children's Press.

4. Kanao, Keiko. (1987). *Kitten up a Tree*. New York: Alfred A. Knopf.

5. McCue, Lisa. (1990). *Kittens Love*. New York: Random House.

6. Mantegazza, Giovanna. (1992). *The Cat*. Boyds Mills Press.

7. Martin, Bengt. (1992). *Olaf the Ship's Cat*. Checkerboard.

8. Parnell, Peter. (1989). *Cats from Away*. New York: Macmillan.

9. Pittman, Helena C. (1990). *Miss Hindy's Cats*. Minneapolis: Carolrhoda Books.

10. Polushkin, Maria. (1990). *Here's That Kitten!* New York: Macmillan.

11. Dupont, Marie. (1991). *Your First Kitten*. Neptune City, NJ: TFH Publications.

12. Nottridge, Rhoda. (1990). *Let's Look at Big Cats*. New York: Franklin Watts, Inc.

13. Petty, Kate. (1992). *Baby Animals: Kittens*. Hauppauge, NY: Barron's Educational Series, Inc.

14. Piers, Helen. (1992). *Taking Care of Your Cat*. Hauppauge, NY: Barron's Educational Series, Inc.

15. Carle, Eric. (1991). *Have You Seen My Cat?* Saxonville, MA: Picture Book Studio, Ltd.

16. Ehlert, Lois. (1990). *Feathers for Lunch*. San Diego: Harcourt Brace.

17. Hutchins, Hazel. (1992). *And You Can Be the Cat*. Buffalo, NY: Firefly Books, Ltd.

18. Moncure, Jane. (1990). *Caring for My Kitty*. Mankato, MN: Children's World, Inc.

19. Farjeon, Eleanor. (1990). *Cats Sleep Anywhere*. New York: Harper Collins Children's Books.

20. Kherdian, David, & Hogrogian, Nonny. (1990). *The Cat's Midsummer Jamboree*. New York: Philomel Books.

21. Bryan, Ashley. (1985). *The Cat's Purr*. New York: Atheneum.

22. Marzello, Jean. (1990). *Pretend You're a Cat*. New York: Dial Books for Young Readers.

23. Simon, Seymour. (1991). *Big Cats*. New York: Harper Collins.

24. Larrick, Nancy (Ed.). (1988). *Cats Are Cats*. New York: Philomel Books.

25. Kuklin, Susan. (1988). *Taking My Cat to the Vet*. New York: Bradbury Press.

26. Aylesworth, Jim. (1989). *Mother Halverson's New Cat*. New York: Macmillan.

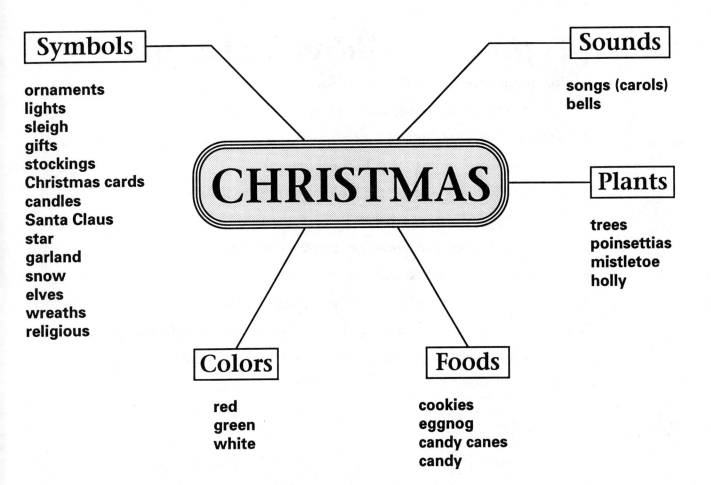

Symbols

ornaments
lights
sleigh
gifts
stockings
Christmas cards
candles
Santa Claus
star
garland
snow
elves
wreaths
religious

CHRISTMAS

Sounds

songs (carols)
bells

Plants

trees
poinsettias
mistletoe
holly

Colors

red
green
white

Foods

cookies
eggnog
candy canes
candy

Here's an exciting new way to turn instant photography into an effective teaching tool. Refer to the full-color insert for the activity entitled Tell Me A Story.

Theme Goals:

Through participating in the experiences provided by this theme, the children may learn:

1. Christmas colors.

2. Christmas foods.

3. Christmas plants.

4. Symbols of Christmas.

5. Sounds heard at Christmas.

Concepts for the Children to Learn:

1. Red, green, and white are Christmas colors.

2. Christmas cookies and candy are special treats for Christmas.

3. Santa Claus, reindeer, stockings, and Christmas trees are symbols of Christmas.

4. Decorating Christmas trees is a Christmas activity.

5. Christmas ornaments and garland are hung on Christmas trees.

6. There are special Christmas songs.

7. Bells and Christmas carols are sounds heard at Christmas.

8. Pointsettias, pine trees, and mistletoe are Christmas plants.

9. Many people spend Christmas with their families and friends.

10. Some people hang special stockings that are filled with candy and small gifts.

11. Christmas for some people is a time for giving and receiving gifts.

12. Christians believe that Jesus was born on Christmas day.

Vocabulary:

1. **Santa Claus**—a jolly man who wears a red suit and symbolizes Christmas.

2. **pine tree**—a tree decorated for the Christmas holidays.

3. **wreath**—a decoration made from evergreen branches.

4. **elf**—Santa's helper.

5. **star**—a treetop decoration.

6. **stocking**—a large Christmas sock.

7. **reindeer**—an animal used to pull Santa's sleigh.

8. **present**—a gift.

9. **ornament**—decoration for the home or tree.

10. **carol**—a Christmas song.

11. **pinata**—brightly colored paper mache figure that is filled with candy and gifts.

Bulletin Board

The purpose of this bulletin board is to foster positive self-concept, as well as name recognition. Construct a stocking out of tagboard for each child in your class. Print the name across the top and punch a hole in the top with a paper punch. Hang a Christmas poster or teacher-made poster in the center of the bulletin board. Next, attach push pins to the bulletin board, allowing enough room for each stocking to hang on a pin. The children can hang their own stocking on the bulletin board as they arrive each day.

Parent Letter

Dear Parents,

The Christmas season is approaching. All we need to do is drive through our neighborhoods to see decorations and busy shoppers everywhere. Songs of Christmas are heard, and Santa is in the thoughts and sentences of many children. At school we will be participating in many Christmas activities. The children will learn the colors, plants, and symbols that are associated with the Christmas season.

At School

A few of the Christmas learning experiences planned include:

- creating ornaments to decorate the classroom Christmas tree.
- painting with pine boughs at the easel.
- making Christmas cookies.
- designing Christmas cards in the art area.
- practicing songs for our Holiday program. Keep your eyes open for a special invitation! The program will be held on December 19th at 3:30. Mark your calendar.

At Home

Music and singing are wonderful ways to communicate our feelings, and we often have many feelings this time of year! When singing Christmas carols, encourage traditional songs as well as this new song:

"I'm a Little Pine Tree"
(Sing to the tune of "I'm a Little Teapot")

I'm a little pine tree tall and straight
Here are my branches for you to decorate.
   (extend arms)
First we'll put the shiny star on top.
   (touch head)
Just be careful the balls don't drop.
   (clap hands)
Now be sure to plug in all the lights
So I will look very cheerful and bright.
Then put all the presents under me.
I'm all set for Christmas, as you can see!

Reminder

Our last day of school will be December 23. We will begin school again on January 3 of the new year.

Happy holidays to you and yours!

FIGURE 12 Santa Claus and Christmas make winter fun.

Music:

1. **"Rudolph the Red-Nosed Reindeer"** (traditional)

2. **"Jingle Bells"** (traditional)

3. **"The Twelve Days of Christmas"** (traditional)

4. **"We Wish You a Merry Christmas"** (traditional)

5. **"Peppermint Stick Song"**

   Oh I took a lick of my
   peppermint stick
   And I thought it tasted yummy.
   Oh it used to hang on my
   Christmas tree,
   But I like it better in my tummy.

6. **"S-A-N-T-A"**
   (Sing to the tune of "B-I-N-G-O")

   There was a man on Christmas Day
   And Santa was his name-o.
   S-A-N-T-A
   S-A-N-T-A
   S-A-N-T-A
   And Santa was his name-o.

7. **"Up on the House Top"** (traditional)

8. **"Santa Claus is Coming to Town"** (traditional)

9. **"Circle Christmas Verse"**

   Two, four, six, eight.
   Santa Claus don't be late;
   Here's my stocking, I can't wait!
   Two, four, six, eight.

10. **"Christmas Chant"**

    With a "hey" and a "Hi" and a "ho-ho-ho,"
    Somebody tickled old Santa Claus' toe.
    Get up ol' Santa, there's work to be done,
    The children must have their holiday fun.
    With a "hey" and a "hi" and a "ho-ho-ho,"
    Santa Claus, Santa Claus,
    GO-GO-GO!

11. **"Santa's in His Shop"**
    (Sing to the tune of "The Farmer in the Dell")

    Santa's in his shop
    Santa's in his shop
    What a scene for Christmas
    Santa's in his shop.

Other verses:

Santa takes a drum
The drum takes a doll
The doll takes a train
The train takes a ball
The ball takes a top
They're all in the shop
The top stays in the shop

Pictures could be constructed for use during
the singing of each toy.

Fingerplays:

SANTA'S WORKSHOP

Here is Santa's workshop.
  (form peak with both hands)
Here is Santa Claus.
  (hold up thumb)
Here are Santa's little elves
  (wiggle fingers)
Putting toys upon the shelves.

HERE IS THE CHIMNEY

Here is the chimney.
  (make fist and tuck in thumb)
Here is the top.
  (cover with hand)
Open it up quick
  (lift hand up)
And out Santa will pop.
  (pop out thumb)

FIVE LITTLE CHRISTMAS COOKIES

(hold up five fingers, take one away as
directed by poem)

Five little Christmas cookies on a plate by the
door,
One was eaten and then there were four.

Four little Christmas cookies, gazing up at me,
One was eaten and then there were three.

Three little Christmas cookies, enough for me
and you,
One was eaten and then there were two.

Two little Christmas cookies sitting in the sun,
One was eaten and then there was one.

One little Christmas cookie, better grab it fast,
As you can see the others surely didn't last.

PRESENTS

See all the presents by the Christmas tree?
  (hand shades eyes)
Some for you,
  (point)
And some for me—
  (point)

Long ones,
  (extend arms)
Tall ones,
  (measure hand up from floor)
Short ones, too.
  (hand to floor—low)
And here is a round one
  (circle with arms)
Wrapped in blue.

Isn't it fun to look and see
  (hand shade eyes)
All of the presents by the Christmas tree?
  (arms open wide)

Science:

1. **Making Candles**

Candles can be made for Christmas gifts. This
experience provides an opportunity for the
children to see how a substance can change
from solid to liquid and back to a solid form.
The children can place pieces of paraffin in a
tin can that is bent at the top, forming a spout.
A red or green crayon piece can be used to add
color.

The bottom of the tin cans should be placed in
a pan of water and heated on the stove until
the paraffin is melted. Meanwhile, the children
can prepare small paper cups.

In the bottom of each paper cup mold place a
wick. Wicks can be made by tying a piece of
string to a paper clip and a pencil. Then lay the
pencil horizontally across the cup allowing the

string to hang vertically into the cup. When the wax is melted, the teacher should carefully pour the wax into the cup. After the wax hardens, the candles can be used as decorations or presents. This activity should be restricted to four- and five-year-old children. Constant supervision of this activity is required for safety.

2. **Add to the Science Area:**

   • pine needles and branches with magnifying glasses
   • pinecones with a balance scale
   • red, green, and white materials representing different textures

3. **Bells**

   Collect bells of various shapes and sizes. Listen for differences in sounds in relation to the sizes of the bells.

4. **Feely Box**

   A feely box containing Christmas items such as bows, cookie cutters, wrapping paper, non-breakable ornaments, stockings, bells, candles, etc., can be placed on the science table.

Dramatic Play:

Gift Wrapping

Collect and place in the dramatic play area empty boxes, scraps of wrapping paper, comic paper, wallpaper books, and scraps. Scissors, tape, bows, and ribbon should also be provided.

Arts and Crafts:

1. **Christmas Chains**

   Cut sheets of red, green, and white construction paper into strips. Demonstrate how to form the links. The links can be pasted, taped, or stapled, depending upon the developmental level of the children.

2. **Cookie Cutter Painting**

   Provide Christmas cookie cutters, paper, and shallow pans containing red and green paint. The children can apply the paint to the paper using the cookie cutters as printing tools.

3. **Rudolph**

   Begin the activity by encouraging the children to trace their shoe. This will be used for Rudolph's face. Then the children should trace both of their hands which will be used as the reindeer's antlers. Finally, cut out a red circle to be used as the reindeer's nose. Have the children paste all the pieces together on a sheet of paper and add facial features.

4. **Designing Wrapping Paper**

   The children can design their own wrapping paper using newsprint, ink stampers, felt-tip colored markers, tempera paint, etc. Glitter can also be glued onto the paper.

5. **Creating Christmas Cards**

   Paper, felt-tip colored markers, and crayons should be available at the art table. Christmas stencils can also be provided.

6. **Pine Branch Painting**

   Collect short pine boughs to use as painting tools. The tools can be placed at the easel or used with a shallow pan of tempera paint at tables.

7. **Candy Cane Marble Painting**

   Cut red construction paper into candy cane shapes. Marble paint with white tempera paint.

8. **Seasonal Stencils**

   Spread glue inside a seasonal stencil. Apply glitter over the glued area.

9. **Glittery Pine Cones**

   Paint pinecones with tempera paint, sprinkle with glitter, and allow the paint to dry. The glittery pinecones can be used for classroom decoration, presents, or taken home.

10. **Paper Wreaths**

Purchase green muffin tin liners. To make the paper wreaths, cut out a large ring from light tagboard or construction paper for each child in the class. The children can glue the green muffin tin liners to the ring, adding small pieces of red yarn, crayons, or felt-tip marker symbols to represent berries if desired.

11. **Playdough Cookies**

Using red, green, and white playdough and Christmas cookie cutters, the children can make playdough cookies.

Favorite Playdough

Combine and boil until dissolved:
2 cups water
1/2 cup salt
food coloring or tempera

Mix while very hot:
2 tablespoons salad oil
2 tablespoons alum
2 cups flour

Knead approximately five minutes until smooth. Store in an airtight covered container.

Sensory:

1. **Add to the Sensory Table:**

   - pine branches, needles, and cones
   - scented red and green playdough
   - icicles or snow (if possible) with thermometers
   - water for a sink and float activity; add different Christmas objects such as bells, plastic stars, and cookie cutters
   - Add scents such as peppermint and ginger to water

2. **Holiday Cubes**

Prepare ice cube trays using water colored with red and green food coloring. Freeze. Place in the sensory table.

Field Trip:

1. **Christmas Tree Farm**

Plan a trip to a Christmas tree farm so the children can cut down a Christmas tree. Check your state's licensing requirements regarding the use of fresh Christmas trees and decorations in the center or classroom.

2. **Caroling**

Plan to go Christmas caroling at a local nursing home or even for another group of children. After caroling, Christmas cookies could be shared.

Math:

1. **Christmas Card Sort**

Place a variety of Christmas cards on a table in the math area. During self-selected or self-initiated periods, the children can sort by color, pictures, size, etc.

2. **Christmas Card Puzzles**

Collect two sets of identical Christmas cards. Cut the covers off the cards. Cut one of each of the identical sets of cards into puzzle pieces. The matching card can be used as a form for the children to match the pieces on.

Group Time (games, language):

1. **Find the Christmas Bell**

For this activity the children should be standing in a circle. One child is given a bell. Then the child should hide, while the remainder of the children cover their eyes. After the child has hidden, he begins to ring the bell, signaling the remainder of the children to listen for the sound and identify where the bell is hidden. Turns should be taken, allowing each child an opportunity to hide and ring the bell.

2. **"Guess What's Inside"**

Wrap a familiar object inside of a box. Let the children shake, feel, and try to identify the object. After this, open the box and show the children the object. This activity works well in small groups as well as large groups.

Cooking:

1. **Candy Canes**

Prepare the basic sugar dough recipe for cookie cutters. Divide the recipe in half. Add red food coloring to one half of the dough. Show the children how to roll a piece of red dough in a strip about 3 inches long by 1/2 inch wide. Repeat this process using the white dough. Then twist the two strips together, shaping into a candy cane. Bake the cookies in a 350-degree oven for 7 to 10 minutes.

2. **Basic Sugar Dough for Cookie Cutters**

1/2 cup butter
1 cup sugar
1 egg
1/2 teaspoon salt
2 teaspoons baking powder
2 cups flour
1/2 teaspoon vanilla

Cut into desired shapes. Place on lightly greased baking sheets. Bake 8 minutes at 400 degrees. This recipe makes approximately 3 to 4 dozen cookies.

3. **Eggnog**

4 eggs
2 teaspoons vanilla
4 tablespoons honey
4 cups milk

Beat all of the ingredients together until light and foamy. Pour into glasses or cups and shake a little nutmeg on the top of the eggnog. This adds color and flavor. The recipe makes one quart. Eggnog should always be served immediately or refrigerated until snack or lunch. It should not be served to children who are allergic to eggs.

GIFTS FOR PARENTS

Wax Paper Placemats
wax paper that is heavily
    waxed
crayon shavings
paper designs
dish towel
scissors

Use at least one of the
    following:
yarn
fabric
lace
dried leaves

Cut the wax paper into 12-inch by 20-inch sheets (2 per mat). Place crayon shavings between the wax paper. Then decorate with other items. Place towel on wax paper and press with warm iron until crayon melts. Fringe the edges.

Popsicle Stick Picture Frames
popsicle sticks (10 per
    frame)
glue
picture

Make a background of sticks and glue picture in place. Add additional sticks around the edges, front, and back for the frame and for support. For a freestanding frame add more popsicle sticks to both the front and the back at the bottom.

Refrigerator Magnets
small magnets
glue
any type of decoration
    (paper cut-outs, plaster
    of paris molds, yarn,
    styrofoam pieces,
    buttons, etc.)

Glue the decorations to the magnet.

Service Certificate
paper
crayons
pencils
lace
ribbon

Have the children write and decorate a certificate that states some service they will do for their parents. (Example: This certificate is good for washing the dishes; sweeping the floor; picking up my toys; etc.)

Ornaments
plaster of paris
any mold
glitter
yarn
straw

Pour the plaster of paris into the mold. Decorate with glitter and let dry. If so desired, place a straw into the mold and string with yarn or thread.

Refrigerator Clothespin
clothespins
glue
sequins/glitter/beads
small magnet

Let the children put glue on one side of the clothespin. Sprinkle this area with glitter, sequins, or beads. Then assist the child in gluing the magnet to the other side.

Patchwork Flowerpot
precut fabric squares
glue
tins (for glue)
flower pots

Let the children soak the fabric squares one at a time in the glue. Press onto the pot in a patchwork design. Let dry overnight.

Snapshot Magnet
snapshot
plastic lid
scissors (preferably pinking shears)
glue
magnet

Using the lid, trace around the back of the picture. Cut the picture out and glue into the lid. Glue the magnet to the underside of the lid.

Holiday Pin
outline of a heart, wreath etc., cut out of tagboard
glue
sequins, beads, buttons, yarn
purchased backing for a pin

Let the children decorate the cardboard figure with glue and other decorating items. Glue onto purchased backing for a pin.

Flowers with Vase
styrofoam egg carton
pipe cleaner
scissors
glass jar or bottle
liquid starch
colored tissue paper (cut into squares)
glue yarn
paintbrush

Cut individual sections from egg carton and punch a hole in the bottom of each. Insert a pipe cleaner through the hole as a stem. Use the scissors to cut the petals.

For the vase: Using the paintbrush, cover a portion of the jar with liquid starch. Apply the tissue paper squares until the jar is covered. Add another coat of liquid starch. Dip the yarn into the glue and wrap it around the jar. Insert the flower for a decoration.

Pinecone Ornament
pinecones
paint
paintbrush
glue
glitter
yarn

Paint the pinecones. Then roll the pinecones in the glue and then into a dish filled with glitter. Tie a loop of yarn for hanging.

Paper Weights
glass furniture glides
crepe paper
crayons
glue
plaster of paris
felt piece
scissors

Children decorate a picture and then cut it to fit the glide. Place the picture face down into the recessed part of the glide. Pour plaster of paris over the top of the picture and let it dry. Glue a felt piece over the plaster.

Rock Paperweight
large rocks
paint

Let the children paint a design on a rock they have chosen and give to their parents as a present.

Soap Balls

1 cup Ivory Snow detergent
1/8 cup of water
food coloring
colored nylon netting
ribbon

Add the food coloring to the water and then add the Ivory Snow detergent. Shape the mixture into balls or any shape. Wrap in colored netting and tie with ribbon.

Closet Clove Scenter

orange
cloves
netting
ribbon

Have the children push the pointed ends of the cloves into an orange. Cover the orange completely. Wrap netting around the orange and tie it with the ribbon. These make good closet or dresser drawer scenters.

Handprint Wreath

colored construction paper
scissors
glue
pencil
cardboard/tagboard circle

Let the children trace their hand and cut it out. Glue the palm of the hand to the cardboard circle. Using a pencil roll the fingertips of the hand until curly.

Bird's Nest

1 can sweetened condensed milk
2 teaspoons vanilla
3 to 4 cups powdered milk
1 cup confectioners' sugar
yellow food coloring

Mix all the ingredients together and add food coloring to tint the mixture to a yellow-brown color. Give each child a portion and let him mold a bird's nest. Chill for 2 hours. If so desired, green tinted coconut may be added for grass and put in the nest. Add small jelly beans for bird's eggs.

Flower Pots

plaster of paris
1/2-pint milk containers
straws (3 to 4 for each container)
scissors
construction paper
paint
paintbrush
stapler

Cut the cartons in half and use the bottom half. Pour 1 to 3 inches of plaster into the containers. Stick 3 or 4 straws into the plaster and let harden. After plaster has hardened, remove the plaster very carefully from the milk carton. Let the children paint the plaster pot and make flowers from construction paper and staple the flowers to the straws.

Cookie Jar

coffee can with lid or oatmeal box
construction paper
crayons or felt-tip markers
glue
scissors

Cover the can with construction paper and glue to seal. Let the children decorate their cans with crayons or felt-tip markers. For an added gift, make cookies in the classroom to send home in the jars.

Felt Printing

felt
glue
wood block
tempera paint
scissors

Let the children cut the felt pieces into any shape. Glue the shape onto the wood block. Dip into a shallow pan of tempera paint. Print on newspaper to test.

Napkin Holder

paper plates
scissors
yarn
paper punch
crayons
clear shellac

Cut one paper plate in half. Place the inside together and punch holes through the lower half only. Use yarn to lace the plates together. Punch a small hole at the top for hanging. Decorate with crayons or felt-tip markers. Coat with shellac. May be used as a potholder, napkin, or card holder.

Clay Figures

4 cups flour
1 1/2 cup water
1 cup salt paint
paintbrush

Combine flour, water, and salt. Knead for 5 to 10 minutes. Roll and cut dough into figures. (Cookie cutters work well.) Make a hole at the top of the figure. Bake in a 250-degree oven for 2 hours or until hard. When cool, paint to decorate.

Key Holder
8 popsicle sticks
construction paper or a
    cutout from a greeting
    card
self-adhesive picture
    hanger
yarn

Glue five sticks together
    edge to edge. Cut a 1
    3/4-inch piece of stick
    and glue it across the 5
    sticks. Glue 2 sticks
    across the top parallel to
    the 5 sticks. Turn the
    sticks over. Cut paper or
    a greeting card to fit
    between the crossed
    sticks. Place on the self-
    adhesive hanger and tie
    yarn to the top for hang-
    ing.

Planter Trivets
7 popsicle sticks
glue

Glue four popsicle sticks
    into a square, the top
two overlapping the bot-
tom ones. Fill in the
open space with the
remaining three and
glue into place.

Pencil Holder
empty soup cans
construction paper or
    contact paper
crayons or felt-tip markers
glue
scissors

Cover the can with
    construction or contact
    paper. Decorate with
    crayons or markers and
    use as a pencil holder.

Plaster Hand Prints
plaster of paris
1-inch-deep square
    container
paint
paintbrush

Pour plaster of paris into
    the container. Have the
    child place his hand in
the plaster to make a
mold. Let the mold dry
and remove it from the
container. Let the child
paint the mold and give
as a gift with the following poem:

My Hands

Sometimes you get
    discouraged
Because I am so small
And always have my
    fingerprints
on furniture and walls.
But everyday I'm growing
    up
and soon I'll be so tall
that all those little
    handprints
will be hard for you to
    recall.
So here's a little handprint
just for you to see
Exactly how my fingers
    looked
When I was little me.

Books:

The following books can be used to complement the theme:

1. Schumacher, Claire. (1987). *Santa's Hat*. New York: Prentice Hall Books.

2. Shuttleworth, Cathie (Illus.). (1987). *The Twelve Days of Christmas*. New York: Derrydale Books.

3. Poulet, Virginia. (1987). *Blue Bug's Christmas*. Chicago: Children's Press.

4. Bokich, Obren. (1987). *A Christmas Card for Mr. McFizz*. Chicago: Children's Press.

5. Dubanevich, Arlene. (1989). *Pigs at Christmas*. New York: Macmillan.

6. Gerver, Jane E. (1990). *Happy Bear, Christmas Star*. New York: Random House.

7. Goffin, Jesse. (1991). *Silent Christmas*. Boyds Mills Press.

8. Hayes, Sarah. (1992). *Happy Christmas, Gemma*. New York: Morrow.

9. McCully, Emily A. (1992). *A Christmas Gift*. New York: Harper Collins.

10. Naylor, Phyllis R. (1989). *Keeping a Christmas Secret*. New York: Macmillan.

11. Radzinski, Kandy. (1992). *The Twelve Cats of Christmas*. San Francisco: Chronicle Books.

12. Clifton, Lucille. (1993). *Everett Anderson's Christmas Coming*. New York: Holt.

13. Bishop, Adela. (1991). *The Christmas Polar Bear*. Union City, CA: DOT Garnet.

14. dePaola, Tomie. (1992). *Jingle the Christmas Clown*. New York: Putnam Publishing Group.

15. Garcia-Bengochea, Debbie. (1992). *Gumdrop the Christmas Bear*. Hazelwood, MO: Masterson Publishing Corp.

16. Haung, Benrei. (1992). *Pop-up Merry Christmas*. New York: Putnam Publishing Group.

17. Jerris, Tony. (1991). *The Littlest Spruce*. Caldeonia, NY: Little Spruce Productions.

18. Shpakow, Tanya. (1991). *On the Way to Christmas*. New York: Alfred A. Knopf Books for Young Readers.

19. Jordan, Sandra. (1993). *Christmas Tree Farm*. New York: Orchard Books.

20. Hague, Michael. (1990). *We Wish You a Merry Christmas*. New York: Henry Holt & Co.

21. Kelley, Emily. (1986). *Christmas Around the World*. Minneapolis: Lerner.

22. Angel, Marie. (1991). *Woodland Christmas*. New York: Dial Books.

23. Aloia, Gregory F. (1989). *The Legend of the Golden Straw: A Christmas Story*. Chicago: Loyola.

24. Palangi, Paula. (1992). *Last Straw*. Elgin, IL: Cook.

25. Hague, Michael. (1991). *We Wish You a Merry Christmas*. New York: Henry Holt & Co.

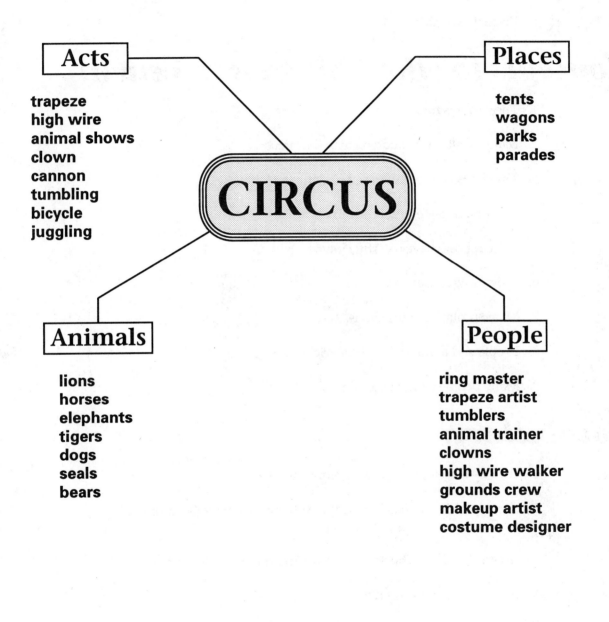

Acts

trapeze
high wire
animal shows
clown
cannon
tumbling
bicycle
juggling

Places

tents
wagons
parks
parades

CIRCUS

Animals

lions
horses
elephants
tigers
dogs
seals
bears

People

ring master
trapeze artist
tumblers
animal trainer
clowns
high wire walker
grounds crew
makeup artist
costume designer

Polaroid
Education
Program

Here's an exciting new way to turn instant photography into an effective teaching tool. Refer to the full-color insert for the activity entitled Spatial Relations.

Theme Goals:

Through participating in the experiences provided by this theme, the children may learn:

1. Different circus acts.

2. People who work for a circus.

3. Animals that perform in a circus.

4. Places to watch a circus.

Concepts for the Children to Learn:

1. The circus is fun.

2. Many adults and children enjoy the circus.

3. The circus can be performed under a big tent.

4. An animal trainer teaches animals tricks.

5. Circus shows have colorful clowns.

6. Clowns wear makeup.

7. Music is played at the circus.

8. People and animals do special tricks in the circus.

9. Many people work at the circus.

Vocabulary:

1. **circus**—traveling show with people and animals.

2. **circus parade**—a march of people and animals at the beginning of the performance.

3. **clowns**—people who wear makeup and dress in silly clothes.

4. **trapeze**—short bar used for swinging.

5. **ring master**—person in charge of the circus performance.

6. **makeup**—colored face paint.

7. **stilts**—long sticks a performer stands on to be taller.

Bulletin Board

The purpose of this bulletin board is to develop color recognition and matching skills. Construct eight clown faces with collars out of tagboard. Color each collar a different color using felt-tip markers. Hang these pieces on the bulletin board. Next, construct eight hat pieces out of tagboard. Color each one a different color, to correspond with the colors of the clowns' collars. Punch holes in the hats, and use push pins to hold the hats above the appropriate clown. The children can match the colored hats to the clown wearing the same-colored collar.

Parent Letter

Dear Parents,

We are starting a unit that is fun for everyone—the circus! It will be a very exciting unit! Developing an awareness of special people and animals enhances an appreciation of others. It also stimulates children's curiousity to learn more about other people and jobs people have. The children will be learning about the many acts and performances people and animals do at the circus.

At School

Some of the many fun and exciting things we will be doing include:

- listening to the story, *Harriet Goes to the Circus* by Betsy and Guilio Maestro.
- dressing up in clown suits and applying makeup in the dramatic play area.
- acting out a small circus of our own.
- making clown face puppets.

We will have a very special visitor come to our room on Friday—a clown! He will show us how he applies his makeup and will perform for us. You are invited to join us for the fun at 3:00 p.m. to share in this activity.

At Home

It has been said that the circus is perhaps the world's oldest form of entertainment. Pictures of circus acts drawn over 3,000 years ago have been discovered on walls of caves. Most children enjoy clowns and dressing up as clowns. Prepare clown makeup with your child by adding a few drops of food coloring to cold cream. Have your child use his fingers or a clean paintbrush to paint his face. This activity will help develop an awareness of colors, as well as help him or her realize that appearances can change but the person remains the same!

Enjoy your child!

FIGURE 13 Clowns like to make people laugh.

Music:

1. **"Circus"**
   (Sing to the tune of "Did You Ever See a Lassie")

   Let's pretend that we are clowns, are clowns, are clowns.
   Let's pretend that we are clowns.
   We'll have so much fun.
   We'll put on our makeup and make people laugh hard.
   Let's pretend that we are clowns.
   We'll have so much fun.

   Let's pretend that we are elephants, are elephants, are elephants.
   Let's pretend that we are elephants.
   We'll have so much fun.
   We'll sway back and forth and stand on just two legs.
   Let's pretend that we are elephants.
   We'll have so much fun.

   Let's pretend that we are on a trapeze, a trapeze, a trapeze.
   Let's pretend that we are on a trapeze.
   We'll have so much fun.
   We'll swing high and swoop low and make people shout "oh!"
   Let's pretend that we are on a trapeze.
   We'll have so much fun!

2. **"The Ring Master"**
   (Sing to tune of "The Farmer and the Dell")

   The ring master has a circus.
   The ring master has a circus.
   Hi-ho the clowns are here.
   The ring master has a circus.

   The ring master takes a clown.
   The ring master takes a clown.
   Hi-ho the clowns are here.
   The ring master takes a clown.

   The clown takes an elephant...

   Use clowns, elephants, lions, tigers, tightrope walker, trapeze artist, acrobat, etc.

Fingerplays:

GOING TO THE CIRCUS

   Going to the circus to have a lot of fun.
      (hold closed fist, and raise fingers to indicate number)
   The animals parading one by one.
   Now they are walking 2 by 2,
   A great big lion and a caribou.
   Now they are walking 3 by 3,
   The elephants and the chimpanzee.
   Now they are walking 4 by 4,
   A striped tiger and a big old bear.
   Now they are walking 5 by 5,
   It makes us laugh when they arrive.

ELEPHANTS

   Elephants walk like this and like that.
      (sway body back and forth)
   They're terribly big; they're terribly fat.
      (spread arms wide in a circular motion)
   They have no hands, they have no toes,

And goodness gracious, what a NOSE!
  (put arms together and sway for elephant nose)

FIVE LITTLE CLOWNS

Five little clowns running through the door.
  (hold up one hand, put down one finger at each verse)
One fell down and then there were four.
Four little clowns in an apple tree.
One fell out and then there were three.
Three little clowns stirring up some stew.
One fell in and then there were two.
Two little clowns having lots of fun.
One ran away and then there was one.
One little clown left sitting in the sun.
He went home and then there were none!

CIRCUS CLOWN

I'd like to be a circus clown
And make a funny face,
  (make a funny face)
And have all the people laugh at me
As I jump around the place.
  (act silly and jump around)

THE CIRCUS IS COMING

The circus is coming hurray, hurray!
  (clap hands)
The clowns are silly; see them play.
  (make a face)
The animals parade one by one
  (walk fingers on lap)
While clowns juggle balls for fun.
  (pretend to juggle)
The lion growls; the tigers roar,
  (paw in the air)
While the elephant walks on all fours.
  (swing arms like an elephant trunk)
The circus is coming hurray, hurray!
  (clap hands)

Source: Rountree, Barbara, et al. (1981). *Creative Teaching with Puppets*. Alabama: The Learning Line, Inc.

Science:

1. **Circus Balloons**

   Cut several pieces of tagboard into circles. If desired, cover the balloons with transparent contact or lamination paper. On each table have three cups of colored water—red, yellow, and blue—with a brush in each cup. The child can mix all or any two colors and see which colors they can create for their circus balloons.

2. **Shape the Clown**

   Cut several large outlines of clowns' heads from tagboard or construction paper and many eyes, hats, ears, noses, ruffles, and bowties. Make a large die with an ear, nose, hat, eye, ruffle, and bow tie. (One on each of the six sides.) The children can take turns rolling the die to construct their clown face. If a child rolls a die with the shape they already have, they must wait for their next turn.

   Source: *Teacher-made Games*. (1980). Missouri: Parent-Child Early Education.

3. **Seal and Ball Color/Word Match**

   Cut several seals out of different-colored tagboard. Out of the same colors cut several balls. Write the correct color on each ball. The children match each ball with the word on it to the correct seal.

4. **Sizzle Fun**

   Pour 1 inch of vinegar in a soda or catsup bottle. Put 2 teaspoons of baking soda inside a balloon. Quickly slip the open end of the balloon over the soda bottle. Watch the balloon fill with gas created by the interaction of the vinegar with the baking soda.

5. **Texture Clown**

   Construct a large clown from tagboard. Use different textured materials to create the clown's features. Make two sets. Place the extra set in a box or a bag. The children may pick a piece of textured material from the bag and match it to the identical textured piece used as a clown feature.

6. **Make Peanut Butter**

Take the shells off of fresh peanuts. Blend peanuts in a blender until smooth. Add 1 1/2 to 2 tablespoons of oil per cup of peanuts and blend well. Add 1/2 teaspoon salt per cup if desired. Spread on bread or crackers and eat for snack.

Dramatic Play:

1. **Clown Makeup**

Prepare clown makeup by mixing 1 part facial cream with 1 drop food coloring. Place clown makeup by a large mirror in the dramatic play area. The children apply makeup to their faces. Clown suits can also be provided if available.

2. **Circus**

Set up a circus in your classroom. Make a circle out of masking tape on the floor. The children can take turns performing in the ring. The addition of Hula Hoops, animal and clown costumes, tickets, and chairs would extend the children's play in this area.

3. **Animal Trainers**

Each child can bring in their favorite stuffed animals on an assigned day. The children can pretend to be animal trainers for the circus. They may select to act out different animal performances.

Arts and Crafts:

1. **Clown Stencils**

Cut several clown figures out of tagboard. Place felt-tip markers, crayons, pencils, and stencils on the art table. The children can trace the stencils.

2. **Easel Ideas**

- clown face-shaped paper
- circus tent-shaped paper

3. **Circus Wagons**

Collect old cardboard boxes and square food containers. The children can make circus wagons by decorating the boxes. When each child is through making their wagon, all of the boxes can be placed together for a circus train.

4. **Clown Face Masks**

Provide paper plates and felt-tip markers to make paper plate clown masks. Glue the plate to a tongue depressor. The children can use the masks as puppets.

5. **Playdough Animals**

Prepare playdough by combining:

2 cups flour
1 cup salt
1 cup hot water
2 tablespoons oil
4 teaspoons cream of tartar
food coloring

Mix the ingredients. Then knead the mixture until smooth. This dough may be kept in a plastic bag or covered container. If the dough becomes sticky, add additional flour.

6. **Peanut Shell Collages**

Provide peanut shells, glue, and paper for the children to create collages.

Sensory:

Provide rubber or plastic animal figurines for the children to play with in the water table.

Large Muscle:

1. **Tightrope Walker**

Provide a balance beam and a stick for the children to hold perpendicular to their bodies.

2. Dancing Elephants

Provide each child a scarf and play music. The children can pretend to be dancing elephants.

3. Bean Bag Toss

Make a large clown or other circus person or animal bean bag toss out of thick cardboard. Cut the eyes, nose, and mouth holes all large enough for the bean bags to go through. For older children, assign each hole a certain number of points and maintain a score chart or card.

4. Can Stilts

Provide large tin cans with prebored holes on sides and thick string or twine for the children to make can stilts. Once completed, the children stand on the cans and walk around the room.

5. Tightrope Transition

As a transition, place a 10-foot line of masking tape on the floor. The children can pretend to tightrope walk over to the next activity.

6. Monkey, Monkey, Clown

Play Duck, Duck, Goose but change the words to Monkey, Monkey, Clown.

These games are most appropriate for older children—four-, five-, six-, and seven-year-olds.

Field Trips/Resource People:

1. Clown Makeup

Invite a clown to demonstrate putting on makeup. Then have the clown put on a small skit and talk about the circus.

2. The Circus

If possible, go to a circus or circus parade in your area.

Math:

1. Clown Hat Match

Make sets of matching colored hats. On one set print a numeral. On the matching hats print an identical number of dots. The children match the dots to the numbers.

2. Circus Sorting

Find several pictures of symbols that represent a circus. Also include other pictures. Place all pictures in a pile. The children can sort pictures into two piles. One pile will represent circus objects.

3. Growing Chart

Make a giraffe growing chart. If desired, another animal can be substituted. Record each child's height on the chart at various times during the year.

Social Studies:

1. Circus Life

Read *You Think It's Fun to be a Clown!* by David A. Adler. When finished, discuss the lives of circus people.

2. Body Parts

Make a large clown out of tagboard. Make corresponding matching body parts such as arms, legs, ears, shoes, hands, and fingers. The children can match the parts.

Group Time (games, language):

1. Making a Clown

Give each child a paper and one crayon. Have children draw as you recite this fingerplay:

Draw a circle round and big,
Add a few hairs as a wig.
Make a circle for a nose,

Now a smile, broad and wide.
Put an ear on either side.
Add some eyes, but not a frown.
Now you have your very own clown.

This activity should only be used with older children when it is developmentally appropriate and when self-selected during small group time.

Source: Indenbaum, Valerie & Shapiro, Marcia. (1985). *The Everything Book for Teachers of Young Children*. Michigan: Partner Press.

2. **Circus Pictures**

Place pictures of clowns and circus things around the room at the children's eye level. Introduce the pictures at group time and discuss each picture.

3. **Who Took My Nose?**

Prepare red circles from construction paper. Seat the children in a circle. Give each child a red circle to tape on their nose. Then, have everyone close their eyes. Tap one child. This child should get up and go to another child and take his nose. When the child returns to his place the teacher claps her hands and all the children open their eyes. The children then try to identify the child who took the nose.

4. **Clown Lotto**

Adhere clown face stickers, or draw simple clown faces, on several 2-inch x 2-inch pieces of tagboard. Also, prepare lotto boards using the same stickers or drawings. To play, turn all cards face down. Children take turns choosing a card from the table and seeing if it matches a picture on their game boards.

Cooking:

1. **Clown Snack**

Place a pear in the middle of a plate. Sprinkle grated cheese on the pear for hair. Add raisin eyes, a cherry nose, and a raisin mouth. Finally, make a ruffle collar from a lettuce leaf.

2. **Cheese Popcorn**

1/4 cup butter
1/4 cup dry cheddar cheese
3 cups popped popcorn

Melt butter and grate cheese. Mix together and pour over popcorn. Stir until well coated. Salt to taste if desired.

Source: Warren, Jean. (1982). *Super Snacks*. Alderwood Manor, WA: Warren Publishing House.

Multimedia:

The following resources can be found in preschool educational catalogs:

1. Palmer, Hap. *Pretend* [record].

2. Wood, Lucille. *Animals and Circus* [record].

3. Wood, Lucille & Tanner. "Circus Parade" on *Rhythm Time* [record].

4. *Kindergarten Carnival* [record]. Melody House.

5. *Do It Yourself Kid's Circus* [record]. Kimbo.

Books:

The following books can be used to complement the theme:

1. McCully, Emily. (1992). *Mirette on the High Wire*. New York: Putnam.

2. Doty, Roy. (1991). *Wonderful Circus Parade*. New York: Simon and Schuster Trade.

3. Ehlert, Lois. (1992). *Circus*. New York: Harper Collins Children's Books.

4. Goennel, Heidi. (1992). *The Circus*. New York: William Morrow and Co.

5. DeHieronymis, Elve F. (1989). *A Night at the Circus*. New York: Barron.

6. Hill, Eric. (1986). *Spot Goes to the Circus*. New York: Putnam.

7. Moncure, Jane B. (1987). *A Color Clown Comes to Town*. Mankato, MN: Child's World.

8. Peppe, Rodney. (1985). *Circus Numbers: A Counting Book*. New York: Delacorte.

9. Peppe, Rodney. (1989). *Thumbprint Circus*. New York: Delacorte.

10. Petersham, Maud, & Petersham, Miska. (1989). *The Circus Baby*. New York: Macmillan.

11. Prelutsky, Jack. (1989). *Circus!* New York: Macmillan.

THEME 14

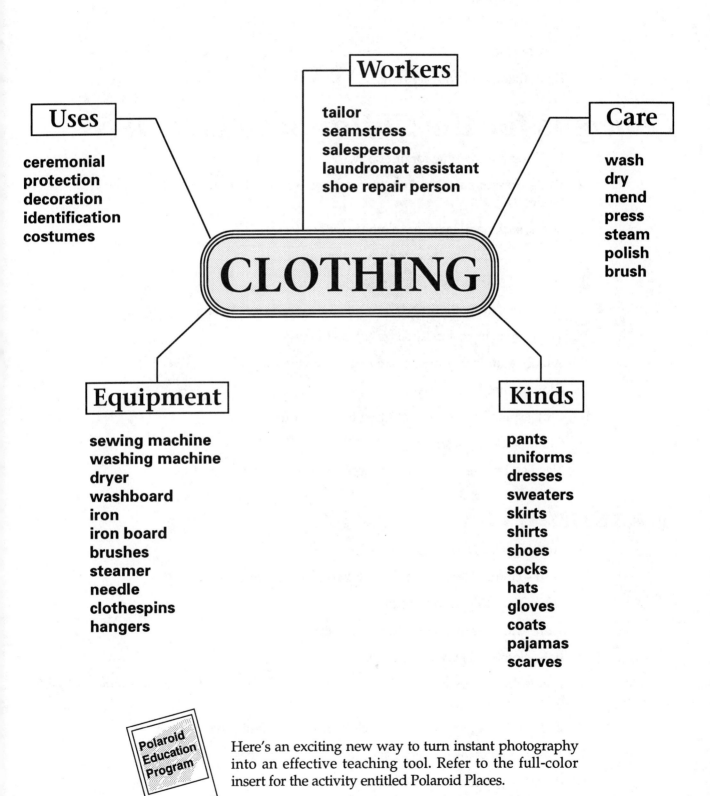

Uses

ceremonial
protection
decoration
identification
costumes

Workers

tailor
seamstress
salesperson
laundromat assistant
shoe repair person

Care

wash
dry
mend
press
steam
polish
brush

CLOTHING

Equipment

sewing machine
washing machine
dryer
washboard
iron
iron board
brushes
steamer
needle
clothespins
hangers

Kinds

pants
uniforms
dresses
sweaters
skirts
shirts
shoes
socks
hats
gloves
coats
pajamas
scarves

Polaroid Education Program

Here's an exciting new way to turn instant photography into an effective teaching tool. Refer to the full-color insert for the activity entitled Polaroid Places.

Theme Goals:

Through participating in the experiences provided by this theme, the children may learn:

1. Types of clothing.
2. Clothing workers.
3. Uses of clothing.
4. Care of clothing.
5. Equipment used with clothing.

Concepts for the Children to Learn:

1. Clothing is a covering for our body.
2. Pants, dresses, shirts, and sweaters are some of the clothing we wear on our bodies.
3. Shoes, socks, and boots are clothing for our feet.
4. Gloves and mittens are coverings for our hands.
5. Hats and scarves are coverings for our head.
6. Protection, decoration, and identification are uses for clothing.
7. There are many colors and sizes of clothing.
8. A tailor and a seamstress make and mend clothing.
9. Clothing needs to be cleaned.
10. Clothespins and hangers are used to hang clothes.
11. Clothes identify workers.
12. Needles, brushes, and irons are needed to care for clothing.

Vocabulary:

1. **clothing**—a covering for the body.
2. **shirt**—clothing that covers the chest and sometimes arms.
3. **shoes**—clothing for our feet.
4. **skirt**—clothing that hangs from the waist.
5. **hat**—clothing that covers our head.
6. **coat/jacket**—a piece of clothing that is often used for warmth and is worn over other clothing.
7. **clothespin**—a clip used to hang clothes on a clothesline or a hanger.
8. **washing machine**—an appliance used to clean clothes.
9. **dryer**—an appliance that dries clothes.
10. **laundromat**—a place to clean clothes.

Bulletin Board

The purpose of this bulletin board is to develop visual perception and discrimination skills. A "Sort the Clothes" bulletin board can be an addition to the clothing unit. Construct shorts and shirt pieces out of tagboard. The number used will be dependent upon the size of the bulletin board and the age of the children. Draw a pattern on a pair of shorts and the same pattern on one of the shirts. Continue, drawing a different pattern for each shorts and shirt set. Hang the shorts on the bulletin board, and hang a push pin on top of the shorts, so the children can hang the corresponding patterned shirt on top of the shorts.

Parent Letter

Dear Parents,

We will be beginning a unit on clothing. Through participating in this unit, the children will learn about many different kinds of clothing. They will also become aware of the care of clothing and purposes of clothing.

At School

Some of the learning experiences planned for this unit include:

- sorting clothes hangers by color.
- going to a laundromat in the dramatic play area.
- making newspaper skirts at the art table.
- washing doll clothes in the sensory table.

We will also be taking a walk to the Corner Laundromat on Tuesday afternoon. We will be looking at the big laundry carts, washers and dryers, and folding tables. If you would like to join us, please contact me. We will be leaving the center at 3:00 p.m.

At Home

You can foster the concepts introduced in this unit by letting your child select what he will wear to school each day. To promote independence, begin by placing your child's clothes in a low drawer allowing easy access to the clothes. To make mornings more enjoyable, encourage your child to select clothes at night that can be worn the next day. Find a location to place the clothes. Also, if your child has doll clothes, fill the kitchen sink or a tub with soapy water, and let your child wash the doll clothes. This will help your child become aware of the care of clothes.

Have fun exploring concepts related to clothing.

FIGURE 14 We take turns washing the clothes.

Fingerplay:

DRESS FOR THE WEATHER

If you go without your coat
   (put on coat)
When the wind is damp and chill,
   (hug self)
You could end up in bed, my friend,
   (shake finger)
Feverish, sneezing, and ill.
   (look sick, sneeze)
Wear your boots through snow and mud
   (put on boots)
And during a thunderstorm.
Also wear a waterproof coat and hat
   (put on coat and hat)
To keep yourself dry and warm.

Source: Cromwell, Hibner, & Faitel. (1983).
Finger Frolics. Michigan: Partner Press.

Science:

Fabric Sink and Float

Provide various kinds of clothing and fabric on
the science table along with a large tub of
water. The children can test the different types
of clothing to see which will sink and which
will float. Some clothing articles will sink
while other clothing articles float until they
become saturated with water. After a test has
been made, the clothes can be hung to dry.

Dramatic Play:

1. **Clothing Store**

   Place dress-up clothing on hangers and a rack.
   A cash register, play money, bags, and small
   shopping carts can also be provided to extend
   the play.

2. **Party Clothes**

   Provide dressy clothes, jewelry, shoes, hats,
   and purses.

3. **Uniforms**

   Collect occupational clothing and hats, such as
   police officer shirts and hats, a fire fighter's
   hat, nurse and doctor lab coats, and artist
   smocks. High school athletic uniforms can also
   be provided. After use, store this box so the
   uniforms are available upon request for other
   units.

4. **Hanging Clothes**

String a low clothesline in the classroom or outdoors. Provide clothespins and doll clothes for the children to hang up.

5. **Laundromat**

Collect two large appliance-sized boxes. Cut a hole in the top of one to represent a washing machine, and cut a front door in the other to represent a dryer. A laundry basket, empty soap box, and play clothing may be welcome additions to extend the play.

Arts and Crafts:

1. **Dress the Paper Doll**

Prepare clothing to fit paper dolls out of construction paper scraps. For younger children, the dolls can be pre-cut. Older children may be able to cut their own dolls if the lines are traced on paper, and a simple pattern is provided.

2. **Newspaper Skirts**

Depending upon the developmental level of the children, newspaper skirts can be constructed in the classroom. Begin by stapling about 10 sheets of newspaper across at the top. Draw a bold line about two inches from the staples. Then instruct the children to vertically cut from the bottom edge of the paper, all the way up to the bold line, creating strips. String pieces can be attached by stapling to the top of both sides to enable the skirt to be tied in the back.

3. **Easel Ideas**

- feature clothes-shaped easel paper
- paint using tools created by attaching small sponges to a clothespin

Sensory:

1. **Washing Clothes**

Fill the sensory table with soapy water and let the children wash doll clothing. After being

washed, the clothes can be hung on a low clothesline.

2. **Add to the Sensory Table**

- clothespins

Large Muscle:

1. **Clothespin Drop**

Collect clothespins and a series of jars with mouth openings of varying widths. The children can stand near the jar and drop the clothespins into it. To ensure success, the younger children should be guided to try the jar with the largest opening.

2. **Bean Bag Toss**

Bean bags can be tossed into empty laundry baskets.

3. **Clothes Race**

Fill bags with large-sized clothing items. Give a bag to each child. Signal the children to begin dressing up with the clothing. The object is to see how quickly they can put all of the clothes items in the bag over their own clothing. This activity is more appropriate for five-, six-, and seven-year-olds who have better large motor coordination and development.

Field Trips/Resource People:

1. **Clothing Store**

Visit a children's clothing store. Look at the different colors, sizes, and types of clothing.

2. **Tailor/Seamstress**

Invite a seamstress to visit your classroom to show the children how they make, mend, and repair clothing. The seamstress can demonstrate tools and share some of the clothing articles they have made.

3. **Laundromat**

Take a walk to a local laundromat. Observe the facility. Point out the sizes of the different kinds of washing machines and dryers. Explain the use of the laundry carts and folding tables.

Math:

1. **Clothes Seriation**

   Provide a basketful of clothes for the children to line up from largest to smallest. Include hats, sweatshirts, shoes, and pants. Use clothing items whose sizes are easily distinguishable.

2. **Line 'em Up**

   Print numerals on clothespins. The children can attach the clothespins on a low clothesline and sequence them in numerical order.

3. **Hanger Sort**

   Colored hangers can be sorted into laundry baskets or on a clothesline by color.

4. **Sock Match**

   Collect many different pairs of socks. Combine in a laundry basket. The children can find the matching pairs and fold them.

Social Studies:

1. **Weather Clothing**

   Bring in examples of clothing worn in each of the four seasons. Provide four laundry baskets. Label each basket with a picture representing a sunny hot day, a rainy day, a cold day, and a fall or spring day. Then encourage the children to sort the clothing according to the weather label on the basket.

2. **Who Wears It?**

   At group time, hold up clothing items and ask the children who would wear it. Include baby clothes, sports uniforms and occupational clothing, ladies clothes, men's clothes, etc.

Group Time:

Look Closely

While the children are sitting on the floor in a circle, call out the clothes items that one child is wearing. For example, say, "I see someone who is wearing a red shirt and pants." The children can look around the circle and say the name of the child who is wearing those items.

Cooking:

1. **Graham Crackers**

   Wear chef uniforms, and make your own graham crackers for snack.

   1/2 cup margarine
   2/3 cup brown sugar
   1/2 cup water
   2 3/4 cups graham flour
   1/2 teaspoon salt
   1/2 teaspoon baking powder
   1/8 teaspoon cinnamon

   Beat margarine and sugar till smooth and creamy. Add the remainder of the ingredients and mix well. Let the mixture sit for 30 to 45 minutes. Sprinkle flour on a board or tabletop. Roll out dough to 1/8 inch thick. Cut the dough into squares, logs, or whatever. Place on an oiled cookie sheet. Bake at 350 degrees for 20 minutes until lightly brown. This recipe should produce a sufficient quantity for eight children.

2. **Irish Gingerbread**

   1 or 2 teaspoons butter
   2 cups flour
   1 1/2 teaspoon baking soda
   1 teaspoon cinnamon
   1 teaspoon ground ginger
   3/4 teaspoon salt
   1 egg
   2 egg yolks
   1 cup molasses
   1/2 cup soft butter
   1/2 cup sugar
   1/2 cup quick-cooking oatmeal
   1 cup hot water

Preheat the oven to 350 degrees. Grease the bottom of the baking pan with 1 or 2 teaspoons of butter. Measure the flour, baking soda, cinnamon, ginger, and salt; sift them together onto a piece of waxed paper. In a mixing bowl, combine the butter with the sugar by stirring them with the mixing spoon until they are blended. Add the egg and egg yolks. With the mixing spoon, beat the mixture until it is fluffy. Stir in the molasses.

Add the sifted dry ingedients, the oatmeal, and the hot water one fourth at a time to the egg and molasses mixture, stirring after each addition. Pour the mixture into the greased pan. Bake 50 to 55 minutes. Test with a toothpick. Make gingerbread people with cookie cutters. Decorate: make clothes for the gingerbread people using coconut, nuts, raisins, etc.

Source: Touff, Terry, & Ratner, Marilyn. (1974). *Many Hands Cooking*. New York: Thomas Y. Crowell Co.

3. **Pita or Pocket Bread**

1 package of yeast
1/4 cup of lukewarm water
3 cups of flour
   (white, whole wheat, or any combination)
2 teaspoons of salt

Dissolve the yeast in the water and add the flour and salt. Stir into a rough sticky ball. Knead on a floured board or table until smooth, adding more flour, if necessary. Divide the dough into 6 balls and knead each ball until smooth and round. Flatten each ball with a rolling pin until 1/4 inch thick and about 4 to 5 inches in diameter.

Cover the dough with a clean towel and let it rise for 45 minutes. Arrange the rounds upside down on baking sheets. Bake in a 500-degree oven for 10 to 15 minutes or until brown and puffed in the center. The breads will be hard when they are removed from the oven, but will soften and flatten as they cool. When cooled, split or cut the bread carefully and fill with any combination of sandwich filling.

DRAMATIC PLAY CLOTHES

The following list contains names of clothing articles to save for use in the dramatic play area:

aprons	socks	coats
boots	purses	earmuffs
pajamas	jewelry— rings	raincoats
shirts	bracelets	snow pants
dresses	necklaces	shorts
skirts	clip-on earrings	sweatsuits
hats	shoes	suspenders
gloves/mittens	slippers	billfolds
scarves	robes	ties
leotards	slacks	belts
swimsuits	sweaters	

Multimedia:

The following resource can be found in educational catalogs:

Palmer, Hap. "What Are You Wearing?" on *Learning Basic Skills through Music* [record].

Books:

The following books can be used to complement the theme:

1. Corey, Dorothy. (1985). *New Shoes!* Niles, IL: Albert Whitman & Co.

2. Tyrrell, Anne. (1987). *Elizabeth Jane Gets Dressed*. Woodbury, NY: Barron's.

3. Daly, Niki. (1986). *Not So Fast, Songololo*. New York: Atheneum.

4. Winthrop, Elizabeth. (1986). *Shoes*. New York: Harper and Row.

5. Hill, Ari. (1986). *The Red Jacket Mix-up*. New York: Golden Press.

6. Hoban, Tara. (1987). *Dots, Spots, Speckles and Stripes*. New York: Greenwillow Books.

7. Fitz-Gerald, Christine Maloney. (1987). *I Can Be a Textile Worker*. Chicago: Children's Press.

8. Shreckhise, Roseva. (1985). *What Was It Before It Was a Sweater?* Chicago: Children's Press.

9. Flournoy, Valerie. (1985). *The Patchwork Quilt*. New York: Dial Press.

10. Oliver, Stephen. (1991). *Clothes*. New York: Random House Books for Young Readers.

11. Pluckrose, Henry. (1990). *Wear It!* New York: Franklin Watts, Inc.

12. Allen, Jonathan. (1992). *Purple Sock, Pink Sock*. New York: William Morrow and Co.

13. Gaban, Jesus. (1992). *Harry Dresses Himself*. Milwaukee: Gareth Stevens, Inc.

14. Neitzel, Shirley. (1992). *The Dress I'll Wear to the Party*. New York: Greenwillow Books.

15. Rice, Eve. (1989). *Peter's Pocket*. New York: Greenwillow Books.

16. Roy, Ron. (1991). *Whose Shoes are These?* Boston: Houghton Mifflin Co.

17. Hilton, Nettle. (1990). *The Long Red Scarf*. Minneapolis: Carolrhoda Books.

18. Blackman, Marjorie. (1992). *A New Dress for Maya*. Milwaukee: Gareth Stevens Children's Books.

19. Brett, Jan. (1989). *The Mitten*. New York: G. P. Putnam.

20. Peek, Merle. (1985). *Mary Wore Her Red Dress and Henry Wore His Green Sneakers*. New York: Clarion.

21. Borden, Louise. (1989). *Caps, Hats, Socks, and Mittens*. New York: Scholastic.

22. Carlstrom, Nancy White. (1986). *Jesse Bear, What Will You Wear?* New York: Macmillan.

23. Hest, A. (1986). *The Purple Coat*. New York: Four Winds.

24. Brown, Marc. (1989). *One, Two Buckle My Shoe*. New York: Dutton.

THEME 15

Alarm

flashing light
car horn
fire
sirens

Verbal

talking
singing
sounds
foreign accents
disabilities

Equipment

telephone
television
typewriter
telegraph
FAX
radio
records
video recorder
cassette player
computer

COMMUNICATION

Visual

letters
numbers
signs
pictures
art
artifacts

Written

books
newspapers
magazines
letters
cards
words

Nonverbal

listening
body movements
sign language
dancing
pantomime
drawings

Here's an exciting new way to turn instant photography into an effective teaching tool. Refer to the full-color insert for the activity entitled Photo Face.

Theme Goals:

Through participating in the experiences provided by this theme, the children may learn:

1. Visual communication skills.
2. Nonverbal communication skills.
3. Verbal communication skills.
4. Communication equipment.

Concepts for the Children to Learn:

1. Talking is a form of communication.
2. Listening is a way to communicate.
3. Our hands can communicate.
4. Our faces can communicate.
5. Sign language is a way of communication.
6. The telephone is a communication tool.
7. Letters and cards are a way of communicating.
8. Machines can transmit messages.
9. Typewriters, televisions, radios, and computers are equipment for communicating.
10. Signs are a way of communicating.
11. Books are a form of communication.

Vocabulary:

1. **communication**—sharing information.
2. **typewriter**—a machine that prints letters.
3. **newspaper**—words printed on paper.
4. **sign language**—making symbols with our hands to communicate.
5. **Braille**—a system of printing for blind people.
6. **alphabet**—letter symbols that are used to write a language.
7. **signs**—symbols.
8. **card**—a piece of folded paper with a design. Cards are sent to people on special occasions: birthdays, holidays, celebrations, or when ill.
9. **letter**—paper with a written or typed message.

Bulletin Board

The purpose of this bulletin board is to assist older children in learning their home telephone number. Construct a telephone and receiver for each child. See the illustration. Affix each child's telephone number to the telephone. Laminate this card. For younger children, receivers can be attached to the telephones but left off the hook. The children can hang up their receiver when they arrive at school. Older children can match their receiver to their number and correct themselves by the color match. Later, white receivers for each child could be used to see if they know their telephone number. Telephones can be prepared for dialing by fastening the rotary dial with a brass fastener. Then the children can practice calling home by dialing their own number.

Parent Letter

Dear Parents,

We will begin talking about communication or how we get our ideas across to others. Through this unit the children will become aware of the different ways we communicate: through our voices, letters, using hands, and our bodies. They will also become familiar with machines that are used to communicate such as the television, radio, computer, typewriter, and telephone.

At School

Some of the learning experiences planned for this unit include:

- a sign language demonstration.
- a phone booth in the dramatic play area.
- a typewriter in the writing center.
- songs and books about communication.

At Home

It is important for children to know their telephone number for safety reasons. Help your children learn your home telephone number. (This is also something we will be practicing at school.) To make practicing more fun, construct a toy telephone with your child. Two paper cups or empty tin cans and a long piece of rope, string, or yarn are needed to make a telephone. Thread the string through the two cups and tie knots on the ends. Have two people hold the cups and pull the string taut. Take turns talking and listening. The sound vibrations travel through the string—and you won't hear a busy signal!

Enjoy your children as you share concepts and experiences related to communication.

FIGURE 15 Computers are one way to communicate.

Music:

1. **"Call a Friend"**
   (Sing to the tune of "Row, Row, Row Your Boat")

   Call, call, call a friend.
   Friend, I'm calling you.
   Hi, hello, how are you?
   Very good, thank you!

2. **"A Letter, A Letter"**
   (Sing to the tune of "A Tisket, A Tasket")

   A letter, a letter, I can make a letter.
   I take my arms and take my legs and I can
   make a _____.

   Encourage the children to make letters of the
   alphabet with their body parts.

   Source: Wirth, Stassevitch, Shotwell, and
   Stemmler. *Musical Games, Fingerplays and
   Rhythmic Activities for Early Childhood.*

3. **"Twinkle, Twinkle Traffic Light"**
   (Sing to the tune of "Twinkle, Twinkle Little
   Star")

   Twinkle, twinkle traffic light
   Standing on the corner bright.

   Green means go, we all know
   Yellow means wait, even if you're late.
   Red means STOP!
      (pause)
   Twinkle, twinkle traffic light
   Standing on the corner bright.

4. **"I'm a Little Mail Carrier"**
   (Sing to the tune of "I'm a Little Teapot")

   I'm a little mail carrier, short and stout.
   Here is my hat, and here is my pouch.
      (point to head, point to side)
   I walk around from house to house,
   Delivering mail from my pouch.
      (pretend to take things out of a bag)

Fingerplays:

BODY TALK

When I smile, I tell you I'm happy.
   (point at the corner of mouth)
When I frown I tell you that I'm sad.
   (pull down corners of mouth)
When I raise my shoulders and tilt my head I
tell you "I don't know."
   (raise shoulders, tilt head, raise hands, shake
   head)

HELPFUL FRIENDS

Mail carriers carry a full pack
Of cards and letters on their backs.
   (hold both hands over one shoulder)
Step, step, step! Now ring, ring, ring!
   (step in place and pretend to ring bell)
What glad surprises do they bring?

MY HANDS

My hands can talk
In a special way.
These are some things
They help me to say.
"Hello"
   (wave)
"Come Here"
   (beckon toward self)
"It's A–OK"
   (form circle with thumb and pointer)
"Now Stop"
   (hand out–palm up)
"Look"
   (hands shading eyes)
"Listen"
   (cup hand behind ear)
Or "It's far, far away"
   (point out into the distance)
And "Glad to meet you, how are you today."
   (shake neighbor's hand)

Science:

1. **Telephones**

   Place telephones, real or toy, in the classroom to encourage the children to talk to each other. Also, make your own telephones by using two large empty orange juice concentrate cans, removing one end for the removal of content. After washing the cans, connect with a long string. The children can pull the string taut. Then they can take turns talking and listening to each other.

2. **Sound Shakers**

   Using identical small orange juice cans, pudding cups, or empty film containers, fill pairs of the containers with different objects.

Included may be sand, coins, rocks, rice, salt, etc. Replace the lids. Make sure to secure the lids with glue or heavy tape to avoid spilling. To make the containers self-correcting, place numbers or like colors on the bottoms of the matching containers.

3. **Feely Box**

   Prepare a feely box which includes such things as tape cassette, pen, pencil, block letters, an envelope, and anything else that is related to communication. The children can place their hand in the box and identify objects using their sense of touch.

4. **Training Telephones**

   Contact your local telephone company to borrow training telephones. Place the telephone on the science table along with a chart listing the children's telephone numbers. The children can sort, match, and classify the wires.

5. **Vibrations**

   Encourage the children to gently place their hand on the side of the piano, guitar, record player, radio, television, etc., in order to feel the vibrations. Then have the children feel their own throats vibrate as they speak. A tuning fork can also be a teaching aid when talking about vibrations.

6. **Telephone Parts**

   Dismantle an old telephone and put it on the science table for the children to discover and explore the parts.

Dramatic Play:

1. **Post Office**

   In the dramatic play area place a mailbox, envelopes, old cards, paper, pens, old stampers, ink pads, hats, and mailbags. During self-selected or self-initiated play periods, the children can play post office.

2. Telephone Booth

Make a telephone booth from a large refrigerator-sized cardboard box. Inside, place a toy phone. Place in the dramatic play area.

3. Television

Obtain a discarded television console to use for puppetry or storytelling experiences. Remove the back and set, leaving just the wooden frame. If desired, make curtains.

4. Radio Station

Place an old microphone, or one made from a styrofoam ball and cardboard, with records in the dramatic play area.

5. Puppet Show

Place a puppet stand and a variety of puppets in the dramatic play area for the children to use during the self-selected or self-directed play period.

Arts and Crafts:

1. Record Player Art

Place a piece of round paper or a paper plate with a hole punched in the center on a record player turntable. Turn the record player on. The children can use crayons or markers to draw softly on the paper while the record player is spinning.

2. Easel Idea

Cut easel paper in the shape of a book, record, radio, or other piece of communication equipment.

3. Traffic Lights

Provide red, yellow, and green circles, glue, and construction paper for the children to create a traffic light.

4. Stationery

Provide the children with various stencils or stamps to make their own stationery. It can be used for a gift for a parent or a special person. Children could then dictate a letter to a relative or friend.

Large Muscle:

Charades

Invite children one at a time to come to the front of the group. Then whisper something in the child's ear, like "You're very happy." The child then uses his hands, face, feet, arms, etc., to communicate this feeling to the other children. The group of children then identifies the demonstrated feeling.

Field Trips/Resource People:

1. Post Office

Visit a local post office. Encourage the children to observe how the mail is sorted.

2. Phone Company

Visit a local phone company.

3. Radio Station

Visit a local disc jockey at the radio station.

4. Television Station

If available, visit a local television station. Observe the cameras, microphones, and other communication devices.

5. Sign Language Demonstration

Invite someone to demonstrate sign language.

Math:

Phone Numbers

Make a list of the children's names and telephone numbers. Place the list by a toy, trainer, or unhooked telephone.

Social Studies:

Thank You

Let the children dictate a group thank-you letter to one of your resource visitors or field trip representatives. Before mailing the letter, provide writing tools for children to sign their names.

Group time (games, language):

1. **Telephone**

   Play the game "telephone" by having the children sit in a circle. Begin by whispering a short phrase into a child's ear. That child whispers your message to the next child. Continue until the message gets to the last child. The last child repeats the message out loud. It is fun to see how much it has changed. (This game is most successful with older children.)

2. **What's Missing?**

   Place items that are related to communication on a tray. Include a stamp, a telephone, a record, a pocket radio, etc. The children can examine the objects for a few minutes. After this they should close their eyes while you remove an object. Then let the children look at the tray and identify which object is missing.

3. **Household Objects Sound Like...**

   Make a tape of different sounds around the house. Include a radio, television, alarm clock, telephone, vacuum cleaner, flushing toilet, door bells, egg timer, etc. Play the tape for the children, letting them identify the individual sounds.

Cooking:

Edible Envelope

Spread peanut butter on a graham cracker. Add raisins to represent an address and a stamp.

FINGERPAINT RECIPES

Liquid Starch Method

liquid starch (put in
    squeeze bottles)
dry tempera paint in
    shakers

Put about 1 tablespoon of liquid starch on the surface to be painted. Let the child shake the paint onto the starch. Mix and blend the paint. Note: If this paint becomes too thick, simply sprinkle a few drops of water onto the painting.

Soap Flake Method

Mix in a small bowl:
soap flakes
a small amount of water

Beat until stiff with an egg-beater. Use white soap on dark paper, or add colored tempera paint to the soap and use it on light-colored paper. This gives a slight three-dimensional effect.

Wheat Flour Paste

3 parts water
1 part wheat paste flour
coloring

Stir flour into water. Add coloring. (Wallpaper paste can be bought at low cost in wallpaper stores or department stores.)

Uncooked Laundry Starch

A mixture of 1 cup laundry/liquid starch, 1 cup

cold water, and 3 cups soap flakes will provide a quick fingerpaint.

Flour and Salt I

1 cup flour
1 1/2 cups salt
3/4 cup water
coloring

Combine flour and salt. Add water. This has a grainy quality, unlike the other fingerpaints, providing a different sensory experience. Some children enjoy the different touch sensation when 1 1/2 cups salt are added to the other recipes.

Flour and Salt II

2 cups flour
2 teaspoons salt
3 cups cold water
2 cups hot water
coloring

Add salt to flour, then pour in cold water gradually and beat mixture with egg beater until it is smooth. Add hot water and boil until it becomes clear. Beat until smooth, then mix in coloring. Use 1/4 cup food coloring to 8 to 9 ounces of paint for strong colors.

Instantized Flour Uncooked Method

1 pint water (2 cups)
1 1/2 cups instantized flour (the kind used to thicken gravy)

Put the water in the bowl and stir the flour into the water. Add color. Regular flour may be lumpy.

Cooked Starch Method

1 cup laundry starch dissolved in a small amount of cold water
5 cups boiling water added slowly to dissolve starch
1 tablespoon glycerine (optional)

Cook the mixture until it is thick and glossy. Add 1 cup mild soap flakes. Add color in separate containers. Cool before using.

Cornstarch Method

Gradually add 2 quarts water to 1 cup cornstarch. Cook until clear and add 1/2 cup soap flakes (like Ivory Snow). A few drops of glycerine or oil of wintergreen may be added.

Flour Method

Mix 1 cup flour and 1 cup cold water. Add 3 cups boiling water and bring all to a boil, stirring constantly. Add 1 tablespoon alum and coloring. Paintings from this recipe dry flat and do not need to be ironed.

TIPS

1. Be sure you have running water and towels nearby or provide a large basin of water where children can rinse off.

2. Fingerpaint on smooth table, oil cloth, or cafeteria tray. Some children prefer to start fingerpainting with shaving cream on a sheet of oil cloth.

3. Food coloring or powdered paint may be added to mixture before using, or allow child to choose the colors he wants sprinkled on top of paint.

4. Sometimes reluctant children are more easily attracted to paint table if the fingerpaints are already colored.

Multimedia:

The following resources can be found in educational catalogs:

1. Jenkins, Ella. *Jambo Songs and Chants* [record].

2. *Community Helpers* [record]. Bowmar/Noble Publishers.

3. Palmer, Hap. *Creative Movement and Rhythmic Exploration* [record].

4. *Listening Skills for Pre-readers* [record]. Classroom Materials, Inc.

5. Jenkins, Ella. *You'll Sing a Song and I'll Sing a Song* [record].

6. *Starting to Read* [54-minute video]. Edu-vid.

7. *Alphie's Alphabet* [60-minute video]. Edu-vid.

8. *Getting Ready to Read* [video]. Random House.

9. *Learning about Letters* [video]. Random House.

10. *Reader Rabbit's Ready for Letters* [IBM/Mac software, PK–1]. The Learning Company.

11. *Reading Maze* [Mac software, PK–2]. Great Wave.

12. *Mario's Early Years: Fun with Letters* [IBM software, PK–1]. Software Tools.

13. *Reading Rodeo* [Apple/IBM/Mac software, PK–1]. Heartsoft.

Books:

The following books can be used to complement the theme:

1. Chaplin, Susan Gibbons. (1986). *I Can Sign My ABC's.* Washington, DC: Gallaudet University Press.

2. Baker, Pamela. (1986). *My First Book of Sign.* Washington, DC: Gallaudet University Press.

3. Kalman, Bobbie. (1986). *How We Communicate.* New York: Crabtree Publishing Company.

4. Hughes, S. (1985). *Noisy.* New York: Lothrop, Lee & Shepard Company.

5. Everett, Louise. (1988). *Amigo Means Friend.* Mahwah, NJ: Troll Associates.

6. Hutchins, Pat. (1991). *The Surprise Party.* New York: Macmillan Children's Book Group.

7. Leedy, Loreen. (1990). *The Furry News: How to Make a Newspaper.* New York: Holiday House, Inc.

8. Brown, Ann. (1992). *TV or Not TV.* Racine, WI: Western Publishing Co.

9. Levine, Ellen. (1989). *I Hate English!* New York: Scholastic.

10. Hayes, Sarah. (1988). *Clap Your Hands: Finger Rhymes.* New York: Lothrop, Lee & Shepard.

11. Bulla, Clyde R. (1989). *Singing Sam.* New York: Random House.

12. Morris, Winifred. (1990). *Just Listen.* New York: Macmillan.

THEME 16

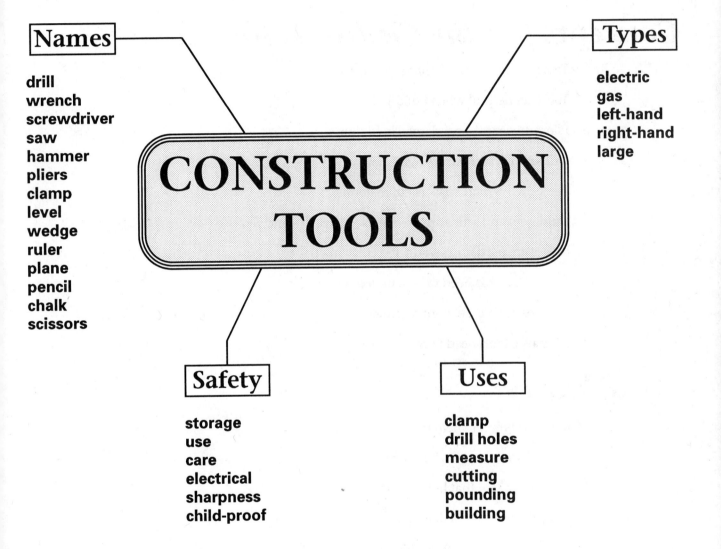

Names

drill
wrench
screwdriver
saw
hammer
pliers
clamp
level
wedge
ruler
plane
pencil
chalk
scissors

CONSTRUCTION TOOLS

Types

electric
gas
left-hand
right-hand
large

Safety

storage
use
care
electrical
sharpness
child-proof

Uses

clamp
drill holes
measure
cutting
pounding
building

Here's an exciting new way to turn instant photography into an effective teaching tool. Refer to the full-color insert for the activity entitled Polaroid Places.

Theme Goals:

Through participating in the experiences provided by this theme, the children may learn:

1. Types of tools.
2. Names of common tools.
3. Functions of tools.
4. Tool safety.

Concepts for the Children to Learn:

1. Tools can be electric or hand-powered.
2. Tools are helpful when building.
3. Pliers, tweezers, and clamps hold things.
4. Drills, nails, and screws make holes.
5. Planes, saws, and scissors cut materials.
6. Hammers and screwdrivers are used to put in and remove nails and screws.
7. Rulers are used for measuring.
8. To be safe, tools need to be handled with care.
9. Goggles should be worn to protect our eyes when using tools.
10. After use, tools need to be put away.

Vocabulary:

1. **tool**—an object to help us.
2. **drill**—a tool that cuts holes.
3. **wrench**—a tool that holds things.
4. **screwdriver**—a tool that turns screws.
5. **saw**—a cutting tool with sharp edges.
6. **hammer**—a tool used to insert or remove objects such as nails.
7. **pliers**—a tool used for holding.
8. **clamp**—a tool used to join or hold things.
9. **ruler**—a measuring tool.
10. **wedge**—a tool used for splitting.
11. **plane**—a tool used for shaving wood.

Bulletin Board

The purpose of this bulletin board is to develop awareness of types of tools, as well as foster visual discrimination skills. A shadow tool match bulletin board can be constructed by drawing about six or seven tool pieces on tagboard. See the illustration. These pieces can be colored and cut out. Next, trace the pieces on black construction paper to make shadows of each piece. These shadow pieces can be attached to the bulletin board. Magnet pieces can be applied to both the shadows and the colored tool pieces, or a push pin can be placed above the shadow and a hole can be punched in the colored tool piece. The children can match the colored tool piece to its corresponding-shaped shadow.

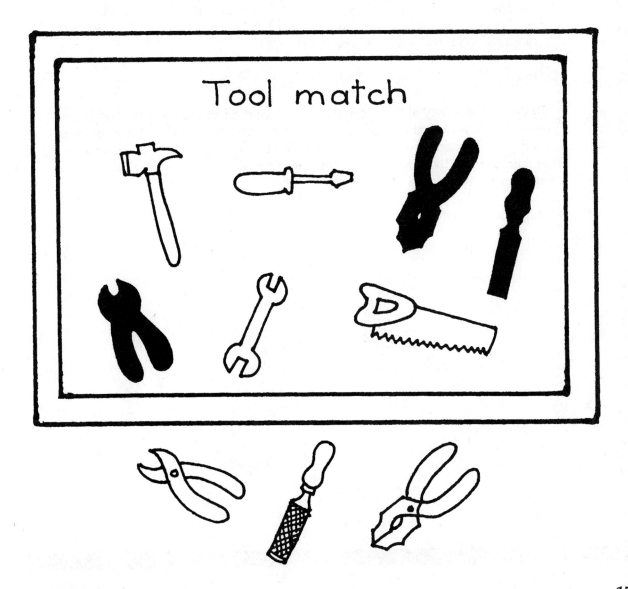

Parent Letter

Dear Parents,

Construction tools will be the focus of our next unit. This unit will help your child become more aware of many kinds of tools, their purposes, and tool safety. While exploring this unit, the children will have opportunities to use many hand tools at the woodworking bench.

At School

Some of the activities the children will participate in include:

- painting with screwdrivers and wrenches.
- exploring wood shavings in the sensory table.
- setting up a mechanic's shop where the children can pretend to fix cars.
- a visit on Wednesday from Mr. Smith, a local shoe repairer. Mr. Smith will show us the tools he uses to repair shoes.

At Home

To develop memory skills, recall with your child all of the tools we use in our homes—from cooking and cleaning tools to gardening tools. Count the number of tools that are in each room of your house. Which room contains the most tools? This will promote the mathematical concepts of rational counting and vocabulary of most and least.

Have fun with your child!

FIGURE 16 Construction tools help people build tall buildings.

Music:

"This Is the Way"
(Sing to the tune of "Mulberry Bush")

This is the way we saw our wood,
saw our wood, saw our wood.
This is the way we saw our wood,
so early in the morning.

Other verses: pound our nails
                 drill a hole
                 use a screwdriver

Fingerplays:

CARPENTER'S HAMMER

The carpenter's hammer goes rap, rap, tap
   (make hammer motion)
And his saw goes see, saw, see.
   (make saw motions)
He planes and measures and hammers and
saws
   (act out each one)
While he builds a house for me.
   (draw house with index fingers)

JOHNNY'S HAMMER

Johnny works with one hammer, one hammer,
one hammer.
Johnny works with one hammer, then he
works with two.

Say the same words adding one hammer each
time. Children are to pretend to hammer using
various body parts.

Verse 1: 1 hand hitting leg.
Verse 2: 2 hands hitting legs.
Verse 3: use motions for verses 1 and 2, plus
             tap one foot.
Verse 4: verses 1, 2, and 3 plus tap other foot.
Verse 5: verses 1 to 4, plus nod head. At the
             end of verse 5 say, "Then he goes to
             sleep," and place both hands by side
             of head.

You can also change the name used in the
fingerplay to include names of children in
your classroom.

THE COBBLER

Cobbler, cobbler, mend my shoe.
   (point to shoe)
Get it done by half past two.
   (hold up two fingers)

Half past two is much too late.
Get it done by half past eight.
  (hold up eight fingers)

Science:

1. **Exploring Levels**

   Place levels and wood scraps on a table for the children to explore while being closely supervised.

2. **Hammers**

   Collect a variety of hammers, various-sized nails, and wood scraps or styrofoam. Allow the children to practice pounding using the different tools and materials.

3. **The Wide World of Rulers**

   Set up a display with different types and sizes of rulers. Include the reel type. Paper and pencils can also be added to create interest.

Dramatic Play:

1. **The Carpenter**

   Place a carpentry box with scissors, rulers, and masking tape in the woodworking area. Also, provide large cardboard boxes and paint, if desired.

2. **Shoemaker Store**

   Set up a shoemaker's store. Provide the children with shoes, toy hammers, smocks, cash registers, and play money. The children can act out mending, buying, and selling shoes.

Arts and Crafts:

1. **Rulers**

   Set rulers and paper on the table. The children can then experiment creating lines and geometric shapes.

2. **Tool Print**

   Pour a small amount of thick colored tempera paint in a flat pan. Also, provide the children with miniature tools such as wrenches, screwdrivers, and paper. The children then can place the tools in the paint pan, remove them, and print on paper.

Sensory:

1. **Scented Playdough**

   Prepare playdough and add a few drops of extract such as peppermint, anise, or almond. Also, collect a variety of scissors, and place in the art area with the playdough.

2. **Wood Shavings**

   Place wood shavings in the sensory table along with scoops and pails.

Large Muscle:

The Workbench

In the woodworking area place various tools, wood, and goggles for the children to use. It is very important to discuss the safety and limits used when at the workbench prior to this activity. An extra adult is helpful to supervise this area.

Field Trips/Resource People:

1. **Shoe Repair Store**

   Visit a shoe repair store. Observe a shoe being repaired.

2. **Wood Worker**

   Invite a parent or other person into the classroom who enjoys woodworking as a hobby.

Math:

1. Use of Rulers

Discuss how rulers are used. Provide children with rulers so that they may measure various objects in the classroom. Allow them to compare the lengths. Also, measure each child and construct a chart including each child's height.

2. Weighing Tools

Place scales and a variety of tools on the math table. Let the children explore weighing the tools.

Social Studies:

1. Tool Safety

Discuss the safe use of tools. Allow the children to help decide what classroom rules are necessary for using tools. Make a chart containing these rules to display in the woodworking area.

2. Helper Chart

Design a helper chart for the children to assist with cleanup and care of the classroom tools. Each day select new children to assist, assuring that everyone gets a turn. To participate, the children can be responsible for cleaning the dirty tools and putting them away.

Group Time (games, language):

1. Tool of the Day

Each day of this unit, introduce a "tool of the day." Explain how each tool is used and who uses it. If possible, leave the tool out for children to use on the woodworking bench.

2. Thank-You Letter

Using a pencil as a tool, let the children dictate a thank-you note to any resource person or field trip site coordinator who has contributed to the program.

Cooking:

"Hands On" Cookies

3 cups brown sugar
3 cups margarine or butter
6 cups oatmeal
1 tablespoon baking soda
3 cups flour

Place all of the ingredients in a bowl. Let the children use clean child-size wooden hammers to mash and knead. Form into small balls and place on ungreased cookie sheet. Butter the bottom of a glass. Dip the bottom of the glass into a saucer with sugar. Use the glass to flatten the balls. Bake in an oven preheated to 350 degrees for 10 to 12 minutes. Makes 15 dozen.

SCIENCE MATERIALS AND EQUIPMENT

Teachers need to continuously provide science materials for the classroom. Materials that can be collected include:

acorns and other nuts	bones	drinking straws
aluminum foil	bowls and cups	drums
ball bearings	cocoon	egg cartons
balloons	corks	eggbeaters
binoculars	discorded clock	eyedroppers and basters
bird nests	dishpans	fabric scraps

filter paper	musical instruments	scales
flashlight	newspapers	scissors—assorted sizes
flowers	nails, screws, bolts	screen wire
gears	paper bags	sieves, sifters, and funnels
insect nests	paper of various types	seeds
insects	paper rolls and spools	spatulas
jacks	plants	sponges
kaleidoscope	plastic bags	stones
locks and keys	plastic containers with	string
magnets—varying	lids—many sizes	styrofoam
strengths, sizes	plastic tubing	tape
magnifying glasses—good	pots, pans, trays, muffin	thermometers
lenses	tins	tongs and tweezers
marbles	prisms	tools—hammer, pliers
measuring cups and	pulleys	tuning forks
spoons	rocks	waxed paper
microscope	rubber tubing	weeds
milk cartons	ruler	wheels
mirrors—all sizes	safety goggles—child size	wood and other building
moths	sandpaper	materials

Multimedia:

The following resources can be found in educational catalogs:

1. *Moving Machines* [25-minute video]. Bo Peep Productions.

2. *Alphabet Blocks* [IBM/Mac/Windows software, PK–1]. Bright Star.

Books:

The following books can be used to complement the theme:

1. Screckhise, Roseva. (1985). *What Was It Before It Was a Chair?* Chicago: Children's Press.

2. Jennings, Terry. (1993). *Cranes, Dump Trucks, Bulldozers and Other Building Machines.* New York: Kingfisher Books

3. Krasilovsky, Phyllis. (1992). *The Man Who Was Too Lazy to Fix Things.* New York: William Morrow and Co.

4. Miller, Margaret. (1990). *Who Uses This?* New York: Greenwillow Books.

5. Sandow, Lyn. (1990). *My Drill.* New York: Little, Brown and Co.

6. Sandow, Lyn. (1990). *My Pliers.* New York: Little, Brown and Co.

7. Sandow, Lyn. (1990). *My Saw*. New York: Little, Brown and Co.

8. Sandow, Lyn. (1990). *My Screwdriver*. New York: Little, Brown and Co.

9. Sandow, Lyn. (1990). *My Wrench*. New York: Little, Brown and Co.

10. Stone, Venice. (1991). *Tools*. New York: Scholastic, Inc.

11. *Ernie's Little Toolbook: A Sesame Street Book*. (1991). New York: Random House Books for Young Readers.

12. Morris, Ann. (1992). *Tools*. New York: Lothrop, Lee & Shepard.

13. Butterworth, Brent, & Green, Tie. (1991). *The Big Book of How Things Work*. Lincolnwood, IL: Publications International.

14. Macauley, David. (1988). *The Way Things Work*. Boston: Houghton Mifflin.

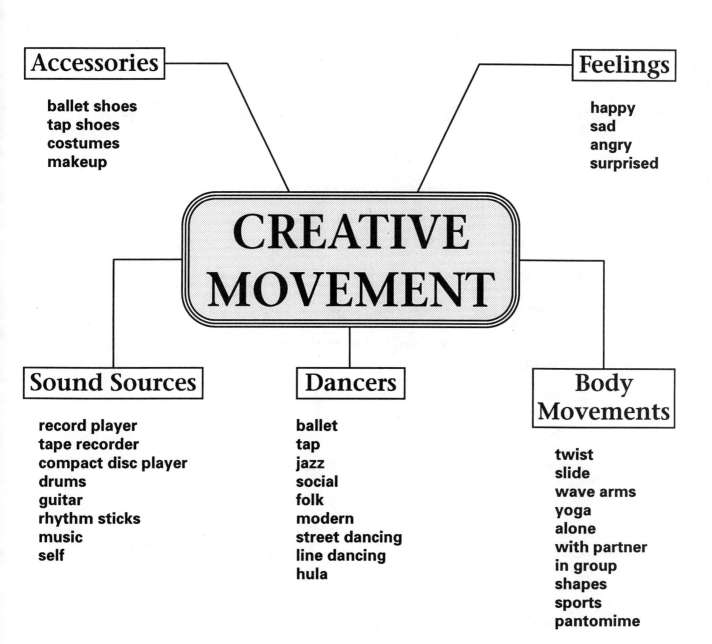

CREATIVE MOVEMENT

Accessories

ballet shoes
tap shoes
costumes
makeup

Feelings

happy
sad
angry
surprised

Sound Sources

record player
tape recorder
compact disc player
drums
guitar
rhythm sticks
music
self

Dancers

ballet
tap
jazz
social
folk
modern
street dancing
line dancing
hula

Body Movements

twist
slide
wave arms
yoga
alone
with partner
in group
shapes
sports
pantomime

Polaroid Education Program

Here's an exciting new way to turn instant photography into an effective teaching tool. Refer to the full-color insert for the activity entitled Photo Open House.

Theme Goals:

Through participating in the experiences provided by this theme, the children may learn:

1. Creative movement accessories.

2. Creative movement sound sources.

3. Body movements used in creative movement.

4. Expression of feelings through creative movement.

5. Types of dancers.

Concepts for the Children to Learn:

1. People can dance to music.

2. The record player, tape recorder, and compact disc player are all sound sources used for dance.

3. Dancing and moving can be done alone, with a partner, or in a group.

4. Our bodies can move in many different ways.

5. Ballet, tap, jazz, and social are some types of dances.

6. Happy, sad, angry, and surprised are feelings that can be expressed through dance.

7. Some dancers wear special costumes and makeup.

8. Ballet and tap dancers wear special shoes.

9. Our bodies can move to the sound of drums, guitars, and rhythm sticks.

10. We can twist, slide, and wave our arms during dance.

Vocabulary:

1. **dance**—a pattern of body movements.

2. **movement**—change in body position.

3. **ballet**—movement that usually tells a story.

4. **music**—sounds made by instruments or voices.

Bulletin Board

The purpose of this bulletin board is to develop one-to-one correspondence skills and the ability to match a set to the matching written numeral. Construct tank tops, each a different color, from a sheet of tagboard. See the illustration. Print a numeral that would be developmentally appropriate for the group of children on each tank top. Draw a corresponding number of black dots below each numeral. Construct a tutu ruffle from white tagboard for each top. Place colored dots on each ruffle. Trace ruffles onto black construction paper. Laminate all pieces. Staple tank tops and shadow ruffles to bulletin board. The children can match the ruffles with dots to the corresponding tank top, using holes in white ruffles and push pins in shadow ruffles.

Parent Letter

Dear Parents,

Children love to dance, and they are constantly on the move. We will begin a unit on creative movement. Throughout the activities provided in the unit the children will discover the different ways our bodies move, and also learn about various forms of dance. Some of the activities include:

- singing songs and moving to music.
- dancing in the dance studio that will be set up in the dramatic play area.
- watching other people move.
- participating in an aerobics class.

Field Trip

On Thursday, at 2:30 p.m., we will be taking a bus to a dance studio. At the studio, we will observe dancers and learn a few steps from a dance instructor. To assist with the trip, we need several parents to accompany us. Please call the school if you are available.

At Home

As your child develops, he will show increased control and interest in perfecting and improving motor skills. To foster the development of large muscle skills, balance, and body coordination, provide opportunities each day for vigorous play. Give suggestions, such as "How fast can you hop?" "How far can you hop on one foot?" etc. Also, ask your child to walk on a curved line, a straight line, or a balance beam.

Enjoy your child!

FIGURE 17 Exercise can be a form of creative movement.

Fingerplays:

The following circle games are from *Finger Frolics: Fingerplays for Young Children* by Cromwell, Hibner, and Faitel. (Partner Press: 1983).

HOP AND TWIRL

Make a circle and we'll go around.
First walk on tiptoe so we don't make a sound.
Tip, toe, around we go.
Then hop on our left foot, and then on our right.
Then hop together. What a funny sight!
Now stop hopping and twirl around
Now we're ready to settle down.

A CIRCLE

Around in a circle we will go.
Little tiny baby steps, make us go very slow.

And then we'll take some great giant steps,
As big as they can be.
Then in our circle we'll stand quietly.

STAND IN A CIRCLE

Stand in a circle and clap your hands.
Clap, clap, clap, clap.
Now put your hands over your head.
Slap, slap, slap, slap.
Now hands at your sides and turn around.
Then in our circle we'll all sit down.

ONE TO TEN CIRCLE

Let's make a circle and around we go,
Not too fast and not too slow.
One, two, three, four, five, six, seven, eight, nine, ten,
Let's face the other way and go around again.
One, two, three, four, five, six, seven, eight, nine, ten.

PARTNER GAME

Pick a partner, take a hand.
Then in a circle partners stand.
Take two steps forward,
And two steps back.
Then bow to your partner
And clap, clap, clap.
Wrap your elbows
And around you go.
Not too fast and not too slow.
Change elbows.
Go around again.
Then stand in a circle
And count to ten.

Science:

1. **Magnet Dancers**

On a piece of tagboard, draw pictures of three-inch dancers. Stickers or pictures from magazines can also be used. Cut the dancers out and attach paper clips to the back side. Use a small box and a magnet to make these dancers move. Hold the dancers up on one side of the box and move the dancer up by holding and moving a magnet on the other side of the box.

2. **Kaleidoscopes**

On the science table, put a number of kaleidoscopes. The tiny figures inside appear to be dancing.

3. **Dancing Shoes**

Place various types of dancing shoes at the science table. Let the children compare the shape, size, color, and texture of the shoes. The children may also enjoy trying the shoes on for size and dancing in them.

Dramatic Play:

1. **Dance Studio**

Add to the dramatic play area tap shoes, tutus, ballet shoes, tights, and leotards. Provide a record player with records or tape player with tapes.

2. **Fitness Gym**

Add to the dramatic play area a small mat, head bands, wrist bands, sweat shirts, sweat pants, leotards, and music.

Arts and Crafts:

1. **Stencils**

The teacher can construct stencils from tagboard. Shapes such as shoes, ballerinas, circles, etc., can be made and added to the art table for use during self-selected activity periods.

2. **Musical Painting**

Provide a tape recorder with headphones and a tape of children's music or classical music at the easel. The children can listen and move their brushes to the music if desired.

Large Muscle:

1. **Streamer/Music Activity**

In the music area provide streamers. Play a variety of music, allowing the children, if desired, to move to the different rhythms.

2. **Do As I Say**

Provide the children verbal cues for moving. For example, say, "Move like you are sad," "Show me that you are tired," "You just received a special present," or "Show me how you feel."

3. **Animal Movement**

Ask a child to act out the way a certain animal moves. Examples include: frog, spider, caterpillar, butterfly, etc.

4. **Balance**

Add a balance beam or balance strip to the indoor or outdoor environment.

5. **Roly-Poly**

The children can stretch their bodies out on the floor. When touched by a teacher, the child rolls into a tight ball.

6. **Dancing Cloud**

Using an inflated white balloon or ball, let the children stand in a circle and bounce or hit it to each other.

7. **Obstacle Course**

Set up an obstacle course indoors or outdoors depending on the weather. Let the children move their bodies in many different ways. They can run or crawl through the course. Older children may enjoy hopping or skipping.

Field Trips/Resource People:

1. **Field Trips**

   - dance studio
   - health club
   - gymnasium

2. **Resource People**

Invite the following people to class to talk with the children:

   - a dancer or dance instructor
   - gymnast
   - aerobics instructor

Math:

1. **Matching Leotards to Hangers**

   Using plastic hangers, prepare a numeral on each of the hangers. Provide the children with a box of leotards. Have a printed numeral on each. Encourage the children to match the numbered leotard with the identically numbered hanger.

2. **Following Steps**

   Using tagboard, cut out some left feet and right feet. Write the numerals from one to ten on the feet and arrange them in numerical order. Place the footprints on the floor, securing them with masking tape. Encourage the children to begin the walk on the numeral one and continue in the correct sequence.

3. **Ballet Puzzle**

   Purchase a large poster of a ballet dancer. Laminate the poster or cover it with clear contact paper. Cut the poster into several large shapes. Place the puzzle in the manipulative area. During self-selected play periods, the children can reconstruct the puzzle.

Social Studies:

Social Dancing

   Let each child choose a partner. Encourage the children to hold hands. Play music as a background, so the partners can move together.

Group Time (games, language):

1. **Balloon Bounce**

   Blow up balloons for the children to use at group time. Play music and have children bounce the balloons up in the air. Let the balloons float to the ground when the music ends. Supervision is required for this activity. Broken balloons should be immediately removed from the environment.

2. **Toy Movements**

   Form a circle and move like different toys. Try to include as many actual toys as you can, so that the children can observe each toy moving, and then can more easily pretend to be that toy.

   - jack-in-the-box
   - wind-up dolls
   - roll like a ball
   - skates

3. **Rag Doll**

   Repeat the following poem as the child creates a dance with a rag doll.

   If I were a rag doll
   And I belonged to you,
   Whenever I would try to dance,
   This is what I'd do.

Cooking:

1. **Orange Buttermilk Smoothie**

   1 quart buttermilk
   3 cups orange juice
   1/2 teaspoon cinnamon
   1/4 cup honey

   Blend in a blender until the mixture is smooth. Enjoy!

2. **Indian Flat Bread**

   2 cups all-purpose flour
   1/4 cup unflavored yogurt
   1 egg, slightly beaten
   1 1/2 teaspoons baking powder
   1 teaspoon sugar
   1/4 teaspoon salt
   1/4 teaspoon baking soda
   1/2 cup milk
   vegetable oil
   poppy seeds

   Mix all ingredients except milk, vegetable oil, and poppy seeds. Stir in enough milk to make a soft dough. Turn dough onto lightly floured surface. Knead until smooth, about 5 minutes.

Place in greased bowl; turn greased side up. Cover and let rest in warm place 3 hours.

Divide dough into 6 or 8 equal parts. Flatten each part on lightly floured surface, rolling it into 6-inch x 4-inch leaf shape about 1/4 inch thick. Brush with vegetable oil; sprinkle with poppy seeds.

Place 2 cookie sheets in oven; heat oven to 450 degrees. Remove hot cookie sheets from oven; place breads on cookie sheets. Bake until firm, 6 to 8 minutes. Makes 6 to 8 breads.

Source: *Betty Crocker's International Cookbook.* (1980). New York: Random House.

MOVEMENT ACTIVITIES

Listen to the Drum

Accessory: drum
fast
slow
heavy
soft
big
small

Choose a Partner

Make a big shape
go over
go under
go through
go around

To Become Aware of Time

Run very fast
Walk very slowly
Jump all over the floor quickly
Sit down on the floor slowly
Slowly grow up as tall as you can
Slowly curl up on the floor as small as possible

To Become Aware of Space

Lift your leg up in front of you
Lift it up backwards, sideways
Lift your leg and step forward, backwards, sideways, and around and around

Reach up to the ceiling
Stretch to touch the walls
Punch down to the floor

To Become Aware of Weight

To feel the difference between heavy and light, the child should experiment with his own body force.
Punch down to the floor hard
Lift your arms up slowly and gently
Stomp on the floor
Walk on tiptoe
Kick out one leg as hard as you can
Very smoothly and lightly slide one foot along the floor

Moving Shapes

1. Try to move about like something huge and heavy: elephant, tug boat, bulldozer.
2. Try to move like something small and heavy: a fat frog, a heavy top.
3. Try moving like something big and light: a beach ball, a parachute, a cloud.
4. Try moving like something small and light: a feather, a snowflake, a flea, a butterfly.

Put Yourself Inside Something

(bottle, box, barrel)
You're *outside* of something—now get into it
You're *inside* of something—now get out of it
You're *underneath* something
You're *on top of* something
You're *beside* or *next to* something
You're *surrounded* by it

Pantomime

1. You're going to get a present. What is the shape of the box? How big is the box? Feel it. Hold it. Unwrap it. Take it out. Put it back in.
2. Think about an occupation. How does the worker act?
3. Show me that it is cold, hot.
4. You are two years old (sixteen, eighty, etc.)
5. Show me: It's very early in the morning, late in the afternoon.
6. Show me: What is the weather like?
7. Pretend you are driving, typing, raking leaves.
8. Take a partner. Pretend you're playing ball.

Multimedia:

The following resources can be found in educational catalogs:

1. Nelson, Esther, & Haack, Bruce. *Dance, Sing, and Listen* [record].

2. Palmer, Hap. *Creative Movement and Rhythmic Exploration* [record].

3. Jenkins, Ella. *Songs, Rhythms and Chants for the Dance* [record].

4. *Music for Creative Movement* [record]. Kimbo Records.

5. *Simple Folk Dances* [record]. Kimbo Records.

6. *Tempo for Tots* [record]. Melody House.

7. *Preschool Fitness* [record]. Melody House.

8. *Channel 3* [record]. Melody House.

9. *Up & Down, In & Out, Big & Little* [30-minute video]. Edu-vid.

10. *Mario's Early Years: Preschool Fun* [IBM software, PK–1]. Software Tools.

Books:

The following books can be used to complement the theme:

1. Raffi. (1987). *Shake My Sillies Out*. New York: Crown Publishers, Inc.

2. Jonas, Ann. (1989). *Color Dance*. New York: Greenwillow Books.

3. Alpert, Lou. (1991). *Emma's Turn to Dance*. Ipswich, MA: Whispering Coyote Press.

4. Jabar, Cynthia (Comp.). (1992). *Shimmy Shake Earthquake: Don't Forget to Dance Poems*. New York: Little, Brown and Co.

5. Nicklaus, Carol. (1991). *Come Dance with Me*. Eden Prairie, MN: Silver Press.

6. Slater, Teddy. (1992). *The Bunny Hop*. New York: Scholastic, Inc.

7. Martin, Bill, Jr., & Archambalt, John. (1986). *Barn Dance*. New York: Henry Holt & Company.

8. Coombs, Linda. (1992). *Pow Wow*. Cleveland, OH: Modern Curriculum Press.

9. Brown, Marc. (1985). *Hand Rhymes*. New York: E. P. Dutton.

10. Oxenbury, Helen. (1987). *All Fall Down*. New York: Macmillan.

11. Ackerman, Karen. (1988). *Song and Dance Man*. New York: Alfred A. Knopf.

12. Shannon, George. (1991). *Dance Away*. New York: Morrow.

13. Giff, Patricia R. (1989). *The Almost Awful Play*. New York: Live Oak Media.

14. Brown, Judith G. (1989). *The Mask of the Dancing Princess*. New York: Macmillan.

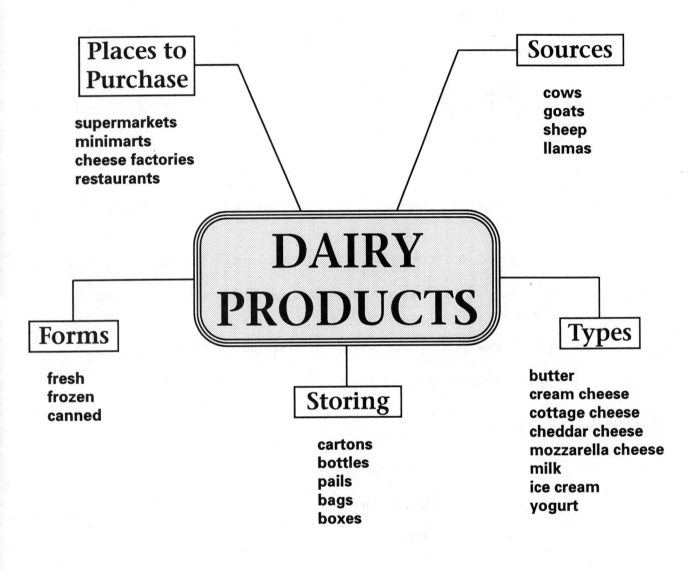

Places to Purchase

supermarkets
minimarts
cheese factories
restaurants

Sources

cows
goats
sheep
llamas

DAIRY PRODUCTS

Forms

fresh
frozen
canned

Storing

cartons
bottles
pails
bags
boxes

Types

butter
cream cheese
cottage cheese
cheddar cheese
mozzarella cheese
milk
ice cream
yogurt

Polaroid Education Program

Here's an exciting new way to turn instant photography into an effective teaching tool. Refer to the full-color insert for the activity entitled Photo Open House.

Theme Goals:

Through participating in the experiences provided by this theme, the children may learn:

1. Sources of dairy products.

2. Types of dairy products.

3. Forms of dairy products.

4. Places dairy products can be purchased.

5. Containers used to hold dairy products.

Concepts for the Children to Learn:

1. Cows, goats, sheep, and llamas provide milk.

2. Milk can be used to make butter, cheese, ice cream, and yogurt.

3. There are many kinds of cheese such as cottage cheese, cream cheese, cheddar cheese, mozzarella, and colby.

4. Dairy products can be purchased fresh, frozen, canned, or processed.

5. We can buy dairy products at supermarkets, minimarts, cheese factories, and restaurants.

6. Cartons, bottles, pails, bags, and boxes are used to store dairy products.

7. Dairy products are good food choices.

Vocabulary:

1. **dairy product**—a product made from milk.

2. **can**—to prepare food for future use.

3. **frozen**—food that is kept cold.

4. **cheese factory**—a place where cheese is made or sold.

5. **carton**—a box or container to hold food or other objects.

6. **cream**—the yellowish part of milk.

7. **yogurt**—a milk product that can be flavored with fruit.

8. **minimart**—a very small store.

Bulletin Board

The purpose of this bulletin board is to help children become aware of ice cream as a dairy product, as well as recognize the printed word. This is designed as a check-in bulletin board. Each child is provided a bulletin board piece with his name on it. When the children arrive each day at school, they place their name on the bulletin board.

To create the bulletin board, cut an ice cream cone out of tagboard or construction paper for each child in the class. Color or decorate each cone as desired. Print the child's name on the ice cream cone. Laminate the pieces or cover with clear contact paper. Use push pins or adhesive magnet pieces to attach the ice cream cones to the bulletin board.

Parent Letter

Dear Parent:

Did you know that on the average each person in the United States consumes about 550 pounds of dairy products each year? Dairy products provide us with one of our main sources of protein. We will study dairy products in our classroom. The children will learn sources of dairy products, types of dairy products, forms of dairy products, places dairy products can be purchased, and containers used to hold dairy products.

At School

Some of the learning activities the children will participate in include:

- Preparing milkshakes, homemade vanilla pudding, and strawberry yogurt in the cooking area.
- Creating a dairy collage, yogurt print cups, and ice cream cone sponge paints in the art area.
- Hearing stories related to the story theme.
- Visiting the dairy department of a grocery store.

At Home

At home you can reinforce the dairy product concepts by:

- Encouraging your child to prepare instant pudding with you for snack or a desert.
- At mealtimes have your child identify the foods being served that are dairy products.
- Browse through newspaper ads or magazines and have your child identify dairy products.
- Take your child grocery shopping and have him show you where the dairy section of the store is located.

Enjoy your child!

FIGURE 18 Milk is a dairy product.

Music:

1. **"The Farmer in the Dell"**

   The farmer in the dell,
   The farmer in the dell,
   Hi-ho, the dairy-o
   The farmer in the dell.

   Continue with additional verses:

   The farmer takes the wife/husband
   The wife/husband takes the nurse.
   The nurse takes the dog.
   The dog takes the cat.
   The cat takes the rat.
   The rat takes the cheese.

   The final verse:

   The cheese stands alone.
   The cheese stands alone.
   Hi-ho, the dairy-o,
   The cheese stands alone.

2. **"Old McDonald Had a Farm"** (traditional)

3. **"We Like Ice Cream"**
   (Sing to the tune of "Are You Sleeping?")

   We like ice cream, we like ice cream.
   Yes, we do! Yes, we do!
   Vanilla and strawberry,
   Chocolate and mint.
   Yum, yum, yum.
   Yum, yum, yum!

4. **"Drink Your Milk"**
   (Sing to the tune of "My Darling Clementine")

   Drink your milk.
   Drink your milk.
   Drink your milk everyday.
   It is good for your teeth and bones.
   Drink your milk everyday.

5. **"Cows"**
   (Sing to the tune of "Mulberry Bush")

   This is the way we feed the cows,
   Feed the cows, feed the cows.
   This is the way we feed the cows,
   On the dairy farm each day.

   This is the way we milk the cows,
   Milk the cows, milk the cows.
   This is the way we milk the cows,
   On the dairy farm each day.

Fingerplays:

ICE CREAM

I'm licking my ice cream.
I'm licking it fast.
It's dripping down my arm.
It's disappearing fast.

LITTLE MISS MUFFET

Little Miss Muffet
Sat on a tuffet
Eating her curds and whey.
Along came a spider
And sat down beside her
And frightened Miss Muffet away!

THIS LITTLE COW

This little cow eats grass.
    (hold up fingers of one hand, bend down
    one finger)
This little cow eats hay.
    (bend down another finger)
This little cow drinks water.
    (bend down another finger)
And this little cow does nothing.
    (bend down another finger)
But lie and sleep all day.

Science:

1. Make Butter

Fill baby food jars half-full with whipping cream and replace lids. The children can take turns shaking the jars until the cream separates. (The mixture will first look like whipping cream, then like overwhipped cream, and finally it will be obvious that separation has occurred.) Pour off the remaining liquid. Rinse the butter in cold water several times and drain. Add salt to taste. Let the children spread the butter on crackers or bread.

2. Making Ice Cream

Collect the following ingredients:

1 cup milk
1/2 cup sugar
1/4 teaspoon salt

3 beaten egg yolks
1 tablespoon vanilla
2 cups whipping cream

In a saucepan, combine milk, sugar, salt, and egg yolks. Stir constantly over medium heat until bubbles appear around the edge of the pan. Cool mixture at room temperature. Stir in vanilla and whipping cream. Pour into an ice cream maker and follow the manufacturer's directions. (Recipe makes 1 quart of ice cream.)

3. Science Table Additions

Additions to the science table may include:

- pictures of dairy cows.
- books about milking cows and dairy animals.
- containers of grain, corn, and hay along with magnifying glasses.
- pictures of goats, sheep, and llamas.

Dramatic Play:

1. Ice Cream Shop

Clothes and props for an ice cream shop can be placed in the dramatic play area. Include items such as empty, clean ice cream pails and cartons, ice cream scoops, plastic parfait glasses and bowls, plastic spoons, empty ice cream cone boxes, napkins, aprons, and a cash register with play money. Prepare and display posters in the area that portray various ice cream products and flavors.

2. Dairy Farm

Turn the dramatic play center into a dairy farm where the children can pretend to do chores. Display pictures of farms and cows and provide overalls, boots, hats, pails, hoses, and other appropriate props.

3. Grocery Store—Dairy Department

Set up the dramatic play area to resemble the dairy department of a grocery store. Include props such as milk cartons, cottage cheese containers, yogurt cups, sour cream containers, ice cream pails and cartons, butter boxes, cheese packages, and a cash register. Display pictures of dairy foods.

Arts and Crafts:

1. Buttermilk Chalk Pictures

Dip colored chalk into a small container of buttermilk or brush construction paper with buttermilk. Use the chalk to create designs on construction paper.

2. Dairy Product Paint Containers

Use empty dairy product containers to hold paint for use at the art table or easel. Examples include milk cartons, yogurt cups, and cottage cheese containers.

3. Whipped Soap Painting

The following mixture can be made to represent ice cream or cottage cheese. Mix one cup of Ivory Snow flakes with 1/2 cup of warm water in a bowl. The children can beat the mixture with a hand eggbeater until it is fluffy. Add more water, if necessary. Apply mixture with paint brushes or fingers to construction paper. For a variation, food coloring can be added to the paint mixture.

4. Ice Cream Cone Sponge Painting

Cut sponges into shapes of ice cream cones and scoops of ice cream. Provide shallow trays of various colors of paints. Designs are created by dipping the sponge in the paint and then pressing it onto a piece of construction paper.

5. Yogurt Cup Prints

Collect empty yogurt cups of various shapes and sizes. Wash them thoroughly. Prepare shallow trays of paint. Create designs by inverting a yogurt cup, dipping it into the paint, and then applying it to construction paper. Repeat the process as desired.

6. Dairy Collage

Provide magazines that contain pictures of dairy products for the children to cut out. The pictures can be glued to a piece of construction paper, tagboard, or a paper plate for the children to create a collage.

Sensory:

Add to the sensory table:

- sand, scoops, and empty milk cartons.
- water and empty, clean yogurt and cottage cheese containers.
- cotton balls, spoons, ice cream scoops, bowls, and empty, clean ice cream pails.

Field Trips:

1. The Grocery Store

Visit a grocery store and locate the dairy section. Look at the types of dairy products available.

2. Ice Cream Shop

Take a trip to an ice cream shop. Count the flavors of ice cream available. Purchase a cone for each of the children.

3. Dairy Farm

Visit a dairy farm. Ask the farmer to show the housing, equipment, and food supplies needed to care for dairy cows.

Math:

1. Dairy Sort

Collect different types of food product containers, including dairy products. Place all of the containers in a basket. Encourage the children to sort out the containers representing dairy products from the other food product containers.

2. Dairy Lids

Collect lids and caps from milk jugs. They can be recycled and used for game pieces, creating patterns, and counting activities.

3. Favorite Ice Cream Graph

The children can assist in making a graph of their favorite ice cream flavors. Begin by printing the caption, "Our Favorite Ice Cream Flavors," across the top of a piece of tagboard. Draw or paste pictures of different flavors of ice cream along the left-hand side of the tagboard. Each child's name or picture is placed next to the picture of his favorite ice cream flavor. The results of the graph should be shared with the children using math vocabulary words: most, more, fewer, least, etc. Display the graph for further reference.

Additional graphs could be made depicting the children's favorite flavors of yogurt, cheese, or milk.

Social Studies:

1. Sharing a Treat

Prepare a dairy food with the children and share it with another class, senior citizens group, or other community group.

2. Role of the Dairy Farmer

Invite a dairy farmer to the classroom to discuss his occupation. The equipment and tools used to farm could also be shown and discussed.

Group Time (games, language):

1. Dairy Charts

Print the caption, "Foods Made from Milk," across the top of a piece of tagboard. During group time, present the chart and record the children's responses. Display the chart and refer to it throughout the theme.

Additional language charts could be made about types of cheeses, ice cream, and yogurt.

2. Cheese Tasting Party

Cut various types of cheese into small slices or pieces. Place the cheese pieces on paper plates for the children to taste. Discuss types of cheeses, textures, flavors, and colors.

Cooking:

1. Milk Shake

For each shake, combine 1/2 cup of vanilla ice cream and one cup of milk in a blender. If desired, flavor the shake with one of the following: 1/2 cup fresh berries, 1/2 banana, two tablespoons of peanut butter, or two tablespoons chocolate syrup.

2. Grilled Cheese Sandwich

Assist the children in making cheese sandwiches. Provide plastic knives for the children to spread soft butter or margarine on the outside of sandwiches. Turn over and place a cheese slice between the two pieces of bread.

Under adult supervision, place the sandwiches on a heated skillet or electric grill until golden brown, turning once.

3. Homemade Vanilla Pudding

1/8 teaspoon salt
2 cups milk
2 slightly beaten egg yolks
1 tablespoon softened butter or margarine
2 teaspoons vanilla

Combine cornstarch, sugar, and salt in a medium saucepan. Stir in the milk. Over medium heat, cook and stir constantly until the mixture thickens and comes to a boil. Stir and boil one minute. In a small bowl, blend half of the hot mixture into the egg yolks. Pour the egg mixture back into the saucepan and cook until the mixture boils, stirring constantly. Remove the pan from the heat and add the butter and vanilla. Allow the pudding to cool slightly and spoon into a serving bowl or individual dishes. Refrigerate. (This recipe makes four servings.)

4. Strawberry Yogurt Surprise

3-oz. package strawberry-flavored gelatin
1 cup boiling water
1/2 cup cold water
1 cup strawberry yogurt

Dissolve gelatin in the boiling water. Stir in cold water. Chill until thickened but not set. Beat gelatin and fold in yogurt. Pour into serving dish. Refrigerate until firm. (This recipe makes four servings.)

Multimedia:

The following resources can be found in educational catalogs:

1. Raffi. "Down on Grandpa's Farm" on *One Light, One Sun* [record].

2. Raffi. "Corner Grocery Store" on *The Corner Grocery Store* [record].

3. Sharon, Lois, & Bram. "Did You Feed My Cow?" on Smorgasbord [record].

Books:

The following books can be used to complement the theme:

1. Ziegler, Sandra. (1987). *A Visit to the Dairy Farm*. Chicago: Children's Press.

2. Fowler, Allan. (1992). *Thanks to Cows*. Chicago: Children's Press.

3. Moncure, Jane. (1987). *Ice Cream Cows and Mitten Sheep*. Mankato, MN: Child's World, Inc..

4. Royston, Angela. (1990). *Cow*. New York: Franklin Watts, Inc..

5. Gibbons, Gail. (1985). *The Milk Makers*. New York: Macmillan Publishing Co.

6. Carrick, Donald. (1985). *Milk*. New York: Greenwillow Books.

7. Robbins, Ken. (1992). *Make Me a Peanut Butter Sandwich and a Glass of Milk*. New York: Scholastic, Inc.

8. Rice, Colleen. (1985). *What Was It Before It Was Ice Cream?* Mankato, MN: Child's World, Inc.

9. Asch, Frank. (1991). *Milk and Cookies*. New York: Putnam Publishing.

10. Modell, Frank. (1988). *Ice Cream Soup*. New York: Greenwillow.

11. Geringer, Laura. (1993). *The Cow Is Mooing Anyhow*. New York: Harper Collins.

12. Grossman, Bill. (1992). *Tommy at the Grocery Store Big Book*. New York: Harper Collins.

13. Peterson, Katherine. (1993). *Smallest Cow in the World*. New York: Harper Collins.

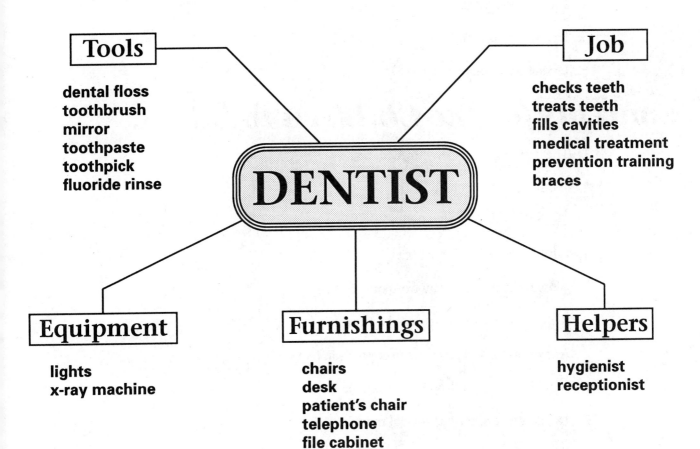

Tools

dental floss
toothbrush
mirror
toothpaste
toothpick
fluoride rinse

Job

checks teeth
treats teeth
fills cavities
medical treatment
prevention training
braces

DENTIST

Equipment

lights
x-ray machine

Furnishings

chairs
desk
patient's chair
telephone
file cabinet

Helpers

hygienist
receptionist

Polaroid
Education
Program

Here's an exciting new way to turn instant photography into an effective teaching tool. Refer to the full-color insert for the activity entitled People and Uniforms.

Theme Goals:

Through participating in the experiences provided by this theme, the children may learn:

1. How the dentist helps us.

2. Dentist's tools.

3. The name of a dental assistant.

4. Proper tooth care.

5. Dental equipment.

6. Dental office furnishings.

Concepts for the Children to Learn:

1. The dentist helps keep our teeth healthy.

2. Teeth are used to chew food.

3. Teeth should be brushed after each meal.

4. A hygienist helps the dentist.

5. A dentist removes decay from our teeth.

6. Pictures of our teeth are called x-rays.

7. A toothbrush and paste are used to clean teeth.

8. Dental floss helps clean between teeth.

9. The dentist's office has special machines.

Vocabulary:

1. **toothbrush**—a brush to clean teeth.

2. **toothpaste**—a paste to clean our teeth.

3. **dentist**—a person who helps keep our teeth healthy.

4. **teeth**—used to chew food.

5. **hygienist**—the dentist's assistant.

6. **cavity**—tooth decay.

7. **toothpick**—a stick-like tool used for removing food parts between our teeth.

8. **dental floss**—a string used to clean between the teeth.

184

Bulletin Board

The purpose of this bulletin board is to develop a positive self-concept and assist in name recognition. Prepare an attendance bulletin board by constructing a toothbrush out of tagboard for each student and teacher. See the illustration. Color the toothbrushes and print the children's names on them! Laminate. Punch holes in each toothbrush. Observe who brushed by observing who hung their toothbrush on a push pin on the bulletin board.

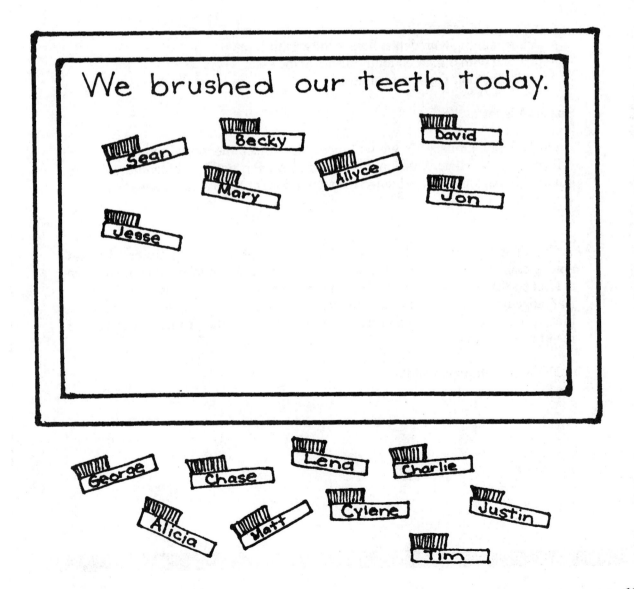

Parent Letter

Dear Parents,

We are continuing our study of community helpers with a unit on the dentist. The dentist is an important helper for us because our teeth are very important. Children are very aware of their teeth at this age. Many of the older five-year-olds will soon begin losing their baby teeth. Through the experiences provided in this unit the children may learn that the dentist is a person who helps us to keep our teeth healthy. They will also spend some time learning about the importance of tooth care.

At School

Some of the experiences planned for the unit include:

- making toothpaste.
- string painting with dental floss at the art table.
- painting with discarded toothbrushes at the easel.
- exploring tools that a dentist uses.

Special Visitor

On Tuesday, January 13, we will meet Mrs. Jones, the dental hygienist at Dr. Milivitz's dental clinic. Mrs. Jones will discuss proper toothbrushing and will pass out toothbrush kits. You are invited to join our class at 10:00 a.m. for her visit.

At Home

Good habits start young! Dental cavities are one of the most prevalent diseases among children. It has been estimated that 98 percent of school-aged children have at least one cavity. You and your child can spend some time each day brushing your teeth together. Sometimes a child will more effectively brush if someone else is with him. It is important for children to realize that they are the primary caretakers of their teeth!

Have fun with your child!

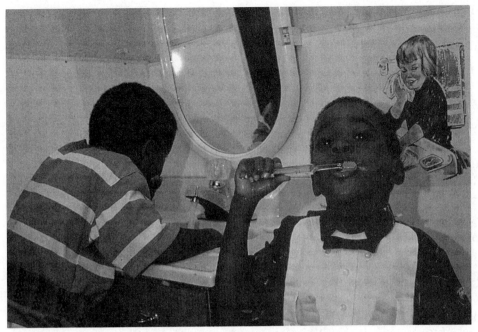

FIGURE 19 Children usually enjoy brushing their teeth.

Music:

1. **"Brushing Teeth"**
   (Sing to the tune of "Mulberry Bush")

   This is the way we brush our teeth,
   brush our teeth, brush our teeth.
   This is the way we brush our teeth,
   so early in the morning.

2. **"Clean Teeth"**
   (Sing to the tune of "Row, Row, Row Your Boat")

   Brush, brush, brush your teeth
   Brush them everyday.
   We put some toothpaste on our brush
   To help stop tooth decay.

Fingerplays:

MY TOOTHBRUSH

I have a little toothbrush.
(use pointer finger)

I hold it very tight.
(make hand into fist)
I brush my teeth each morning,
and then again at night.
(use pointer finger and pretend to brush)

MY FRIEND THE TOOTHBRUSH

My toothbrush is a tool.
I use it every day.
I brush and brush and brush and brush
to keep the cavities away.
(pretend to brush teeth)

Science:

1. **Tools**

   Place some safe dental products on the sensory table. Include a mirror, dental floss, tooth-brush, toothpaste, etc. A dentist may even lend you a model of a set of teeth.

2. **Acid on Our Teeth**

   Show the children how acid weakens the enamel of your teeth. Place a hard-boiled egg into a bowl of vinegar for 24 hours. Observe how the egg shell becomes soft as it decalcifies. The same principle applies to our teeth if the acid is not removed by brushing. (This activity is only appropriate with older children.)

3. **Making Toothpaste**

   In individual plastic bags, place 4 teaspoons of baking soda, 1 teaspoon salt, and 1 teaspoon water. Add a drop of food flavoring extract such as peppermint, mint, or orange. The children can mix their own toothpaste.

4. **Sugar on Our Teeth**

   Sugar found in sweet food can cause cavities on tooth enamel if it is not removed by rinsing or brushing. To demonstrate the effect of brushing, submerge white eggshells, which are made of enamel, into a clear glass of cola for 24 hours. Observe the discoloration of the eggshell. Apply toothpaste to toothbrush. Brush the eggshell removing the stain. Ask the children, "What caused the stain?"

Arts and Crafts:

1. **Easel Ideas**

   - paint with discarded toothbrushes
   - paint on tooth-shaped easel paper

2. **Toothbrushes and Splatter Screen**

   Provide construction paper, splatter screens, and discarded toothbrushes. The children can splatter paint onto the paper using the toothbrush as a painting tool.

3. **Dental Floss Painting**

   Provide thin tempera paint, paper, and dental floss. The child can spoon a small amount of paint onto their paper and can hold on to one end of the dental floss while moving the free end through the paint to make a design.

Sensory:

Additions to the Sensory Table

- toothbrushes and water
- peppermint extract added to water

Large Muscle:

1. **Drop the Toothbrush**

   Set a large plastic open-mouth bottle on the floor. Encourage the children to try to drop the toothbrushes into the mouth of the bottle.

2. **Sugar, Sugar, Toothbrush**

   Play like "Duck, Duck, Goose." The toothbrush tries to catch the "sugar" before it gets around the circle to where the "toothbrush" was sitting. Game can continue until interest diminishes.

Field Trips/Resource People:

1. **The Dentist**

   Visit the dentist's office. Observe the furnishings and equipment.

2. **The Hygienist**

   Invite a dental hygienist to visit the classroom. Ask the hygienist to discuss tooth care and demonstrate proper brushing techniques. After the discussion, provide each child with a disclosing tablet to check their brushing habits.

Group Time (games, language):

Pass the Toothpaste

Play music and pass a tube of toothpaste around the circle. When the music stops, the person who is holding the toothpaste stands up and claps his hands three times (or some similar action). Repeat the game.

Cooking:

1. Happy Teeth Snacks

- apple wedges
- orange slices
- asparagus
- cheese chunks
- milk
- cucumber slices
- cauliflower pieces

2. Smiling Apples

apples, cored and sliced
peanut butter
mini-marshmallows, raisins, or peanuts

Spread peanut butter on one side of each apple slice. Place 3 to 4 mini-marshmallows, raisins, or peanuts on the peanut butter of one apple slice. Top with another apple slice, peanut butter side down.

Multimedia:

The following resources can be found in educational catalogs:

1. Kangaroo, Captain. *Let's Go to the Dentist* [record]. Columbia.

2. Palmer, Hap. "Brush Away" on *Health and Safety* [record].

3. Raffi. "Brush Your Teeth" on *Singable Songs for the Very Young* [record]. Kimbo.

Books:

The following books can be used to complement the theme:

1. Quinlan, Patricia. (1992). *Brush Them Bright*. New York: Walt Disney Books Publishing Group.

2. Borgardt, Marianne. (1991). *Going to the Dentist*. New York: Simon and Schuster Trade.

3. Rogers, Fred. (1989). *Going to the Dentist*. New York: Putnam Publishing Group.

4. Mitra, Annie. (1990). *Tusk! Tusk!* New York: Holiday House Inc.

5. Luttrell, Ida. (1992). *Milo's Toothache*. New York: Dial Books for Young Readers.

6. McPhail, David. (1986). *The Bear's Toothache*. New York: Live Oak Media.

7. Kroll, Steven. (1992). *Loose Tooth*. New York: Scholastic.

8. Linn, Margot. (1988). *A Trip to the Dentist*. New York: Harper Collins.

9. Pohl, Linda. (1991). *The Wiggly Tooth Book*. L. P. Pohl.

10. West, Colin. (1988). *The King's Toothache*. New York: Harper Collins.

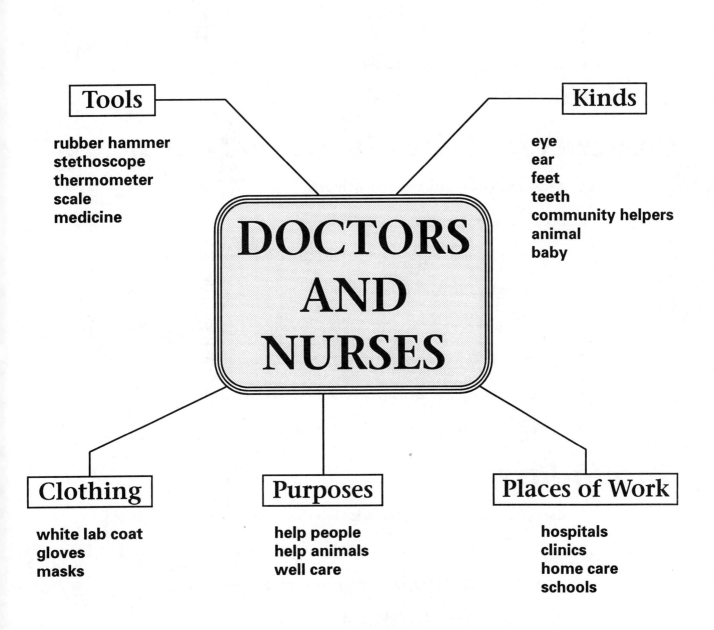

Tools

rubber hammer
stethoscope
thermometer
scale
medicine

Kinds

eye
ear
feet
teeth
community helpers
animal
baby

DOCTORS AND NURSES

Clothing

white lab coat
gloves
masks

Purposes

help people
help animals
well care

Places of Work

hospitals
clinics
home care
schools

Here's an exciting new way to turn instant photography into an effective teaching tool. Refer to the full-color insert for the activity entitled Photo Expectations.

Theme Goals:

Through participating in the experiences provided by this theme, the children may learn:

1. Kinds of doctors and nurses.

2. Places doctors and nurses work.

3. Tools used by doctors and nurses.

4. Clothing worn by doctors and nurses.

5. How doctors and nurses help people and animals.

Concepts for the Children to Learn:

1. A man or woman can be a doctor or nurse.

2. Doctors and nurses are community helpers.

3. Doctors and nurses help to keep people and animals healthy.

4. Doctors and nurses work in hospitals and clinics.

5. Lab coats, gloves, and masks are clothing doctors and nurses may wear.

6. Special doctors and nurses care for our eyes, ears, feet, and teeth.

7. A stethoscope is a tool used to check heartbeats and breathing.

8. Thermometers are used to check body temperature.

Vocabulary:

1. **doctor**—a man or woman who helps keep our bodies healthy.

2. **nurse**—a man or woman who usually assists the doctor.

3. **stethoscope**—a tool used for checking heartbeat and breathing.

4. **thermometer**—tool for checking body temperature.

5. **patient**—a person who goes to see a doctor.

6. **pediatrician**—a children's doctor.

7. **veterinarian**—an animal doctor.

8. **ophthalmologist**—an eye doctor.

Bulletin Board

The purpose of this bulletin board is to develop skills in identifying written numerals and matching sets to numerals. Construct bandages out of manilla tagboard as illustrated or use purchased adhesive bandages. Laminate. Collect small boxes and cover with white paper if necessary. The number will be dependent upon the developmental age of children. Plastic bandage boxes or 16-count crayon boxes may be used. On each box place a numeral. Affix the box to a bulletin board by stapling. The children can place the proper number of bandages in each box.

Parent Letter

Dear Parents,

I hope everyone in your family is happy and healthy! Speaking of healthy, we are starting a unit on doctors and nurses. The children will be learning about the different types of doctors and nurses and how they help people. They also will be introduced to some of the tools used by doctors and nurses.

At School

A few of the learning experiences planned include:
* listening to the story, *Tommy Goes to the Doctor*.
* taking our temperatures with forehead strips and recording them on a chart in the science area.
* dressing up as doctors and nurses in the dramatic play area.
* experimenting with syringes (no needles!) and water at the sensory table.

At Home

There are many ways to integrate this unit into your home. To begin, discuss the role of your family doctor. Talk about your child's visit to a physician. This will help to alleviate anxiety and fears your child may have about the procedures and setting.

Let your child help you prepare this nutritious snack at home. We will be making it for Wednesday's snack as well.

Peanut Butter Balls

1/2 cup peanut butter
1/2 cup honey
3/4 to 1 cup powdered milk

Combine all of the ingredients in a bowl. Shape the mixture into small balls and roll in chopped nuts, coconut, or graham cracker crumbs, if desired.

Model positive attitudes toward health for your child.

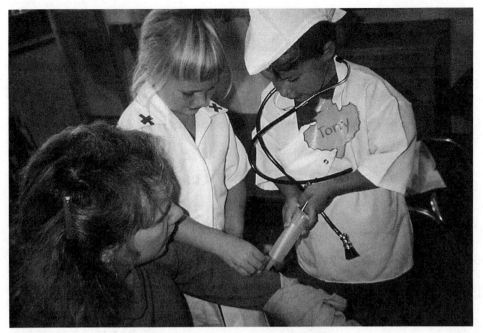

FIGURE 20 Girls and boys can be doctors or nurses.

Music:

1. **"The Doctor in the Clinic"**
   (Sing to the tune of "Farmer in the Dell")

   The doctor in the clinic.
   The doctor in the clinic.
   Hi-ho the derry-o,
   The doctor in the clinic.

   The doctor takes a nurse…
   The nurse takes a patient…
   The patient gets help…
   The patient gets better…

2. **"To the Hospital"**
   (Sing to the tune of "Frere Jacques")

   To the hospital, to the hospital,
   We will go, we will go.
   We will see the doctors,
   And we'll see the nurses,
   Dressed in white, dressed in white.

Fingerplays:

MISS POLLY'S DOLLY

Miss Polly had a dolly that was sick, sick, sick.
   (cradle arms and look sad)

She called for the doctor to come quick, quick, quick.
   (clap hands three times)
The doctor came with his coat and his hat.
   (point to your shirt and head)
And rapped on the door with a rap, rap, rap.
   (pretend to knock three times)
He looked at the dolly and he shook his head
   (shake head)
And he said, "Miss Polly, put her straight to bed."
   (shake finger)
Then he wrote on a paper for some pills, pills, pills.
   (hold left hand out flat, pretend to write with right hand)
I'll be back in the morning with my bill, bill, bill.
   (hold left hand out flat, wave it up and down as if waiting to be handed cash)

Note: The doctor may be male or female. Substitute pronouns.

DOCTOR DAY

My father said,
"It's doctor day,"
Then he and I
We're on our way
To see our friend

The doctor who
Would check me out
As doctors do.
She had more things
Than I can tell
To help her keep
The people well.
She checked me up
And all the while
She wore a big
And friendly smile.
So now I hope
That someday you
May go to see
The doctor too!

Source: Wilmes, Liz & Dick. (1983). *Everyday Circle Times*. Illinois: Building Blocks Publishing.

Science:

1. **Thermometer**

   Place a variety of unbreakable thermometers on the science table. Include a candy, meat, and an outdoor thermometer. Also include a strip thermometer that can be safely used on children's foreheads.

2. **Casts**

   Ask personnel at a local hospital to save clean, discarded casts. Place the casts on the science table, allowing the children to observe the materials, try them on for size, as well as feel their weight. The children may also enjoy decorating the casts.

3. **Stethoscope**

   Place a stethoscope on the science table for the children to experiment with. After each child uses it, wipe the ear plugs with alcohol to prevent the transmission of disease.

4. **Doctors' Tools**

   In a feely box place several tools that a doctor uses. Include a thermometer, gauze, stethoscope, rubber hammer, and a tongue depressor.

5. **Making Toothpaste**

   Mix four teaspoons baking soda, one teaspoon salt, and one teaspoon peppermint flavoring. Then add just enough water to form a thick paste.

Dramatic Play:

1. **Doctors and Nurses**

   Make a prop box for a doctor and nurse. Include a white coat, rubber gloves, a thermometer, gauze, tape, masks, eye droppers, tongue depressors, eye chart, cots, blankets, pencil and paper, empty and washed medicine bottles, a stethoscope, a scale, and syringes without needles. A first-aid kit including gauze and tape, bandages, butterflies, a sling, and ace bandages can be placed in this box. Place the prop boxes in the dramatic play area.

2. **Animal Clinic**

   Place stuffed animals with the doctor tools in the dramatic play area.

3. **Eye Doctor Clinic**

   Ask a local eye doctor for discontinued eye glass frames. Place the frames with a wall chart in the dramatic play area.

Arts and Crafts:

1. **Cotton Swab Painting**

   Place cotton swabs, cottonballs, and tempera paint on a table in the art area. The cotton swabs and balls can be used as painting tools.

2. **Body Tracing**

   Trace the children's bodies by having them lie down on a large piece of paper. The body shape can be decorated at school by the child with crayons and felt-tip markers. The shapes could also be taken home and decorated with parental assistance.

3. Eye Dropper Painting

Provide eye droppers, thin tempera paint, and absorbent paper. Designs can be made by using the eye dropper as a painting tool. Another method is to prepare water colored with food coloring in muffin tins. Using heavy paper towels with construction paper underneath for protection, the children will enjoy creating designs with the colored water.

Field Trips/Resource People:

1. Doctor's Office

Visit a doctor's office.

2. Resource Person

Invite a nurse or doctor to visit the classroom. Encourage them to talk briefly about their jobs. They can also share some of their tools with the children.

3. The Hospital

Visit a local hospital.

Math:

1. Weight and Height Chart

Prepare a height and weight chart out of tagboard. Record each child's height and weight on this chart. Repeat periodically throughout the year to note physical changes.

2. Tongue Depressor Dominoes

Make a set of dominoes by writing on tongue depressors. Divide each tongue depressor in half with a felt-tip marker. On each half place a different number of dots. Consider the children's developmental level in determining the number of dots to be included. Demonstrate to interested children how to play dominoes.

3. Bandage Lotto

Construct a bandage lotto game using various sizes and shapes of bandages. Place it on a table for use during self-selected activity time.

Social Studies:

Pictures

Display various health-related pictures in the room at the children's eye level, including doctors and nurses. Pictures should depict males and females in these health-related fields.

Group Time (games, language):

1. Doctor, Doctor, Nurse

Play "Duck, Duck, Goose" inserting the words, "Doctor, Doctor, Nurse."

2. What's Missing?

Place a variety of doctors' and nurses' tools on a large tray. Tell the children to close their eyes. Remove one item from the tray. Then have the children open their eyes and guess which item has been removed. Continue playing the game using all of the items as well as providing an opportunity for each child.

Cooking:

1. Mighty Mixture

Mix any of the following:
A variety of dried fruit (apples, apricots, pineapple, raisins)
A variety of seeds (pumpkin, sunflower)
A variety of nuts (almond, walnuts, pecans)

2. Vegetable Juice

Prepare individual servings of vegetable juice in a blender by adding 1/2 cup of cut-up vegetables and 1/4 cup water. Salt to taste. Vegetables that can be used include: celery, carrots, beets, tomatoes, cucumbers, and zucchini.

Books:

The following books can be used to complement the theme:

1. Reit, Seymour. (1984). *Jenny's in the Hospital*. Racine, WI: Western Publishing Company, Inc.

2. Rogers, Fred. (1986). *Going to the Doctor*. New York: G.P. Putnam's Sons.

3. Lumley, Kathryn Wentzel. (1985). *I Can Be an Animal Doctor*. Chicago: Children's Press.

4. Bauer, Judith. (1990). *What's It Like to Be a Doctor?* Mahwah, NJ: Troll Associates.

5. Fine, Anne. (1992). *Poor Monty*. Boston: Houghton Mifflin Co.

6. Bauer, Judith. (1990). *What's It Like to Be a Nurse?* Mahwah, NJ: Troll Associates.

7. Bauer, Judith. (1990). *Kevin and the School Nurse*. Mahwah, NJ: Troll Associates.

8. Davidson, Martine. (1992). *Maggie and the Emergency Room*. New York: Random House Books for Young Readers.

9. Davidson, Martine. (1992). *Rita Goes to the Hospital!* New York: Random House Books for Young Readers.

10. Bucknall, Caroline. (1991). *One Bear in the Hospital*. New York: Dial Books for Young Readers.

11. Rockwell, Anne. (1985). *The Emergency Room*. New York: Macmillan.

12. Kuklin, Susan. (1988). *Taking My Dog to the Vet*. New York: Macmillan.

13. Linn, Margot. (1988). *A Trip to the Doctor*. New York: Harper Collins.

Food

water
dog food
scraps

Supplies

collars
bones
leashes
brushes

Homes

dog houses
kennels
house

Sizes

large
medium
small

DOGS

Body Parts

fur
four legs
paws
tail
ears
eyes
nose
mouth

Colors

yellow
brown
black
white
mixed

Safety

diseases
rabies
wild dogs
strange dogs

Care

exercise
food
water
sleep
grooming
medical
fleas

Occupational Uses

police/security dog
seeing eye dog
hunting
farming

Here's an exciting new way to turn instant photography into an effective teaching tool. Refer to the full-color insert for the activity entitled Graphing.

Theme Goals:

Through participating in the experiences provided by this theme, the children may learn:

1. Dog's body parts.

2. Types of dogs.

3. Dogs need special care.

4. Dogs can be trained to do special tasks and tricks.

Concepts for the Children to Learn:

1. There are many different sizes of dogs.

2. Dogs have a keen sense of smell and hearing.

3. Dogs growl and bark to communicate.

4. Dogs may bark at strangers to protect their owners and their space.

5. Dogs have legs, eyes, ears, a mouth, nose, and tail.

6. Dogs have fur on their skin.

7. Dogs enjoy being handled carefully and gently.

8. Some dogs help people.

9. There are many different colors, sizes, and kinds of dogs.

10. Dogs need food, water, and exercise every day.

11. Dogs can be taught to do tricks.

Vocabulary:

1. **puppy**—a baby dog.

2. **pet**—an animal kept for pleasure.

3. **paw**—the dog's foot.

4. **veterinarian**—an animal doctor.

5. **guide dog**—a dog trained to help blind people.

6. **leash**—a rope, chain, or cord that attaches to a collar.

7. **collar**—a band worn around the dog's neck.

8. **obedience school**—a school where dogs are taught to obey.

9. **whiskers**—stiff hair growing around the dog's nose, mouth, and eyes.

10. **bone**—an object a dog uses to chew on.

11. **coat**—hair or fur covering the skin.

12. **doghouse**—a place for dogs to sleep and keep warm.

Bulletin Board

The purpose of this bulletin board is to develop color recognition and matching skills. Prepare the bulletin board by cutting dog shapes out of tagboard or construction paper. Use rubber cement to attach a different colored paper collar to each dog's neck. Also, cut out dog dishes from colored construction paper. Attach the pieces to the bulletin board as illustrated. Use lengths of yarn or string for children to match the color of each dog's collar to the corresponding dog dish.

Parent Letter

Dear Parents,

We will begin a unit on a favorite subject of children of all ages—dogs! We will be learning about their basic physical features such as coat and body. We will also learn about caring for a dog, the roles of dogs in people's lives, dog training, as well as things families need to consider when choosing a dog. This unit is designed so that the children will develop an awareness of and respect for dogs as pets.

At School

Some of the learning experiences planned include:

- creating paw prints at the art table (dipping paw-shaped sponges into paint and applying them to paper).
- sorting various-sized dog biscuits.
- listening to the children's stories about their own dogs.
- setting up a "pet store" in the dramatic play area, complete with stuffed animals and many dog accessories.
- baking dog biscuits!

At Home

To foster parent-child interaction and reinforce some of the concepts we are working on at school, try some of the following ideas:

- Look through magazines to find pictures of dogs and puppies. Help your child tear out pictures of dogs and puppies. This activity is good for the development of fine motor and visual discrimination skills. An interesting collage can be made by gluing these pictures onto a piece of paper.
- If you don't have access to a dog, visit a pet shop to observe the puppies. At the same time note all of the dog supplies available.

Enjoy your child!

FIGURE 21 What is your favorite breed of dog?

Music:

1. **"Bingo"**

   There was a farmer who had a dog
   And Bingo was his name-o.
   B-I-N-G-O
   B-I-N-G-O
   B-I-N-G-O
   And Bingo was his name-o.

2. **"Six Little Dogs"**
   (Sing to the tune of "Six Little Ducks")

   Six little dogs that I once knew,
   fat ones, skinny ones, fair ones too.
   But the one little dog with the brown curly fur,
   He led the others with a grr, grr, grr.
   Grr, grr, grr
   Grr, grr, grr
   He led the others with a grr, grr, GRR!

Fingerplays:

FRISKY'S DOGHOUSE

This is Frisky's doghouse;
(pointer fingers touch to make a roof)
This is Frisky's bed;
(motion of smoothing)
Here is Frisky's pan of milk;
(cup hands)
So that he can be fed.

Frisky has a collar
(point to neck with fingers)
With his name upon it, too;
Take a stick and throw it,
(motion of throwing)
He'll bring it back to you.
(clap once)

FIVE LITTLE PUPPIES

Five little puppies were playing in the sun.
(hold up hands, fingers extended)
This one saw a rabbit, and he began to run.
(bend down first finger)
This one saw a butterfly, and he began to race.
(bend down second finger)
This one saw a cat, and he began to chase.
(bend down third finger)
This one tried to catch his tail, and he went
round and round.
(bend down fourth finger)
This one was so quiet, he never made a sound.
(bend down thumb)

FIVE LITTLE PUPPIES

Five little puppies jumping on the bed,
(hold up five fingers)
One fell off and bumped his head,
(hold up one finger—tap head)
Mama called the doctor and the doctor said,
"No more puppies jumping on the bed."
(shake index finger)

Science:

1. Additions to the science table or area may
   include:

   • a magnifying glass with bones, dog hair,
   and dog food.

- dog tags of different sizes, including some with squeakers.
- a balance scale and dry dog food.

2. During a cooking activity, prepare dog biscuits. The recipe is listed under cooking.

Dramatic Play:

1. **Pet Store**

   Using stuffed animals simulate a pet store. Include a counter complete with cash register and money. Post a large sign that says, "Pet Store." Set out many stuffed dogs with collars and leashes. Children will enjoy pretending they have a new pet.

2. **Veterinarian's Office**

   Use some medical equipment and stuffed dogs to create a veterinarian's office.

3. **Pet Show**

   Encourage the children to bring a stuffed animal to school. Children can pretend that their stuffed animals can do tricks. Have ribbons available for them to look at and award to each other.

4. **Dog House**

   Construct a dog house from a large cardboard box. Provide dog ears and tails for the children to wear as they imitate the pet.

Arts and Crafts:

1. **Paw Prints**

   Make stamps out of erasers, sponges, or with the child's fist.

2. **Dog Puppets**

   Provide socks, paper bags, and/or paper plates to make dog puppets.

3. **Dog Masks**

   Use fake fur ears and pipe cleaners for whiskers.

4. **Bone Printing**

   Provide different meat bones, a tray of tempera paint, and paper to make prints.

5. **Bone Painting**

   Cut easel paper in bone shapes.

6. **Dog Collages**

   Provide dog pictures cut out of magazines to make a collage.

Large Muscle:

1. Encourage the children to dramatize the following movements:

   - a big dog
   - a tiny dog
   - a dog with heavy steps
   - a dog with light steps
   - a happy dog
   - a sad dog
   - a mad dog
   - a loud dog
   - a quiet dog
   - a hungry dog
   - a tired dog
   - a curious dog
   - a sick dog

2. **Dog Hoops**

   Provide hoops for the children to jump through as they imitate dogs.

3. **Scent Walk**

   Place prints of dog paws on the play yard leading to different activities. Encourage the child to crawl to each activity.

4. **Tracks**

   If snow is available, make tracks with boots that have different treads. Encourage children to follow one track.

5. **Bean Bag Bones**

   Provide round bean bags or make special bone-shaped bean bags. Encourage the children to throw them into a large dog food bowl.

Field Trips/Resource People:

1. **Pet Store**

   Take a field trip to a pet store. While there ask the manager how to care for dogs. Observe the different types of cages, collars, leashes, food, and toys.

2. **Veterinarian Office**

   Take a field trip to a veterinarian's office or animal hospital. Compare its similarities and differences to a doctor's office.

3. **Kennel**

   Visit a kennel and observe the different sizes of cages and dogs.

4. **Variety Store**

   Visit a variety store and observe pet accessories.

5. **Grocery Store**

   Take a field trip to the grocery store and purchase the ingredients needed to make dog biscuits.

6. **Dog Trainer**

   Invite an obedience trainer to talk about teaching dogs.

7. **Additional Resource People**

   - veterinarian
   - pet store owner
   - parents (bring in family dogs)
   - humane society representative
   - representative from a kennel
   - dog groomer
   - person with a seeing eye dog (guide dog)

Math:

1. **Dog Bones**

   Cut dog bone shapes of four different sizes from tagboard. Encourage the children to sequence them.

2. **Classifying Dog Biscuits**

   Purchase three sizes of dog biscuits. Using dog dishes, have the children sort them according to size and type.

3. **Weighing Biscuits**

   Using the scale, encourage the children to weigh different sizes and amounts of dog biscuits.

Social Studies:

1. **Share Your Dog**

   Individually invite the parents to bring their child's pet to school.

2. **Pictures of Dogs**

   Display pictures of different types of dogs.

3. **Bulletin Board**

   Prepare a bulletin board with pictures of the children's dogs.

4. **Slides**

   Take slides of field trips and of resource people. Share them at group time. (This slide series may be shared with parents at meetings or coffees.)

5. **Dog Biscuits**

   Prepare dog biscuits and donate to the local animal shelter. (See Cooking.)

6. **Chart**

   Make a chart including the children's name, type of pet, size of pet, and the name of the pet. Count the number of dogs, cats, birds, etc. Discuss the most popular names.

7. **Dogs**

Using pictures or a real dog, talk about a dog's body. Some dogs have long noses so they can smell things very well; others have short hair to live in hot climates. Discuss why some dogs are good guard dogs. Discuss how dogs' tongues help them to cool off on hot days. Also talk about what else a dog's rough tongue is used for.

Group Time (games, language):

1. **The Dog Catcher**

Hide stuffed dogs or those cut from construction paper around the classroom and have children find them.

2. **Child-created Stories**

Bring in a picture of a dog or stuffed dog. Encourage the children to tell you a story about the picture or the stuffed dog. While the child speaks, record the words. Place the story in the book corner.

3. **Dog Chart**

Make a chart listing the color of each child's dog. A variation would be to have the children state their favorite color of dog. This activity can be repeated using size.

4. **Doggie, Doggie, Where's Your Bone?**

Bring in a clean bone or a bone cut from construction paper. Sit the children in a circle. Choose one child to be the dog. Have the child pretending to be the dog sit in the middle. The doggie closes his eyes. A child from the circle sneaks up and takes the bone. Children call, "Doggie, doggie, where's your bone? Someone stole it from your home!" The "dog" gets three guesses to find out who has the bone.

5. **The Lost Dog**

(This is a variation of the "Dog Catcher" game.) Using the children's stuffed animals from home, have the children trade dogs so that each is holding another's pet. One child begins by hiding the dog he is holding while the other children cover their eyes. He tells the owner, "Your dog is lost, but we can help you find it." As the dog owner looks, he can put the pet he is holding on his carpet square to free both hands. The group gives "hot" and "cold" clues to indicate whether the child is close to or far away from the pet. When the child finds his pet, he is the next one to hide a pet.

Cooking:

1. **Hot "Dog" Kebabs on a Stick**

    paper plates and napkins
    skewers
    1 package hot dogs
    2 green peppers, cut up
    cherry tomatoes

Place 2 pieces of green pepper, 2 cherry tomatoes, and 2 hot dog pieces on each child's plate. Show the children how to thread the ingredients on skewers. Bake the kabobs in a preheated oven for 15 minutes at 350 degrees.

2. **Dog Biscuits**

    2 1/2 cups whole wheat flour
    1/2 cup powdered dry milk
    1/2 teaspoon salt
    1/2 teaspoon garlic powder
    6 tablespoons margarine, shortening, or meat
        drippings
    1 egg
    1 teaspoon brown sugar
    1/2 cup ice water

Combine flour, milk, salt, and flour. Cut in the shortening. Mix in egg. Add enough water until mixture forms a ball. Pat the dough to a half-inch thickness on a lightly oiled cookie sheet. Cut with cutters and remove scraps. Bake 25 to 30 minutes at 350 degrees. This recipe may be varied by adding pureed soup greens, liver powder, etc.

3. **Dogs-in-a-Blanket**

    cheese crust
        1/2 teaspoon salt
        pinch baking powder
        1 cup white flour
        1/4 cup shortening

206

1/4 cup water
1/4 cup finely shredded cheddar cheese
hot dogs

Stir the dry ingredients in a large bowl. Cut in shortening and then add 1/4 cup water. Stir with a fork and add more water only if necessary to work in flour. Add cheese and knead together. Cut the cheese pie crust in strips and wrap each around a whole or half of a hot dog. Bake at 350 degrees until crust is light brown.

Source: Warren, Jean. (1982). *Super Snacks*. Alderwood Manor, WA: Warren Publishing House.

4. Hush Puppies

vegetable oil
2 1/4 cups yellow cornmeal
1 teaspoon salt
2 tablespoons finely chopped onion
3/4 teaspoon baking soda
1 1/2 cups buttermilk

Heat oil (about 1 inch deep) to 375 degrees. Mix cornmeal, salt, onion, and baking soda in a bowl. Add buttermilk. Drop by spoonfuls into hot oil. Fry until brown about 2 minutes.

Multimedia:

The following resources can be found in educational catalogs:

1. McCurdy, Ed. "I Had a Little Dog" on *Children's Stories and Songs* [record].

2. Barduhn, Art. "Animals" on *Children's Creative Play Songs* [record].

3. Mc Laughlin, Roberta & Wood, Lucille. "Kitty and Puppy" on *The Small Singer*. (Vol. 2.) [record].

4. Stewart, Georgiana Liccione. "Puppy Dog" on *Walk Like the Animals* [record].

Books:

The following books can be used to complement the theme:

1. Barrett, Norman. (1990). *Dogs*. New York: Franklin Watts, Inc.

2. Cole, Joanna. (1991). *My Puppy Is Born* (rev. ed.). New York: Morrow Junior Books.

3. Hanes, Harriet. (1992). *My New Puppy*. New York: Dorling Kindersley, Inc.

4. Perry, Kate. (1992). *Baby Animals: Puppies*. Hauppauge, NY: Barron's Educational Series, Inc.

5. Crozat, Francois. (1990). *I Am a Little Dog*. Hauppauge, NY: Barron's Educational Series, Inc.

6. Gottlieb, Dale. (1992). *Big Dog*. New York: Puffin Books.

7. Holland, Margaret. (1991). *Look Around Puppies and Dogs*. Pinellas Park, FL: Willowisp Press.

8. Johnson, Audean. (1993). *Fuzzy as a Puppy*. New York: Random House for Young Readers.

9. Pepin, Muriel. (1992). *Little Puppy Saves the Day*. New York: Readers Digest Association, Inc.

10. Robertus, Polly. (1992). *The Dog Who Had Kittens*. New York: Holiday House, Inc.

11. Weller, Frances Ward. (1990). *Riptide*. New York: Philomel Books.

12. Bridwell, Norman. (1988). *Clifford, the Big Red Dog*. New York: Scholastic.

13. Day, Alexandra. (1991). *Good Dog Carl*. New York: Simon & Schuster.

14. Dodd, Lynley. *Dogs & Puppies*. New York: Checkerboard Press.

15. McCue, Lisa. (1990). *Puppies Love*. New York: Simon & Schuster.

16. Taylor, Judy. (1989). *My Dog*. New York: Macmillan.

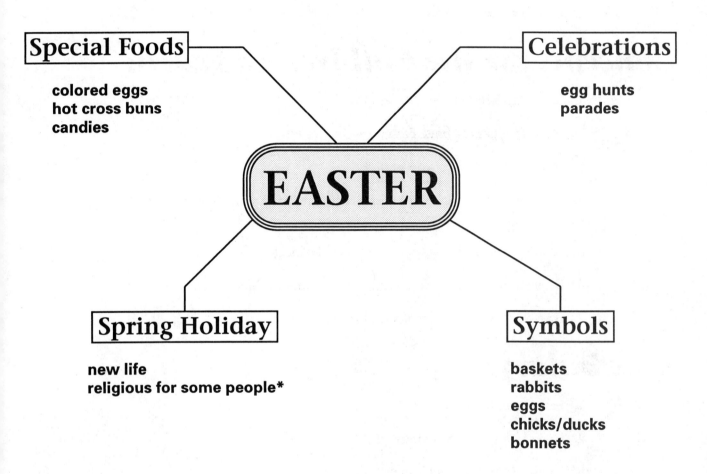

Special Foods

colored eggs
hot cross buns
candies

Celebrations

egg hunts
parades

EASTER

Spring Holiday

new life
religious for some people*

Symbols

baskets
rabbits
eggs
chicks/ducks
bonnets

* Some center personnel may elect to include an Easter
theme with an emphasis on the spring holiday as
opposed to the traditional religious emphasis.

Polaroid
Education
Program

Here's an exciting new way to turn instant photography
into an effective teaching tool. Refer to the full-color
insert for the activity entitled Tell Me A Story.

Theme Goals:

Through participating in the experiences provided by this theme, the children may learn:

1. Easter traditions.

2. Easter symbols.

3. Boiled eggs can be dyed and decorated for Easter.

4. Care of rabbits.

Concepts for the Children to Learn:

1. Easter is a holiday.

2. Many families celebrate Easter.

3. At Eastertime eggs are decorated.

4. There are many symbols of Easter, including baby animals, baskets, rabbits, and eggs.

5. Baskets filled with eggs and candy may be hidden.

6. Baby animals born in the Spring are a sign of new life.

7. Bonnets (hats) may be worn at Easter time.

Vocabulary:

1. **Easter**—a holiday in Spring.

2. **basket**—a woven container.

3. **hatch**—to break out of a shell.

4. **dye**—to change the color.

5. **duckling**—a baby duck.

6. **chick**—a baby chicken.

7. **lamb**—a baby sheep.

8. **bunny**—a baby rabbit.

9. **holiday**—a day of celebration.

10. **Spring**—the season of the year when plants begin to grow.

11. **bonnet**—a kind of hat.

Bulletin Board

The purpose of this bulletin board is to promote correspondence of sets to the written numeral. Construct baskets out of stiff tagboard. Write a numeral beginning with the number one on each basket as illustrated. Carefully attach these to the bulletin board stapling all the way around the round bottom of the baskets. Construct many small Easter eggs. Encourage the children to deposit the corresponding number of Easter eggs in the numbered baskets. Care needs to be taken when removing the eggs. The number of baskets should reflect the developmental level of the children. If available, you might want to try using lightweight Easter baskets. They are harder to hang up, but may prove to be more sturdy.

Parent Letter

Dear Parents,

"Here comes Peter Cottontail, hopping down the bunny trail..." Easter is on its way, and is the theme we will explore this unit. This is an exciting holiday for children. Through learning experiences planned for the unit, the children will find out about ways that some families celebrate Easter and symbols that represent Easter. Included will be the Easter bunny, Easter baskets, and foods that are associated with Easter.

At School

Learning experiences planned to reinforce concepts of Easter include:

- a special visitor for the week—a rabbit! The children will assist in taking care of the rabbit.
- a hat shop in the dramatic play area with materials to create Easter bonnets.
- Easter grass and plastic eggs in the sensory table.
- an egg hunt! On Friday, we will search our play yard for hidden eggs and place them in our baskets.

At Home

To establish a sense of family history, recall family Easter celebrations that you have had in the past with your child. What special things does your family do together on this holiday? And, of course, dye some Easter eggs!

Be adventurous and try some dyes from natural materials. Natural dying is not new; natural dyes were the original Easter egg colors the world over. To make purple eggs purchase a box of frozen blackberries. Thaw and place in a saucepan. Add eggs and cover with water plus 1 tablespoon of vinegar. Bring the water to a boil and simmer for 20 minutes. Afterward, take the pan off the heat source and let stand for approximately 20 minutes.

To make gold eggs use powdered tumeric. Place eggs in a saucepan and add enough water to cover. Then, add 3 tablespoons of tumeric and bring to a boil. Simmer for 20 minutes. Remove from heat source and cool.

To create pale green eggs, cut spinach and place in the bottom of a pan. Add enough water to cover and add eggs. Bring to a boil and simmer for 20 minutes. Remove from heat and allow to set for more intense color.

From all of us,

FIGURE 22 Children enjoy being read Easter stories.

Music:

1. **"Did You Ever See a Rabbit?"**
   (Sing to the tune of "Did You Ever See a Lassie?")

   Did you ever see a rabbit, a rabbit, a rabbit?
   Did you ever see a rabbit, a rabbit on Easter morn?
   He hops around so quietly
   And hides all the eggs.
   Did you ever see a rabbit, on Easter morn?

2. **"Easter Bunny"**
   (Sing to the tune of "Ten Little Indians")

   Where, oh, where is the Easter Bunny,
   Where, oh, where is the Easter Bunny,
   Where, oh, where is the Easter Bunny,
   Early Easter morning?

   Find all the eggs and put them in a basket,
   Find all the eggs and put them in a basket,
   Find all the eggs and put them in a basket,
   Early Easter morning.

3. **"Easter Eggs"**
   (Sing to the chorus of "Jingle Bells")

   Easter eggs, Easter eggs,
   Hidden all around.

   Come my children look about
   And see where they are found.

   Easter eggs, Easter eggs
   They're a sight to see.
   One for Tom and one for Ann
   And a special one for me!

   Insert names of children in your classroom.

4. **"Easter Eggs"**
   (Sing to the tune of "Mama's Little Baby Loves Shortnin'")

   Easter eggs here and there,
   Easter eggs everywhere.
   What's the color of the
   Easter egg here?

Fingerplays:

FIVE LITTLE EASTER EGGS

Five little Easter eggs lovely colors wore;
Mother ate the blue one and then there were four.
Four little Easter eggs, two and two, you see;
Daddy ate the red one, and then there were three.
Three little Easter eggs; before I knew
Sister ate the yellow one, then there were two.

Two little Easter eggs; oh what fun.
Brother ate the purple one, then there was one.
One little Easter egg; see me run!
I ate the very last one, and then there were none!

This could be a fingerplay or could be done with colored finger puppet eggs with the children holding a particular color going down when that color is named.

Source: Peck, Don. (1975). *Fingerplays that Motivate*. Minneapolis: T.S. Denison and Company.

KITTY AND BUNNY

Here is a kitty.
   (make a fist with one hand)
Here is a bunny.
   (hold up other hand with pointer and middle fingers up straight)
See his tall ears so pink and funny?
   (wiggle the two extended fingers)
Kitty comes by and licks his face;
   (extend thumb and wiggle near the bunny)
And around and around the garden they race.
   (make circular motions with hands)
And then without a single peep,
They both lie down and go to sleep.
   (fold hands)

Source: Peck, Don. (1975). *Fingerplays that Motivate*. Minneapolis: T.S. Denison and Company.

EASTER BUNNY

Easter Bunny, Easter Bunny
   (make "ears" at head with arms outstretched)
Pink and white
Come fill my basket
   (make filling motion)
Overnight
   (pretend to sleep, lay head on hands)

Source: Overholser, Kathy. (1979). *Let Your Fingers Do the Talking*. Minneapolis: T.S. Denison and Company.

THE DUCK

I waddle when I walk.
   (hold arms elbow high and twist trunk side to side, or squat down)
I quack when I talk.
   (place palms together and open and close)
And I have webbed toes on my feet.
   (spread fingers wide)
Rain coming down
Makes me smile, not frown
   (smile)
And I dive for something to eat.
   (put hands together and make diving motion)

MY RABBIT

My rabbit has two big ears
   (hold up index and middle fingers for ears)
And a funny little nose.
   (join other three fingers for nose)
He likes to nibble carrots
   (move thumb away from other two fingers)
And he hops wherever he goes.
   (move whole hand jerkily)

Science:

1. **Incubate and Hatch Eggs**

    Check the yellow pages of your telephone book to see if any hatcheries are located in your area.

2. **Dying Eggs**

    Use natural products to make egg dye. Beets—deep red, onions—yellow (add soda to make bright yellow), cranberries—light red, spinach leaves—green, and blackberries—blue. To make dyed eggs pick two or three colors from the list. Make the dye by boiling the fruit or vegetable in small amounts of water. Let the children put a cool hard-boiled egg in a nylon stocking and dip it into the dye. Keep the egg in the dye for several minutes. Pull out the nylon and check the color. If it is dark enough, place the egg on a paper towel to dry. If children want to color the eggs with crayons before dying, you can show how the wax keeps liquid from getting on the egg.

3. **Science Table Additions**

    - bird nests
    - empty bird eggs

- different kinds of baskets
- an incubator
- newly planted seeds
- flowers still in bud (children can watch them open)
- pussy willows

4. **Basket Guessing**

Do reach-and-feel using a covered basket. Place an egg, a chick, a rabbit, a doll's hat, some Easter grass, etc., in a large Easter basket. Let the children place their hands into the basket individually and describe the objects they are feeling.

Dramatic Play:

1. **Flower Shop**

Plan a flower shop for the dramatic play area. Include spring plants, baskets, and Easter lilies.

2. **Egg Center**

Create a colored egg center to be used during self-directed play. Some children put stickers on plastic eggs, some sell the eggs, and others buy them.

3. **Costume Shop**

Place costumes for bunny use, Easter baskets, and Easter eggs in the dramatic play area. The children can take turns hiding the eggs and going on hunts.

4. **A Bird Nest**

Place a nest with eggs in the dramatic play area. Also provide bird masks, a perch, and other bird items in the area for use during self-initiated play.

5. **Easter Clothes**

Bring in Easter clothes for the children to dress up in. Suits, dresses, hats, purses, gloves, and dress-up shoes should be included.

6. **Hat Shop**

Make a hat shop. Place hats with ribbons, flowers, netting, and other decorations in the dramatic play area. The children can decorate the hats. If the children are interested, plan an Easter Parade.

Arts and Crafts:

1. **Easter Collages**

Collect eggshells, straw, Easter grass, or plant seeds for making collages. Place on art table with sheets of paper and glue.

2. **Colorful Collages**

Use pastel-colored sand and glue to make collages.

3. **Wet Chalk Eggs**

Use wet chalk to decorate paper cut in the shape of eggs in pastel colors. Show the children the difference between wetting the chalk in vinegar and water. The vinegar color will be brighter.

4. **Easel Ideas**

Cut egg-shaped easel paper or basket-shaped paper. Clip to the easel. Provide pastel paints at the easel. To make the paint more interesting add glitter.

5. **Milk Carton Easter Baskets**

Cut off the bottom four inches of milk cartons. Provide precut construction or wallpaper to cover the baskets, and yarn. Include small bits of paper or bright cloth to glue on. Make a handle using a thin strip of paper that is stapled to the carton. Use the baskets for the children's snack.

6. **Plastic Easter Baskets**

Easter baskets can be made by using the green plastic baskets that strawberries and blueberries come in from the grocery store. Cut thin strips of paper that children can practice weaving through the holes. This activity is most successful with older children.

7. **Color Mixing**

Provide red, yellow, and blue dyed water in shallow pans. Provide the children with medicine droppers and absorbent paper cut in the shape of eggs. Also, the children can use medicine droppers to apply color to the paper. Observe what happens when the colors blend together.

8. **Rabbit Ears**

Construct rabbit ears out of heavy paper. Attach them to a band that can be worn around the head, fitting it for size. These ears may stimulate creative movement as well as dramatic play.

9. **Shape Rabbit**

Provide a large, a medium, and four small circles cut from white paper, as well as two tall thin triangles. Show the children how to put these shapes together to make a rabbit.

Sensory:

1. **Sensory Table Activities**

Add to the sensory table:

- cotton balls with scoops and measuring cups
- birdseed or beans
- straw or hay and plastic eggs
- plastic chicks and ducks with water
- Easter grass, eggs, small straw mats
- dirt with plastic flowers and/or leaves
- dyed, scented water and water toys
- sand, shovels, and scoops

2. **Clay Cutters**

Make scented clay. Place on the art table with rabbit, duck, egg, and flower cookie cutters for the children to use during self-directed or self-initiated play.

Large Muscle:

1. **Bunny Trail**

Set up a bunny trail in the classroom. Place tape on the floor and have children hop over the trail. To make it more challenging, add a balance beam to resemble a bridge.

2. **Eggs in the Basket**

The children can practice throwing egg-shaped or regular bean bags into a large basket or bucket.

3. **Rabbit Tag**

Make the egg-shaped bean bags to play rabbit tag. To play the game, the children stand in a circle, with one child being the rabbit. The rabbit walks around the circle with a bean bag balanced on his head, and drops a second bean bag behind the back of another child. The second child must put the bean bag on his head and follow the rabbit around the circle once. Each child must keep the bean bag balanced—if it drops, it must be picked up and replaced on the head. If the rabbit is tagged, he chooses the next rabbit. If the rabbit returns to the empty spot in the circle, the second child becomes the rabbit. This is an unusual game in that the action is fairly slow, but it's still very exciting.

4. **Egg Rolling**

Place mats on the floor and have children roll across with their arms at their sides. For older children, you can place the mat on a slightly inclined plane and have children roll down, then try to have them roll back up, which is more challenging.

Field Trips:

1. **The Farm**

Take a trip to a farm to see the new baby animals.

2. **The Hatchery**

Visit a hatchery on a day that they are selling baby chicks.

3. **Neighborhood Walk**

   Take a walk around the neighborhood and look for signs of new life.

4. **Rabbit Visit**

   Bring some rabbits to school for the children to observe.

Math:

1. **Egg Numerals**

   Collect five large plastic eggs, such as the kind that nylon stockings can be purchased in. Put numerals from one to five (or ten, for older children) on the eggs. Let the children place the correct number of cotton balls or markers into each egg.

2. **Easter Seriation**

   Cut different-sized tagboard eggs, chicks, ducks, and rabbits. The children can place the items in a row from the smallest to the largest.

Social Studies:

1. **Family Easter Traditions**

   During large group, ask the children what special activities their families do to celebrate Easter. Their families may go to church, eat together, have egg hunts, or do other things that are special on this day.

2. **Sharing Baskets**

   Decorate eggs or baskets to give to a home for the elderly. If possible, take a walk and let the children deliver them.

Group Time (games, language):

1. **The Last Bunny**

   This is a game for ten or more players. It is more fun with a large number. An Easter rabbit is chosen by counting out or drawing straws. All the other players stand in a circle.

The Easter rabbit walks around the circle and taps one player on the back saying, "Have you seen my bunny helper?" "What does it look like?" asks the player and the Easter rabbit describes the bunny helper. He may say, "She is wearing a watch and blue shoes." The player tries to guess who it is. When he names the right person, the Easter rabbit says, "That's my helper!" and the other player chases the bunny helper outside and around the circle. If the chaser catches the bunny helper before he can return to his place the chaser becomes the Easter rabbit. If the bunny helper gets there first then the first Easter rabbit must try again. The Easter rabbit takes the place in the circle of whoever is the new Easter rabbit.

Source: Rockwell, Anne. (1973). *Games and How to Play Them*. New York: Thomas Y. Crowell Co.

2. **Outdoor Egg Hunt**

   Plan an egg hunt outdoors, if possible. Hide the boiled eggs that the children have decorated, candy eggs in wrappers, or small Easter candies in clear plastic bags. The children can use the baskets they have made to collect their eggs, then, weather permitting, eat the boiled eggs for a snack outdoors.

Cooking:

1. **Decorating Cupcakes**

   Let the children use green frosting, dyed coconut shreds, and jelly beans to decorate cupcakes and put them into an Easter basket. As a last touch, add a pipe cleaner handle. Cake mixes can be used to make the cupcakes. Follow the directions on the box. Place paper liners in a muffin pan to ensure easy removability.

2. **Bunny Food**

   Carrot sticks, celery, and lettuce can be available for snack.

3. **Egg Sandwiches**

   Use the boiled eggs the children have decorated to make egg salad or deviled eggs for snack time.

4. Carrot and Raisin Salad

4 cups grated carrots
1 cup raisins
1/2 cup mayonnaise or whipped salad
   dressing

Place ingredients in a bowl and mix
thoroughly.

5. Bunny Salad

For each serving place one lettuce leaf on a
plate. Put one canned pear half with the cut
side down on top of the lettuce leaf. Add
sections of an orange to represent the ears.
Decorate the bunny face by adding grated
carrots, raisins, nuts, or maraschino cherries to
make eyes, a nose, and a mouth.

EASTER EGGS

Where did the custom of coloring Easter eggs come from? No one knows for sure. In any
case, the Easter holiday centers around eggs for young children. Here are some projects
you might like to try.

To hard cook eggs: Place eggs in a saucepan and add enough cold water to cover at least 1 inch above the eggs. Heat rapidly to boiling and remove from heat. Cover the pan and allow to stand for 22 to 24 minutes. Immediately cool the eggs in cold water.

- Make a vegetable dye solution by adding a teaspoon of vinegar to 1/2 cup of boiling water. Drop in food coloring and stir. The longer the egg is kept in the dye, the deeper the color will be.

- Add a teaspoonful of salad oil to a dye mixture and mix in the oil well. This results in a dye that produces swirls of color. Immerse the egg in the dye for a few minutes.

- Draw a design on an egg with a crayon before dying it. The dye will not take to the areas with the crayon marks and the design will show through.

- Wrap rubber bands, string, yarn, or narrow strips of masking tape around an egg to create stripes and other designs. Dip the egg in a dye and allow to dry before removing the wrapping.

- Drip the wax of a lighted birthday candle over an egg or draw a design on the egg using a piece of wax. Place the egg in dye. Repeat process again, if desired, dipping the egg in another color of dye. (Note: The lighted candle is to be used by an adult only.)

- Felt-tip markers can be used to decorate dyed or undyed eggs.

- Small stickers can be used on eggs.

- Craft items such as sequins, glitter, and ribbons and small pom poms can be used with glue to decorate eggs.

- Apply lengths of yarns, string, or thread to the eggs with glue, creating designs, and allow to dry.

- Egg creatures can be created by using markers, construction paper, feathers, ribbon, lace, cotton balls, fabric, and buttons. To make an egg holder, make small cardboard or construction paper cylinders. A toilet paper or paper towel tube can be cut to make stands as well.

- Save the shells from the eggs to use for eggshell collages. Crumble the shells and sprinkle over a glue design that has been made on paper or cardboard.

218

Multimedia:

The following resource can be found in educational catalogs:

Palmer, Hap. "Easter Time Is Here Again" on *Holiday Songs and Rhythms* [record]. Freeport, NY: Educational Activities, Inc.

Books:

The following books can be used to complement the theme:

1. Wilhelm, Hans. (1985). *Bunny Trouble.* New York: Scholastic Books.

2. Winthrop, Elizabeth. (1985). *Happy Easter, Mother Duck.* New York: Golden Press.

3. Auch, Mary J. (1992). *The Easter Egg Farm.* New York: Holiday House, Inc.

4. Devlin, Wende, & Devlin, Harry. (1990). *Cranberry Easter.* New York: Macmillan Children's Book Group.

5. Fittro, Charlene C. (1992). *Happy, The Easter Bunny.* Sabina, OH: Children's Books and Music.

6. Gambling, Lois G. (1991). *Elephant and Mouse Get Ready for Easter.* Hauppauge, NY: Barron's Educational Series, Inc.

7. Miller, Edna. (1989). *Mousekin's Easter Basket.* New York: Simon and Schuster Trade.

8. Pienkowski, Jan. (1992). *Easter.* New York: Alfred A. Knopf, Books for Young Readers.

9. Stevenson, James. (1990). *The Great Big Especially Beautiful Easter Egg.* New York: William Morrow and Co.

10. Burgess, Beverly C. (1985). *Is Easter Just for Bunnies?* Tulsa, OK: Harrison House.

11. Gibbons, Gail. (1989). *Easter.* New York: Holiday.

12. Ross, Bill. (1992). *Easter Bunnyheads.* Nashville, TN: Ideals.

13. Ross, Bill. (1992). *Easter Eggheads.* Nashville, TN: Ideals.

14. Stock, Catherine. (1991). *Easter Surprise.* New York: Macmillan Child Group.

15. Tangvald, Christine H. (1993). *The Best Thing About Easter.* Cincinnati, OH: Standard Publishing.

16. Bowman, Pete. (1992). *A Surprise for Easter: A Revolving Picture Book.* New York: Macmillan.

17. Friedrich, Priscilla & Otto. (1993). *The Easter Bunny That Overslept.* New York: Morrow.

18. Moncure, Jane B. (1987). *Word Bird's Easter Words.* Mankato, MN: Child's World.

19. Tudor, Tasha. (1989). *A Tale for Easter*. New York: Random House.

20. Wilhelm, Hans. (1991). *Bunny Trouble*. New York: Scholastic.

21. Adams, Adrienne. (1991). *The Easter Egg Artists*. New York: Macmillan.

Changes

**leaves turn color
temperature cooler
darker earlier**

Clothing

**sweaters
scarves
long-sleeved shirts
long pants
blankets**

FALL

Holidays

**Labor Day
Halloween
Thanksgiving**

Activities

**football
raking leaves
walks
bike rides
harvesting foods
camping
soccer**

Here's an exciting new way to turn instant photography into an effective teaching tool. Refer to the full-color insert for the activity entitled Presto-Chango-Photo.

Theme Goals:

Through participating in the experiences provided by this theme, the children may learn:

1. Characteristics of fall weather.

2. Fall holidays.

3. Fall clothing.

4. Fall activities.

Concepts for the Children to Learn:

1. Fall is one of the four seasons.

2. Fall is the season between summer and winter.

3. Some trees change color in the fall.

4. In some places the weather becomes cooler in the fall.

5. The day becomes shorter in the fall.

6. Leaves fall from some trees in the fall.

7. Labor Day, Halloween, and Thanksgiving are some fall holidays.

8. Scarfs and sweaters may need to be worn in the fall in some areas.

9. Pumpkins and apples can be harvested in the fall.

10. Football is a fall sport.

11. Blankets are usually needed on our beds in the fall in some places.

Vocabulary:

1. **fall**—the season between summer and winter.

2. **Halloween**—the holiday when people wear costumes and go trick or treating.

3. **Thanksgiving**—a holiday to express thanks.

4. **Labor Day**—a holiday to honor working people.

5. **season**—a time of the year.

Bulletin Board

The purpose of this bulletin board is to foster a positive self-concept as well as develop skills of name recognition. Construct an acorn for each child. Print the children's names on the acorns. See illustration. Laminate and punch holes in the acorns. Children can hang their acorns on a push pin on the bulletin board when they arrive.

Parent Letter

Dear Parents,

Where we live, the days are getting shorter, the temperature is getting colder, and the leaves are changing color. It's the perfect time to introduce our next unit—fall. By participating in the experiences provided throughout this unit, children will become more aware of changes that take place in the fall and common fall activities.

At School

A few of this week's learning experiences include:

- recording the temperature and the changing colors of the leaves.
- making leaf rubbings in the art area.
- raking leaves on our playground during outdoor time.

We will also be taking a fall walk around the neighborhood to observe the trees in their peak changes. We will be leaving Thursday at 10:00 a.m. Please feel free to join us. It will be a scenic tour.

At Home

To develop classification skills help your child sort leaves by their color, type, or size.

Fingerplays promote language and vocabulary skills. This fingerplay is one we will be learning this week. Enjoy it with your child at home!

Autumn

Autumn winds begin to blow.
   (blow)
Colored leaves fall fast and slow.
   (make fast and slow motions with hands)
Twirling, whirling all around,
   (turn around)
`Til at last, they touch the ground.
   (fall to the ground)

Enjoy your child as you explore experiences related to the unit on fall.

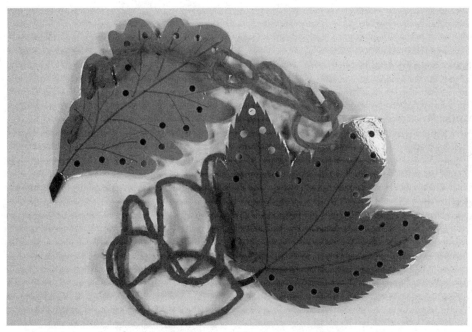

FIGURE 23 Leaves turn different colors during the Fall.

Music:

1. **"Little Leaves"**
   (Sing to the tune of "Ten Little Indians")

   One little, two little, three little leaves.
   Four little, five little, six little leaves.
   Seven little, eight little, nine little leaves.
   Ten little leaves fall down.

2. **"Happy Children Tune"**
   (Sing to the tune of "Did You Ever See a Lassie?")

   Happy children in the autumn,
   In the autumn, in the autumn.
   Happy children in the autumn
   Do this way and that.

   While singing the song, children can keep time by pretending to rake leaves, jump in the leaves, etc.

3. **"Pretty Leaves Are Falling Down"**
   (Sing to the tune of "London Bridges")

   Pretty leaves are falling down, falling down, falling down.

   Pretty leaves are falling down, all around the town.
      (wiggle fingers)

   Let's rake them up in a pile, in a pile, in a pile.
   Let's rake them up in a pile, all around the town.
      (make raking motions)

   Let's all jump in and have some fun,
   have some fun, have some fun.
   Let's all jump in and have some fun, all around the town.
      (jump into circle)

Fingerplays:

AUTUMN

Autumn winds begin to blow.
   (blow)
Colored leaves fall fast and slow.
   (make fast and slow falling motions with hands)
Twirling, whirling all around
   (turn around)
'Til at last, they touch the ground.
   (fall to the ground)

LEAVES

Little leaves fall gently down
Red and yellow, orange and brown.
　　(flutter hands as leaves falling)
Whirling, whirling around and around.
　　(turn around)
Quietly without a sound.
　　(put finger to lips)
Falling softly to the ground
　　(begin to fall slowly)
Down and down and down and down.
　　(lie on floor)

LITTLE LEAVES

The little leaves are falling down
　　(use hands to make falling motion)
Round and round, round and round.
　　(turn around)
The little leaves are falling down,
　　(use hands to make falling motion)
Falling to the ground.
　　(fall to ground)

TWIRLING LEAVES

The autumn wind blows—Oooo Oooo Oooo.
　　(make wind sounds)
The leaves shake and shake then fly into the
sky so blue.
　　(children shake)
They whirl and whirl around them, twirl and
twirl around.
　　(turn around in circles)
But when the wind stops, the leaves sink
slowly to the ground.
Lower, lower, lower, and land quietly without
a sound.
　　(sink very slowly and very quietly)

Science:

1. **Leaf Observation**

   Collect leaves from a variety of trees. Place
   them and a magnifying glass on the science
   table for the children to explore.

2. **Temperature Watch**

   Place a thermometer outside. A large
   cardboard thermometer can also be
   constructed out of tagboard with movable

elastic or ribbon for the mercury. The children
can match the temperature on the cardboard
thermometer with the outdoor one.

3. **Weather Calendar**

   Construct a calendar for the month. Record the
   changes of weather each day by attaching a
   symbol to the calendar. Symbols should
   include clouds, sun, snow, rain, etc.

4. **Color Change Sequence**

   Laminate or cover with contact paper, several
   leaves of different colors. The children can sort,
   count, and classify the leaves.

Dramatic Play:

1. **Fall Wear**

   Set out warm clothes such as sweaters, coats,
   hats, and blankets to indicate cold weather
   coming on. The children can use the clothes for
   dressing up.

2. **Football**

   Collect football gear including balls, helmets,
   and jerseys and play on the outdoor
   playground.

Arts and Crafts:

1. **Fall Collage**

   After taking a walk to collect objects such as
   grass, twigs, leaves, nuts, and weeds, collages
   can be made in the art area.

2. **Leaf Rubbings**

   Collect leaves, paper, and crayons and show
   the children how to place several leaves under
   a sheet of paper. Using the flat edge of crayon
   color rub over paper. The image of the leaves
   will appear.

3. **Pumpkin Seed Collage**

   Wash and dry pumpkin seeds and place them
   in the art area with glue and paper. The
   children can make pumpkin seed collages.

4. **Leaf Spatter Painting**

Use a lid from a box that is approximately 9 inches x 12 inches x 12 inches. Cut a rectangle from top of lid leaving a 1 1/2-inch border. Invert the lid and place a wire screen over the opening. Tape the screen to the border. Arrange the leaves on a sheet of paper. Place the lid over the arrangement. Dip a toothbrush into thin tempera paint and brush across screen. When the tempera paint dries, remove the leaves.

Sensory:

Leaves

Place a variety of leaves in the sensory table. Try to include moist and dry examples for the children to compare.

Large Muscle:

Raking Leaves

Child-sized rakes can be provided. The children can be encouraged to rake leaves into piles.

Field Trips:

1. **Neighborhood Walk**

Take a walk around the neighborhood when the leaves are at their peak of changing colors. Discuss differences in color and size.

2. **Apple Orchard**

Visit an apple orchard. Observe the apples being picked and processed. If possible let children pick their own apples from a tree.

3. **Pumpkin Patch**

Visit a pumpkin patch. Discuss and observe how pumpkins grow, their size, shape, and color. Let the children pick a pumpkin to bring back to the classroom.

Math:

1. **Weighing Acorns and Pinecones**

A scale, acorns, and pinecones for the children to weigh can be added to the science table.

2. **Leaf Math**

Out of construction paper or tagboard, prepare pairs of various-shaped leaves. The children can match the identical leaves.

Social Studies:

Bulletin Board

Construct a bulletin board using bare branches to represent a tree. Cut out leaves from colored construction paper and print one child's name on each. At the beginning of the day, children can hang their name on the tree when they arrive.

Cooking:

1. **Apple Banana Frosty**

1 golden delicious apple, diced
1 peeled sliced banana
1/4 cup milk
3 ice cubes

Blend all the ingredients in a blender. Serves 4 children.

2. **Apple Salad**

6 medium apples
1/2 cup raisins
1/2 teaspoon cinnamon
1/2 cup chopped nuts
1/4 cup white grape juice

Peel and chop the apples. Mix well and add the remaining ingredients. Serves 10 children.

NATURE RECIPES

Cattails

Use them in their natural color or tint by shaking metallic powder over them. Handle carefully. The cattail is dry and feels crumbly. It will fall apart easily.

Crystal Garden*

Place broken pieces of brick or terra cotta clay in a glass bowl or jar. Pour the following solution over this:

4 teaspoons water
1 teaspoon ammonia
4 teaspoons bluing
1 teaspoon Mercurochrome
4 teaspoons salt

Add more of this solution each day until the crystal garden has grown to the desired size. (Adult supervision required.)

* This activity should be carefully observed if in a classroom with preschool children.

Drying Plants for Winter Bouquets

Strip the leaves from the flowers immediately. Tie the flowers by their stems with string and hang them with the heads down in a cool dry place away from the light. Darkness is essential for preserving their color. Thorough drying takes about 2 weeks.

Preserving Fall Leaves

Place alternate layers of powdered borax and leaves in a box. The leaves must be completely covered. Allow them to stand for four days. Shake off the borax and wipe each with liquid floor wax. Rub a warm iron over a cake of paraffin, then press the iron over front and back of leaves.

Preserving Magnolia Leaves

Mix two parts of water with one part of glycerine. Place stems of the magnolia leaves in the mixture and let them stand for several days. The leaves will turn brown and last several years. Their surface may be painted or sprayed with silver or gold paint.

Pressing Wild Flowers

When gathering specimens, include the roots, leaves, flowers and seed pods. Place between newspapers, laying two layers of blotters underneath the newspaper and two on top to absorb the moisture. Change the newspapers three times during the week. Place between two sheets of corrugated cardboard and press. It usually takes seven to ten days to press specimens. Cardboard covered with cotton batting is the mounting base. Lay the flower on the cotton and cover with cellophane or plastic wrap to preserve the color.

Treating Gourds

Soak gourds for two hours in water. Scrape them clean with a knife. Rub with fine sandpaper. While still damp cut an opening to remove seeds.

Multimedia:

The following resources can be found in educational catalogs:

1. James, Dixie, & Becht, Linda. *The Singing Calendar* [record].

2. McLaughlin, Roberta, & Wood, Lucille. *Sing a Song of Holidays and Seasons* [record]. Bowman Records.

Books:

The following books can be used to complement the theme:

1. Tejima, Keizaburo. (1986). *The Bears' Autumn*. Chicago: Children's Press.

2. Allington, Richard L., & Kroll, Kathleen. (1985). *Autumn*. Milwaukee: Raintree.

3. Maass, Robert. (1990). *When Autumn Comes*. New York: Henry Holt & Co.

4. Updike, David. (1988). *An Autumn Tale*. New York: Pippin Press.

5. Hains, Harriet. (1993). *My New School*. New York: Dorling Kindersley.

6. Baer, Edith. (1990). *This Is the Way We Go to School: A Book about Children around the World*. New York: Scholastic.

7. Arnosky, Jim. (1993). *Ever Autumn Comes the Bear*. New York: Putnam.

8. Fowler, Allan. (1992). *How Do You Know It's Fall?* Chicago: Children's Press.

9. Moncure, Jane B. (1990). *Step Into Fall: A New Season*. Mankato, MN: Child's World, Inc.

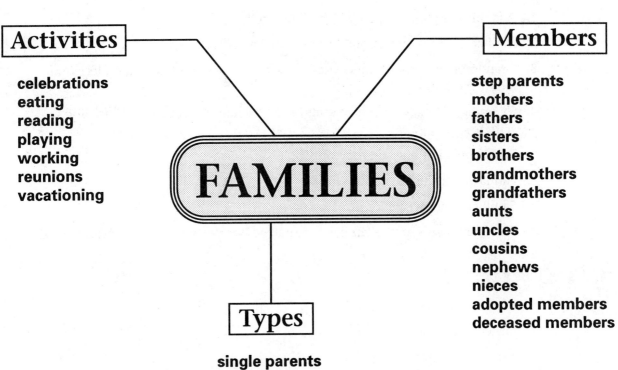

Activities

celebrations
eating
reading
playing
working
reunions
vacationing

Members

step parents
mothers
fathers
sisters
brothers
grandmothers
grandfathers
aunts
uncles
cousins
nephews
nieces
adopted members
deceased members

FAMILIES

Types

single parents
two parents
blended
extended

Polaroid
Education
Program

Here's an exciting new way to turn instant photography into an effective teaching tool. Refer to the full-color insert for the activity entitled Photo Peek-A-Boo.

Theme Goals:

Through participating in the experiences provided by this theme, the children may learn:

1. The members in a family.
2. Roles of family members.
3. Family activities.

Concepts for the Children to Learn:

1. A family is a group of people who live together.
2. Mothers, fathers, sisters, and brothers are family members.
3. Grandmothers, grandfathers, aunts, uncles, cousins, nephews, and nieces are family members.
4. Camping, eating, working, reading, and watching television are all family activities.
5. Each family is a special group of people.
6. Families teach us about our world.
7. Family members care for us.
8. There are many types of families: one parent, two parent, blended, and extended.

Vocabulary:

1. **mother**—female parent.
2. **father**—male parent.
3. **children**—young people.
4. **sister**—a girl having the same parents as another person.
5. **brother**—a boy having the same parents as another person.
6. **grandmother**—mother of a parent.
7. **grandfather**—father of a parent.
8. **cousin**—son or daughter of an uncle or aunt.
9. **aunt**—sister of a parent.
10. **uncle**—brother of a parent.
11. **nephew**—son of a brother or sister.
12. **niece**—daughter of a brother or sister.
13. **love**—feeling of warmth toward another.
14. **family**—people living together.
15. **one-parent family**—a child or children who lives with only one parent, a father or mother.
16. **blended**—people from two or more families living together.
17. **extended**—includes aunts, uncles, grandparents, and cousins.

Bulletin Board

The purpose of this bulletin board is to foster awareness of various family sizes, as well as to identify family members. From tagboard construct a name card for each child. Print each child's name on one of the tagboard pieces. Then cut people figures as illustrated. Laminate the name cards and people. Staple the name cards to a bulletin board. Individually, the children can affix the people in their family after their name using tape, sticky putty, or a stapler.

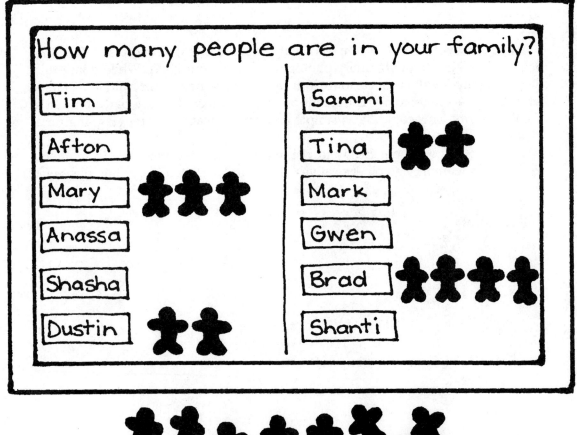

Parent Letter

Dear Parents,

Our next unit will focus on families. Through this unit, the children will develop an understanding of various family patterns. They will also discover what family members do for each other, as well as activities that families can participate in together.

At School

A few of this unit's highlights include:

- creating pictures of our families on a bulletin board.
- looking at photographs of classmates' families. To assist us with this unit, please send a picture of your family to school with your child. We will place the photograph in a special photo album to look at in the reading area.

At Home

There are several activities you can do at home to foster the concepts of this unit. Begin by looking through family photographs with your child. While doing this discuss family traditions or customs. You can also encourage your child to dictate a letter to you to write to a grandparent or other relative. Plan and participate in a family activity. This could be as simple as taking a walk together or going on a picnic.

We invite you and your family to visit us. This includes moms, dads, brothers, sisters, grandparents, and other relatives! If you are interested in coming, please let me know!

From all of us,

FIGURE 24 Families are an important part of life.

Music:

"Family Helper"
  (Sing to the tune of "Here We Are Together")

  It's fun to be a helper, a helper, a helper.
  It's fun to be a helper, just any time.
  Oh, I can set the table, the table, the table.
  Oh, I can set the table at dinner time.
  Oh, I can dry the dishes, the dishes, the dishes.
  Oh, I can dry the dishes, and make them shine.

Fingerplays:

MY FAMILY

  If you peek in my room at night,
    (stand on toes as if peeking)
  My family you will see,
    (nod head)

They kiss my face and tuck me in tight,
  (kiss into the air)
Why? Because they love me!
  (hug yourself)

SEE MY FAMILY

See my family? See them all?
  (hold up all five fingers)
Some are short
  (hold up thumb)
Some are tall
  (hold up middle finger)

Let's shake hands. "How do you do?"
  (grasp hands and shake)
See them bow? "How are you?"
  (bend fingers)

Father,
  (hold up middle finger)
Mother,
  (hold up pointer finger)
Sister,
  (hold up ring finger)
Brother
  (hold up thumb)
And me.
  (hold up pinky finger)

THIS IS THE MOTHER

This is the mother, kind and dear.
  (make a fist then point to the thumb)
This is the father sitting near.
  (show each finger in turn)
This is the brother strong and tall.
This is the sister, who plays with her ball.
This is the baby, the littlest of all.
See my whole family large and small?
  (wiggle all fingers)

I LOVE MY FAMILY

Some families are large.
  (spread arms out wide)
Some families are small.
  (bring arms close together)
But I love my family
  (cross arms over chest)
Best of all!

A GOOD HOUSE

This is the roof of the house so good.
  (make roof with hands)
These are the walls that are made of wood.
  (hands straight, palms parallel)
These are the windows that let in the light.
  (thumbs and forefingers form window)
This is the door that shuts so tight.
  (hands straight by side)
This is the chimney so straight and tall.
  (arms up straight)
Oh! What a good house for one and all!

All fingerplays taken from Cromwell, Faitel &
Hibner. (1983). *Finger Frolics: Fingerplays for
Young Children.* Michigan: Partner Press.

Science:

1. **Sounds**

   Tape different sounds from around the house
   that families hear daily, such as a crying baby,
   brushing teeth, telephone ringing, toilet
   flushing, doorbell ringing, water running,
   electric shaver, alarm clock, etc. Play the tape
   for the children to identify the correct sound.

2. **Feely Box**

   Place objects pertaining to a family into a box.
   Include items such as a baby rattle, a toothbrush, a comb, baby bottle, etc. The children
   feel the objects and try to identify them.

3. **Animal Families**

   Gerbils or hamsters with young babies in a
   cage can be placed on the science table.
   Observe daily to see how they raise their
   babies. Compare the animal behavior to the
   children's own families.

Dramatic Play:

1. **Baby Clothing**

   Arrange the dramatic play area for washing
   baby dolls. Include a tub with soapy water,
   washcloths, drying towels, play clothes, brush,
   and comb.

2. **Family Picnic**

   Collect items to make a picnic basket. Include
   paper napkins, cups, plates, plastic eating
   utensils, etc.

3. **Dollhouse**

   Set up a large dollhouse for children to play
   with. These can be constructed from cardboard. Include dolls to represent several
   members of a family.

Arts and Crafts:

1. **Family Collage**

   The children can cut out pictures of people
   from magazines. The pictures can be pasted on
   a sheet of paper to make a collage.

2. **My Body**

   Trace each child's body on a large piece of
   paper. The children can use crayons and felt-
   tip markers to color their own body picture.
   When finished, display the pictures around the
   room or in the center's entrance.

Sensory:

1. Washing baby dolls in lukewarm, soapy water
2. Washing dishes in warm water
3. Washing doll clothes and hanging them up to
   dry
4. Cars and houses placed on top of several
   inches of sand

Large Muscle:

Neighborhood Walk

   Take a walk through a neighborhood and have
   children identify different homes. Observe the
   colors and sizes of the homes.

Resource People:

Family Day

Invite moms, dads, sisters, brothers, grandfathers, grandmothers, and other family members to a tea at your center.

Math:

1. **Families—Biggest to Smallest**

   Cut out from magazines several members of a family. The children can place the members from largest to smallest, and then smallest to largest. They can also identify each family member as the biggest and the smallest.

2. **Family Member Chart**

   Graph the number of family members for each child's family in the classroom.

Social Studies:

Family Pictures

1. Display posters of all types of families. Discuss at group time ways that families help and care for each other.

2. Ask each child to bring in a family picture. Label each child's picture and place on a special bulletin board with the caption, "Our Families."

3. Discuss the Muslim celebration of Ramadan. Each year Muslims around the world observe the religious period of Ramadan by refraining from food, water, television, and other activities from sunrise to sunset. The fasting lasts for 28 days. Fasting teaches patience, discipline, and humility. Families and friends gather before sunrise (*Suhour*) and after sunset for meals. When it is time to break the fast (*Iftar*), the first thing one should eat is dates. Children learn that the Prophet Mohammed broke his fast on dates. Families then mostly have soup, because it is easy on the stomach and also helps rehydrate the thirsty.

Group Time (games, language):

A Hundred Ways to Get There

During outdoor play or large group, form a large circle. Begin the game by choosing a child to cross the circle by skipping, hopping, jumping, crawling, running, etc. Once the circle has been crossed the child takes the place of another person who then goes across the circle in another manner. Each child can try to think of something new.

Cooking:

1. **Peanut Butter and Jelly**

   Cut whole wheat bread into house shapes for snack one day. Put peanut butter, raisins, and jelly on the table with knives. Let children choose their own topping.

2. **Gingerbread Families**

   Use the following recipe to create gingerbread families.

   1 1/2 cups whole wheat pastry flour
   1 teaspoon baking soda
   1/2 teaspoon salt
   1/2 teaspoon ginger
   1 teaspoon cinnamon
   1/4 cup oil
   1/4 cup maple syrup
   1/4 cup honey
   1 large egg

   Preheat oven to 350 degrees. Measure all of the dry ingredients into a bowl and mix well. Measure all wet ingredients into a second bowl and mix well. Add the two mixtures together. Pour the combined mixture into an 8-inch square pan and bake for 30 to 35 minutes. When cool, roll the gingerbread dough into thin slices and provide cookie cutters for children to cut their family. Decorate the figures with raisins, peanut butter, wheat germ, etc. Enjoy for snack time.

3. **Raisin Bran Muffins**

4 cups raisin bran cereal
2 1/2 cups all-purpose flour
1 cup sugar
1/2 cup chopped walnuts
2 1/2 teaspoons baking soda
1 teaspoon salt
2 eggs, beaten
2 cups buttermilk
1/2 cup cooking oil

Stir the cereal, flour, sugar, nuts, baking soda, and salt together in a large mixing bowl. In a separate bowl beat the eggs, buttermilk, and oil together. Add this mixture to the dry ingredients and stir until moistened. The batter will be thick. Spoon the batter into greased or lined muffin cups, filling 3/4 full. Bake in a 375-degree oven for 20 to 25 minutes and remove from pans.

4. **Kabbat hamudth** (Meatball soup served during Ramadan, a Muslim celebration)

For the meatballs:

1 pound choice ground beef
14-oz. box cream of rice
1/2 teaspoon salt

Combine ingredients and mix well. Add a little water if necessary. Puree in small batches. Divide mixture into 30 balls. Cover and chill.

For the stuffing:

1 medium onion, chopped
1/2 pound choice ground beef
1 cup drained chickpeas, cut in half
1/4 cup chopped fresh parsley
1 scant teaspoon ground allspice

Brown onions and beef in a 10-inch skillet. Drain fat and add remaining stuffing ingredients. Set aside.

To form meatballs flatten each ball with your fingertips. Place 2–3 teaspoons of the stuffing in the center and reform beef into a ball around the stuffing. Cover and chill.

For the soup:

2–3 medium onions, quartered
1 pound turnips, chopped
2 tablespoons olive oil
16 cups beef broth
1 pound Swiss chard, coarsely chopped
1 cup drained canned chickpeas
1 teaspoon ground allspice (optional)
Salt and pepper to taste
3–4 tablespoons finely chopped fresh mint
    leaves or 2 teaspoons dried
1/2 cup lemon juice

Sauté onions and turnips in olive oil until onions are translucent. Bring broth to boil, lower heat, add onions, turnips, Swiss chard, and chickpeas. Season with allspice, salt, and pepper. Simmer until turnips are soft. Add mint and lemon juice. About 20 minutes before serving add meatballs.

Serve in bowls with 2–3 meatballs per serving. Caution must be taken regarding the temperature of the soup.

SNACK IDEAS

MILK

1. Dips (yogurt, cottage cheese, cream cheese)
2. Cheese (balls, wedges, cutouts, squares, faces, etc.)
3. Yogurt and fruit
4. Milk punches made with fruits and juices
5. Conventional cocoa
6. Cottage cheese (add pineapple, peaches, etc.)
7. Cheese fondues (pre-heated, no open flames in classroom)
8. Shakes (mix fruit and milk in a blender)

MEAT

1. Meat strips, chunks, cubes (beef, pork, chicken, turkey, ham, fish)

238

2. Meatballs, small kabobs
3. Meat roll-ups (cheese spread, mashed potatoes, spinach, lettuce leaves, or tortillas)
4. Meat salads (tuna, other fish, chicken, turkey, etc.) as spreads for crackers, stuffing for celery, rolled in spinach or lettuce
5. Sardines
6. Stuffing for potatoes, tomatoes, squash

EGGS

1. Hard boiled
2. Deviled (use different flavors)
3. Egg salad spread
4. Eggs any style that can be managed
5. Egg as a part of other recipes
6. Eggnog

FRUITS

1. Use standard fruits, but be adventurous: pomegranates, cranberries, pears, peaches, apricots, plums, berries, pineapples, melons, grapes, grapefruit, tangerines
2. Kabobs and salads
3. Juices and juice blends
4. In muffins, yogurt, milk beverages
5. Fruit "sandwiches"
6. Stuffed dates, prunes, etc.
7. Dried fruits (raisins, currants, prunes, apples, peaches, apricots, dates, figs)

VEGETABLES

1. Variety—sweet and white potatoes, cherry tomatoes, broccoli, cauliflower, radishes, peppers, mushrooms, zucchini, all squashes, rutabaga, avocados, eggplant, okra, pea pods, turnips, pumpkin, sprouts, spinach
2. Almost any vegetable can be served raw with or without dip
3. Salads, kabobs, cutouts
4. Juices and juice blends
5. Soup in a cup (hot or cold)
6. Stuffed—celery, cucumbers, zucchini, spinach, lettuce, cabbage, squash, potatoes, tomatoes
7. Vegetable spreads
8. Sandwiches

DRIED PEAS AND BEANS

1. Peanuts, kidney beans, garbanzos, limas, lentils, yellow and green peas, pintos, black beans
2. Beans and peas mashed as dips or spreads
3. Bean, pea, or lentil soup in a cup
4. Roasted soybean-peanut mix
5. Three-bean salad

PASTAS

1. Different shapes and thicknesses
2. Pasta with butter and poppy seeds

3. Cold pasta salad
4. Lasagne noodles (cut for small sandwiches)
5. Chow mein noodles (wheat or rice)

BREADS

1. Use a variety of grains— whole wheat, cracked wheat, rye, cornmeal, oatmeal, bran, grits, etc.
2. Use a variety of breads—tortillas, pocket breads, crepes, pancakes, muffins, biscuits, bagels, popovers, English muffins
3. Toast—plain, buttered, with spreads, cinnamon
4. Homemade yeast and quick breads
5. Fill and roll up crepes, pancakes
6. Waffle sandwiches

CEREALS, GRAINS, SEEDS

1. Granola
2. Slices of rice loaf or rice cakes
3. Dry cereal mixes (not pre-sweetened)
4. Seed mixes (pumpkin, sunflower, sesame, poppy, caraway, etc.)
5. Roasted wheat berries, wheat germ, bran as roll-ins, toppers, or as finger mix
6. Popcorn with toppers of grated cheese, flavored butters, mixed nuts
7. Stir into muffins or use as a topper

Multimedia:

The following resources can be found in educational catalogs:

1. Rogers, Fred. *A Place of Our Own* [record].

2. "Around the House" on *Sounds Around Us* [record]. Glenview, IL: Scott Foresman.

3. *The Sleepy Family* [record]. New York: Young People's Records.

4. *Small Voice, Big Voice with Dick, Laurie, and Jed* [record]. Folkway Records and Service Corp.

5. *The Playroom* [Apple/IBM/Mac software, PK-2]. Broderbund.

6. *Learning to Tell Time* [video]. Tele-Story.

Books:

The following books can be used to complement the theme:

1. Greenspun, Adele A. (1991). *Daddies*. New York: Putnam Publishing Group.

2. Hallinan, P. K. (1990). *We're Very Good Friends, My Father and I*. Nashville, TN: Ideals Publishing Corp.

3. Hallinan, P. K. (1990). *We're Very Good Friends, My Mother and I*. Nashville, TN: Ideals Publishing Corp.

4. Corey, Dorothy. (1992). *Will There Be a Lap for Me?* Morton Grove, IL: Albert Whitman and Co.

5. Asch, Frank, & Vagin, Vladmir. (1992). *Dear Brother*. New York: Scholastic, Inc.

6. Birdseye, Tom. (1991). *Waiting for Baby*. New York: Holiday House, Inc.

7. Franklin, Jonathan. (1991). *Don't Wake Baby*. New York: Farrar, Straus and Giroux, Inc.

8. Holabird, Katharine. (1991). *Angelina's Baby Sister*. New York: Crown Books for Young Readers.

9. Hutchins, Pat. (1992). *Silly Billy*. New York: Greenwillow Books.

10. Levinson, Riki. (1991). *Me Baby!* New York: Dutton Children's Books.

11. Mcphail, David. (1990). *Sisters*. San Diego: Harcourt Brace Jovanovich.

12. Steptoe, John. (1992). *Baby Says*. New York: William Morrow and Co.

13. Henkes, Kevin. (1990). *Julius, The Baby of the World*. New York: Greenwillow.

14. Crews, Donald. (1991). *Big Mama's*. New York: Greenwillow.

15. Dorros, Arthur. (1992). *This Is My House*. New York: Scholastic.

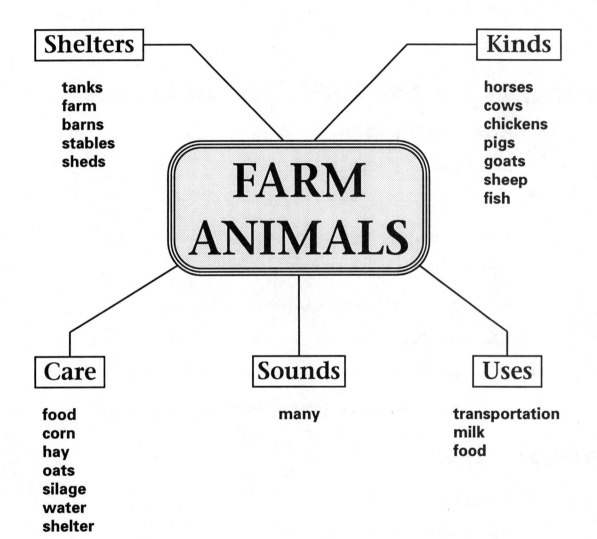

Shelters

tanks
farm
barns
stables
sheds

Kinds

horses
cows
chickens
pigs
goats
sheep
fish

FARM ANIMALS

Care

food
corn
hay
oats
silage
water
shelter

Sounds

many

Uses

transportation
milk
food

Here's an exciting new way to turn instant photography into an effective teaching tool. Refer to the full-color insert for the activity entitled Photo Bingo.

Theme Goals:

Through participating in the experiences provided by this theme, the children may learn:

1. Names of farm animals.

2. Uses for farm animals.

3. Farm animal shelters.

4. Food for farm animals.

5. Sounds of farm animals.

Concepts for the Children to Learn:

1. A farm animal lives on a farm.

2. Barns, stables, and sheds are homes for farm animals.

3. Horses are farm animals that can be used for transportation.

4. Cows, chickens, pigs, sheep, and goats are farm animals.

5. Some cows and goats give milk.

6. Farm animals eat corn, hay, oats, and silage.

7. A farmer cares for farm animals.

8. We can recognize some farm animals by their sounds.

9. Some farm animals supply us with food such as milk, meat, and eggs.

Vocabulary:

1. **herd**—a group of animals.

2. **stable**—building for horses and cattle.

3. **farmer**—person who cares for farm animals.

4. **barn**—building to house animals and store grain.

Bulletin Board

The purpose of this bulletin board is to foster one-to-one correspondence skills and matching sets to written numerals. Out of tagboard construct red barns as illustrated. The number of barns constructed will depend upon the maturity of your group of children. Place a numeral on each red barn. Construct the same number of black barns by tracing around the red barns onto black construction paper. After cutting out, place small white circles (dots from paper punch) onto the black barns. Laminate all barns. Staple black barns to the board. Punch a hole in each red barn window. During self-selected activity periods the children can hang red barns on push pins of corresponding black barns.

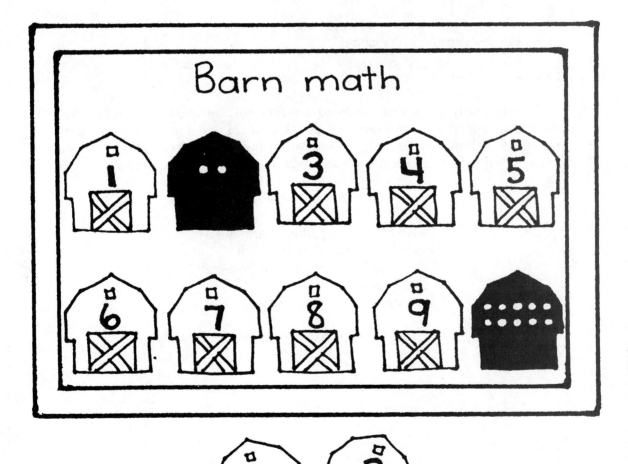

Parent Letter

Dear Parents,

Farm animals will be the focus of our next unit. The children will be learning the many different ways that farm animals help us. They will also become aware of the difference between pets and farm animals. The children will also discover that farm animals need homes and food.

At School

Some of the learning activities scheduled for this week include:

- making a barn out of a large cardboard box for the dramatic play area
- tasting different kinds of eggs, milk, and cheese for breakfast one day
- observing and comparing the many grains and seeds farm animals eat at the science table
- dressing up like farmers and farm animals
- making buttermilk chalk pictures

At Home

There are many ways you can integrate this unit into your family life. To stimulate imagination and movement skills ask your child to imitate different farm animals by walking and making that animal's noise. Also, your child will be learning this rhyme at school. You can also recite it at home to foster language skills.

If I Were a Horse

If I were a horse, I'd gallop all around.
(slap thighs and gallop in a circle)
I'd shake my head and say "Neigh, neigh."
(shake head)
I'd prance and gallop all over town.

Enjoy your child as you explore experiences related to farm animals.

FIGURE 25 Seesaws can be pretend horses.

Music:

1. **"Old Mac Donald Had a Farm"**
   (traditional)

2. **"The Animals on the Farm"**
   (Sing to the tune of "The Wheels on the Bus")

   The cows on the farm go moo, moo, moo.
   Moo, moo, moo, moo, moo, moo.
   The cows on the farm go moo, moo, moo
   all day long.

   The horses on the farm go neigh, neigh, neigh.
   Neigh, neigh, neigh, neigh, neigh, neigh.
   The horses on the farm go neigh, neigh, neigh
   all day long.

   (pigs—oink)
   (sheep—baa)
   (chicken—cluck)
   (turkeys—gobble)

3. **"The Farmer in the Dell"**
   (traditional)

   The farmer in the dell,
   The farmer in the dell,
   Hi-ho the dairy-o
   The farmer in the dell.

   The farmer takes a wife/husband.
   The farmer takes a wife/husband.
   Hi-ho the dairy-o
   The farmer in the dell.

   (The other verses are:)
   The wife/husband takes the child
   The child takes the nurse
   The nurse takes the dog
   The dog takes the cat
   The cat takes the rat
   The rat takes the cheese.

   (The final verse:)
   The cheese stands alone.
   The cheese stands alone.
   Hi-ho the dairy-o
   The cheese stands alone.

Fingerplays:

THIS LITTLE COW

This little cow eats grass.
   (hold up one hand, fingers erect, bend down
   one finger)
This little cow eats hay.
   (bend down another finger)

This little cow drinks water.
    (bend down another finger)
And this little cow does nothing.
    (bend down another finger)
But lie and sleep all day.

IF I WERE A HORSE

If I were a horse, I'd gallop all around.
    (slap thighs and gallop in a circle)
I'd shake my head and say "Neigh, neigh."
    (shake head)
I'd prance and gallop all over town.

THIS LITTLE PIG

This little pig went to market.
    (point to one finger at a time)
This little pig stayed home.
This little pig had roast beef.
This little pig had none.
This little pig cried, "Wee, wee, wee"
And ran all the way home.

EIGHT BABY PIGS

Two mother pigs lived in a pen.
    (thumbs)
Each had four babies and that made ten.
    (fingers of both hands)
These four babies were black and white.
    (fingers of one hand)
These four babies were black as night.
    (fingers of other hand)
All eight babies loved to play
    (wiggle fingers)
And they rolled in the mud all day!
    (roll hands)

THE FARM

The cows on the farm go, "Moo-oo, moo-oo";
The rooster cries, "Cock-a-doodle-doo";
The big brown horse goes, "Neigh, neigh";
The little lamb says, "Baa," when he wants to play.
The little chick goes, "Peep, peep, peep";
The cat says, "Meow," when it's not asleep;
The pig says, "Oink," when it wants to eat.
And we all say, "Hello," when our friends we meet.

Source of fingerplays: Cromwell, Hibner & Faitel. (1983). *Finger Frolics: Fingerplays for Young Children*. Michigan: Partner Press.

Science:

1. **Sheep Wool**

   Place various types of wool on a table for the children to observe. Included may be wool clippings, lanolin, dyed yarn, yarn spun into thread, wool cloth, wool articles such as mittens and socks.

2. **Feathers**

   Examine various types of feathers. Use a magnifying glass. Discuss their purposes such as keeping animals warm and helping ducks to float on water. Add the feathers to the water table to see if they float. Discuss why they float.

3. **Tasting Dairy Products**

   Plan a milk-tasting party. To do this, taste and compare the following types of milk products: cow milk, goat milk, cream, skimmed milk, whole milk, cottage cheese, sour cream, butter, margarine, and buttermilk.

4. **Eggs**

   Taste different kinds of eggs. Let children choose from scrambled, poached, deviled, hard-boiled, and fried. This could also be integrated as part of the breakfast menu.

5. **Cheese Types**

   Observe, taste, and compare different kinds of cheese. Examples include swiss, cheddar, colby, cottage cheese, and cheese curds.

6. **Egg Hatching**

   If possible, contact a hatchery to borrow an incubator. Watch the eggs hatch in the classroom.

7. **Feels from the Farm**

   Construct a feely box containing farm items. Examples may include an ear of corn, hay, sheep wool, a turkey feather, hard-boiled egg, etc.

Dramatic Play:

1. **Farmer**

   Clothes and props for a farmer can be placed in the dramatic play area. Include items such as hats, scarves, overalls, boots, etc.

2. **Saddle**

   A horse saddle can be placed on a bench in the classroom. The children can take turns sitting on it, pretending they are riding a horse.

3. **Barn**

   A barn and plastic animals can be added to the classroom. The children can use blocks as accessories to make pens, cages, etc.

4. **Veterinarian**

   Collect materials to make a veterinarian prop box. Stuffed animals can be used as patients.

Arts and Crafts:

1. **Yarn Collage**

   Provide the children with several types and lengths of yarn. Include clipped yarn, yarn fluffs, frayed yarn in several different colors, along with paper.

2. **Texture Collage**

   On the art table provide several colors, shapes, and types of fabric for creating a texture collage during the self-selected activity period for the children.

3. **Grain and Seed Collage**

   Corn, wheat, hay, oats, barley, and grains that farm animals eat can be placed on the art table. Paper and glue or paste should also be provided.

4. **Buttermilk Chalk Picture**

   Brush a piece of cardboard with 2 to 3 table-spoons of buttermilk or dip chalk in buttermilk. Create designs using colored chalk as a tool.

5. **Farm Animal Mobiles**

   Cut pictures of farm animals from magazines and hang them from hangers or branches.

6. **Eggshell Collages**

   Collect eggshells and crush into pieces. Place the eggshells in the art area for the children to glue on paper. Let dry. If desired, the shells can be painted. If preparation time is available, eggshells can be dyed with food coloring by teacher prior to the activity.

7. **Sponge Prints**

   Cut farm animal shapes out of sponges. If a pattern is needed, cut out of a coloring book. Once cut, the sponge forms can be dipped into a pan of thick tempera paint and used as a tool to apply a design.

Sensory:

Add to the Sensory Table:

- different types of grain, such as oats, wheat, barley, and corn, and measuring devices
- wool and feathers
- sand and plastic farm animals
- provide materials to make a barnyard. Include soil, hay, farm animals, barns, farm equipment toys, etc.

Large Muscle:

1. **Trikes**

   During outdoor play, encourage children to use trikes and wagons for hauling.

2. **Barn**

   Construct a large barn out of a large cardboard box. Let all the children help paint it outdoors. When dry, the children can play in it.

Field Trips/Resource People:

1. **Farmer**

   Invite a farmer to talk to the children. If possible, have him bring a smaller farm animal for the children to touch and observe.

2. **The Farm**

Visit a farm. Observe the animals and machinery.

3. **Milk Station**

Visit a milk station if there is one in your area.

4. **Grocery Store**

Visit the dairy section of a grocery store. Look for dairy products.

Math:

1. **Puzzles**

Laminate several pictures of farm animals; coloring books are a good source. Cut the pictures into puzzles for the children.

2. **Grouping and Sorting**

Collect plastic farm animals. Place in a basket and let the children sort them according to size, color, where they live, how they move, etc.

Social Studies:

Farm Animal of the Day

Throughout the week let children take care of and watch baby farm animals. Suggestions include a piglet, chicks, small ducks, rabbit, or lamb.

Group Time (games, language):

1. **"Duck, Duck, Goose"**

Sit the children in a circle. Then choose one child to be "it." This child goes around the circle and touches each of the other children on the shoulder and says "Duck, Duck, Goose." The child who is tapped as "goose" gets up and chases the other child around the circle. The first child who returns back to the empty spot sits down and the other child proceeds with the game of tapping children on the shoulder until someone else is tapped as the goose.

2. **Thank You**

Write a thank-you note as a follow-up activity after a field trip or a visit from a resource person.

Miscellaneous:

Transition

During transition time encourage the children to imitate different farm animals. They may gallop like a horse, hop like a bunny, waddle like a duck, move like a snake, etc.

Cooking:

1. **Make Butter**

Fill baby food jars half-full with whipping cream. Allow the children to take turns shaking the jars until the cream separates. First it will appear like whipping cream, then like overwhipped cream, and finally an obvious separation will occur. Then pour off liquid and taste. Wash the butter in cold water in a bowl several times. Drain off milky liquid each time. Taste and then wash again until nearly clear. Work the butter in the water with a wooden spoon as you wash. Add salt to taste. Let the children spread the butter on crackers or bread.

2. **Make Cottage Cheese**

Heat one quart of milk until lukewarm. Dissolve one rennet tablet in a small amount of the milk. Stir the rennet mixture into remaining milk. Let the mixture stand in a warm place until set. Drain the mixture through a strainer lined with cheesecloth. Bring the corners of the cloth together and squeeze or drain the mixture. Rinse the mixture with cold water and drain again. Add a small amount of butter and salt.

3. **Purple Cow Drink Mix**

   1/2 gallon milk
   1/2 gallon grape juice
   6 ice cubes
   blender

   Mix the ingredients in a blender for one minute. Drink. Enjoy! This recipe will serve approximately 20 children.

4. **Animal Crackers**

   Serve animal crackers and peanut butter for snack.

5. **Hungry Cheese Spread**

   1 8-ounce goat cheese or 8-ounce soft cream cheese
   1/4 cup soft butter
   1 teaspoon salt
   1 tablespoon paprika
   1 teaspoon dry mustard
   1 1/2 tablespoons caraway seeds

   Blend the cheese and butter in the mixing bowl. Add the remaining ingredients. Mix them well. Put the blended cheese into a small serving bowl. Chill in the refrigerator for at least 30 minutes before serving.

   Source: Cooper, Terry Touff, & Ratner, Marilyn. (1974). *Many Hands Cooking*. New York: Thomas Y. Crowell Company.

6. **Corn Bread**

   2 cups cornmeal
   1 teaspoon salt
   1/2 teaspoon baking soda
   1 1/2 teaspoons baking powder
   1 tablespoon sugar
   2 eggs
   1 1/2 cups buttermilk
   1/4 cup cooking oil

   Heat oven to 400 degrees. Sift cornmeal, salt, soda, baking powder, and sugar into a bowl. Stir in unbeaten eggs, buttermilk, and cooking oil until all ingredients are mixed. Pour the batter into a greased 9-inch x 9-inch pan or cob-formed pans. Bake for 30 minutes until lightly browned.

Multimedia:

The following resources can be found in educational catalogs:

1. Poelker, Kathy Lecinski. "My Pony Stop and Go" on *Look at My World* [record]. Look at Me Company.

2. *McDonald's Farm* [47-minute video]. Edu-vid.

3. *Doing Things* [27-minute video]. Bo Peep Productions.

4. *Good Morning, Good Night* [17-minute video]. Bo Peep Productions.

Books:

The following books can be used to complement the theme:

1. Gibbons, Gail. (1985). *The Milk Makers*. New York: Macmillan.

2. Brura, Dick. (1984). *Farmer Brown*. Los Angeles: Price, Stern, Sloan.

3. Ziegler, Sandra. (1987). *A Visit to the Dairy Farm*. Chicago: Children's Press.

4. *Baby Animals on the Farm*. (1989). Auburn, ME: Ladybird Books, Inc.

5. Brown, Craig. (1991). *My Barn*. New York: Greenwillow Books.

6. Cousins, Lucy. (1991). *Farm Animals*. New York: Morrow, Williams and Co.

7. Sweet, Melissa. (1992). *Fiddle - I - Fee: A Farm Yard Song for the Very Young*. New York: Little, Brown and Co.

8. Wells, Donna K. (1990). *What Animals Give Us: So Many Things*. Mankato, MN: Child's World, Inc.

9. Carroll, Kathaleen S. (1992). *One Red Rooster*. Boston: Houghton Mifflin Co.

10. Lewison, Wendy C. (1992). *Going to Sleep on the Farm*. New York: Dial Books for Young Readers.

11. Most, Bernard. (1990). *The Cow That Went Oink*. San Diego: Harcourt Brace Jovanovich.

12. Curran, Ellen. (1985). *Hello, Farm Animals*. Mahwah, NJ: Troll.

13. Galdone, Paul. (1985). *The Little Red Hen*. Boston: Houghton Mifflin.

14. Hammar, Asa. (1992). *Fit for Pigs*. New York: Checkerboard Press.

15. Hellen, Nancy. (1990). *Old MacDonald Had a Farm*. New York: Orchard Books.

16. Archambault, John. (1989). *Counting Sheep*. New York: Henry Holt.

17. Cross, Verda. (1992). *Great Grandma Tells of Threshing Day*. Morton Grove, IL: Albert Whitman.

18. McPhail, David. (1992). *Farm Boy's Year*. New York: Macmillan.

19. Mother Goof. (1992). *The Sheep Who Was Allergic to Wool*. Sunflower Hill.

20. Snow, Nancy. (1991). *Sheep In a Shop*. Boston: Houghton Mifflin.

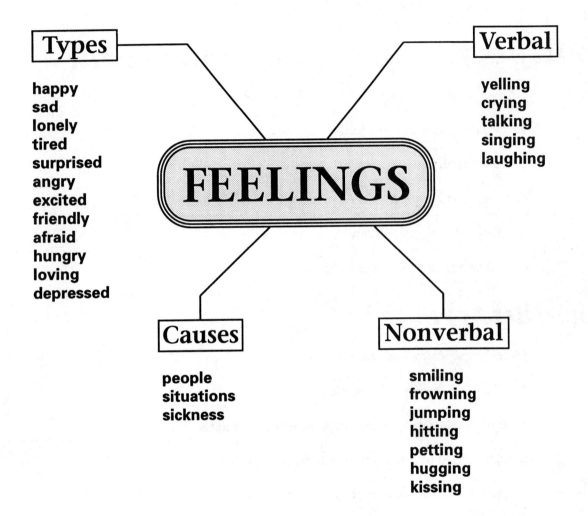

Types

happy
sad
lonely
tired
surprised
angry
excited
friendly
afraid
hungry
loving
depressed

Verbal

yelling
crying
talking
singing
laughing

FEELINGS

Causes

people
situations
sickness

Nonverbal

smiling
frowning
jumping
hitting
petting
hugging
kissing

Polaroid Education Program

Here's an exciting new way to turn instant photography into an effective teaching tool. Refer to the full-color insert for the activity entitled Photo Face.

Theme Goals:

Through participating in the experiences provided by this theme, the children may learn:

1. Types of feelings.

2. Verbal expressions of feelings.

3. Nonverbal expressions of feelings.

4. Causes for our feelings.

Concepts for the Children to Learn:

1. Everyone has feelings.

2. Feelings show how we feel.

3. Feelings change.

4. Happy, sad, excited, and surprised are types of feelings.

5. Happy people usually smile.

6. Sad people sometimes cry.

Vocabulary:

1. **feelings**—expressed emotions.

2. **happy**—a feeling of being glad.

3. **smile**—a facial expression of pleasure or happiness.

4. **surprise**—a feeling from something unexpected.

5. **sad**—the feeling of being hurt or unhappy.

6. **afraid**—the feeling of being unsure of or frightened about something.

Bulletin Board

The purpose of this bulletin board is to help the children become aware of feelings, as well as recognize their printed names. Prepare individual name cards for each child. Then prepare different expression faces such as happy, sad, and angry. Staple faces to top of bulletin board. See the illustration for an example. If available, magnetic strips may be added to the bulletin board under faces and pieces affixed to name cards, or push pins may be placed on the board and holes punched in name cards. The children may place their names under the face they decide they feel when arriving at school. Later, during large group time, the board can be reviewed to see if any of the children's feelings have changed.

Parent Letter

Dear Parents,

Emotions and feelings will be the focus of our next unit. Throughout each day, the children experience many feelings, ranging from happiness to sadness. The purpose of this unit is to have the children develop an understanding of feelings. Feelings are something we all share, and feelings are acceptable. We will also be exploring ways of expressing different feelings.

At School

Some of the learning experiences planned for this unit include:

* listening and discussing the book, *Alexander and the Terrible, Horrible, No Good, Very Bad Day* by Judith Viorst.
* singing songs about our feelings.
* drawing and painting to various types of music.

Our Special Visitor

"Clancy the Clown" will be visiting the children on Thursday at 3:00 p.m. The children are all looking forward to this special visitor. You are encouraged to join us and share their excitement.

At Home

To help your child identify situations that elicit feelings, have your child cut or tear pictures from discarded magazines that depict events or situations that make your child feel happy or sad. These pictures can then be glued or pasted on paper to create a feelings collage.

Talking with your child about your feelings will encourage parent-child communication. Tell your child what things make you feel various ways. Then ask your child to share some feelings.

Make your child happy today!

FIGURE 26 How do you feel today?

Music:

1. **"Feelings"**
   (Sing to the tune of "Twinkle, Twinkle Little Star")

   I have feelings.
   You do, too.
   Let's all sing about a few.

   I am happy.
     (smile)
   I am sad.
     (frown)
   I get scared.
     (wrap arms around self)
   I get mad.
     (make a fist and shake it)

   I am proud of being me.
     (hands on hips)
   That's a feeling too you see.

   I have feelings.
     (point to self)
   You do, too.
     (point to someone else)
   We just sang about a few.

2. **"If You're Happy and You Know It"**
   (traditional)

   If you're happy and you know it
   Clap your hands.
     (clap twice)
   If you're happy and you know it
   Clap your hands.
     (clap twice)
   If you're happy and you know it
   Then your face will surely show it.
   If you're happy and you know it
   Clap your hands.
     (clap twice)

   For additional verses, change the emotions and actions.

Fingerplays:

FEELINGS

   Smile when you're happy.
   Cry when you are sad.
   Giggle if it's funny.
   Get angry if you're mad.

   Source: Wilems, Dick. *Everyday Circle Times*.

I LOOKED INSIDE MY LOOKING GLASS

   I looked inside my looking glass
   To see what I could see.
   It looks like I'm happy today,
   Because that smiling face is me.

STAND UP TALL

   Stand up tall
   Hands in the air.
   Now sit down
   In your chair.
   Clap your hands
   And make a frown.
   Smile and smile.
   Hop like a clown.

Science:

1. **Sound Tape**

   Tape various noises that express emotions; suggestions include sounds such as laughter, cheering, growling, shrieking, crying, etc. Play these sounds for the children letting them identify the emotion. They may also want to act out the emotion.

2. **Communication Without Words**

   Hang a large screen or sheet with a bright light behind it. The children can go behind the screen and act out various emotions. Other children guess how they are feeling.

3. **How Does It Feel?**

   Add various pieces of textured materials to the science table. Include materials such as soft fur, sandpaper, rocks, and cotton. Encourage the children to touch each object and explain how it feels.

Dramatic Play:

1. **Flower Shop**

   Plastic flowers, vases, and wrapping paper can be placed in the dramatic play area. Make a sign that says "Flower Shop." The children may want to arrange, sell, deliver, and receive flowers among one another.

2. **Post Office**

   Collect discarded greeting cards and envelopes. The children can stamp and deliver the cards to one another.

3. **Puppet Center**

   A puppet center can be added to the dramatic play area. Include a variety of puppets and a stage.

Arts and Crafts:

1. **Drawing to Music**

   Play various types of music including jazz, classical, and rock and let the children draw during the self-selected activity period. Different tunes and melodies might make us feel a certain way.

2. **Playdough**

   Using playdough is a wonderful way to vent feelings. Prepare several types and let the children feel the different textures. Color each type a different color. Add a scent to one and to another add a textured material such as sawdust, rice, or sand. A list of playdoughs can be found later in this theme.

3. **Footprints**

   Mix tempera paint. Pour the paint into a shallow jelly roll pan approximately 1/4 inch deep. The children can dip their feet into the pan. After this, they can step directly onto paper. Using their feet as an application tool, footsteps can be made. This activity actually could be used to create a mural to hang in the hall or lobby.

Sensory:

Texture Feelings

Various textures can create feelings. Let the children express their feelings by adding the following to the sensory table:

- cotton
- water (warm or with ice)
- black water
- blue water
- sand
- pebbles
- dirt with scoops
- plastic worms with water

Large Muscle:

1. **Mirrors**

   The children should sit as pairs facing each other. Select one child to make a "feeling face" at the partner. Let the other child guess what feeling it is. A variation of this activity would be to have partners face each other. When one child smiles, the partner is to imitate his feelings.

2. **Simon Says**

   Play "Simon Says" using emotions:
   "Simon Says walk in a circle feeling happy…"
   "Simon Says walk in a circle feeling sad…"

Resource People:

1. **A Clown**

   Invite a clown to the classroom. You may ask the clown to dress and apply makeup for the children. After the clown leaves provide makeup for the children.

2. **Musician**

   Invite a musician to play a variety of music for the children to express feelings.

3. **Florist**

   Invite a florist to visit your classroom and show how flowers are arranged. Talk about why people send flowers. If convenient the children could visit the florist, touring the greenhouses.

Math:

Face Match

Collect two small shoe boxes. On one shoe box draw a happy face. On the other box, draw a sad face. Cut faces of people from magazines. The children can sort the pictures accordingly.

Social Studies:

Pictures

Share pictures of individuals engaged in different occupations such as doctors, fire fighters, beauticians, florists, nurses, bakers, etc. Discuss how these individuals help us and how they make us feel.

Group Time (games, language):

Happy Feeling

Discuss happiness. Ask each child one thing that makes him happy. Record each answer on a "Happiness Chart." Post the chart for the parents to observe as they pick up their children.

Cooking:

1. **Happy Rolls**

   1 package of fast-rising dry yeast
   1 cup warm water
   1/3 cup sugar
   1/3 cup cooking oil
   3 cups flour
   a dash of salt

   Measure the warm water and pour it into a bowl. Sprinkle the yeast on top of the water. Let the yeast settle into the water. Mix all of the ingredients in a large bowl. Place the dough on a floured board to knead it. Demonstrate how to knead, letting each of the children take turns kneading the bread. This is a wonderful activity to work through emotions. After kneading it for about 10 minutes, put the ball of dough into a greased bowl. If kneaded sufficiently, the top of the dough should have blisters on it. Cover the bowl and put in the sun or near heat. Let it rise for about an hour or until doubled. Take the dough out of the bowl. Punch it down, knead for several more minutes and then divide the dough into 12 to 15 pieces. Roll each piece of dough into a ball. Place each ball on a greased cookie sheet. Let the dough rise again until doubled. Bake at 450 degrees for 10 to 12 minutes. A happy face can be drawn on the roll with frosting.

2. **Berry "Happy" Shake—Finland**

10 fresh strawberries or 6 tablespoons sliced
   strawberries in syrup, thawed
2 cups cold milk
1 1/2 tablespoons sugar or honey

Wash the strawberries (if fresh) and cut out the stems. Cut the strawberries into small pieces. (If you are using frozen strawberries, drain the syrup into a small bowl or cup and save it.) Pour the milk into the mixing bowl. Add the strawberries. If you are using fresh strawberries, add the sugar or honey. If you are using frozen strawberries, add 3 tablespoons of the strawberry syrup instead of sugar. Beat with the egg beater for 1 minute. Pour the drink into glasses.

Source: Touff, Terry, & Ratner, Marilyn. (1974). *Many Hands Cooking*. New York: Thomas Y. Crowell Company.

3. **Danish Smile Berry Pudding**

1 10-ounce package frozen raspberries, thawed
1 10-ounce package frozen strawberries,
   thawed
1/4 cup cornstarch
2 tablespoons sugar
1/2 cup cold water
1 tablespoon lemon juice
slivered almonds

Puree berries in blender or press through sieve. Mix cornstarch and sugar in 1 1/2-quart saucepan. Gradually stir in water; add puree. Heat to boiling, stirring constantly. Boil and stir 1 minute. Remove from heat. Stir in lemon juice. Pour into dessert dishes or serving bowl. Cover and refrigerate at least 2 hours. Sprinkle with almonds; serve with half-and-half if desired. Makes 6 servings.

Source: *Betty Crocker's International Cookbook*. (1980). New York: Random House.

RECIPES FOR DOUGHS AND CLAYS

Clay Dough

3 cups flour
3 cups salt
3 tablespoons alum

Combine ingredients and
   slowly add water, a little
   at a time. Mix well with
   spoon. As mixture thickens, continue mixing
   with your hands until it
   has the feel of clay. If it
   feels too dry, add more
   water. If it is too sticky,
   add equal parts of flour
   and salt.

Play Dough

2 cups flour
1 cup salt
1 cup hot water
2 tablespoons cooking oil
4 teaspoons cream of tartar
food coloring

Mix well. Knead until
   smooth. This dough
   may be kept in a plastic
   bag or covered container
   and used again. If it gets
   sticky, more flour may
   be added.

Favorite Playdough

Combine and boil until
   dissolved:

2 cups water
1/2 cup salt
food coloring or tempera
   paint

Mix in while very hot:

2 tablespoons cooking oil
2 tablespoons alum
2 cups flour

Knead (approximately 5
   minutes) until smooth.
   Store in covered airtight
   containers.

Oatmeal Dough

2 cups oatmeal
1 cup flour
1/2 cup water

Combine ingredients. Knead well. This dough has a very different texture, is easily manipulated, and looks different. Finished projects can be painted when dry.

Baker's Clay #1

1 cup cornstarch
2 cups baking soda
1 1/2 cups cold water

Combine ingredients. Stir until smooth. Cook over medium heat, stirring constantly until mixture reaches the consistency of slightly dry mashed potatoes.

Turn out onto plate or bowl, covering with damp cloth. When cool enough to handle, knead thoroughly until smooth and pliable on cornstarch-covered surface.

Store in tightly closed plastic bag or covered container.

Baker's Clay #2

4 cups flour
1 1/2 cups water
1 cup salt

Combine ingredients. Mix well. Knead 5 to 10 minutes. Roll out to 1/4-inch thickness. Cut with decorative cookie cutters or with a knife. Make a hole at the top.

Bake at 250 degrees for 2 hours or until hard. When cool, paint with tempera paint and spray with clear varnish or paint with acrylic paint.

Cloud Dough

3 cups flour
1 cup oil
scent (oil of peppermint, wintergreen, lemon, etc.)
food coloring

Combine ingredients. Add water until easily manipulated (about 1/2 cup).

Sawdust Dough

2 cups sawdust
3 cups flour
1 cup salt

Combine ingredients. Add water as needed. This dough becomes very hard and is not easily broken. It is good to use for making objects and figures that one desires to keep.

Salt Dough

4 cups salt
1 cup cornstarch

Combine with sufficient water to form a paste. Cook over medium heat, stirring constantly.

Peanut Butter Playdough

2 1/2 cups peanut butter
2 tablespoons honey
2 cups powdered milk

Mix well with very clean hands. Keep adding powdered milk until the dough feels soft, not sticky. This is a dough that can be eaten.

Variations:

1. Cocoa or carob powder can be added for chocolate flavor.
2. Raisins, miniature marshmallows, or chopped peanuts may be added or used to decorate finished shapes.

Each child can be given dough to manipulate and then eat.

Cooked Clay Dough

1 cup flour
1/2 cup cornstarch
4 cups water
1 cup salt
3 or 4 pounds flour
coloring if desired

Stir slowly and be patient with this recipe. Blend the flour and cornstarch with cold water. Add salt to the water and boil. Pour the boiling salt and water solution into the flour and cornstarch paste and cook over hot water until clear. Add the flour and coloring to the cooked solution and knead. After the clay has been in use, if too moist, add flour; if dry, add water. Keep in covered container. Wrap dough with damp cloth or towel. This dough has a very nice texture and is very popular with all age groups. May be kept 2 or 3 weeks.

Play Dough

5 cups flour
2 cups salt
4 tablespoons cooking oil
add water to right consistency

Powdered tempera may be added in with flour, or food coloring may be added to finished dough. This dough may be kept in plastic bag or covered container for approximately 2 to 4 weeks. It is better used as playdough rather than leaving objects to harden.

Used Coffee Grounds

2 cups used coffee grounds
1/2 cup salt
1 1/2 cups oatmeal

Combine ingredients and add enough water to moisten. Children like to roll, pack, and pat this mixture. It has a very different feel and look, but it's not good for finished products. It has a very nice texture.

Mud Dough

2 cups mud
2 cups sand
1/2 cup salt

Combine ingredients and add enough water to make pliable. Children like to work with this mixture. It has a nice texture and is easy to use. This cannot be picked up to save for finished products easily. It can be used for rolling and cutouts.

Soap Modeling

2 cups soap flakes

Add enough water to moisten and whip until consistency to mold. Use soap such as Ivory Snow, Dreft, Lux, etc. Mixture will have very slight flaky appearance when it can be molded. It is very enjoyable for all age groups and is easy to work. Also, the texture is very different from other materials ordinarily used for molding. It may be put up to dry, but articles are very slow to dry.

Soap and Sawdust

1 cup whipped soap
1 cup sawdust

Mix well together. This gives a very different feel and appearance. It is quite easily molded into different shapes by all age groups. May be used for 2 to 3 days if stored in tight plastic bag.

Multimedia:

The following resources can be found in educational catalogs:

1. Rosenshontz, Gary & Bill. *Tickles You* [record].

2. Palmer, Hap. *Happy Hour* [record].

3. *I'm Glad I'm Me* [video]. Random House.

Books:

The following books can be used to complement the theme:

1. Keyworth, C. L. (1986). *New Day*. New York: Morrow.

2. Lionni, Leo. (1986). *It's Mine—A Fable*. New York: Alfred A. Knopf.

3. Amos, Janine. (1991). *Afraid*. Madison, NJ: Raintree Steck—Vaughn Publishing.

4. Amos, Janine. (1991). *Angry*. Madison, NJ: Raintree Steck—Vaughn Publishing.

5. Amos, Janine. (1991). *Hurt*. Madison, NJ: Raintree Steck—Vaughn Publishing.

6. Amos, Janine. (1991). *Jealous*. Madison, NJ: Raintree Steck—Vaughn Publishing.

7. Amos, Janine. (1991). *Lonely*. Madison, NJ: Raintree Steck—Vaughn Publishing.

8. Amos, Janine. (1991). *Sad*. Madison, NJ: Raintree Steck—Vaughn Publishing.

9. Dombrower, Jan. (1990). *Getting to Know Your Feelings*. Pleasanton, CA: Heartwise Press.

10. Moddy, Marlys. (1991). *ABC Books of Feelings*. Saint Louis, MO: Concordia Publishing House.

11. Modesitt, Jeanne. (1992). *Sometimes I Feel Like a Mouse*. New York: Scholastic, Inc.

12. Colin, Susan, & Friedman, Susan Levine. (1991). *Nathan's Day at Preschool*. Seattle, WA: Parenting Press.

13. Carlson, Nancy. (1988). *I Like Me!* New York: Viking Kestrel.

14. Hazen, Barbara Shook. (1992). *Even If I Did Something Awful*. New York: Macmillan.

15. Hines, Anna Grossnickle. (1988). *Grandma Gets Grumpy*. New York: Clarion.

16. Morris, Ann. (1990). *Loving*. New York: Lothrop, Lee, & Shepard.

17. Simon, Norma. (1986). *The Saddest Time*. Niles, IL: Albert Whitman.

18. Wilhelm, Hans. (1985). *I'll Always Love You*. New York: Crown.

19. Prelutsky, Jack (Ed.). (1991). *For Laughing Out Loud: Poems to Tickle Your Funnybone*. New York: Alfred A. Knopf.

20. Duncan, Riana. (1989). *When Emily Woke Up Angry*. New York: Barron.

Presenting
Bright Ideas
for
Child Development

Julie Korklan
Ann Cason

Photo Face

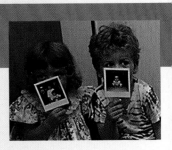

Aim
Gain a better under-
standing of emotions and
the facial expressions
which usually accompany
them. Vocabulary related
to emotional states is
developed, as well as
increased awareness of an
individual's emotional
condition.

Group Size
Small to whole group.

Materials
Polaroid Camera,
600 High Definition
film, craft sticks or paint
sticks, and glue or mask-
ing tape.

Activity
Take at least two pictures
of each child with different facial expressions.
Label each photo with
the child's name and
emotional state. *Be sure to
check with the child to
make sure that the label is
correct.* For instance, ask
the child to make a
happy face. Model the
expression, if necessary,
and use a mirror to help
the child achieve the
appropriate expression.
Attach a stick to the back
of each picture so the
children may hold up
their pictures like signs.

During circle time,
initiate a discussion on
feelings. Explore feelings
and their related expres-
sions. Children can study
their pictures, imitate the
expressions, and hold up
their appropriate picture.

Remember
This activity should help
the children learn more
about themselves and
increase their under-
standing of others. Allow
children to take pictures
home so that they can
discuss what they have
learned with their parents.

Photo Expectations

Aim

Reinforce appropriate behavior, cooperation, and independence.

Activity

In the early childhood setting, children are learning how to get along with their peers, follow directions, and become independent. Teachers create a pleasant learning atmosphere by making their expectations clearly understood. Rules are an important part of running a smooth classroom. Early childhood educators understand the importance of keeping rules simple and stating them in a positive manner; what to do, not just what NOT to do! Often, rules are posted in a prominent place in classrooms, however, many youngsters are not yet readers. Take a picture of children in class following each direction. Post the pictures with a simple label on a poster board or bulletin board so that everyone in the class can view them. For instance, the rule: TAKE TURNS could be illustrated with a Polaroid of two children on a slide, one at the top and one at the bottom.

Remember

At the early childhood level, most children are beginning to work on internalizing rules and developing impulse control. A concrete visual aid like a Polaroid can help prompt their memory. Also, this is a nice way to acknowledge and reward children for following the rules.

Group Size

Whole group.

Materials

Polaroid camera, 600 High Definition film, and poster board or bulletin board.

Photo Lotto

Aim

Teach children to recognize concepts, themes, or similarities through imagery.

Group Size

Small to whole group.

Materials

Polaroid camera, 600 High Definition film, and poster board.

Activity

Take duplicate images of objects that represent a theme or a concept (e.g., objects that represent winter, different types of cars, different parts of cars, etc.).

Paste one set of images on a poster board. Ask children to identify the content of each of the images. Then ask them if they can describe what is common to all of the images. Ask them if they can describe additional things that would also be similar or representative of the theme.

For younger children, hand out a second set of pictures so that each child has at least one photograph. Ask the children to match their photograph to one on the poster board. Ask them if they can identify the content of the photograph.

Extending the Activity

For children who are learning their alphabet or who are learning words, write the beginning letter of each object on the photograph. Ask them to find the object that begins with a specific letter.

Concentration Game

Aim
Increase language development, comprehension, and memory skills.

Activity
Take two pictures of the same objects around the school, indoors or outdoors, such as toys, cars, books, desks, crayons, balls, swings, etc.

Students mix the pictures up, place them face down on the table or floor, and alternate turning the cards over to match two pictures. This game is played like regular Concentration except with objects from the students' environment. After all the pictures have been matched, the game is over.

Extending the Activity
The teacher may want to integrate picture/letter/sound association into this game. Use a medium point permanent marker to write the beginning letter of each object in the corner of the picture.

Depending on the skill level of the player, the teacher may say the name of the object and ask for the beginning letter, or she may state the letter and name when the image is turned over.

Group Size
Partners or whole group.

Materials
Polaroid camera and 600 High Definition film.

Mathematics

Graphing

Aim

Introduce basic mathematic concepts.

Activity

Use a bulletin board or poster board to make graphs.

Begin by gathering one close-up and one full body image of each student. Place pictures of students in a row by eye color. This graph will show how many students have brown, blue, black eyes, etc.

Try a variation of graphs using: Color of eyes; Types of clothes (pants, dresses, shorts); Month of birthday; Hair.

Integrate other concepts into the lesson such as more or less than, counting, sets, sorting, similarities, and differences.

Extending the Activity

The teacher may guide students in a multi-cultural discussion of how everyone is special despite differences.

Group Size

Small or whole group.

Materials

Polaroid camera and 600 High Definition film.

Grouping

Aim

Enhance the students' perception, visual judgement, and language development skills, as well as the subject of math, dealing with sets.

Activity

Have students gather objects from outdoor and indoor sources. Objects may also be brought from home for this activity. Group sets of objects on the floor, table, or wall. The same object can be used several times. Grouping can be done in a variety of ways:

- Objects with similarities
- Objects with similar functions
- Objects of the same color, size, or shape
- A mixed grouping of objects

Take pictures of sets of objects arranged in various ways. Then take a second picture of the same set, taking something away, or putting something new in. You may also take pictures of objects with the same function, shape, color, or size in a set, then add an object that is different, or one that does not belong.

Have students sit in small groups. Place a pair of the pictures on the table or floor. First students discuss the pictures with each other. Many times students will discover the objective of the activity on their own. Allow time for this discovery learning through student interaction. Guide students through each pair of pictures, allowing them to discuss differences and similarities in the pictures.

Group Size
Small or whole group.

Materials
Polaroid camera and 600 High Definition film.

Language Arts

Photo Bingo

Aim
Introduce the alphabet and develop vocabulary in a visual game format. Children participate in a group activity which requires listening and visual judgement skills.

Group Size
Small to whole group.

Materials
Polaroid camera, 600 High Definition film, poster board, and poker chips for markers.

Activity
Cut poster board into game boards for each child and mark off a grid with 3" x 3" or 5" x 5" squares. In each square, print the letter that will be reinforced in the game by visual images. Give each child enough poker chips to cover several letters on their game board.

To play the game, hold up a picture of an object or person. Say the name of the person or object, and then say what letter that name begins with. Children should mark that letter on their game board with a poker chip.

A more difficult version is to hold up the image and say the name of the person or object. The children then must identify the first letter on their own.

Remember
The game boards are quite versatile. For example, the initial consonant game boards can be used with different Polaroids to identify ending or middle consonant sounds. Also, this is a great way to use those Polaroid pictures that might be leftovers from another activity.

Spatial Relations

Aim

Demonstrate various prepositions such as over, under, on, in, beside, behind, between, first, last, and second using visuals. Children can comprehend concepts easier when they are directly involved.

Activity

Have students pose and take pictures in various positions such as:

- Standing *on* a box or chair
- Sitting *under* the table
- Jumping *over* a candle or toy
- Standing *between* two objects
- Lying *beside* the stuffed animal
- Standing *in* line (with three or four students)

Once the pictures have been taken, show the pictures to children one-on-one or in small groups. Have them dialogue with each other as to the children's position in each picture. Use the appropriate vocabulary as children describe where they are positioned in the picture.

Extending the Activity

Integrate concepts like opposites such as up-down, in-out, first-last, boy-girl, etc.

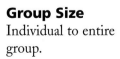

Group Size

Individual to entire group.

Materials

Polaroid camera and 600 High Definition film.

Story Books

My Friends and Me

Aim
Encourage language development, enjoyment of reading, social interaction, and enhance positive relations in the classroom.

Group Size
Small to whole group.

Materials
Polaroid camera, 600 High Definition film, paper, and paste or glue stick.

Activity
Take pictures of children. Use the copy machine to make enough copies so that each child can have a picture of each other. Paste or glue pictures to construction paper in a book format stapled together. The children can then write or dictate something that they like to do with each other:
- I like to play in the building blocks center with Susan.
- I like to read books with Carlos.
- Mary and I can color together.
- I like to push Jack in his wheelchair.

Write the phrases opposite the images. After completing their books, encourage children to read them aloud or read along with them.

Extending the Activity
Children can draw on the page as an extension of the photograph to depict the activity they like to do with their friends.

Create images of the children interacting with their favorite things (e.g., hugging "teddy"). Place the pictures in photo mounts, or construct books by folding paper in half, then stapling or sewing the paper along the fold. Create an appropriate cover for each book, with the title: **My I Like Book**.

Tell Me A Story

Aim

Record events of the day and special activities throughout the year with pictures. Children may use the pictures to recall those events and activities during circle time. Verbal expression is emphasized, as well as sequencing, listening, and recall. Vocabulary words may be introduced and reinforced.

Activity

Get double mileage out of special events at school by photographing them from the beginning to the end. Use these pictures soon after the event to display one picture at a time and allow a child to explain the event portrayed. Try to get agreement from the group as to the correct sequence of all the images. Then date the pictures in a classroom photo album. Throughout the year, you can use the album during circle time to generate discussion, look for familiar objects, find all of the details in an image, and learn about sequencing.

Group Size

Small to whole group.

Materials

Polaroid camera, 600 High Definition film, and photo album.

Creative Thinking

Photo Peek-A-Boo

Aim
Teach children how parts relate to a whole and how details compose an entire image. Also, skills of visualization and hypotheses will be developed.

Activity
Utilizing the close-up feature, take pictures of objects and people that the children will recognize. Mount the pictures on a tagboard behind paper doors that will reveal the image. The door should have a peekhole, displaying some portion of the picture. Children will try to guess what the whole object is by peering through the peekhole, formulating their hypotheses with the bit of image they can see. Baseball card boxes also work well to construct this activity. They are sturdy and the perfect size to hold the Polaroid pictures.

Remember
This is a great activity to mount on a bulletin board. The game can be altered by simply changing the pictures under the doors. Use photos with seasonal themes or concepts being presented in the class.

Group Size
Individuals to whole group.

Materials
Polaroid camera, 600 High Definition film, and baseball card sized boxes or tagboard.

Presto-Chango-Photo

Aim

Enhance visual processing skills and teach children to formulate hypotheses in a game-like format.

Activity

Mount Polaroid pictures on sturdy board with adhesive. Apply a clear overlay of plastic on top of the picture and staple. The plastic should be attached on only one side, so children can lift it. On this plastic overlay, draw or paint over the picture to add to the overall image. For instance, take a picture of a child wearing warm-weather clothes. The overlay should be drawn so that when situated on the photo, it appears that the child has on a winter cap and coat. The children can lift the overlay to reveal the warm-weather look. Another idea is to take a picture of some portion of the room, recognizable to the children. Outline basic shapes that can be seen in the picture, such as rectangles on the bookshelves, on the overlay.

Group Size

Individuals or pairs.

Materials

Polaroid camera, 600 High Definition film, sheets of clear plastic, Modge-Podge or similar adhesive, stapler, mounting boards, craft paints, and/or pens.

Polaroid Places

Aim

Teach children to organize their materials and become responsible for their own possessions.

Group Size

Whole group.

Materials

Polaroid camera, 600 High Definition film, and tape.

Activity

Most early childhood settings have an area designated for the children to hang up their outdoor gear and backpacks and store other materials. Sometimes this area includes a hook, shelf, locker, and/or a "cubby" space. To help children find their spot every day, place their pictures at their stations so that recognition is made easier. Be sure to write each child's name on the Polaroid picture. While many youngsters cannot read, they may recognize their own name. Seeing it every day at his space is added exposure to the letters if the child is working on the skill of learning to read his name.

Remember

Children learn better in an environment that is not only rich but also well-organized. Most early childhood educators teach organization and self-help skills leading to more productive, aware, and cooperative children.

People and Uniforms

Aim

Acquaint children with uniforms and the people in their community who wear them. This exercise promotes parental involvement and encourages children to learn the contemporary meaning of various uniforms and what they represent.

Activity

At least a day before the activity begins, discuss the uses for and role of uniforms. Talk about the people who wear them and the services they provide. Ask the children to talk with their parents about the various uniforms they wear.

Mount close-up photographs that the children have created of one another on individual pieces of construction paper. Using pictures of people drawn from magazines and newspapers, cut out their uniforms or create uniforms using colored construction paper. Attach the cutout to the photograph so that it extends beyond the photo itself to create the illusion that the children are wearing the uniform. Ask the children to choose the uniforms that they might like to wear. Discuss their feelings about that choice.

Group Size
Whole group.

Materials
Polaroid camera, 600 High Definition film, construction paper, magazines, scissors, and glue stick or clear tape.

Photo Open House

Aim
Give parents a better understanding of what goes on during the day at their child's preschool or day care facility.

Activity
Take Polaroid pictures of classroom activities which occur in specific parts of the room and at certain times of the day. For instance, take a picture of children playing at the water table, then mount the picture in that area and label the event and its purpose in the program. (Try using magnetic tape when applying Polaroid pictures to a metal surface.)

To display, post a large schedule with time slots, labels, and Polaroid pictures to illustrate each daily activity. These pictures will show the parents the various activities that their children are engaged in during the day. During Open House, the teacher may refer to the pictures to visually explain the program to parents. These pictures may stimulate further dialogue between parents and program personnel.

Extending the Activity
Parents are automatically drawn to pictures of their own children. Polaroid pictures of the children "in action" offer parents a real glimpse of their child's activities. Polaroid pictures can serve as springboards to later discussions between parents and children. For instance, "I saw that picture of you at the easel. You sure looked interested in your painting. Tell me what you like about painting."

Remember
Send pictures home to parents. Let children embellish the pictures with drawings or stickers.

Group Size
Small to whole group.

Materials
Polaroid camera, 600 High Definition film, mounting boards, tacks, and tape.

Clothing

hats
coats
masks
boots
gloves
uniforms

Job

fight fires
inspect buildings
teach fire safety
provide medical treatment

Fire Station

garage
workroom
kitchen
bedroom
dalmatians

FIRE FIGHTERS

Safety

when to use
house
person
how to get them
false alarms
matches
cooking
smoking

Vehicles

fire trucks
water trucks
fire chief car
ambulance
police car

Equipment

fire hydrant
fire extinguisher
hose
nozzles
ax
ladders
telephone
communication radios
water

Polaroid Education Program

Here's an exciting new way to turn instant photography into an effective teaching tool. Refer to the full-color insert for the activity entitled People and Uniforms.

Theme Goals:

Through participating in the experiences provided by this theme, the children may learn:

1. The fire fighter's job.

2. Fire fighter's clothing.

3. Vehicles used by fire fighters.

4. Fire fighting equipment.

5. Areas inside of a fire station.

Concepts for the Children to Learn:

1. Men and women who fight fires are called fire fighters.

2. Fire fighters help keep our community safe.

3. Fire fighters wear special hats and clothing.

4. The fire station has a garage, kitchen, workroom, and sleeping rooms.

5. The fire station has a special telephone number.

6. Ladders and water hoses are needed to fight fires.

7. Fire and water trucks are driven to fires.

8. Fire fighters check buildings to make sure they are safe.

9. Fire fighters teach us fire safety.

10. Fire extinguishers can be used to put out small fires.

11. Fire drills teach us what to do in case of a fire.

Vocabulary:

1. **fire alarm**—a sound warning people about fire.

2. **fire drill**—practice for teaching people what to do in case of a fire.

3. **fire extinguisher**—equipment that puts out fires.

4. **hose**—a tube that water flows through.

5. **helmet**—a protective hat.

6. **fire engine**—trucks carrying tools and equipment needed to fight fires.

7. **fire station**—a building that provides housing for fire fighters and fire trucks.

Bulletin Board

The purpose of this bulletin board is to develop an awareness of clothing worn by fire fighters and to reinforce color matching skills. From tagboard construct five fire fighter hats. Color each hat a different color. Then construct five fire fighter boots from tagboard. Color coordinate boots to match the hats. Laminate all of the pieces. Staple hats in two rows across the top of the bulletin board as illustrated. Staple boots in a row across the bottom of the bulletin board. Affix matching yarn to each hat. Children can match each hat to its corresponding colored boot by winding the string around a push pin in the top of the boot.

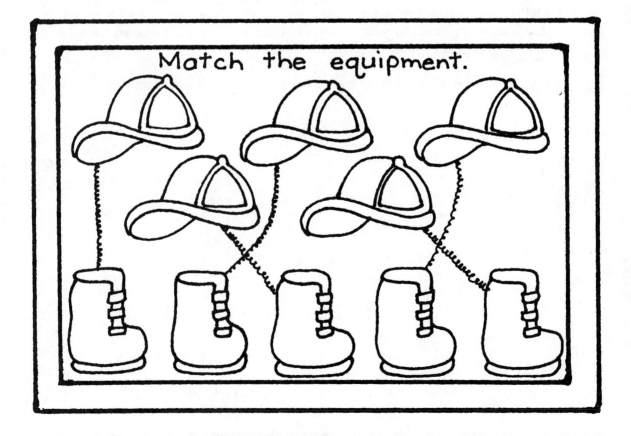

Parent Letter

Dear Parents,

Because next week is Fire Prevention Week, we have decided that it would be fun and educational to focus on some very important community helpers—fire fighters. The children will become more aware of the role of the fire fighter, clothing worn by fire fighters, and parts of the fire station. We will also be talking about how to use the telephone to call the emergency fire number.

At School

We have many activities planned for this unit! On Monday, we will paint a large box to create our own fire engine to use during the week in the dramatic play area. On Tuesday, a real fire engine will visit the parking lot, so the children can see how many tools fire fighters need to take along on the job. We'll also be making fire helmets, and practicing our fire drill procedures.

At Home

To ensure your family's safety, talk with your child about what would happen in the event of a fire at your house. You can do this calmly, without frightening your child. Practice taking a fire escape route from the child's bedroom, the playroom, kitchen, and other rooms of your house. Establish a meeting place so that family members can go to the same location in the event of a fire.

Enjoy your child as you share the importance of safety in the event of a fire.

FIGURE 27 A unit on fire fighters provides an opportunity to practice fire drills.

Music:

"Down By the Station"

Down by the station early in the morning
See the great big fire trucks all in a row.
Hear the jangly fire bell sound a loud alarm now—
Chug chug, clang clang, off we go!

Fingerplay:

TEN BRAVE FIRE FIGHTERS

Ten brave fire fighters sleeping in a row.
   (fingers curled to make sleeping men)
Ding, dong, goes the bell
   (pull down on the bell cord)
And down the pole they go.
   (with fists together make hands slide down
   the pole)
Off on the engine, oh, oh, oh!
   (pretend you are steering the fire engine
   very fast)
Using the big hose, so, so, so.
   (make a nozzle with fist to use hose)

When all the fire's out, home so slow.
Back to bed, all in a row.
   (curl all fingers again for sleeping fire
   fighters)

Source: Adapted from Cromwell, Liz, & Hibner, Dixie. (1976). *Finger Frolics*. Mt. Ranier, MD: Gryphon House.

Dramatic Play:

1. **Fire Fighters**

   Place fire fighting clothes such as hats, boots, and coats for children to wear. Sometimes fire station personnel will allow schools to borrow some of their clothing and equipment. Also, provide a bell to use as an alarm. A vacuum cleaner hose or a length of garden hose can be included to represent a water hose to extend play.

2. **Fire Truck**

   A fire truck can be cut from a cardboard refrigerator box. The children may want to paint the box yellow or red. A steering wheel and chairs may be added.

Arts and Crafts:

1. Fire Fighters' Hats

Provide materials for the children to make fire hats. The hats can be decorated with foil, crayons, or paint. The emergency number 911 may be printed on the crown.

2. Charcoal Drawings

Provide real charcoal at the easels to be used as an application tool.

3. Crayon Melting

Place waxed crayons and paper on the art table for the children to create a design during self-initiated or self-directed play. Place a clean sheet of paper over the picture. Apply a warm iron. Show the children the effect of heat. This activity needs to be carefully supervised. The caption "crayon melting" may be printed on a bulletin board. On the board place the children's pictures, identifying each by name in the upper left-hand corner.

Sensory:

1. Fill the sensory table with water. Provide cups and rubber tubing to resemble hoses and funnels.

2. Place sand in the sensory table. Add fire engines, fire fighter dolls, popsicle sticks to make fences, and blocks to make buildings or houses.

Large Muscle:

1. Fire Fighter's Workout

Lead children in a fire fighter's workout. Do exercises like jumping jacks, knee bends, leg lifts, and running in place. Ask children why they think fire fighters need to be in good physical condition for their jobs.

2. Obstacle Course

Make an obstacle course. Let children follow a string or piece of tape under chairs or tables, over steps, and across ladders. This activity can be planned for indoors or outdoors.

Field Trips/Resource People:

1. Fire Station

Take a trip to a fire station. Observe the clothing worn by fire fighters, the building, the vehicles, and the tools.

2. Fire fighter

Invite a fire fighter to bring a fire truck to your school. Ask the fire fighter to point out the special features such as the hose, siren, ladders, light, and special clothing kept on the truck. If permissable and safe, let the children climb onto the truck.

Math:

1. Sequencing

Cut a piece of rubber tubing into various lengths. The children can sequence the pieces from shortest to longest.

2. Emergency Number

Contact your local telephone company for trainer telephones to use. If developmentally appropriate, teach the children how to dial a local emergency number.

Social Studies:

1. Safety Rules

Discuss safety rules dealing with fire. Let children generate ideas about safety. Write their ideas on chart paper and display. Discuss why fire drills are a good idea.

2. Fire Inspection Tour

Tour the classroom or building looking for fire extinguishers, emergency fire alarm boxes, and exits.

3. Fire Drill

Schedule a fire drill. Prior to the drill talk to the children about fire drill procedures.

Group Time (games, language):

Language Experience

Review safety rules. Write the rules on a large piece of paper. These rules can also be included in a parent letter as well as posted in the classroom.

Cooking:

Firehouse Baked Beans

Purchase canned baked beans. To the beans, add cut-up hot dogs and extra catsup. Heat and serve for snack.

Multimedia:

The following resources can be found in educational catalogs:

1. *Little Firemen* [record]. Young People's Records.

2. "Let's Be Firemen" on *Men Who Come to Our House* [record]. Young People's Records.

3. Poelker, Kathy Lecinski. "At the Firehouse" on *Look At My World* [record]. Look at Me Company.

Books:

The following books can be used to complement the theme:

1. Rey, Margaret, & Shalleck, Alan J. (1985). *Curious George at the Fire Station*. New York: Scholastic.

2. Rius, Marie. (1985). *Fire*. Woodbury, NY: Barron's.

3. Maas, Robert. (1989). *Fire Fighters*. New York: Scholastic Inc.

4. Leonard, Marcia. (1990). *Jeffrey Lee, Future Fireman*. Morristown, NJ: Silver, Burdett and Ginn.

5. Marion, Kenneth P. (1990). *Volunteer Firefighter*. Kings Park, NY: JK Publishing.

6. Seymour, Peter. (1990). *Fire Fighters*. New York: Dutton Children's Books.

7. Barrett, Norman. (1991). *Picture World of Fire Engines*. New York: Watts, Franklin, Inc.

8. Pellowski, Michael. (1989). *Fire Fighter*. Tarrytown, NY: Troll Associates.

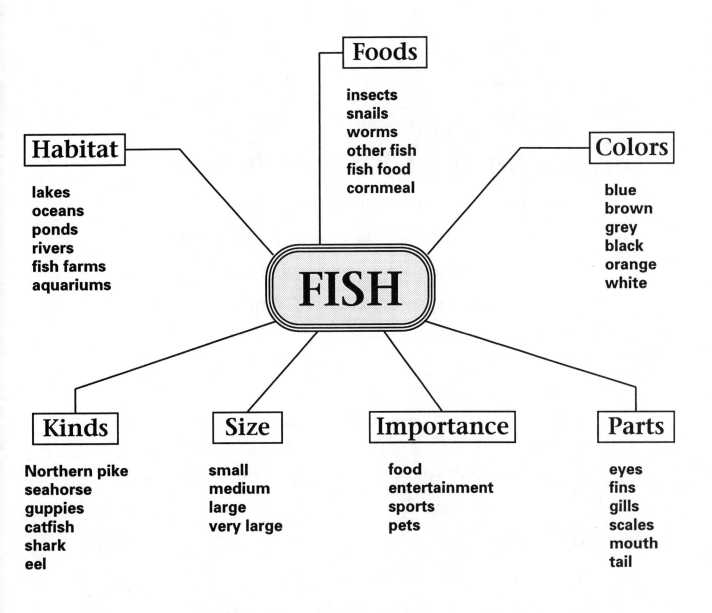

Foods

insects
snails
worms
other fish
fish food
cornmeal

Habitat

lakes
oceans
ponds
rivers
fish farms
aquariums

Colors

blue
brown
grey
black
orange
white

FISH

Kinds

Northern pike
seahorse
guppies
catfish
shark
eel

Size

small
medium
large
very large

Importance

food
entertainment
sports
pets

Parts

eyes
fins
gills
scales
mouth
tail

Polaroid
Education
Program

Here's an exciting new way to turn instant photography into an effective teaching tool. Refer to the full-color insert for the activity entitled Grouping.

Theme Goals:

Through participating in the experiences provided by this theme, the children may learn:

1. Homes for fish.

2. The importance of fish.

3. Colors of fish.

4. Care of fish.

5. Kinds of fish.

6. Sizes of fish.

7. Parts of fish.

Concepts for the Children to Learn:

1. Most fish have eyes, fins, gills, scales, a mouth, and tail.

2. Fish vary in size. They may be small, medium, large, or very large.

3. Blue, brown, grey, white, black, and orange are colors of fish.

4. Fish may live in lakes, oceans, ponds, rivers, fish farms, and aquariums.

5. Fish need food and water to live.

6. Insects, snails, other fish, plants, worms, fish food, and cornmeal are foods fish eat.

7. There are many kinds of fish. Some kinds include Northern pike, seahorse, guppies, catfish, shark, and eel.

8. Fish are important to people. (They provide food, entertainment, pets, and sport.)

Vocabulary:

1. **scales**—skin covering of fish and other reptiles.

2. **gills**—the part of the fish body that helps it get air.

3. **fin**—the part that moves to help fish swim.

4. **tail**—the end body part that helps fish move.

5. **fish farm**—a place to raise fish for food.

6. **school**—a group of fish.

Bulletin Board

The purpose of this bulletin board is to promote identification of written numerals, as well as matching a set to a written numeral. To prepare the bulletin board begin by drawing and cutting fish shapes from construction paper. Decorate the fish as desired and print a numeral on each fish. Make another set of identical fish shapes from black construction paper to create fish "shadows." Cut small circles out of white construction paper to represent the fish air bubbles. Staple the fish shadows to the bulletin board. Above each fish shadow, staple a set of air bubbles. Children can then match the numerals on the fish to the corresponding set of air bubbles. The fish can be attached to the bulletin board with push pins or small adhesive magnet pieces.

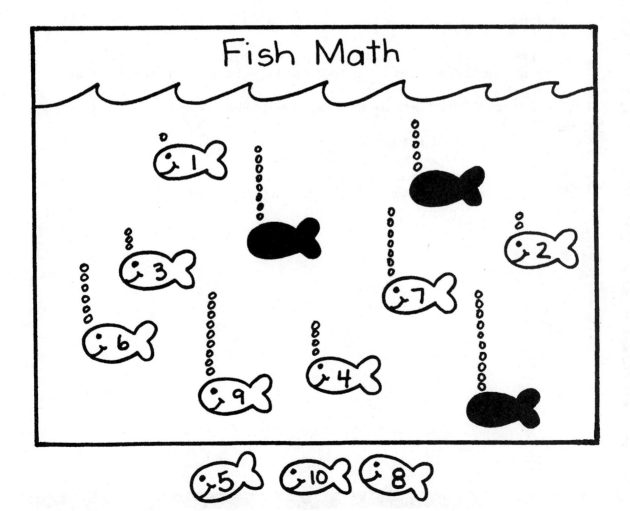

Parent Letter

Dear Parents,

Our next theme will focus on fish. Through participating in the experiences provided by this theme, the children will learn the color, size, kinds, and parts of a fish. They will also learn where fish live and the role fish play in our lives.

At School

Learning experiences that have been planned to complement this theme include:

- Visiting a pet store to observe different types and colors of fish. We will also purchase fish to bring back to our classroom.
- Listening to the story *Fish Eyes* by Lois Ehlert.
- Sorting, counting, and eating various fish-shaped crackers.
- Fishing in the dramatic play area.
- Observing minnows in the sensory table.

At Home

- Prepare a tuna salad using a favorite recipe with your child.
- Point out fishing gear in the sports section of a department store or in a catalog.
- Check out children's books about fish from the library. Look for:

     Fishes by Brian Wildsmith.
     Fish Is Fish and *Swimmy* by Leo Lionni.
     Gone Fishing by Earlene R. Long.
     A Million Fish…More or Less by Patricia C. McKissack.

FIGURE 28 How many fish can you catch?

Music:

1. **"I'm a Little Fish"**
   (Sing to the tune of "I'm a Little Teapot")

   I'm a little fish in the lake so blue,
   There are so many things that I can do.
   I can swim around with my tail and fin.
   The water's fine—just jump right in.

2. **"Goldfish"**
   (Sing to the tune of "Have You Ever Seen a Lassie?")

   Have you ever seen a goldfish, a goldfish, a goldfish?
   Have you ever seen a goldfish, just swimming all around?
   He swims this way and that way,
   And this way and that way.
   Have you ever seen a goldfish, just swimming all around?

3. **"Six Little Fish"**
   (Sing to the tune of "Six Little Ducks")

   Six little fish that I once knew,
   Fat ones, skinny ones, fair ones, too.

But the one little fish who was the leader of the crowd.
He led the other fish around and around.

Fingerplays:

FISH STORY

One, two, three, four, five
   (hold up fingers while counting)
Once I caught a fish alive.
Six, seven, eight, nine, ten
   (hold up additional fingers)
Then I let it go again.
Why did I let it go?
Because it bit my finger so.
Which finger did it bite?
The little finger on the right.
   (hold up pinky on the right hand)

DIVE LITTLE GOLDFISH

Dive, little goldfish one.
   (hold up one finger)
Dive, little goldfish two.
   (hold up two fingers)
Dive, little goldfish three
   (hold up three fingers)

Here is food, you see!
    (sprinkling motion with fingers)
Dive, little gold fish four.
    (hold up four fingers)
Dive, little gold fish five.
    (hold up five fingers)
Dive, little goldfish six.
    (hold up six fingers)
I like your funny tricks.

Source: Scott, Louise Binder. *Rhymes for Learning Times.*

GOLD FISH PETS

One little goldfish lives in a bowl.
    (hold up one finger)
Two little goldfish eat their food whole.
    (hold up two fingers)
Three little goldfish swim all around.
    (hold up three fingers)
Although they move, they don't make a sound.
Four little goldfish have swishy tails.
    (hold up four fingers)
Five little goldfish have pretty scales.
    (hold up five fingers)

Source: Scott, Louise Binder. *Rhymes for Learning Times.*

Science:

1. **Aquarium**

    Set up an aquarium to place on the science table. Let the children take turns feeding the fish. Provide pictures and books about fish.

2. **Balance Scale**

    Place on the science table a balance scale and clean aquarium rocks. The children can use spoons and measuring cups to transfer the rocks into the scale containers. After this, they can experiment with the balance.

3. **Fish Tasting Party**

    Plan a tasting party. Prepare fish using different methods such as baked, broiled, fried, and prepared in a casserole. The results of the

children's favorite fish preparation can be discussed and charted.

Dramatic Play:

1. **Gone Fishing**

    Set up a fishing area in the dramatic play center. Provide props such as a wooden rocking boat, small wading pool, life vests, hats, tackle boxes, nets, and fishing poles. Fishing poles can be made by attaching string to a short dowel or paper towel tube. Tie a small magnet to the end of the string. Attach paper clips to the construction paper fish. Then, go fishing!

2. **Bait and Tackle Shop**

    Provide props to simulate a bait and tackle shop in the dramatic play area. Items can include a cash register, play money, plastic or paper fish of varying sizes, nets, fishing lures (remove hooks), tackle boxes, coolers, fishing poles, and life vests. Display pictures of fish and people fishing.

Arts and Crafts:

1. **Aquarium Crayon Resist**

    After observing fish or listening to stories about fish, encourage the children to use crayons to draw fish on a piece of white construction paper. Then, the children can paint over their crayon drawing with a thin wash of blue tempera or water color. The wax will repel the water paints leaving an interesting effect.

2. **Fish Sponge Painting**

    Cut sponges into fish shapes. Place the sponges on the art table with paper and several shallow trays of paint. Use thick tempera paint the color of fish. Also provide paper. The children can make prints by dipping the sponges into the paint and then pressing them onto paper.

3. Fish Rubbings

Cut fish shapes out of tagboard, adding details as desired. Place the fish shapes on the art table along with paper and crayons. The children can create designs by placing a tagboard fish beneath a piece of paper and rubbing over the top of the paper with a crayon. Repeat as discussed.

4. Tackle Box Paint Container

Use a discarded, clean tackle box as a container to hold paints at the art table. Paints can be placed in individual compartments, providing several choices for the children.

Sensory:

1. Aquarium Rocks

Place a bag of clean aquarium rocks in the sensory table. Provide cups, bowls, and pails for the children's use. Add water, if desired.

2. Plastic Fish

Purchase small plastic fish and place in the sensory table with water, strainers, and pails.

3. Minnows

Purchase minnows from a bait store. Place the minnows in a sensory table filled with cold water. Stress the importance of being gentle with the fish and follow through with limits set for the activity. After participating in this activity, the children need to wash their hands.

4. Plastic Boats

Place small plastic boats in a sensory table filled with water. Also provide small plastic people to ride and fish in the boats.

Field Trips/Resource People:

1. Lake, Pond, or Stream

If possible, visit a small body of water to observe fish habitat. Watch for people fishing.

(For safety purposes, the body of water will have to be carefully chosen. Likewise, additional supervision may be required.)

2. Pet Store

Visit a pet store to see many types of fish, as well as aquariums and fish supplies. Purchase one or more goldfish to take back to your classroom.

3. Bait and Tackle Shop

Make arrangements to visit a bait and tackle shop. Observe the many types of fishing poles and lures, as well as boat safety items.

4. State or National Fish Hatchery

These make a wonderful field trip. They also have coloring books, etc., for the children.

5. Fish Sportsman or Sportswoman

Invite a parent or another person who enjoys fishing to come talk with the children. Ask the person to bring fishing gear and pictures of fishing trips as well as fish caught.

Math:

1. Sort the Fish

Purchase a variety of small plastic fish or construct some out of tagboard. Put them in a large pail. The children can sort the fish by size, color, and type.

2. Fish Seriation/Measurement

Trace and cut shapes out of construction paper. Encourage the children to place them in order from smallest to largest. If developmentally appropriate, provide rulers and yardsticks for the children to measure the fish.

3. Fishbowl Math

Print numerals or sets of dots on small plastic fish. Place the fish in a clean bowl or container. The children can use small nets to take turns scooping out a fish and stating the numeral or counting the dots.

4. Fish Cracker Sort

Purchase a variety of flavors of small fish-shaped crackers. For each child, place a few of each kind of cracker in a paper cup. Before eating the crackers, encourage the children to sort the crackers. If appropriate, the children can count the number of each cracker flavor.

Group Time (games, language):

1. Fish Memory Game

Collect items associated with fish and place on a tray. At group time, show the tray containing the items and name them. To play the game, cover the tray with a towel. Then ask the children to recall the names of items on the tray. To vary the game, play again, this time removing an item from the tray while covered. The children then try to name the item missing from the tray. To ensure success, begin the activity with few objects. Additional objects can be added depending upon the developmental maturity of the children.

2. Go Fish!

Cut fish shapes out of various colors of construction paper. Attach a paper clip to each fish. Make a fishing pole by tying a string to a short dowel. Attach a small magnet to the end of the string. At group time, present the fishing pole and fish. Place the fish on the floor and allow the children to take turns fishing. As a fish is caught, the child removes it from the magnet and names the color. Repeat until all of the children have had a turn. The game can be varied by drawing a basic shape and printing a numeral or a letter on each fish for the children to identify.

Cooking:

1. Swimming Fish Snack

8 ounces soft cream cheese
blue food coloring

1 box rectangular-shaped crackers
2 cups small fish-shaped crackers (any flavor)

Add a few drops of blue food coloring to the cream cheese and stir. For each serving, spread cream cheese on a large, rectangular cracker. Place a few fish-shaped crackers on top of the cream cheese.

2. Fish Mix Snack

2 cups toasted oat cereal
2 cups pretzel sticks
2 cups small fish-shaped crackers (any flavor)
1/4 cup melted margarine
2 teaspoons Worcestershire sauce

Combine oat cereal, pretzels, and fish-shaped crackers in a bowl. In a small bowl, stir together melted margarine and Worcestershire sauce. Drizzle over cereal mixture and toss to coat evenly. Transfer into 13 x 9 baking pan and bake in a 300-degree oven for 30 minutes, stirring occasionally. Remove from oven and cool. Makes approximately 6 cups.

3. Tuna Salad

1 can of tuna (3 1/4-ounce), drained
1/4 cup mayonnaise, salad dressing, or plain yogurt
1/4 cup finely chopped apple
3 tablespoons sunflower seeds
4 slices of bread or 2 English muffins

Combine the tuna, mayonnaise, apple, and sunflower seeds in a bowl. Chill if desired. Toast the bread or English muffins. Spread tuna mixture on toasted muffins. (Makes four servings.)

4. Tartar Sauce for Fish Sticks

1/2 cup mayonnaise or salad dressing
1 tablespoon finely chopped pickle or pickle relish
1 teaspoon dried parsley
1/2 teaspoon grated onion or onion flakes

Combine all ingredients and chill. Bake frozen fish sticks as directed on the package and serve with tartar sauce.

Multimedia:

The following resources can be found in educational catalogs:

1. Poelker, Kathy. "A Pretty Little Fish" on *Amazing Musical Moments* [record].

2. Diamond, Charolette. "Octopus" on *Ten Carrot Diamond* [record].

3. *Undersea Adventure* [IBM software PK+]. Knowledge Adventure.

Books:

The following books can be used to complement the theme:

1. Adams, Georgie. (1993). *Fish Fish Fish*. New York: Dial Books for Young Readers.

2. Wildsmith, Brian. (1987). *Fishes*. New York: Oxford University Press.

3. Cazet, Denys. (1987). *A Fish in This Pocket*. New York: Orchard Books.

4. Seuss, Dr. (1987). *One Fish Two Fish Red Fish Blue Fish*. New York: Random House Books for Young Readers.

5. Ehlert, Lois. (1990). *Fish Eyes: A Book You Can Count On*. San Diego: Harcourt Brace Jovanovich.

6. Erickson, Gina C., & Foster, Kelli C. (1991). *Sometimes I Wish*. Hauppauge NY: Barron's Educational Series.

7. Luenn, Nancy. (1990). *Nessa's Fish*. New York: Macmillan Children's Book Group.

8. Wylie, Joanne, & Wylie, David. (1987). *A Big Fish Story Book*. Chicago: Children's Press.

9. Alexander, Sally H. (1992). *Maggie's Whopper*. New York: Macmillan Children's Book Group.

10. Long, Earlene R. (1987). *Gone Fishing*. Boston, MA: Houghton Mifflin Co.

11. McKissack, Patricia C. (1992). *A Million Fish...More or Less*. New York: Alfred A. Knopf Books for Young Readers.

12. Ward, Sally G. (1991). *Punky Goes Fishing*. New York: Dutton Children's Books.

13. George, William T., & George, Lindsay B. (1991). *Fishing at Long Pond*. New York: Greenwillow Books.

14. Bush, John, & Korky, Paul. (1991). *The Fish Who Could Wish*. Brooklyn, NY: Kane/Miller.

15. Edwards, Roberta. (1989). *Five Silly Fisherman: A Step One Book*. New York: Random House.

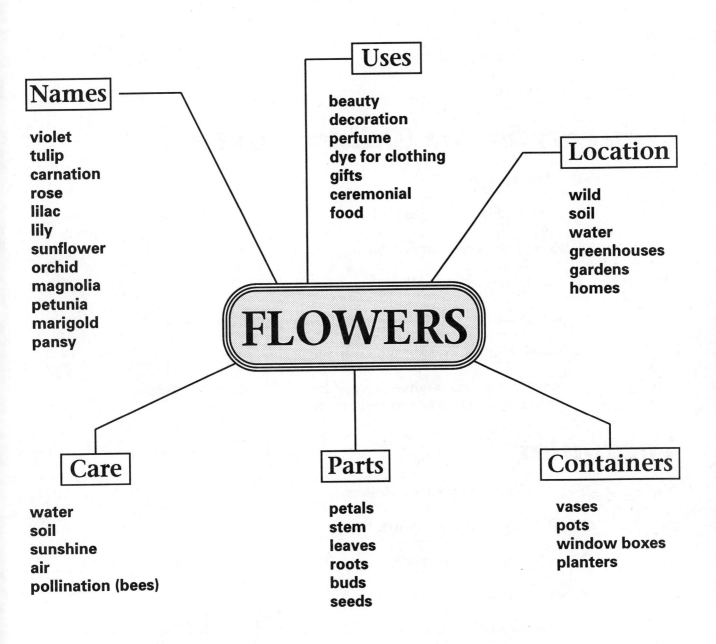

Names

violet
tulip
carnation
rose
lilac
lily
sunflower
orchid
magnolia
petunia
marigold
pansy

Uses

beauty
decoration
perfume
dye for clothing
gifts
ceremonial
food

Location

wild
soil
water
greenhouses
gardens
homes

FLOWERS

Care

water
soil
sunshine
air
pollination (bees)

Parts

petals
stem
leaves
roots
buds
seeds

Containers

vases
pots
window boxes
planters

Here's an exciting new way to turn instant photography into an effective teaching tool. Refer to the full-color insert for the activity entitled *Photo Lotto.*

Theme Goals:

Through participating in the experiences provided by this theme, the children may learn:

1. Parts of the flower.

2. Flowers have names.

3. Places flowers grow.

4. Uses of flowers.

5. Containers that hold flowers.

6. Care of flowers.

Concepts for the Children to Learn:

1. A flower is a plant.

2. Flowers add beauty to our world.

3. Flowers can be used for decoration.

4. Most flowers have a smell.

5. Vases, pots, window boxes, and planters are all flower containers.

6. Flowers need soil, water, sunshine, and air to grow.

7. Sometimes flowers are given to people for special reasons, such as holidays, birthdays, or if someone goes to the hospital.

Vocabulary:

1. **flower**—part of a plant that blossoms.

2. **petal**—colored part of a flower.

3. **seed**—produces a new plant.

4. **stem**—the trunk of the plant.

5. **leaves**—growth from the stem.

6. **greenhouse**—a glass house for growing plants.

7. **root**—the part of the plant that usually grows down into the soil.

Bulletin Board

The purpose of this bulletin board is to develop color matching skills, as well as foster the correspondence of sets to written numerals. A math skills bulletin board can be created by cutting large numerals out of tagboard. Color each number a different color. Next, create tulips out of tagboard. The number will be dependent upon the maturity of the children. Color one tulip the same color as the numeral one. Color two tulips the same color as the numeral two. Continue with the numerals three and four. The children can hang the appropriate number of tulips on the bulletin board next to each numeral. The children can also match the colored tulips next to the corresponding colored numeral to make this activity self-correcting.

Flower math

283

Parent Letter

Dear Parents,

Hello! As spring arrives and all the flowers begin to bloom, we will begin a unit on flowers. Through this unit the children will learn about the care, uses, and parts of a flowering plant.

At School

Some of the learning experiences planned to help the children make discoveries about flowers include:

* listening to the story, *Dandelion* by Ladislav Svatos.
* observing and measuring the growth of various flowers.
* visiting a floral shop.
* playing a flower beanbag toss game.

At Home

You can integrate the concepts included in this unit into your home in many ways. If you are planning to plant a garden in your yard this spring, let your child help you. It might even be fun to section off a small part of your garden for your child to grow flowers and care for them. Another activity would be to examine the plants and flowers you have growing in your house. Also, let your child send flowers to someone special.

To develop language skills, we will be learning this fingerplay in school. Let your child teach it to you.

Daisies

One, two, three, four, five
    (pop up fingers, one at a time)
Yellow daisies all alive.
Here they are all in a row.
    (point to fingers standing)
The sun and the rain will help them grow.
    (make a circle with fingers, flutter fingers for rain)

Enjoy your child!

FIGURE 29 Children learn science concepts by growing flowers.

Music:

"Flowers"
(Sing to the tune of "Pop! Goes the Weasel")

All around the forest ground
There's flowers everywhere.
There's pink, yellow, and purple, too.
Here's one for you.

Fingerplays:

MY GARDEN

This is my garden
   (extend one hand forward, palm up)
I'll rake it with care
   (raking motion with fingers)
And then some flower seeds
   (planting motion)

I'll plant in right there.
The sun will shine
   (make circle with hands)
And the rain will fall
   (let fingers flutter down to lap)
And my garden will blossom
   (cup hands together, extend upward slowly)
And grow straight and tall.

DAISIES

One, two, three, four, five
   (pop up fingers, one at a time)
Yellow daisies all alive.
Here they are all in a row.
   (point to fingers standing)
The sun and the rain will help them grow.
   (make a circle with fingers, flutter fingers for rain)

FLOWER PLAY

If I were a little flower
Sleeping underneath the ground,
   (curl up)
I'd raise my head and grow and grow
   (raise head and begin to grow)
And stretch my arms and grow and grow
   (stretch arms)
And nod my head and say,
   (nod head)
"I'm glad to see you all today."

Science:

1. **Flowers**

   Place a variety of flowers on the science table. Encourage the children to compare the color, shape, size, and smell of each flower.

2. **Planting Seeds**

   Plant flower seeds in a styrofoam cup. Save the seed packages and mount on a piece of tagboard. Place this directly behind the containers on the science table. Encourage the children to compare their plants. When the plant starts growing, compare the seed packages to the plant growth.

3. **Carnation**

Place a white carnation in a vase containing water with red food coloring added. Watch the tips of the carnation petals gradually change colors. Repeat the activity using other flowers and colors of water.

4. **Observing and Weighing Bulbs**

Collect flower bulbs and place in the science table. Encourage the children to observe the similarities and differences. A balance scale can also be added.

5. **Microscopes**

Place petals from a flower under a microscope for the children to observe.

Dramatic Play:

1. **Garden**

Aprons, small garden tools, a tin of soil, seeds, watering cans, pots, and vases can all be provided. Pictures of flowers with names on them can be hung in the classroom.

2. **Gardener**

Gather materials for a gardener prop box. Include gloves, seed packets, sun hat, hoe, stakes for marking, watering cans, etc.

3. **Flower Shop**

In the dramatic play area, set up a flower shop complete with plastic flowers, boxes, containers, watering cans, misting bottle, and cash register. Artificial corsages would also be a fun addition.

4. **Flower Arranging**

Artificial flowers and containers can be placed in the dramatic play area. The children can make centerpieces for the lunch table. Also, a centerpiece can be made for the science table, the lobby, and the secretary, director, or principal.

Arts and Crafts:

1. **Muffin Cup Flowers**

For younger children, prepare shapes of flowers and leaves. The older children may be able to do this themselves. Attach the stems and leaves to muffin tin liners. Add a small amount of perfume to the flower for interest.

2. **Collage**

Cut pictures of flowers from seed catalogs. With these flowers, create a collage.

3. **Easel**

Cut easel paper into flower shapes.

4. **Seed Collages**

Place a pan containing a variety of seeds in the middle of the art table. In addition, supply glue and paper for the children to form a collage.

5. **Egg Carton Flowers**

Cut the sections of an egg container apart. Attach pipe cleaners for stems and decorate with watercolor markers.

6. **Flower Mobile**

Bring in a tree branch and hang from the classroom ceiling. Let the children make flowers and hang them on the branch for decoration.

7. **Paper Plate Flowers**

Provide snack-sized paper plates, markers, crayons, and colored construction paper. The children may use these materials to create a flower.

Sensory:

Add to the sensory table:

- soil and plastic flowers
- water and watering cans

Field Trips/Resource People:

1. **Florist**

   Arrange to visit a local floral shop. Observe the different kinds of flowers. Then watch the florist design a bouquet or corsage.

2. **Walk**

   Walk around the neighborhood observing different types and colors of flowers.

Math:

1. **Flower Growth**

   Prepare sequence cards representing flowers at various stages of growth. Encourage the children to sequence them.

2. **Flower Match**

   Cut pictures of flowers from magazines or seed catalogs. If desired, mount the pictures. The children can match them by kind, size, color, and shape.

3. **Measuring Seed Growth**

   Plant several types of seeds. At determined intervals, measure the growth of various plants and flowers. Maintain a chart comparing the growth.

Group Time (games, language):

Hide the Flower

Choose one child to look for the flower. Ask him to cover his eyes. Ask another child to hide a flower. After the flower is hidden and the child returns to the group, instruct the first child to uncover his eyes and find the flower. Clues can be provided. For example, if the child aproaches the area where the flower is hidden, the remainder of the children can clap their hands.

Cooking:

1. **Fruit Candy**

   Some fruits start with a flower. Discuss which of the following fruits begin with a flower from the ingredients below.

   1 pound dried figs
   1 pound dried apricots
   1/2 pound dates
   2 cups walnuts
   1/2 cup raisins
   1/2 cup coarsely chopped walnuts

   Put fruits and 2 cups of walnuts through a food grinder. Mix in the 1/2 cup of chopped walnuts and press into a buttered 9-inch x 13-inch pan. Chill and enjoy!

2. **China—Egg Flower Soup**

   Watch an egg turn into a flower. Chinese cooks say that the cooked shreds of egg afloat in this soup look like flower petals.

   1 tablespoon cornstarch
   2 tablespoons cold water
   1 egg
   3 cups clear canned chicken broth
   1 teaspoon salt
   1 teaspoon chopped scallion or parsley (optional)

   Put the cornstarch into a small bowl and gradually add water, stirring it with a fork until you no longer see any lumps. Break the egg into another small bowl and beat it with the fork. Pour the broth into the saucepan. Bring it to a boil over high heat. Add the salt. Give the cornstarch and water mixture a quick stir with the fork. Add it to the soup. Stir the soup with a spoon until it thickens and becomes clear (about one minute). Slowly pour the beaten egg into the soup. The egg will cook in the hot soup and form shreds. When all the egg has been added, stir once. Turn off the heat. Pour the soup into 4 soup bowls. Top if desired with chopped scallion or parsley for decorations.

   Source: Touff, Terry, & Ratner, Marilyn. (1974). *Many Hands Cooking*. New York: Thomas Y. Crowell Company.

3. **Dandelion Salad**

6 cups young dandelion leaves, picked before
   flower blossoms
croutons, hard-boiled eggs, vegetables (optional)
dressing

Thoroughly wash the dandelion greens,
removing stems and roots. Tear the leaves into
small pieces and place in bowls. Add optional
ingredients. Toss with salad dressing.

Multimedia:

The following resources can be found in educational catalogs:

1. Follman, Ilene, & Jackson, Helen. "Dandelion Seed" on *Science in a Nutshell* [record].

2. *Daisy Quest* [Mac software, PK–2]. Great Wave.

Books:

The following books can be used to complement the theme:

1. Braithwaite, Althea. (1988). *Flowers*. Chicago: Dearborn Financial Publishing, Inc.

2. Butterfield, Moira. (1992). *Flower*. New York: Simon and Schuster Trade.

3. Wexler, Jerome. (1990). *Flowers Fruits Seeds*. New York: Simon and Schuster Trade.

4. Ehlert, Lois. (1992). *Planting a Rainbow*. San Diego: Harcourt Brace Jovanovich.

5. Turner, Ann, & Blake, Robert J. (1992). *Rainflowers*. New York: Harper Collins Children's Books.

6. Jordan, Helene J. (1992). *How a Seed Grows*. New York: Crowell Junior Books.

7. Demi. (1990). *The Empty Pot*. New York: Henry Holt.

8. Fowler, Allan. (1993). *What's Your Favorite Flower?* Children's Books.

9. dePaola, Tomie. (1988). *The Legend of the Indian Paintbrush*. New York: G. P. Putnam's Sons.

Activities

play
share
learn
talk
listen
work

Who

self
mothers
fathers
brothers
sisters
cousins
relatives
boys
girls
neighbors
pets

FRIENDS

Places

school
neighborhood
home
park

Why

to help
to enjoy

Polaroid
Education
Program

Here's an exciting new way to turn instant photography into an effective teaching tool. Refer to the full-color insert for the activity entitled My Friends and Me.

Theme Goals:

Through participating in the experiences provided by this theme, the children may learn:

1. Who friends are.

2. Why we have friends.

3. Activities we can do with our friends.

4. Places we can make friends.

Concepts for the Children to Learn:

1. A friend is someone who I like and who likes me.

2. My friends are special to me.

3. We have friends at school.

4. Our brothers and sisters can be our friends.

5. Friends can help us with our work.

6. We play with our friends.

7. We share and learn with friends.

8. Friends talk and listen to us.

9. A pet can be a friend.

10. Friends can be boys or girls.

Vocabulary:

1. **friend**—a person we enjoy.

2. **sharing**—giving and taking turns.

3. **like**—feeling good about someone or something.

4. **giving**—sharing something of your own with others.

5. **cooperating**—working together to help someone.

6. **togetherness**—being with one another and sharing a good feeling.

7. **pal or buddy**—another word for friend.

Bulletin Board

The purpose of this bulletin board is to help the children with recognition of their own and their friends' names. The bulletin board can also be used by the teacher as an attendance check. Prepare the board by constructing name cards for each child as illustrated. Then laminate and punch holes in each card. When the children arrive at school, they can attach their name card to the bulletin board with a push pin.

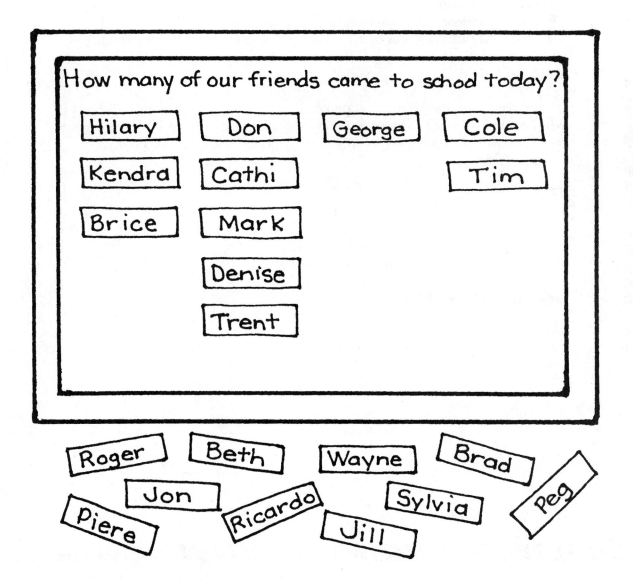

Parent Letter

Dear Parents,

We will be starting a unit on friends, which will include discovering people of all ages and even animal friends. The children have made many new friends at school with whom they are learning to take turns, cooperate, work, and play. Through this unit, the children will become more aware of what a friend is and activities friends can do together.

At School

Highlights of the learning experiences in this unit include:

- making friendship fortune cookies.
- sending notes to pen pals.
- creating a friendship chain with strips of paper.
- looking at pictures of our friends at school in our classroom photo album.

At Home

Your child may enjoy looking at photo albums of family and friends. Perhaps a friend could be invited to come and play with your child. Here is a poem about friends we will be learning to promote an enjoyment of language and poetry.

Friends

I like my friends.
So when we are at play,
I try to be very kind,
and nice in every way.

Be your child's best friend!

FIGURE 30 Tina is my best friend!

Music:

1. **"Do You Know This Friend of Mine"?**
   (Sing to the tune of "The Muffin Man")

   Do you know this friend of mine,
   This friend of mine,
   This friend of mine?
   Do you know this friend of mine?
   His name is _____.

   Yes, we know this friend of yours,
   This friend of yours,
   This friend of yours.
   Yes, we know this friend of yours.
   His name is _____.

2. **"The More We Are Together"**
   (Sing to the tune of "Have You Ever Seen a Lassie?")

   The more we are together, together, together,
   The more we are together, the happier we'll be.
   For your friends are my friends, and my friends are your friends.
   The more we are together the happier we'll be.

   We're all in school together, together, together,
   We're all in school together, and happy we'll be.
   There's Mary and Peter and Janet and Joshua

   There's _____ and _____ and _____ and _____.
   We're all in school together and happy we'll be.

   Insert names of children in your classroom.

3. **"Beth Met a Friend"**
   (Sing to the tune of "The Farmer in the Dell")

   Beth met a friend,
   Beth met a friend,
   When she came to school today,
   Beth met a friend.

   Insert names of children in your classroom for each verse.

Fingerplays:

FRIENDS

I like my friends.
So when we are at play,
I try to be very kind
and nice in every way.

FIVE LITTLE FRIENDS
(hold up five fingers; subtract one with each action)

Five little friends playing on the floor,
One got tired and then there were four.

Four little friends climbing in a tree,
One jumped down and then there were three.
Three little friends skipping to the zoo,
One went for lunch and then there were two.
Two little friends swimming in the sun,
One went home and then there was one.
One little friend going for a run,
Decided to take a nap and then there were none.

Science:

1. **Comparing Heartbeats**

   Provide stethoscopes for the children to listen to their friends' heartbeats.

2. **Fingerprints**

   Ink pads and white paper can be provided for the children to make fingerprints. Also, a microscope can be provided to encourage the children to compare their fingerprints.

3. **Friends' Voices**

   Tape the children's voices throughout the course of the day. The following day, leave the tape recorder at the science table. The children can listen to the tape and try to guess which classmate is talking.

4. **Animal Friends**

   Prepare signs for the animal cages listing the animal's daily food intake and care.

Dramatic Play:

1. **Puppet Show**

   Set up a puppet stage with various types of puppets. The children can share puppets and act out friendships using the puppets in various situations.

2. **A Tea Party**

   Provide dress-up clothes, play dishes, and water in the dramatic play area.

Arts and Crafts:

1. **Friendship Chain**

   Provide strips of paper for the older children to print their names on. For those children who are not interested or unable, print their names for them. When all the names are on the strips of paper, the children can connect them to make a chain. The chain should symbolize that everyone in the class is a friend.

2. **Friendship Collage**

   Encourage the children to find magazine pictures of friends. These pictures can be pasted on a large sheet of paper for a collage. Later the paper can be used for decoration and discussion in the lobby or hallway.

3. **Friendship Exchange Art**

   Provide each child with a piece of construction paper with "To: _____" printed in the upper left corner and "From: _____" printed on the bottom. The teacher assists the children in printing their names on the bottom and the name of the person to their right on the top of the paper. Using paper scraps, tissue paper squares, fabric scraps, and glue, each child will construct a picture for a friend. When finished, have each child pass the paper to the friend it was made for.

Sensory:

The sensory table is an area where two to four children can make new friends and share. Materials that can be added to the sensory table include:

- shaving cream
- playdough
- sand with toys
- water with boats
- wood shavings
- silly putty
  Mix equal parts of white glue and liquid starch. Food coloring can be added for color. Store in an airtight container.

- dry pasta with scoops and a balance scale
- goop
  Mix water and cornstarch. Add cornstarch to the water until you get the consistency that you want.

Large Muscle:

1. **Double Balance Beam**

   Place two balance beams side by side and encourage two children to hold hands and cross together.

2. **Bowling Game**

   Set up pins or plastic bottles. With a ball, have the children take turns knocking down the pins.

3. **Outdoor Obstacle Course**

   Design an obstacle course outdoors that is specifically designed for two children to go through at one time. Use balance beams, climbers, slides, etc. Short and simple obstacle courses seem to work the best.

Field Trips/Resource People:

1. **The Zoo**

   Take a trip to the zoo to observe animals.

2. **The Nursing Home**

   Visit a nursing home allowing the children to interact with elderly friends.

3. **Resource People**

   Invite the following community helpers into the classroom:

   - police officer
   - trash collector
   - janitor/custodian
   - fire fighter
   - doctor, nurse, dentist
   - principal or director

Math:

1. **Group Pictures**

   Take pictures of the children in groups of 2, 3, 4, etc. Make separate corresponding number cards. The children then can match the correct numeral to the picture card.

2. **Friend Charts**

   Take individual pictures of the children and chart them according to hair color, eye color, etc. Encourage the children to compare their looks to the characteristics of their friends.

Social Studies:

Friends Bulletin Board

Ask the children to bring pictures of their friends into the classroom. Set up a bulletin board in the classroom where these pictures can be hung for all to see. Remind the children that friends can be family members and animals too.

Cooking:

1. **Pound Cake Brownies**

   3/4 cup butter or margarine, softened
   1 cup sugar
   3 eggs
   2 1-ounce squares unsweetened chocolate, melted and cooled
   1 teaspoon vanilla
   1 1/4 cups all-purpose flour
   1/2 teaspoon baking powder
   1/4 teaspoon salt
   1/2 cup chopped nuts

   Cream butter and sugar; beat in eggs. Blend in chocolate and vanilla. Stir flour with baking powder and salt. Add to creamed mixture. Mix well. Stir in nuts. Spread in a greased 9- x 9- x 2-inch baking pan. Bake at 350 degrees for 25 to 30 minutes. Cool. If desired, sift powdered sugar over the top. Cut into bars. Yields 24 bars.

Clean-Up

"Do You Know What Time It is?"
(Sing to the tune of "The Muffin Man")

Oh, do you know what time it is,
What time it is, what time it is?
Oh, do you know what time it is?
It's almost clean-up time.
(Or, it's time to clean up.)

"Clean-up Time"
(Sing to the tune of "London Bridge")

Clean-up time is already here,
Already here, already here.
Clean-up time is already here,
Already here.

"This Is the Way"
(Sing to the tune of "Mulberry Bush")

This is the way we pick up our toys,
Pick up our toys, pick up our toys.
This is the way we pick up our toys,
At clean-up time each day.

"Oh, It's Clean-up Time"
(Sing to the tune of "Oh, My Darling Clementine")

Oh, its clean-up time,
Oh, it's clean-up time,
Oh, it's clean-up time right now.
It's time to put the toys away,

It is clean-up time right now.

"A Helper I Will Be"
(Sing to the tune of "The Farmer in the Dell")

A helper I will be.
A helper I will be.
I'll pick up the toys and put them away.
A helper I will be.

"We're Cleaning Up Our Room"
(Sing to the tune of "The Farmer in the Dell")

We're cleaning up our room.
We're cleaning up our room.
We're putting all the toys away.
We're cleaning up our room.

"It's Clean-up Time"
(Sing to the chorus of "Looby Loo")

It's clean-up time at school.
It's time for boys and girls
To stop what they are doing
And put away their toys.

"Time to Clean-up"
(Sing to the tune of "Are You Sleeping?")

Time to clean-up.
Time to clean-up.
Everybody help.
Everybody help.
Put the toys away, put the toys away.
Then sit down. (Or, then come here.)

Specific toys can be mentioned in place of "toys."

"Clean-up Time"
(Sing to the tune of "Hot Cross Buns")

Clean-up time.
Clean-up time.
Put all of the toys away.
It's clean-up time.

ROUTINES

"Passing Around"
(Sing to the tune of "Skip to My Loo")

Brad, take a napkin and pass them to Sara.
Sara, take a napkin and pass them to Tina.
Tina, take a napkin and pass them to Eric,
Passing around the napkins.

Fill in appropriate child's name and substitute napkin for any object that needs to be passed at meal time.

"Put Your Coat On"
(Sing to the tune of "Oh, My Darling Clementine")

Put your coat on.
Put your coat on.
Put your winter coat on now.
We are going to play outside.
Put your coat on right now.

Change coat to any article of clothing.

"Time to Go Outside"
(Sing to the tune of "When Johnny Comes Marching Home")

When it's time for us to go outside
To play, to play,
We find a place to put our toys
Away, away.
We'll march so quietly to the door.
We know exactly what's in store
When we go outside to play for a little while.

"We're Going on a Walk"
(Sing to the tune of "The Farmer in the Dell")

We're going for a walk.
We're going for a walk.
Hi-ho, the dairy-o,
We're going for a walk.

Additional verses:
What will we wear?

What will we see?
How will we go?
Who knows the way?

"Find a Partner"
(Sing to the tune of "Oh, My Darling Clementine")

Find a partner, find a partner,
Find a partner right now.
We are going for a walk.
Find a partner right now.

"Walk Along"
(Sing to the tune of "Clap Your Hands")

Walk, walk, walk along,
Walk along to the bathroom.
____ and ____ walk along,
Walk along to the bathroom.

Change walk to any other types of movement—jump, hop, skip, crawl.

"We're Going...."
(Sing to the tune of "Go in and out the Window")

We're going to the bathroom,
We're going to the bathroom,
We're going to the bathroom,
And then we'll wash our hands.

"It's Time to Change"
(Sing to the tune of "Hello, Everybody")

It's time to change, yes indeed,
Yes indeed, yes indeed.
It's time to change, yes indeed
Time to change groups.
(Or, Time to go outside.)

Multimedia:

The following records can be found in educational catalogs:

1. Thomas, Marlo, & Friends. *Free to Be You and Me* [record]. Arista.

2. Palmer, Hap. *Getting to Know Myself* [record].

3. Palmer, Hap. *Ideas, Thoughts, and Feelings* [record].

4. Poelker, Kathy Lecinski. *Look at My World* [record]. Look at Me Company.

5. Rogers, Fred. *Let's Be Together Today* [record].

6. *Toddlers on Parade* [record]. Kimbo Records.

7. *Children's Songs Around the World* [record]. Alphabetical.

8. *Play-Along Games & Songs* [video]. Random House.

9. *Scruffy and Friends* [Mac/IBM/Apple Software]. Hartley. Age: 6.

Books:

The following books can be used to complement the theme:

1. Newman, Nanette. (1990). *Sharing*. New York: Doubleday and Co., Inc.

2. Daniel, Becky. (1991). *Count on Your Friends*. Carthage, IL: Good Apple.

3. Adams, Pam. (1991). *Playmates*. New York: Child's Play International.

4. Aliki. (1987). *We Are Best Friends*. New York: Morrow, William and Co., Inc.

5. dePaola, Tomie. (1992). *Bill and Pete*. New York: Putnam Publishing Group.

6. Isadora, Rachel. (1990). *Friends*. New York: Greenwillow Books.

7. Mason, Margo. (1990). *Two Good Friends*. New York: Bantam Books, Inc.

8. Rogers, Fred. (1987). *Making Friends*. New York: Putnam Publishing Group.

9. Kellogg, Steven. (1990). *Best Friends*. New York: Dial Books for Young Readers.

10. Wilheim, Hans. (1986). *Let's Be Friends Again*. New York: Crown.

11. Winthrop, Elizabeth. (1989). *The Best Friends Club*. New York: Lothrop, Lee, & Shepard.

12. Hutchins, Pat. (1989). *The Doorbell Rang*. New York: Morrow.

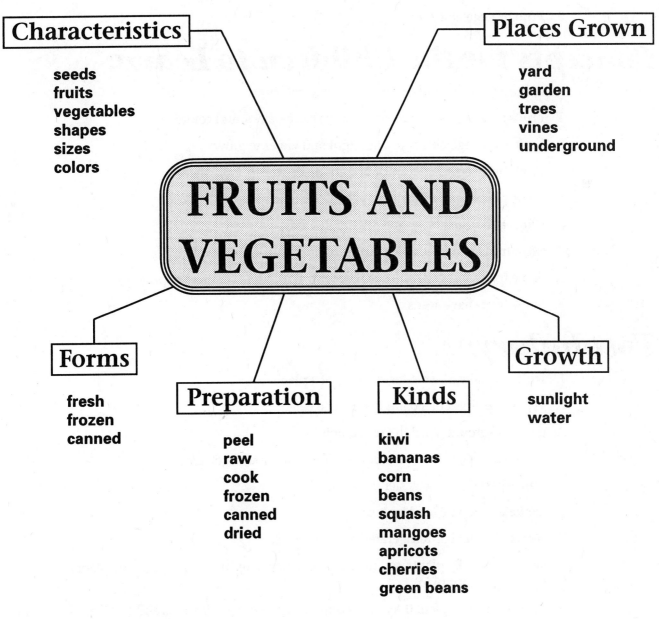

Characteristics

seeds
fruits
vegetables
shapes
sizes
colors

Places Grown

yard
garden
trees
vines
underground

FRUITS AND VEGETABLES

Forms

fresh
frozen
canned

Preparation

peel
raw
cook
frozen
canned
dried

Kinds

kiwi
bananas
corn
beans
squash
mangoes
apricots
cherries
green beans

Growth

sunlight
water

Polaroid Education Program

Here's an exciting new way to turn instant photography into an effective teaching tool. Refer to the full-color insert for the activity entitled Grouping.

Theme Goals:

Through participating in the experiences provided by this theme, the children may learn:

1. Names of common fruits and vegetables.
2. Purposes of fruits and vegetables.
3. Places fruits and vegetables are grown.
4. Preparation of fruits and vegetables.
5. Tastes of fruits and vegetables.
6. Fruit or vegetable seeds.

Concepts for the Children to Learn:

1. There are many kinds of fruits and vegetables.
2. Fruits and vegetables come in many shapes, sizes, and colors.
3. Fruits and vegetables need sunlight and water to grow.
4. Fruits and vegetables can be bought fresh, frozen, or canned.
5. Some people grow fruits and vegetables in gardens.
6. Fruits and vegetables have different names.
7. Most fruits and vegetables can be eaten raw or cooked.
8. Some fruits and vegetables we eat with skin; some we need to peel first.
9. Some fruits have seeds.

Vocabulary:

1. **fruit**—usually a sweet-tasting part of a plant.
2. **vegetable**—part of a plant that can be eaten.
3. **garden**—ground used to grow plants.
4. **produce**—agriculture products such as fruits and vegetables.
5. **vine**—plant with long, slender stem.
6. **cooked**—prepare food by heating.
7. **frozen**—chilled or refrigerated to make solid.
8. **seeds**—part of a plant used for growing a new crop and; edible in some plants (sunflower, pumpkin).
9. **roots**—part of a plant that grows downward into the soil and is edible in some plants (potatoes, turnips, radishes, onions, and carrots).
10. **soil**—portion of earth; dirt used for growing.
11. **sprout**—to begin to grow.
12. **stems**—part of a plant used for transporting food and water and edible in some plants (celery).

Bulletin Board

The purpose of this bulletin board is to observe the growth of a lima bean seed. To prepare the bulletin board, place a moist paper towel in a small plastic bag and place a lima bean on top of the towel for each child. Staple each bag to the bulletin board as illustrated; place each child's name by his bag. Sprouting will occur faster if seeds have been pre-soaked overnight. Additional watering may be needed throughout the unit.

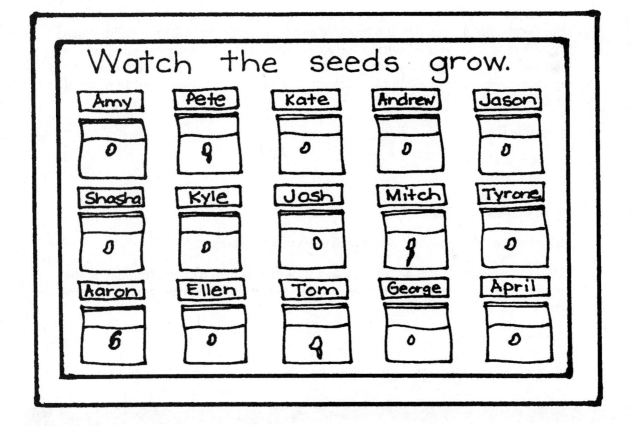

Parent Letter

Dear Parents,

Hello again! We hope that everyone in your family is healthy and happy. Speaking of health, we are starting a new unit on fruits and vegetables. Through the experiences planned for this unit, the children will become aware of many fruits and vegetables and how they are grown. Also, they will discover how many fruits and vegetables taste.

At School

Some of the many fun-filled learning activities scheduled for this unit are:

* planting lima bean seeds to sprout. Take a look at our bulletin board this week.
* playing the role of a gardener/farmer in the dramatic play area.
* matching pictures of vegetables to where they are grown (trees, vines, underground, etc.).
* having a fruit and vegetable tasting party during snack.
* visiting a produce section at the grocery store.
* listening to a story called *What Was It Before It Was Orange Juice?* by Jane Belk Moncure.

At Home

There are many ways that you can integrate concepts included in this unit into your family life. To help develop memory and language skills, ask your child which vegetables or fruit he tried during the week. Then let your child help you prepare them at home. Cooking often tempts a child to try new foods. Also, here is a great dip recipe we will be making for snack on Tuesday that you may want to make at home also.

Vegetable Dip

1 cup yogurt
1 cup mayonnaise
1 tablespoon dill weed
1 teaspoon seasoned salt

Mix all ingredients and chill. Serve with fresh raw vegetables.

We still need two more helpers to assist us with our field trip on Thursday to the grocery store. Let me know if you are available. The children enjoy having parents join in our activities.

Enjoy your child!

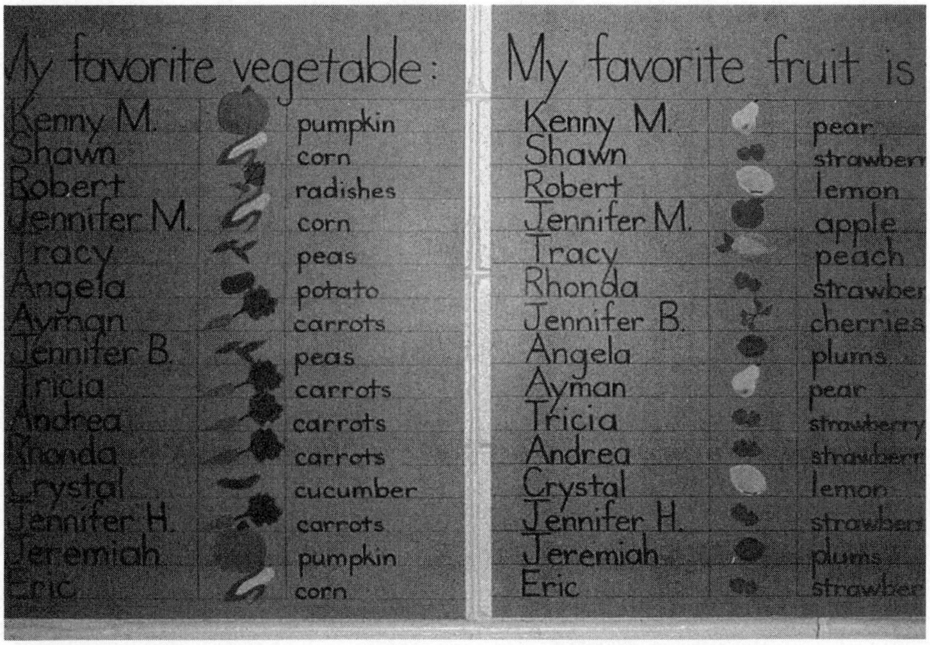

FIGURE 31 Trying different fruits and vegetables and listing favorites is a good activity.

Music:

1. **"The Vegetable Garden"**
   (Sing to the tune of "Mulberry Bush")

   Here we go 'round the vegetable garden,
   The vegetable garden, the vegetable garden,
   Here we go round the vegetable garden,
   So early in the morning.

   Other verses:
   This is the way we pull the weeds…
   This is the way we water the plants…
   This is the way we eat the vegetables…

2. **"Vegetables"**
   (Sing to the tune "Mary Had a Little Lamb")

   I'm a tomato, red and round,
   Red and round, red and round.
   I'm a tomato, red and round,
   Seated on the ground.

   I'm a corn stalk, tall and straight,
   Tall and straight, tall and straight.
   I'm a corn stalk, tall and straight
   And I taste just great.

Fingerplays:

MY GARDEN

This is my garden
   (extend one hand forward, palm up)
I'll rake it with care
   (make raking motion on palm with three
   fingers of other hand)
And then some seeds
   (planting motion)
I'll plant in there.
The sun will shine
   (make circle with arms)
And the rain will fall
   (let fingers flutter down to lap)
And my garden will blossom
   (cup hand together, extend upward slowly)
And grow straight and tall.

DIG A LITTLE HOLE

Dig a little hole.
   (dig)
Plant a little seed.
   (drop seed)
Pour a little water.
   (pour)

Pull a little weed.
  (pull and throw)
Chase a little bug.
  (chasing motion with hands)
Heigh-ho, there he goes.
  (shade eyes)
Give a little sunshine
  (circle arms over head)
Grow a little bean!
  (hands grow upward)

APPLE TREE

Way up high in the apple tree
  (hold arms up high)
Two little apples smiled at me.
  (look at 2 hands up high)
I shook that tree as hard as I could.
  (shake arms)
Down came the apples,
  (arms fall)
Mmm, were they good!
  (rub tummy)

BANANAS

Bananas are my favorite fruit.
  (make fists as if holding banana)
I eat one every day.
  (hold up one finger)
I always take one with me
  (act as if putting one in pocket)
When I go out to play.
  (wave good-bye)
It gives me lots of energy
  (make a muscle)
To jump around and run.
  (move arms as if running)
Bananas are my favorite fruit.
  (rub tummy)
To me they're so much fun!
  (point to self and smile)

VEGETABLES AND FRUITS

The food we like to eat that grows
On vines and bushes and trees.
Are vegetables and fruits my friends
Like cherries, grapes, and peas.
Apples and oranges and peaches are fruits
And so are tangerines,
Lettuce and carrots are vegetables,
Like squash and beans.

Science:

1. **Cut and Draw**

   Cut out or draw many different fruits and vegetables from tagboard or construction paper scraps. Also make a tree, a vine, and some soil. Have children classify the fruit to where it's grown—on a tree, on vines, or underground.

2. **Tasting Center**

   Cut small pieces of various fruits and set up a tasting center. Encourage the children to taste and compare different fruits and vegetables.

3. **Tasting Party**

   Plan a vegetable tasting party. Cut small pieces of vegetables. Also, have children taste raw vegetables compared to the same vegetable cooked.

4. **Identify by Smelling**

   Place one each of several fruits and vegetables in small cups and cover with aluminum foil. Punch a small hole in the top of the aluminum foil. Then have the children smell the cups and try to identify each fruit or vegetable.

5. **Growing a Seed**

   Give each child a plastic sealable bag, a moistened paper towel, and a lima bean. Demonstrate how to place the bean in the paper towel and close bag. After the children have finished planting their beans, place each child's bag on a bulletin board. Check the bulletin board on a daily basis to see when the seed sprouts.

6. **Carrot Tops in Water**

   Cut off the top of a carrot and place it in a shallow dish of water. Observe what happens day to day. Given time the top of the carrot should sprout.

304

7. **Colored Celery Stalks**

Place celery stalks into water colored with food coloring. Observe what happens to the leaves of celery.

Dramatic Play:

Grocery Store

Plan a grocery store containing many plastic fruits and vegetables, a cash register, grocery bags, and play money if available. The children can take turns being a produce clerk, cashier, and price tagger.

Arts and Crafts:

1. **Fruit and Vegetable Collage**

Make a fruit and vegetable collage. Have children draw or cut their favorite fruits and vegetables from magazines and paste on paper.

2. **Seeds**

Save several seeds from fruits and vegetables for the children to make a seed collage. When seeds are securely glued, children can also paint them if desired. The collage can be secured to a bulletin board.

3. **Cutting Vegetable and Fruit Shapes**

Cut easel paper into a different shape of fruit or vegetable every day.

4. **Mold with Playdough**

The children can mold and create fruits and vegetables out of clay and playdough. Another option would be to color and scent the play-dough. Examples might include orange-smelling orange, lemon-smelling yellow, banana-smelling yellow.

5. **Potato Prints**

Cut potatoes in half. The children can dip in paints and stamp the potatoes on a large sheet of paper.

6. **Paint with Celery Leaves**

Mix some thin tempera paint. Use celery leaves as a painting tool.

Sensory:

Preparing Fruits and Vegetables

Wash vegetables and fruits to prepare for eating at snack time.

Large Muscle:

Place hoes, shovels, rakes, and watering cans around the outdoor sand area.

Field Trips:

1. **Grocery Store**

Take a trip to the grocery store to visit the produce department. Ask the clerk to show the children how the food is delivered.

2. **Visiting a Farm**

Visit a farm. Ask the farmer to show the children the fruits and vegetables grown on the farm.

3. **Visit a Farmers' Market**

Visit a farmers' market. Purchase fruits and vegetables that can be used for snacks.

4. **Visit an Orchard**

Visit an apple or fruit orchard. Observe how the fruit is grown. If possible, pick some fruit to bring back to the classroom.

Math:

1. **Fruit and Vegetable Match**

Cut out various fruits and vegetables from a magazine. Trace their shapes onto tagboard. Have children match the fruit or vegetable to the correct shape on the tagboard.

2. **Seriation**

Make five sizes of each vegetable or fruit you want to use. Have children place in order from smallest to largest, or largest to smallest.

3. **Measuring**

The children can measure their bean sprouts. Maintain a small chart of their measurements.

4. **Parts and Wholes**

Cut apples in half at snack time to introduce the concepts of parts and whole.

5. **Grouping Pictures**

Cut pictures of fruits and vegetables for the children to sort according to color, size, and shape.

Social Studies:

1. **Field Trip to a Garden**

Plan a field trip to a large garden. Point out different fruits and vegetables. If possible, have the children pull radishes and carrots.

2. **Hang Pictures**

On a bulletin board in the classroom hang pictures of fruits and vegetables.

3. **Fruit and Vegetable Book**

The children can make a fruit and vegetable book. Possible titles include "My favorite fruit is," "My favorite vegetable is," "I would like to grow," and "I would most like to cook." The children can paste pictures or adhere stickers to the individual pages.

Group Time (games, language):

1. **Carrot, Carrot, Corn**

Play "Duck, Duck Goose," but substitute "Carrot, Carrot, Corn."

2. **Hot Potato**

The children sit in a circle and the teacher gives one child a potato. Teacher then plays lively music and the children pass potato around the circle. When the music suddenly stops, the child with the potato must stand up and say the name of a fruit or vegetable. Encourage children to think of a fruit or vegetable that hasn't been named yet. Play the game until almost all fruits and vegetables have been named.

Cooking:

1. **Vegetable Dip**

1 cup plain yogurt
1 cup mayonnaise
1 tablespoon dill weed
1 teaspoon seasoned salt

Mix all the ingredients together and chill. Serve with fresh raw vegetables.

2. **Ants on a Log**

Cut celery into pieces and spread with peanut butter. Top with raisins, coconut, or grated carrots. (Celery is difficult for younger children to chew.)

3. **Applesauce**

4 apples
1 tablespoon water
2 tablespoons brown sugar or honey

Wash the apples and cut into small pieces. Dip the pieces into water and roll in brown sugar or honey. Serves 8.

4. **Banana Rounds**

4 medium bananas
1/2 cup yogurt
3 tablespoons honey
1/8 teaspoon nutmeg
1/8 teaspoon cinnamon
1/4 cup wheat germ

The children can participate by peeling the bananas and slicing into "rounds." Measure the spices, wheat germ, and honey. Blend this mixture with yogurt and bananas. Chill prior to serving. Serves 8.

5. **Middle East Date and Banana Dessert**

4 ounces (1 cup) pitted dates, cut up
2 bananas, thinly sliced
2 to 3 teaspoons finely shredded lemon peel
1/2 cup half and half
sliced almonds (optional)

Alternate layers of dates and bananas in serving dish or dessert dishes. Sprinkle with lemon peel. Pour half and half over top. Cover and refrigerate at least 4 hours. Just before serving sprinkle with almonds. Makes 3 to 4 servings.

Source: *Betty Crocker's International Cookbook.* (1980). New York: Random House.

6. **Finnish Strawberry Shake**

20 fresh strawberries
4 cups milk
3 tablespoons sugar

Wash strawberries and remove stems. Cut strawberries into small pieces. Combine milk, sugar, and strawberries in a large mixing bowl or blender. Beat with an eggbeater or blend for 2 minutes. Pour strawberry shakes into individual glasses. Makes 4 to 8 servings.

Variation: Raspberries or other sweet fruit may be used instead.

7. **Banana Sandwiches**

1/2 or 1 banana per child
peanut butter

Peel the bananas and slice them in half lengthwise. Spread peanut butter on one half of the banana and top with the other half.

COOKING VOCABULARY

The following vocabulary words can be introduced through cooking experiences:

bake	garnish	scrape
beat	grate	scrub
boil	grease	shake
broil	grill	shread
brown	grind	sift
chop	heat	simmer
cool	knead	spread
core	marinate	sprinkle
cream	measure	squeeze
cube	mince	stir
cut	mix	strain
dice	pare	stuff
dip	peel	tear
drain	pit	toast
freeze	pour	whip
frost	roast	
fry	roll	

Multimedia:

The following resources can be found in preschool educational catalogs:

1. Palmer, Hap. *Learning Basic Skills Through Music—Health and Safety* [record]. #EA AR526R.

2. Avni, Fran. *Artichokes & Brussels Sprouts* [record]. Alphabetical.

Books:

The following books can be used to complement the theme:

1. Moncure, Jane Belk. (1985). *What Was It Before It Was Orange Juice?* Chicago: Children's Press.

2. *Eating the Alphabet: Fruits and Vegetables A to Z.* (1989). San Diego: Harcourt Brace Jovanovich.

3. Robinson, Fay. (1992). *We Love Fruit.* Chicago: Children's Press.

4. de Bourgoing, Pascale. (1991). *Fruit.* New York: Scholastic, Inc.

5. Wexler, Jerome. (1990). *Flower Fruit Seeds.* New York: Simon and Schuster.

6. Watts, Barrie. (1990). *Tomato.* Morristown, NJ: Silver Burdett Press.

7. Politi, Leo. (1993). *Three Stalks of Corn.* New York: Macmillan.

8. Berger, Thomas. (1990). *The Mouse and the Potato.* Edinburgh, Scotland: Floris Books.

9. Ehlert, Lois. (1987). *Growing Vegetable Soup.* San Diego, CA: Harcourt Brace Jovanovich.

10. Weiss, Ellen. (1989). *Oh Beans! Starring Wax Beans.* Mahwah, NJ: Troll.

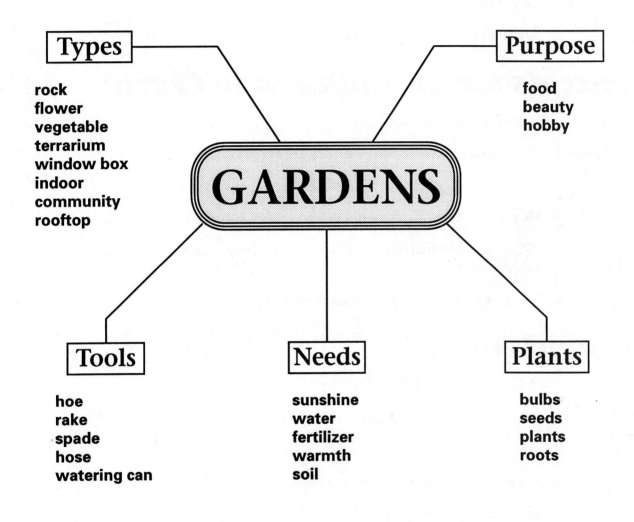

Types

rock
flower
vegetable
terrarium
window box
indoor
community
rooftop

Purpose

food
beauty
hobby

GARDENS

Tools

hoe
rake
spade
hose
watering can

Needs

sunshine
water
fertilizer
warmth
soil

Plants

bulbs
seeds
plants
roots

Here's an exciting new way to turn instant photography into an effective teaching tool. Refer to the full-color insert for the activity entitled Spatial Relations.

Theme Goals:

Through participating in the experiences provided by this theme, the children may learn:

1. Purposes of gardens.

2. Types of gardens.

3. Tools used for gardening.

4. Care of gardens.

5. Types of plants grown in a garden.

Concepts for the Children to Learn:

1. Plants are living things.

2. Plants need sunshine, water, soil, fertilizer, and warmth to grow.

3. Gardens produce food and beautiful flowers.

4. We plant gardens by placing bulbs, seeds, plants, or roots in the ground.

5. Weeds are plants that do not bear fruit. They take water and food from our garden plants.

6. Fruits, vegetables, and flowers can be planted in our gardens.

Vocabulary:

1. **bulb**—a type of seed.

2. **flower**—part of the plant that has colored petals.

3. **garden**—a place to grow plants.

4. **greenhouse**—building for growing plants and flowers.

5. **leaf**—flat green part of a plant.

6. **rake**—a tool with teeth or prongs.

7. **soil**—top of the ground.

8. **root**—part of the plant that grows into the ground.

9. **seed**—part of the plant from which a new plant will grow.

10. **stem**—part of the plant that holds the leaves and flowers.

11. **vegetable**—a plant that can be eaten.

12. **weed**—plant that is not needed.

Bulletin Board

The purpose of this bulletin board is to foster visual discrimination skills. To prepare the bulletin board, construct five or six watering cans out of tagboard. Color each one a different color with felt-tip markers and hang on the bulletin board. Attach a string to each watering can. Next, construct the same number of small rakes out of tagboard. Color each one using the same colors you used for the watering cans. Attach a push pin to the top of each rake. The children can match each watering can to the corresponding colored rake by winding the string around the correct push pin.

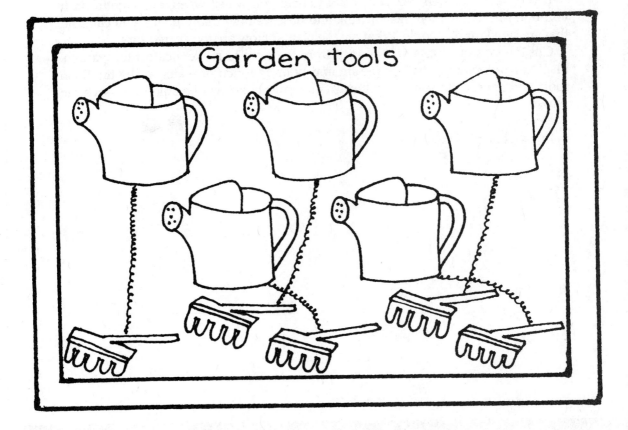

Parent Letter

Dear Parents,

"Mary, Mary, quite contrary, how does your garden grow?" That familiar nursery rhyme sums up our next theme—gardens! We will be exploring flower and vegetable gardens, as well as finding out about the work involved in planning and maintaining gardens and garden tools.

At School

Some of the learning experiences planned to foster concepts related to gardens include:

- a flower shop set up in the dramatic play area.
- dramatizing the story of *The Big Turnip*.
- preparing a section of our play yard for a garden. The children will help decide which seeds to plant.
- mud in the sensory table.

At Home

If you have a garden, ask your child to help you water, weed, and care for it. If you don't have a garden, take a walk and observe how many plants you can find that are cared for by people. What are the plants? How are they cared for?

Cut the tops of carrots off 1/4 inch from the stem to make a carrot-top garden. Place carrot tops in a shallow pie tin and pour 1/4 inch of water in the tin. Soon roots will appear, the greens will grow, and your child will be able to observe the growth.

Enjoy your child!

FIGURE 32 Watching a garden grow is a long-term science experience.

Music:

"A Little Seed"
(Sing to the tune of "I'm a Little Teapot")

Here's a little seed in the dark, dark ground.
Out comes the warm sun, yellow and round.
Down comes the rain, wet and slow.
Up comes the little seed, grow, grow, grow!

Fingerplays:

SEEDS

Some little seeds have parachutes
To carry them around
   (cup hand downward)
The wind blows them swish, swish, swish.
   (flip fingers outward from parachute)

Then gently lays them on the ground.
   (let hand gently float down and rest on lap)

RELAXING FLOWERS

Five little flowers standing in the sun
   (hold up five fingers)
See their heads nodding, bowing one by one?
   (bend fingers several times)
Down, down, down comes the gentle rain
   (raise hands, wiggle fingers, and lower arms
   to simulate falling rain)
And the five little flowers lift their heads up
again!
   (hold up five fingers)

HOW IT HAPPENS

A muddy hump,
   (make a fist using both hands)
A small green lump,
   (poke up thumbs together as one)
Two leaves and then
Two leaves again
   (raise forefinger of each hand from fist, then
   middle fingers)
And shooting up, a stem and cup.
   (put elbows, forearms, and hands together,
   fingers slightly curved)
One last shower,
   (rain movements with spread arms and
   fingers)
Then a flower.
   (elbows, forearms together with hands wide
   apart, palms up)

LITTLE FLOWERS

The sun comes out and shines so bright
   (join hands over head in circle)
Then we have a shower.
   (wiggle fingers coming down)
The little bud pushes with all its might
   (one hand in fist; other hand clasped over,
   move hands up slowly)
And soon we have a flower.
   (join thumbs and spread fingers for flower)

MR. CARROT

Nice Mr. Carrot
Makes curly hair.
   (hand on head)

His head grows underneath the ground,
  (bob head)
His feet up in the air.
  (raise feet)
And early in the morning
I find him in his bed
  (close eyes, lay head on hands)
And give his feet a great big pull
  (stretch legs out)
And out comes his head.

Science:

1. **Growing Grass**

   Germinate grass seeds by placing a damp sponge in a pie tin of water and sprinkling seeds on the sponge. The children will notice tiny sprouts after a few days. Experiment by putting one sponge in the freezer, one near a heat source, and one in a dark closet. Discuss what happens to each group of seeds.

2. **Plants Contain Water**

   Cut off 1/4 inch from the bottom of a celery stalk. Fill a clear vase with water containing food coloring. Place the celery stalk in the vase. Encourage the children to observe color changes in the celery stalk. This activity can be repeated using a white carnation.

3. **Planting Seeds**

   Purchase bean and radish seeds. If space permits, plant outdoors. Otherwise, place soil in planters indoors. Plant the seeds with the children. Identify the plants by pasting the seed packages on the planters. This will help the children to recognize the plants as they emerge from the soil.

4. **The Science Table**

   Place a magnifying glass with different types of seeds and bulbs on the science table. During the week add fresh flowers, plant leaves, and dried plants.

5. **Rooting a Sweet Potato**

   To root a sweet potato in water, push toothpicks halfway into the potato. Then place the potato in a glass of water with the toothpicks resting on the top rim. Make sure the end of the potato is immersed in water. Place the glass where it will receive adequate light. Maintain the water level so that the bottom of the potato is always immersed. Note that in a few weeks roots will grow out of the sides and bottom of the potato, and leaves will grow out of the top. The plant can be left in the water or replanted in soil. This activity provides the children an opportunity to observe root growth.

6. **Worm Farm**

   Collect the following materials: large clear jar with a wide mouth, soil, earthworms, gravel, food for worms (lettuce, cornmeal, cereals). Place gravel and soil in the jar. Add the worms. Add food on the top of the dirt and keep the soil moist, but not wet. Tape black construction paper around outside of jar. The paper can be temporarily removed to observe the worms and see their tunnels.

Dramatic Play:

1. **Flower Shop**

   Introduce a flower shop by gathering plastic flowers and plants. If desired, flowers can be made from tissue paper and pipe cleaners. Collect different kinds of vases and also styrofoam or sponge blocks so the children can make flower arrangements. A cash register, aprons, money, and sacks can also be provided to encourage play.

2. **Gardening Center**

   Gather tools, gloves, hats, seeds, and plastic flowers or plants. The children can pretend to plant and grow seeds. Provide seed catalogs and order blanks for children to choose seeds to order.

3. **Fruit Stand**

   Set up a fruit stand by using plastic fruits and vegetables. Aprons, a cash register, market baskets or bags, and play money can also be used to encourage play. The children can take turns being the owner and the shopper.

314

4. Sandbox

The children can experiment with gardening tools in the sandbox.

Arts and Crafts:

1. Collage

Make collages using all types of seeds and beans. This activity can also be used by cutting pictures from seed catalogs.

2. Leaf Rubbings

Take the children on a leaf walk. The children choose a couple of large leaves to bring back to school. Place the leaves between two sheets of paper and rub with flat, large crayons across the top sheet of paper.

3. Stencils

Cut stencils out of tagboard of various-shaped leaves or vegetables (see patterns). Laminate the stencils. The children can use crayons, pencils, or marking pens to make the leaf or vegetable outlines. These stencils can be used as the front of the "soup and salad" party invitations listed under social studies activities.

4. Decorating Vases

Collect tin cans or milk cartons for the children to use as vases. If cans are used, file the sharp edges or cover them with masking tape. The children can decorate the containers with colored paper, gift wrapping paper, or wallpaper. Greeting cards may also be useful for this activity.

Sensory:

1. Sensory Activities

In the sensory table place:

- soil
- seeds
- plastic plants
- beans

- measuring cups
- balance scales
- worms
- miniature garden tools
- cut grass or hay

2. Fill and Guess

After showing and discussing several kinds of fruits or vegetables with children, place the fruits or vegetables in a bag. Individually let children reach in and touch one item. See if they can guess what it is before pulling it out of the bag. Older children may also be able to describe the item.

Large Muscle:

Leaf Jumping

This is an active skill game that can be played indoors or outdoors. Cut out large cardboard leaves and arrange them in an irregular line, as they might appear on a stem. The closer they are together, the harder the game will be. Beginning at one end, each player tries to jump over the leaves without touching them. Older children may try to skip or hop over the leaves.

Field Trips/Resource People:

1. Field Trips

Take a field trip to:

- a flower garden
- a vegetable garden
- a flower shop
- a farmers' market
- a greenhouse
- a conservatory
- a park
- the produce section of a grocery store
- a natural food store

2. Resource People

- gardeners
- florist to demonstrate flower arranging

Math:

1. **Sorting Beans**

   Mix together several shapes and colors of large, dried beans. The children can sort the beans by size and color.

2. **Inchworm Measuring**

   A good introduction for this activity is the story *Inch by Inch* by Leo Lionni. Cut 2 or 3 dozen inchworms out of felt. Then cut out flowers of various heights—with long or short stems. Encourage the children to place worms along stem from bottom to top of flower. How many inchworms tall is each flower? After this, have the children count the inchworms.

Social Studies:

1. **Salad and Soup Party**

   The children can plan and participate in a salad and soup party for their parents. The groceries will need to be purchased, cleaned, and prepared.

2. **Plant Hunt**

   Go on a hunt to discover how many non-flowering plants such as algae, fungi, lichens, mosses, and ferns are found in the school yard. Make a display. How are these plants different from garden plants?

Group Time (games, language):

1. **Huckle Buckle Bean Stalk**

   A small object such as a plastic flower or acorn may be used for hiding. All the players cover their eyes, except the one who hides the object. After it is hidden, the players stand up and begin to look for it. When one locates it, he doesn't let others know the placement. Instead he quietly takes a seat saying "Huckle Buckle Bean Stalk." The game continues until all players have located the object. The first child

to find the object usually hides it the next time. This game is appropriate for older children.

2. **The Big Turnip—Creative Dramatics**

   First tell the story of *The Big Turnip*. Then pass out an identifying piece of clothing for each character. Hats work well for people and collars or signs for the animals. Retell the story, letting the children act the story out. Use as many characters as you have children. This would be a good outdoors activity.

Cooking:

1. **Vegetable Soup**

   Begin with consomme or soup base. Add whatever vegetables, beans, etc., children want to add and can help to prepare. Make soup a day ahead so that all of the vegetables will be cooked thoroughly.

2. **Indian—Cucumbers and Tomatoes with Yogurt**

   2 medium cucumbers
   2 green onions with tops, chopped
   1 teaspoon salt
   2 tomatoes chopped
   1/2 clove garlic, finely chopped
   2 tablespoons snipped parsley
   1/2 teaspoon ground cumin
   1/8 teaspoon pepper
   1 cup unflavored yogurt

   Cut cucumbers lengthwise into halves. Scoop out seeds. Chop cucumbers. Mix cucumbers, green onions, and salt. Let stand 10 minutes. Add tomatoes. Mix remaining ingredients except yogurt. Toss with cucumber mixture. Cover and refrigerate at least 1 hour. Drain thoroughly. Just before serving, fold in yogurt. Makes 6 servings.

   Source: *Betty Crocker's International Cookbook*. (1980). New York: Random House.

3. **Lettuce or Spinach Roll-ups**

   On clean lettuce or spinach leaves, spread softened cream cheese or cottage cheese. If desired, sprinkle with grated carrots or chopped nuts. Roll them up. Chill and serve.

4. **Carrot Cookies**

   1/2 cup honey
   1 egg
   1/2 cup margarine
   1 cup whole wheat flour
   1 1/4 teaspoons baking powder
   1/4 teaspoon salt

   1/2 cup rolled oats
   1/2 cup wheat germ
   1/2 cup grated raw carrots
   1/2 cup raisins
   1/2 cup nuts (optional)
   1 teaspoon vanilla

   Mix all ingredients in a bowl. Drop mixture by spoonfuls onto a lightly greased cookie sheet. Flatten each ball slightly. Bake in a 350-degree oven for approximately 12 minutes.

Multimedia:

The following resources can be found in educational catalogs:

1. Palmer, Hap. *Walter the Waltzing Worm* [record].

2. Raffi. "Oats and Beans and Barley Grow" and "Over in the Meadow" on *Baby Beluga* [record].

3. Seeger, Pete. "Jimmy Crack Corn" on *American Folk Songs* [record].

Books:

The following books can be used to complement the theme:

1. Titherington, Jeanne. (1990). *Pumpkin Pumpkin*. New York: Morrow.

2. Ehlert, Lois. (1990). *Growing Vegetable Soup*. San Diego: Harcourt Brace Jovanovich.

3. Buria, Maria E. (1989). *Billy the Bean*. Downey, CA: Colorful Learnings.

4. Krementz, Jill. (1991). *A Very Young Gardener*. New York: Dial Books for Young Readers.

5. McCann, Sean. (1989). *Growing Things*. Chester Springs, PA: Dufour Editions, Inc.

6. Sanchez, Isidro, & Peris, Carme. (1991). *The Garden*. Hauppauge, NY: Barron's Educational Series, Inc.

7. Stagg, Mildred A., & Lamb, Cecile. (1992). *Song of the Seed*. Cincinnati, OH: Standard Publishing Co.

8. Wilner, Isabel. (1991). *A Garden Alphabet*. New York: Dutton Children's Books.

9. Cooke, Tom (Illus.). (1991). *Bert's Little Garden: A Sesame Street Book*. New York: Random House Books for Young Readers.

10. Florian, D. (1991). *Vegetable Garden*. San Diego: Harcourt Brace Jovanovich.

11. Gerstein, Mordicai. (1993). *Maggies Garden*. New York: Harper Collins Children's Books.

12. McKissack, Patricia, & McKissack, Frederick. (1991). *Messy Bessy's Garden*. Chicago: Children's Press.

13. Slote, Elizabeth. (1991). *Nelly's Garden*. New York: William Morrow and Co.

14. Christini, Ermanno, & Puricelli, Luigi. (1991). *In My Garden*. Saxonville, MA: Picture Book Studios.

15. Kemp, Moira. (1992). *Round & Round the Garden*. New York: Dutton.

16. Ryder, Joanne. (1992). *The Snail's Spell*. New York: Viking.

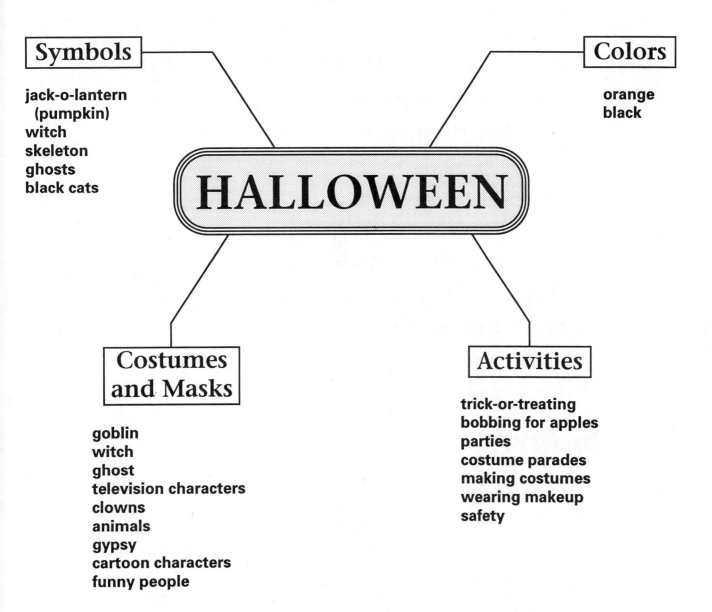

Symbols

jack-o-lantern
  (pumpkin)
witch
skeleton
ghosts
black cats

Colors

orange
black

HALLOWEEN

Costumes and Masks

goblin
witch
ghost
television characters
clowns
animals
gypsy
cartoon characters
funny people

Activities

trick-or-treating
bobbing for apples
parties
costume parades
making costumes
wearing makeup
safety

Here's an exciting new way to turn instant photography into an effective teaching tool. Refer to the full-color insert for the activity entitled Tell Me A Story.

Theme Goals:

Through participating in the experiences provided by this theme, the children may learn:

1. Halloween colors.

2. Halloween costumes and masks.

3. Halloween activities.

4. Halloween symbols.

Concepts for the Children to Learn:

1. Orange and black are Halloween colors.

2. Costumes and masks are worn on Halloween.

3. Some children make their costumes and wear makeup.

4. A costume is clothes for pretending.

5. A mask is a covering we put over our face.

6. A pumpkin can be cut to look like a face.

7. Ghosts, black cats, and witches are symbols of Halloween.

8. People go trick-or-treating on Halloween.

9. A costume parade is a march with many children who are dressed up.

10. Bobbing for apples is an activity at Halloween parties.

Vocabulary:

1. **Halloween**—a day when children dress up and go trick-or-treating.

2. **jack-o-lantern**—a pumpkin cut to look like a face.

3. **trick-or-treat**—walking from house to house to ask for candy or treats.

4. **witch**—a make-believe person who wears black.

5. **ghost**—a make-believe person who wears all white.

6. **goblin**—a Halloween character.

7. **costume**—clothing worn to pretend.

8. **mask**—face covering worn when pretending.

9. **pretending**—acting like someone else.

Bulletin Board

The purpose of this bulletin board is to have the children practice visual discrimination skills. To prepare the bulletin board, construct pumpkins out of orange-colored tagboard. The number will depend upon the developmental appropriateness for the group of children. An alternative would be to use white tagboard colored orange with paint or markers. Divide the pumpkins into pairs. Draw a different kind of face for each pair of pumpkins. Hang one pumpkin from each pair on the left side of the bulletin board as illustrated. Attach an orange string to each pumpkin. On the right side of the bulletin board, hang the matching pumpkins. See illustration. Attach a push pin to each of these pumpkins. The child can match the faces on the pumpkins by winding the correct string around the correct push pin.

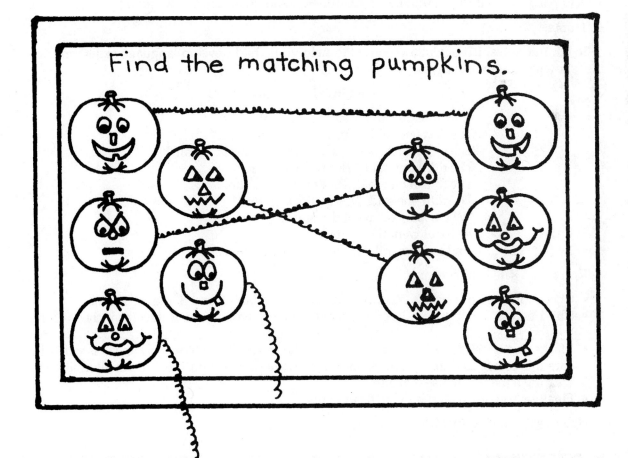

Parent Letter

Dear Parents,

The month of October has a special holiday for children—Halloween! Consequently, our next theme will center on Halloween. Many learning experiences have been planned to promote an awareness of colors that are associated with Halloween, as well as symbols that represent Halloween such as pumpkins, black cats, bats, and witches.

At School

Some of the Halloween activities planned include:

- discussing Halloween safety procedures, especially while trick-or-treating.
- carving a jack-o-lantern for the classroom.
- roasting pumpkin seeds and baking a pumpkin pie.
- trying on a variety of costumes in the dramatic play area.
- creating designs with pumpkin seeds and glue on paper.

Halloween Party!

We will be having a Halloween party on Friday. You are welcome to send a costume to school with your child that day. The costume can be simple. A funny hat, a pair of silly glasses, a wig, or a little makeup would be fine Halloween attire. We would appreciate it if you could send the costume and accessories in a bag that is labeled with your child's name. This will prevent a mix-up of belongings. We will dress in our costumes about 2:00 p.m. Then we will have a small party and parade around in our costumes. It should be a fun day. Join us!

At Home

To get into the spirit of Halloween and to help your child develop language skills, practice the following Halloween rhyme:

"Five Little Pumpkins"

Five little pumpkins sitting on a gate.
The first one said, "Oh my, it's getting late."
The second one said, "There are witches in the air."
The third one said, "But we don't care."
The fourth one said, "Let's run. Let's run."
The fifth one said, "It's Halloween fun!"
"Wooooooooo," went the wind,
And out went the lights.
And the five little pumpkins rolled out of sight.

To ensure a safe Halloween:

- Check to see if your child's costume is flame resistant or at least flame retardant.
- Children can easily trip in long garments. Be sure the hemline is several inches off the ground.
- Masks and hoods can slip and make it difficult for your child to see. If a mask is worn, be sure it is secure and that the holes for the eyes are properly positioned. An alternative to wearing a mask is to use makeup.
- Finally, check the batteries in the flashlight!

Have a safe and happy Halloween.

FIGURE 33 Masks and pumpkins are symbols of Halloween.

Music:

1. **"Flying Witches"**
   (Sing to the tune of "When the Saints Come Marching In")

   Oh, when the witches
   Come flying by.
   Oh, when the witches come flying by,
   It will be Halloween night,
   When the witches come flying by.

2. **"One Little, Two Little, Three Little Pumpkins"**
   (Sing to the tune of "One Little, Two Little, Three Little Indians")

   One little, two little, three little pumpkins,
   Four little, five little, six little pumpkins,
   Seven little, eight little, nine little pumpkins,
   Ready for Halloween night!

3. **"Have You Made a Jack-O-Lantern?"**
   (Sing to the tune of "Muffin Man")

   Have you made a jack-o-lantern,
   A jack-o-lantern, a jack-o-lantern?
   Have you made a jack-o-lantern
   For Halloween night?

Fingerplays:

JACK-O-LANTERN

   I am a pumpkin, big and round.
      (show size with arms)
   Once upon a time, I grew on the ground.
      (point to ground)
   Now I have a mouth, two eyes, and a nose.
      (point to each)
   What are they for do you suppose?
      (point to forehead and "think")
   Why—I'll be a jack-o-lantern on Halloween night.

FIVE LITTLE WITCHES

   Five little witches standing by the door.
      (hold up five fingers)
   One flew out and then there were four.
      (flying motion with hand)
   Four little witches standing by a tree.
      (four fingers)
   One went to pick a pumpkin and then there were three.
      (picking motion, then three fingers)
   Three little witches stirring their brew.
      (stir)
   One fell in and then there were two.
      (two fingers)
   Two little witches went for a run.
      (run with fingers)
   One got lost and then there was one.
      (one finger)
   One little witch, yes, only one.
      (one finger)
   She cast a spell and now there are none.
      (make motions as if to cast spell and then put hands in lap)

HALLOWEEN FUN

   Goblins and witches in high pointed hats,
      (hands above head to form hat)

Riding on broomsticks and chasing black cats.
(ride broomstick)
Children in costumes might well give a fright.
(look frightened)
Get things in order for Halloween night.
We like our treats
(nod head)
And we'll play no mean pranks.
(shake head)
We'll do you no harm and we'll only say,
"Thanks!"

THE JACK-O-LANTERN

Three little pumpkins growing on a vine.
(three fingers)
Sitting in the sunlight, looking just fine.
(arms up like sun)
Along came a ghost who picked just one
(one finger)
To take on home for some Halloween fun.
(smile)
He gave him two eyes to see where he goes.
(paint two eyes)
He gave him a mouth and a big handsome
nose.
(point to mouth and nose)
Then he put a candle in.
(pretend to put in candle)
Now see how he glows.
(wiggle fingers from center of body out until
arms are extended)

I'VE A JACK-O-LANTERN

I've a jack-o-lantern
(make a ball with open fist, thumb at top)
With a great big grin.
(grin)
I've got a jack-o-lantern
With a candle in.
(insert other index finger up through bottom
of first)

HALLOWEEN WITCHES

One little, two little, three little witches,
(hold up one hand, nod fingers at each count)
Fly over the haystacks
(fly hand in up-and-down motion)
Fly over ditches
Slide down moonbeams without any hitches
(glide hand downward)
Heigh-ho! Halloween's here!

THE FRIENDLY GHOST

I'm a friendly ghost—almost!
(point to self)
And I chase you, too!
(point to child)
I'll just cover me with a sheet
(pretend to cover self ending with hands
covering face)
And then call "scat" to you.
(uncover face quickly and call out "scat")

WITCHES' CAT

I am the witches' cat.
(make a fist with two fingers extended for
cat)
Meoow. Meoow.
(stroke fist with other hand)
My fur is black as darkest night.
My eyes are glaring green and bright.
(circle eyes with thumb and forefingers)
I am the witches' cat.
(make a fist again with two fingers extended
and stroke fist with other hand)

MY PUMPKIN

See my pumpkin round and fat.
(make circle with hands, fingers spread
wide, touching)
See my pumpkin yellow.
(make a smaller circle)
Watch him grin on Halloween.
(point to mouth, which is grinning wide)
He is a very funny fellow.

Science:

1. **Carve Pumpkins**

Purchase several pumpkins. Carve them and
save the seeds for roasting. An alternative
activity would be to use a black felt-tip marker
to draw facial features on the pumpkin.
Pumpkins can also have added accessories.
For example, a large carrot can be used for a
nose, parsley for hair, cut green peppers for
ears, radishes for eyes, and a small green onion
can be placed in a cut mouth for teeth.

2. **Roasting Pumpkin Seeds**

Wash and dry pumpkin seeds. Then spread the seeds out on a cookie sheet to dry. Bake the seeds in a preheated oven at 350 degrees until brown. Salt, cool, and eat at snack time.

3. **Plant Pumpkin Seeds**

Purchase a packet of pumpkin seeds. Plant the pumpkin seeds in small paper cups. Set the paper cups with the pumpkin seeds in a sunny place. Water as needed. Observe to see if there is growth on a daily basis.

Dramatic Play:

Costume

Add Halloween costumes to the dramatic play area. (Some teachers purchase these at thrift stores or sales. From year to year they are stored in a Halloween prop box.)

Arts and Crafts:

1. **Spooky Easel**

Provide orange and black paint at the paint easels.

2. **Pumpkin Seed Pictures**

Dye pumpkin seeds many colors. Place the seeds with paste and paper on a table in the art area. The children then can create their own pictures.

3. **Crayon Wash**

On the art table, place paper, light-colored crayons, tempera paint, and brushes. The children can draw on paper with light-colored crayons. After this, they can paint over the entire picture.

4. **Masks**

Yarn, paper plates, felt tip markers, and any other accessories needed to make masks

interesting can be placed on a table in the art area. If desired, yarn can be used as hair on the mask.

Sensory:

1. **Measuring Seeds**

Pumpkin seeds and measuring cups can be added to the sensory table. The children will enjoy feeling and pouring seeds.

2. **Goop**

Add dry cornstarch to the sensory table. Slowly add enough water to make it a "goopy" consistency. If desired, add coloring to make it black or orange.

Large Muscle:

Ghost, Ghost, Witch

This game is played like "Duck, Duck, Goose." Form a circle and kneel. Choose one child to walk around the outside of the circle chanting, "Ghost, ghost, ghost." When the child taps another child and says "witch," the child tapped chases the initiator around the circle, attempting to tag the child. If the child who is "it" returns to the tapped child's spot before the other, he can lose his turn. If not, the child continues walking around the circle, repeating the same procedure.

Field Trips/Resource People:

1. **Pumpkin Patch**

Visit a pumpkin patch. During the tour point out various-sized pumpkins. Discuss how the pumpkins grow, as well as their shapes, sizes, etc.

2. **Halloween Safety**

A police officer can be invited to talk with the children about Halloween safety.

Math:

1. **Counting Pumpkin Seeds**

   Cut circles from construction paper. The number needed will depend upon the developmental level of the children. Write a numeral on each paper circle and place each into a pie tin. The children may count pumpkin seeds into the tins matching the circles.

2. **Weighing Pumpkin Seeds**

   In the math area, place a scale and pumpkin seeds. The children may elect to experiment by balancing the scale with the pumpkin seeds.

Group Time (games, language):

1. **Thank-you Note**

   Write a thank-you note to any resource person. Encourage all of the children to participate by sharing what they liked or saw.

2. **Costume Parade**

   On Halloween day, the children can dress up in costumes and march around the room and throughout the school to music. If available, a walk to a local nursing home may be enjoyed by the children as well as the elderly.

Cooking:

1. **Pumpkin Pie**

   1 unbaked pie shell
   2 cups (16–17 ounces) pumpkin
   1 can sweetened condensed milk
   1 egg
   1/2 teaspoon salt
   2 teaspoon pumpkin pie spice

   Blend all of the ingredients in a large mixing bowl. Pour the mixture into the pie shell. Bake the pie in an oven preheated to 375 degrees for 50 to 55 minutes or until a sharp knife blade inserted near center of pie is clean when removed. Cool and refrigerate the pie for 1 hour before serving. Top with whipped cream if desired.

2. **Pumpkin Patch Muffins**

   3 cups flour
   1 cup sugar
   4 teaspoons baking powder
   1 teaspoon salt
   1 teaspoon pumpkin pie spice
   1 cup milk
   1 cup canned pumpkin
   1/2 cup (1 stick) butter or margarine, melted
   2 eggs, beaten

   Sift the flour, sugar, baking powder, salt, and pumpkin pie spice into a large mixing bowl. Add the milk, pumpkin, melted butter, and eggs. Mix with a wooden spoon just until flour is moist. (Batter will be lumpy.) Place paper liners in the muffin tins and fill 2/3 full with batter. Bake in a preheated 400-degree oven 20 minutes or until muffins are golden. Cool in muffin tins 10 minutes on a wire rack. Remove muffins from muffin tins and finish cooling on wire racks. Pile into serving baskets and serve warm for snack.

3. **Witches' Brew**

   5 cups cranberry juice, unsweetened
   5 cups apple cider, unsweetened
   1 or 2 cinnamon sticks
   1/4 teaspoon ground nutmeg

   Place ingredients in a large saucepan. Cover, heat, and simmer for 10 minutes. Serve warm.

4. **Roasted Pumpkin Seeds**

   Soak pumpkin seeds for 24 hours in saltwater (1/4 cup salt to 1 cup water). Spread on cloth-covered cookie sheet and roast at 100 degrees for 2 hours. Turn oven off and leave seeds overnight.

5. **Non-bake Pumpkin Pie**

   1 can prepared pumpkin pie
   1 package vanilla instant pudding
   1 cup milk

   Mix and pour into baked pie shell or graham cracker pie shell.

DECORATING A PUMPKIN

In carving or decorating a pumpkin with the children you can discuss:

- the physical properties of pumpkins—color, texture, size, shape (both outside and inside).
- food category to which pumpkins belong.
- what other forms pumpkins can be made into after scooped out of the shell.
- where pumpkins grow (plant some of the seeds).

- what size and shape to make the features of the pumpkin, including eyes, nose, mouth, and what kind of expression to make.

Accessories:

1 bunch parsley (hair)
1 carrot (nose)
2 string beans (eyebrows)
2 radishes (eyes)

1 green pepper (ears)
1 stalk celery (teeth)
1 large pumpkin (head)

Prepare the pumpkin in the usual manner; that is, cut off the cap and scoop out the seeds inside. Save the seeds for roasting. If desired, individual vegetable pieces may be attached by carving or inserting toothpicks.

Multimedia:

The following resources can be found in educational catalogs:

1. Palmer, Hap. *Holiday Songs and Rhythms* [record].

2. *Holiday Songs for All Occasions* [record]. Kimbo Records.

3. *Holiday Action Songs* [record]. Kimbo Records.

4. *Why We Celebrate* [30-minute video]. Edu-Vid.

Books:

The following books can be used to complement the theme:

1. Alexander, Sue. (1990). *Who Goes Out on Halloween*. New York: Bantam Books, Inc.

2. Berenstain, Stan & Janice. (1989). *The Berenstain Bears Trick or Treat*. New York: Random House Books for Young Readers.

3. Barkan, Jeanne. (1991). *The Very Scary Jack 'O Lantern*. New York: Scholastic Inc.

4. Cassedy, Sylvia. (1990). *Best Cat Suit of All*. New York: Dial Books for Young Readers.

5. Craig, Janet. (1988). *Joey the Jack-O'-Lantern*. Mahwah, NJ: Troll Associates.

6. Gardner, Beau. (1990). *Whooo's a Fright on Halloween Night*. New York: Putnam Publishing Group.

7. George, Diann. (1992). *The Peanut Butter Witch*. New York: Carlton Press, Inc.

8. Silverman, Erica. (1992). *Big Pumpkin*. New York: Macmillan Children's Book Group.

9. Titherington, Jeanne. (1990). *Pumpkin Pumpkin*. New York: William Morrow and Co., Inc.

10. Wojciechowski, Susan. (1992). *The Best Halloween of All*. New York: Crown Books for Young Readers.

11. Ziefert, Harriet. (1992). *Halloween Parade*. New York: Viking Children's Books.

12. Gantos, Jack. (1988). *Rotten Ralph's Trick or Treat*. Boston: Houghton Mifflin.

13. Himmelman, John. (1987). *Amanda & The Witch Switch*. New York: Puffin.

14. Merriam, Eve. (1987). *Halloween ABC*. New York: Macmillan.

15. Moncure, Jane B. (1987). *Word Bird's Halloween Words*. Mankato, MN: Child's World.

16. Nerlove, Miriam. (1989). *Halloween*. Morton Grove, IL: Albert Whitman.

17. Reeves, Mona R. (1989). *The Spooky Eerie Night*. New York: Macmillan.

18. Stock, Catherine. (1990). *Halloween Monster*. New York: Bradbury Press.

19. Leaf, Margaret. (1987). *Eyes of the Dragon*. New York: Lothrop, Lee & Shepard.

20. Bauer, Caroline F. (Ed.). (1989). *Halloween: Stories & Poems*. New York: Harper Collins.

21. Ziefert, Harriet. (1992). *What Is Halloween?* New York: Harper Collins.

22. Bunting, Eve. (1989). *Ghost's Hour, Spook's Hour*. Boston: Houghton Mifflin.

Symbols

menorah
Star of David
dreidel
synagogue/temple

Foods

latkes
honey-spice cookies
ka'achei sumsum
matzo

HANUKKAH
(CHANUKAH)

Celebrations

lighting the menorah
gift giving
family togetherness

Here's an exciting new way to turn instant photography into an effective teaching tool. Refer to the full-color insert for the activity entitled Photo Expectations.

Theme Goals:

Through participating in the experiences provided by this theme, the children may learn:

1. The story of Hanukkah.

2. Symbols of Hanukkah.

3. Hanukkah celebrations.

Concepts for the Children to Learn:

1. Hanukkah is a Jewish holiday.

2. Hanukkah is a time for giving and sharing with others.

3. The menorah and the dreidel are symbols of Hanukkah.

4. Hanukkah is celebrated for eight days.

5. Some foods eaten during Hanukkah include latkes, honey-spice cookies, ka'achei sumsum, and matzo.

Vocabulary:

1. **latkes**—potato pancakes eaten during Hanukkah.

2. **dreidel**—four-sided toy that spins like a top.

3. **Star of David**—six-sided star-shaped figure, is a Jewish symbol.

4. **menorah**—eight-branched candlestick. The middle or ninth candle is taller than the other eight and is called the shammash.

5. **Hanukkah**—eight-day Jewish festival of lights. A celebration of the Jewish people's fight long ago to retain/keep the right to practice their religion. One candle is lighted on the menorah each day.

Bulletin Board

The purpose of this bulletin board is to develop an awareness of the passage of time as well as the math concept of sets. This bulletin board starts out with the base of the menorah. Each day of Hanukkah the children work together to construct a candle and a flame to add to the menorah. Candles and flames are most interesting when made using a wide variation of mediums: sequins, feathers, cut construction paper, yarn, etc.

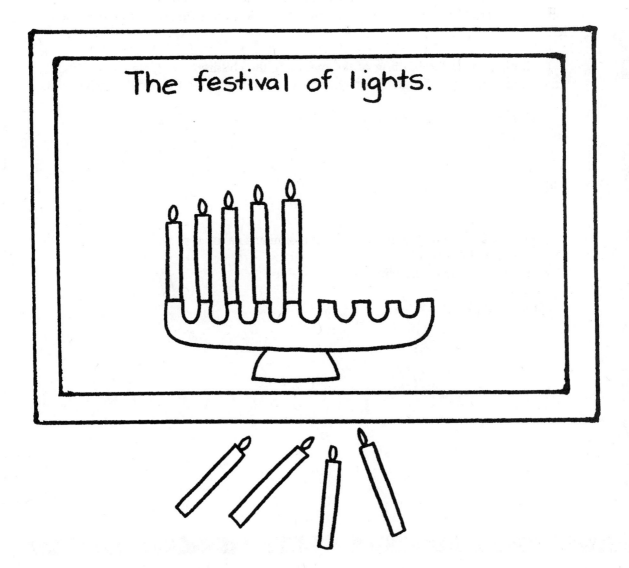

The festival of lights.

Parent Letter

Dear Parents,

For the next eight days, we will be celebrating Hanukkah. Hanukkah commemorates the victory of the Jews over the Syrians. Hanukkah, also known as the Festival of Lights, is celebrated for eight days in either November or December. In 175 B.C. a Syrian King, Antiochus, ordered the Jewish Temple defiled. After the Syrians desecrated the Temple, Judah Maccabee formed a small but powerful army to defend the Jews. The Maccabees rebuilt the Temple and the legend states that when it was time to light the Temple lamp for rededication, there was only enough sacred oil to burn for one day. Miraculously, it burned for eight days!

Hanukkah is celebrated by the lighting of a special candelabra called a menorah. On the menorah there is one holder for each of the eight nights and one for the shammash. Shammash means helper in Hebrew; this is the candle that is used to light the others. The candles are lit beginning on the right side and moving to the left.

Each night, after the lighting of the menorah, the children are given small gifts. Traditionally this gift was gelt, money to be used while playing the dreidel game.

Unlike most Jewish holidays, work and schooling continues during the eight-day celebration.

At School

Some of the learning experiences the children will participate in include:

- playing a game with a dreidel, which is similar to a toy top.
- preparing latkes (potato pancakes) for snack.
- creating wax-resist drawings at the art table.

Happy Hanukkah!

FIGURE 34 Learning about Hanukkah and other religious holidays is an important social studies activity.

Music:

"Menorah Candles"
    (Sing to the tune of "Twinkle, Twinkle, Little Star")

    Twinkle, twinkle candles in the night,
    Standing on the menorah bright,
    Burning slow we all know,
    Burning bright to give us light.
    Twinkle, twinkle candles in the night,
    Standing on the menorah bright.

Fingerplays:

THE MENORAH CANDLE

    I'm a menorah candle
        (stand, point at self)
    Growing shorter you can see
        (bend down slowly)
    Melting all my wax
        (go down more)
    Until there's nothing left to see.
        (sit down)

HANUKKAH LIGHTS

    One light, two lights, three lights, and four
        (hold up four fingers, one at a time)
    Five lights, six lights, and three more,
        (hold up five fingers on other hand)
    Twinkle, twinkle nine pretty lights,
        (move fingers)
    In a golden menorah bright!
        (make cup with palm of hand)

MY DREIDEL

    I have a little dreidel.
        (cup hands to form a square)
    I made it out of clay.
        (move fingers in a molding motion)
    And when it's dry and ready
        (flatten hands as if to hold in hand—palm up, pinkies together)
    Then with it I will play.
        (pretend to spin dreidel on the floor)

Science:

1. **Potato Sprouts**

    Provide each child with a clear plastic cup. Fill the plastic cup half-full with water. Place a potato part way in the water supported by toothpicks to keep it from dropping into the jar. Put the end with tubers into the water. The other end should stick out of the water. Refill with fresh water as it evaporates and watch the roots begin to grow and leaves start to sprout.

2. **Candle Snuffer**

Demonstrate how a candle snuffer is used to put out a flame. (Check licensing regulations prior to the activity.)

3. **Light**

Light a candle. Discuss other sources of light. (Examples: sun, lamp, flashlight, traffic lights, etc.)

4. **Sunlight Power**

Fill two glasses half-full of warm water. Stir some flour into one glass. In the other, dissolve a little yeast in the water, then add flour. Now set them both in a warm place for an hour and watch the results.

Dramatic Play:

1. **Family Celebration**

Collect materials for a special family meal. These may include dresses, hats, coats, plates, cups, plastic food, napkins, etc. The children can have a holiday meal.

2. **Gift Wrapping Center**

Collect various-sized boxes, wrapping paper, tape, and ribbon. The children can wrap presents for Hanukkah.

Sensory:

Sand Temples

Fill the sensory table with sand and moisten until the sand begins to adhere. The children may pack sand into cans to mold into desired shapes and build sand temples from the molded forms.

Arts and Crafts:

1. **Star of David**

Provide the children with triangles cut from blue construction paper. Demonstrate to the children how to invert one triangle over the other to form a star. The stars may be glued to construction paper.

2. **Potato Art**

Slice potatoes in half. The children may dip the potato halves in shallow pans containing various colors of tempera paint and then create designs on construction paper.

3. **Hanukkah Handprints**

Provide the children with construction paper, brushes, and tempera paint in shallow pans. Paint each of the children's hands with a brush that has been dipped in tempera paint. The children then may place their hands on the construction paper, creating handprints.

4. **Dreidel Top**

Collect and wash out 1/2-pint milk containers. Tape the top down so that the carton forms a square. Provide construction paper squares for the children to paste to the sides of the milk carton. The children may decorate with crayons or felt-tip markers. Upon completion, punch an unsharpened pencil through the milk container so that the children may spin it like a top.

5. **Star of David Mobile**

Provide each child with two drinking straws. Demonstrate to the children how to bend the straws so that they make triangles. Glue the straw triangles together, inverting one over the other to make a six-pointed star. Tie string to the star and hang from a window or ceiling. This activity is appropriate for 6-, 7-, and 8-year-olds.

Resource People:

Invite a rabbi or parent of the Jewish faith to come and talk about Hanukkah and how it is celebrated.

Large Muscle:

1. Dreidel Dance

The children can dance the dreidel dance by standing in a circle and spinning as they sing this song to the tune of "Row, Row, Row, Your Boat."

Dreidel, dreidel, dreidel,
A-spinning I will go.
Speed it up and slow it down,
And on the ground I'll go!

2. Frying Donuts—Dramatic Play

Children can act out frying donuts as they sing this song to the tune of "I Have a Little Turtle."

I have a little donut,
It is so nice and light,
And when it's all done cooking,
I'm going to take a bite!

Frying donuts usually pop up and out of the frying oil when they are finished cooking. The children can act out these motions. The oil used in frying the donuts is significant in the Hanukkah celebration. It signifies the oil burned in the Temple lamp.

Math:

1. Sort the Stars

Provide children with various-colored stars. The children can match the colors. A variation would be to have stars of various sizes. The children could sequence the stars from largest to smallest.

2. Hanukkah Puzzles

Mount pictures of a menorah and the Star of David on tagboard. Cut into pieces. Laminate. The number of pieces will depend upon the children's developmental age.

3. Candle Holder and Candle Match

Have a variety of candle holders set out with candles. The children will have to match the candles to the correct-sized candle holder.

Group Time (games, language):

1. Hot Potato

Ask the children to sit in a circle. Provide one child with a real, a plastic, or a potato constructed from tagboard. Play music. As the music is playing, the children pass the potato around the circle until the music stops. The one holding the potato is out of the circle. Game continues until one child is left or the children no longer wish to play.

2. Dreidel Game

Each player starts with 10 to 15 pennies, nuts, or raisins. Each player places an object in the center of the circle. The dreidel is spun by one of the players, while the following verse is chanted:

I have a little dreidel.
I made it out of clay.
And when it's dry and ready.
Then with it I will play.

Whether the spinning player wins or loses depends on which side of the dreidel lands upward when it falls. The following may be used as a guide:

Nun (N) means nothing: player receives nothing from the pot.
Gimmel (G) means all: player receives everything from the pot.
Hay (H) means half: player takes 1/2 of the pot.
Shin (S) means put in: player adds two objects to the pot.

When one player has won all of the objects, the game is completed.

3. Gelt Hunt

Make a silver coin by cutting out a 4-inch round piece of cardboard and covering it with aluminum foil. Hide the coin (gelt) in the classroom and play a hide-and-seek game. For younger children hide the gelt in an obvious place.

(Gelt is the Yiddish word for money. Traditionally, small amounts of gelt are given to children each night of Hanukkah.)

Social Studies:

1. Menorah

Glue eight wooden or styrofoam spools of equal size to a piece of wood, leaving a space in the middle. Glue a larger spool in the middle, thus having four smaller spools on each side. Spray with gold or silver paint. The menorah can be lit during the eight days of Hanukkah during group time. Explain the meaning of the menorah to the group as well.

2. Hanukkah Celebration

Display pictures at the child's eye level of the Hanukkah celebration. Examples would include such pictures as lighting the menorah, a family meal, etc.

3. Human Menorah

The children can make a human menorah by positioning themselves to resemble a menorah. A menorah is a lamp with nine flames that is used to celebrate Hanukkah. Two children can lie head-to-toe on the floor to form the base. Have nine children stand behind the base to form the candles. The tallest child can stand in the middle and be the shammash. The shammash is the center candle that lights the other candles. The children can make pretend flames out of construction paper for the candles to hold as if they are lit.

Cooking:

1. Latkes

6 medium-sized potatoes washed, pared, and grated
1 egg
3 tablespoons flour
1/2 teaspoon baking powder

In a large bowl, mix the egg and the grated potatoes. Add the flour and baking powder. Drop by spoonfuls into hot cooking oil in a frying pan. Brown on both sides. Drain on paper towel. Latkes may be served with a spoonful of applesauce or sour cream.

2. Hanukkah Honey and Spice Cookies

1/2 cup (1 stick) margarine, softened
1/2 cup firmly packed dark brown sugar
1/2 cup honey
2 1/2 cups unsifted flour
2 teaspoons ground ginger
1 teaspoon baking soda
1 teaspoon ground cinnamon
1 teaspoon ground nutmeg
1/2 teaspoon salt
1/4 teaspoon ground cloves

In a large mixing bowl cream margarine and sugar. Beat in honey and egg until well combined. In a small bowl combine flour, ginger, baking soda, cinnamon, nutmeg, salt, and cloves. Add to honey mixture. Beat on low speed until well blended. Cover dough and chill at least 1 hour or up to 3 days. Heat oven to 350 degrees. Grease cookie sheets. Set aside. Working quickly with 1/4 of the dough at a time, roll out on floured surface to 1/4-inch thickness. Cut into desired shapes, including a dreidel, menorah, or star. Using a spatula, place cookies on prepared cookie sheets 1 inch apart. Reroll scraps. Bake for 7 minutes. Transfer to wire racks to cool. Makes about 4 dozen cookies.

3. Ka'achei Sumsum—Bagel Cookies

4 cups of flour
1 cup margarine
1 teaspoon salt
3 tablespoons cake-form yeast
1 egg
1 cup lukewarm water
1/4 teaspoon sugar

Place yeast and sugar in a bowl. Pour over lukewarm water. Put in a warm place for 10 minutes or until yeast rises. Prepare a dough from the flour, margarine, salt, and dissolved yeast mixture. Cover dough with a towel, put in a warm place for 2 hours. When dough rises, take small pieces and roll into strips about 4 inches long. Join the ends to form a bagel. Brush each one with beaten egg and place on a greased baking sheet. Bake in a 350-degree oven for 20 to 30 minutes.

Source: Nahoum, Aldo (Ed.). (1970). *The Art of Israeli Cooking*. New York: Holt, Rinehart and Winston.

4. K'naidlach Soup

3 eggs
3 1/2 cups matzo meal
1/2 chicken bouillon cube
1 teaspoon celery leaves, chopped
nutmeg
juice of 1/2 lemon
salt
pepper

Beat eggs well. Add bouillon cube, salt, pepper, and a pinch of nutmeg. Add lemon juice and celery leaves. Continue to beat. Slowly add matzo meal, using a wooden spoon to stir. When matzo meal thickens, knead by hand. After matzo meal has been thoroughly kneaded, form small balls (1 inch). Arrange in a deep dish and leave in refrigerator for at least 3 hours. Prepare a clear chicken soup and when it reaches boiling, drop in matzo balls. Let cook for 10 to 12 minutes. Serve 3 to 4 balls per bowl of soup. Add lemon juice to taste.

Source: Nahoum, Aldo (Ed.). (1970). *The Art of Israeli Cooking*. New York: Holt, Rinehart and Winston.

Multimedia:

The following resources can be found in educational catalogs:

1. Palmer, Hap. "Hanukkah" in *Holiday Songs and Rhythms* [record].

2. "Hanukkah" in *Holiday Songs for All Occasions* [record]. Kimbo Records.

3. "My Dreidel" in *Kindergarten Songs, Record 1* [record]. Bowmar.

4. "O Hannukah" in *Folk Songs of Israel* [record]. Bowmar.

5. Ben Ezra. *Israeli Children's Songs* [record]. Folkways.

6. *Songs to Share* [record]. United Synagogue Book Service.

Books:

The following books can be used to complement the theme:

1. Fisher, Aileen. (1985). *My First Hanukkah Book*. Chicago: Children's Press.

2. Shostak, Myra. (1986). *Rainbow Candles*. Rockville, MD: Kar Ben.

3. Gellman, Ellie. (1985). *It's Chanukah*. Rockville, MD: Kar Ben.

4. Chaikin, Miriam. (1990). *Hanukkah*. New York: Holiday House, Inc.

5. dePaola, Tomie. (1989). *My First Chanukah*. New York: Putnam Publishing Group.

6. Ehrlich, Amy. (1989). *Story of Hanukkah*. New York: Dial Books for Young Readers.

7. Gertz, Susan E. (1992). *Hanukkah and Christmas at My House*. Middleton, OH: Willow and Laurel Press.

8. Groner, Judye, & Wikler, Madeline. (1992). *Hanukkah Fun: For Little Hands*. Rockville, MD: Kar-Ben Copies, Inc.

9. Katz, Bobbi. (1992). *A Family Hanukkah*. New York: Random House Books for Young Readers.

10. Kimmelman, Leslie, & Kimmelman, John. (1992). *Hanukkah Lights, Hanukkah Nights*. New York: Harper Collins Children's Books.

11. Schotter, Roni. (1990). *Hanukkah*. New York: Little, Brown and Co.

12. Sidi, Smadar S. (1988). *Chanukah A–Z*. Bellmore, NY: Modan/Adama Books.

13. Adler, David A. (1989). *Happy Hanukkah Rebus*. New York: Viking Children's Books.

14. Kimmel, Eric A. (1990). *The Chanukah Guest*. New York: Holiday House, Inc.

15. Manushkin, Fran. (1990). *Latkes and Applesauce: A Hanukkah Story*. New York: Scholastic, Inc.

16. Wolfberg, Carrie. (1991). *The Happy Dreidels: Hanukkah Adventure*. Clearwater, FL: Peartree.

17. Levine, Abby (Ed.). (1989). *Hanukkah*. Morton Grove, IL: Whitman.

18. Zalben, Jane B. (1988). *Beni's First Chanukah*. New York: Holt.

19. Sholem, Aleichem. (1991). *Hanukkah Money*. New York: Morrow.

20. Backman, Aidel. (1990). *One Night, One Hanukkah Night*. Philadelphia: JPS.

21. Rosenberg, Amy. (1991). *Melly's Menorah*. New York: Simon & Schuster.

22. Zwebner, Janet. (1989). *Animated Menorah*. New York: Shapolsky Publications.

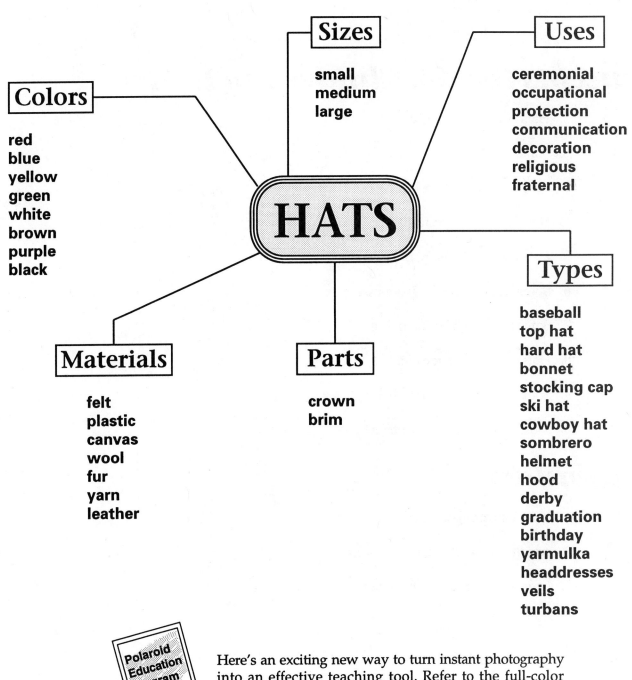

Colors

red
blue
yellow
green
white
brown
purple
black

Sizes

small
medium
large

Uses

ceremonial
occupational
protection
communication
decoration
religious
fraternal

HATS

Types

baseball
top hat
hard hat
bonnet
stocking cap
ski hat
cowboy hat
sombrero
helmet
hood
derby
graduation
birthday
yarmulka
headdresses
veils
turbans

Materials

felt
plastic
canvas
wool
fur
yarn
leather

Parts

crown
brim

Polaroid Education Program

Here's an exciting new way to turn instant photography into an effective teaching tool. Refer to the full-color insert for the activity entitled Polaroid Places.

Theme Goals:

Through participating in the experiences provided by this theme, the children may learn:

1. Types of hats.

2. Uses for hats.

3. Materials used to make hats.

4. Parts of a hat.

5. Colors and sizes of hats.

Concepts for the Children to Learn:

1. Hats are worn on our heads.

2. Some hats keep us warm.

3. Felt, plastic, cloth, and yarn are all materials used to make hats.

4. Hats come in different sizes.

5. Hats come in different colors.

6. Some hats have special names.

7. Some hats can keep us cool.

8. Hats can be worn for fun.

9. Some people wear hats when they are working.

10. Most hats have a crown and a brim.

Vocabulary:

1. **hat**—a covering for the head.

2. **crown**—top part of the hat.

3. **brim**—the part of a hat that surrounds the crown.

Bulletin Board

The purpose of this bulletin board is to have the children match the colored pieces to their corresponding shadow, thereby developing visual discrimination skills. To construct the bulletin board, draw different types of hats on white tagboard. Color the hats with watercolor markers and cut out. Trace the cut-out hats onto black construction paper to create shadows. Then cut the shadows out and attach to the bulletin board. A magnet piece or a push pin can be fastened to the shadow. A magnet piece or a hole can be applied to the colored hats.

Parent Letter

Dear Parents,

Hats will be the focus of our next curriculum. Through this unit the children will become familiar with occupations and sports for which hats are worn, materials used to make hats, and purposes of hats such as for protection, decoration, and identification.

At School

Some of the learning activities planned include:

- playing in the Hat Store located in the dramatic play area.
- making paper plate hats at the art table.
- listening to and dramatizing the story, *Caps for Sale*, by Esphyr Slobodkina.

Special Request!

On Friday we will have a Hat Day. The children will show and wear hats that they have brought from home. If your child wishes to share a special hat, please label it and send it to school with your child in a paper bag. This will help us to keep track of which hat belongs to each child. Thank you for your help.

At Home

Ask your child to help you search the closets of your home for hats. To develop classification skills, discuss the colors and types of hats with your child. Are there more seasonal hats or sports hats? What are the hats made from? Why were those materials used?

Hats off to a fun unit!

FIGURE 35 Hats serve many different functions and represent many different areas of the world.

Music:

"My Hat"
(traditional song)

My hat it has three corners.
(point to head, hold up three fingers)
Three corners has my hat.
(hold up three fingers, point to head)
And had it not three corners
(hold up three fingers)
It wouldn't be my hat.
(shake head, point to head)

Variation: Make three-cornered paper hats to wear while acting out this song.

Science:

What's It Made Of?

Hats representing a variety of styles and materials can be placed on the science table.

Magnifying glasses can also be provided to allow the children to explore. They can look at, feel, and try on the hats.

- Before letting the children try on the hats, make sure the children do not have head lice.

Dramatic Play:

1. **Sports Hats**

   Provide football helmets and jerseys, baseball hats, batters' helmets, and uniforms. Encourage the children to pretend they are football and baseball players.

2. **Construction Site**

   Provide the children with toy tools, blocks, and construction hard hats.

3. **Hat Store**

   Fire fighter hats, bonnets, top hats, hard hats, bridesmaids' hats, baby hats, etc., can all be available in the hat store. Encourage the children to buy and sell hats using a cash register and play money.

Arts and Crafts:

1. **Easel Ideas**

   - top hat-shaped paper
   - baseball cap-shaped paper
   - football helmet-shaped paper
   - graduation cap-shaped paper

2. **Paper Plate Hats**

   Decorate paper plates with many different kinds of scraps, glitter, construction paper, and crepe paper. Punch a hole, using a paper punch, on each side of the hat. Attach strings so that the hat can be tied on and fastened under the chin.

Large Muscle:

Hat Bean Bag Toss

Lay several large hats on the floor. Encourage the children to stand about two feet from the hats and try to throw the beanbags into the hats.

Field Trips:

1. **Hat Store**

   Visit a hat store or hat department of a store. Examine the different kinds, sizes, and colors of hats.

2. **Sports Store**

   Visit a sporting goods store. Locate the hat section. Observe the types of hats used for different sports.

Math:

1. **Hat Match**

   Construct pairs of hat puzzles out of tagboard. On each pair, draw a different pattern. Encourage the children to mix the hats up and sort them by design.

2. **Hat Seriation**

   Collect a variety of hats. The children can arrange them from smallest to largest and largest to smallest. Also, they can classify the hats by colors and uses.

Social Studies:

Many of these activities lend themselves to group time situations.

1. **"Weather" or Not to Wear a Hat**

   Discuss the different kinds of hats that are worn in cold weather. Ask questions such as, "What parts of our body does a hat keep warm?" "What kind of hats do we wear when it is warm outside?" "How does a hat help to keep us cool?"

2. **Sports Hats**

   Make an arrangement of different sports hats. Place a mirror close by. The children can try on the hats.

3. **Community Helpers**

   Many people in our community wear hats as part of their uniform. Collect several of these hats such as fire fighter, police officer, mail carrier, baker, etc., and place in a bag for a small group activity. Identify one child at a time to pull a hat out of the bag. Once the hat is removed, the children can identify the worker. Older children may be able to describe the activities of the identified worker.

Group Time (games, language):

1. **"My Favorite Hat Day"**

   Encourage the children to share their favorite hats with the class on a specific day. Talk about each hat and ask where it was bought or found. Colors, sizes, and shapes can also be discussed.

2. **Dramatization**

   Read the story, *Caps for Sale*. After the children are familiar with the storyline, they may enjoy acting out the story.

Cooking:

The children may enjoy wearing baker's hats for the cooking experiences! Ask a bakery or fast-food restaurant to donate several for classroom use.

1. **Cheese Crunchies**

   1/2 cup butter or margarine
   1 cup all-purpose flour
   1 cup shredded cheddar cheese

344

pinch of salt
1 cup rice cereal bits

Cut the butter into 6 or 8 slices and mix together with the flour, cheese, and salt. Use fingers or fork to mix. Knead in the cereal bits; then roll the dough into small balls or snakes. Press them down flat and place onto an ungreased cookie sheet. Bake at 325 degrees for approximately 10 minutes. Cool and serve for snack.

2. **Hamantaschen from Israel**

Children in Israel eat hamantaschen on the holiday of Purim. A hamantaschen is a pastry that represents the hat worn by the evil Haman, who plotted against the ancient Jews. Today, Israeli children dress in costumes, parade in the streets, and have parties on Purim.

7 tablespoons butter or margarine
1/3 cup sugar

2 eggs
2 1/2 cups flour
1/4 cup orange juice
1 teaspoon lemon juice
1 jar prune or plum jam

Cream the butter or margarine and sugar together in a large mixing bowl. Separate the eggs. Discard the whites. Add the yolk to the mixture and stir. Add the flour and juices to the mixture and mix to form dough. On a floured board, roll the dough to about 1/8-inch thickness. Use a cookie cutter to cut into 4-inch circles. Spoon a tablespoon of jam into the center of each circle and fold up 3 edges to create a triangle shape. Leave a small opening at the center. (Other fillings, such as poppy seeds or apricot jam, can be used.) Place the shaped dough on a cookie sheet and bake for 20 minutes in a 350-degree preheated oven. Serve for snack.

HATS

A variety of hats can be collected for use in the dramatic play area. Some examples are:

fire fighter	railroad engineer	ski caps
police officer	motorcycle helmet	berets
visor	cloche	top hat
sunbonnets	sports:	cowboy
sombrero	football	stocking cap
straw hats	baseball	mail carrier
mantilla	chef	bicycle helmet
party (birthday)	sailor	pillbox
nurse's cap	hard hats	

Books:

The following books can be used to complement the theme:

1. Cooke, Tom (Illus.). (1987). *I Want a Hat Like That*. New York: Golden Press.

2. Geringer, Laura. (1987). *A Three Hat Day*. New York: Harper Collins.

3. Mark, Jan. (1986). *Fur*. New York: Harper and Row.

4. Schumacher, Claire. (1987). *Santa's Hat*. New York: Prentice Hall Books.

5. Morris, Ann. (1993). *Hats, Hats, Hats*. New York: Morrow.

6. Barkan, Joanne. (1992). *That Fat Hat*. New York: Scholastic Inc.

7. Cushman, Dough. (1988). *Uncle Foster's Hat Tree*. New York: Dutton Children's Books.

8. Hindley, Judy. (1991). *Uncle Harold and the Green Hat*. New York: Farrar, Straus and Girous.

9. Howard, Elizabeth F. (1991). *Aunt Flossie's Hats (and Crab Cakes Later)*. Boston: Houghton Mifflin.

10. Leemis, Ralph. (1991). *Mister Momboo's Hat*. New York: Dutton Children's Books.

11. Miller, Margaret. (1988). *Whose Hat?* New York: Greenwillow Books.

12. Scarry, Richard. (1990). *Be Careful! Mr. Fumble!* New York: Random House Books for Young Readers.

13. Walbrecker, Dirk. (1991). *Benny's Hat*. Wilmington, DE: Atonium Books, Inc.

14. Borden, Louise. (1989). *Caps, Hats, Socks, and Mittens*. New York: Scholastic.

15. Roy, Ron. (1987). *Whose Hat Is That?* Boston: Houghton Mifflin.

16. Schneider, Howie. (1993). *Uncle Lester's Hat*. New York: Putnam.

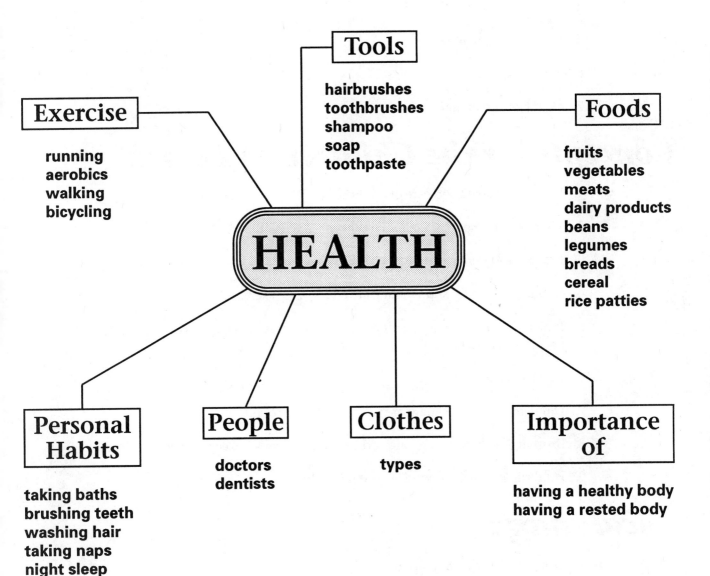

Tools

hairbrushes
toothbrushes
shampoo
soap
toothpaste

Exercise

running
aerobics
walking
bicycling

Foods

fruits
vegetables
meats
dairy products
beans
legumes
breads
cereal
rice patties

HEALTH

Personal Habits

taking baths
brushing teeth
washing hair
taking naps
night sleep

People

doctors
dentists

Clothes

types

Importance of

having a healthy body
having a rested body

Polaroid Education Program

Here's an exciting new way to turn instant photography into an effective teaching tool. Refer to the full-color insert for the activity entitled Presto-Chango-Photo.

Theme Goals:

Through participating in the experiences provided by this theme, the children may learn:

1. Importance of good health.

2. Health foods.

3. Exercise clothes.

4. Tools used for health needs.

5. Exercises for health.

6. Health habits.

7. Health occupations.

Concepts for the Children to Learn:

1. We need to take good care of our bodies.

2. Vitamins, shampoo, soap, and toothpaste are health aids.

3. Doctors and dentists provide health checkups.

4. Running, aerobics, and walking are all forms of exercise.

5. Fruits, vegetables, dairy products, beans, legumes, meat, breads, and cereals keep our bodies healthy.

6. Our bodies need rest.

7. Different types of clothing are worn during exercise.

8. Brushing teeth, washing hair, and bathing are ways to keep our bodies clean.

9. Hairbrushes and toothbrushes are health tools.

Vocabulary:

1. **exercise**—moving body parts.

2. **health**—feeling good.

3. **nutrition**—eating foods that are good for our body.

4. **cleanliness**—keeping our body parts free from dirt.

5. **diet**—the food we eat.

6. **checkup**—a visit to a doctor to make sure you are healthy.

Bulletin Board

The purpose of this bulletin board is to have the children match the health aids to their corresponding shadow. Construct health aids from white tagboard such as a toothbrush, toothpaste, comb, brush, and soap. Color the objects with colored felt-tip markers and laminate. Trace each of the health aids onto black construction paper to construct shadows as illustrated. Staple the shadow aids on the bulletin board either by affixing magnets or using push pins. Then punch a hole in the health aids for the children to hang them on the appropriate shadow.

Parent Letter

Dear Parents,

We will be starting a unit on health. This unit will include many aspects of health. We will be discussing foods that are good for us, important personal habits, and exercise. Through this unit the children will develop an awareness of how important it is to keep their bodies healthy.

At School

Some of the learning experiences planned for the week include:

- tracing our bodies at the art center.
- visiting Dr. Thomas, the dentist, at her office.
- having a visit by an aerobics instructor.
- creating healthy snacks.
- weighing and measuring ourselves.

Field Trip

Arrangements have been made to visit Dr. Thomas's office on Thursday of this week. Dr. Thomas will give us a tour of the dental clinic and show us various pieces of dental equipment. We will walk to her office, leaving school at 10:00 a.m., and return just in time for lunch. Please have your child at school by 10:00 a.m. if he wishes to participate. Parents, please feel free to join us.

Just a Reminder

If your child's toothbrush at school is missing, please send another one. We teach the importance of dental hygiene by brushing our teeth after all meals and snacks at school.

At Home

Cotton swabs may be used instead of brushes for painting. They may also be used to dot paper with different colors. Painting is a valuable sensory experience for a child. It provides an opportunity to experiment with color.

Teach your child healthy habits today!

FIGURE 36 Clean hands can prevent the spread of germs.

Music:

1. **"Brush Your Teeth"** by Raffi.

2. **"My Body"**
   (Sing to the tune of "Where is Thumbkin?")

   This is my body.
   This is my body.
   It's the only one I've got.
   It's the only one I've got.
   I'm going to take good care of it.
   I'm going to take good care of it.
   Yes I am. Yes I am.

Fingerplay:

BRUSHING TEETH

I jiggle the toothbrush again and again.
   (pretend to brush teeth)

I scrub all my teeth for awhile.
I swish the water to rinse them and then
   (puff out cheeks to swish)
I look at myself and I smile.
   (smile at one another)

Science:

Soap Pieces

Add different kinds of soaps and a magnifying glass to the science area. Talk about what each one is used for.

Dramatic Play:

1. **Health Club**

   Mats, fake weights (made from large tinker toys), headbands, and music to represent a health club can be placed in the dramatic play area.

2. **Doctor's Office (Hospital)**

   White clothing, stethoscopes, strip thermometers, magazines, bandages, cots, sheets, and plastic syringes without needles can be placed in the dramatic play area to represent a hospital.

3. **Restaurant**

   Tables, tablecloths, menus, and tablets for taking orders can be placed in the dramatic play area. Paste pictures of food on the menus. A sign for the area could be "Eating for Health."

Arts and Crafts:

1. **Paper Plate Meals**

   Magazines for the children to cut food pictures from the five food groups should be provided. The pictures can be pasted on a paper plate to represent a balanced meal. Plates from microwave dinners, if thoroughly cleaned, work well, too.

2. Body Tracing

Instruct each child to lie on a large piece of paper. Trace the child's body and let him take the tracing home and decorate it with his parents. After this, it can be returned to school for display. This activity should help the children become aware of individual uniqueness and fosters parent-child interaction.

Sensory:

Add shampoo or dish detergent to the sensory table.

Large Muscle:

1. Weight Awareness

The object of this activity is to become aware of weight and to feel the difference between heavy and light. To do this, the child should experiment with body force. Exercise in the following ways: lift arms slowly and gently, stomp on the floor, walk on tiptoes, kick out one leg as hard as possible, very smoothly and lightly slide one foot along the floor. Music can be added to imitate aerobics.

2. Mini-Olympics

Set up various areas for jumping jacks, jogging, relays, and a "beanbag launch." For the "launch" put a beanbag on the top edge of a child's foot and launch it by kicking. Observe the distance each beanbag goes.

Field Trips/Resource People:

1. Take a field trip to:

- hospital
- health care facility
- doctor's office
- dentist's office
- beauty shop
- health club
- drugstore

2. Invite the following resource people to visit the classroom:

- doctor
- nurse
- dentist
- dietician
- aerobics instructor
- beautician

Math:

1. Food Group Sorting

Create a food group display. To do this, encourage the children to bring empty food containers. The food containers can be sorted into food groups. This could be a small group activity or a choice during the self-selected play period.

2. Height and Weight Chart

Weigh and measure each of the children at various times throughout the year. Record the data on a chart. This chart can be posted in the classroom.

Group Time (games, language):

Tasting Party

Prepare for a tasting party. Collect a wide variety of foods. For example, the children could experiment with bananas by dipping them in wheat germ, peanut butter, honey, raisins, etc. To extend this activity, charts can be prepared listing the children's favorite foods.

Cooking:

Fruit Tree Salad

On a plate place a lettuce leaf. On the center of the lettuce, place a pineapple slice. In the hole of the pineapple, place two peeled bananas. Drain 1 small can of fruit cocktail. Spoon the fruit over the bananas.

Multimedia:

The following resources can be found in educational catalogs:

1. Stewart, Georgiana Liccione. *Aerobics for Kids* [record]. Kimbo Educational Records.

2. Johnson, Laura. *Fun Activities for Toddlers* [record]. Kimbo Educational Records.

3. Caesar, Irving. "Songlets for Project Head," *Health-Cleanliness-Safety* [record]. Cleanliness Bureau.

4. *Children's Body Awareness and Movement Exercises* [record]. Stallman Records.

5. *Learning Basic Skills* [25-minute video]. Edu-vid.

6. *The Clean Machine* [video]. Marshfilm.

Books:

The following books can be used to complement the theme:

1. Kalman, Bobbie, & Hughes, Susan. (1986). *The Food We Eat*. New York: Crabtree Publishing Company.

2. Woodruff, Elvira. (1990). *Tubtime*. New York: Holiday House, Inc.

3. Adams, Pam. (1990). *Six in a Bath*. New York: Child's Play International.

4. Berry, Joy. (1987). *Teach Me About Bathtime*. Chicago: Children's Press.

5. Cobb, Vicki. (1989). *Keeping Clean*. New York: Harper Collins Children's Books.

6. McDonnell, Janet. (1990). *Good Health: A Visit from Droopy*. Mankato, MN: Child's World, Inc.

7. Edwards, Frank B., & Bianchi, John. (1990). *Mortimer Mooner Stopped Taking a Bath*. Buffalo, NY: Firefly Books.

8. Hutchins, Pat. (1991). *Tidy Titch*. New York: Greenwillow Books.

9. Moncure, Jane B. (1990). *Caring for My Body*. Mankato, MN: Child's World, Inc.

10. Rockwell, Harlow. (1992). *My Doctor*. New York: Macmillan.

11. Rogers, Alison. (1987). *Luke Has Asthma*. Burlington, VT: Waterfront Books.

12. Scott, Ann Herbert. (1992). *On Mother's Lap*. Boston: Houghton Mifflin.

13. Cowen-Fletcher, Jane. (1993). *Mama Zooms*. New York: Scholastic.

— T H E M E 37 —

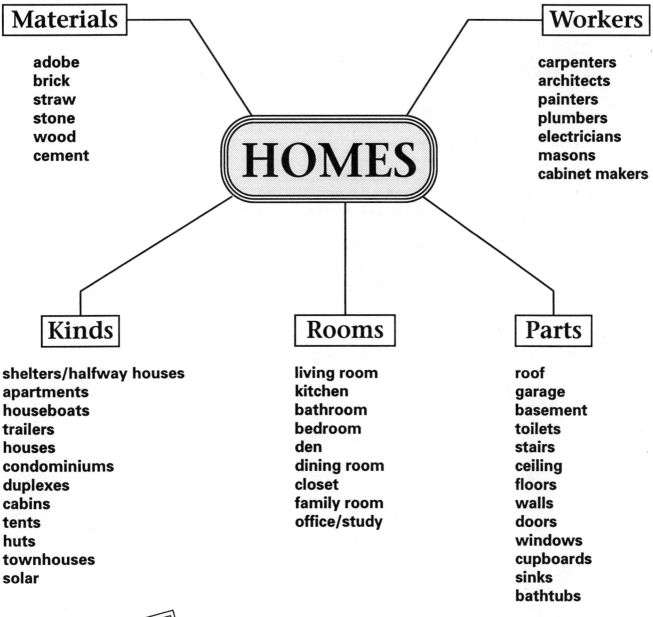

Materials

adobe
brick
straw
stone
wood
cement

Workers

carpenters
architects
painters
plumbers
electricians
masons
cabinet makers

HOMES

Kinds

shelters/halfway houses
apartments
houseboats
trailers
houses
condominiums
duplexes
cabins
tents
huts
townhouses
solar

Rooms

living room
kitchen
bathroom
bedroom
den
dining room
closet
family room
office/study

Parts

roof
garage
basement
toilets
stairs
ceiling
floors
walls
doors
windows
cupboards
sinks
bathtubs

Polaroid Education Program

Here's an exciting new way to turn instant photography into an effective teaching tool. Refer to the full-color insert for the activity entitled Photo Bingo.

Theme Goals:

Through participating in the experiences provided by this theme, the children may learn about:

1. Home builders.

2. Parts of a home.

3. Rooms in a home.

4. Kinds of homes.

5. Building materials.

Concepts for the Children to Learn:

1. A home is a place to live.

2. Apartments, condominiums, trailers, and houses are all kinds of homes.

3. Most homes have a kitchen, bedroom, bathroom, and living room.

4. Homes can be built from brick, stone, wood, or cement.

5. The ceiling, floor, roof, and windows are parts of a home.

6. Construction workers build houses.

7. Homes come in many sizes.

8. Homes can be decorated many ways.

Vocabulary:

1. **apartment**—a building including many homes.

2. **duplex**—a house divided into two separate homes.

3. **house**—a place to live.

4. **construction worker**—a person who builds.

5. **kitchen**—a room for cooking.

6. **bedroom**—a room for sleeping.

7. **architect**—a person who designs homes.

Bulletin Board

The purpose of this bulletin board is to develop classification skills. Draw an unfurnished model of a home on a large sheet of tagboard as illustrated. Include the basic rooms such as kitchen, bedroom, and living room. Draw and cut furnishings to add to the home. Laminate home and furnishings. The children can place the furnishings in the proper room by using "fun tack" or magnetic strips on the furnishings.

Parent Letter

Dear Parents,

Homes will be the focus of our next curricular theme. Since everyone's home is unique we will be discussing how homes differ. We will also be discussing activities we do in our home and the rooms in our homes.

At School

Some of our activities will include:

- constructing homes out of cardboard boxes and paper in the art area.
- acting out the story of *The Three Little Pigs* in the dramatic play area.
- building at the workbench.

A special activity will include making placemats, but we need your help. For our placemats we will need a few pictures of your family, home, or both. These will be glued to construction paper and laminated during our project. They will not be returned in their original form. Thank you!

This week we will also be taking a neighborhood tour to observe the various types of homes in the area. We will be taking our walk at 10:00 a.m. on Thursday. Please feel free to join us!

At Home

To develop observation skills, take your child on a walk around your neighborhood to look at the houses in your area. Talk about the different colors and sizes of dwellings.

Enjoy the time you spend with your child!

FIGURE 37 Playing house is an activity that builds interpersonal skills.

Music:

"This is the Way We Build Our House"
  (Sing to the tune of "Here We Go 'Round the Mulberry Bush")

  This is the way we build our house
  So early in the morning.

  Other suggestions:
  This is the way we paint the house.
  This is the way we wash the car.
  This is the way we rake the leaves.

Fingerplays:

MY HOUSE

  I'm going to build a little house
      (fingers make roof)
  With windows big and bright
      (stand with arms in air)
  Drifting out of sight.
  In winter when the snowflakes fall
      (hands flutter down)

Or when I hear a storm
    (hand cupped to ear)
I'll go sit in my little house
    (sit down)
Where I'll be snug and warm.
    (cross arms over chest)

WHERE SHOULD I LIVE?

Where should I live?
In a castle with towers and a moat?
    (make a point with arms over head)
Or on a river in a houseboat?
    (make wave like motions)
A winter igloo made of ice may be just the thing
    (pretend to pack snow)
But what would happen when it turned to spring?
    (pretend to think)
I like tall apartments and houses made of stone,
    (stretch up tall)
But I'd also like to live in a blue mobile home.
    (shorten up)
A cave or cabin in the woods would give me lots of space
    (stretch out wide)
But I guess my home is the best place!
    (point to self)

KNOCKING

Look at _____ knocking on our door.
   (knock)
Look at _____ knocking on our door.
   (knock)
Come on in out of the cold
   (shiver)
Into our nice, warm home.
   (rub hands together to be warm)

MY CHORES

In my home, I wash the dishes
   (pretend to wash)
Vacuum the floor
   (push vacuum)
And dust the furniture.
   (dust)
Outside my home, I rake the leaves
   (rake)
Plant the flowers
   (plant)
And play hard all day.
   (wipe sweat from forehead)
When the day is over
I eat my supper,
   (eat)
Read a story
   (read)
And go to sleep.
   (put head on hands)

Science:

Building Materials

Building materials with magnifying glasses should be placed in the science area. The children may observe and examine materials. Included may be wood, brick, canvas, tar paper, shingles, etc.

Dramatic Play:

1. **Tent Living**

A small tent can be set up indoors or outdoors depending upon weather and space. Accessories such as sleeping bags, flashlights, rope, cooking utensils, and backpacks should also be provided if available.

2. **Cardboard Houses**

Collect large cardboard boxes. Place outdoors or in an open classroom area. The children may build their own homes. If desired, tempera paint can be used for painting the homes. Wallpaper may also be provided.

3. **Cleaning House**

Housecleaning tools such as a vacuum cleaner, dusting cloth, sponges, mops, and brooms can be placed in the dramatic play area. During the self-selected play periods the children may choose to participate in cleaning.

Arts and Crafts:

1. **Shape Homes**

An assortment of construction paper shapes such as squares, triangles, rectangles, and circles should be placed on a table in the art area. Glue and large pieces of paper should also be provided.

2. **Tile Painting**

Ask building companies to donate cracked, chipped, or discontinued tiles. The children can paint tiles.

3. **Homes I Like**

The children can cut pictures of homes, rooms, appliances, and furniture from magazines. They can glue these pieces on large construction paper pieces. The construction paper can be stapled. A cover can also be added and labeled, "Things in My Home."

4. **Household Tracings**

Several household items such as a spatula, wooden spoon, pizza cutter, or cookie cutter can be placed on the art table. Also include paper, scissors, and crayons. These items can be traced. Some of the older children may color and cut their tracings.

Sensory:

1. Identifying Sounds

Record several sounds found in the home such as a vacuum cleaner, television, water running, and a toilet flushing. Encourage children to name sounds. For older children, this could also be played as a lotto game. Make cards containing pictures of sounds, vary pictures from card to card. When a sound is heard, cover the corresponding picture with a chip.

2. Sand Castles

Add wet sand to the sensory table. Provide forms to create buildings, homes, etc. Examples may include empty cans, milk cartons, plastic containers, etc.

Large Muscle:

Pounding Nails

Collect building materials such as soft pine scraps and styrofoam for the workbench. Adult supervision is always required with this activity.

Field Trips/Resource People:

1. Neighborhood Walk

Walk around the neighborhood. Observe the construction workers' actions and tools.

2. Construction Site

If available visit a local construction sight. Discuss the role of the construction worker.

3. Resource People

The following resource people could be invited to the classroom:

- builder
- architect
- plumber
- painter
- electrician

Math:

My House

Construct a "My House" book for each child. On the pages write things like

"My home has _____ steps."
My home is the color _____.
My home has _____ windows.
There are _____ doors in my home.
My home has _____ keyholes.

Other ideas could include the number of beds, people, pets, etc. Send this home with the child to complete with parents.

Social Studies:

Room Match

Collect several boxes. On one box print kitchen; on another print bathroom; on another print living room; and on another print bedroom. Then cut objects related to each of these rooms from catalogs. The children may sort objects by placing them in the appropriate boxes. To illustrate, dishes, silverware, and a coffee pot would be placed in the box labeled kitchen.

Group Time (games, language):

Construct a "My home is special because…" chart. Encourage the children to name a special thing about their homes. Display the chart at the children's eye level in the classroom for the week.

Cooking:

Individual Pizza

English muffins
pizza sauce
grated mozzarella cheese

Spread a tablespoon of sauce on each muffin half. Sprinkle the top with grated cheese. Bake in a preheated oven at 375 degrees until cheese melts.

Multimedia:

The following resources can be found in educational catalogs:

1. Seeger, Pete. *American Folk Songs for Children* [record]. Folkway Records.

2. Rogers, Fred. *A Place of Our Own* [record]. Dickwick International, Inc.

3. Jenkins, Ella. *My Street Begins at My House* [record].

4. *Fisher-Price Classics* [Apple/IBM software, PK–1]. Gametek.

5. *Early Learning* [IBM/Mac/Apple software, PK–2]. Compu-Tech.

6. *Early Games* [Apple/IBM software, PK–1]. Queue.

Books:

The following books can be used to complement the theme:

1. North, Carol. (1985). *The House Book*. Racine, WI: Western Publishing Company, Inc.

2. Durham, Robert. (1987). *Around the House*. Chicago: Children's Press.

3. Dorros, Arthur. (1992). *This Is My House*. New York: Scholastic, Inc.

4. Brown, Richard (Illus.). (1989). *One Hundred Words About My House*. San Diego: Harcourt Brace Jovanovich.

5. Emberly, Rebecca. (1990). *My House, Mi Casa: A Book in Two Languages*. New York: Little Brown and Co.

6. Gibbons, Gail. (1990). *How a House Is Built*. New York: Holiday House, Inc.

7. Ackerman, Karen. (1992). *This Old House*. New York: Macmillan Children's Book Group.

8. Hoberman, Mary A. (1982). *A House Is a House for Me*. New York: Puffin Books.

9. Rockwell, Anne. (1991). *In Our House*. New York: Harper Collins Children's Books.

10. Ringgold, Faith. (1991). *Tar Beach*. New York: Crown Publishers.

11. Wagon, Crescent Dragon. (1990). *Home Place*. New York: Macmillan.

12. Rosen, Michael J. (Ed.). (1992). *Home: A Collaboration*. New York: Harper Collins.

13. Barton, Byron. (1990). *Building a House*. New York: Morrow.

14. Brown, Margaret Wise. (1989). *Big Red Barn*. New York: Harper & Row.

15. Bowden, Jane. (1992). *Where Does Our Garbage Go?* New York: Bantam Doubleday Dell Publishing.

16. Kuklin, Susan. (1992). *How My Family Lives in America*. New York: Bradbury Press.

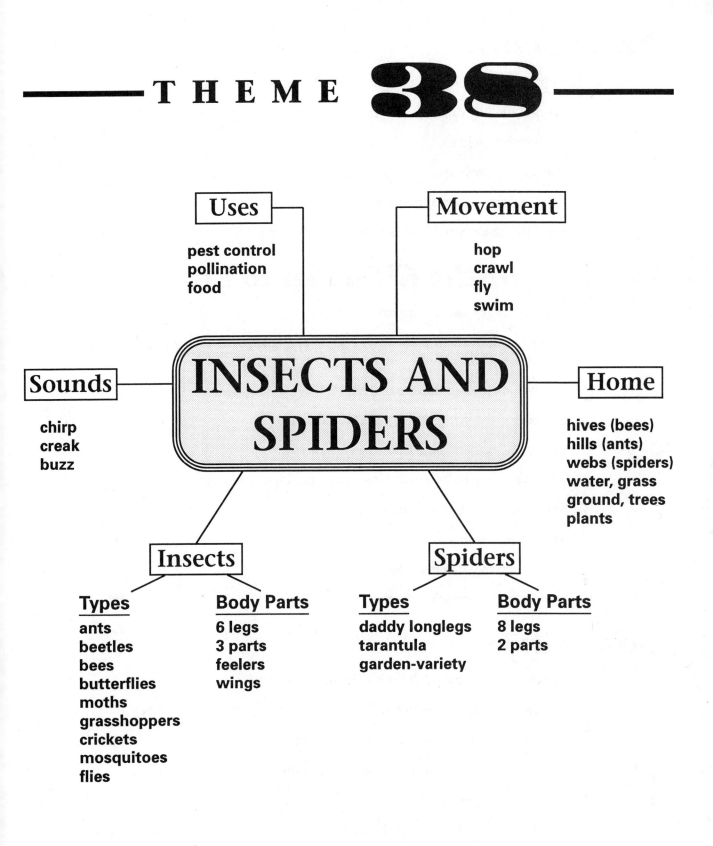

Uses

pest control
pollination
food

Movement

hop
crawl
fly
swim

Sounds

chirp
creak
buzz

INSECTS AND SPIDERS

Home

hives (bees)
hills (ants)
webs (spiders)
water, grass
ground, trees
plants

Insects

Types
ants
beetles
bees
butterflies
moths
grasshoppers
crickets
mosquitoes
flies

Body Parts
6 legs
3 parts
feelers
wings

Spiders

Types
daddy longlegs
tarantula
garden-variety

Body Parts
8 legs
2 parts

Polaroid Education Program

Here's an exciting new way to turn instant photography into an effective teaching tool. Refer to the full-color insert for the activity entitled Concentration Game.

Theme Goals:

Through participating in the experiences provided by this theme, the children may learn:

1. Ways to identify different insects and spiders.

2. Ways insects help us.

3. Ways spiders help us.

4. Places where spiders and insects live.

5. Ways that spiders and insects move from place to place.

Concepts for the Children to Learn:

1. There are many kinds of insects.

2. Insects are different in many ways: size, shape, color, eyes, mouths, and number of wings.

3. Insects have six legs (three pairs) and, if winged, four wings.

4. Spiders have eight legs (four pairs) and no wings.

5. Insects and spiders come from eggs.

6. Insects can help us by making honey and pollinating fruits and flowers.

7. Spiders can help us by eating insect pests.

8. Most spiders spin a web.

9. Some insects fly, others walk.

10. Spiders spin a web to catch other insects to eat.

Vocabulary:

1. **insect**—small animal with three pairs of jointed legs.

2. **spider**—small animal with four pairs of legs.

3. **caterpillar**—the wormlike larvae of a butterfly or moth.

4. **pollinate**—the way insects help flowers to grow.

5. **spiderling**—a baby spider.

6. **antennae**—feelers on an insect that stick out from the head.

7. **pupa**—intermediate stage of an insect; chrysalis.

8. **moth**—night-flying insect with four wings related to the butterfly.

9. **wasp**—winged insect with a poisonous sting.

10. **cricket**—small leaping insect known for its chirping.

Bulletin Board

The purpose of this bulletin board is to develop visual discrimination skills. Construct several butterflies, each of a different shape, out of tagboard. Trace on black construction paper for shadows. Laminate. Staple shadow butterflies to bulletin board. Punch holes in colored butterflies for children to hang on the push pin of the corresponding shadow butterfly.

Parent Letter

Dear Parents,

We are continuing our study of animals. We are moving to a new category—insects and spiders. The children will become aware of the difference between insects and spiders and the ways that those creatures are helpful. Do you know the difference between insects and spiders? Most insects have three body parts and six legs. Spiders have two body parts and eight legs.

At School

Some of the learning experiences planned include:

- singing and acting out the song, "One Elephant Went Out to Play." It's about an elephant that plays on a spider web!
- listening to a flannel board version of the story, *The Very Hungry Caterpillar* by Eric Carle.
- watching and observing an ant farm set up in the science area.
- creating spiders and insects out of a variety of materials in the art area.

At Home

There are many ways to bring this unit into your home. Take a walk with your child and see how many spiders and insects you can find. Avoid touching unknown types of insects or spiders with your fingers. Instead, use a clear jar with a lid to observe the creature close up. Release the insect or spider after the observation.

We will be having a snack this week called ants on a log. Let your child make some for you! Spread peanut butter on pieces of celery. Top with raisins. Enjoy!

Enjoy your child!

FIGURE 38 Children enjoy observing bugs.

Music:

1. **"The Eensie Weensie Spider"**
   (traditional)

   The eensie weensie spider crawled up the water spout.
   (walk fingers of one hand up other hand)
   Down came the rain and washed the spider out.
   (lower hands to make rain, wash out spider by placing hands together in front and extending out to either side)
   Out came the sun and dried up all the rain
   (form sun with arms in circle over head)
   And the eensie weensie spider went up the spout again.
   (walk fingers up other arm)

2. **"The Elephant Song"**

   One elephant went out to play
   On a spider's web one day.
   He had such enormous fun,
   That he called for another elephant to come.

   Elephant! Elephant! Come out to play!
   Elephant! Elephant! Come out to play!

   Two elephants…

3. **"The Insects and Spiders"**
   (Sing to the tune of "The Wheels on the Bus")

   The bugs in the air fly up and down,
   up and down, up and down.
   The bugs in the air fly up and down all through the day.

   The spiders on the bush spin a web.
   The crickets in the field hop up and down.
   The bees in their hive go buzz, buzz, buzz.

Fingerplays:

ANTS

Once I saw an ant hill, with no ants about.
So I said "Little ants, won't you please come out?"
Then as if they heard my call, one, two, three, four, five came out.
And that was all!

BUMBLEBEE

Brightly colored bumblebee
Looking for some honey.
Flap your wings and fly away
While it still is sunny.

THE CATERPILLAR

A caterpillar crawled to the top of a tree.
(index finger of left hand moves up right arm)
"I think I'll take a nap," said he.
So under a leaf, he began to creep
(wrap right hand over left fist)
To spin his chrysalis and he fell asleep.

All winter long he slept in his chrysalis bed,
   (keep right hand over left fist)
Till spring came along one day, and said,
"Wake up, wake up little sleepy head."
   (shake left fist with right hand).
"Wake up, it's time to get out of bed!"
So, he opened his eyes that sun shiny day
   (shake fingers and look into hand)
Lo—he was a butterfly and flew away!
   (move hand into flying motion)

LITTLE MISS MUFFET

Little Miss Muffet
Sat on a tuffet
Eating her curds and whey.
Along came a spider
And sat down beside her
And frightened Miss Muffet away!

Spiders can be prepared in the art area.

Science:

1. Observe an ant farm.
   The children can watch the ants dig tunnels, build roads and tunnels, build roads and rooms, eat and store food, etc. (Ant farms are available in some commercial play catalogs.)

2. Go outside and observe anthills in the playground area.

3. Observe deceased flies and ants under a microscope.

4. Observe insects and spiders in a caged bug keeper or plastic jars with holes in the lids.

5. Listen to a cricket during quiet time.

6. Capture a caterpillar and watch it spin a chrysalis and turn into a butterfly.

Dramatic Play:

1. **Scientist**

   The children can dress up in white lab coats and observe spiders and insects with magnifying glasses.

2. **Spider Web**

   Tie together a big piece of rope to resemble a spider web. Have children pretend they are spiders playing on their web.

3. **Spider Sac**

   Tape together a 10-foot by 25-foot piece of plastic on the sides. Blow it up with a fan to make a big bubble. Make a slit in the plastic for the entrance. The children can pretend to be baby spiders coming out of the spider sac when they are hatching.

4. The children can act out "Little Miss Muffet."

Arts and Crafts:

1. Cut easel paper in the shape of a butterfly.

2. Fingerpaint creepy crawly pictures.

3. Make insects and spiders out of clay. Use toothpicks, straws, and pipe cleaner segments for the appendages.

4. Make insects and spiders with thumbprints. Children can draw crayon legs to make prints look like insects and spiders.

5. Egg carton caterpillars. Cut egg cartons in half, lengthwise. Each child paints a carton half. When dry, children can make a face on the end of the carton and insert pipe cleaners or straws for feelers.

6. Have children make spiders from black construction paper—one large black circle for a body and eight strips for legs. Children can paste on two yellow circles for eyes. Hang by a string around the room.

7. Make ladybug shapes out of red and orange construction paper. Have children sponge paint dots and legs on the bugs.

8. Make butterfly templates.

9. Use butterfly templates and place crayon shavings between two pieces of waxed paper and iron. Put a butterfly template over the

waxed paper and glue it on. A pretty butterfly will be the final product!

10. Tissue paper butterflies. Have children lightly paint white tissue paper or use colored tissue paper. Fasten a pipe cleaner around the middle. Add circles on the ends for antennaes.

11. Balloon bugs. Blow up several long balloons. Cover them with strips of paper dipped in wallpaper paste. Put on three to four layers of this sticky paper. Let dry for two to three days. Then paint your own giant bug!

12. Have insect and spider stencils set out for the children to draw and trace.

Sensory:

Add soil and plastic insects to the sensory table.

Large Muscle:

Have children pretend to walk as different insects when in transition from one activity to another.

Field Trips/Resource People:

1. Go on a walk to a nearby park to find bugs. Look under rocks, in cracks, in sidewalks, in bushes, etc.

2. Have someone who has a butterfly collection come in.

3. Visit a pet store. Ask them to show you what kind of insects they feed to the animals in the store. Do they sell any insects?

4. Invite a zoologist to come in and talk about insects and how important they are.

5. Invite an individual who raises bees to talk to the children. Ask him to bring in a honeycomb for the children to taste.

Math:

1. **Butterfly Match**

   Make several triangles of different colors. On one triangle put the numbers 1 to 10; on the other make dots to correspond to the numbers 1 to 10. Have the children match the dots to the numbers and clip them together with a clothespin to form a butterfly.

2. **Ladybug Houses**

   Paint several 1/2-pint milk cartons red. Write the numerals 1 to 10 on each. Make 50 small ladybugs dotting 5 sets of 1 to 10. Have children put ladybugs in their correct houses by matching dots to numerals.

3. **Numeral Caterpillar**

   Make a caterpillar with 10 body segments and a head. Have the children put the numbers in order to complete the caterpillar's body.

4. Sing the song, "The Ants Go Marching One by One," and have the children act out the song using their fingers as numbers.

5. Make an insect and spider lotto or concentration game with stickers for children to play.

Social Studies:

1. Take the children on an insect hunt near your school. When children are finished, have everyone show the rest of the class what they found. Talk about where they found the insects (on a tree, under a log, etc.).

2. Have children make homes for all the insects they found. They can put dirt, grass, twigs, and small rocks in plastic jars and cans.

3. Discuss what it is like to be a member of a family. Ask the children if each member of their family has a certain job. Then focus on ant colonies or families. Ants live together

much like people do, except that ants live in a larger community. Each ant has a certain task within the community. Some of the jobs are:

- nurse: to look after the young
- soldier: defend colony and attack the enemies
- others: search for food; enlarge and clean the nest (house)

Group Time (games, language):

1. **Matching Insects**

   Divide children into two groups. Hand out pictures of different spiders and insects, one to each group that matches one in the other group. Point to a child from one group and have that child act out the insect they have in some way (movement or noises). The child that has the same insect from the other group must go and meet the child in the middle and act out the insect also.

2. Have many pictures of insects and spiders on display. Talk about a different insect or spider every day. Include where it lives, how it walks, what it might eat, etc.

Cooking:

1. **Honey Bees**

   1/2 cup peanut butter
   1 tablespoon honey
   1/3 cup nonfat dry milk
   2 tablespoons toasted wheat germ
   unsweetened cocoa powder
   sliced almonds

   In a mixing bowl, mix peanut butter and honey. Stir in dry milk and wheat germ until well mixed. Lay waxed paper on a baking sheet. Using 1 tablespoon at a time, shape peanut butter mixture into ovals to look like bees. Put on baking sheet. Dip a toothpick in cocoa powder and press lightly across the top of the bees to make stripes. Stick on almonds for wings. Chill for 30 minutes.

   Source: *Better Homes and Gardens Kids Snacks*. (1979). Iowa: Meredith Corporation.

2. **Ants on a Log** (traditional)

   Cut celery pieces into 3-inch strips. Fill the cavity of the celery stick with peanut butter. Garnish with raisins. (As with all recipes calling for celery, this might be more appropriate for older children.)

Multimedia:

The following resources can be found in educational catalogs:

1. Seeger, Pete. *Birds, Beasts, Bugs, and Little Fishies* [record].

2. Norfolk, Bobby. *Why Mosquitoes Buzz in People's Ears* [record].

3. *Bugs Don't Bug Us* [35-minute video]. Bo Peep Productions.

Books:

The following books can be used to complement the theme:

1. Carle, Eric. (1985). *The Very Busy Spider*. New York: Philomel Books.

2. Heller, Ruth. (1992). *How to Hide a Butterfly and Other Insects*. New York: Putnam.

3. Arvetis, Chris. (1987). *What Is a Butterfly?* Chicago: Children's Press.

4. de Bourgoing, Pascale. (1991). *Ladybug and Other Insects*. New York: Scholastic, Inc.

5. Fowler, Allen. (1990). *It's a Good Thing There Are Insects*. Chicago: Children's Press.

6. Kindersley, Dorling. (1992). *Insects and Crawly Creatures*. New York: Macmillan Children's Book Group.

7. Morris, Dean. (1990). *Insects That Live in Families*. Madison, NJ: Raintree Steck—Vaughn Publishers.

8. National Wildlife Federation Staff. (1991). *Incredible Insects*. Vienna, VA: Author.

9. Aylesworth, Jim. (1992). *Old Black Fly*. New York: Henry Holt and Co.

10. Carle, Eric. (1990). *The Very Quiet Cricket*. New York: Putnam Publishing Group.

11. Inkpen, Mick. (1992). *Billy's Beetle*. San Diego: Harcourt Brace Jovanovich.

12. Pienkowski, Jan. (1990). *Oh My a Fly*. Los Angeles: Price Stern Sloan, Inc.

13. Ross, Katharine. (1991). *Twinkle, Twinkle, Little Bug: A Sesame Street Book*. New York: Random House for Young Readers.

14. McDonald, Suse. (1991). *Space Spinners*. New York: Dial Books for Young Readers.

15. Patent, Dorothy H. (1989). *Looking at Ants*. New York: Holiday House, Inc.

16. Moses, Amy. (1992). *If I Were an Ant*. Chicago: Children's Press.

17. Butterfield, Moira. (1992). *Butterfly*. New York: Simon and Schuster Trade.

18. Gibbons, Gail. (1989). *Monarch Butterfly*. New York: Holiday House, Inc.

19. Van Allsburg, Chris. (1988). *Two Bad Ants*. Hoston: Houghton Mifflin.

20. Lunn, Carolyn. (1989). *Spiders & Webs*. Chicago: Children's Press.

21. Kimmel, Eric. (1992). *Anansi Goes Fishing*. New York: Doubleday.

22. Rodanas, Kristina. (1992). *Dragonfly's Tale*. New York: Clarion.

23. Hopkins, Lee Bennett (Ed.). (1992). *Flit, Flutter, Fly: Poems About Bugs and Other Crawly Creatures*. New York: Doubleday.

24. Henwood, Chris. (1988). *Earthworms*. New York: Watts.

25. Giganti, Paul, Jr. (1988). *How Many Snails?* New York: Greenwillow.

26. Parker, Nancy Winslow, & Wright, Joan Richards. (1987). *Bugs*. New York: Mulberry Books.

27. Ryder, Joanne. (1989). *Where Butterflies Grow*. New York: Lodestar.

28. Rounds, Glen. (1990). *I Know an Old Woman Who Swallowed a Fly*. New York: Holiday House.

29. Selsam, Millicent E. (1988). *Backyard Insects*. New York: Scholastic.

30. Thomson, Ruth. (1991). *Creepy Crawlies*. New York: Macmillan.

31. Fleming, Denise. (1993). *In the Tall, Tall Grass*. New York: Holt.

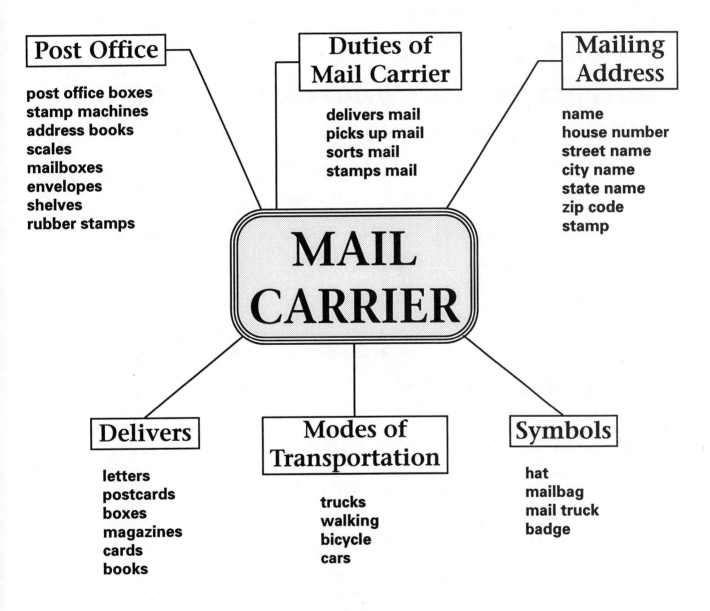

Post Office

post office boxes
stamp machines
address books
scales
mailboxes
envelopes
shelves
rubber stamps

Duties of Mail Carrier

delivers mail
picks up mail
sorts mail
stamps mail

Mailing Address

name
house number
street name
city name
state name
zip code
stamp

MAIL CARRIER

Delivers

letters
postcards
boxes
magazines
cards
books

Modes of Transportation

trucks
walking
bicycle
cars

Symbols

hat
mailbag
mail truck
badge

Here's an exciting new way to turn instant photography into an effective teaching tool. Refer to the full-color insert for the activity entitled People and Uniforms.

Theme Goals:

Through participating in the experiences provided by this theme, the children may learn:

1. Duties of a mail carrier.

2. Symbols identifying a mail carrier.

3. Objects found in a post office.

4. Parts of a mailing address.

5. Types of postal deliveries.

Concepts for the Children to Learn:

1. A man or woman who delivers mail is a mail carrier.

2. The mail carrier usually wears a badge and a hat.

3. A mail carrier sometimes drives a truck or jeep.

4. Mail carriers deliver cards, letters, postcards, boxes, books, and magazines.

5. Stamps are used for mailing.

6. Names, house numbers, street names, city names, state names, and zip codes are on mailing labels.

7. A post office has stamp machines, address books, mailboxes, and envelopes.

8. Scales are used to weigh mail.

Vocabulary:

1. **post office**—place where mail is sorted.

2. **letter**—a printed message.

3. **zip code**—the last numbers on a mailing address.

4. **address**—directions for the mail carrier.

5. **mail**—letters, cards, postcards, and packages.

6. **envelope**—a cover for a letter.

7. **stamp**—a sticker put on mail.

8. **mail carrier**—person who delivers mail.

9. **mail bag**—bag that holds letters and postcards.

Bulletin Board

The purpose of this bulletin board is to reinforce the mathematical skill of matching a set to its written numeral. Construct mailboxes out of tagboard. Each mailbox should include a flag, which is red-colored and contains a numeral. The number will depend upon the maturity of the children. A set of dots, corresponding to the numeral on the flag, should be placed on the mailbox. Hang the mailboxes on the bulletin board. Next, construct letters by using small cards with sets of dots on them. The children can match the dots on the cards with the dots and numerals on the mailboxes. If desired, magnet pieces can be attached to both the mailboxes and the cards.

Parent Letter

Dear Parents,

We have been busy discussing the roles of a variety of community helpers these past weeks. Next we will focus the curriculum on the role of the mail carrier. The children will be learning about letters, stamps, and addresses, and will be able to identify objects found in a post office. They will also become aware of how mail is delivered and what needs to be on a letter or package before it is delivered.

At School

Some of the many learning activities scheduled include:

- listening to the story, *Adventures of a Letter*, by Warren G. Schloat.
- playing in a post office set up in the classroom.
- making mailboxes and postcards.
- weighing letters and packages.
- delivering mail to our friends in our room.

At Home

Let your children help or watch you open the mail. Give your child the "junk mail" to play with. Show your child where your address is on your house and mailbox. You may also enjoy having your children dictate a letter to a grandparent, favorite aunt, or cousin. As you write the letter, show your child the printed alphabet letters to develop an awareness of alphabet letters. After you finish the letter, address an envelope. Let your child lick the stamp and show the proper placement. Then it's off to the post office!

Enjoy your child!

FIGURE 39 The mail used to be delivered by pony.

Music:

1. **"Mailing Letters"**
(Sing to the tune of "The Mulberry Bush")

This is the way we mail a letter,
Mail a letter, mail a letter.
This is the way we mail a letter,
So early in the morning.

2. **"Let's Pretend"**
(Sing to the tune of "Here We Are Together"
and "Did You Ever See a Lassie")

Let's pretend that we are mail carriers,
Are mail carriers, are mail carriers.
Let's pretend that we are mail carriers,
We'll have so much fun.
We'll carry the letters and put them in boxes.
Let's pretend that we are mail carriers,
We'll have so much fun.

Fingerplays:

LITTLE MAIL CARRIER

I am a little mail carrier
(point to self)
Who can do nothing better.
I walk.
(walk in place)
I run.
(run in place)
I hop to your house.
(hop in place)
To deliver your letter.

FIVE LITTLE LETTERS

Five little letters lying on a tray.
(extend fingers of right hand)
Mommy came and took the first one away.
(bend down thumb)
Daddy said, "This one's for me!"
I counted them twice, now there are three.
(bend down pointer finger)
Brother Bill asked, "Did I get any mail?"
He found one and cried, "A letter from Gail."
(bend down middle finger)
My sister Jane took the next to the last
And ran upstairs to open it fast.
(bend down ring finger)
As I can't read, I am not able to see,
Whom the last one is for, but I hope it's for me!
(wiggle last finger, clap hands)

THE MAIL CARRIER

I come from the post office
(walk from post office)
My mail sack on my back.
(pretend to carry sack on back)
I go to all the houses
(pretend to go up to a house)
Leaving letters from my pack.
(pretend to drop letters into mailbox)
One, two, three, four
(hold up fingers as you count)
What are these letters for?
(pretend to hold letters as you count)
One for John. One for Lou.
(pretend to hand out letters)
One for Tom and one for you!
(pretend to hand out letters to others)

LETTER TO GRANDMA

Lick them, stamp them
    (make licking and stamping motions)
Put them in a box.
    (extend arms outward)
Hope that Grandma
Loves them alot!
    (hug self)

Dramatic Play:

1. **Post Office**

   Develop the dramatic play area into a post office. Provide a mailbox, mail carrier hats, mailbag, stamps, cash register, rubber date stamps, and a letter scale. The children may enjoy acting out the role of a mail carrier or a post office worker.

2. **Letters**

   Provide a variety of writing materials. Include different colors of paper, writing tools, and envelopes. The children can dictate a letter to a friend or a family member. After all interested children have completed dictation, apply stamps and walk to the nearest mailbox or post office. (Contact a local printer, office supply store, or card shop and ask for discontinued samples or misprinted envelopes.)

Science:

1. **Dress the Mail Carrier**

   Place flannel board pieces representing seasonal clothing for a mail carrier. Let the children select the appropriate clothing for the weather. This may be an interesting activity to introduce daily during group time.

2. **Weighing Mail**

   A variety of letters, boxes, stamps, and a scale can be placed in the science area. The children can weigh letters and packages. This activity can be extended by placing materials in the boxes and weighing them, noting the difference.

3. **How Does the Mail Feel?**

   Place different types of envelopes and stationery on the sensory table for the children to explore. Include airmail paper, onionskin, bond paper, typing paper, and different kinds of stationery. Also, provide a magnifying glass.

Field Trips/Resource People:

1. **Post Office**

   Plan a field trip to the local post office. Observe the mailboxes, stamp machines, address books, scales, and rubber stamps with the children. Mail a postcard back to the center. Count the number of days it takes to arrive.

2. **Mail Carrier**

   Invite the mail carrier who delivers mail or the local postmaster to your center or school to visit in the classroom. Ask the mail carrier to share his mailbag, hat, etc., with the children.

Social Studies:

Mailboxes

   Plan a walk around the neighborhood. Observe the different types of mailboxes and addresses.

Math:

The number of items and numerals used in these activities needs to be adjusted to reflect the developmental appropriateness of the children.

1. **Dominoes**

   Create dominoes out of envelopes. Have the children match the numbers and dots.

2. **How Many Stamps?**

   Write an individual numeral on an envelope. Make or collect many stamps. The children can place the correct number of stamps in the

378

envelope with the corresponding numeral. A variation of this activity is to make mailboxes from shoeboxes. Again, write a numeral on each box. Make or collect many different envelopes. The children can put the correct number of letters in the corresponding mailboxes.

3. **Package Seriation**

Prepare several packages and letters of different sizes. The children can place the letters and packages in order from largest to smallest or smallest to largest.

Arts and Crafts:

1. **Easel Ideas**

Cut easel paper in the shape of envelopes, letters, stamps, or mailbags.

2. **Postcards**

Have children make postcards at school to send to family and friends. Provide index cards. Let the children design the postcards.

3. **Mailboxes**

Make mailboxes out of old shoeboxes. Each child can decorate his own box. Names can be added by the child or teacher. Include a home address for older children.

4. **Mail Truck**

Construct a mail truck out of a large cardboard box. Provide paint for the children to decorate it. When dried, place chairs and, if available, a steering wheel inside for the children to drive.

5. **Stamps**

Collect assorted stamps or stickers. Cancelled stamps can be reglued. The children can make a stamp collage.

Group Time (games, language):

Thank You

Write a thank-you note to the postmaster or mail carrier after visiting.

Cooking:

Zip Code Special

1 1/2 cups nonfat dry milk
2 cups fresh or frozen berries
1 teaspoon vanilla
1 cup water
1 tray ice cubes

Blend all ingredients in a blender. Serve and enjoy.

Books:

The following books can be used to complement the theme:

1. Matthews, Morgan. (1990). *What's It Like to Be a Postal Worker?* Mahwah, NJ: Troll Associates.

2. Ziegler, Sandra. (1989). *A Visit to the Post Office*. Chicago: Children's Press.

3. Hedderwick, Mairi. (1988). *Kathie Morag Delivers the Mail*. New York: Little, Brown and Co.

4. Henri, Adrian. (1990). *The Postman's Palace*. New York: Macmillan Children's Book Group.

5. Skurzynski, Gloria. (1992). *Here Comes the Mail*. New York: Macmillan Children's Book Group.

6. Casely, Judith. (1991). *Dear Annie*. New York: Greenwillow Books.

7. Johnson, Jean. (1987). *Postal Workers: A to Z*. New York: Walker & Co.

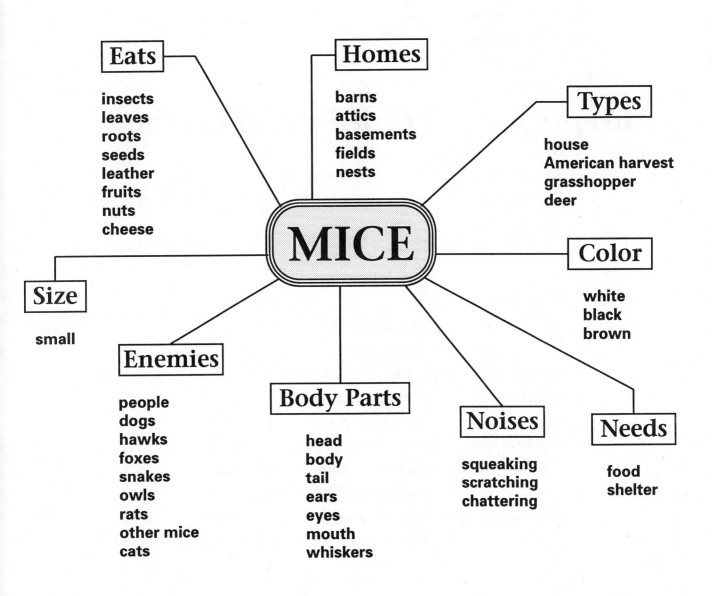

Eats
insects
leaves
roots
seeds
leather
fruits
nuts
cheese

Homes
barns
attics
basements
fields
nests

Types
house
American harvest
grasshopper
deer

MICE

Color
white
black
brown

Size
small

Enemies
people
dogs
hawks
foxes
snakes
owls
rats
other mice
cats

Body Parts
head
body
tail
ears
eyes
mouth
whiskers

Noises
squeaking
scratching
chattering

Needs
food
shelter

Polaroid
Education
Program

Here's an exciting new way to turn instant photography into an effective teaching tool. Refer to the full-color insert for the activity entitled Photo Face.

Theme Goals:

Through participating in the experiences provided by this theme, the children may learn:

1. Body parts of mice.
2. Size of mice.
3. Care of mice.
4. Color of mice.
5. Sounds made by mice.
6. Foods mice eat.
7. Homes mice make.
8. Enemies of mice.
9. Use of mice.

Concepts for the Children to Learn:

1. A mouse is a small animal.
2. Mice is the word to use when you refer to more than one mouse.
3. There are four main types of mice: house, American harvest, grasshopper, and deer.
4. The body of a mouse is 2 1/2 to 3 1/2 inches long. The tail is almost as long as the body.
5. The body of a mouse is covered with fur.
6. Mice may have white-, brown- or black-colored fur.
7. Mice need water, food, and shelter to live.
8. Mice eat plants, insects, leaves, roots, seeds, leather, fruits, and nuts.
9. Barns, attics, basements, fields, and nests are homes for mice.
10. Mice live where they can find food and shelter.
11. Mice have good hearing but poor sight.
12. Mice have strong, sharp front teeth that keep growing.
13. Mice have a head, body, tail, ears, eyes, mouth, and whiskers.
14. A house mouse has a brown back and white belly.
15. People can sometimes hear mice squeak, scratch, and chatter.
16. House mice are good climbers. People sometimes hear them running inside the walls of their homes.
17. Mice are sometimes used for pets and for health care discoveries.
18. People, cats, dogs, hawks, foxes, snakes, owls, rats, and other mice can be enemies of mice.

Vocabulary:

1. **mouse**—a small furry animal that has a head, ears, eyes, a mouth, whiskers, four legs, body, and tail.
2. **squeaking**—a clear, sharp sound made by a mouse.
3. **scratching**—a noise a mouse makes by rubbing his nails against a surface.

Bulletin Board

The purpose of this bulletin board is to promote the identification of written numerals as well as matching a set to a written numeral. Construct cheese and mice shapes out of construction paper or tagboard. Draw a set of dots on each piece of cheese. The number of dots used should correspond to the developmental level of the children. Print a corresponding numeral on each mouse. Staple the cheese pieces to the bulletin board along the side edges and the bottom, creating a pocket. The children should be encouraged to match the written numeral of each mouse to the corresponding set of dots on the cheese pieces and place the mice in the pockets.

Parent Letter

Dear Parents:

Squeak! Squeak! Squeak! We will be enjoying a new theme that will provide us with discoveries about small animals called mice. The children will be learning about types and colors of mice, care of mice, and enemies of mice.

At School

Learning experiences planned for this unit include:

- Visiting the pet store to observe mice.
- Pretending to be mice in the dramatic play area.
- Listening to the stories titled, *Mouse Paint* and *Mouse Count*, by Lois Ehlert.

At Home

Go to the library and check out some children's books about mice. Some titles to look for include:

- *If You Give a Mouse a Cookie* by Laura Numeroff
- *Mouse Poems* by John Foster

Have a nice week!

FIGURE 40 Can you squeak like a mouse?

Music:

1. **"Ten Little Mice"**
(Sing to the tune of "Ten Little Indians.")

    One little, two little, three little mice.
    Four little, five little, six little mice.
    Seven little, eight little, nine little mice.

2. **"Two Little Brown Mice"**
(Sing to the tune of "Two Little Blackbirds" or "Baa Baa Black Sheep.")

    Two little brown mice,
    Scampering through the hall.
    One named Sarah.
    One named Paul.

    Run away Sarah.
    Run away Paul.
    Come back, Sarah.
    Come back, Paul.

    Two little brown mice,
    Scampering through the hall.
    One named Sarah.
    One named Paul.

3. **"Find the Mouse"**
(Sing to the tune of "The Muffin Man.")

    Oh, can you find the little mouse.
    The little mouse, the little mouse.
    Can you find the little mouse,
    He's somewhere in the house.

4. **"One Little Mouse"**
(Sing to the tune of "Six Little Ducks.")

    One little brown and whiskery mouse
    Lived in a hole in a cozy house.
    When the cat came along to
    Take a little peek,
    The mouse ran away with a "Squeak, squeak, squeak."
    "Squeak, squeak, squeak."
    "Squeak, squeak, squeak."
    "The mouse ran away with a "Squeak, squeak, squeak."

5. **"Three Little Brown Mice"**
(Sing to the tune of "Three Blind Mice.")

    Three brown mice, three brown mice.
    See how they run. See how they run.
    They were chased through the house by the big black cat.
    Lucky for them, she was lazy and fat.
    Did you ever see such a sight as that?
    Three brown mice, three brown mice.

Fingerplays:

WHERE ARE THE BABY MICE?

Where are the baby mice?
(hide fists behind back)
Squeak, squeak, squeak!
I cannot see them.
Peek, peek, peek.
(show fist)
Here they come out of their hole in the wall.
One, two, three, four, five, and that is all!
(show fingers one at a time)

FIVE LITTLE BABY MICE

Five little mice on the kitchen floor.
(hold up five fingers)
This little mouse peeked behind the door.
(point to thumb)
This little mouse nibbled at the cake.
(point to index finger)
This little mouse not a sound did he make.
(point to middle finger)
This little mouse took a bite of cheese.
(point to ring finger)
This little mouse heard the kitten sneeze.
(point to pinky)
"Ah-choo!" sneezed the kitten,
And "squeak" they cried.
As they found a hole and ran inside.
(move hand behind back)

LITTLE MOUSE

See the little mousie.
(place index and middle finger on thumb to
represent a mouse)
Creeping up the stair,
(creep mouse slowly up the forearm)
Looking for a warm rest.
There—Oh! There!
(spring mouse into a elbow corner)

HICKORY DICKORY DOCK

Hickory, dickory, dock.
(bend arm at elbow; hold up and open
palm)
The mouse ran up the dock.
(run fingers up the arm)
The clock struck one,
(hold up index finger)

The mouse ran down,
(run fingers down arm)
Hickory, dickory, dock.

MOUSE

Here is a mouse with ears so funny,
(place index and middle finger on thumb to
represent a mouse)
And here is a hole in the ground.
(make a hole with the other fist)
When a noise he hears, he pricks up his ears.
And runs to his hole in the ground.
(jump mouse into hole in other fist)

Science:

Mice

Purchase or borrow mice from a pet store to
keep as classroom pets. Place the cage on the
science table for the children to observe. Allow
the children to assist in caring for the animals.

Dramatic Play:

1. **Mouse House**

   The children can pretend to be mice! Construct
   mouse ears out of fabric or construction paper
   and attach to headbands. Provide large cardboard boxes to represent houses for the mice.

2. **Pet Store**

   Arrange the dramatic play area as a pet store.
   Provide props such as a cash register, play
   money, stuffed animals, animal cages, animal
   toys, and empty pet food boxes. Display
   posters of pets, including mice.

Arts and Crafts:

1. **Mouse Sponge Painting**

   Cut sponges into mice shapes. Place on the art
   table with paper and a shallow pan of thick
   tempera paint. The children can make designs
   by pressing the sponge into the paint and then
   on a piece of paper.

2. Seed Collage

Place a variety of seeds, glue, and paper on a table in the art area. The children can create designs with the materials.

Sensory:

Add to the sensory table:

- grains with scoops, cups, and spoons.
- seeds with pails and shovels.
- clean cedar chips (animal bedding) with measuring cups, scoops, and pails.

Field Trips:

1. Pet Store

Visit a pet store to observe the colors of pet mice and animal accessories. Photographs can be taken during the trip and later displayed in the classroom.

2. Mouse Walk

Take a walk around your school and look for places mice might live.

Group Time (games, language):

1. "Mouse, Mouse, Where's Your Cheese?"

This game is played in a circle formation. Arrange the chairs and place one in the center of the circle. Place a block to represent the cheese under the chair. Select one child, the "mouse," to sit on the chair and close his eyes. Then point to another child. This child must try to remove the cheese without making a sound. After the child returns to his chair in the circle, instruct all of the children to place their hands behind their backs. Then in unison the children say, "Mouse, Mouse, where is your cheese?" The mouse then opens his eyes and tries to guess who is holding the cheese.

2. Language Chart

Across the top of a piece of tagboard, print the question, "Where would you like to live if you were a mouse?" During group time introduce the chart and record the children's responses. Display the chart in the classroom.

Cooking:

1. Macaroni and Cheese

Purchase prepackaged macaroni and cheese. Prepare following the directions provided on the container. Compare the flavor to the recipe that follows:

3–3 1/2 cups of cooked macaroni
1/4 cup of butter or margarine
1/4 cup chopped onion (optional)
1/2 teaspoon salt
1/4 cup flour
1 1/2 cups of milk
1/2 pound of Swiss or American cheese cut into small cubes

Combine butter, onion, salt, and pepper in a saucepan; cook over medium heat until onion is tender. Blend in the flour. Lower heat and stir constantly until the mixture is smooth and bubbly. Add milk and heat to boiling, stirring constantly. Stir and boil one minute. Remove from heat. Add cheese and stir until melted.

Place macaroni in ungreased 1 1/2 quart casserole. Stir cheese sauce into the macaroni. Bake in an oven heated to 375 degrees for 30 minutes. (Makes five servings.)

2. Mouse Cookies

With the children, prepare a batch of drop cookie dough according to the recipe. Demonstrate how to drop three spoonfuls of dough onto a cookie sheet so that it will resemble a mouse head with two ears when baked. The mouse cookies can be frosted or details can be added with raisins, chocolate chips, and string licorice.

Multimedia:

The following resources can be found in educational catalogs:

1. Palmer, Hap. "The Mice Go Marching," *Rhythms on Parade* [record].

2. Sharon, Lois, & Bram. "Three Blind Mice" and "Hickory, Dickory, Dock," *Mainly Mother Goose* [record].

Books:

The following books can be used to complement the theme:

1. Cartlidge, Michelle. (1991). *Mouse in the House*. New York: Dutton Children's Books, Inc.

2. Watts, Barrie. (1992). *Mouse*. New York: Dutton Children's Books, Inc.

3. Baker, Alan. (1991). *Two Tiny Mice*. New York: Dail Books for Young Readers.

4. Walsh, Ellen S. (1991). *Mouse Court*. San Diego: Harcourt Brace Jovanovich.

5. Cartlidge, Michelle. (1990). *Mouse House*. New York: Dutton Children's Books, Inc.

6. Duerrstein, Richard (Illus.). (1992). *Mickey Is Happy: A Disney Book of Feelings*. New York: Walt Disney Book Publishing Group.

7. Dunbar, Joyce. (1990). *Ten Little Mice*. San Diego: Harcourt Brace Jovanovich.

8. Geraghty, Paul. (1990). *Look Out Patrick!* New York: Macmillan Children's Book Group.

9. Holabird, Katharine. (1989). *Angelina Ballerina*. New York: Crown Books for Young Readers.

10. Holabird, Katharine. (1989). *Angelina on Stage*. New York: Crown Books for Young Readers.

11. Holabird, Katharine. (1989). *Angelina's Birthday Surprise*. New York: Crown Books for Young Readers.

12. Lionni, Leo. (1992). *A Busy Year*. New York: Alfred A.Knopf Books for Young Readers.

13. Lionni, Leo. (1987). *Frederick*. New York: Alfred A. Knopf Books for Young Readers.

14. Lionni, Leo. (1987). *Mr. McMouse*. New York: Alfred A. Knopf Books for Young Readers.

15. Majewski, Joe. (1991). *A Friend For Oscar Mouse*. New York: Puffin Books.

16. Shories, Pat. (1991). *Mouse Around*. New York: Farrar, Straus, and Giroux.

17. Foster, John. (1992). *Mouse Poems*. New York: Oxford University Press.

18. Beguinot, Brigitte. (1992). *Mouse Part: An Open-the-Door Book*. Honesdale, PA: Boyds Mills Press.

19. Brown, Marcia. (1989). *Once a Mouse*. New York: Macmillan.

20. *Cottage Mouse: Village Mouse Stories*. (1992). Los Angeles: Price Stern Sloan.

21. Lobel, Arnold. *Martha the Movie Mouse*. (1993). New York: Harper Collins.

22. Wohl, Lauren. (1993). *Matzoh Mouse*. New York: Harper Collins.

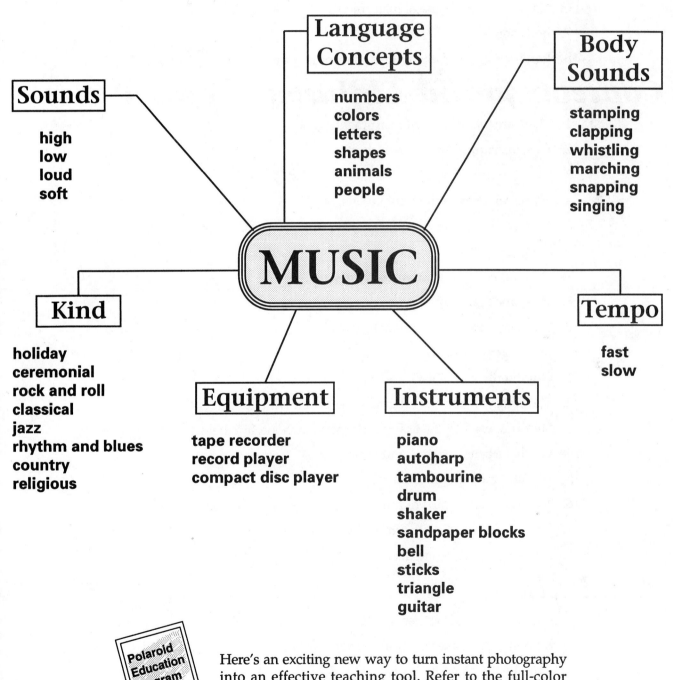

Language Concepts

numbers
colors
letters
shapes
animals
people

Body Sounds

stamping
clapping
whistling
marching
snapping
singing

Sounds

high
low
loud
soft

MUSIC

Kind

holiday
ceremonial
rock and roll
classical
jazz
rhythm and blues
country
religious

Tempo

fast
slow

Equipment

tape recorder
record player
compact disc player

Instruments

piano
autoharp
tambourine
drum
shaker
sandpaper blocks
bell
sticks
triangle
guitar

Polaroid Education Program

Here's an exciting new way to turn instant photography into an effective teaching tool. Refer to the full-color insert for the activity entitled Concentration Game.

Theme Goals:

Through participating in the experiences provided by this theme, the children may learn:

1. Music is a language.
2. Kinds of music.
3. Music tempos.
4. Language concepts.
5. Different sounds.
6. Names of many musical instruments.
7. Body sounds.
8. Equipment used for playing and recording music.

Concepts for the Children to Learn:

1. There are many types of instruments.
2. Each instrument has its own sound.
3. Music sounds can be high, low, loud, and soft.
4. Music can express different moods.
5. Music can be played in different rhythms.
6. Songs can tell stories.
7. Our bodies are musical instruments.
8. Our hands can clap.
9. Our feet can stamp and march.
10. Our fingers can snap.
11. Our mouths can whistle and sing.
12. The piano, autoharp, and guitar are played with our fingers.
13. Sticks are used on the triangle, drum, xylophone, and bells.
14. We shake bells, shakers, and tambourines.
15. We rub sandpaper blocks.
16. There are many kinds of music.
17. We can tape music with a recorder.
18. A record, tape, or compact disc player can play music.

Vocabulary:

1. **music**—a way of expressing ideas and feelings.
2. **instrument**—makes musical sounds.
3. **tempo**—the speed of music.
4. **body sounds**—sounds made by moving one or more body parts.
5. **mallets**—special sticks used to play the xylophone and bells.

Bulletin Board

The purpose of this bulletin board is to develop visual discrimination skills. Create a musical bulletin board by drawing musical instruments on tagboard as illustrated. Color the instruments with markers, cut out, and laminate. Trace these pieces onto black construction paper. Cut out the pieces and attach to the bulletin board. A magnet should be attached to both the colored pieces and the black shadow pieces. The children can match the appropriately shaped instrument piece to its shadow on the bulletin board.

Parent Letter

Dear Parents,

We will be singing and playing instruments during our unit on music. Music is a way of communicating and expressing oneself. For young children, singing is not that much different from talking—as I'm sure you've noticed from observing the children! Throughout the unit the children will be making discoveries about the many sounds that we can make with our voices, body parts, and musical instruments.

At School

A few highlights of our scheduled musical learning activities include:

- making musical instruments.
- painting at the easel while listening to music with headphones.
- trying on band uniforms (courtesy of Mead School) in the dramatic play area.
- forming a rhythm band outside in the play yard.

At Home

To stimulate creativity and language, create verses with your child for this song to the tune of "Old McDonald Had A Farm:"

Mr. Roberts had a band,
E-I-E-I-O.
And in his band he had a drum
E-I-E-I-O.
With a boom, boom here, and a boom, boom, there,
Here a boom, there a boom,
Everywhere a boom, boom.
Mr. Roberts had a band,
E-I-E-I-O.

And in his band he had a horn…
Continue adding instruments that your child can think of.

Provide materials for your child to make simple musical instruments. A drum can be made using an empty oatmeal carton or coffee can. Your child can personalize the instrument by decorating the outside of the container with paper, crayons, and markers. A kazoo can also be made with a cardboard tube and a small piece of waxed paper attached to the end of the tube with a rubber band. Poke a small hole in the waxed paper and your child will be ready to blow up a storm! The sounds produced by the different instruments can be compared to develop auditory discrimination skills.

Keep a song in your heart!

FIGURE 41 Children enjoy listening to and creating their own music.

Music:

Music for this unit should consist of the children's favorite and well-known songs. The children will enjoy singing these songs, and you will be able to focus on the sound of the music. Here are some suggestions of traditional songs that most children enjoy:

1. "Old MacDonald Had a Farm"

2. "Five Green Speckled Frogs"

3. "The Farmer in the Dell"

4. "Row, Row, Row Your Boat"

5. "Mary Had a Little Lamb"

6. "Hickory Dickory Dock"

7. "If You're Happy and You Know It"

8. "ABC Song"

9. "The Little White Duck"

10. "Six Little Ducks"

Fingerplays:

I WANT TO LEAD A BAND

I want to lead a band
With a baton in my hand.
   (wave baton in air)
I want to make sweet music high and low.
Now first I'll beat the drum
   (drum-beating motion)
With a rhythmic tum-tum-tum,
And then I'll play the bells
A-ting-a-ling-a ling,
   (bell-playing motion)
And next I'll blow the flute
With a cheery toot-a-toot.
   (flute-playing motion)
Then I'll make the violin sweetly sing.
   (violin-playing motion)
Now I'm leading a band
With a baton in my hand.
   (wave baton in air again)

IF I COULD PLAY

If I could play the piano
This is the way I would play.
   (move fingers like playing a piano)

If I had a guitar
I would strum the strings this way.
　　(hold guitar and strum)

If I had a trumpet
I'd toot to make a tune.
　　(play trumpet)

But if I had a drum
I'd go boom, boom, boom.
　　(pretend to play a drum)

MUSICAL INSTRUMENTS

This is how a horn sounds
Toot! Toot! Toot!
　　(play imaginary horn)

This is how guitars sound
Vrrroom, Vrrroom, Vrrroom
　　(strum imaginary guitar)

This is how the piano sounds
Tinkle, grumble, brring.
　　(run fingers over imaginary keyboard)

This is how the drum sounds
Rat-a-tat, grumble, brring.
　　(strike drum, include cymbal)

JACK-IN-THE-BOX

Jack-in-the-box all shut up tight
　　(fingers wrapped around thumb)
Not a breath of air, not a ray of light.
　　(other hand covers fist)
How tired he must be all down in a heap.
　　(lift off)
I'll open the lid and up he will leap!
　　(thumbs pop out)

Science:

1. **Water Music**

Fill four identically sized crystal glasses each
with a different amount of water. The children
can trace their wet finger around the rim of
each glass. Each glass will have a different
tune. Older children may enjoy reordering the
glasses from the highest to the lowest tone.

2. **Pop Bottle Music**

Fill six 12-ounce pop bottles, each with a
different amount of water. For effect, in each
bottle place a drop of food coloring, providing
six different colors. Younger children can tap
the bottles with a spoon as they listen for the
sound. Older children may try blowing
directly into the opening for sound production.

3. **Throats**

Show the children how to place their hands
across their throat. Then have them whisper,
talk, shout, and sing feeling the differences in
vibration.

4. **Jumping Seeds**

Set seeds or something small on top of a drum.
Then beat the drum. What happens? Why?
This activity can be extended by having the
childen jump to the drum beat.

5. **Identifying Instruments**

Prepare a tape recording of classroom musical
instruments. Play the tape, encouraging the
children to identify the correct instrument
related to each sound.

6. **Matching Sounds**

Collect 12 containers, such as film canisters,
milk cartons, or covered baby food jars, that
would be safe to use with the children. Fill 2
containers with rice, 2 cans with beans, 2 cans
with pebbles, 2 cans with water, and the
remaining cans with dry pasta. Coins, such as
pennies, could be substituted. Color code each
pair of containers on the bottom. Let the
children shake the containers, listening to the
sounds, in an attempt to find the matching
pairs.

Dramatic Play:

1. **Band**

Collect materials for a band prop box, which
may include band uniforms, a baton, music
stand, cassette player, and tapes with marching
music. The children can experiment with
instruments.

2. **Dramatizing**

   Add a cassette recorder and a small microphone to the dramatic play area. The children may enjoy using it for singing and recording their voices.

3. **Disc Jockey**

   In the music area, provide a tape recorder and cassettes for the children.

Arts and Crafts:

1. **Drums**

   Create drums out of empty coffee cans with plastic lids, plastic ice cream pails, or oatmeal boxes. The children can decorate as desired with paper, paint, felt-tip markers, or crayons.

2. **Shakers**

   Collect a variety of egg-shaped panty hose containers. Fill each egg with varying amounts of sand, peas, or rice, and securely tape or glue them shut. To compare sounds, empty film containers can also be filled.

3. **Cymbals**

   Make cymbals out of old tin foil pans. Attach a string for the handles.

4. **Tambourines**

   Two paper plates can be made into a tambourine. Begin by placing pop bottle caps or small stones between the plates. Staple the paper plates together. Shake to produce sound.

5. **Easel Ideas**

   Cut easel paper into the shape of different instruments such as a drum, guitar, or tambourine.

6. **Musical Painting**

   On a table in the art area, place a tape recorder with headphones. The children can listen to music as they paint.

7. **Kazoos**

   Kazoos can be made with empty paper towel rolls and waxed paper. The children can decorate the outside of the kazoos with colored felt-tip markers. After this, place a piece of waxed paper over one end of the roll and secure it with a rubber band. Poke two or three small holes into the waxed paper allowing sound to be produced.

8. **Rhythm Sticks**

   Two wooden dowels should be given to each interested child. The sticks can be decorated with paint or colored felt-tip markers.

Large Muscle:

1. **Body Movement Rhythms**

   Introduce a simple body movement. Then have the children repeat it until they develop a rhythm. Examples include:

   - stamp foot, clap hands, stamp foot, clap hands
   - clap, clap, stamp, stamp
   - clap, stamp, clap, stamp
   - clap, clap, snap fingers
   - clap, snap, stamp, clap, snap, stamp
   - clap, clap, stamp, clap, clap, stamp

2. **Body Percussion**

   Instruct the children to stand in a circle. Repeat the following rhythmic speech:

   We walk and we walk and we stop (rest)
   We walk and we walk and we stop (rest)
   We walk and we walk and we walk and we walk
   We walk and we walk and we stop. (stop)

3. **March**

   Play different rhythm beats on a piano or another instrument. Examples include hopping, skipping, gliding, walking, running, tiptoeing, galloping, etc. The children can move to the rhythm.

Field Trips/Resource People:

1. **Band Director**

   Visit a school band director. Observe the different instruments available to students. Listen to their sounds.

2. **Who Can Play?**

   Invite parents, grandparents, brothers, sisters, relatives, friends, etc., to visit the classroom and demonstrate their talent.

3. **Radio Station**

   Visit a local radio station.

4. **Taping**

   Videotape the children singing and using rhythm instruments. Replay the video for the children. Save this for a future open house, parent meeting, or holiday celebration.

Math:

1. **Colors, Shapes, and Numbers**

   Sing the song, "Colors, Shapes, and Numbers," mentioned in the shapes unit or make up a song about shapes. Hold up different colors, shapes, and numbers while you sing the song for the children to identify.

2. **Number Rhyme**

   Say the following song to reinforce numbers:

   One, two, three, four
   Come right in and shut the door.
   Five, six, seven, eight
   Come right in. It's getting late.
   Nine, ten, eleven, twelve
   Put your books upon the shelves.
   Will you count along with me?
   It's as easy as can be!

3. **Ten in the Bed**

   Chant the following words to reinforce numbers:

There were 10 in the bed and the little one said, "Roll over, roll over."
So they all rolled over and one fell out.

There were 9 in the bed and the little one said, "Roll over, roll over."
So they all rolled over and one fell out.

Continue until there is only one left. The last line will be "…and the little one said, "Good night!"

4. **Music Calendar**

   Design a calendar for the month of your music unit. The different days of the week can be made out of musical notes and different instruments.

Social Studies:

1. **Our Own Songs**

   Encourage the children to help you write a song about a common class experience. Substitute the words into a melody that everyone knows ("Twinkle, Twinkle, Little Star" or "The Mulberry Bush").

2. **Pictures**

   Put up pictures of instruments and band players in the room to add interest and stimulate discussion.

3. **Sound Tapes**

   Make a special tape of sounds heard in a home. Homes are full of different sounds. Included may be:

   • people knocking on doors
   • wind chimes
   • telephone ringing
   • teakettle whistling
   • clock ticking
   • toilet flushing
   • popcorn popping
   • vacuum cleaner
   • doorbell
   • running water
   • car horn

Play the tape and have the children listen carefully to identify the sounds.

Group Time (games, language):

1. **Name Game**

   Say the following rhythmic chant as the whole class claps.

   "Names, names we all have names
   Play a game as we say our names
   Scott (class echoes) Scott
   Melanie (class echoes) Melanie
   Tommy (class echoes) Tommy."

   Repeat until all the children have had their name repeated.

   Source: *The Kinder-Music House.* (1982). Fairfax County Public Schools.

2. **Are You Here?**

   Sing the following song to the tune of "Twinkle, Twinkle, Little Star."

Hello, children, here we are,
At our school from near and far.
Today we are going to play a game,
Please stand when I call your name.

Source: Beckman, Simmons, & Thomas. (1982). *Channels to Children.* Colorado: Channels to Children Publishing Company.

Miscellaneous:

Instrument of the Day

Focus on a different instrument each day. Talk about the construction and demonstrate the instrument's sound.

Cooking:

Popcorn

Make popcorn and have the children listen to the sounds of the oil as well as the corn popping. Supervise this activity closely since the corn popper will become hot. This activity is most appropriate for older children—younger children may choke on popcorn.

Multimedia:

The following resources can be found in educational catalogs:

1. *Simplified Lummi Stick Activities* [record]. Kimbo.

2. Palmer, Hap. *Getting to Know Myself* [record].

3. *Color Me a Rainbow* [record]. Melody House.

4. *Music Skills* [record]. Melody House.

5. "Scat Like That," *On the Move with Greg and Steve* [record]. Youngheart Records.

6. "Sing a Happy Song," *We All Live Together Series—Vol. 3* [record]. Youngheart Records.

7. *Family Folk Festival: A Multicultural Sing-Along* [record]. Scholastic.

8. *Rhythm Band Time* [record]. Melody House Records.

9. *Shake It to the One That You Love the Best: Play Songs and Lullabies from Black Musical Tradition* [record]. Mattox.

Books:

The following books can be used to complement the theme:

1. Lillegard, Dee. (1987). *Percussion*. Chicago: Children's Press.

2. Lillegard, Dee. (1987). *Woodwinds*. Chicago: Children's Press.

3. Raffi. (1987). *Down by the Bay*. New York: Crown Publishers.

4. Greenfield, Eloise. (1991). *I Make Music*. New York: Writers and Readers Publishing, Inc.

5. Gregorich, Barbara. (1991). *A Different Tune*. Grand Haven, MI: School Zone Publishing Co.

6. Keats, Ezra J. (1989). *Louie's Search*. New York: Macmillan Children's Book Group.

7. Komaiko, Leah. (1987). *I Like the Music*. New York: Harper Collins Children's Books.

8. Kraus, Robert. (1990). *Musical Max*. New York: Simon and Schuster Trade.

9. McCurdy, Michael. (1992). *The Old Man and the Fiddle*. New York: Putnam Publishing Group.

10. Micucci, Charles. (1989). *A Little Night Music*. New York: Morrow Junior Books.

11. Muntean, Michaela. (1991). *Grover's Overtunes*. Astor, FL: Astor Publications.

12. Rubin, Mark. (1992). *The Orchestra*. Buffalo, NY: Firefly Books, Ltd.

13. Sage, James. (1991). *The Little Band*. New York: Macmillan Children's Book Group.

14. Sharmat, Marjorie W. (1991). *Nate the Great and the Musical Note*. New York: Dell Publishing Co., Inc.

15. Lillegard, Dee. (1989). *Brass*. Chicago: Children's Press.

16. Lillegard, Dee. (1988). *Strings*. Chicago: Children's Press.

17. Williams, Vera B. (1989). *Music, Music for Everyone*. New York: Morrow.

18. Ziefert, Harriet. (1992). *Music Lessons*. New York: Harper Collins.

19. Kherdian, David, & Hogrogian, Nonny. (1990). *The Cat's Midsummer Jamboree*. New York: Philomel.

20. Medearis, Angela S. (1992). *The Zebra-Riding Cowboy: A Folk Song From the Old West*. New York: Henry Holt & Co.

21. Hart, Avery, & Mantell, Paul. (1993). *Kids Make Music! Clapping & Tapping from Bach to Rock*. Charlotte, VT: Williamstown.

22. Weil, Lisl. (1989). *The Magic of Music*. New York: Holiday.

23. Hart, Jane (Ed.). (1989). *Singing Bee!: A Collection of Favorite Children's Songs*. New York: Lothrop, Lee, & Shepard.

24. Ackerman, Karen. (1988). *Song and Dance Man*. New York: Alfred A. Knopf.

25. deRegniers, Beatrice Schenk (Ed.). (1988). *Sing a Song of Popcorn: Every Child's Book of Poems*. New York: Scholastic.

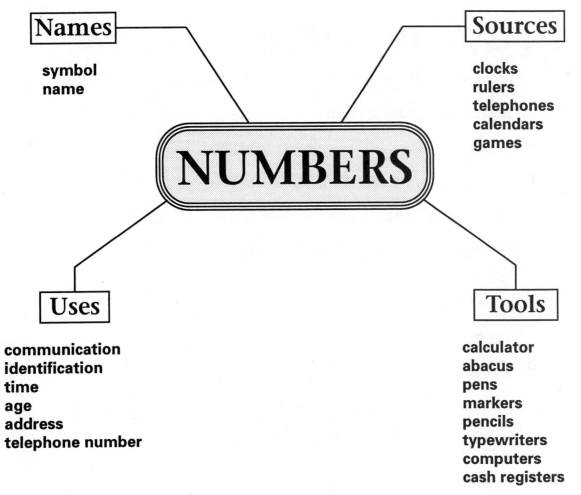

Names

symbol
name

Sources

clocks
rulers
telephones
calendars
games

NUMBERS

Uses

communication
identification
time
age
address
telephone number

Tools

calculator
abacus
pens
markers
pencils
typewriters
computers
cash registers

Polaroid Education Program

Here's an exciting new way to turn instant photography into an effective teaching tool. Refer to the full-color insert for the activity entitled Graphing.

Theme Goals:

Through participating in the experiences provided by this theme, the children may learn:

1. Uses of numbers.

2. Sources of numbers.

3. Number names.

4. Tools for recording numbers.

Concepts for the Children to Learn:

1. A number is a symbol.

2. Each number symbol has a name.

3. Pencils, typewriters, and computers are tools used to make numbers.

4. Numbers can be found on clocks, rulers, telephones, and calendars.

5. Communication, identification, time, and age are uses for numbers.

6. Adding machines and cash registers have numerals.

Vocabulary:

1. **numeral**—a symbol that represents a number.

2. **number**—a symbol used to represent an amount.

Bulletin Board

The objective of this bulletin board is for the children to match the numeral to the set by winding the string around the other push pin. Construct the numerals out of tagboard. Construct objects familiar to the child to correspond to one type of object to each numeral. The number of objects and numerals should be developmentally appropriate for the group of children. Laminate. Staple 1, 2, 3, 4, and 5 down the left side of bulletin board. Staple the sets of objects in random order (3, 5, 1, 2, 4) down the right side of the bulletin board as illustrated. Affix a push pin with an attached long string by each numeral. Affix a push pin in front of each set row.

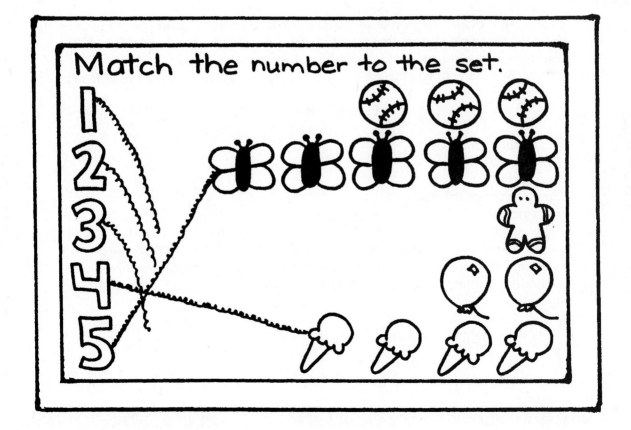

Parent Letter

Dear Parents,

Our next unit will focus on numbers. The children will be exposed to concepts of pairs, sets, and halves and wholes. They will also be participating in activities that include the concepts of heavy/light, bigger/smaller, and more/less.

At School

Some of the play-related activities include:

- measuring with scales and rulers at the science table.
- charting our weight and height.
- listening to the book titled, *I Can Count*, by Lynn Grundy.
- using number cookie cutters with playdough.
- bowling with numbered pins.

Personnel from the telephone company will be visiting us Tuesday. They will show us a variety of phones. They will also stress the importance of knowing our telephone number. Feel free to join us for this activity.

At Home

Cooking provides a concrete foundation for mathematical concepts. It involves amounts, fractions, and measures. While you are cooking, have your child help. Count how many spoonfuls it takes to fill a one-cup measurer.

Your child can help you make this simple no-bake recipe for peanut butter treats.

Peanut Butter Treats

1/4 cup margarine
1/4 cup peanut butter
1 cup raisins
40 regular-size marshmallows
5 cups rice cereal

Melt margarine over low heat. Add marshmallows and melt. Add the peanut butter and stir. Add the rice cereal and raisins; stir until everything is mixed well. Spread the mixture into a buttered pan and press into a firm layer. Cool and cut into squares.

Enjoy counting with your child.

FIGURE 42 Developmentally appropriate software can be an effective strategy for teaching children numbers.

Music:

1. **"Hickory Dickory Dock"**
   (traditional)

   Hickory dickory dock.
   The mouse ran up the clock.
   The clock struck one,
   The mouse ran down.
   Hickory dickory dock.

2. **"Two Little Blackbirds"**
   (traditional)

   Two little blackbirds sitting on a hill
   One named Jack,
   One named Jill.
   Fly away, Jack,
   Fly away, Jill.
   Come back, Jack,
   Come back, Jill.
   Two little blackbirds sitting on a hill
   One named Jack,
   One named Jill.

Fingerplays:

I CAN EVEN COUNT SOME MORE

One, two, three, four
I can even count some more.
Five, six, seven, eight
All my fingers stand up straight
Nine, ten are my thumb men.

FIVE LITTLE MONKEYS SWINGING FROM A TREE

Five little monkeys swinging from the tree
Teasing Mr. Alligator, "You can't catch me."
Along comes Mr. Alligator as sneaky as can be
SNAP
4 little monkeys swinging from the tree.
3 little monkeys swinging from the tree.
2 little monkeys swinging from the tree.
1 little monkey swinging from the tree.
No more monkeys swinging from the tree!

ONE, TWO, THREE

1, 2 How do you do?
1, 2, 3 Clap with me.
1, 2, 3, 4 Jump on the floor.

1, 2, 3, 4, 5 Look bright and alive!
1, 2, 3, 4, 5, 6 Pick up your sticks.
1, 2, 3, 4, 5, 6, 7 We can count up to eleven.
1, 2, 3, 4, 5, 6, 7, 8 Draw a circle around your plate.
1, 2, 3, 4, 5, 6, 7, 8, 9 Get the trunks in the line.
1, 2, 3, 4, 5, 6, 7, 8, 9, 10 Let's do it over again.

Source: Wilmes, Liz & Dick. (1983). *Everyday Circle Times*. Elgin, IL: Building Blocks Publications.

FIVE LITTLE BIRDS

Five little birds without any home.
   (hold up five fingers)
Five little trees in a row.
   (raise hands high over head)
Come build your nests in our branches tall.
   (cup hands)
We'll rock them to and fro.

TEN LITTLE FINGERS

I have 10 little fingers and 10 little toes.
   (children point to portions of body as they
   repeat words)
Two little arms and one little nose.
One little mouth and two little ears.
Two little eyes for smiles and tears.
One little head and two little feet.
One little chin, that makes _____ complete.

Science:

1. **Height and Weight Chart**

   Design a height and weight chart for the classroom. The children can help by measuring each other. Record the numbers. Later in the year measure the children and record their progress. Note the differences.

2. **Using a Scale**

   Collect a variety of small objects and place on the science table with a balancing scale. The children can measure with the scale, noting the differences.

3. **Temperature**

   Place an outdoor thermometer on the playground. Encourage the children to examine the thermometer. Record the temperature. Mark the temperature on the thermometer with masking tape. Bring the thermometer into the classroom. Check the thermometer again in half an hour. Show the children the change in temperature.

Dramatic Play:

1. **Grocery Store**

   In the dramatic play area, arrange a grocery store. To do this, collect a variety of empty boxes, paper bags, sales receipts, etc. Removable stickers can be used to indicate the grocery prices. A cash register and play money can also be added to create interest.

2. **Clock Shop**

   Collect a variety of clocks for the children to explore. Using discarded clocks, with the glass face removed, is an interesting way to let the children explore numerals and internal mechanisms.

3. **Telephoning**

   Prepare a classroom telephone book with all the children's names and telephone numbers. Contact your local telephone company to borrow the training system. The children can practice dialing their own numbers as well as their classmates'.

Arts and Crafts:

1. **Marker Sets**

   Using rubber bands, bind two watercolor markers together. Repeat this procedure making several sets. Set the markers, including an unbound set, on the art table. The children can use the bound marker sets for creating designs on paper.

2. **Clipping Coupons**

   Collect coupon flyers from the Sunday edition of the paper and magazines for this activity. Place the flyers with scissors on a table in the art area. If interested, the children can cut coupons from the paper.

3. **Coupon Collage**

   Clipped coupons, paste, and paper can be placed on a table in the art area.

4. **Ruler Design**

   Collect a variety of rulers that are of different colors, sizes, and types. Using paper and a marking tool, the children can create designs.

5. **Numeral Cookie Cutter**

   Numeral cookie cutters should be provided with playdough.

Sensory:

Add to the sensory table colored water and a variety of measuring tools.

Math:

1. **Number Chain**

   Cut enough strips of paper to make a number chain for the days of the month. During group time each day, add a link to represent the passage of time. Another option is to use the chain as a countdown by removing a link per day until a special day. This is an interesting approach to an upcoming holiday.

2. **Silverware Set**

   Provide a silverware set. The children can sort the pieces according to sizes, shapes, and/or use.

3. **Constructing Numerals**

   Provide each interested child with a ball of playdough. Instruct children to form some numerals randomly. It is important for the teacher to monitor work and correct reversals. Then children can add the proper corresponding number of dots for that numeral just formed.

   An extension of this activity would be to make cards with numerals. The children roll their playdough into long ropes that could be placed over the lines of the numerals.

Group Time (games, language):

1. **Squirrels in the Park**

   Choose five children to be squirrels. The children should sit in a row while one child pretends to go for a walk in the park carrying a bag of peanuts. When the child who is walking approaches the squirrels, provide directions. These may include: feeding the first squirrel, the fifth, the third, etc.

2. **Block Form Board**

   On a large piece of cardboard trace around one of each of the shapes of the blocks in the block area. Let children match blocks to the shape on the board.

3. **Match Them**

   Show the child several sets of identical picture cards, squares, objects, or flannel board pictures. Mix the items. Then have the children find matching pairs. One method of doing this is to hold up one item and have the children find the matching one.

4. **Follow the Teacher**

   At group time, provide directions containing a number. For examples say 1 jump, 2 hops, 3 leaps, 4 tiptoe steps, etc. The numbers used should be developmentally appropriate for the children.

Cooking:

Peanut Butter Treats

   1/4 cup margarine
   1/4 cup peanut butter
   1 cup raisins
   40 regular-size marshmallows
   5 cups rice cereal

   Melt the margarine over low heat. Add marshmallows and melt. Add the peanut butter and stir. Add the rice cereal and raisins. Stir until all ingredients are well mixed. Spread the mixture onto a buttered pan and press into a firm layer. Let cool and cut into squares.

MANIPULATIVES FOR MATH ACTIVITIES

buttons	checkers	small toy cars
beads	crayons	plastic bread ties
bobbins	golf tees	marbles
craft pompoms	plastic caps from markers,	cotton balls
spools	milk containers, plastic	bottle caps
shells	bottles	poker chips
seeds (corn, soybeans)	stickers	paper clips
shelled peanuts	fishing bobbers	clothespins
toothpicks	keys	erasers
pennies		

Multimedia:

The following resources can be found in educational catalogs:

1. *Number Fun* [record]. Melody House Records.

2. "The Number Rock," *We All Live Together Series—Vol. 2.* [record]. Youngheart Records.

3. "1, 2, Buckle My Shoe," *We All Live Together Series—Vol. 3.* [record]. Youngheart Records.

4. *Numbers* [record]. Sesame Street Records.

5. *Early Math* [IBM/Mac/Windows software, PK–2]. Bright Star.

6. *Mathosaurus.* [IBM software PK–K and K–2]. Micrograms.

7. *Numbers…What They Mean* [30-minute video]. Edu-vid.

8. *Learning Your Numbers* [30-minute video]. Edu-vid.

9. *Hello Number* [30-minute video]. Edu-vid.

10. *Ten Little Robots* [Apple/IBM software, PK and lower]. Unicorn.

11. *Math and Me* [Apple/IBM software, PK–2]. Davidson.

12. *Stickybear Numbers* [Apple/IBM software, PK–1]. Optimum Resources.

Books:

The following books can be used to complement the theme:

1. Hutchins, Pat. (1986). *The Doorbell Rang.* New York: Scholastic.

2. Aker, Suzanne. (1990). *What Comes in Twos, Threes, & Fours?* New York: Simon & Schuster.

3. Anno, Mitsumasa. (1992). *Anno's Counting Book Big Book*. New York: Harper Collins.

4. Carle, Eric. (1985). *My Very First Book of Numbers*. New York: Harper Collins.

5. Gillen, Patricia B. (1987). *My Signing Book of Numbers*. Washington, DC: Gallaudet University Press.

6. Holmes, Stephen. (1990). *Hidden Numbers*. San Diego: Harcourt Brace Jovanovich.

7. Oliver, Stephen. (1990). *My First Look at Numbers*. New York: Random House.

8. Pomerantz, Charlotte. (1987). *How Many Trucks Can a Tow Truck Tow?* New York: Random House.

9. Bang, Molly. (1986). *Ten, Nine, Eight*. New York: Greenwillow.

10. Giganti, Paul, Jr. (1988). *How Many Snails?* New York: Greenwillow.

11. Hort, Lenny. (1991). *How Many Stars in the Sky?* New York: Tambourine.

12. Grossman, Virginia, & Long, Sylvia. (1991). *Ten Little Rabbits*. San Francisco: Chronicle Books.

13. Bryant-Mole, K. (1992). *Numbers*. Tulsa, OK: EDC Publishing.

14. *Moja Means One: A Swahili Counting Book*. (1987). New York: Dial Books for Young Readers.

15. Lottridge, Celia B. (1900). *One Watermelon Seed*. New York: Oxford University Press, Inc.

16. Moss, David. (1989). *Numbers*. Avenal, NJ: Outlet Book Inc.

17. Tucker, Sian. (1992). *Numbers*. New York: Simon and Schuster Trade.

18. Tudor, Tasha. (1988). *One Is One*. New York: Macmillan Children's Book Group.

19. Walsh, Abigail. (1992). *Exploring the Numbers One to Ten*. Mankato, MN: Capstone Press, Inc.

20. Zimmerman, H. Werner. (1990). *Alphonse Knows...Zero Is Not Enough*. New York: Oxford University Press.

Characters

animals
people
objects

Forms

written
spoken
sung

NURSERY RHYMES

Uses

enjoyment
learning words
bedtime rituals

Favorites

Little Bo Peep
Mary Had a Little Lamb
Old Mother Hubbard
Hey Diddle Diddle
Little Miss Muffet
Humpty Dumpty
Jack and Jill
Mary Mary Quite Contrary

Jack Be Nimble
Rub-A-Dub-Dub
The Muffin Man
Little Jack Horner
Old MacDonald Had A Farm
Two Little Blackbirds
Hickory Dickory Dock
Three Kittens' Mittens

Here's an exciting new way to turn instant photography into an effective teaching tool. Refer to the full-color insert for the activity entitled Photo Bingo.

Theme Goals:

Through participating in the experiences provided by this theme, the children may learn:

1. Favorite nursery rhymes.

2. Uses of nursery rhymes.

3. Forms of nursery rhymes.

4. Characters portrayed in nursery rhymes.

Concepts for the Children to Learn:

1. Nursery rhymes are fun to listen to and say.

2. Nursery rhymes can contain real or pretend words.

3. Some nursery rhymes are about animals.

4. Some nursery rhymes help us learn numbers and counting.

5. Some nursery rhymes teach us about different people.

Vocabulary:

nursery rhyme—short, simple poem or rhyme.

Bulletin Board

The purpose of this bulletin board is to promote name recognition and call attention to the printed word. This is a check-in bulletin board. Each child is provided a bulletin board piece with his name printed on it. When the children arrive each morning at school, they hang their name on the bulletin board. To create a "Find Your Mitten" bulletin board, cut a mitten out of tagboard for each child in the class. Three kittens can be constructed and attached to the bulletin board to represent the three little kittens who lost their mittens. Use a paper punch to cut a hole in the top of each mitten. Hang push pins on the bulletin board for the children to hang their mittens on during the course of the day.

Parent Letter

Dear Parents,

Nursery rhymes will be the focus of our next theme. These rhymes can serve as a bridge between the home and school. I'm sure many of you have shared favorite nursery rhymes with your child at home. Nursery rhymes are an easy introduction to poetry, as well as the concept of rhyming words.

At School

We have a fun-filled curriculum planned for our unit on nursery rhymes. A few highlights include:

- acting out various rhymes with puppets that represent different characters from familiar nursery rhymes.
- unraveling the riddle of the "Humpty Dumpty" nursery rhyme. (Why couldn't Humpty be put back together? Because Humpty was an egg!)
- creating "Little Miss Muffet" spiders in the art area.
- taking turns being nimble and quick as we jump over a candlestick to dramatize the rhyme of "Jack Be Nimble."

At Home

To foster concepts of the unit at home, try the following:

- Let your child help you crack eggs open to make scrambled eggs. Children like to feel that they have accomplished a grown-up task when they crack the eggs.
- Sing or recite some of the many rhymes your child already knows such as, "Jack and Jill," and, "Mary Had a Little Lamb." These also develop an enjoyment of music and singing.

Share a nursery rhyme with your child today!

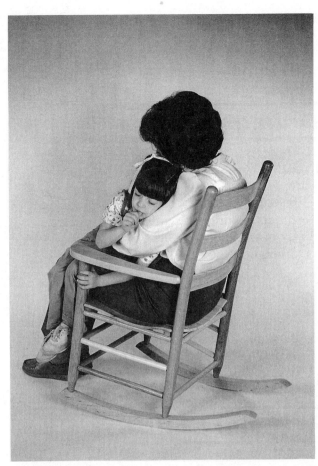

FIGURE 43 Reciting nursery rhymes can help relax a child.

Music:

1. **"Hickory Dickory Dock"** (traditional)

   Hickory dickory dock
   The mouse ran up the clock.
   The clock struck one, the mouse ran down,
   Hickory dickory dock.

2. **"The Muffin Man"** (traditional)

   Oh, do you know the muffin man,
   The muffin man, the muffin man?
   Oh, do you know the muffin man
   Who lives on Dreary Lane?

   Yes, I know the muffin man…

3. **"Two Little Blackbirds"** (traditional)

   Two little blackbirds sitting on a hill
   One named Jack. One named Jill.

   Fly away, Jack. Fly away, Jill.
   Come back, Jack. Come back, Jill.
   Two little blackbirds sitting on a hill.
   One named Jack. One named Jill.

4. **"Jack and Jill"** (traditional)

   Jack and Jill went up a hill
   To fetch a pail of water.
   Jack fell down and broke his crown
   And Jill fell tumbling after.

Fingerplays:

LITTLE JACK HORNER

Little Jack Horner
Sat in a corner
Eating a Christmas pie.
   (pretend you're eating)
He put in his thumb,
   (thumb down)
And pulled out a plum
   (thumb up)
And said, "What a good boy am I!"
   (say out loud)

PAT-A-CAKE

Pat-a-cake, pat-a-cake, baker's man.
Bake me a cake as fast as you can!
   (clap hands together lightly)
Roll it
   (roll hands)
And pat it
   (touch hands together lightly)
And mark it with a "B"
   (write "b" in the air)
And put it in the oven for baby and me.
   (point to baby and to yourself)

WEE WILLIE WINKLE

Wee Willie Winkle runs through the town
   (pretend to run)
Upstairs, downstairs in his nightgown,
   (point up, point down, then point to clothes)
Rapping at the window, crying through the lock
   (knock in the air, peek through a hole)
"Are the children all in bed, for now it's eight o'clock?"
   (shake finger)

OLD KING COLE

Old King Cole was a merry old soul
   (lift elbows up and down)
And a merry old soul was he.
   (nod head)
He called for his pipe.
   (clap two times)
He called for his bowl.
   (clap two times)
And he called for his fiddlers three.
   (clap two times then pretend to play violin)

HICKORY DICKORY DOCK

Hickory dickory dock
   (swing arms back and forth together, bent down low)
The mouse ran up the clock.
   (run fingers up your arm)
The clock struck one
   (clap, and then hold up one finger)
The mouse ran down.
   (run fingers down your arm)
Hickory dickory dock.
   (swing arms back and forth together, bent down low)

Science:

1. **Mary's Garden**

   A styrofoam cup with the child's name printed on it and a scoop of soil should be provided. Then let everyone choose a flower seed. Be sure to save the seed packages. The children can plant their seed, water, and care for it. When the plant begins to grow, try to identify the names of the plants by comparing them to pictures on the seed packages.

2. **Hickory Dickory Dock Clock**

   Draw and cut a large Hickory Dickory Dock clock from cardboard. Move the hands of the clock and see if the children can identify the numeral.

3. **Wool**

   Pieces of wool fabric mounted on cardboard can be matched with samples.

4. **Pumpkin Tasters**

   Plan a Peter, Peter, Pumpkin Eater pumpkin-tasting party.

Dramatic Play:

1. **Baker**

   Baking props such as: hats, aprons, cookie cutters, baking pans, rolling pins, mixers, spoons, and bowls can be placed in the dramatic play area.

2. **Puppets**

   A puppet theater can be placed in the dramatic play area for the duration of the unit. To add variety, each day a different set of puppets can be added for the children.

Arts and Crafts:

1. **Spiders**

   Add black tempera paint to a playdough mixture. In addition to the playdough, provide black pipe cleaners or yarn. Using these materials, spiders or other objects can be created.

2. **Spider Webs**

   Cut circles of black paper to fit in the bottom of a pie tin. Mix thin silver or white tempera paint. Place a marble and two teaspoons of paint on the paper. Gently tilt the pie tin, allowing the marble to roll through the paint, creating a spider web design.

3. **Twinkle Twinkle Little Stars**

   The children can decorate stars with glitter and sequins. The stars can be hung from the ceiling and during group time sing "Twinkle, Twinkle, Little Star."

4. **Little Boy Blue's Horn**

   Collect paper towel tubes. The tubes can be painted with tempera. When the tubes are dry, cover one end with tissue paper and secure with a rubber band. The children can use them as horns.

Sensory:

Water and Pails

Add water, pails, and scoopers to the sensory table.

Large Muscle:

1. Jack Be Nimble's Candlestick

Make a candlestick out of an old paper towel holder and tissue paper for the flame. Repeat the rhyme by substituting each child's name.

Jack be nimble. Jack be quick.
Jack jump over the candlestick.

2. Wall Building

Encourage the children to create a large wall out of blocks for Humpty Dumpty. Act out the rhyme.

Field Trips/Resource People:

1. Candlemaking

Invite a resource person to demonstrate candlemaking, or take a field trip to a craft center so that the children can view candles being made.

2. Greenhouse

Visit a florist or greenhouse to observe flowers and plants.

Math:

1. Puzzles

Draw or cut out several pictures of different nursery rhymes ("Jack and Jill," "Jack Be Nimble," etc.) and mount on tagboard. Laminate and cut each picture into five to seven pieces. The children can match nursery rhyme puzzle pieces.

2. Rote Counting

Say or sing the following nursery rhyme to help the children with rote counting.

1, 2 buckle my shoe
3, 4 shut the door
5, 6 pick up sticks
7, 8 lay them straight
9, 10 a big fat hen.

3. Matching

Draw from one to 10 simple figures from a nursery rhyme (mittens, candlesticks, pails, etc.) on the left side of a sheet of tagboard and the corresponding numeral on the right side. Laminate the pieces and cut each in half creating different-shaped puzzle pieces. The children can match the number of figures to the corresponding numeral.

4. Mitten Match

Collect several matching pairs of mittens. Mix them up and have children match the pairs.

Social Studies:

Table Setting

On a sheet of tagboard, trace the outline of a plate, cup, knife, fork, spoon, and napkin. Laminate. The children can match the silverware and dishes to the outline on the placemat in preparation for snack or meals. This activity can be extended by having the children turn the placemat over, and arrange the place setting without the aid of an outline.

Group Time (games, language):

Old Mother Hubbard's Doggie Bone Game

Save a bone or construct one from tagboard. Ask one child to volunteer to be the doggie.

Seat the children in a circle with the doggie in the center and the bone in front of him. The doggie closes his eyes. A child from the circle quietly comes and steals the bone. When the child is reseated with the bone out of sight, the children will call,

"Doggie, doggie, where's your bone? Someone took it from your home!"

The doggie gets three chances to guess who has the bone. If he guesses correctly, the child who took the bone becomes the doggie.

Cooking:

1. Bran Muffins

(Use with the "Muffin Man" rhyme)

3 cups whole wheat bran cereal
1 cup boiling water
1/2 cup shortening or oil
2 eggs
2 1/2 cups unbleached flour
1 1/2 cups sugar
2 1/2 teaspoons baking soda
2 cups buttermilk

Preheat the oven to 400 degrees. Line the muffin tins with paper baking cups. In a large bowl combine the cereal and boiling water. Stir in the shortening and eggs. Add the remaining ingredients. Blend well. Spoon the batter into cups about 3/4 full. Bake at 400 degrees for 18 to 22 minutes or until golden brown. Eat at snack and sing the "Muffin Man" song.

2. Humpty Dumpty Pear Salad

For each serving provide 1/2 pear, 1 lifesaver, 1 tablespoon mayonnaise, 2 cherries, 1 raisin, and a lettuce leaf. The children can prepare their own salad. To do this each child puts a lettuce leaf on a plate and places a pear half on top of it, round side up. Then add the two cherries for eyes, a raisin for a nose and the piece of lifesaver candy for a mouth. Add mayonnaise to taste.

Source: Graham, Terry. (1982). *Let Loose on Mother Goose*. Terry Graham. Incentive Publishing Company.

3. Cottage Cheese*

2 quarts pasteurized skim milk (to make 1 to 3/4 pounds of cottage cheese)
salt
liquid rennet or a junket tablet

Heat the water to 80 degrees Fahrenheit in the bottom part of a double boiler. Use a thermometer to determine the water temperature. Do not guess.

Pour the skim milk into the top of the double boiler. Dilute 1 or 2 drops of liquid rennet in a tablespoon of cold water and stir it into the milk. If rennet is not available, add 1/8 of a junket tablet to a tablespoon of water and add it to the milk. Allow the milk to remain at 80 degrees until it curdles, in about 12 to 18 hours. During this period no special attention is necessary. If desired, the milk may be placed in a warm oven overnight. Place the curd in a cheese cloth over a container to drain the whey. Occasionally, pour out the whey that collects in the container so that the draining will continue. In 15 to 20 minutes, the curd will become mushy and will drain more slowly. When it is almost firm and the whey has nearly ceased to flow, the cheese is ready for salting and eating. Salt the cheese to taste. The cottage cheese can be spread on crackers for a snack.

* This activity is time-consuming; consequently, it may be more appropriate for older children.

4. Miss Muffet's Curds and Whey

2 cups whole milk
1 teaspoon vinegar

Warm milk and add vinegar. Stir as curds separate from the whey. Curds are the milk solids and the whey is the liquid that is poured off. You can let your children taste the whey but they probably will not be thrilled by it. Strain the curds from the whey, then dump the curds onto a paper towel and gently press the curds with more towels to get out the liquid. Sprinkle with salt and refrigerate. Eat as cottage cheese. You can also serve the curds at room temperature. Stir them until they are smooth. Add different flavorings (such as cinnamon, orange flavoring, vanilla, etc.). Use as a spread on crackers. Curds mixed with peanut butter is great. Serves 12 (2 crackers each).

Multimedia:

The following resources can be found in educational catalogs:

1. *More Mother Goose with the Play-Along at Home Rhythm Band* [record]. (1962). A Disney Land Record, Walt Disney Production.

2. Jenkins, Ella. *Nursery Rhymes—Rhyming and Remembering* [record].

3. *Mother Goose* [record]. Melody House.

Books:

The following books can be used to complement the theme:

1. Aylesworth, Jim. (1992). *The Cat & the Fiddle & More*. New York: Macmillan.

2. Baker, Keith. (1994). *Big Fat Hen*. San Diego: Harcourt Brace Jovanovich.

3. Beck, Ian. (1993). *Five Little Ducks*. New York: Henry Hold & Co.

4. Craig, Helen. (1993). *I See the Moon & the Moon Sees Me*. New York: Harper Collins.

5. Demi. (1986). *Dragon Kites & Dragonflies: A Collection of Chinese Nursery Rhymes*. San Diego: Harcourt Brace Jovanovich.

6. Langley, Jonathan. (1991). *Rain, Rain, Go Away! A Book of Nursery Rhymes*. New York: Dial.

7. Lewis, J. Patrick. (1991). *Two Legged, Four-Legged, No Legged Rhymes*. New York: Alfred A. Knopf.

8. Officer, Robyn. (1992). *Mother Goose's Nursery Rhymes*. Kansas City: Andrews & McMeel.

9. Wyndham, Robert. (1989). *Chinese Mother Goose*. New York: Putnam.

10. Young, Ed. (1989). *Lon Po Po: A Red Riding Hood Story from China*. New York: Putnam.

11. Hale, Sarah J. (1990). *Mary Had a Little Lamb*. New York: Scholastic Inc.

12. Hennessy, B. G. (1991). *The Missing Tarts*. New York: Puffin Books.

13. Hopkins, Lee B. (1989). *Animals from Mother Goose*. San Diego: Harcourt Brace Jovanovich.

14. Hopkins, Lee B. (1989). *People from Mother Goose*. San Diego: Harcourt Brace Jovanovich.

15. Kemp, Moira (Illus.). (1991). *Baa, Baa, Black Sheep*. New York: Dutton Children's Books.

16. Kemp, Moira (Illus.). (1991). *Hey Diddle Diddle*. New York: Dutton Children's Books.

17. Kemp, Moira (Illus.). (1991). *Hickory Dickory Dock*. New York: Dutton Children's Books.

18. Kemp, Moira (Illus.). (1991). *This Little Piggy*. New York: Dutton Children's Books.

19. Langley, Jonathan. (1991). *Rain, Rain, Go Away! A Book of Nursery Rhymes*. New York: Dial Books for Young Readers.

20. McGee, Shelagh. (1992). *I'm a Little Teapot*. New York: Doubleday and Co.

21. Marshall, James. (1991). *Old Mother Hubbard and Her Wonderful Dog*. New York: Farrar, Straus and Giroux, Inc.

22. Wildsmith, Brian. (1987). *Mother Goose: Nursery Rhymes*. New York: Oxford University Press, Inc.

THEME 44

Other

homemaker
unemployed
seasonal
part-time
self-employed
shift
cottage
migrant

Construction

carpenter
plumber
cabinetmaker
architect

Transportation

taxi driver
bus driver
car salesperson
pilot
ambulance driver
truck driver
gas station attendant
astronaut

Service Workers

teacher
librarian
waitress/waiter
banker
cashier
custodian
secretary
auto mechanic
butcher
clerk
sanitation engineer

OCCUPATIONS

Production

farmer
factory worker
cook/chef
baker
miner

Health

doctor
nurse
dentist
hygienist
paramedic
child care

Communications

computer operator
television reporter
telephone operator
newspaper reporter
actor

Community Helpers

police officer
fire fighter
mail carrier
judge

Sports

announcer
umpire
coach
athlete

Polaroid Education Program

Here's an exciting new way to turn instant photography into an effective teaching tool. Refer to the full-color insert for the activity entitled People and Uniforms.

Theme Goals:

Through participating in the experiences provided by this theme, the children may learn:

1. Occupations of community helpers.

2. Sports figure occupations.

3. Health occupations.

4. Transportation occupations.

5. Communications occupations.

6. Construction occupations.

7. Production occupations.

8. Service occupations.

Concepts for the Children to Learn:

1. An occupation is a job a person performs.

2. There are many different kinds of occupations.

3. Taxi drivers, pilots, and ambulance drivers are transportation occupations.

4. Doctors, nurses, and dentists are health occupations.

5. A community helper is someone who helps us.

6. Teachers, librarians, and custodians are service occupations.

7. Cooks, factory workers, and farmers are production occupations.

8. Football and baseball players are sports occupations.

9. Television and newspaper reporters are in communications occupations.

10. Builders and architects are in construction occupations.

Vocabulary:

1. **occupation**—the job a person performs to earn money.

2. **job**—type of work.

3. **service**—helping people.

420

Bulletin Board

The purpose of this bulletin board is to stress that men and women can be doctors, farmers, construction workers, teachers, judges, etc. To prepare the bulletin board, construct a boy and girl out of tagboard. Design several occupational outfits that may be worn by either sex. Color and laminate the pieces. Magnet pieces or push pins and holes could be used to affix clothing on children.

Parent Letter

Dear Parents,

Hello! We will be exploring a new unit on occupations. Through experiences provided by this theme the children will become aware of a great number of occupations and the way these workers help us today.

At School

Some learning experiences include:

- listening to books and records about people in our neighborhoods.
- making occupation hats.
- visiting a police station on Wednesday at 2:00 p.m. Join us if you can!
- observing an ambulance and talking with a paramedic.
- designing a job chart for our classroom.

At Home

Page through magazines with your child. Discuss equipment and materials that are used in various occupations. Questions such as the following can be asked to stimulate thinking skills: Who might use a typewriter to perform a job? What occupations involve the use of a cash register? Your child might be interested in visiting your place of employment!

Enjoy your child!

FIGURE 44 Abduraham likes cookies; someday he wants to be a bakery chef.

Fingerplays:

FARM CHORES

Five little farmers woke up with the sun.
    (hold up hand, palm forward)
It was early morning and the chores must be done.
The first little farmer went out to milk the cow.
    (hold up hand, point to thumb)
The second little farmer thought he'd better plow.
    (hold up hand, point to index finger)
The third little farmer cultivated weeds.
    (point to middle finger)
The fourth little farmer planted more seeds.
    (point to fourth finger)
The fifth little farmer drove his tractor round.
    (point to last finger)
Five little farmers, the best that can be found.
    (hold up hand)

TRAFFIC POLICEMAN

The traffic policeman holds up his hand.
    (hold up hand, palm forward)
He blows the whistle,
    (pretend to blow whistle)
He gives the command.
    (hold up hand again)
When the cars are stopped
    (hold up hand again)
He waves at me.
Then I may cross the street, you see.
    (wave hand as if indicating for someone to go)

THE CARPENTER

This is the way he saws the wood
    (right hand saws left palm)
Sawing, sawing, sawing.
This is the way he nails a nail
    (pound right fist on left palm)
Nailing, nailing, nailing.
This is the way he paints the house
    (right hand paints left palm)
Painting, painting, painting.

Dramatic Play:

1. **Hat Shop**

Police officer hats, fire fighter hats, construction worker hats, business person hats, and other occupation-related hats should be placed in the dramatic play area.

2. **Classroom Cafe**

Cover the table in the dramatic play area with a tablecloth, provide menus, a tablet for the waitress to write on, a space for a cook, etc. A cash register and play money may also be added to encourage play.

3. **Hairstylist**

Collect empty shampoo bottles, combs, barrettes, ribbons, hair spray containers, and magazines. Cut the cord off a discarded hair dryer and curling iron and place in the dramatic play area.

4. **Our Library**

Books on a shelf, a desk for the librarian, stamper and ink pad to check out books should be placed in the dramatic play area. A small table for children to sit and read their books would also add interest.

5. **Workbench**

A hammer, nails, saws, vises, a carpenter's apron, etc., should be added to the workbench. Eye goggles for the children's safety should also be included. Constant supervision is needed for this activity.

6. **An Airplane**

Create an airplane out of a large cardboard refrigerator box. If desired, the children can paint the airplane.

7. **Post Office**

A mailbox, letters, envelopes, stamps, and mail carrier bags can be set up in the dramatic play or art area.

8. **Fast-Food Restaurant**

Collect bags, containers, and hats to set up a fast-food restaurant.

9. **A Construction Sight**

Hard hats, nails, a hammer, large blocks, and scrap wood can be provided for outdoor play. Cardboard boxes and masking tape should also be available.

10. **Prop Boxes**

The following prop boxes can be made by collecting the materials listed.

Police Officer

- badge
- hat
- uniform
- whistle
- walkie-talkie

Mail Carrier

- letter bag
- letter/stamps
- uniform
- mailbox
- envelopes
- paper
- pencil
- rubber stamp
- ink pad
- wrapped cardboard boxes

Fire Fighter

- boots
- helmet
- hose
- uniform
- gloves
- raincoat
- suspenders
- goggles

Doctor

- stethoscope
- medicine bottles
- adhesive tape
- cotton balls
- Red Cross armband
- chart holder

Arts and Crafts:

1. **Mail Truck**

Pre-cut mail truck parts including: 1 rectangle, 1 square, and 2 circles. The children can paste the pieces together and decorate. This activity is most appropriate for older children.

2. **Occupation Vests**

Cut a circle out of the bottom of a large paper grocery bag. Then from the circle cut a slit down the center of the bag. Cut out arm holes. Provide felt-tip colored markers for the children to decorate the vests. They may elect to be a pilot, police officer, mail carrier, baker, flight attendant, doctor, fire fighter, etc.

3. **Mail Pouch**

Cut the top half off a large grocery bag. Use the cutaway piece to make a shoulder strap. Staple it to the bag. The children can decorate the bag with crayons or markers.

Sensory:

The following materials can be added to the sensory table:

- sponge hair rollers with water
- wood shavings with scoops and scales
- sand with toy cars, trucks, airplanes
- pipes with water

Large Muscle:

Cut large cardboard boxes to make squad cars. Take the boxes and spray paint them either blue or white. Emblems can be constructed for the sides.

Field Trips/Resource People:

1. Take field trips to the following:

- bank
- library
- grocery store
- police station
- doctor/dentist office
- beauty salon/barber

- courthouse
- television/radio station
- airport
- farm
- restaurant

2. Invite the following resource people to school:

- police officer with squad car
- fire fighter with truck
- ambulance driver with ambulance
- truck driver with truck
- taxi driver with cab
- librarian with books

Social Studies:

1. **Occupation Pictures**

Pin occupation pictures on classroom bulletin boards and walls.

2. **A Job Chart**

Make a chart containing classroom jobs. Include tasks such as feeding the class pet, watering plants, sweeping the floor, wiping tables, etc.

Group Time (games, language):

1. **Brushes as Tools**

Collect all types of brushes and place in a bag. The children can reach into the bag and feel one. Before removing it, the child describes the kind of brush. When using with younger children, limit the number of brushes. Also, before placing the brushes in the bag, show the children each brush and discuss its use.

2. **Machines as Helpers Chart**

Machines and tools help people work and play. Ask the children to think of all of the machines they or their parents use around the house. As they name a machine, list it on a chart and discuss how it is used.

3. Mail It

Play a variation of "Duck, Duck, Goose." The children can sit in a circle. One child holds an envelope and walks around the circle saying, "letter," and taps each child on the head. When he gets to the one he wants to chase him, have the child drop the letter and say, "Mail it!" Then both children run around the circle until they return to the letter. The chaser gets to "mail" the letter by walking around and repeating the game.

Cooking:

Cheese Treats

cheese chunks
pretzel sticks

Cut cheese into small squares. Poke a pretzel into each cheese chunk.

Source: Wilmes, Liz & Dick. *Everyday Circle Times.*

EXCURSIONS

Special excursions and events in an early childhood program give opportunities for widening the young child's horizons by providing children exciting direct experiences. The following places or people are some suggestions:

train station	tree farm	airport
dentist office	car wash	riding stable
post office	children's houses	barber shop
grocery store	garage mechanic	college dormitory
zoo	television studio	shoe repair shop
dairy	drugstore	print shop
family garden	bakery	artist's studio
poultry house	hospital	bowling alley
construction site	meat market	department store windows
beauty shop	library	potter's studio
offices	apple orchard	teacher's house
animal hospital	farm	street repair site
fire station		

Multimedia:

The following resources can be found in educational catalogs:

1. Rogers, Fred. *These are the People in My Neighborhood* [record].

2. *We All Live Together*. Youngheart Records.

3. Jenkins, Ella. *My Street Begins at My House* [record].

4. Palmer, Hap. *Pretend* [record].

Books:

The following books can be used to complement the theme:

1. Lillegard, Dee. (1987). *I Can Be a Secretary*. Chicago: Children's Press.

2. Durham, Robert. (1987). *World At Work*. Chicago: Children's Press.

3. Merriam, Eve. (1991). *Daddies at Work*. New York: Simon and Schuster Trade.

4. Merriam, Eve. (1991). *Mommies at Work*. New York: Simon and Schuster Trade.

5. Civardi, Anne. (1986). *Things People Do*. Tulsa, OK: EDC Publishing.

6. Imershein, Betsy. (1990). *The Work People Do* (3 books). New York: Simon and Schuster Trade.

7. Moncure, Jane B. (1987). *What Can We Play Today?* Mankato, MN: Child's World, Inc.

8. Butterworth, Nick. (1992). *Busy People*. Cambridge, MA: Candlewick Press.

9. Grossman, Patricia. (1991). *The Night Ones*. San Diego: Harcourt Brace Jovanovich.

10. Hazen, Barbara Shook. (1992). *Mommie's Office*. New York: Macmillan.

11. Pringle, Laurence. (1989). *Jesse Builds a Road*. New York: Macmillan.

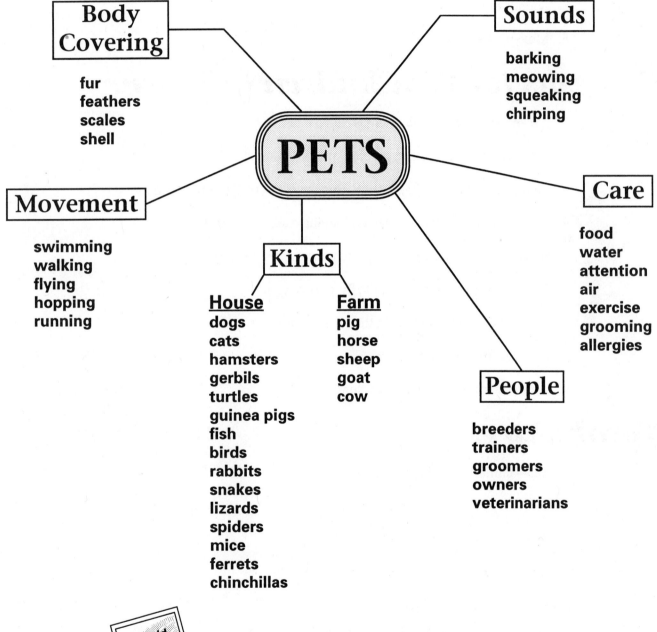

Body Covering

fur
feathers
scales
shell

Sounds

barking
meowing
squeaking
chirping

PETS

Movement

swimming
walking
flying
hopping
running

Care

food
water
attention
air
exercise
grooming
allergies

Kinds

House
dogs
cats
hamsters
gerbils
turtles
guinea pigs
fish
birds
rabbits
snakes
lizards
spiders
mice
ferrets
chinchillas

Farm
pig
horse
sheep
goat
cow

People

breeders
trainers
groomers
owners
veterinarians

Polaroid Education Program

Here's an exciting new way to turn instant photography into an effective teaching tool. Refer to the full-color insert for the activity entitled Polaroid Places.

Theme Goals:

Through participating in the experiences provided by this theme, the children may learn:

1. Some animals are kept as pets.

2. Pet care.

3. Places pets live.

4. Body coverings of pets.

5. Sounds of pets.

6. Movements of pets.

Concepts for the Children to Learn:

1. An animal kept for enjoyment is called a pet.

2. Dogs, cats, fish, hamsters, gerbils, and birds can all be house pets.

3. Pigs, ponies, horses, sheep, goats, and cows can be pets on a farm.

4. Pets need food, water, shelter, and loving care.

5. Barking, meowing, squeaking, and chirping are pet sounds.

6. To move, pets may swim, walk, fly, hop, or run.

7. The care of a pet depends on the type of animal.

8. Skin coverings on pets differ.

9. A veterinarian is an animal doctor.

Vocabulary:

1. **pet**—animal that is kept for pleasure.

2. **fur**—hairy coating of some animals.

3. **feathers**—skin covering of birds.

4. **scales**—skin covering of fish and other reptiles.

5. **veterinarian**—an animal doctor.

6. **collar**—a band worn around an animal's neck.

7. **leash**—a cord that attaches to a collar.

8. **whiskers**—stiff hair growing around the animal's nose, mouth, and eyes.

Bulletin Board

The purpose of this bulletin board is to encourage the development of mathematical skills. The children can count the fish in each water piece and match it to the corresponding numbered fishbowl. To prepare the bulletin board, construct fishbowls out of white tagboard or construction paper. Write a numeral beginning with one on each fishbowl and the corresponding number of dots. Hang the fishbowls on the bulletin board. Next, construct pieces as illustrated that will fit on top of the fishbowl to represent water in the bowl. Draw fish to match the numerals in each bowl. The pieces can be attached to each other to hang on the bulletin board by using magnet pieces, or push pins and a paper punch.

Parent Letter

Dear Parents,

Children are naturally curious about animals. Keeping that in mind, we will be starting a unit on pets, and I'm sure that we'll be busy! The children will discover the kinds of animals most people keep as pets. They will also learn the care that is involved in having a pet.

At School

The following are some of the learning experiences your child will participate in during our pet unit:

- making a special treat for Greta, our classroom gerbil.
- creating a large doghouse out of an appliance box for the dramatic play area.
- interacting with a variety of pets. Dani and Donny will bring their rabbit on Tuesday, and Cindy will bring her bird on Wednesday. If you are willing to bring your family pet to school to show the children, we welcome you. Contact me and we can arrange a time that would be convenient for you (and your pet).
- listening to the story, *Clifford, The Big Red Dog*, by Norman Bridwell.

At Home

Is your family considering adding a pet to your household? If so, there are many variables to be taken into consideration because not all households are meant to include pets. Allergies, fears, and life-styles are three things that need to be considered. Also, you will need to consider your child's readiness for a pet.

To develop fine motor skills, provide magazines and newspapers for your child to cut or tear out pictures of animals. These can be used to create an animal alphabet book or a collage to hang in your child's bedroom.

Enjoy your child!

FIGURE 45 Children enjoy feeding baby animals.

Music:

1. **"Rags"**
(Sing this song to one of the children's favorite tunes)

   I have a dog and his name is Rags.
   (point to self)
   He eats so much that his tummy sags.
   (hold tummy)
   His ears flip-flop and his tail wig-wags.
   (flip hands by ears and wag hands at back)
   And when he walks he zigs and zags.
   (put hands together and zig-zag them)

   Flip-flop
   Wiggle-waggle
   Zig-zag   (Repeat the same actions)
   Flip-flop
   Wiggle-waggle
   Zig-zag

2. **"Six Little Pets"**
(Sing to the tune of "Six Little Ducks," a traditional early childhood song)

   Six little gerbils I once knew, fat ones, skinny ones, fair ones too. But the one little gerbil was so much fun. He would play until the day was done.

   Six little dogs that I once knew, fat ones, skinny ones, fair ones too. But the one little dog with the brown curly fur, he led the others with a grr, grr, grr.

   Six little fish that I once knew, fat ones, skinny ones, fair ones too. But the one little fish who was the leader of the crowd, he led the others around and around.

   Six little birds that I once knew, fat ones, skinny ones, fair ones too. But the one little bird with the pretty little beak, he led the others with a tweet, tweet, tweet.

   Six little cats that I once knew, fat ones, skinny ones, fair ones too. But the one little cat who was as fluffy as a ball, he was the prettiest one of all.

3. **"Have You Ever Seen a Rabbit?"**
(Sing to the tune of "Have You Ever Seen A Lassie?")

   Have you ever seen a rabbit, a rabbit, a rabbit?
   Have you ever seen a rabbit go hopping around?
   Go hopping, go hopping, go hopping, go hopping
   Have you ever seen a rabbit go hopping around?

Fingerplays:

MY PUPPY

I like to pet my puppy.
   (pet puppy)
He has such nice soft fur.
   (pet puppy)
And if I don't pull his tail
   (pull tail)
He won't say "Grr!"
   (make face)

IF I WERE

If I were a dog
I'd have four legs to run and play.
   (down on all four hands and feet)
If I were a fish
I'd have fins to swim all day.
   (hands at side fluttering like wings)
If I were a bird
I could spread my wings out wide.
And fly all over the countryside.
   (arms out from sides fluttering like wings)
But I'm just me.
I have two legs, don't you see?
And I'm just as happy as can be.

THE BUNNY

Once there was a bunny
   (fist with two fingers tall)
And a green, green cabbage head.
   (fist of other hand)
"I think I'll have some breakfast," this little
bunny said.
So he nibbled and he cocked his ears to say,
"I think it's time that I be on my way."

SAMMY

Sammy is a super snake.
   (wave finger on opposite palm)
He sleeps on the shore of a silver lake.
   (curl finger to indicate sleep)
He squirms and squiggles to snatch a snack
   (wave finger and pounce)
And snoozes and snores till his hunger is back.
   (curl finger on palm)

NOT SAY A SINGLE WORD

We'll hop, hop, hop like a bunny
   (make hopping motion with hand)
And run, run, run like a dog.
   (make running motion with fingers)
We'll walk, walk, walk like an elephant
   (make walking motion with arms)
And jump, jump, jump like a frog.
   (make jumping motions with arms)
We'll swim, swim, swim like a goldfish
   (make swimming motion with hand)
And fly, fly, fly like a bird.
   (make flying motion with arms)
We'll sit right down and fold our hands
   (fold hands in lap)
And not say a single word!

Science:

1. **Pet Foods**

   Cut pictures of pets and pet foods and place on
   the science table. Include different foods such
   as meat, fish, carrots, lettuce, nuts, and acorns.
   The children can match the food to a picture of
   the animal that would eat each type of food.

2. **Bird Feathers**

   Bird feathers with a magnifying glass can be
   placed on the science table for the children to
   examine.

3. **Hamster and Gerbil Pet Food**

   The children can assist in preparing the pet
   food for hamsters or gerbils. The recipe is as
   follows:

   1/2 cup cracked corn
   1/2 cup flour
   1/4 cup water
   1/2 teaspoon salt

   Mix the water with flour in a bowl. Add salt.
   Form into balls and roll into cracked corn. Cool
   to harden. Serve once a day.

   Source: Reynolds, Michelle. (1979). *Critter's
   Kitchen.* New York: Athenum Publishing
   Company.

Dramatic Play:

1. **Pet Store**

   The children can all bring in their stuffed animals to set up a pet store. A counter, a cash register, and several empty pet food containers should be provided to stimulate play.

2. **Veterinarian Prop Box**

   Collect materials for a veterinarian prop box. Include a stethoscope, empty pill bottles, fabric cut as bandages, splints, and stuffed animals.

Arts and Crafts:

1. **Pet Sponge Painting**

   Cut sponges into a variety of pet shapes. Place on the art table with paper and a shallow pan of tempera paint.

2. **Doghouse**

   Provide an old large cardboard box for the children to make a doghouse with adult supervision. They can cut holes, paint, and decorate it. When dry, the doghouse can be moved into the dramatic play area or to the outdoor play yard.

3. **Cookie Cutters and Playdough**

   Pet-shaped cookie cutters and playdough can be placed on the art table.

Sensory:

Minnows

Fill the sensory table with cold water. Place minnows purchased from a bait store into the water. The children will attempt to catch the minnows. Teachers should stress the importance of being gentle with the fish and follow through with limits set for the activity. After participating in this activity, the children should wash their hands.

Field Trips/Resource People:

1. **Pet Show**

   Plan a pet show. Each child who wants to show a pet should sign up for a time and day. If children can all bring in a pet the same day, have a big pet show. Award prizes for longest tail, longest ears, biggest, smallest, best groomed, loudest barker, most obedient, etc. Children who do not have a pet or cannot arrange to bring it to school can bring a stuffed toy.

2. **Veterinarian**

   Invite a veterinarian to talk to the children about how a veterinarian helps pets and animals. Pet care can also be addressed.

3. **Pet Store**

   Visit a pet store to observe types of pets, their toys, and other accessories. Pictures can be taken on the trip and later placed on the bulletin board of the classroom.

4. **Pet Groomer**

   Visit a pet groomer. Observe how the pet is bathed and groomed.

Social Studies:

1. **Animal Sounds**

   Tape several animal sounds and play them back for the children to identify.

2. **Feeding Chart**

   Design and prepare a feeding chart for the classroom pets.

3. **Weekend Visitor**

   Let children take turns bringing class pets home on weekends. Prepare a card for each animal's cage outlining feeding and behavioral expectations.

Cooking:

Animal Cookies

1 1/2 cups powdered sugar
1 cup butter or margarine
1 egg
1 teaspoon vanilla extract
1/2 teaspoon almond extract
2 1/2 cups flour
1 teaspoon baking soda
1 teaspoon cream of tartar

Mix powdered sugar, margarine, egg, and vanilla and almond extracts. Mix in flour, baking soda, and cream of tartar. Cover and refrigerate for 2 hours. Preheat oven to 375 degrees. Divide dough into halves. Roll out 1/2-inch thick on a lightly floured, cloth-covered board. Cut the dough into animal shapes with cookie cutters or let children cut. Place on lightly greased cookie sheet. Bake 7 to 10 minutes. Serve for snack.

Multimedia:

The following resources can be found in educational catalogs:

1. Palmer, Hap. *Walk Like the Animals* [record].

2. Palmer, Hap. *Walter the Waltzing Worm* [record].

Books:

The following books can be used to complement the theme:

1. Blacker, Terrance. (1990). *Herbie Hamster, Where Are You?* New York: Random House.

2. Robbins, Sandra. (1990). *How the Turtle Got Its Shell: An African Tale. New York: Berrent* Publications.

3. Yolen, Jane. (1990). *Sky Dog.* San Diego: Harcourt Brace Jovanovich.

4. Szekeres, Cyndy. (1990). *What Bunny Loves.* Racine, WI: Western Publishing Co.

5. Cohen, C. (1988). *The Mud Pony: A Traditional Skidi Pawnee Tale.* New York: Scholastic.

6. Brown, Marc. (1990). *Arthur's Pet Business.* Boston: Joy Street Books.

7. Rogers, Fred. (1988). *When a Pet Dies.* New York: G. P. Putnam.

8. Berry, Joy. (1987). *Teach Me About Pets.* Chicago: Children's Press.

9. Cousins, Lucy. (1991). *Pet Animals.* New York: William Morrow and Co.

10. Dupont, Marie. (1991). *Your First Kitten.* Neptune City, NJ: TFH Publications, Inc.

11. Pienkowski, Jan. (1992). *Pets.* New York: Simon and Schuster Trade.

12. Smith, Lane. (1991). *The Big Pets.* New York: Viking Children's Books.

13. Davies, Andrew, & Davies, Diana. (1990). *Poonam's Pets*. New York: Viking Children's Books.

14. Erickson, Gina C., & Foster, Kelli C. (1992). *The Best Pets Yet*. Hauppauge, NY: Barron's Educational Series, Inc.

15. Garland, Sarah. (1992). *Billy and Belle*. New York: Viking Children's Press.

16. Tusan, Stan. (1992). *Who Will Be My Pet?* Racine, WI: Western Publishing Co.

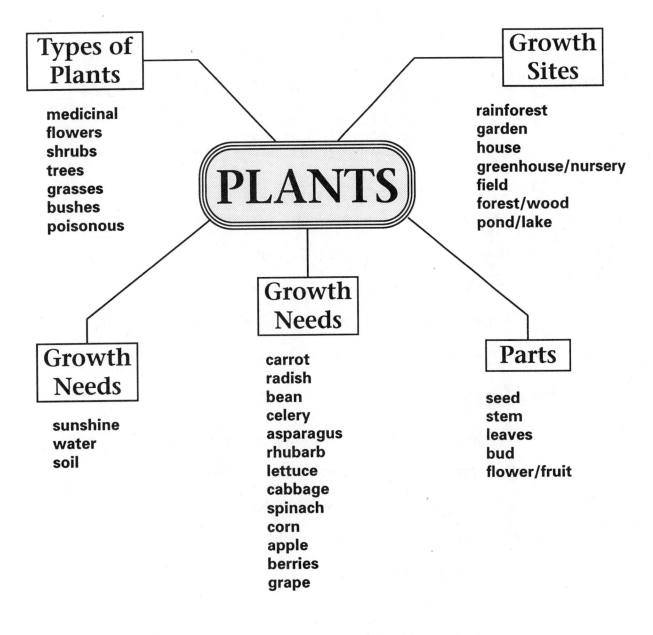

Types of Plants

medicinal
flowers
shrubs
trees
grasses
bushes
poisonous

Growth Sites

rainforest
garden
house
greenhouse/nursery
field
forest/wood
pond/lake

PLANTS

Growth Needs

carrot
radish
bean
celery
asparagus
rhubarb
lettuce
cabbage
spinach
corn
apple
berries
grape

Growth Needs

sunshine
water
soil

Parts

seed
stem
leaves
bud
flower/fruit

Polaroid Education Program

Here's an exciting new way to turn instant photography into an effective teaching tool. Refer to the full-color insert for the activity entitled Photo Peek-A-Boo.

Theme Goals:

Through participating in the experiences provided by this theme, the children may learn:

1. Types of plants.

2. Growth of plants.

3. The parts of a plant.

4. Plant growth sites.

5. Plants that provide food.

Concepts for the Children to Learn:

1. Plants are living things that grow.

2. There are many kinds of plants.

3. Some plants grow from seeds.

4. Some plants grow from another plant.

5. Plants need water, sunlight, and soil to grow.

6. People and animals eat some types of plants.

7. The parts of a plant are the stem, roots, leaves, flower/fruit, and seeds.

8. There are different sizes, colors, and shapes of seeds.

Vocabulary:

1. **plant**—living thing, usually green, that grows and changes.

2. **stem**—part of the plant that supports the leaves and grows upward.

3. **leaf**—part of the plant that grows on the stem.

4. **root**—part of the plant that grows into the soil.

5. **seed**—part of plant that can grow into another plant.

6. **vegetable**—a plant grown for food.

7. **fruit**—edible plant product that has seeds.

8. **flower**—a colored plant part that contains seeds.

9. **garden**—ground for growing plants.

10. **sprout**—first sign of growth.

Bulletin Board

The purpose of this bulletin board is to foster numeral recognition. To prepare the bulletin board, construct flowerpots out of construction paper. Color each pot and draw dots on it as illustrated. Hang the pots on the bulletin board. Next, construct the same number of flowers with stems as pots. In the center of each flower, write a numeral. The children can place each flower in the flowerpot with the corresponding number of dots.

Parent Letter

Dear Parents,

Plants will be the focus of our next unit. Through the unit the children will become aware of the parts of a plant as well as discover where plants can be grown and what plants can be eaten.

At School

Some of the learning experiences planned related to plants include:

- listening to the story, *The Plant Sitter*, by Gene Zion.
- sprouting alfalfa seeds to add to a salad.
- walking around our play yard to collect plants.
- playing hopscotch in the shape of a flower.

At Home

There are many ways to foster the concepts of this unit at home. If you have plants, let your child help water them. If you are planning to start a garden, section off a small portion for your child to grow plants.

At mealtimes, identify various parts of plants that are eaten. For example, we eat the leaves of lettuce, the stems of celery, the root of a carrot, and so on.

Plant some flower seeds with your child!

FIGURE 46 Which flower do you like best?

Music:

1. **"The Seed Cycle"**
   (Sing to the tune of "The Farmer in the Dell")

   The farmer sows his seeds.
   The farmer sows his seeds.
   Hi-ho the dairy-o
   The farmer sows his seeds.

   Other verses:
   The wind begins to blow…
   The rain begins to fall…
   The sun begins to shine…
   The seeds begin to grow…
   The plants grow big and tall…
   The farmer cuts his corn…
   He puts it in his barns…
   And now the harvest is in…

   Children can dramatize the parts for each verse.

2. **"This is the Way We Rake the Garden"**
   (Sing to the tune of: "Here We Go Round the Mulberry Bush")

   This is the way we rake the garden,
   Rake the garden, rake the garden.
   This is the way we rake the garden,
   So early in the morning.

   Other verses:
   This is the way we plant the seeds…
   This is the way the rain comes down…
   This is the way we hoe the weeds…
   This is the way the garden grows…
   This is the way we pick the vegetables…
   This is the way we eat the vegetables…

3. **"The Farmer in the Dell"** (traditional)

Fingerplays:

MY GARDEN

This is my garden.
   (extend one hand forward, palm up)
I'll rake it with care
   (make raking motion on palm with other hand)
And then some flower seeds
   (make planting motion with thumb and index fingers)
I'll plant in there.
The sun will shine
   (make circle above head)
And the rain will fall
   (let fingers flutter down to lap)
And my garden will blossom
   (cup hands together, extend upward slowly until fingers stand straight)
And grow straight and tall.

PLANTS

Plants need care to help them grow
   (make fist with hand)
Just like boys and girls you know.
Good soil, water, sunshine bright.
Then watch them pop overnight.
   (extend fingers from fist)

Science:

1. **Watch Seeds Grow**

   Two identical plastic transparent plates and blotting paper are needed for this activity. Moisten the blotting paper. Then lay the wet paper on one of the plates. On the top of the paper plate place various seeds—corn, peas, squash, bean, etc. Place the other plate over the seeds to serve as a cover. Tie the plates together tightly. Stand the plate on its edge in a pan containing 1/2 inch water. Watch the seeds sprout and grow.

2. **Colored Celery**

   In clear containers place several celery stalks with leaves. In each container add 3 inches of water and drop a different color of food coloring. The leaves of the celery should turn colors in a few hours. Try splitting a celery stalk in half, but do not split the stalk all the way up to the top. Put one half of the stalk in red water, and the other half in blue water. Watch what happens to the leaves.

3. **Sunlight Experiment**

   Place seeds in two jars with a half-inch of soil. Place one jar in a dark place such as a closet or cupboard and avoid watering it. Keep the other jar in a sunny area and water it frequently. Which one grew? Why?

4. **Growing Bean Plants**

   Each child can grow a bean plant.

5. **Tasting Plants**

   Various fruits and vegetables grown from plants should be provided for the children to taste and smell.

6. **Feely Box**

   In the feely box, place different parts of a plant such as root, stem, leaves, flowers, fruit, and buds. The children can feel and verbally identify the part of the plant before looking at it.

7. **Root a Vegetable**

   Place a potato or carrot in a jar, root end down so that one-third is covered by water. A potato can be held upright by inserting toothpicks or nails at three points. This can be rested on the rim of the jar. The children can water as needed. Roots should grow out from the bottom and shoots from the top. Then plant the root in soil for an attractive plant.

8. **Beans**

   Soak dry navy beans in a jar of water overnight. The next day compare soaked beans with dry beans. Note the difference in texture and color. Open some bean seeds that were soaked. A tiny plant should be inside the seed. These can be placed under a microscope for closer observation.

9. **Budding Branches**

   Place a branch that has buds ready to bloom in a jar of water on the science table. Let the children observe the buds bloom. Notice that after all the stored food of the plant is used the plant will die.

Dramatic Play:

1. **Greenhouse**

   Provide materials for a greenhouse. Include window space, pots, soil, water, watering cans, seeds, plants, posters, work aprons, garden gloves, a terrarium, and seed packages to mount on sticks.

2. **Jack and the Beanstalk**

   Act out the story, *Jack and the Beanstalk*. The children can dramatize a beanstalk growing.

3. **Vegetable-Fruit Stand**

   Display plastic fruits and vegetables. Set up a shopping area with carts, cash registers, and play money. Provide a balance scale for children to weigh the produce.

4. Garden Planting

Plant a small garden outdoors. Provide seeds, watering cans, garden tools, gloves, and garden hats.

Arts and Crafts:

1. Grass Hair

Save 1/2-pint milk cartons. The children can decorate the outside of the carton like a face. Place soil in the cartons and add grass seeds. After approximately 7 days the grass will start to grow, and it will look like hair. If the grass becomes too long, have the child give it a haircut.

2. Flower Collage

Collect flowers and weeds. Press the flowers and weeds between paper and books. Old telephone directories can be used. Dry them for 7 to 10 days. The children can use the pressed foliage to create their own collages on paper plates or construction paper.

3. Seed Pictures

Supply the children with paper, paste or glue, and various kinds of seeds. Included may be grass, beans, and unpopped popcorn kernels. The children can express their own creativity through self-created designs.

4. Nature Tree

Cut a branch off a tree and place in a pail of plaster of paris. The children can decorate the tree with a ribbon and different forms of plant life that they have collected or made. Included may be flowers, plants, fruits, vegetables, and seeds.

5. Leaf Rubbings

Place a thin piece of paper over a leaf. Rub gently with the long side of a crayon.

6. Easel Ideas

Cut easel paper into different shapes such as:

- leaves
- flowers
- flowerpots
- fruits and vegetables

7. Egg Carton Flowers

Use egg cartons and pipe cleaners to make flowers. To make the flower stand up, place a pipe cleaner into the egg carton as well as a styrofoam block.

8. Muffin Liner Flowers

Use paper muffin tin liners to make flowers.

9. Hand and Foot Flowers

Create a flower by using the child's hands and feet. Trace and cut two left and right hands and one set of left and right feet. Put one set of hands together to form the top of the flower and the other set (facing down) to form the bottom side. Add a circle to the middle. Cut a stem from green paper and add the green feet, as leaves. This makes a cute Mother's Day idea. Mount on white paper.

Math:

1. Charting Growth

The children can observe the growth of a small plant by keeping a chart of its growth. Record the date of the observation and the height. For convenience, place the chart near the plant table.

2. Flowerpot Match Game

Construct flowerpots. The number constructed will depend upon the developmental appropriateness. Write a numeral on each, beginning with the numeral one. Then make the same number of flowers, varying from one petal to the total number of flowerpots constructed. The children match the flowerpot to the flower with the same number of petals.

3. Counting and Classifying Seeds

Place a variety of seeds on a table. Encourage the children to count and classify them into groups. To assist in counting and classifying, an egg carton with each section given a number from 1 to 12 may be helpful. Encourage the children to observe the numeral and place a corresponding number of seeds in each section.

4. **Plant Growth Seriation**

Construct pictures of plants through stages of growth. Begin with a seed, followed by the seed sprouting. The third picture should be the stem erupting from the soil surface. Next a stem with leaves can be constructed. Finally, flowers can be added to the last picture. This could also be made into a bulletin board.

5. **Seed Match**

Collect a variety of seeds such as corn, pumpkin, orange, apple, lima bean, watermelon, pea, and peach. Cut several rectangles out of white tagboard. On the top half of each rectangle glue one of the seed types you have collected. Encourage the children to sort the seeds, matching them to those seeds glued on the individual cards.

Social Studies:

1. **Plant Walk**

Walk around the neighborhood and try to identify as many plants as you can.

2. **Play Yard Plants**

Make a map of the play yard. The children can collect a part of each plant located in the playground. The plant samples can be mounted on the map.

3. **Planting Trees**

Plant a tree on your playground. Discuss the care needed for trees.

4. **Family Tree**

Make a Family Tree by mounting a bunch of branches in a pail of dirt. Each child can bring in a family picture to be placed on a leaf shape and hung on the tree branches.

Large Muscle:

1. **Leaf Jumping**

Cut out eight large leaves from tagboard. Arrange the leaves in a pattern on the floor. Encourage the children to jump from one leaf to another. This game could also be played outdoors by drawing the leaves on the sidewalk with chalk.

2. **Flower Hopscotch**

Design a hopscotch in the form of a flower. Use chalk on a sidewalk outdoors or masking tape can be used indoors to make the form.

3. **Vegetable, Vegetable, Plant**

Play "Vegetable, Vegetable, Plant" as a variation of "Duck, Duck, Goose."

4. **Raking and Hoeing**

Provide the children with hoes and rakes to tend to the play yard.

Field Trips:

1. **Greenhouse**

Visit a greenhouse or a tree nursery to observe the different plants and trees and inquire about their care.

2. **Farm**

Plan a visit to a farm. While there, observe the various forms of plant life.

3. **Florist**

Visit a florist. Observe the different colors, types, and sizes of flowering plants.

446

Group Time (games, language):

Feltboard Fun

Construct felt pieces representing the stages of a flower's growth. Include a bulb, seed, cuttings, root, stem, leaves, and a flower. During group time, review the name and purpose of each part with the children. The children can take turns coming up to the flannel board and adding the pieces. After group time, the felt pieces should be left out so that the child can reconstruct the growth during self-selected activity period.

Cooking:

1. **Vegetable-Tasting Party**

   Prepare raw vegetables for a tasting party. Discuss the color, texture, and flavor of each vegetable.

2. **Sprouts**

   Provide each interested child with a small jar. Fill the bottom with alfalfa seeds. Fill the jar with warm water and cover with cheesecloth and a rubberband. Each day rinse and fill the jar with fresh warm water. In three or four days the seeds will sprout. The sprouts may be used on sandwiches or salads at lunchtime.

3. **Latkes (Potato Pancakes)**

   2 potatoes, peeled and grated 1 egg, slightly beaten
   1/4 cup flour
   1 teaspoon salt
   cooking oil

   Mix the ingredients in a bowl. Drop the mixture by tablespoons into hot oil in an electric skillet. Brown on both sides. Drain on paper towels.

4. **Ground Nut Soup (Nigeria)**

   1 large tomato
   1 large potato
   1 onion
   2 cups water
   1 beef boullion cube
   1 cup shelled, unsalted roasted peanuts
   1/2 cup milk
   2 tablespoons rice

   Peel potato and onion. Dice potato, tomato, and onion. Place in saucepan with the water and boullion cube. Boil, covered, for 30 minutes. Chop and add the peanuts, milk, and rice to the boiling mixture. Stir. Lower heat and simmer 30 minutes. Serves 6 to 8.

Multimedia:

The following resources can be found in educational catalogs:

1. "Oats, Peas, Beans and Barley Grow," *Let's Sing Along with Mother Goose* [record]. Farmingdale, NY: Record Guild of America.

2. *Great Bedtime Stories: Jack and the Beanstalk* [record]. New York: A.A. Records Inc.

3. "The Little Nut Tree," [record]. Walt Disney Productions.

Books:

The following books can be used to complement the theme:

1. Fife, Dale H. (1991). *The Empty Lot*. Boston: Little Brown.

2. Politi, Leo. (1993). *Three Stalks of Corn*. New York: Macmillan.

3. Cherry, Lynne. (1990). *The Great Kapok Tree*. San Diego: Harcourt Brace Jovanovich.

4. Bunting, Eve. (1993). *Someday a Tree*. New York: Clarion.

5. Allard, Harry. (1993). *The Cactus Flower Bakery*. New York: Harper Collins.

6. Gibbons, Gail. (1991). *From Seed to Plant*. New York: Holiday House, Inc.

7. Heller, Ruth. (1992). *Plants That Never Ever Bloom*. New York: Putnam Publishing Group.

8. Riehecky, Janet. (1990). *What Plants Give Us: The Gift of Life*. Mankato, MN: Child's World, Inc.

9. Wexler, Jerome. (1991). *Flowers Fruits and Seeds*. New York: Simon and Schuster Trade.

10. Blos, Joan W. (1992). *A Seed, a Flower, a Minute, an Hour*. New York: Simon and Schuster Trade.

11. Taylor, Barbara. (1991). *Growing Plants*. New York: Franklin Watts Inc.

Stages

tables
bookcases
cardboard boxes
blankets
sheets

Purposes

express feelings
entertainment
communication

Kinds

finger
hand
stick
cloth
rod
shadow
marionette
dummy

PUPPETS

Materials

cloth
paper/paper bags
novelty sticks
socks
wooden spoons
string
felt
coat hangers
pot holders
mittens
gloves
paper plates
flyswatters

Movement

string
wire
rods
hands
fingers

Types

animals
people
pretend creatures

Here's an exciting new way to turn instant photography into an effective teaching tool. Refer to the full-color insert for the activity entitled Tell Me A Story.

Theme Goals:

Through participating in the experiences provided by this theme, the children may learn:

1. The purpose of using puppets.

2. Kinds of puppets.

3. Types of puppets.

4. Materials used to make puppets.

5. Ways of moving puppets.

6. Types of puppet stages.

Concepts for the Children to Learn:

1. Puppets can be fun.

2. Puppets can be used for communicating and entertainment.

3. We can use puppets to express feelings.

4. People talk for puppets.

5. Puppets can be made from paper, cloth, or even wood.

6. Puppets can be made to look like animals, people, or pretend creatures.

7. Puppets can be moved with hands or fingers.

8. Mittens, gloves, and paper plates can all be made into puppets.

9. Large boxes can be used for puppet stages.

Vocabulary:

1. **puppet**—a toy that is moved by the hand or finger.

2. **marionette**—a puppet with strings for movement.

3. **puppet show**—a story told with puppets.

4. **puppeteer**—a person who makes a puppet move and speak.

5. **puppet stage**—a place for puppets to act.

6. **entertainment**—things we enjoy seeing and listening to.

7. **imaginary**—something that is not real.

Bulletin Board

The purpose of this bulletin board is to show a variety of puppets. The children's expressive language skills will be stimulated by interacting with the puppets. Design the bulletin board by constructing about five or six simple puppets for the children to take off the bulletin board to play with. Include a flyswatter puppet, a paper bag puppet, hand puppet, sock puppet, and a wooden spoon puppet. Hooks or push pins can be used to attach the puppets to the bulletin board.

Parent Letter

Dear Parents,

Our new unit will focus on puppets. They are magical and motivating to young children. Sometimes a child will respond or talk to a puppet in a situation when he might not talk to an adult or other child. Through learning experiences involving puppets, the children will become aware of the different types of puppets and materials that can be used to make puppets. They will express themselves creatively and imaginatively.

At School

Some of the activities related to puppets include:

* creating our own puppets with a variety of materials.
* using the puppet stage throughout the week, putting on puppet shows for one and all.
* exploring various types of puppets, including finger, hand, stick, shadow, and marionette puppets.

At Home

The children enjoy retelling familiar stories and making up original stories for puppet characters. To stimulate this type of play, you and your child can make simple puppets at home with objects found around the house.

Paper Bag Puppets—Using small paper lunch bags, children can use crayons or markers to create a puppet. The fold in the bag can be used as the mouth. After the child's hand is in the bag, the puppet can talk. Yarn scraps can easily be glued on for hair and construction paper scraps can add a decorative touch.

Sock Puppets—I'm sure you have a couple of socks around the house that seem to have lost their mates. (Does your dryer eat socks, too?) Depending on your child's skills and how much supervision you can provide—eyes, a nose, and hair of a variety of materials (yarn, buttons, fabric) can either be sewn or glued on. Insert your hand and your puppet is ready!

Stick Puppets—Make story characters' faces or bodies on heavy paper or on cardboard with crayons, markers, or paint. Cut the figures out and attach them with strong glue or tape to a ruler, popsicle stick, tongue depressor, or any stick that can be used to hold the puppet and move it. A large box or table can serve as the puppet stage.

Enjoy your child!

FIGURE 47 Young children become engrossed in puppet shows.

Music:

"Eensy Weensy Spider" (traditional)

Fingerplays:

CATERPILLAR CRAWLING

One little caterpillar crawled on my shoe.
Another came along and then there were two.
Two little caterpillars crawled on my knee.
Another came along and then there were three.
Three little caterpillars crawled on the floor.
Another came along and then there were four.
Four little caterpillars watch them crawl away.
They'll all turn into butterflies some fine day.

This fingerplay can be told using puppets
made from felt or tagboard.

Source: Indenbaum, Valerie, & Shapior,
Marcia. (1983). *The Everything Book*. Chicago:
Partner Press.

SPECKLED FROGS

Five green-speckled frogs
Sitting on a speckled log

Eating the most delicious bugs,
Yum, yum!
    (rub tummy)

One jumped into the pool
Where it was nice and cool
Now there are four green-speckled frogs.

Repeat until there are no green-speckled frogs.

This fingerplay can be told using puppets
made from felt or tagboard.

CHICKADEES

Five little chickadees sitting in a door
    (hold up hand)
One flew away and then there were four
    (put down one finger at a time)
Four little chickadees sitting in a tree
One flew away and then there were three.
Three little chickadees looking at you.
One flew away and then there were two.
Two little chickadees sitting in the sun.
One flew away and then there was one.
One little chickadee sitting all alone.
He flew away and then there were none.

This fingerplay can be told using puppets
made from felt or tagboard.

453

Science:

1. **Classify Puppets**

   During group time let the children classify the various puppets into special categories such as animals, people, insects, imaginary things, etc.

2. **Button Box**

   A large box of buttons should be provided. The children can sort the buttons according to color, size, or shape into a muffin tin or egg carton.

Dramatic Play:

1. **Puppet Show**

   A puppet stage should be available throughout the entire unit in the dramatic play area. Change or add the puppets on a regular basis using as many different kinds of puppets as possible.

2. **Puppet Shop**

   A variety of materials should be provided for the children to construct puppets. Include items such as buttons, bows, felt, paper bags, cloth pieces, socks, tongue depressors, etc.

Arts and Crafts:

1. **Making Puppets**

   Puppets can be made from almost any material. Some suggestions are listed here:

   - cotton covered with cloth attached to a tongue depressor.
   - paper sacks stuffed with newspaper.
   - a cork for a head with a hole in it for a finger.
   - socks.
   - cardboard colored with crayon attached to a tongue depressor.
   - flyswatter.
   - oatmeal box attached to a dowel.

   - nylon panty hose stretched over a hanger bent into an oval shape.
   - empty toilet paper and paper towel rolls.

2. **Puppet Stages**

   Puppet stages can be made from the following materials:

   - boxes, including tempera paint and markers for decorating.
   - large paper bags.
   - half-gallon milk carton.
   - towel draped over an arm.
   - towel draped over the back of a chair.
   - blanket covering a card table.

Sensory:

Sensory Table

During this unit add to the sensory table all of the various materials that puppets are made of:

- string
- buttons
- felt
- toilet paper rolls
- cardboard
- paper
- sticks
- wood shavings

Large Muscle:

1. **Creative Movement**

   Demonstrate how to manipulate a marionette. Then have the children pretend that they are marionettes and that they have strings attached to their arms and legs. Say, "Someone is pulling up the string that is attached to your arm, what would happen to your arm?" Allow the children to make that movement. Continue with other movements.

2. **Large Puppets**

   Large puppets such as stick or rod puppets can provide the children with a lot of large muscle movement.

3. **Pin the Nose on the Puppet**

This game is a variation of the traditional "Pin the Tail on the Donkey." (This game would be more appropriate for five-, six-, seven-, and eight-year-old children.)

Field Trips/Resource People:

1. **Puppet Show**

Place puppets by the puppet stage to encourage the children to put on puppet shows.

2. **Puppeteer**

Invite a puppeteer to visit the classroom and show the children the many uses of puppets.

Math:

1. **Examine a Puppet**

With the children, examine a puppet and count all of its various parts. Count its eyes, legs, arms, stripes on its shirt, etc. Discuss how it was constructed.

2. **Puppet Dot-to-Dot**

Draw a large puppet on a sheet of tagboard. Laminate or cover the tagboard sheet with clear adhesive paper. A grease pencil or felt-tip watercolor marker should be provided for the children to draw. Also, felt scraps should be available to remove grease markings. Otherwise, a damp cloth or paper towel should be available.

Social Studies:

Occupation Puppets

Introduce various types of occupation puppets. Ask the children to describe each.

Group Time (games, language):

Puppet Show

Using your favorite classroom stories, put on a puppet show. The children can volunteer to be the various characters. Pre-tape the story so that the children can listen to it while they practice. This might be a good activity to invite parents to attend.

Cooking:

1. **Puppet Faces**

Make open-faced sandwiches using peanut butter or cream cheese spread onto a slice of bread or a bun. Carrot curls can be used to represent hair. Raisins and green or purple grape halves can be used for the eyes, nose, and mouth.

2. **Dog Puppet Salad**

Place a pear half onto the plate. Two apple slices can be added to resemble a dog's ears hanging down. Then raisins or grape halves can be used to represent the eyes and nose of a dog.

Multimedia:

The following resource can be found in educational catalogs:

"The Little Red Hen Operetta," *Puppet Parade* [record]. Melody House Records.

Books:

The following books can be used to complement the theme:

1. Hoyt-Goldsmith, Diane. (1991). *Pueblo Storyteller.* New York: Holiday.

2. Poskanzer, Susan C. (1989). *Puppeteer.* Mahwah, NJ: Troll Associates.

3. Bridwell, Norman. (1991). *Hello Clifford: A Puppet Book.* New York: Scholastic Inc.

4. Chaney, Steve. (1989). *The Puppet in the Big Black Box.* Sunnyvale, CA: Stiff Lip Productions.

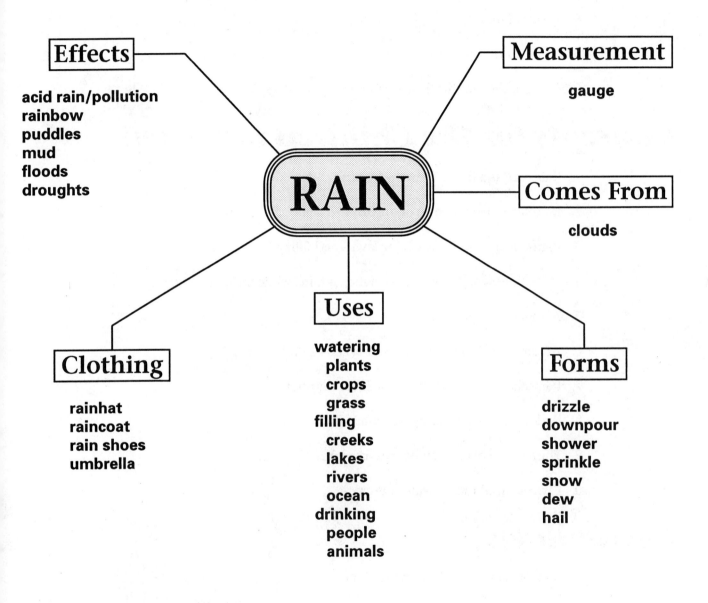

Effects

acid rain/pollution
rainbow
puddles
mud
floods
droughts

Measurement

gauge

RAIN

Comes From

clouds

Clothing

rainhat
raincoat
rain shoes
umbrella

Uses

watering
    plants
    crops
    grass
filling
    creeks
    lakes
    rivers
    ocean
drinking
    people
    animals

Forms

drizzle
downpour
shower
sprinkle
snow
dew
hail

Polaroid
Education
Program

Here's an exciting new way to turn instant photography into an effective teaching tool. Refer to the full-color insert for the activity entitled Presto-Chango-Photo.

Theme Goals:

Through participating in the experiences provided by this theme, the children may learn:

1. Uses of rain.

2. Effects of rain.

3. Clothing worn for protection from the rain.

4. Forms of rain.

5. Origin of rain.

6. The tool used for the measurement of rain.

Concepts for the Children to Learn:

1. Rain falls as a liquid from the clouds.

2. Rain can fall in the form of drizzle, hail, snow, or a shower.

3. Rain can be used for watering lawns and filling lakes.

4. A rainbow sometimes appears when it rains while the sun is shining.

5. A rainbow is colorful.

6. An umbrella is used in the rain to keep us dry.

7. Raincoats, hats, and rubber shoes are rain clothing.

8. Puddles can form during a rainfall.

9. The amount of rain can be measured in a water gauge.

10. Farmers need rain to water the crops.

Vocabulary:

1. **rain**—water that falls from the clouds.

2. **rainbow**—a colorful arc formed when the sun shines while it is raining.

3. **puddle**—rain collection on the ground.

4. **umbrella**—a shade for protection against rain.

5. **snow**—frozen rain.

6. **gauge**—a tool for measuring rain.

Bulletin Board

The purpose of this bulletin board is to develop an awareness of sets, as well as to identify written numerals. Construct clouds out of gray tagboard. Write a numeral on each cloud. Cut out and laminate. Next, trace and cut cloud shadows from construction paper. Attach the shadows to the bulletin board. A set of raindrops, from one to 10, should be attached underneath each cloud shadow. Magnet pieces or push pins and holes in the cloud piece can be used for the children to match each cloud to a corresponding shadow, using the raindrops as a clue.

Parent Letter

Dear Parents,

"Rain, rain, go away. Come again some other day," is a familiar nursery rhyme. It is one that we may often hear as a unit on rain begins. Through the experiences provided, the children will become aware of the uses and forms of rain as well as how rainbows are created.

At School

The following activities are just a few that have been planned for the rain unit:

- a visit by TV 8's weatherman. Tom Hector will be coming at 2:00 pm on Tuesday to show us a video made for preschoolers that depicts various weather conditions.
- finding out about evaporation by setting out a shallow pan of water and marking the water level each day.
- creating a rainbow on a sunny day outdoors with a garden hose.

At Home

To develop language skills practice this rain poem with your child:

> Rain on the green grass
> And rain on trees.
> Rain on the rooftops,
> But not on me!!

Use an empty can or jar to make a rain gauge. Place the container outdoors to measure rainfall. Several gauges could be placed in various places in your yard.

Enjoy your child!

FIGURE 48 Rain serves many purposes.

Music:

"Rainy"
(Sing to the tune of "Bingo")

There was a day when we got wet
and rainy was the weather
R-A-I-N-Y R-A-I-N-Y R-A-I-N-Y
and rainy was the weather.

Repeat each verse eliminating a letter and
substituting it with a clap until the last chorus
is all claps to the same beat.

Fingerplays:

LITTLE RAINDROP

This is the sun, high up in the sky.
  (hold hands in circle above head)
A dark cloud suddenly comes sailing by.
  (slide hands to side)
These are the raindrops.
  (make raining motion with fingers)
Pitter patter down.
Watering the flowers,
  (pouring motion)
Growing on the ground.
  (hands pat the ground)

RAINY DAY FUN

Slip on your rain coat.
  (pretend to put coat on)
Pull up your galoshes.
  (pull up galoshes)
Wade in puddles,
Make splishes and sploshes.
  (make stomping motions)

THUNDERSTORM

Boom, bang, boom, bang!
  (clap hands)
Rumpety, lumpety, bump!
  (stomp feet)
Zoom, zam, zoom, zam!
  (swish hands together)
Rustles and bustles
  (pat thighs)
And swishes and zings!
  (pat thighs)
What wonderful noises
A thunderstorm brings.

RAIN

From big black clouds
  (hold up arms)
The raindrop fell.
  (pull finger down in air)

Drip, drip, drip one day,
  (hit one finger on palm of hand)
Until the bright sunlight changed them
Into a rainbow gay!
  (make a rainbow with hands)

Source of first four fingerplays: Wilmes, Dick & Liz. *Everyday Circle Times*. Building Block Publications.

THE RAIN

I sit before the window now
  (seat yourself, if possible)
And I look out at the rain.
  (shade your eyes and look around)
It means no play outside today
  (shake head, shrug)
So inside I remain.
  (rest chin on fist, look sorrowful)
I watch the water dribble down
  (follow up-to-down movements with eyes)
And turn the brown grass green.
  (sit up, take notice)
And after a while I start to smile
At Nature's washing machine.
  (smile, lean back, relax)

Source: Cromwell, Hibner, & Faitel. *Finger Frolics—Finger Plays for Young Children*.

Science:

1. **Tasting Water**

   Collect tap water, soda water, mineral water, and distilled water. Pour the different types of water into paper cups and let children taste them. Discuss the differences.

2. **Evaporation**

   The children can pour water into a jar. Mark a line at the water level. Place the jar on a window ledge and check it every day. The disappearance is called evaporation.

3. **Catching Water**

   If it rains one day during your unit, place a bucket outside to catch the rain. Return the bucket to your science table. Place a bucket of tap water next to the rainwater and compare.

4. **Color Mixing**

   Using water and food coloring or tempera, mix the primary colors. Discuss the colors of the rainbow.

Dramatic Play:

1. **Rainy Day Clothing**

   Umbrellas, rain coats, hats, rain shoes, and a tape containing rain sounds should be added to the dramatic play area. Use caution when selecting umbrellas for this activity. Some open quickly and can be dangerous.

2. **Weather Station**

   A map, pointer, adult clothing, and pretend microphone should be placed in the dramatic play area. The children can play weather person. Pictures depicting different weather conditions can be included.

Arts and Crafts:

1. **Eyedropper Painting**

   Use eyedroppers filled with colored water as applicators.

2. **Waxed Paper Rainbows**

   Cut waxed paper in the shape of large rainbows. Then prepare red, yellow, green, and blue crayon shavings. After this, the children can sprinkle the crayon shavings on one sheet of waxed paper. Place another sheet of waxed paper on the top of the sheet with sprinkled crayon. Finally, the teacher should place a linen towel over the top of the waxed paper sheets. A warm iron should be applied to melt the two pieces together. Cool and attach a string. Hang from the window. (This activity needs constant adult supervision.)

3. **Rainbow Yarn Collage**

   Using rainbow-shaped paper and rainbow-colored yarn, the children can make rainbow yarn collages.

4. Thunder Painting

Tape record a rain or thunderstorm. Leave this tape with a tape recorder and earphones at the easel. Grey, black, and white paint can be provided. Let the children listen to the rainstorm and paint to it. Ask the children how the music makes them feel.

5. Rainbow Mobiles

Pre-cut rainbow arcs. On these, the children can paste styrofoam packing pieces. After this, they can paint the pieces. Display the mobiles in the room.

Sensory:

Add to the sensory table:

- water with scoops, cups, and spoons.
- sand and water (make puddles in the sand).
- rainbow-colored sand, rice, and pasta.
- rainwater

Large Muscle:

Worm Wiggle

The purpose of this game is to imitate worm motions. Show the children how to lie on their stomachs, holding their arms in at their sides. The children should try to move forward without using their hands or elbows like a worm would wiggle.

Field Trips/Resource People:

1. Reflection

Take a walk after it rains. Enjoy the puddles, overflowing gutters, and swirls of water caught by sewers. Look in the puddles. Does anyone see a reflection? Look up in the sky. Do you see any clouds, the sun, or a rainbow? What colors are in a rainbow?

2. The Weather Person

Take a field trip to a television station and see what equipment a weather person uses.

Math:

Rainbow Match

Fabrics of all the colors of the rainbow can be cut into pieces. The children can sort these and group them into different colors, textures, and sizes.

Group Time (games, language):

1. Creative Thinking

Read this poem to your children and then ask them, "Why didn't I get wet?" You may have to read the poem again or you may have to encourage the children to use their imagination since the answer is not in the poem.

RAIN

Rain on green grass
and rain on the tree.
Rain on the rooftop,
But not on me!

Source: Wilmes, Liz & Dick. *Everyday Circle Times*. Building Block Publications.

2. Jump in Puddles

This game is played like "Musical Chairs." The puddles are made from circles on the floor with one child in each and one less circle than children so one child is out of the circles. On the signal, "Jump in the puddles," the children have to switch puddles. The child who was out has a chance to get in a puddle. The child who does not get into a puddle waits until the next round. This can be played indoors or outdoors. Hula hoops could also be used in small groups of four children using three hoops. (This activity is most appropriate for older children.)

Miscellaneous:

1. **Cut and Tell Story: "The Rainbow's End"**

   Source: Warren, Jean. *Cut and Tell Scissor Stories for Spring*. Everett, WA: Totline Press, Warren Publishing House.

2. **Flannelboard Stories**

   Source: Stangl, Jean. *Flannel Graphs—Flannel Board Fun for Little Ones*. Belmont, CA: David S. Lake Publishers.

Cooking:

Rainbow Fruits

Serve a different colored snack each day. An example would be to correspond with the colors of the rainbow.

- strawberries
- oranges
- lemon finger gelatin (see a gelatin box for recipe)
- blueberries added to yogurt
- grape juice
- grapes or blackberries
- lettuce salad

Multimedia:

The following resources can be found in educational catalogs:

1. *Color Me a Rainbow* [record]. Melody House Records.

2. *Follow the Clouds* [record]. Melody House Records.

3. *Raindrops* [record]. Melody House Records.

4. *Adventures in Sound* [record]. Melody House Records.

Books:

The following books can be used to complement the theme:

1. Szilagyi, Mary. (1985). *Thunderstorm*. New York: Bradbury.

2. Gay, Marie-Louise. (1989). *Rainy Day Magic*. Morton Grove, IL: Albert Whitman.

3. Stevenson, James. (1988). *We Hate Rain!* New York: Greenwillow.

4. Stolz, Mary. (1990). *Storm in the Night*. New York: Harper Collins.

5. Wiesner, David. (1990). *Hurricane*. New York: Clarion Books.

6. O'Neill, Mary. (1989). *Hailstones and Halibut Bones*. New York: Doubleday.

7. Markle, Sandra. (1993). *A Rainy Day*. New York: Orchard Books.

8. Kachenmeister, Cheryl. (1989). *On Monday When it Rains*. Boston: Houghton Mifflin.

9. Koch, Michele. (1993). *World Water Watch*. New York: Greenwillow.

10. Martin, Bill, Jr., & Archambault, John. (1988). *Listen to the Rain*. New York: Henry Holt.

11. Polacco, Patricia. (1990). *Thunder Cake*. New York: Putnam.

12. Moncure, Jane B. (1990). *Rain: A Great Day for Ducks*. Mankato, MN: Child's World, Inc.

13. Wyler, Rose. (1989). *Raindrops and Rainbows*. New York: Simon and Schuster Trade.

14. Cole, Sheila. (1991). *When the Rain Stops*. New York: Lothrop, Lee, & Shepard Books.

15. Corrin, Ruth. (1990). *It Always Rains for Jackie*. New York: Oxford University Press.

16. Ehlert, Lois. (1988). *Planting a Rainbow*. San Diego: Harcourt Brace Jovanovich.

17. Hallinan, P. K. (1991). *My Very Best Rainy Day*. Nashville, TN: Ideals Publishing Corp.

18. Serfozo, Mary. (1990). *Rain Talk*. New York: Macmillan Children's Books Group.

THEME 49

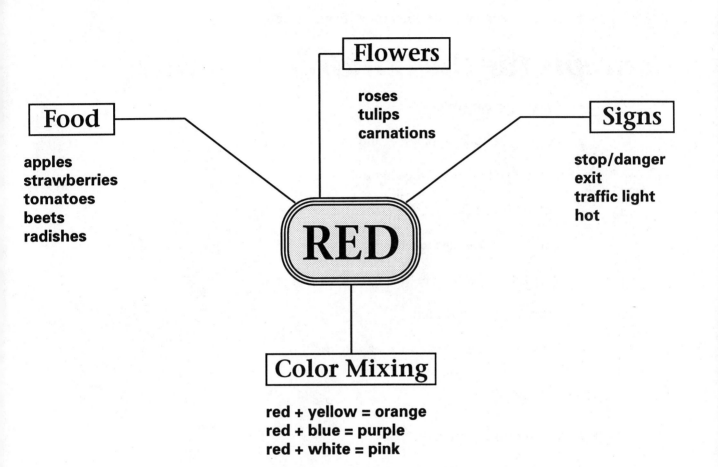

Flowers

roses
tulips
carnations

Food

apples
strawberries
tomatoes
beets
radishes

RED

Signs

stop/danger
exit
traffic light
hot

Color Mixing

red + yellow = orange
red + blue = purple
red + white = pink

Polaroid
Education
Program

Here's an exciting new way to turn instant photography into an effective teaching tool. Refer to the full-color insert for the activity entitled Concentration Game.

Theme Goals:

Through participating in the experiences provided by this theme, the children may learn:

1. Red is a color.

2. Some foods are red.

3. Many objects are red.

4. Red can be mixed with other colors to make different colors.

Concepts for the Children to Learn:

1. Red is a primary color.

2. Some foods, such as tomatoes and strawberries, are red.

3. Red and yellow mixed together make orange.

4. Red and blue mixed together make purple.

5. Red and white mixed together make pink.

6. Some fire trucks and fire hydrants are red.

7. A stop sign is colored red.

8. Some roses, tulips, and carnations are red.

Vocabulary:

1. **red**—a primary color.

2. **primary colors**—red, yellow, and blue.

Bulletin Board

The purpose of this bulletin board is to reinforce the mathematical skills of matching sets of objects to a written numeral. Green produce baskets or other small baskets can be hung on the bulletin board for a strawberry-counting bulletin board. Attach baskets to the bulletin boards using staples or push pins. Collect small plastic strawberries, or make strawberries out of tagboard. On each basket mark a numeral. The children can place the appropriate number of strawberries into each basket.

Parent Letter

Dear Parents,

Colors are everywhere and they make our world beautiful. That's why we'll focus on a specific color—red! It's a popular color with young children and many objects in our world are red. The experiences provided will also help the children become aware of colors that are formed when mixed with red.

At School

A few of the curriculum experiences include:

- mixing the color red with yellow and blue to make orange and purple.
- setting up an art store in the dramatic play area where the children can act out the buying and selling of art supplies.
- exploring red-colored crayons, markers, pencils, chalk, paint, and paper.
- filling the sensory table with red goop.

At Home

To reinforce the concepts in this unit, try the following activities at home with your child:

- To develop observation skills look around your house with your child for red items. How many red objects can you find in each room?
- Prepare red foods for meals such as apples, strawberries, tomatoes, and jam.
- Prepare red ice cubes to cool your drinks. To do this, just add a few drops of red food coloring to the water before freezing it.

Enjoy making colorful discoveries with your child.

FIGURE 49 Sponges and red paint can make interesting designs.

Fingerplays:

TULIPS

Five little tulips–red and bright
   (hold up hand)
Let us water them every day.
   (make sprinkle motion with other hand)
Watch them open in the bright sunlight.
   (cup hand, then open)
Watch them close when it is night.
   (close hand again).

MY APPLE

Look at my apple, it's red and round.
   (make ball shape with hands)
It fell from a tree down to the ground
   (make downward motion)
Come let me share my apple, please do!
   (beckoning motion)

My mother can cut it right in two—
   (make slicing motion)
One half for me and one half for you
   (hold out 2 hands, sharing halves)

FIVE RED APPLES

Five red apples in a grocery store.
   (hold up five fingers)
Bobby bought one, and then there were four.
   (bend down one finger)
Four red apples on an apple tree.
Susie ate one, and then there were three.
   (bend down one finger)
Three red apples. What did Alice do?
Why, she ate one, and then there were two.
   (bend down one finger)
Two red apples ripening in the sun;
Timmy ate one, and then there was one
   (bend down one finger)
One red apple and now we are done;
I ate the last one, and now there are none.
   (bend down last finger)

Science:

Mixing Colors

Place 2 or 3 ice cube trays and cups filled with red-, yellow-, and blue-colored water on the science table. Using an eyedropper, the children can experiment mixing colors in the ice cube trays. Smocks should be provided to prevent stained clothing.

Dramatic Play:

1. **Art Store**

    Set up an art supply store. Include paints, crayons, markers, paper, chalk, brushes, money, and cash register.

2. **Fire Station**

    Fire fighter hats can be added to the dramatic play area.

3. **Colored Hats**

    After reading *Caps for Sale* by Esphyr Slobodykina, set out colored hats for children to retell the story.

Arts and Crafts:

1. **Red Paint**

   Red and white paint can be provided at the easels. By mixing these colors, children can discover shades of red.

2. **Red Crayons, Markers, etc.**

   Red markers, crayons, and chalk can be placed on a table in the art area. The children can observe the similarities and differences between these various items.

3. **Red Paper**

   Watercolors and red paper can be placed on a table in the art area.

4. **Red Crayon Rubbings**

   Red crayons, red paper, or both can be used to do this activity. Place an object such as a penny, button, or leaf under paper. Use the flat edge of a crayon to color over the item. An image of the object will appear on the paper.

5. **Paint Blots**

   Fold a piece of paper in half. Open up and place a spoon of red paint on the inside of the paper. Refold paper and press flat. Reopen and observe the design. Add two colors such as blue and yellow and repeat process to show color mixing.

6. **Paint Over Design**

   Paint over a crayon picture with watery red paint. Observe how the paint will not cover it.

7. **Glitter Pictures**

   The children make a design using glue on a piece of paper. Then shake red glitter onto glue. Shake the excess glitter into a pan.

8. **Red Fingerpaint**

   Red fingerpaint and foil should be placed on an art table. Yellow and blue paint can be added to explore color mixing.

Sensory:

1. **Red Water**

   Fill the sensory table with water and red food coloring. The children can add coloring and observe the changes.

2. **Red Shaving Cream**

   Shaving cream with red food coloring added can be placed in the sensory table. During self-selected play the children can explore the shaving cream.

3. **Red Goop**

   Mix together red food coloring, 1 cup corn-starch, and 1 cup water in sensory table.

4. **Red Silly Putty**

   Mix together red food coloring, 1 cup liquid starch, and 2 cups white glue. This mixture usually needs to be stirred continuously for an extended period of time before it jells.

Large Muscle:

1. **Ribbon Dance**

   Attach strips of red crepe paper to short wooden dowels or unsharpened pencils to make ribbons. The children can use the ribbons to move to their favorite songs.

2. **Red Bird, Red Bird**

   The children should form a circle by holding hands. Then choose a child to be a bird and start the game. Children chant:

   Red bird, red bird through my window
   Red bird, red bird through my window
   Red bird, red bird through my window
   Oh!

   The bird goes in and out, under the children's arms. The bird stops on the word "Oh" and bows to the child facing him. This child becomes the new bird. The color of the bird can be determined by the color of the clothing of each child picked to be the bird.

472

Field Trips/Resource People:

1. **Art Store**

   Visit an art store. Observe all the red items for sale.

2. **Take a Walk**

   Take a walk around the neighborhood and look for red objects.

3. **Floral Shop**

   Visit a floral shop and specifically observe red flowers.

4. **Fire Station**

   Visit a fire station. Note the color of the engine, hats, sirens, etc.

5. **Resource People**

   Invite the following resource people to the classroom:

   - artist
   - gardener
   - fire fighter

Math:

1. **Color Cards**

   Construct color cards that start with white and gradually become cherry red. The children can sequence the cards from white to red or red to white. Discontinued sample color cards could be obtained from a paint store.

2. **Bead Stringing**

   Yarn and a variety of colored beads should be available to the children. After initial exploration, the children can make patterns with beads. Example: red, yellow, red, yellow, red.

3. **Colored Bags**

   Place three bags labeled red, yellow, and blue and a variety of blocks on a table. The children can sort the blocks by placing them in the matching colored bag.

Social Studies:

1. **Discussion about Colors**

   During group time discuss colors and how they make us feel. Hold up a color card and ask a child how it makes him feel.

2. **Color Chart**

   Construct a "My Favorite Color Is…" chart. Encourage each child to name his favorite color. After each child's name, print his favorite color with a colored marker. Display the chart in the classroom.

3. **Colored Balloons**

   Each child should be provided with a balloon. The balloons should be the colors of the rainbow: red, orange, yellow, green, blue, and purple. Arrange the children in the formation of a rainbow. Children with red balloons should stand together, etc. Take a picture of the class. Place the picture on the bulletin board.

Group Time (games, language):

1. **Colored Jars**

   Collect five large clear jars. Fill 3 with red water, 1 with yellow water, and 1 with blue water. Show children the 3 red jars. Discuss the color red. Discuss that it can make other colors too. Show them the yellow jar. Add yellow to red. What happens? Add blue water to other red jar. What happens? Discuss color mixing.

2. **Play "Red Light, Green Light"**

   Pick one child to be your traffic light. Place the "traffic light" about 30 feet away from the other children facing away from children who have formed a long line. With back to children, the traffic light says, "green light." Children try to creep toward the traffic light. Traffic light may then say, "red light" and turn toward the children. Children must freeze. The traffic light tries to see if any children are still at the starting line. The game continues with "green light." The first child to reach the traffic light becomes the new light.

Cooking:

1. **Raspberry Slush**

   Thaw and cook 4 packages of 10-ounce frozen raspberries for 10 minutes. Rub the cooked raspberries through strainer with wooden spoon. Cool. Add 1 can (6 ounces) of frozen lemonade concentrate, thawed. Just before serving, stir in 2 quarts of ginger ale, chilled. Makes 24 servings, about 1/2 cup each.

2. **Red Pepper Paste—West Africa**

   1/4 cup dry red cooking wine
   1 teaspoon ground red pepper
   3/4 teaspoon salt
   1/4 teaspoon ground ginger
   1/8 teaspoon ground cardamom
   1/8 teaspoon ground coriander
   1/8 teaspoon ground nutmeg
   1/8 teaspoon cloves
   1/8 teaspoon ground cinnamon
   1/8 teaspoon black pepper
   1/8 of a medium onion
   1 small clove garlic
   1/4 cup paprika

   Place all ingredients except paprika in blender container. Cover and blend on high speed until smooth, scraping the sides of the blender frequently. Heat paprika in 1 quart saucepan for 1 minute. Add spice mixture gradually, stirring until smooth. Heat, stirring occasionally, until hot, about 3 minutes. Cool.

3. **Pink Dip**

   Mix 2/3 cup mayonnaise or salad dressing, 2 tablespoons Red Pepper Paste, and 1 tablespoon lemon juice. Serve with celery sticks.

   Source: *Betty Crocker's International Cookbook.* (1980). New York: Random House.

Multimedia:

The following resources can be found in educational catalogs:

1. Jenkins, Ella. *I Know the Colors in the Rainbow* [record].

2. *Play & Learn Colors* [IBM software, PK–1]. Remarkable.

Books:

The following books can be used to complement the theme:

1. Graham, Bob. (1987). *The Red Woolen Blanket.* Boston: Little, Brown & Co.

2. Hill, Ari. (1986). *The Red Jacket Mix-Up.* New York: Golden Press.

3. Brown, Margaret Wise. (1989). *Big Red Barn.* New York: Harper & Row.

4. Williams, Vera B. (1988). *Three Days on a River in a Red Canoe.* New York: Morrow.

5. Reiss, John J. (1987). *Colors.* New York: Macmillan.

6. Lundell, Margaretta. (1989). *The Land of Colors.* New York: Putnam.

7. *Baby's Red Picture Book*. (1989). Arburn, ME: Ladybird Books.

8. DeVito, Pam. (1989). *Lydia & the Purple Paint*. Mount Desert, ME: Windswept House.

9. Sklenitzha, Franz S. (1988). *The Red Sports Car*. New York: Barron.

10. Imershein, Betsy. (1989). *Finding Red Finding Yellow*. San Diego: Harcourt Brace Jovanovich.

11. Yardley, Joanna. (1991). *The Red Ball*. San Diego: Harcourt Brace Jovanovich.

12. Rikys, Bodel. (1992). *Red Bear*. New York: Dial Books for Young Readers.

13. Carroll, Kathleen S. (1992). *One Red Rooster*. Boston: Houghton Mifflin Co.

14. Woolfitt, Gabrielle. (1992). *Red*. Minneapolis: Carolrhoda Books, Inc.

15. Broger, Achium. (1991). *Red Armchair*. Wilmington, DE: Atonium Books.

16. Serfozo, Mary. (1988). *Who Said Red?* New York: Macmillan Children's Book Group.

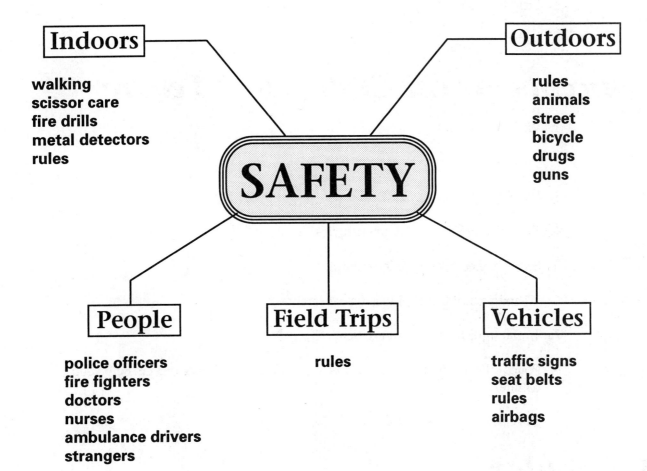

Indoors

walking
scissor care
fire drills
metal detectors
rules

Outdoors

rules
animals
street
bicycle
drugs
guns

SAFETY

People

police officers
fire fighters
doctors
nurses
ambulance drivers
strangers

Field Trips

rules

Vehicles

traffic signs
seat belts
rules
airbags

Polaroid Education Program

Here's an exciting new way to turn instant photography into an effective teaching tool. Refer to the full-color insert for the activity entitled Polaroid Places.

477

Theme Goals:

Through participating in the experiences provided by this theme, the children may learn:

1. Indoor safety precautions.

2. Play yard safety.

3. People who keep us safe.

4. Field trip safety.

5. Vehicle safety.

Concepts for the Children to Learn:

1. We walk indoors.

2. Play yard rules help keep us safe.

3. We have special rules for field trips.

4. Fire drills prepare us for emergencies.

5. Scissors need to be handled carefully.

6. Wearing a seat belt is practicing car safety.

7. Traffic signs help prevent accidents.

8. Police officers, fire fighters, doctors, nurses, and ambulance drivers help keep us safe.

9. Only talk to people you know.

Vocabulary:

1. **safety**—freedom from danger.

2. **sign**—a lettered board.

3. **seat belt**—strap that holds a person in a vehicle.

4. **rule**—the way we are to act.

5. **fire drill**—practicing leaving the building in case of a fire.

Bulletin Board

The purpose of this bulletin board is to call attention to safety signs. The children are to match the safety sign with its outline on the board. To prepare this bulletin board, construct six safety signs out of tagboard, each a different shape. Color appropriately and laminate. Trace the outline of these signs onto black construction paper to create shadow signs as illustrated. Staple the shadow signs to the bulletin board. Punch holes in the safety signs using a hole punch. The children can match the shape of the safety signs to the shadow signs by hanging them on the appropriate push pins.

Parent Letter

Dear Parents,

Safety will be the focus of our next unit. We will be learning about safety at school, at home, and outdoors. Through this unit the children will also become more aware of traffic signs and their importance.

At School

A few of the activities planned for this unit include:

- taking a safety walk to practice crossing streets.
- counting the number of traffic signs that are in our school neighborhood.
- visiting the fire station on Tuesday morning. We will be leaving at 9:30 and should return to school by 11:00.

At Home

One of the songs we will be learning follows. It will help your child become aware of the purpose and colors of a traffic light. You may enjoy singing the song at home with your child. The song is sung to the tune of "Twinkle, Twinkle, Little Star." The words are as follows:

> Twinkle, twinkle, traffic light,
> Standing on the corner bright.
> When it's green it's time to go.
> When it's red it's stop, you know.
> Twinkle, twinkle, traffic light,
> Standing on the corner bright.

During your daily routines, share safety tips with your child.

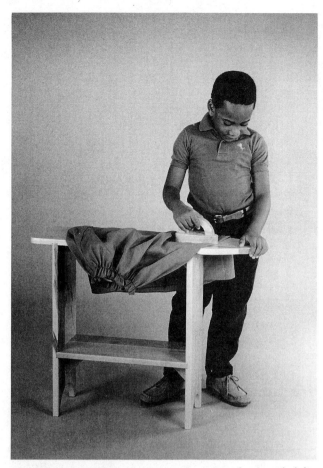

FIGURE 50 Safety in even the simplest activities must be reinforced.

Music:

1. **"Twinkle, Twinkle, Traffic Light"**
   (Sing to the tune of "Twinkle, Twinkle, Little Star")

   Twinkle, twinkle, traffic light,
   Standing on the corner bright.
   When it's green it's time to go.
   When its red it's stop, you know.
   Twinkle, twinkle, traffic light,
   Standing on the corner bright.

2. **"Do You Know the Police Officer"**
   (Sing to the tune of "The Muffin Man")

   Oh, do you know the police officer,
   The police officer, the police officer?
   Oh, do you know the police officer
   Who helps me cross the street?

This song can be extended. For example, the song can be continued substituting "who helps me when I'm lost" or "who helps one cross the street."

3. **"We Are Safe"**
   (Sing to the tune of "Mulberry Bush")

   This is the way that we are safe
   We are safe, we are safe.
   This is the way that we are safe
   Every day of the year.

   This is the way we cross the street—
   Look left, then right, left then right.
   This is the way we cross the street—
   Look left, then right for safety.

   This is the way we ride in the car—
   Sit up straight, buckle your belt.
   This is the way we ride in the car—
   Buckle your belt for safety.

   Resource: Wilmes, Liz & Dick. (1983). *Everyday Circle Time*. IL: Building Blocks Publication.

Fingerplays:

SILLY TEDDY BEAR

Silly little teddy bear
Stood up in a rocking chair.
   (make rocking movement)
Now he has to stay in bed
   (lay head on hands)
With a bandage round his head.
   (circular movement of hand around head)

CROSSING STREETS

At the curb before I cross
I stop my running feet
   (point to feet)
And look both ways to left and right
   (look left and right)
Before I cross the street.
Lest autos running quietly
Might come as a surprise.
I just don't listen with my ears
   (point to ears)
But look with both my eyes.
   (point to eyes)

RED LIGHT

Red light, red light what do you say?
I say, "Stop and stop right away!"
    (hold palms of both hands up)
Yellow light, yellow light what do you say?
I say, "Wait till the light turns green."
    (hold one palm of hand up)
Green light, green light what do you say?
I say "Go, but look each way."
    (circle arm in forward motion and turn head
    to the right and left)
Thank you, thank you, red, yellow, green
Now I know what the traffic light means.

FIVE POLICE OFFICERS

Five strong police officers standing by a store.
    (hold up the one hand)
One became a traffic cop, then there were four.
    (hold up four fingers)
Four strong police officers watching over me.
One took a lost boy home, then there were
three.
    (hold up three fingers)
Three strong police officers all dressed in blue.
One stopped a speeding car and then there
were two.
    (hold up two fingers)
Two strong police officers, how fast they can
run.
One caught a bad man and then there was one.
    (hold up one finger)
One strong police officer saw some smoke one
day.
He called a fire fighter who put it out right
away.

THE CROSSING GUARD

The crossing guard keeps us safe
As he works from day to day.
He holds the stop sign high in the air.
    (hold palm of hand up)
For the traffic to obey.
And when the cars have completely stopped
And its as safe as can be,
He signals us to walk across
    (make a beckoning motion)
The street very carefully.

Science:

1. **Sorting for Safety**

   Collect empty household product containers.
   Include safe and dangerous items such as
   cleaning supplies, orange juice containers, etc.
   Place all the items in one large box. The
   children can separate the containers into "safe"
   and "dangerous" categories. Younger children
   may be ableto separate the containers into
   edible and nonedible categories.

2. **All About Me**

   On a table place identification items. Prepare a
   separate card for each child. Record the
   following information on the cards:

   - height
   - weight
   - color hair
   - color eyes
   - fingerprint
   - signature (if child can or a teacher can help)

Dramatic Play:

1. **Fire Engine**

   A large cardboard box can be decorated by the
   children as a fire engine with yellow or red
   tempera paint. When the fire engine is dry,
   place it in the dramatic play area with short
   hoses and fire fighter hats. This prop could
   also be placed outdoors, weather permitting.

2. **Prop Boxes**

   Develop prop boxes such as:

   Fire Fighter
   bell
   jacket/uniform
   boots
   whistle
   hose
   oxygen mask
   hat

   Police Officer
   hat
   badges

482

handcuffs
stop sign (for holding)

3. **Fire Fighter Jackets**

Construct fire fighter jackets out of large paper bags. Begin by cutting three holes. One hole is used for the child's head at the top of the bag. Then cut two large holes for arms. These props may encourage the children to dramatize the roles of the fire fighters.

4. **Seat Belts**

Collect child-sized car seats. Place them around like chairs, letting the children adjust them for themselves or their dolls.

Arts and Crafts:

1. **Fire Fighter Hats**

Cut fire fighter hats out of large sheets of red construction paper for the children to wear.

2. **Easel Painting**

On the easel, place cut-out shapes of fire hats or boots.

3. **Traffic Lights**

Construct stop and go lights out of shoeboxes. Tape the lid to the bottom of the box. Cover with black construction paper and have children place green, yellow, and red circles in correct order on the box. The red circle should be placed on the top, yellow in the middle, and green on the bottom.

4. **Officer Hats and Badges**

Police officer hats and badges can be constructed out of paper and colored with crayons or felt-tip watercolor markers.

Sensory:

1. **Pumps and Hoses**

Water pumps, hoses, and water can be placed in the sensory table.

2. **Trucks**

Small toy fire trucks and police cars can be placed in the sensory table with sand.

Large Muscle:

1. **Safety Walk**

Take a safety walk. Practice observing traffic lights when crossing the street. Point out special hazards to the children.

2. **Stop, Drop, and Roll**

Practice "Stop, Drop, and Roll" with the children. This will be valuable to them if they are ever involved in a fire and their clothes happen to catch on fire. Usually a fire fighter will teach them this technique while visiting the fire station.

Field Trips/Resource People:

1. **Fire Fighter**

Invite a fire fighter to the classroom. Ask him to bring fire fighter clothing and equipment and to discuss each item.

2. **Police Car**

Invite a police officer to visit the classroom. Ask him to bring a police car to show the children.

Math:

1. **Sequencing Hats**

Draw pictures of three police hats. Make each picture identical except design three different sizes. The children can sequence the objects from largest to smallest or smallest to largest. Discuss the sizes and ask which is largest, smallest, middle.

2. **Safety Items**

Walk around the school and observe the number of safety items. Included may be exit signs, fire drill posters, fire extinguishers, sprinkler systems, fire alarm/drill bells, etc.

Social Studies:

1. **Safety Pictures and Signs**

   Post safety pictures and signs around the room.

2. **Stop and Go Light**

   Draw a large stop and go light on a piece of tagboard. Color with felt-tip markers. Print the following across from the corresponding colors:

   Green means go we all know
   Yellow means wait even if you're late,
   Red means stop!

3. **Safety Signs**

   Take a walk and watch for safety signs. Discuss the colors and letters on each sign.

Group Time (games, language):

Toy Safety

Collect a variety of unsafe toys that may have sharp edges, a broken wagon, etc. During group time discuss the dangers of each toy.

Cooking:

1. **Banana Rounds**

   4 medium bananas
   1/2 tablespoon honey
   1/8 teaspoon nutmeg
   1/8 teaspoon cinnamon
   1/4 cup wheat germ

   The children can peel the bananas and then slice them with a plastic knife. Measure the spices, wheat germ, and honey. Finally, mix them with the bananas. Chill. Serves 8.

2. **Stop Signs**

   eight-sided crackers
   peanut butter
   jelly

   Spread a thin layer of peanut butter and jelly on each cracker.

3. **Yield Signs**

   triangle crackers
   yellow cheese

   Cut yellow cheese into triangles. Put the cheese on the crackers.

Multimedia:

The following resources are available through educational catalogs:

1. *Learning Basic Skills Through Music, Health and Safety* [record]. Freeport, NY: Activity Records, Inc.

2. Poelker, Kathy Lencinski. "Fire Station," *Look at My World Record* [record].

3. Moore, Thomas. *Safe Not Sorry* [record].

4. *Bean Bag Activities & Coordination Skills* [record]. Kimbo Records.

Books:

The following books can be used to complement the theme:

1. Hoban, Tana. (1987). *I Read Signs*. New York: Morrow.

2. Chacon, Rick. (1985). *You Can Say "No!"* Huntington Beach, CA: Teacher Created Materials, Inc.

3. Chlad, Dorothy. (1987). *Playing on the Playground*. Chicago: Children's Press.

4. Molnar, Dorothy E., & Fenton, Stephen H. (1991). *Who Will Pick Me Up When I Fall?* Morton Grove, IL: Albert Whitman.

5. Patz, Nancy. (1990). *No Thumping No Bumping No Rumpus Tonight!* New York: Macmillan.

6. Wilson, Sarah. (1988). *Beware the Dragon!* New York: Harper Collins.

7. Chlad, Dorothy. (1992). *Bicycles Are Fun to Ride*. Chicago: Children's Press.

8. Crary, Elizabeth. (1985). *I'm Lost*. Seattle, WA: Parenting Press.

9. Klingel, Cynthia F. (1986). *Safety First-School*. Mankato, MN: Creative Education, Inc.

10. Reihecky, Janet. (1990). *Carefulness*. Mankato, MN: Child World, Inc.

11. Perry, Kate. (1992). *Mr. Toad to the Rescue*. Hauppauge, NY: Barron's Educational Series, Inc.

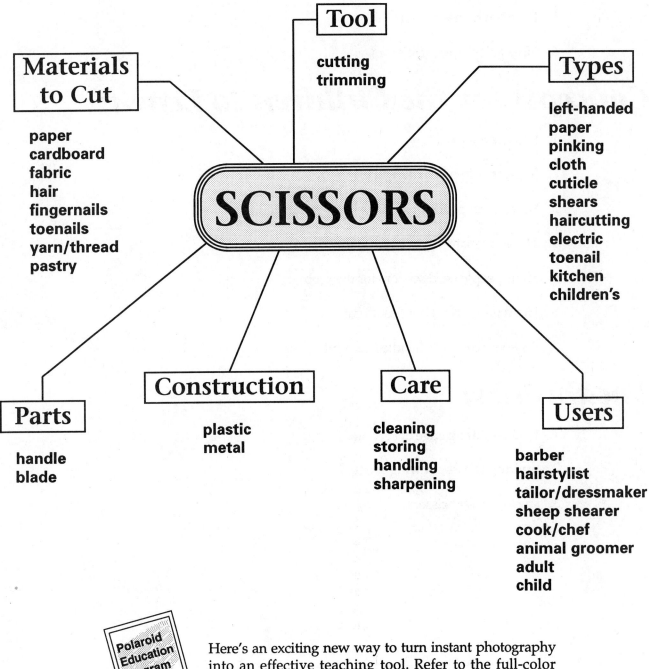

Tool

cutting
trimming

Materials to Cut

paper
cardboard
fabric
hair
fingernails
toenails
yarn/thread
pastry

Types

left-handed
paper
pinking
cloth
cuticle
shears
haircutting
electric
toenail
kitchen
children's

SCISSORS

Parts

handle
blade

Construction

plastic
metal

Care

cleaning
storing
handling
sharpening

Users

barber
hairstylist
tailor/dressmaker
sheep shearer
cook/chef
animal groomer
adult
child

Polaroid
Education
Program

Here's an exciting new way to turn instant photography into an effective teaching tool. Refer to the full-color insert for the activity entitled Photo Open House.

Theme Goals:

Through participating in the experiences provided by this theme, the children may learn:

1. Parts of scissors.

2. Uses of scissors.

3. Materials that can be cut with scissors.

4. Care of scissors.

5. People who use scissors.

6. Sizes and shapes of scissors.

Concepts for the Children to Learn:

1. Scissors are tools.

2. Scissors help us do our work.

3. Scissors cut paper, fingernails, hair, and material.

4. There are many types of scissors.

5. Some people need scissors for their job.

6. Hand motions make scissors cut.

7. Scissors need to be handled carefully.

Vocabulary:

1. **blade**—cutting edge of scissors.

2. **pinking shears**—sewing scissors.

3. **shears**—large scissors.

Bulletin Board

The purpose of this bulletin board is to have the children match the colored scissors to the corresponding colored skein. To prepare the bulletin board, construct six scissors out of tagboard. With felt-tip markers, color each one a different color and laminate. Fasten the scissors to the top of the bulletin board. Next, construct six skeins of yarn out of tagboard. Color each skein a different color to correspond with the scissors. Attach the skeins to the bottom part of the bulletin board. Fasten a string to each of the scissors and a push pin to each of the skeins of yarn.

Parent Letter

Dear Parents,

Snip, snip, snip! This sound will be heard frequently in the classroom as we start a unit on scissors. Through the experiences provided the children will be introduced to various kinds and uses of scissors. They will also learn the proper care and safety precautions to consider when handling and using scissors.

At School

Some activities related to scissors will include:

- discussing safety and proper uses of scissors.
- experimenting cutting with different kinds of scissors.
- cutting a variety of materials such as yarn, fabric, paper, wallpaper, and aluminum foil.
- visiting Tom's Barber Shop on Wednesday morning. We will be leaving at 10:00 am and expect to watch a haircut demonstration. Also, we will observe the tools and equipment used by a barber.

At Home

Children need many experiences working with scissors before they are able to master cutting skills. Each child will learn this skill at his own rate. To assist your child, save scraps of paper and allow your child to practice cutting them using child-sized scissors. Once the cutting skills have been mastered, your child may enjoy cutting coupons out of newspaper sections or magazines.

Have fun with your child!

FIGURE 51 Some children need left-handed scissors; others can use right-handed scissors.

Fingerplay:

OPEN SHUT THEM

Open, shut them, open, shut them.
   (use index and middle finger to make scissors motion)
Give a little snip, snip, snip.
   (three quick snips with fingers)
Open, shut them, open, shut them.
   (repeat scissors motion)
Make another clip.
   (make another scissor motion)

Science:

1. **Scissor Show**

   Place a variety of scissors on an overhead projector. Encourage the children to describe each by naming it and explaining its use.

2. **Shadow Profiles**

   Tape a piece of paper on a wall or bulletin board. Stand a child in front of the paper. Shine a light source to create a shadow of the head. Trace each child's shadow. Provide scissors for the children to cut out their own shadows.

3. **Weighing Scissors**

   On the science table, place a variety of scissors and a scale. The children should be encouraged to note the differences in weight.

Dramatic Play:

1. **Beauty Shop**

   Set up a beauty shop in the dramatic play area. Include items such as curling irons, hair dryers, combs, and wigs. Also, include a chair, plastic covering, and Beauty Shop sign. A cash register and money can be added to encourage play. (For safety purposes, cut the cords off the hair dryer and curling irons.)

2. **Tailor/Dressmaking Shop**

   Materials that are easy to cut should be provided. Likewise, a variety of scissors should be placed next to the material. Older children may want to make doll clothes.

3. **Bake Shop**

   Playdough, scissors, and other cooking tools can be placed on a table. If desired, make paper baker hats and a sign.

4. **Dog Groomer**

   A dog grooming area can be set up in the dramatic play corner with stuffed animals, brushes, and combs. If available, cut off the cord of an electric dog shaver and provide for the children.

Arts and Crafts:

1. **Scissor Snip**

   Strips of paper with scissors can be provided for snipping.

2. Cutting

For experimentation, a wide variety of materials and types of scissors can be added to the art area for the children.

Sensory:

Playdough

Scissors can be placed next to the playdough in the sensory area.

Field Trips/Resource People:

1. Hairstylist

Visit a hairstylist. While there, observe a person's hair being cut. Notice the different scissors that are used and how they are used.

2. Pet Groomer

Invite a pet groomer to class. If possible, arrange for a dog to be groomed.

Math:

Shape Sort

Cut out different-colored shapes. Place the shapes on a table for the children to sort by color, shape, and size.

Group Time (games, language):

Scissor Safety

Discuss safety while using scissors. The children can help make a list of "How we use our scissors safely." Display chart in room.

Cooking:

Pretzels

1 1/2 cups warm water
1 envelope yeast
4 cups flour
1 teaspoon salt
1 tablespoon sugar
coarse salt
egg

Mix the warm water, yeast, and sugar together. Set this mixture aside for 5 minutes. Pour salt and flour into a bowl. Add the yeast mixture to make dough. Roll the dough into a long snake form. Cut the dough into smaller sections using scissors. The children can then form individual shapes with dough. Brush egg on the shapes with pastry brush and sprinkle with salt. Preheat the oven and bake pretzels at 425 degrees for 12 minutes.

PASTES

Bookmaker's Paste

1 teaspoon flour
2 teaspoons cornstarch
1/4 teaspoon powdered
   alum
3 ounces water

Mix dry ingredients. Add water slowly, stirring out all lumps. Cook over slow fire (preferably in a double boiler), stirring constantly. Remove when paste begins to thicken. It will thicken more as it cools. Keep in covered jars. Thin with water if necessary.

Cooked Flour Paste

1 cup boiling water

1 tablespoon powdered
   alum
1 pint cold water
1 pint flour
1 heaping teaspoon oil of
   cloves
oil of wintergreen (optional)

To 1 cup boiling water add powdered alum. Mix flour and fold in water until smooth; pour

492

mixture gradually into boiling alum water. Cook until it has a bluish cast, stirring all the time. Remove from fire, add oil of cloves, and stir well. Keep in airtight jars. Thin when necessary by adding water. A drop or two of oil of wintergreen may be added to give the paste a pleasing aroma.

Colored Salt Paste

Mix 2 parts salt to 1 part flour. Add powdered paint and enough water to make a smooth heavy paste. Keep in airtight container.

Crepe Paper Paste

Cut or tear 2 tablespoons crepe paper of a single color. The finer the paper is cut, the smoother the paste will be. Add 1/2 tablespoon flour, 1/2 tablespoon salt, and enough water to make a paste. Stir and squash the mixture until it is as smooth as possible. Store in airtight container.

Books:

The following books can be used to complement the theme:

1. Girard, Linda Walvoord. (1986). *Jeremy's First Haircut*. Niles, IL: Albert Whitman and Co.

2. Lillegard, Dee. (1987). *I Can Be a Beautician*. Chicago: Children's Press.

3. Brown, Laurene, & Brown, Marc. (1986). *Visiting the Art Museum*. New York: Dutton.

4. dePaola, Tomie. (1989). *Haircuts for the Woolseys*. New York: Putnam.

5. Reiss, John J. (1987). *Shapes*. New York: Macmillan.

6. Frandsen, Karen G. (1986). *Michael's New Haircut*. Chicago, IL: Children's Press.

7. Tusa, Tricia. (1991). *Camilla's New Hairdo*. New York: Farrar, Straus and Giroux.

Names

circle
triangle
rectangle
square
oval

Construction

lines
round
four sides
three sides

SHAPES

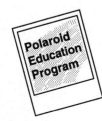

Polaroid
Education
Program

Here's an exciting new way to turn instant photography into an effective teaching tool. Refer to the full-color insert for the activity entitled Grouping.

Theme Goals:

Through participating in the experiences provided by this theme, the children may learn:

1. The names of basic shapes.

2. Identification of basic shapes.

3. Objects have shapes.

Concepts for the Children to Learn:

1. There are many shapes of different sizes and colors in our world.

2. Some shapes have names.

3. A circle is round.

4. Triangles have three sides.

5. Rectangles and squares have four sides.

6. All objects contain one or more shapes.

7. We can draw lines to make shapes.

Vocabulary:

1. **circle**—a shape that is round.

2. **rectangle**—a shape with four sides.

3. **square**—a shape with four sides of equal length.

4. **triangle**—a shape with three sides.

5. **line**—a mark made with a pencil, crayon, etc., to make a shape.

6. **oval**—shaped like an egg.

Bulletin Board

The purpose of this bulletin board is to have the child make a shape train. To prepare the bulletin board use the model shown to construct a train using basic shapes. Color the shapes and laminate. Trace laminated shapes onto black construction paper to construct shadow shapes. Staple shadow shapes onto board in train pattern. By using magnets the children can affix the colored shape pieces to the shadows.

Parent Letter

Dear Parents,

Hello again! Shapes will be the focus of our new unit. Our world consists of shapes. The children will become aware of this on an introductory walk around the block. They will become familiar with the names of shapes and will also classify objects according to shape. Consequently, the children will be more aware of all the shapes in our world. In addition, the children who are developmentally ready will practice drawing some of the basic shapes.

At School

Some of the fun-filled learning activities scheduled for this unit include:

- playing a game called "Shape Basket Upset."
- listening to the story, *Shapes and Things*, by Tana Hoban.
- feeling and identifying objects by shape in a feely box.
- making and baking cookies of various shapes.

At Home

You can reinforce the activities included in this unit at home by observing shaped objects in your house. Each day at school we will have a special shape theme. Your child can bring in an object from home to fit the shape of the day. I will send home the shape the night before so you and your child will have time to look for an object. The following fingerplay can be recited to foster language and memory skills.

Circle and Square

Close my eyes, shut them tight.
(close eyes)
Make a circle with my one hand.
(make a circle with one hand)
Keep them shut; make it fair.
(keep eyes shut)
With my other hand, make a square.
(make a square with other hand)

Enjoy your child!

FIGURE 52 What can you make with these shapes?

Music:

The following songs can be found in Butler, Talmadge, Kirkland, Terry, & Leach. (1975). *Music for Today's Young Children.* Broadman Press.

1. "Colors, Shapes, and Numbers"

2. "Different Shapes"

Fingerplays:

RIGHT CIRCLE, LEFT SQUARE

Close my eyes, shut them tight.
 (close eyes)
Make a circle with my one hand.
 (make circle with one hand)
Keep them shut; make it fair.
 (keep eyes shut)
With my other hand, make a square.
 (make square with other hand)

LINES

One straight finger makes a line.
 (hold up one index finger)
Two straight lines make one "t" sign.
 (cross index fingers)

Three lines made a triangle there
 (form triangle with index fingers touching
 and thumbs touching)
And one more line will make a square.
 (form square with hands)

DRAW A SQUARE

Draw a square, draw a square
Shaped like a tile floor.
Draw a square, draw a square
All with corners four.

DRAW A TRIANGLE

Draw a triangle, draw a triangle
With corners three.
Draw a triangle, draw a triangle
Draw it just for me.

DRAW A CIRCLE

Draw a circle, draw a circle
Made very round.
Draw a circle, draw a circle
No corners can be found.

WHAT AM I MAKING?

This is a circle.
 (draw circle in the air)
This is a square.
 (draw square in the air)

Who can tell me
What I'm making there?
    (draw another shape in the air)

Science:

1. **Feely Box**

   Cut many shapes out of different materials such as felt, cardboard, wallpaper, carpet, etc. Place the shapes into a feely box. The children can be encouraged to reach in and identify the shape by feeling it before removing it from the box.

2. **Evaporation**

   Pour equal amounts of water into a large round and a small square cake pan. Mark the water level with a grease pencil. Allow the water to stand for a week. Observe the amount of evaporation.

3. **Classifying Objects**

   Collect four small boxes. Mark a different shape on each box. Include a circle, triangle, square, and rectangle. Then cut shapes out of magazines. The children can sort the objects by placing them in the corresponding boxes.

4. **What Shape Is It?**

   Place objects with distinct shapes in the feely box such as marbles, dice, pyramid, deck of cards, book, ball, button, etc. Encourage the children to reach in and identify the shape of the object they are feeling before they pull it out.

Dramatic Play:

1. **Baker**

   Provide playdough, cake pans, and cookie cutters.

2. **Puppets**

   A puppet prop box should be placed in the dramatic play area. If available a puppet stage should be added. Otherwise a puppet stage can be made from cardboard.

Arts and Crafts:

1. **Sponge Painting**

   Cut sponges into the four basic shapes. The children can hold the sponges with a clothespin. The sponge can be dipped in paint and printed on the paper. Make several designs and shapes.

2. **Shape Mobiles**

   Trace shapes of various sizes on colored construction paper. If appropriate, encourage the children to cut the shapes from the paper and punch a hole at the top of each shape. Then, put a piece of string through the hole and tie onto a hanger. The mobiles can be hung in the classroom for decoration.

3. **Easel Ideas**

   Feature a different shape of easel paper each day at the easel.

4. **Shape Collage**

   Provide different-colored paper shapes and glue for the children to create collages from shapes.

5. **Stencils**

   Prepare individual stencils of the basic shapes. The children can use the stencils for tracing.

6. **My Shape Book**

   Stickers, catalogs, and magazines should be placed on the art table. Also, prepare booklets cut into the basic shapes. Encourage the children to find, cut, and glue the objects in each shape book.

Sensory:

Add the following items to the sensory table:

1. marbles and water
2. different-shaped sponges and water
3. colored water
4. scented water
5. soapy water

500

© 1995, Delmar Publishers

Large Muscle:

1. Walk and Balance

Using masking tape, outline the four basic shapes on the floor. The children can walk and balance on the shapes. Older children may walk forwards, backwards, and sideways.

2. Hopscotch

Draw a hopscotch with chalk on the sidewalk outdoors. Masking tape can be used to form the grid on the floor indoors.

Field Trip:

Shape Walk

Walk around the school neighborhood. During the walk, observe the shapes of the traffic signs and houses. After returning to the school, record the shapes observed on a chart.

Math:

1. Wallpaper Shape Match

From scraps of old wallpaper, cut out two sets of basic shapes. Then mix all of the pieces. The children can match the sets by pattern and shape.

2. Shape Completion

On several pieces of white tagboad draw a shape, leaving one side, or part of a circle, unfinished or dotted. Laminate the tagboard. The children can complete the shape by drawing with watercolor markers or grease pencils. Erase with a damp cloth.

Group Time (games, language):

1. Shape Hunt

Throughout the classroom hide colorful shapes. Each of the children can find a shape.

2. Twister

On a large old bed sheet, secure many shapes of different colors, or draw the shapes on with magic markers. Make a spinner. Have children place parts of their bodies on the different shapes.

3. Shape Day

Each day highlight a different shape. Collect related items that resemble the shape of the day and display throughout the classroom. During group time, have each child find an object in the classroom that is the same shape as the shape of the day.

Cooking:

1. Shaped Bread and Peanut Butter

The children can cut bread with different-shaped cookie cutters. Spread peanut butter or other toppings on the bread.

2. Fruit Cut-outs

1/2 cup sugar
4 envelopes unflavored gelatin
2 1/2 cups pineapple juice, apple juice, orange juice, grape juice, or fruit drink

In a mixing bowl, stir the sugar and gelatin with rubber scraper until well mixed. Pour fruit juice into a 1-quart saucepan. Put the pan on the burner. Turn the burner to high heat. Cook until the juice boils. Turn burner off. Pour boiling fruit juice over sugar mixture. Stir with a rubber scraper until all the gelatin is dissolved. Pour into a 13-inch x 9-inch x 2-inch pan. Place in the refrigerator and chill until firm. Cookie cutters can be used to make shapes. Enjoy! This activity requires close supervision.

3. Shape Snacks

Spread cheese or peanut butter onto various-shaped crackers and serve.
Serve cheese cut into circles, triangles, squares, and rectangles.

Serve vegetable circles—cucumbers, carrots, zucchini.
Cut fruit snacks into circles—bananas, grapefruit wedges, apple slices, grapes—serve.

4. **Nachos**

4 flour tortillas
3/4 cup grated cheese
1/3 cup chopped green pepper (optional)

With clean kitchen scissors, cut each tortilla into 4 or 6 triangle wedges. Place on a cookie sheet and sprinkle the tortilla wedges with the cheese. Garnish with green pepper if desired. Bake in a 350-degree oven for 4 to 6 minutes or until the cheese melts. Makes 16 to 20 nachos.

5. **Swedish Pancakes**

3 eggs
1 cup milk
1 1/2 cups flour

1 tablespoon sugar
1/2 teaspoon salt
4 tablespoons butter
1 cup heavy cream
2 tablespoons confectioner's sugar or a 12-ounce jar of fruit jelly

Using a fork or whisk, beat the eggs lightly in a large mixing bowl. Add half the milk. Fold in the flour, sugar, and salt. Melt the butter and add it, the cream, and the remaining milk to the mixture. Stir well. Lightly grease a frying pan or griddle, and place it over medium-high heat on a hot plate or stove. Carefully pour small amounts of the mixture onto the frying pan or griddle. Cook until the pancakes are golden around the edges and bubbly on top. Turn the pancakes over with a spatula and cook until the other sides are golden around the edges. Remove to a covered plate. Repeat until all the mixture is used. Sprinkle pancakes lightly with confectioner's sugar, or spread fruit jelly over them. Makes 3 dozen pancakes.

TO TEACH MATH CONCEPTS

Before a child can learn the more abstract concepts of arithmetic, he must be visually, physically, and kinesthetically aware of basic quantitative concepts. Included could be:

Form Discrimination	over	middle
	under	near
circle	top	far
square	bottom	above
triangle	long	below
rectangle	short	many
	tall	few
Vocabulary	high	more
	low	less
big	thick	through
little	thin	around
small	front	fast
smaller	back	slow
large	behind	up
larger	all	down
heavy	none	most
light	some	least
in	first	
out	last	

Multimedia:

The following resources can be found in educational catalogs:

1. "Round in a Circle," *We All Live Together Series, Vol. 1* [record]. Youngheart Records.

2. "Shapes," *We All Live Together Series—Vol. 3* [record]. Youngheart Records.

3. *My World Is Round* [record]. Melody House Records.

4. *Mr. Al Sings Colors and Shapes* [record]. Melody House Records.

5. *Shapes in Action* [record]. Kimbo Records.

6. *Shapes* [30-minute video]. Edu-vid.

7. *Talking Stickybear Shapes* [Apple/IBM/IIGS software, PK–1]. Optimum Resources.

8. *Talking Stickbear Opposites* [Apple/IBM/IIGS software, PK–1]. Optimum Resources.

9. *Play & Learn Shapes* [IBM software, PK–1]. Remarkable.

10. *Learning My ABC's/Shapes* [video]. Tele-Story.

Books:

The following books can be used to complement the theme:

1. Hoban, Tana. (1986). *Shapes, Shapes, Shapes.* New York: Greenwillow Books.

2. Hill, Eric. (1986). *Spot Looks at Shapes.* New York: Putnam.

3. Mahan, Ben. (1992). *See a Circle.* New York: McClanahan Books.

4. Mahan, Ben. (1992). *See a Square.* New York: McClanahan Books.

5. Mahan, Ben. (1992). *See a Star.* New York: McClanahan Books.

6. Mahan, Ben. (1992). *See a Triangle.* New York: McClanahan Books.

7. Falwell, Cathryn. (1992). *Shape Space.* Boston: Houghton Mifflin.

8. Bradbury, Lynee. (1992). *Shapes and Colors.* Auburn, ME: Ladybird Books, Inc.

9. Callinan, Karen. (1992). *Rectangles.* Mankato, MN: Capstone Press, Inc.

10. Rikys, Bodel. (1993). *Red Bear's Fun with Shapes.* New York: Dial Books for Young Readers.

11. Pienkowski, Jan. (1989). *Shapes.* New York: Simon and Schuster Trade.

12. Bryant-Mole, K. (1991). *Shapes*. Tulsa, OK: EDC Publishing.

13. Hoban, Tana. (1992). *Spirals, Curves, Fanshapes, and Lines*. New York: Greenwillow Books.

14. Karlan, Bernie. (1992). *Shapes: Circle*. New York: Simon and Schuster Trade.

15. Karlan, Bernie. (1992). *Shapes: Square*. New York: Simon and Schuster Trade.

16. Karlan, Bernie. (1992). *Shapes: Triangle*. New York: Simon and Schuster Trade.

17. MacKinnon, Debbie. (1992). *What Shape?* New York: Dial Books for Young Readers.

18. Oliver, Stephen (Photog.). (1990). *My First Look at Shapes*. New York: David McKay Co.

19. Parramon, J. M. (1991). *My First Shapes*. Hauppauge, NY: Barron's Educational Series, Inc.

20. Weissman, Bari. (1992). *Dial Playshapes: Circles*. New York: Dial Books for Young Readers.

21. Weissman, Bari. (1992). *Dial Playshapes: Square*. New York: Dial Books for Young Readers.

22. Weissman, Bari. (1992). *Dial Playshapes: Triangle*. New York: Dial Books for Young Readers.

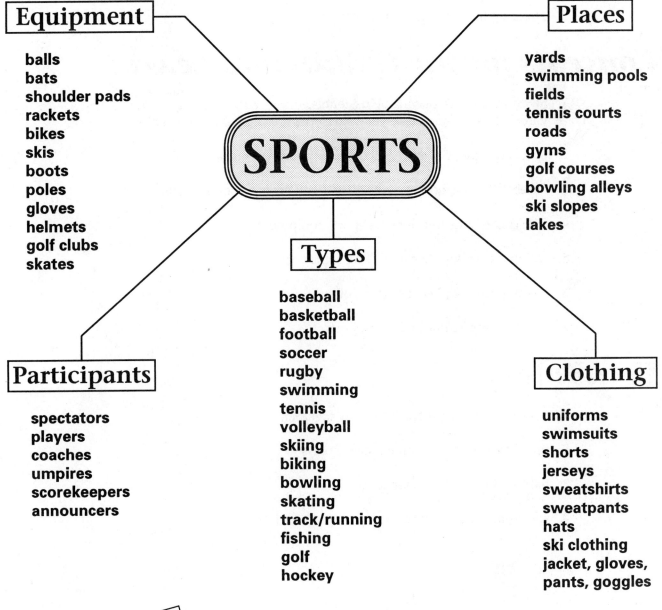

Equipment

balls
bats
shoulder pads
rackets
bikes
skis
boots
poles
gloves
helmets
golf clubs
skates

Places

yards
swimming pools
fields
tennis courts
roads
gyms
golf courses
bowling alleys
ski slopes
lakes

SPORTS

Types

baseball
basketball
football
soccer
rugby
swimming
tennis
volleyball
skiing
biking
bowling
skating
track/running
fishing
golf
hockey

Participants

spectators
players
coaches
umpires
scorekeepers
announcers

Clothing

uniforms
swimsuits
shorts
jerseys
sweatshirts
sweatpants
hats
ski clothing
jacket, gloves,
pants, goggles

Polaroid
Education
Program

Here's an exciting new way to turn instant photography
into an effective teaching tool. Refer to the full-color
insert for the activity entitled My Friends and Me.

Theme Goals:

Through participating in the experiences provided by this theme, the children may learn:

1. Places used for sports participation.

2. Types of sports people play.

3. Types of equipment used for sports.

4. Kinds of clothing worn for sports participation.

5. There are many people who participate in sports.

Concepts for the Children to Learn:

1. Swimming pools, playing fields, tennis courts, roads, gyms, golf courses, backyards, bowling lanes, lakes, and ski slopes are all places that are used for sports.

2. Spectators, players, and coaches are all sports participants.

3. Baseball, biking, hockey, football, and golf are all types of sports.

4. Balls, bikes, and golf clubs are sports equipment.

5. Uniforms are worn when playing some sports.

6. Some sports are played indoors, others outdoors.

7. There are individual and team sports.

Vocabulary:

1. **team**—a group of people who play together.

2. **uniform**—clothing worn for some sports.

3. **ball**—equipment used for sports.

4. **sport**—an activity played for fun.

Bulletin Board

The purpose of this bulletin board is to have the children hang the numeral ball on the glove that has the corresponding number of dots. To prepare the bulletin board construct baseball mitts out of brown tagboard. Attach dots starting with one on each of the gloves. The number of gloves prepared and dots will depend upon the developmental maturity of the children. Hang the gloves on the bulletin board. Next construct white baseballs. Write a numeral, starting with one, on each of the balls.

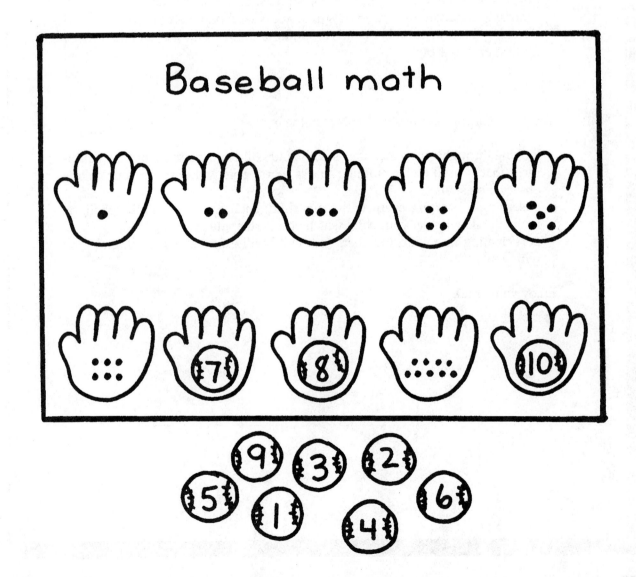

Parent Letter

Dear Parents,

Sports will be the focus of our next unit. Through the experiences provided, the children will become familiar with sports equipment and clothing. They will also recognize sports as a form of exercise.

At School

Activities planned to foster sports concepts include:

- exploring balls used in different sports and classifying them into groups by size, color, and ability to bounce and roll.
- trying on a variety of clothing used in different sports, including a swim cap, goggles, shoulder and leg/knee pads, helmets, gloves, and uniforms.
- skating in the room by wrapping squares of waxed paper around our feet and attaching them with rubber bands around our ankles. Our feet will then easily glide over the carpet!

At Home

You can incorporate sports concepts at home by:

- looking through sports magazines with your child and pointing out the equipment that is used or the clothing that is worn. This will develop your child's observation skills.
- observing a sporting event with your child, such as basketball, baseball, or football. Likewise, let your child watch you participate in a sport!
- participating in a sport together. Your child will enjoy spending special time with you!

Enjoy your child!

FIGURE 53 Soccer is a good physical activity.

Fingerplays:

HERE IS A BALL

Here's a ball
(make a circle with your thumb and pointer finger)
And here's a ball
(make a bigger circle with two thumbs and pointers)
And a great big ball I see.
(make a large circle with arms)
Now let's count the balls we've made,
One, two, three.
(repeat)

FOOTBALL PLAYERS

Five big football players standing in the locker room door.
One had a sore knee
And then there were four.

Four big football players down on their knees.
One made a touchdown
And then there were three.

Three big football players looking up at you.
One made a tackle
And then there were two.

Two big football players running in the sun.
One was offsides
And then there was one.

One big football player standing all alone.
He decided to go home
And then there were none.

Science:

1. **Feely Box**

   Place a softball, hardball, golf ball, and tennis ball in a feeley box. The children can reach into the box, feel, and try to guess the type of ball.

2. **Ball Bounces**

   Observe the way different balls move. Check to see if footballs, basketballs, and soccer balls can be bounced. Observe to see if some go higher than others. Also repeat using smaller balls such as tennis balls, baseballs, and golf balls.

3. **Wheels**

   Observe the wheels on a bicycle. If possible bring a bike to the classroom and demonstrate how peddling makes the wheels move.

4. **Examining Balls**

   Observe the composition of different balls. Ask the children to identify each. Then place the balls in water. Observe to see which ones float and which ones sink.

5. **Types of Grass**

   Place real grass and artifical turf on the science table. The children can feel both types of grass and describe differences in texture.

Dramatic Play:

1. **Baseball**

   Baseball caps, plastic balls, uniforms, catcher's mask, and gloves can be placed in the dramatic play area.

2. **Football**

   Balls, shoulder pads, uniforms, and helmets can be provided for the children to use outdoors.

3. **Tennis**

   Tennis rackets, balls, visors, sunglasses, and shorts for the children can be placed outdoors. A variation would be to use balloons for balls and rackets made from hangers with a nylon pantyhose pulled around the hanger.

4. **Skiing**

   Ski boots and skis can be provided for the children to try on.

5. **Skating**

   Waxed paper squares for children to wrap around their feet and ankles can be provided. The children can attach the waxed paper with rubber bands around their ankles. Encourage the children to slide across the carpeting.

Arts and Crafts:

1. **Easel Ideas**

   Cut easel paper in various sports shapes:

   - baseball glove
   - baseball diamond

   - tennis racket
   - bike
   - tennis shoe
   - football
   - baseball cap
   - football helmet
   - all different sizes of balls

2. **Baseball Glove Lacing**

   Prepare pre-cut baseball gloves out of brown construction paper. The older children might be able to cut them out themselves. Punch holes with a paper punch around the outer edge of the paper. Using yarn, let the children lace in and out of the holes of the gloves. Tie a knot at the end to secure the yarn.

3. **Collages**

   Using sports-related magazines, encourage the children to cut out various pictures. These pictures can be pasted onto another piece of paper.

4. **Ball Collages**

   Balls used in various sports come in all different sizes. Using construction paper or wallpaper, cut the paper in various round shapes, as well as football shapes. Encourage the children to paste them on a large piece of construction paper and decorate.

5. **Golf Ball Painting**

   Place a piece of paper in a shallow tray or pie tin. Spoon two or three teaspoons of thin paint onto the paper. Then, put a golf ball or ping-pong ball in the tray and tilt the pan in a number of directions, allowing the ball to make designs in the paint.

Sensory:

1. **Swimming**

   Add water to the sensory table with dolls or small people figures.

2. **Weighing Balls**

   Fill the sensory table with small balls, such as golf balls, styrofoam balls, wiffle balls, or tennis balls. Add a balance scale so that the children can weigh the balls.

510

3. **Measuring Mud and Sand**

   Add a mud and sand mixture to the sensory table with scoops and spoons.

4. **Feeling Turf**

   Line the bottom of the sensory table with artificial turf.

Large Muscle:

1. **Going Fishing**

   Use a large wooden rocking boat or a large box that two to three children can sit in. Make fish out of construction paper or tagboard, and attach paper clips to the top. Tie a magnet to a string and pole. The magnet will attract the fish.

2. **Kickball**

   Many sports involve kicking a ball. Discuss these sports with the children. Then provide the children with a variety of balls to kick. Let the children discover which balls go the farthest and which are the easiest to kick.

3. **Sports Charades**

   Dramatize various sports including swimming, golfing, tennis, and bike riding.

4. **Golfing**

   Using a child-sized putter and regular golf balls, the children hit golf balls. This is an outdoor activity that requires a lot of teacher supervision.

5. **Beach Volleyball**

   Use a large beach ball and a rope or net in a central spot outdoors. Let the children volley the beach ball to one another.

Field Trips:

Suggested trips include:

1. a football field
2. a baseball field

3. tennis court
4. health (fitness) club
5. stadium
6. a swimming pool
7. the sports facilities of a local high school or college

Math:

1. **Ball Sort**

   Sort various balls by size, texture, and color.

2. **Hat Sorting**

   Sort hats such as baseball cap, football helmet, biking helmet, visor, etc., by color, size, texture, and shape.

Group Time (games, language):

"What's Missing?"

Provide the children in a large group with a tray of sports equipment such as a ball, baseball glove, golf ball, sunglasses, goggles, etc. Let the children examine the tray of items. Then have the children close their eyes and place their heads in their laps. Remove one item from the tray and see if the children can guess what is missing. This activity will be more successful if the numbers are related to the age of the child. For example, with two-year-old children, use only two items. Three-year-olds may be successful with an additional item. If not, remove one.

Cooking:

Cheese Balls

8 ounces cream cheese, softened
1 stick of butter, softened
2 cups grated cheddar cheese
1/2 package of onion soup mix

Blend all of the ingredients together. Shape the mixture into small balls. Roll the balls in chopped nuts if desired.

Multimedia:

The following resources can be found in educational catalogs:

1. *And the Beat Goes on for Physical Education* [record].

2. *Coordination Skills* [record].

3. *Exercise Is Kids' Stuff* [record].

4. *Fitness Fun for Everyone* [record].

5. *Have a Ball!* [record].

6. *Jumpnastics* [record].

Books:

The following books can be used to complement the theme:

1. Koda-Callan, Elizabeth. (1992). *Shiny Skates*. New York: Workman.

2. Kuklin, Susan. (1989). *Going to My Ballet Class*. New York: Macmillan.

3. Scioscia, Mary. (1993). *Bicycle Rider*. New York: Harper Collins.

4. Whitehead, Patricia. (1985). *Arnold Plays Baseball*. Mahwah, NJ: Troll.

5. Blackstone, Margaret. (1993). *This Is Baseball*. New York: Henry Holt.

6. Friend, David. (1992). *Baseball, Football, Daddy and Me*. New York: Puffin Books.

7. Riddle, Tohby. (1991). *Careful with That Ball, Eugene!* New York: Orchard Books.

8. Sanchez, Isidro, & Peris, Carme. (1992). *City Sports*. Hauppauge, NY: Barron's Educational Series, Inc.

9. Curtis, Gavin. (1990). *Grandma's Baseball*. New York: Crown Books for Young Readers.

10. Duffey, Betsy. (1992). *Lucky in Left Field*. New York: Simon and Schuster Trade.

11. McConnachie, Brian. (1992). *Elmer and the Chickens vs. the Big League*. New York: Crown Books for Young Readers.

12. Thayer, Ernest L. (1992). *Casey at the Bat*. New York: Putnam Publishing Group.

13. Real, Rory. (1990). *A Baseball Dream*. Hauppauge, NY: Barron's Educational Series, Inc.

14. Henderson, Kathy. (1991). *I Can Be a Basketball Player*. Chicago: Children's Press.

Plants

flowers
dandelion
grass
tree buds

Activities

flying kites
gardening
fishing
baseball
picnics
golf
tennis
camping
walking
bicycling

Weather

rain
wind
warmer
thunderstorms

SPRING

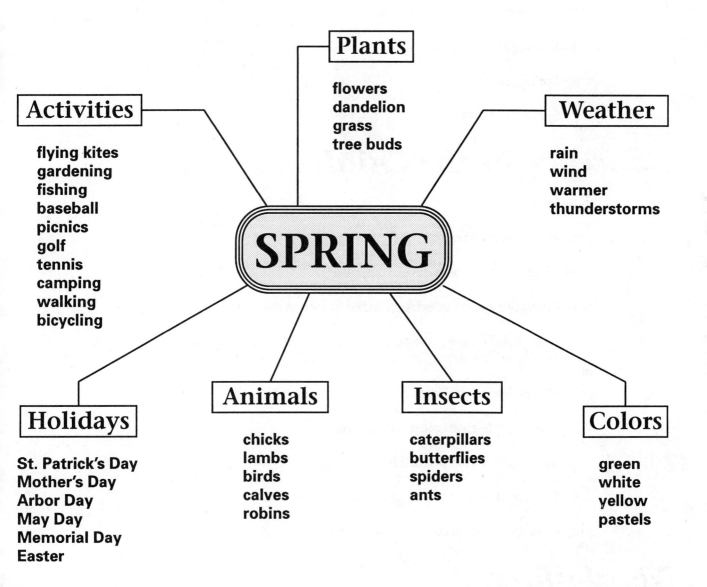

Holidays

St. Patrick's Day
Mother's Day
Arbor Day
May Day
Memorial Day
Easter

Animals

chicks
lambs
birds
calves
robins

Insects

caterpillars
butterflies
spiders
ants

Colors

green
white
yellow
pastels

Polaroid
Education
Program

Here's an exciting new way to turn instant photography into an effective teaching tool. Refer to the full-color insert for the activity entitled Tell Me A Story.

Theme Goals:

Through participating in the experiences provided by this theme, the children may learn:

1. Spring colors.

2. Spring weather.

3. Plants that grow in the spring.

4. Insects seen during the spring.

5. Springtime holidays.

6. Spring animals.

7. Spring activities.

Concepts for the Children to Learn:

1. Spring is a season.

2. It rains in the spring.

3. Light colors are seen during the spring.

4. Caterpillars and butterflies are insects seen in the spring.

5. Some holidays are celebrated in the spring: Mother's Day, Easter, St. Patrick's Day, May Day, Arbor Day, and Memorial Day.

6. Chicks, lambs, and birds are springtime animals.

7. Some people go on picnics in the spring.

8. Many gardens are planted in the spring.

9. Flowers, dandelions, and grass are spring plants.

10. Gardens are often planted in the spring.

Vocabulary:

1. **spring**—the season that comes after winter and before summer.

2. **garden**—a place where plants and flowers are grown.

3. **rain**—water from the clouds.

Bulletin Board

The purpose of this bulletin board is to have the children place the proper number of ribbons on each kite tail. To do this, they need to look at the number of dots on the kite. Construct kites and print the numerals beginning with one and the corresponding number of dots on each. Construct ribbons for the tails of the kites as illustrated. Color the kites and tails and laminate. Staple kites to bulletin board. Affix magnetic strips to each kite as the string. Affix a magnetic piece in the middle of each ribbon.

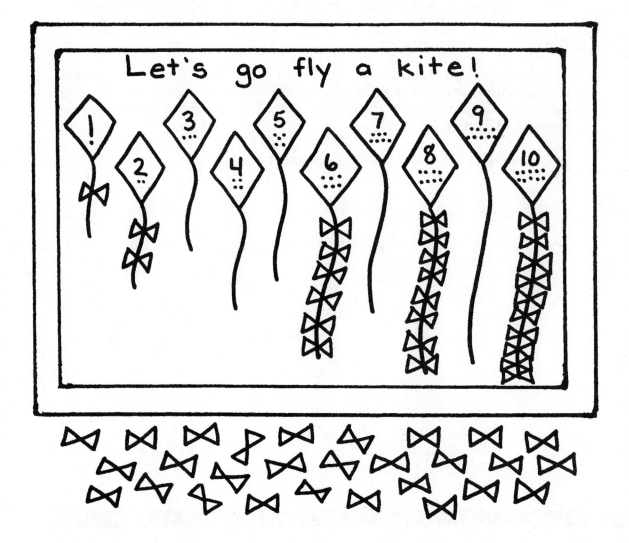

Parent Letter

Dear Parents,

The temperature is slowly rising, and there are patches of green grass on the playground. In other words, spring is here! And spring is the subject we will be exploring at school. Throughout the week, the children will become more aware of the many changes that take place during this season, as well as common spring activities.

At School

Some of the learning experiences for this curriculum unit include:

- finding a suitable place on the playground to plant flowers.
- taking a walk around the neighborhood to observe signs of spring.
- planting grass seed in empty eggshells at the science table.
- creating pictures and designs with pastel watercolor markers in the art area.

At Home

To foster concepts of spring at home, save seeds from fruits such as oranges and apples. Assist your child in planting the seeds. Your child can also sort the seeds by color, size, or type to develop classification skills. The seeds could also be used for counting. Happy seed collecting!

Enjoy your child as you explore concepts related to spring.

FIGURE 54 Bears wake up from long naps in the spring.

Music:

1. **"Catch One If You Can"**
   (Sing to the tune of "Skip to My Lou")

   Butterflies are flying. Won't you try and catch one?
   Butterflies are flying. Won't you try and catch one?
   Butterflies are flying. Won't you try and catch one?
   Catch one if you can.

   Raindrops are falling. Won't you try and catch one?
   Raindrops are falling. Won't you try and catch one?
   Raindrops are falling. Won't you try and catch one?
   Catch one if you can.

2. **"Signs of Spring"**
   (Sing to the tune of "Muffin Man")

   Do you see a sign of spring,
   A sign of spring, a sign of spring?
   Do you see a sign of spring?
   Tell us what you see.

3. **Let's Be Windmills**
   (Sing to the tune of "If I Were a Lassie")

   Oh I wish I were a windmill, a windmill, a windmill.
   Oh I wish I were a windmill. I know what I'd do.
   I'd swing this way and that way, and this way and that way.
   Oh I wish I were a windmill, when the wind blew.

Fingerplays:

SEE, SEE, SEE

See, see, see
   (shade eyes with hands)
Three birds are in a tree.
   (hold up three fingers)
One can chirp
   (point to thumb)
And one can sing.
   (point to index finger)
One is just a tiny thing.
   (point to middle finger, then rock baby bird in arms)
See, see, see
Three birds are in a tree
   (hold up three fingers)

Look, look, look
   (shade eyes)
Three ducks are in a brook.
   (hold up three fingers)
One is white, and one is brown.
One is swimming upside down.
   (point to a finger each time)
Look, look, look
Three ducks are in a brook.
   (hold up three fingers)

THIS LITTLE CALF

(extend fingers, push each down in succession)

This little calf eats grass.
This little calf eats hay.
This little calf drinks water.
This little calf runs away.
This little calf does nothing
But just lies down all day.
    (rest last finger in palm of hand)

RAINDROPS

Rain is falling down.
Rain is falling down.
    (raise arm, flutter fingers to ground, tapping
    the floor)
Pitter-patter
Pitter-patter
Rain is falling down.

CREEPY CRAWLY CATERPILLAR

A creepy crawly caterpiller that I see
    (shade eyes)
Makes a chrysalis in the big oak tree.
    (make body into a ball)
He stays there and I know why
    (slowly stand up)
Because soon he will be a butterfly.
    (flap arms)

MY GARDEN

This is my garden.
    (extend one hand forward, palm up)
I'll rake it with care
    (make raking motion on palm with three
    other fingers)
And then some flower seeds
I'll plant there.
    (planting motion)
The sun will shine
    (make circle with hands)
And the rain will fall.
    (let fingers flutter down to lap)
And my garden will blossom
And grow straight and tall.
    (cup hands together, extend upwards slowly)

CATERPILLAR

The caterpillar crawled from a plant, you see.
    (left hand crawls up and down right arm)

"I think I'll take a nap," said he.
So over the ground he began to creep
    (right hand crawls over left arm)
To spin a chrysalis, and he fell asleep.
    (cover right fist with left hand)
All winter he slept in his bed
Till spring came along and he said,
"Wake up, it's time to get out of bed!"
    (shake fist and pointer finger)
So he opened his eyes that sunny spring day.
    (spread fingers and look into hand)
"Look I'm a butterfly!"…and he flew away.
    (interlock thumbs and fly hands away)

Science:

1. **Alfalfa Sprouts**

   Each child who wishes to participate should be provided with a small paper cup, soil, and a few alfalfa seeds. The seeds and soil can be placed in the cup and watered. Place the cups in the sun and watch the sprouts grow. The sprouts can be eaten for snack. A variation is to plant the sprouts in eggshells as an Easter activity.

2. **Weather Chart**

   A weather chart can be constructed that depicts weather conditions such as sunny, rainy, warm, cold, windy, etc. Attach at least two arrows to the center of the chart so that the children can point the arrow at the appropriate weather conditions.

3. **Thermometers**

   On the science table place a variety of outdoor thermometers. Also, post a thermometer outside of a window, at a low position, so the children can read it.

4. **Sprouting Carrots**

   Cut the large end off a fresh carrot and place it in a small cup of water. In a few days, a green top will begin to sprout.

5. **Nesting Materials**

   Place string, cotton, yarn, and other small items outside on the ground. Birds will collect these items to use in their nest building.

518

6. Grass Growing

Grass seeds can be sprinkled on a wet sponge. Within a few days the seeds will begin to sprout.

7. Ant Farm

An ant farm can by made by using a large jar with a cover. Fill the jar 2/3 full with sand and soil, and add ants. Punch a few air holes in the cover of the jar, and secure the cover to the top of the jar. The children can watch the ants build tunnels.

Dramatic Play:

1. Fishing

Using short dowels prepare fishing poles with a string taped to one end. Attach a magnet piece to the loose end of the string. Construct fish from tagboard and attach a paper clip to each fish. The magnet will attract the paper clip, allowing the children to catch the fish. Add a tackle box, canteen, hats, and life jackets for interest.

2. Garden

A small plastic hoe, rake, and garden shovel can be placed outdoors to encourage gardening. A watering can, flower pots, seed packages, and sun hats will also stimulate interest.

3. Flower Shop

Collect plastic flowers, vases, wrapping paper, seed packages, and catalogs and place in the dramatic play area. A cash register and play money can be added.

4. Spring Cleaning

Small mops, brooms, feather dusters, and empty pails can be placed in the dramatic play area. A spray bottle filled with blue water, which can be used to wash designated windows, can also be provided.

Arts and Crafts:

1. Butterfly Wings

Fold a sheet of light-colored paper in half. Show the children how to paint on only one side of the paper. The paper can be folded again and pressed. The result will be a symmetrical painting. Antennas can be added to make butterflies using crayons and markers.

2. Pussy Willow Fingerprints

Trace around a tongue depressor with a colored marker. Then using ink pads or fingerpaint, the children can press their finger on the ink pad and transfer their fingerprint to the paper. This will produce pussy willow buds.

3. Caterpillars

Horizontally cut egg cartons in half. Place the pieces on the art table with short pieces of pipe cleaners, markers, and crayons. From these materials, the children can make caterpillars.

4. Kites

Provide diamond-shaped construction paper, string, hole punch, crepe paper, glue, glitter, and markers. For older children, provide the paper with a diamond already traced. This provides them an opportunity to practice finger motor skills by cutting out the shapes. Using the triangle shapes, the children can create kites, and use them outdoors.

Sensory:

The following items can be added to the sensory table:

- string, hay, sticks, and yarn to make birds' nests
- tadpoles and water
- dirt with worms
- seeds
- water and boats
- ice cubes to watch them melt

Large Muscle:

1. Windmills

The children can stand up, swing their arms from side to side, and pretend to be windmills. A fan can be added to the classroom for added interest. Sing the song, "Let's Be Windmills," which is listed under music.

2. Puddles

Construct puddles out of tagboard and cover with aluminum foil. Place the puddles on the floor. The children can jump from puddle to puddle. A variation would be to do this activity outside, using chalk to mark puddles on the ground.

3. Caterpillar Crawl

During a transition time, the children can imitate caterpillar movements.

Field Trips:

1. Nature Walk

Walk around your neighborhood, looking for signs of spring. Robins and other birds are often first signs of spring and can usually be observed in most areas of the country.

2. Farm

Arrange a field trip to a farm. It is an interesting place to visit during the spring. Ask the farmer to show you the farm equipment, buildings, crops, and animals.

Math:

1. Seed Counting

On an index card, mark a numeral. The number of cards prepared will depend upon the developmental appropriateness for the children. The children are to glue the appropriate number of seeds onto the card.

2. Insect Seriation

Construct flannel board pieces representing a ladybug, an ant, a caterpillar, a butterfly, etc. The children can arrange them on the flannel board from smallest to largest.

Social Studies:

1. Animal Babies

Collect pictures of animals and their young. Place the adult animal pictures in one basket and the pictures of the baby animals in another basket. The children can match adult animals to their offspring.

2. Spring Cleanup

Each child should be provided with a paper bag to collect litter on a walk to a park, in your neighborhood, or even on your playground. The litter should be discarded when you return to the center. Also, the children should be instructed to wash their hands.

3. Dressing for Spring

Flannel board figures with clothing items should be provided. The children can dress the figures for different kinds of spring weather.

4. Spring Clothing

Collect several pieces of spring clothing such as a jacket, hat, galoshes, and short-sleeved shirts. Add these to the dramatic play area.

Group Time (games, language):

1. What's Inside?

Inside a large box, place many spring items. Include a kite, an umbrella, a hat, a fishing pole, etc. Select an item without showing the children. Describe the object and give clues about how the item can be used. The children should try to identify the item.

2. Insect Movement

During transition time, ask the children to move like the following insects: worm, grasshopper, spider, caterpillar, butterfly, bumblebee, etc.

Cooking:

1. Lemonade

1 lemon
2 to 3 tablespoons sugar
1 1/4 cups water
2 ice cubes

Squeeze lemon juice out of lemon. Add the sugar and water. Stir to dissolve the sugar. This makes one serving. Adjust the recipe to accommodate your class size.

2. Watermelon Popsicles

Remove the seeds and rind from a watermelon. Puree the melon in a blender or food processor. Pour into small paper cups. Insert popsicle sticks and freeze. These fruit popsicles can be served at snack time.

SCIENCE ACTIVITIES

Twenty-five other interesting science activities include:

1. Observe **food forms** such as potatoes in the raw, shredded, or sliced form. Fruits can be juiced, sliced, or sectioned.

2. **Prepare tomatoes** in several ways, such as sliced, juiced, stewed, baked, and pureed.

3. **Show corn** in all forms including on the cob, popcorn, fresh cooked, and canned.

4. **Sort** picture cards into piles, living and non-living.

5. **Tape record voices.** Encourage the children to recognize each others' voices.

6. **Tape record familiar sounds** from their environment. Include a ticking clock, telephone ringing, doorbell, toilet flushing, horn beeping, etc.

7. Take the children on a **sensory walk.** Prepare by filling dishpan-sized containers with different items. Foam, sand, leaves, pebbles, mud, cold and warm water, and grains can be used. Have the children remove their shoes and socks to walk through.

8. **Enjoy a nature walk.** Provide each child with a grocery bag and instructions to collect leaves, rocks, soil, insects, etc.

9. Provide the children with **bubbles.** To make the solution, mix 2 quarts of water, 3/4 cup liquid soap, and 1/4 cup glycerine (available from a local druggist). Dip plastic berry baskets and plastic six-pack holders into the solution. Wave to produce bubbles.

10. Show the children how to feel their **heartbeat** after a vigorous activity.

11. Observe **popcorn** popping.

12. Record **body weights and heights.**

13. Prepare **hair and eye color charts.** This information can be made into bar graphs.

14. If climate permits, **freeze water outdoors.** Return it to the class and observe the effects of heat.

15. **Introduce water absorption** by providing containers with water. Allow the children to experiment with coffee filters, paper towels, newspaper, sponges, dishcloths, waxed paper, aluminum foil, and plastic wrap.

16. Explore **magnets**. Provide magnets of assorted sizes, shapes, and strengths. With magnets, place paper clips, nuts, bolts, aluminum foil, copper pennies, metal spoons, jar lids, feathers, etc.

17. Plan a **seed party**. Provide the children with peanuts, walnuts, pecans, and coconuts. Observe the different sizes, shapes, textures, and flavors.

18. Make a **desk garden**. Cut carrots, turnips, and a pineapple 1 1/2 inches from the stem. Place the stem in a shallow pan of water.

19. Create a **worm farm**. Place gravel and soil in a clear, large-mouth jar. Add worms and keep soil moist. Place lettuce, corn, or cereal on top of the soil. Tape black construction paper around the outside of the jar. Remove the paper temporarily and see the tunnels.

20. Place a **celery stalk** with leaves in a clear container of water. Add blue or red food coloring. Observe the plant's absorption of the colored water. A similar experiment can be introduced with a white carnation.

21. Make a **rainbow** with a garden hose on a sunny day. Spray water across the sun rays. The rays of the sun contain all of the colors, but the water, acting as a prism, separates the colors.

22. Make **shadows**. In a darkened room, use a flashlight. Place a hand or object in front of the light source, making a shadow.

23. Produce **static electricity** by rubbing wool fabric over inflated balloons.

24. Install a **birdfeeder** outside the classroom window.

25. During large group, play the **What's missing game**. Provide children with a variety of small familiar items. Tell them to cover their eyes or put their heads down. Remove one item. Then tell the children to uncover. Ask them what is missing. As children gain skill, remove a second and a third item.

Multimedia:

The following resources can be found in educational catalogs:

1. Jenkins, Ella. *Seasons for Singing* [record].

2. Wood, Lucille. *Springtime Walk* [record].

3. *All About Spring* [record]. Lyons Publishers.

4. Palmer, Hap. "Sunshine," *Modern Tunes for Rhythm and Instruments* [record].

5. *Raindrops* [record]. Melody House Records.

Books:

The following books can be used to complement the theme:

1. Suyenaga, R., et al. (1992). *Korean Children's Day*. Cleveland, OH: Modern Curriculum Press.

2. Good, Elaine W. (1987). *That's What Happens When It's Spring!* Intercourse, PA: Good Books.

3. Updike, David. (1989). *A Spring Story*. Ann Arbor, MI: Pippin.

4. Hautzig, Deborah. (1989). *Happy Mother's Day*. New York: Random House.

5. Brown, Craig. (1993). *In the Spring*. New York: Greenwillow Books.

6. Barker, Cicely M. (1991). *Flower Fairies of the Spring*. New York: Frederick Warne and Co.

7. Fowler, Allan. (1991). *How Do You Know It's Spring?* Chicago: Children's Press.

8. Hirschi, Ron. (1990). *Spring*. New York: Dutton Children's Books.

9. Moncure, Jane B. (1990). *Step into Spring: A New Season*. Mankato, MN: Child's World, Inc.

10. Zimmerman, H. Werner. (1991). *Alphonse Knows…the Colour of Spring*. New York: Oxford University Press, Inc.

11. Chmielarz, Sharon. (1992). *End of Winter*. New York: Crown Books for Young Readers.

12. Tibo, Gilles. (1990). *Simon Welcomes Spring*. Plattsburgh, NY: Tundra Books of Northern New York.

13. Katz, Bobbi (Ed.). (1992). *Puddle Wonderful: Poems to Welcome Spring*. New York: Random House Books for Young Readers.

THEME 55

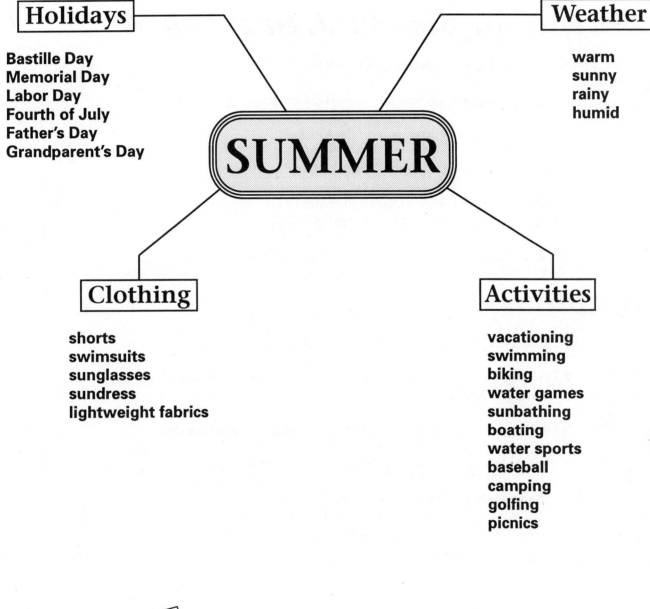

Holidays

Bastille Day
Memorial Day
Labor Day
Fourth of July
Father's Day
Grandparent's Day

Weather

warm
sunny
rainy
humid

SUMMER

Clothing

shorts
swimsuits
sunglasses
sundress
lightweight fabrics

Activities

vacationing
swimming
biking
water games
sunbathing
boating
water sports
baseball
camping
golfing
picnics

Polaroid
Education
Program

Here's an exciting new way to turn instant photography into an effective teaching tool. Refer to the full-color insert for the activity entitled My Friends and Me.

Theme Goals:

Through participating in the experiences provided by this theme, the children may learn:

1. Summer holidays.

2. Types of summer clothing.

3. Summer clothing needs.

4. Summer activities.

Concepts for the Children to Learn:

1. Summer is usually the warmest season.

2. Summer months are usually warm and sunny.

3. Lightweight clothing is worn in the summer.

4. Shade trees protect us from the sun during the summer.

5. Memorial Day, Father's Day, Grandparent's Day, the Fourth of July, Bastille Day, and Labor Day are all summer holidays.

6. Swimming, biking, and camping are all summer activities.

Vocabulary:

1. **shorts**—short pants worn in warm weather.

2. **swimming**—a water sport usually enjoyed by many people during the summer months.

3. **hot**—a warm temperature experienced during summer months.

4. **beach**—a sandy place used for sunbathing and playing.

5. **shade**—being in the shadow of something.

Bulletin Board

The purpose of this bulletin board is to promote the identification of written numerals as well as matching sets of objects to a written numeral. Pairs of pails are constructed out of various scraps of tagboard. Using a black marker print a different numeral on each pail. The number of pairs made and numerals used should depend upon the developmental level of the children. Cut seashells out of tagboard and decorate as desired. Laminate all pieces. Attach pails to the bulletin board by stapling them along the side and bottom edges, leaving the tops of the pails open. The children should place the corresponding sets of shells in each pail.

Parent Letter

Dear Parents,

Summer is the favorite season of most children. As summer approaches, we will be starting a unit on the season. Through this unit, the children will become more aware of summer weather, activities, food, and clothing.

At School

Learning experiences planned to highlight summer concepts include:

- exploring the outside and inside of a watermelon and then eating it!
- trying on shorts, sunglasses, and sandals in the dramatic play area.
- preparing fruit juice popsicles.
- eating a picnic lunch on Wednesday. We will be walking to Wilson Park at 11:45. Please feel free to pack a sack lunch and meet us there!

At Home

To reinforce summer concepts at home, try the following:

- Plan a family picnic and allow your child to help plan what food and items will be needed.
- Take part in or observe any summer activity such as boating, fishing, biking, camping, or taking a bike ride.

Have a good summer!

FIGURE 55 Summer means a lot of outdoor activities.

Music:

1. **"Summer Clothing"**
   (Sing to the tune of "The Farmer in the Dell.")

   Oh, if you are wearing shorts,
   If you are wearing shorts,
   You may walk right to the door,
   If you are wearing shorts.

   Also include: stripes, sandals, tennis shoes,
   flowers, a sundress, blue jeans, belt, barrettes,
   etc.

   This song can be used during transition times
   to point out children's summer clothing.

2. **"Summer Activities"**
   (Sing to the tune of "Skip to My Lou.")

   Swim, swim, swim in a circle.
   Swim, swim, swim in a circle.
   Swim, swim, swim in a circle.
   Swim in a circle now.

   Also include: jump, hop, skip, run, walk, etc.
   Use this song as a transition sone to introduce
   summer activities.

Fingerplays:

HERE IS THE BEE HIVE

Here is the bee hive. Where are the bees?
   (make a fist)
They're hiding away so nobody sees.
Soon they're coming creeping out of their hive,
1, 2, 3, 4, 5. Buzz-z-z-z-z-z.
   (draw fingers out of fist on each count)

GREEN LEAF

Here's a green leaf
   (show hand)
And here's a green leaf.
   (show other hand)
That you see, makes two.

Here's a bud.
   (cup hands together)
That makes a flower;
Watch it bloom for you!
   (open cupped hands gradually)

A ROLY-POLY CATERPILLAR

Roly-poly caterpillar
Into a corner crept.
Spun around himself a blanket
   (spin around)

Then for a long time slept.
(place head on folded hands)

Roly-poly caterpillar
Wakened by and by.
(stretch)
Found himself with beautiful wings
Changed into a butterfly.
(flutter arms like wings)

Science:

1. **Science Table**

   Add the following items to the science table:

   - all kinds of sunglasses with different-colored shades
   - plant grass seeds in small cups of dirt, water daily
   - dirt and grass with magnifying glasses
   - sand with scales and magnifying glasses
   - pinwheels (children use their own wind to make them move)
   - blow bubbles outdoors

2. **Water and Air Make Bubbles**

   Bubble Solution Recipe

   3/4 cup liquid soap
   1/4 cup glycerine (obtain at a drugstore)
   2 quarts water

   Place mixed solution in a shallow pan and let children place the bubble makers in the solution. Bubble makers can be successfully made from the following:

   - plastic six-pack holder
   - straws
   - bent wire with no sharp edges
   - funnels

3. **Flying Kites**

   On a windy day, make and fly kites.

4. **Making Rainbows**

   If you have a hose available the children can spray the hose into the sun. The rays of the sun contain all the colors mixed together. The water acts as a prism and separates the water into colors creating a rainbow.

Dramatic Play:

1. **Juice Stand**

   Set up a lemonade or orange juice stand. To prepare use real oranges and lemons and let the children squeeze them and make the juice. The juice can be served at snack time.

2. **Ice Cream Stand**

   Trace and cut ice cream cones from brown construction paper. Cotton balls or small yarn pompoms can be used to represent ice cream. The addition of ice cream buckets and ice cream scoopers can make this activity more inviting during self-selected play periods.

3. **Indoors or Outdoors Picnic**

   A blanket, picnic basket, plastic foods, purses, small cooler, paper plates, plastic silverware, napkins, etc., can be placed in the classroom to stimulate play.

4. **The Beach**

   In the dramatic play area place beach blankets, lawn chairs, buckets, sunglasses, beach balls, magazines, and books. If the activity is used outdoors, a sun umbrella can be added to stimulate interest in play.

5. **Camping Fun**

   A small freestanding tent can be set up indoors, if room permits, or outdoors. Sleeping bags can also be provided. Blocks or logs could represent a campfire.

6. **Traveling by Air**

   Place a telephone, tickets, travel brochures, and suitcases in the dramatic play area.

Arts and Crafts:

1. **Outdoor Painting**

   An easel can be placed outside. The children choose to use the easel during outdoor play-time. If the sun is shining, encourage the children to observe how quickly the paint dries.

2. **Chalk Drawings**

Large pieces of chalk should be provided for the children to draw on the sidewalks outdoors. Small plastic berry baskets make handy chalk containers.

3. **Foot Painting**

This may be used as an outdoor activity. The children can dip their feet in a thick tempera paint mixture and make prints by stepping on large sheets of paper. Sponges and pans of soapy water should be available for cleanup.

4. **Shake Painting**

Tape a large piece of butcher paper on a fence or wall outdoors. Let the children dip their brushes in paint and stand two feet from the paper. Then show them how to shake the brush, allowing the paint to fly onto the paper.

5. **Sailboats**

Color styrofoam meat trays with markers. Stick a pipe cleaner in the center of the tray and secure by bending the end underneath the carton. Prepare a sail and glue to the pipe cleaner.

Sensory:

Sensory Table

The following items can be added to the sensory table:

- sand with toys
- colored sand
- sand and water
- water with toy boats
- shells
- small rocks and pebbles
- grass and hay

Large Muscle:

1. **Barefoot Walk**

Check the playground to ensure that it is free of debris. Then sprinkle part of the grass and sandbox with water. Go on a barefoot walk.

2. **Balls**

In the outdoor play yard place a variety of large balls.

3. **Catching Balloons**

Balloons can be used indoors and outdoors. Close supervision is required. *If a balloon breaks it should be immediately removed.*

4. **Parachute Play**

Use a real parachute or a sheet to represent one. The children should hold onto the edges. Say a number and then have the children count and wave the parachute in the air that number of times.

5. **Balloon Racket Ball**

Bend coat hangers into diamond shapes. Bend the handles closed and tape for safety. Then pull nylon stockings over the diamond shapes to form swatters. The children can use the swatters to keep the balloons up in the air by hitting them.

Field Trips/Resource People:

1. **Picnic at the Park**

A picnic lunch can be prepared and eaten at a park or in the play yard.

2. **Resource People**

The following resource people may be invited to the classroom:

- A lifeguard to talk about water safety.
- A camp counselor can talk to the children about camping and sing some camp songs with the children.

Math:

Sand Numbers and Shapes

During outdoor play informally make shapes and numbers in the sand and let children identify the shape or number.

Social Studies:

1. Making Floats

To celebrate the Fourth of July, decorate the trikes, wagons, and scooters with crepe paper, streamers, balloons, etc. Parade around the school or neighborhood.

2. Summer at School

Take pictures or slides of community summer activities. Construction workers, parades, children playing, sports activities, people swimming, library hours, picnics, band concerts, and people driving are examples. Show the slides and discuss them during group time.

3. Summer Fun Book

Magazines should be provided for the children to find pictures of summer activities. The pictures can be pasted on a sheet of paper. Bind the pages by stapling them together to make a book.

Group Time (games, language):

1. Exploring a Watermelon

Serve watermelon for snack. Talk about the color of the outside, which is called the rind. Next cut the watermelon into pieces. Give each child a piece to look at. Examine it carefully. "What color is the inside? Are there seeds? Do we eat the seeds? What can we do with them?" The children can remove all the seeds from their piece of watermelon. Then eat the watermelon. Collect all of the seeds. After circle time, wash the seeds. When dry, they can be used for a collage.

2. Puppet Show

Weather permitting, bring puppets and a puppet stage outdoors and have an outdoor puppet show.

Cooking:

1. Popsicles

pineapple juice
grape juice
cranapple juice
popsicle sticks
small paper cups

If frozen juice is used, mix according to the directions on the can. Fill the paper cups 3/4 full of juice. Place the cups in the freezer. When the juice begins to freeze, insert a popsicle stick in the middle of each cup. When frozen, peel the cup away and serve.

2. Watermelon Popsicles

Remove the seeds and rind from watermelon. Puree the melon in a blender. Follow the recipe for popsicles.

3. Zippy Drink

2 ripe bananas
2 cups orange juice
2 cups orange sherbet
ice cubes
orange slices

Peel the bananas, place in a bowl and mash with a fork. Add orange juice and sherbet and beat with a rotary beater until smooth. Pour into pitcher. Add ice cubes and orange slices.

4. Kulfi (Indian Ice Cream)

1 quart milk
1/2 pint heavy cream
1/4 cup sugar
1/2 cup chopped pistachio nuts
1/2 cup chopped almonds
1 tablespoon vanilla
2 drops red food coloring

Combine milk and heavy cream in a saucepan. Simmer over medium heat for about 20 minutes until thick. Add sugar, pistachio nuts, almonds, vanilla, and food coloring. Mix thoroughly. Let cool. Fill small paper cups halfway with kulfi and place in a freezer for 1 hour until the kulfi has the consistency of soft sherbet. Makes 10 servings.

Source: *Wonderful World Macmillan Early Skills Program.* (1985). New York: Macmillan Educational Company.

Multimedia:

The following resources can be found in educational catalogs:

1. *Action Songs for Indoor Days* [record]. Tom Thumb series.

2. *Children's Games* [record]. Kimbo Records.

3. Palmer, Hap. *Modern Marches* [record].

4. *Pretend to Be Me* [record]. Melody House Records.

5. *Adventures in Sounds* [record]. Melody House Records.

6. *Patriotic Songs of the U.S.* [record]. Melody House Records.

Books:

The following books can be used to complement the theme:

1. Sumiko. (1990). *My Summer Vacation*. New York: David McKay Co., Inc.

2. Barker, Cicely M. (1991). *Flower Fairies of the Summer*. New York: Frederick Warne and Co., Inc.

3. Blades, Ann. (1990). *Summer*. New York: Lothrop, Lee, & Shepard Books.

4. Fowler, Allan. (1992). *How Do You Know It's Summer?* Chicago: Children's Press.

5. Moncure, Jane B. (1990). *Step into Summer: A New Season*. Mankato, MN: Child's World, Inc.

6. Sanchez, Isidro, & Peris, Carme. (1992). *Summer Sports*. Hauppauge, NY: Barron's Educational Series, Inc.

7. Schweninger, Ann. (1992). *Summertime*. New York: Viking Children's Books.

8. Komoda, Beverly. (1991). *The Too Hot Day*. New York: Harper Collins Children's Books.

9. Hayward, Linda. (1989). *Grover's Summer Vacation*. New York: Random House.

10. Ransom, Candace F. (1992). *Shooting Star Summer*. Boyds Mills Press.

11. Brown, Margaret W. (1993). *Summer Noisy Book*. New York: Harper Collins.

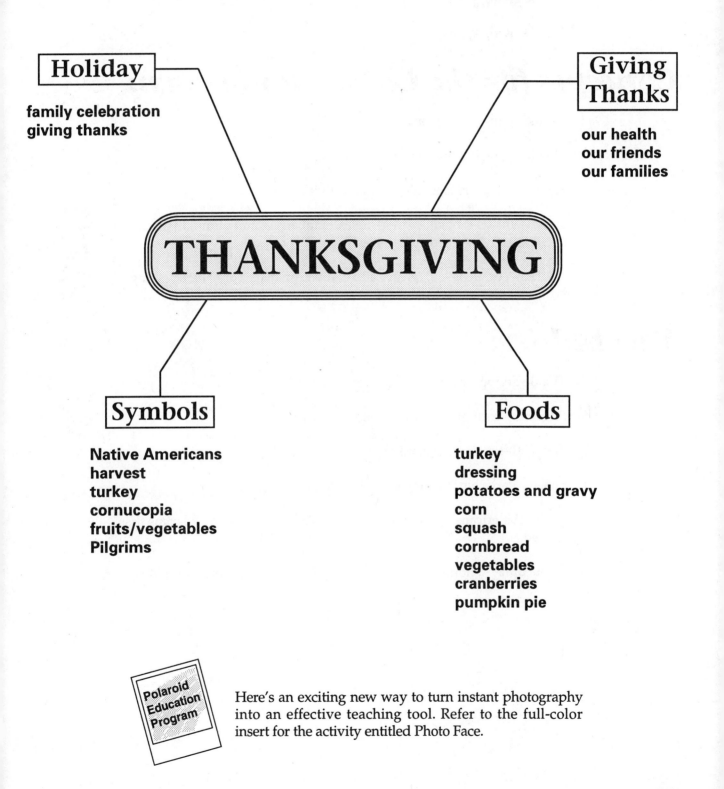

Holiday

family celebration
giving thanks

Giving Thanks

our health
our friends
our families

THANKSGIVING

Symbols

Native Americans
harvest
turkey
cornucopia
fruits/vegetables
Pilgrims

Foods

turkey
dressing
potatoes and gravy
corn
squash
cornbread
vegetables
cranberries
pumpkin pie

Polaroid
Education
Program

Here's an exciting new way to turn instant photography into an effective teaching tool. Refer to the full-color insert for the activity entitled Photo Face.

Theme Goals:

Through participating in the experiences provided by this theme, the children may learn:

1. Purpose of Thanksgiving.

2. Thanksgiving celebration.

3. Thanksgiving foods.

4. Thanksgiving symbols.

Concepts for the Children to Learn:

1. Thanksgiving is a holiday.

2. Thanksgiving is a time for giving thanks.

3. Families celebrate together on Thanksgiving.

4. Turkey, dressing, potatoes, vegetables, cranberries, and pumpkin pie are eaten on Thanksgiving by many families.

5. A turkey, cornucopia, Pilgrims, and Native Americans are Thanksgiving symbols.

Vocabulary:

1. **Thanksgiving**—a holiday in November.

2. **Pilgrims**—early settlers who sailed to America.

3. **thankful**—expressing thanks.

4. **turkey**—large bird that is cooked for Thanksgiving.

5. **Native Americans**—natives who lived in America when the Pilgrims first arrived.

6. **cornucopia**—a horn-shaped container with fruits, vegetables, and flowers.

Bulletin Board

The purpose of this bulletin board is to have the children hang the color-coded card onto the corresponding colored feather. Construct a large turkey out of tagboard. Color each feather a different color. Hang the turkey on the bulletin board. Hang a push pin in each feather. On small index cards, make a circle of each color and write the color name above it. Use a hole punch to make a hole in each card.

Parent Letter

Dear Parents,

During the month of November each year, we celebrate Thanksgiving. To coincide with this holiday at school, we will be focusing our curriculum on Thanksgiving. Through activities provided, the children will develop an understanding of the foods of Thanksgiving, as well as become more aware of the many people and things for which we are thankful.

At School

Planned learning experiences related to Thanksgiving include:

- popping corn.
- creating hand turkeys.
- visiting a turkey farm.
- exploring various types of corn with scales and magnifying glasses.

At Home

There are many ways for you to incorporate Thanksgiving concepts at home. Talk with your child about the special ways your family celebrates Thanksgiving. Involve your child in the preparation of a traditional Thanksgiving dish. Also, emphasize things and people for which you are thankful.

Reminder

There will be no school on Thursday, November 27th.

For those of you who are traveling during the Thanksgiving weekend, drive safely!

Happy Thanksgiving from the staff!

FIGURE 56 Families like to celebrate Thanksgiving.

Music:

1. **"Popcorn Song"**
    (Sing to the tune of "I'm a Little Teapot")

    I'm a little popcorn in a pot.
    Heat me up and watch me pop.
    When I get all fat and white, then I'm done.
    Popping corn is lots of fun.

2. **"If You're Thankful"**
    (Sing to the tune of "If You're Happy")

    If you're thankful and you know it clap your hands.
    If you're thankful and you know it clap your hands.
    If you're thankful and you know it, then your face will surely show it,
    If you're thankful and you know it, clap your hands.

    Additional verses could include stamp your feet, tap your head, turn around, shout hooray, etc.

Fingerplays:

THANKSGIVING DINNER

Everyday we eat our dinner.
Our table is very small.
    (palms of hands close together)
There's room for father, mother, sister, brother, and me—that's all.
    (point to each finger)
But when it's Thanksgiving Day and the company comes,
You'd scarcely believe your eyes.
    (rub eyes)
For that very same reason, the table stretches until it is just this size!
    (stretch arms wide)

THE BIG TURKEY

The big turkey on the farm is so very proud.
    (form fist)
He spreads his tail like a fan
    (spread fingers of other hand being fist)
And struts through the animal crowd.
    (move two fingers of fist as walking)
If you talk to him as he wobbles along;

He'll answer back with a gobbling song.
"Gobble, gobble, gobble."
   (open and close hand)

Science:

1. **Corn**

   Display several types of corn on the science table. Include field corn, popcorn, and popped popcorn.

2. **Wishbone**

   Bring in a wishbone from a turkey and place it in a bottle. Pour some vinegar in the bottle to cover the wishbone. Leave the wishbone in the bottle for 24 hours. Remove it and feel it. It will feel and bend like rubber.

Sensory:

The following items can be placed in the sensory area for the children to discover:

- unpopped or popped popcorn
- pinecones
- cornmeal and measuring cups

Dramatic Play:

Shopping

Set up a grocery store in the dramatic play area. To stimulate play, provide a cash register, shopping bags, as well as empty food containers including boxes, packages, and plastic bottles.

Arts and Crafts:

1. **Thanksgiving Collage**

   Place magazines on the art table for the children to cut out things they are thankful for. After the pictures are cut, they can be pasted on paper to form a collage.

2. **Thanksgiving Feast**

   Place food items cut from magazines and the newspaper on a table along with paste and paper plates. Let the children select the foods they would like to eat for their Thanksgiving feast.

3. **Cornmeal Playdough**

   Make cornmeal playdough. Mix 2 1/2 cups flour with 1 cup cornmeal. Add 1 tablespoon oil and 1 cup water. Additional water can be added to make desired texture. The dough should have a grainy texture. Cooky cutters and rolling pins can extend this activity.

4. **Popcorn Collage**

   Place popped popcorn and dried tempera paint into small sealable bags. Have children shake bags to color the popcorn. Then have them create designs and pictures by gluing the popcorn onto the paper. You can also use unpopped colored popcorn. Make sure the children do not eat any of the popcorn after it has been mixed with paint.

5. **Hand Turkey**

   Paper, crayons, or pencils are needed. Begin by instructing the child to place a hand on a piece of paper. Then tell them to spread their fingers. If possible, have the child trace his own fingers. Otherwise, you need to trace them. The hand can be decorated to create a turkey. Eyes, a beak, and a wattle can be added to the outline of the thumb. The fingers can be colored to represent the turkey's feathers. Then legs can be added below the outline of the palm.

Large Muscle:

Popping Corn

Pretend to be popping corn. Begin by demonstrating how to curl down on the floor, explaining that everyone is a kernel of corn. Then plug in the popcorn popper and listen to the sounds. Upon hearing popping sounds, jump up and down to the sounds.

Field Trip:

Turkey Farm

Visit a turkey farm. The children can observe the behavior of the turkeys as well as the food they eat.

Math:

1. Turkey Shapes

Give children several geometric shapes to create their own turkeys with circles, squares, and triangles. Have children identify the shapes and colors as they create their turkeys.

2. Colored Popcorn

Provide the children with colored popcorn seeds. Place corresponding colored circles in the bottom of muffin tins or egg cartons. Encourage the children to sort the seeds by color.

Group Time (games, language):

1. Turkey Chase

Have the children sit in a circle formation. The game requires two balls of different colors. Vary the size, depending on the age of the children. Generally, the younger the child, the larger the ball size. Begin by explaining that the first ball passed is the "turkey." The second ball is the "turkey farmer." The first ball should be passed from child to child around the circle. Shortly after, pass the second ball in the same direction. The game ends when the turkey farmer, the second ball, catches up to the turkey, the first ball. This game is played like hot potato.

2. Feast

Place several kinds of food on a plate in the middle of the circle. Tell the children to cover their eyes. Choose one child to take something from the plate to eat. The child hides one item, and the others open their eyes and try to guess which food item the child has eaten! The number of items included in this activity should be determined by the children's developmental age. Even to begin the activity, it may be advisable to begin with only two food items.

3. Turkey Keeper

To play this game, a turkey cut from cardboard or even a small plastic replica is needed. Instruct one child to cover his eyes. Then quietly hide the turkey in the classroom. After this, instruct the child to open his eyes and begin to look for the turkey. When the child begins walking in the direction of the turkey, the rest of the children quietly provide a clue by saying, "gobble gobble." As the child approaches the turkey, the children's voices serve as a clue by becoming louder. Once the turkey is located, another child becomes the turkey keeper.

4. Drop the Wishbone

Tell the children to sit in a circle formation. Choose one child to walk around the outside of the circle and drop a wishbone behind another child. (If a real wishbone is unavailable, a wishbone can be cut from cardboard.) The child who had the wishbone dropped behind him must pick it up and chase the first child. If the first child is tagged before he runs around the circle and sits in the second child's place, he is "it" again. If not, the second child is "it." This is a variation of "Drop the Handkerchief."

5. Turkey Waddle

Provide the children with verbal and visual clues to waddle like turkeys. The following terms may be used:

- fat turkey
- little turkey
- fast turkey
- slow turkey
- tired turkey
- happy turkey
- proud turkey
- sad turkey
- hungry turkey
- full turkey

Cooking:

1. **Fu Fu—West Africa**

   3 or 4 yams
   water
   1/2 teaspoon salt
   1/8 teaspoon pepper
   Optional: 3 tablespoons honey or sugar

   Wash and peel yams and cut into 1/2-inch slices. Place slices in a large saucepan and add water to cover them. Bring to a boil over a hot plate or stove. Reduce heat, cover saucepan, and simmer for 20 to 25 minutes, until yams are soft enough to mash. Remove saucepan from stove and drain off liquid into a small bowl. Let yams cool for 15 minutes. Place yam slices in a medium-sized mixing bowl, mash with a fork, add salt and pepper, and mash again until smooth. Roll mixture into small, walnut-sized balls. If mixture is too dry, moisten it with a tablespoon of the reserved yam liquid. For sweeter Fu Fu, roll yam balls in a dish of honey or sugar. Makes 24 balls.

2. **Muffins**

   1 egg
   3/4 cup milk
   1/2 cup vegetable oil
   2 cups all-purpose flour
   1/3 cup sugar
   3 tablespoons baking powder
   1 teaspoon salt

   Heat oven to 400 degrees. Grease bottoms only of 12 medium muffin cups. Beat egg. Stir in milk and oil. Stir in remaining ingredients all at once, just until flour is moistened. Batter will be lumpy. Fill muffin cups about 3/4 full. Bake until golden brown about 20 minutes. For pumpkin muffins: stir in 1/2 cup pumpkin and 1/2 cup raisins with the milk and 2 teaspoons pumpkin pie spice with the flour.

   For cranberry-orange muffins: stir in 1 cup cranberry halves and 1 tablespoon grated orange peel with milk.

3. **Cranberry Freeze**

   16-ounce can (2 cups) whole cranberry sauce
   8-ounce can (1 cup) crushed pineapple, drained
   1 cup sour cream or yogurt

   In a medium bowl, combine all the ingredients and mix well. Pour the mixture into an 8-inch square pan or an ice cube tray. Freeze 2 hours or until firm. To serve cut into squares or pop out of the ice cube tray.

Multimedia:

The following resources can be found in educational catalogs:

1. Palmer, Hap. "Things I Am Thankful For," *Holiday Songs and Rhymes* [record].

2. *Why We Celebrate…Thanksgiving* [30-minute video]. Edu-vid.

Books:

The following books can be used to complement the theme:

1. Nikola-Lisa, W. (1991). *One, Two, Three Thanksgiving!* Morton Grove, IL: Albert Whitman.

2. George, Jean C. (1993). *First Thanksgiving.* New York: Putnam.

3. Ziefert, Harriet. (1992). *What Is Thanksgiving?* New York: Harper Collins.

4. Fradin, Dennis B. (1990). *Thanksgiving Day.* Hillside, NJ: Enslow Publishers.

5. Hoban, Lillian. (1991). *Silly Tilly's Thanksgiving Dinner.* New York: Harper Collins.

6. Parker, Margot. (1988). *What Is Thanksgiving Day?* Chicago: Children's Press.

7. Berenstain, Stan & Janice. (1990). *The Berenstain Bears and the Prize Pumpkin.* New York: Random House Books for Young Readers.

8. Bunting, Eve. (1991). *A Turkey for Thanksgiving.* Boston: Houghton Mifflin Co.

9. Bunting, Eve. (1990). *Daisy's Crazy Thanksgiving.* New York: Henry Hold and Co.

10. Dragonwagon, Crescent. (1992). *Alligator Arrived with Apples: A Potluck Alphabet Feast.* New York: Macmillan Children's Book Group.

11. Pilkey, Dav. (1990). *'Twas the Night Before Thanksgiving.* New York: Orchard Books.

12. Stock, Catherine. (1990). *Thanksgiving Treat.* New York: Macmillan Children's Book Group.

13. Watson, Wendy. (1991). *Thanksgiving at Our House.* Boston: Houghton Mifflin Co.

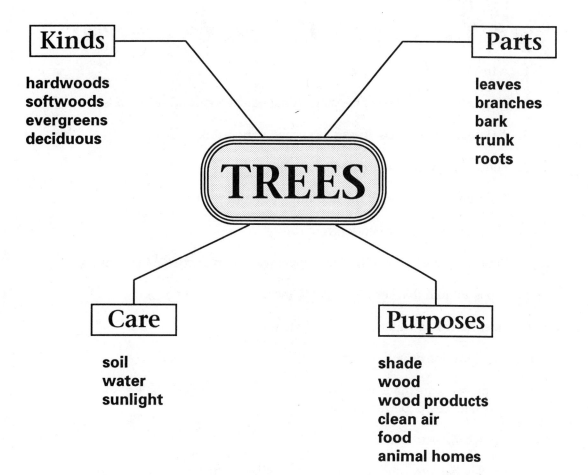

Kinds

hardwoods
softwoods
evergreens
deciduous

Parts

leaves
branches
bark
trunk
roots

TREES

Care

soil
water
sunlight

Purposes

shade
wood
wood products
clean air
food
animal homes

Here's an exciting new way to turn instant photography into an effective teaching tool. Refer to the full-color insert for the activity entitled Graphing.

Theme Goals:

Through participating in the experiences provided by this theme, the children may learn:

1. Parts of a tree.

2. Kinds of trees.

3. Care of trees.

4. How trees help us.

Concepts for the Children to Learn:

1. A tree is a large plant.

2. There are many kinds of trees including hardwoods and softwoods.

3. A tree has many parts: leaves, branches, bark, trunk, and roots.

4. The leaves of some trees are like needles.

5. The trunk is the stem of the tree and is covered with bark.

6. The roots of a tree are underground.

7. Roots help the tree stand; they also get water and nutrients from the soil.

8. Sap is a liquid that supplies food to the tree.

9. Trees need soil, water, and sunlight to grow.

10. Trees provide us with wood.

11. Many items are made from wood, such as houses, chairs, tables, some toys, doors, fences, paper, and paper products.

12. Some fruit grows on trees.

13. Apples, bananas, and oranges are examples of fruits that grow on trees.

14. Trees provide homes for many animals.

15. Trees provide us with shade to keep us cool and protect us from the sun.

Vocabulary:

1. **tree**—a large plant.

2. **trunk**—the main stem and largest part of a tree.

3. **bark**—the tough, outer covering of a tree.

4. **sap**—the fluid part of a tree.

5. **root**—the underground part of a plant.

Bulletin Board

The purpose of this bulletin board is to provide numeral identification as well as matching sets of objects to numerals. To prepare the bulletin board construct tree trunks out of brown tagboard. Print a numeral on each trunk. Next, construct treetops out of green tagboard. Draw sets of leaves on each treetop. Trace and cut out treetop shadows from black construction paper. Using the illustration as a guide, attach the shadows and tree trunks to the bulletin board. Adhesive magnet pieces or map tacks can be used by the children to match each tree trunk to the corresponding treetop.

Parent Letter

Dear Parents,

Did you ever stop to think about what our world would be like without trees? Trees serve many purposes; consequently, we will be exploring a theme on trees beginning this week. Through the experiences provided the children will become aware of the parts of a tree, kinds of trees, and, of course, the importance of trees.

At School

We will use wood to build houses, schools, chairs, tables, and all kinds of other objects. We will make paper. We will talk about foods that grow on trees. The foods served at snack time will be those foods that are grown on trees. Some of the week's activities will include:

- creating leaf and bark rubbings in the art area.
- going on a "tree walk" and recording the number and kinds of trees we see.
- cooking with foods we get from trees.
- creating our own books in the writing center.
- planting citrus fruit seeds and an avocado seed.

At Home

Walk around your home and find all the things that are made from wood. Which room contains the most wood items?

Polish your furniture with your child. Show them how to care for fine wood products.

Try preparing the following recipe with your child:

Apple Bake

Core an apple and place it in a dish with a tablespoon or two of water. Sprinkle with cinnamon and a dash of sugar, if desired. Cover and bake at 350 degrees for 20 minutes. If you prefer microwaving, cover with plastic wrap and cook on "high" for five minutes.

Enjoy your child!

FIGURE 57 Children enjoy a brush as a tool to apply paint.

Music:

1. **"Little Leaves"**
   (Sing to the tune of "Ten Little Indians")

   One little, two little, three little leaves.
   Four little, five little, six little leaves.
   Seven little, eight little, nine little leaves.
   Ten little leaves fall down.

2. **"Foods That Grow on Trees"**
   (Sing to the tune of "The Farmer in the Dell")

   Foods that grow on trees.
   Foods that grow on trees.
   Let's sing a song about
   Foods that grow on trees.

   Apples grow on trees.
   Apples grow on trees.
   Pick them, red and sweet.
   Apples grow on trees.

   Bananas grow on trees.
   Bananas grow on trees.
   Pick them, yellow and long.
   Bananas grow on trees.

   Oranges grow on trees.
   Oranges grow on trees.
   Pick them, sweet and juicy
   Oranges grow on trees.

   Walnuts grow on trees.
   Walnuts grow on trees.
   Pick them, brown and crunchy.
   Walnuts grow on trees.

Fingerplays:

THE APPLE TREE

Way up high in the apple tree
   (raise arms over head)
Two little apples smiled at me.
   (make fists or circles with hands)
I shook that tree as hard as I could
   (move hands as if shaking something)
Down came the apples
   (falling motion with fists)
Mmmmmmmmmmmmmmmmmm—were they good!
   (rub tummy)

ORANGE TREE

This is the orange tree with leaves so green
   (raise arms over head, making a circle)
Here are the oranges that hang in between.
   (make fists)

When the wind blows the oranges will fall.
Here is the basket to gather them all.
   (make circle with arms in front of body)

I AM A TALL TREE

I am a tall tree.
I reach toward the sky
   (reach upward with both hands)
Where the bright stars twinkle
And white clouds float by.
   (sway arms above head)
My branches toss high
As the wild winds blow.
   (wave arms rapidly)
Now they bend forward
Loaded with snow.
   (arms out front swaying)
I like it best
When I rock birds to sleep in their nest.
   (place hands at the side of head and close
   eyes)

THE WIND

Who has seen the wind?
Neither you nor I;
But where the leaves hang trembling,
   (hold hands downward and wiggle fingers)
The wind is passing through.

Who has seen the wind?
Neither you nor I;
But when the trees bow down their heads,
   (move head downward)
The wind is passing by.

Science:

1. **Weighing Nuts**

   Provide a balance scale and acorns, pinecones, or nuts at the science table.

2. **Planting Seeds**

   Collect and plant seeds from fruits that grow on trees such as apples and citrus fruits. Make and record predictions about when the plants will sprout.

3. **Grow An Avocado Tree**

   Remove a seed from an avocado. Peel off the brown outer covering of the seed. Poke three toothpicks into the avocado seed at equal distances from one another. Place the seeds in a glass of lukewarm water with the largest end submerged. Replace the water once a week. Sprouts will appear in about three weeks. When the stem and roots are several inches long, transplant the avocado into a pot that is about 1 inch wider than the avocado.

4. **Leaf Book**

   Collect leaves from various trees. Mount each leaf on a piece of construction paper or tag-board. Then print the name of the tree the leaf represents. Gather the pages and bind with loose-leaf rings. Place the book in the science area for the children to review.

5. **Shade Versus Sun**

   Place an outdoor thermometer in direct sunlight and another beneath the shade of a tree. Compare results. A chart could also be made for this activity and results could be compared for several days.

6. **Pinecone Bird Feeders**

   Collect pinecones. Attach a piece of yarn or string to the stem. Use a plastic knife to spread peanut butter over the pinecone; then roll in birdseed. Hang the bird feeder outside.

7. **Make Paper**

   Cut a piece of screen 7 inches x 11 inches and frame with wood. Tear construction paper or tissues into one-inch pieces. Place the shredded paper pieces in a blender. Add enough water to cover and blend the paper into pulp. Pour the pulp into a 9-inch x 13-inch tray. Use the framed screen to pan the pulp, moving it to get an even layer of pulp. Lift the screen out of the pan in a straight, upward direction. Place the screen on a stack of newspapers. Roll with a rolling pin to squeeze out water. Lift off the newspaper and gently peel the homemade paper from the screen; allow it to dry on paper towels or newspaper.

Dramatic Play:

1. Construction Site

Design a construction site in the dramatic play area. Provide props such as hard hats, blueprints, floor plans, rulers, tape measures, lumber scraps, wooden blocks, and cardboard boxes.

2. Birds

Trace and cut bird masks and wings out of tagboard for the children to wear. Display pictures of trees and birds. Play a tape of bird songs. A variation would be to decorate a climber with green crepe paper to resemble a tree.

Arts and Crafts:

1. Tree Rubbing

Use crayons or chalk to create rubbings of various tree parts. Place leaves under a single sheet of newsprint. Rub the crayon over the top of the paper until the imprint of the leaf appears. Try making additional rubbings using bark and maple seeds.

2. Twig Painting

Twigs from trees can be used as painting tools. Provide the children with trays of tempera paint of a thick consistency and construction paper to create designs. The children may also enjoy experimenting with the twig as a writing tool.

3. Pine Needle Brushes

Cut branches from a pine needle tree. Place the branches at the easel so that the children can use them as brushes to apply paint.

4. Decorating Pinecones

Collect pinecones of different sizes. Place them on the art table with trays of thick colored tempera paints, glitter, glue, yarn, sequins, and strips of paper for the children to decorate the pinecones.

5. Sawdust Playdough

Combine two cups of sawdust, three cups of flour, and one cup of salt. Add water as needed to make a pliable dough. (Sawdust can be obtained, usually at no cost, from a local lumber company.)

6. Textured Paint

Add sawdust to prepared paints for use at the art table or easel.

7. Paper Product Sculptures

Collect magazines, newspapers, boxes, and paper towel rolls for the children to use to create designs and sculptures. Place all of the items on the art table along with glue, scissors, and paint.

8. Make a Tree

Collect paper towel and toilet paper rolls. The children can paint or cover them with construction paper to resemble tree trunks. Branches and leaves can be fabricated from pipe cleaners and construction paper. The branches and leaves can then be attached to the trunk.

Sensory:

1. Wood Shavings

Obtain wood shavings from a local lumber company. Place them in the sensory table along with scoops and pails.

2. Pinecones

Collect pinecones of various sizes and place them in the sensory table. Small boxes, pails, and scoops can be added.

3. Acorns

Collect acorns and allow them to dry thoroughly before placing in the sensory table. Add accessories to encourage participation such as pails, small paper bags, scoops, and spoons.

Large Muscle:

1. **Wooden Climber**

   If available, set up a wooden climber on the playground or in the classroom for the children to practice their climbing skills.

2. **Wooden Balance Beam**

   If available, set up a wooden balance beam in an open area of the classroom. Suggest ways for the children to cross the beam: walking heel to toe, walking sideways, crawling, and walking holding an object. Older children may be able to walk backwards.

Field Trips/Resource People:

The following sources can be contacted for more information:

- area forest industries such as paper mills and logging companies.
- Department of National Resources.
- university or county extension offices.
- national, state, and local parks.
- nature centers.
- university departments of biology, botany, construction, and forestry.

Math:

1. **Trace Walk**

   Record the number of trees observed on a walk. If appropriate, the trees might also be classified as "broadleaf" or "evergreen" or by the type of tree, such as maple, oak, pine, etc.

2. **Sorting and Counting Activities**

   The following items can be collected and used for various sorting and counting activities:

   acorns
   small pinecones
   walnuts
   pecans
   almonds
   apple seeds
   citrus fruit seeds

3. **Items Made From Trees**

   Collect items from around the classroom for children to sort and classify as those made from trees as "wooden items" and "non-wooden items." Label and provide boxes or similar containers for the children to place the items. If appropriate, the children can count the number of items in each category and record the results.

Social Studies:

1. **Family Tree**

   Cut a tree trunk out of brown tagboard. Cut a treetop out of green tagboard. Attach the trunk and treetop to a bulletin board and display on a wall. Ask the children to bring family photographs that can be displayed on the tree.

Group Time (language, games):

1. **Tree Chart**

   On a large piece of tagboard, print the title, "Things Made from Trees." During group time, present the chart and record the children's responses. Display the completed chart and refer to it throughout the theme.

2. **Movement Activity—"Happy Leaves"**

   Cut leaves out of various colors of construction paper. During group time give each child one leaf. When the children hear the color of their leaf in the following rhyme, they may stand up and move like leaves:

   > Little red leaves are glad today,
   > For the wind is blowing them off and away,
   > They are flying here, they are flying there.
   > Oh, little red leaves, you are everywhere.

   Repeat the rhyme and insert additional color words.

Cooking:

1. Guacamole Dip

1 medium avocado
2 tablespoons of chopped onion
1/4 teaspoon chili powder
1/4 teaspoon garlic salt
2 tablespoons mayonnaise or salad dressing

Peel and cut the avocado into pieces and process at medium speed in a blender. Add remaining ingredients and blend. Serve the dip with tortilla or corn chips.

2. Orange Pecan Cookies

1 cup sugar
3/4 cup softened butter or margarine
1/4 cup milk
1 teaspoon vanilla
1 egg
2 cups flour
1/2 cup finely chopped pecans
2 tablespoons grated orange peel
1 teaspoon baking powder
3/4 teaspoon salt

Combine sugar, butter, milk, vanilla, and egg in a large mixing bowl. Add remaining ingredients and blend well. Drop by rounded teaspoonfuls onto ungreased cookie sheets. Bake for 9–12 minutes or until lightly browned in a 370-degree oven. Remove cookies from sheet and cool.

3. Prepare any recipes that include:

almonds	coconuts	nutmeg
apples	dates	olives
apricots	figs	oranges
avocados	grapefruit	peaches
cashews	lemons	pears
cherries	limes	pecans
cinnamon	mangoes	prunes
cloves	maple syrup	walnuts
	nectarines	

Beware of the potential of children choking on nuts. Avoid using them or grind them finely in recipes for young children.

Books:

The following books can be used to complement this theme:

1. Arnotsky, Jim. (1992). *Crinkleroot's Guide to Knowing the Trees.* New York: Macmillan Children's Book Group.

2. Barker, Cicely M. (1991). *Flower Fairies of the Trees.* New York: Warne, Frederick and Co.

3. Braithwaite, Althea. (1988). *Tree.* Chicago: Dearborn Financial Publishing.

4. Brenner, Barbara, & Garelick, May. (1992). *The Tremendous Tree Book.* Honesdale, PA: Boyds Mill Press.

5. Florian, Douglas. (1990). *Discovering Trees.* New York: Macmillian Children's Book Group.

6. Fowler, Allan. (1990). *It Could Still Be a Tree.* Chicago: Children's Press.

7. Lyon, George-Ella. (1989). *A B Cedar: An Alphabet of Trees.* New York: Orchard Books.

8. National Wildlife Federation Staff. (1991). *Trees are Terrific.* Vienna, VA: National Wildlife Federation.

9. Nelson, JoAnne. (1990). *A Home In a Tree.* New York: McClanahan Books Co.

10. Ryder, Joanne. (1991). *Hello, Tree!* New York: Dutton Children's Books.

11. Thornhill, Jan. (1992). *A Tree In a Forest*. New York: Simon and Schuster Trade.

12. Bunting, Eve. (1993). *Someday a Tree*. New York: Clarion.

13. Ehlert, Lois. (1991). *Red Leaf, Yellow Leaf*. San Diego: Harcourt Brace Jovanovich.

14. Ikeda, Daisaku. (1992). *The Cherry Tree*. New York: Alfred A. Knopf Books for Young Readers.

15. Martin, Bill, Jr., & Archambault, Jan. (1989). *Chicka Chicka Boom Boom*. New York: Simon and Schuster Trade.

16. Sato, Saatoru. (1989). *I Wish I Had a Big, Big Tree*. New York: Lothrop, Lee, & Shepard Books.

17. Behn, Harry. (1992). *Trees*. New York: Henry Holt and Co.

18. Arnold, Caroline. (1990). *A Walk in the Woods*. Eden Praire, MN: Silver Press.

19. Pearce, Q. L., & Pearce, W. L. (1990). *In the Forest*. Eden Praire, MN: Silver Press.

20. Greene, Carol. (1989). *I Can Be a Forest Ranger*. Chicago: Children's Press.

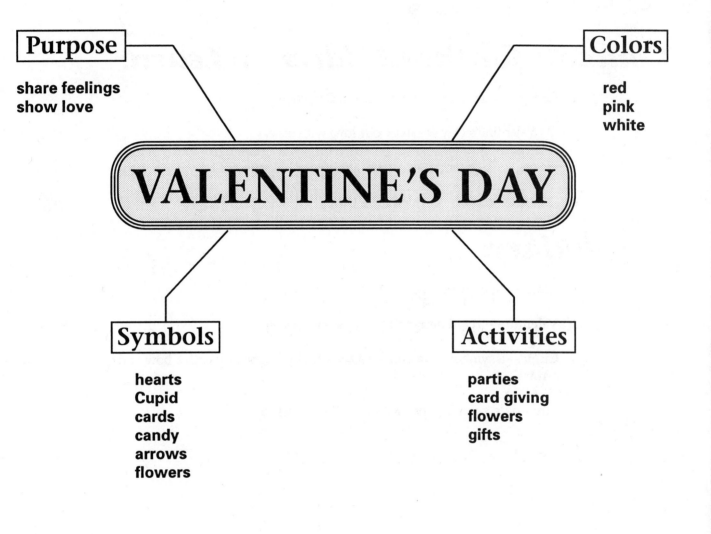

Purpose

share feelings
show love

Colors

red
pink
white

VALENTINE'S DAY

Symbols

hearts
Cupid
cards
candy
arrows
flowers

Activities

parties
card giving
flowers
gifts

Polaroid Education Program

Here's an exciting new way to turn instant photography into an effective teaching tool. Refer to the full-color insert for the activity entitled My Friends and Me.

Theme Goals:

Through participating in the experiences provided by this theme, the children may learn:

1. Valentine's Day colors.

2. Valentine's Day activities.

3. Symbols of Valentine's Day.

4. Purpose of Valentine's Day.

Concepts for the Children to Learn:

1. Red, pink, and white are Valentine's Day colors.

2. On Valentine's Day we share our love with others.

3. Hearts, Cupids, and flowers are symbols of Valentine's Day.

4. People send cards on Valentine's Day.

Vocabulary:

1. **heart**—a symbol of love.

2. **Valentine**—a card designed for someone special.

3. **Cupid**—a symbol of Valentine's Day, usually a baby boy with a bow and arrows.

4. **card**—a decorative paper with a written message.

Bulletin Board

The purpose of this bulletin board is to have the children place the correct number of hearts in the corresponding numbered box. Using boxes as illustrated, a Valentine's Day bulletin board can be made. The bottom of each box should be cut, so it can be taped shut while putting hearts in and easily opened to release the hearts. Mark each box with a numeral and a corresponding number of hearts. The number of numerals will depend upon developmental appropriateness. Attach the boxes to the bulletin board using push pins or staples. Next, construct many small hearts.

Parent Letter

Dear Parents,

Valentine's Day is a special day, so this unit celebrates Valentine's Day. It is a day when we share our good feelings about special people. This day also provides an opportunity to talk about the importance of sharing, giving, loving, and friendship.

At School

Some of the activities related to Valentine's Day will include:

- having a post office in dramatic play to mail valentines to friends.
- constructing valentine mobiles to decorate our room.
- constructing a "What a Friend Is…" chart to hang in our room.
- sending and receiving valentines.

At Home

Try to set aside time to have a heart-to-heart chat with your child. To develop self-esteem talk to your child about feelings and why you are proud of him. Also, help your child make a valentine for a grandparent, aunt, uncle, or other person. A special note could be dictated by your child and written by you.

Have a Happy Valentine's Day!

FIGURE 58 Be my Valentine.

Music:

1. **"My Valentine"**
   (Sing to the tune of "The Muffin Man")

   Oh, do you know my valentine,
   My valentine, my valentine?
   Oh, do you know my valentine?
   His name is _____.

   Chosen valentine then picks another child.

2. **"Ten Little Valentines"**
   (Sing to the tune of "Ten Little Indians")

   One little, two little, three little valentines.
   Four little, five little, six little valentines.
   Seven little, eight little, nine little valentines.
   Ten little valentines here!

3. **"Two Little Cupids"**
   (Sing to the tune of "Two Little Blackbirds")

   Two little cupids sitting on a heart.
       (hold hands behind back)
   One named _____. One named _____.
       (bring out one pointer for each name)
   Fly away, _____. Fly away, _____.
       (place one pointer behind back for each
       name)
   Come back, _____. Come back, _____.
       (bring out pointers one at a time again)
   Two little cupids sitting on a heart.
       (hold up two fingers)
   One named _____. One named _____.
       (wiggle each pointer separately.)

   For each _____ insert a child's name.

Fingerplay:

FIVE LITTLE VALENTINES

   Five little valentines were having a race.
   The first little valentine was frilly with lace.
       (hold up one finger)
   The second little valentine had a funny face.
       (hold up two fingers)
   The third little valentine said, "I love you."
       (hold up three fingers)
   The fourth little valentine said, "I do too."
       (hold up four fingers)
   The fifth little valentine was sly as a fox.
   He ran the fastest to the valentine box.
       (make five fingers run behind back.)

Science:

1. **Valentine's Day Flowers**

   In the science area, place various flowers and
   magnifying glasses. The children can observe
   and explore the various parts of the flowers.

2. **Valentine's Day Colors**

   Mixing red and white tempera paint, the
   children can make various shades of red or
   pink.

Dramatic Play:

1. **Mailboxes**

   Construct an individual mailbox for each child using shoeboxes, empty milk cartons, paper bags, or partitioned boxes. Print each child's name on the box or encourage the child to do so. The children can sort mail, letters, and small packages into the boxes.

2. **Florist**

   Plastic flowers, vases, styrofoam pieces, tissue paper, ribbons, candy boxes, a cash register, and play money can be used to make a flower shop.

3. **Card Shop**

   Stencils, paper, markers, scraps, stickers, etc., can be provided to make a card-making shop.

Arts and Crafts:

1. **Easel Painting**

   Mix red, white, and pink paint and place at the easel.

2. **Chalk Drawings**

   White chalk and red and pink construction paper can be used to make chalk drawings.

3. **Classroom Valentine**

   Cut out one large paper heart. Encourage all children to decorate and sign it. The valentine can be hung in the classroom or be given to a classroom friend. The classroom friend may be the cook, janitor, center director, or principal.

4. **Heart Prints**

   On the art table place white paper and various heart-shaped cookie cutters. Mix pink and red tempera paint and pour into shallow pans. The children can print hearts on white construction paper using the cookie cutters as a tool and then paint them.

5. **Heart Materials**

   The children can cut hearts out of construction paper and decorate them with lace scraps, yarn, and glitter to make original Valentine's Day cards. Pre-cut hearts should be available for children who have not mastered the skill. For other children who have cutting skills, a heart shape can be traced on paper for them to cut.

Sensory:

Soap

   Mix dish soap, water, and red food coloring in the sensory table. Provide egg beaters for children to make bubbles.

Large Muscle:

1. **Hug Tag**

   One child is "it" and tries to tag another child. Once tagged, the child is "frozen" until another child gently hugs him to "unfreeze" him.

2. **Balloon Ball**

   Blow up two or three red, pink, or white balloons. Using nylon paddles made by stretching nylon pantyhose over bent coat hangers, the children can hit the balloons to each other. The object is to try to keep the balloon up off the floor or ground. This activity needs to be carefully supervised. If a balloon breaks, it needs to be immediately removed.

Field Trips:

1. **Visit a Post Office**

   Visit the local post office. Valentine's Day cards made in the classroom can be mailed.

560

2. **Visit a Floral Shop**

Visit a flower store. Observe the different valentine arrangements. Call attention to the beautiful color of the flowers, arrangements, and containers.

Math:

1. **Broken Hearts**

Cut heart shapes out of red and pink tagboard. Print a numeral on one side and a number set of heart stickers or drawings on the other side. Cut the hearts in half as a puzzle. The children can match the puzzle pieces.

2. **Heart Seriation**

Cut various-sized hearts from pink, red, and white construction paper. The children can sequence the heart shapes from small to big or vice versa.

Social Studies:

1. **Sorting Feelings**

Cut pictures of happy and sad people out of magazines. On the outside of two boxes, draw a smiling face on one and a sad face on the other. The children can sort the pictures into the corresponding boxes.

2. **Sign Language**

Show the children how to say, "I love you," in sign language. They can practice with each other. When the parents arrive, the children can share with them.

I	point to self
love	cross arms over chest
you	point outwards

Group Time (games, language):

Valentine March

Place large material hearts with numerals on them on the floor. Include one valentine per child. Play a marching song and encourage children to march from heart to heart. When the music stops, so do the children. Each child then tells the numeral he is standing on. To make the activity developmentally appropriate for young children, use symbols. Examples might include a ball, car, truck, glass, cup, door, etc.

Cooking:

1. **Valentine Cookies**

2/3 cup shortening
1 egg
3/4 cup sugar
1 teaspoon vanilla
1 1/2 cups flour
1 1/2 teaspoons baking powder
4 teaspoons milk
1/4 teaspoon salt

Mix all of the ingredients together. If time permits, refrigerate the dough. Roll out dough. Use heart-shaped cookie cutters. Bake at 375 degrees for 12 minutes. Frost. The children can make two cookies, one for themselves, and one to give to a friend.

2. **Heart-shaped Sandwiches**

1 loaf bread
heart-shaped cookie cutters
strawberry jam or jelly

Give each child 1 or 2 pieces of bread (depending on size of cutter). Cut out 2 heart shapes from bread. Spread on jam or jelly to make a sandwich. Eat at snack time.

MATERIALS TO COLLECT FOR THE ART CENTER

aluminum foil	jars	rug yarn
ball bearings	jugs	safety pins
barrel hoops	lacing	sand
beads	lampshades	sandpaper
belts	leather remnants	seashells
bottles	linoleum	seeds
bracelets	marbles	sheepskin
braiding	masonite	shoelaces
brass	metal foil	shoe polish
buckles	mirrors	snaps
burlap	muslin	soap
buttons	nails	sponges
candles	necklaces	spools
canvas	neckties	stockings
cartons	oilcloth	sweaters
cellophane	ornaments	tacks
chains	pans	tape
chalk	paper bags	thread
chamois	paper boxes	tiles
clay	paper cardboard	tin cans
cloth	paper corrugated	tin foil
colored pictures	paper dishes	tongue depressors
confetti	paper doilies	towels
containers	paper napkins	tubes
copper foil	paper newspaper	twine
cord	paper tissue	wallpaper
cornhusks	paper towels	wax
cornstalks	paper tubes	window shades
costume jewelry	paper wrapping	wire
crayon pieces	phonograph records	wire eyelets
crystals	photographs	wire hairpins
emery cloth	picture frames	wire hooks
eyelets	pinecones	wire mesh
fabrics	pins	wire paper clips
felt	pipe cleaners	wire screen
felt hats	plastic board	wire staples
flannel	plastic paint	wooden beads
floor covering	pocket books	wooden blocks
glass	reeds	wooden clothespins
gourds	ribbon	wooden sticks
hat boxes	rings	wool
hooks	rope	yarn
inner tubes	rubber bands	zippers

Multimedia:

The following resources can be found in educational catalogs:

1. *The Singing Calendar* [record]. Kimbo Records.

2. Palmer, Hap. *Holiday Songs and Rhythms* [record].

Books:

The following books can be used to complement the theme:

1. Modell, Frank. (1987). *One Zillion Valentines*. New York: William Morrow and Company, Inc.

2. St. Pierre, Stephanie. (1990). *Valentine Kittens*. New York: Scholastic, Inc.

3. Watson, Wendy. (1991). *A Valentine for You*. Boston: Houghton Mifflin Co.

4. Blos, Joan W. (1990). *One Very Best Valentine's Day*. New York: Simon and Schuster Trade.

5. Ehrlich, Fred. (1992). *A Valentine for Ms. Vanilla*. New York: Viking Children's Books.

6. Nerlove, Miriam. (1992). *Valentine's Day*. Morton Grove, IL: Albert Whitman and Co.

7. Schweninger, Ann. (1990). *Valentine Friends*. New York: Puffin Books.

8. Stock, Catherine. (1991). *Secret Valentine*. New York: Macmillan Children's Books Group.

9. Bond, Felicia. (1990). *Four Valentines in a Rainstorm*. New York: Harper Collins.

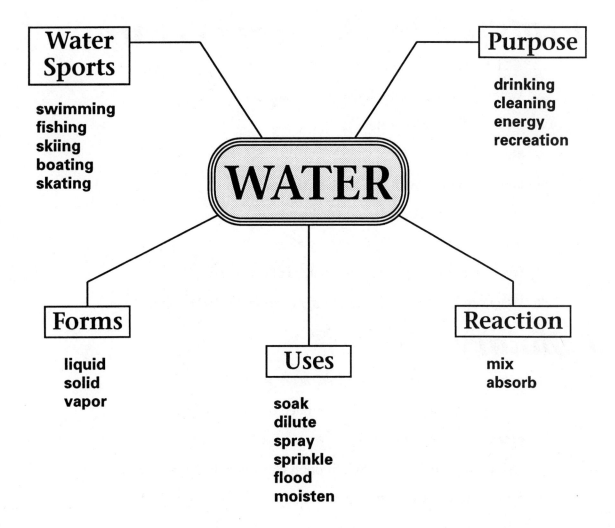

Water Sports

swimming
fishing
skiing
boating
skating

Purpose

drinking
cleaning
energy
recreation

WATER

Forms

liquid
solid
vapor

Uses

soak
dilute
spray
sprinkle
flood
moisten

Reaction

mix
absorb

Here's an exciting new way to turn instant photography into an effective teaching tool. Refer to the full-color insert for the activity entitled Spatial Relations.

Theme Goals:

Through participating in the experiences provided by this theme, the children may learn:

1. Uses of water.
2. Forms of water.
3. Water sports.
4. Purposes of water.

Concepts for the Children to Learn:

1. All living things need water.
2. Water takes three forms: liquid, vapor, and solid.
3. Ice is a solid form of water.
4. Steam is a vapor form of water.
5. Some things mix with water, others do not.
6. Some things absorb water, others do not.
7. Some things float when placed on water.
8. Some animals and plants live in bodies of water.
9. Water can be used to soak, dilute, spray, sprinkle, flood, and moisten.

Vocabulary:

1. **water**—a clear, colorless, odorless, tasteless liquid.
2. **lake**—a large body of water surrounded by land.
3. **ocean**—body of salt water.
4. **swimming**—moving yourself through water with body movements.
5. **cloud**—water droplets formed in the sky.
6. **rain**—water that falls from clouds.
7. **snow**—water that freezes and falls from the sky.
8. **liquid**—substance that can be poured.
9. **freeze**—hardened liquid.
10. **melt**—to change from a solid to a liquid.
11. **ice**—water that has frozen.
12. **sink**—to drop to the bottom of a liquid.
13. **float**—to rest on top of a liquid.

Bulletin Board

The purpose of this bulletin board is to develop visual discrimination and matching skills. Construct and color four or five pictures of swimming and water-related items from tagboard. Laminate. Trace these pictures on black construction paper to make shadows. Staple the shadows on the bulletin board. Encourage the children to hang the colored picture over the correct shadow.

Parent Letter

Dear Parents,

Did you know all living things have something in common? All living things need water to survive. Water will be the subject that we will explore with our next unit. The children will become familiar with the forms, uses, and bodies of water, as well as sports that require water to be played.

At School

Some of the learning experiences planned to include water concepts are:

* placing celery stalks in colored water to observe plants' use of water.
* experimenting with objects that sink or float when placed in water.
* washing doll clothes in the sensory table.
* observing ice with magnifying glasses and watching it change from a solid to a liquid.

At Home

There are many ways that you can reinforce water concepts at home. Try any of the following with your child.

* Allow your child to assist in washing dishes after a meal. This will give your child a sense of responsibility and will develop self-esteem.
* Provide water and large paintbrushes for your child to paint sidewalks and fences outdoors.
* Bubbles made with an eggbeater in a container of soapy water are fun for children of all ages!

Enjoy your child!

FIGURE 59 A water table can be used for science activities.

Music:

"Raindrops"
    (Sing to the tune of "London Bridges")

    Raindrops falling from the sky,
    From the sky, from the sky.
    Raindrops falling from the sky
    On my umbrella.

Fingerplays:

FIVE LITTLE DUCKS

    Five little ducks
        (hold up five fingers)
    Swimming in the lake.
        (make swimming motions)
    The first duck said,
        (hold up one finger)
    "Watch the waves I make."
        (make waves motions)
    The second duck said,
        (hold up two fingers)
    "Swimming is such fun."
        (smile)
    The third duck said,
        (hold up three fingers)

    "I'd rather sit in the sun."
        (turn face to sun)
    The fourth duck said,
        (hold up four fingers)
    "Let's swim away."
        (swimming motions)
    The fifth duck said,
        (hold up five fingers)
    "Oh, let's stay."
    Then along came a motorboat.
    With a Pop! Pop! Pop!
        (clap three times)
    And five little ducks
    Swam away from the spot.
        (put five fingers behind back)

SWIMMING

    I can dive.
        (make diving motion with hands)
    I can swim.
        (swimming motion)
    I can float.
        (hands outstretched with head back)
    I can fetch.
    But dog paddle
        (paddle like dog)
    Is the stroke I do best.

FIVE LITTLE FISHES

    Five little fishes swimming in a pond.
        (wiggle five fingers)

The first one said, "I'm tired," as he yawned.
(yawn)
The second one said, "Well, let's take a nap."
(put hands together on side of face)
The third one said, "Put on your sleeping cap."
(pretend to pull on hat)
The fourth one said, "Wake up! Don't sleep."
(shake finger)
The fifth one said, "Let's swim where it's deep."
(point down and say with a low voice)
So, the five little fishes swam away.
(wiggle fingers and put behind back)
But they came back the very next day.
(wiggle fingers out front again)

THE RAIN

I sit before the window now
(sit down)
And look out at the rain.
(shade eyes and look around)
It means no play outside today,
(shake head)
So inside I remain.
(rest chin on fist; look sad)

I watch the water dribble down
(look up and down)
As it turns the brown grass green.
And after a while I start to smile
At nature's washing machine.
(smile and lean back)

Science:

1. **Painting Sidewalks**

   On a sunny day, allow children to paint sidewalks with water. To do this, provide various paintbrushes and buckets of water. Call attention to the water evaporation.

2. **Measuring Rainfall**

   During spring, place a bucket outside with a plastic ruler set vertically by securing to the bottom. Check the height of the water after each rainfall. With older children, make a chart to record rainfalls.

3. **Testing Volume**

   Containers that hold the same amounts of liquid are needed. Try to include containers that are tall, skinny, short, and flat. Ask the children, "Do they hold the same amount?" Encourage them to experiment by pouring liquids from one container to another.

4. **Freezing Water**

   Freeze a container of water. Periodically, observe the changes. In colder climates, the water can be frozen outdoors. The addition of food coloring may add interest.

5. **Musical Scale**

   Make unique musical tone jars by pouring various levels of water into glass soda bottles. Color each bottle of water differently. Provide the children with spoons, encouraging them to experiment with sounds by tapping each bottle.

6. **Plants Use Water**

   Place celery stalks in colored water. Observe how water is absorbed in its veins.

7. **Chase the Pepper**

   Collect the following materials: water, pepper, shallow pan, piece of soap, sugar. Fill the pan with water and shake the pepper on the water. Then take a piece of wet soap and dip it into the water. What happens? (The pepper moves away from the soapy water to the clear water.) The skin on water pulls and on soapy water the pull is weak. On clear water it is strong and pulls the pepper along. Now take some sugar and shake it into the soapy water. What happens? Sugar gives the skin a stronger pull.

8. **Warm Water/Cold Water**

   Collect the following materials: a small aquarium, a small bottle, food coloring, water. First fill the aquarium with very warm water. Fill the small bottle with colored cold water. Put your thumb on the mouth of the bottle. Hold the bottle sideways and lower it into the warm water. Take away your thumb. What happens? (The cold water will sink to the bottom of the tank. The cold water is heavier than the warm water.) Now fill the tank with cold water and fill the small bottle with colored warm water. What do you predict will happen when you repeat the procedure?

9. **Wave Machine**

Collect the following materials: mineral oil, water, food coloring, transparent jar. Fill the jar 1/2 to 2/3 full with water. Add a few drops of food coloring. Then add mineral oil to completely fill the jar. Secure the lid on the jar. Tilt the jar slowly from side to side to make waves. Notice that the oil and water have separate layers and do not stay mixed after the jar is shaken.

10. **Water and Vinegar Fun**

Collect the following materials: two small jars with lids, water, and white vinegar. Pour water into one jar and an equal amount of vinegar into the other jar. Replace caps. Then let the children explore the jars of liquids and discuss the similarities. Then let the children smell each jar.

Dramatic Play:

1. **Fire Fighter**

Place hoses, hats, coats, and boots in the dramatic play area.

2. **Doll Baths**

Fill the dramatic play sink with water. Children can wash dishes or give dolls baths.

3. **The Beach**

Provide towels, sunglasses, umbrellas, pails, shovels, and beach toys for the children to use indoors or outdoors.

4. **Canoeing**

Bring a canoe into the classroom or onto the play yard. Provide paddles and life vests for the children to wear.

Arts and Crafts:

1. **Liquid Painting**

Paper, straws, thin tempera, and spoons can be placed on the art table. Spoon a small amount of paint onto paper. Using a straw, blow paint on the paper to make a design.

2. **Bubble Prints**

Collect the following materials: 1/2 cup water, 1/2 cup liquid soap, food coloring, straws, and light-colored construction paper. Mix together the water, soap, and food coloring in a container. Place a straw in the solution and blow until the bubbles reach about one to two inches over the top of the container. Remove the straw and place a piece of paper over the jar. The bubbles will pop as they touch the paper, leaving a print.

3. **Wet Chalk Drawings**

Chalk, paper, and water in a shallow pan are needed for this activity. The children can dip chalk into water and then draw on paper. Encourage children to note the difference between wet and dry chalk.

Sensory:

1. **Colored Ice**

Fill the sensory table with colored ice cubes for the children to explore.

2. **Sink and Float**

Fill sensory table with water. Provide the children with a variety of items that will sink and float. Let them experiment. A chart may be prepared listing items that sink and float.

3. **Boating**

Fill the water table. Let the children add blue food coloring. Provide a variety of boats for them to play with.

4. Moving Water

Provide the children with a variety of materials that move water. Include the following:

- sponges
- basters
- eye droppers
- squeeze bottles
- funnels
- measuring cups
- pitchers
- empty film canisters
- plastic tubing

Large Muscle:

Catch Me

Children form a circle with one child in the middle. While walking in a circle they chant:

_____ over the water.
_____ over the sea.
_____ caught a tunafish.
But he can't catch me!

(Insert child's name.)

On "me," all the children stoop quickly. If the child in the middle touches another child, the fish, before he stoops, that child is it. Likewise, he now goes into the middle. This game is for older children.

Math:

Measuring

Assorted measuring cups in a variety of sizes can be added to the sensory table or sandbox.

Group Time (games, language):

Water Fun

Discuss the various recreational uses of water. Included may be swimming, boating, ice fishing, ice skating, fishing, and canoeing. Encourage the children to name their favorite water activities. Prepare a chart using each child's name and favorite water activity along with a small picture of that activity. Display in the room.

Cooking:

1. Fruit Ice

Mix 1/2 can partially thawed juice concentrate with 2 cups of crushed ice in the blender. Liquify until the contents become snowy. Serve immediately.

2. Floating Cake—Philippines

2 cups sweet rice flour
1 cup water
1/2 to 3/4 cup sugar
1/2 cup toasted sesame seeds, hulled
1 cup grated coconut

Mix rice flour and water. Form into 10 to 20 small balls. Flatten each ball into a round or elongated shape and drop into 8 to 10 cups boiling water. As each cake floats to the surface, remove from water with a slotted spoon. Roll in grated coconut and coat with sugar and sesame seeds. Adult supervision is required. Makes 4 servings.

Sensory experiences are especially appealing to young children. They delight in feeling, listening, smelling, tasting, and seeing. They also love to manipulate objects by pulling, placing, pouring, tipping, shoving, as well as dipping. As they interact, they learn new concepts and solutions to old problems. When accompanied by other children, these experiences lead to cooperative, social interactions. As a result, the child's egocentricity is reduced, allowing him to become less self-centered.

Containers

Begin planning sensory experiences by choosing an appropriate container. Remember that it should be large enough so that several children may participate at any given time. If you select a dishpan, due to its size, you may want to use several. Other containers that may be used include a commercially made sensory/water table, baby bathtub, wash tub, pail, wading pool, sink, or bath tub.

Things to Add to Water

A variety of substances can be added to water to make it more inviting. Food coloring is one example. Start by individually choosing and adding one primary color. Later soaps can be added. These may be in liquid or flake form. Baking soda, cornstarch, and salt will affect the feel of the water. Baby and vegetable oil may leave a residue on the child's hand. Extracts add another dimension. Lemon, almond, pine oil, peppermint, anise, and orange all permit a variety for the child. On the other hand, ice cubes allow the child to experience an extreme touch.

Tools and Utensils

A wide variety of household tools can be used in the water play table. Measuring cups, small pitchers, small pots and pans, and film canisters can all be used for pouring. Scoops, spoons, turkey basters, small squeeze bottles, and funnels can be used for transferring the liquid from one container to another. Pipes, rubber hoses, sponges, wire whips, and eggbeaters all can be used for observing water in motion. Plastic toys, corks, spools, strainers, boots, etc., also encourage exploration.

Other Sensory Experiences

There are wide varieties of other materials that can be used in the sensory table. Natural materials such as sand, gravel, rocks, grain, mud, wood chips, clay, corn, and birdseed can be used. Children also enjoy having minnows and worms in the table. They delight in visually tracking the minnow and worm movement. As they attempt to pick them up, eye-hand coordination skills are practiced. Styrofoam pieces and shavings are attractive materials that can lend variety.

A strange mixture called goop is a fun material to play with. To prepare goop empty 1 box of cornstarch into a dishpan or similar container. Sprinkle a few drops of food coloring on the cornstarch. Add small amounts of water (about 1/2 cup) at a time and mix with a spoon or with fingers. (This is a unique sensory experience!) The mixture feels hard when you touch it on the surface, yet melts in your hands when you pick some up! (This will keep for up to one week if kept covered when not in use. You will probably need to add water the next time you use it.)

Silly putty is just as easy to prepare as goop. This mixture is prepared by combining 1 part of liquid starch, 2 parts of white glue, and dry tempera paint for color. Begin by measuring the liquid starch first, as it will prevent the glue from sticking to the measuring cup. Mix with a spoon, adding single tablespoons of liquid starch to get the right consistency. Then knead with hands. Store in an airtight container (such as a zip-lock bag) in the refrigerator. You will be thrilled to find that it will keep for several weeks.

Enjoy yourself with the children, but always change the sensory experiences on a daily basis. In doing so, you stimulate the child's curiosity as well as provide a meaningful curriculum.

For health purposes, children should be encouraged to wash their hands after sensory play.

Multimedia:

The following resources can be found in educational catalogs:

Jenkins, Ella. *Rhythms of Childhood with Ella Jenkins* [record]. Folkway Records.

Books:

The following books can be used to complement the theme:

1. Raffi. (1987). *Down by the Bay*. New York: Crown Publishers, Inc..

2. Blocksma, Mary. (1987). *Rub-a-Dub-Dub-What's in the Tub?* Chicago: Children's Press.

3. Crespo, George. (1993). *How the Sea Began*. New York: Clarion Books.

4. Arnosky, Jim. (1990). *Deer at the Brook*. New York: Morrow.

5. Brown, Marc. (1991). *All Wet*. Boston: Little, Brown.

6. Day, Alexandra. (1992). *River Parade*. New York: Puffin.

7. Gantschev, Ivan. (1991). *The Moon Lake*. Saxonville, MA: Picture Book Studios.

8. Hoban, Julia. (1993). *Amy Loves the Rain*. New York: Harper Collins.

9. Jones, Rebecca C. (1991). *Down at the Bottom of the Deep Dark Sea*. New York: Macmillan.

10. McDowell, Josh, & McDowell, Dottie. (1988). *Katie's Adventure at Blueberry Pond*. Elgin, IL: David Cook.

11. Koch, Michelle. (1993). *World Water Watch*. New York: Greenwillow.

12. Cristini, Ermanno, & Puricelli, Luigi. (1991). *In the Pond*. Saxonville, VA: Picture Book Studio, Ltd.

13. Fowler, Allan. (1992). *It Could Still Be Water*. Chicago: Children's Press.

14. Peters, Lisa. (1991). *Water's Way*. New York: Arcade Publishing, Inc.

15. Russell, Naomi. (1991). *The Stream*. New York: Dutton Children's Books.

——— T H E M E 60 ———

Functions

movement
transportation

Sizes

small
medium
large

Materials

rubber
plastic
wood
metal

WHEELS

Uses

bicycles	wheelbarrows
motorcycles	carts
trikes	chairs
scooters	trailers
cars/trucks	rollerskates/rollerblades
buses	pulleys
planes	gears
unicycles	trains
wagons	wheelchairs

Polaroid Education Program

Here's an exciting new way to turn instant photography into an effective teaching tool. Refer to the full-color insert for the activity entitled Presto-Chango-Photo.

Theme Goals:

Through participating in the experiences provided by this theme, the children may learn:

1. Sizes of wheels.

2. Purposes of wheels.

3. Materials used to make wheels.

4. Movement of wheels.

Concepts for the Children to Learn:

1. Wheels are round.

2. Wheels can help us to do our work.

3. Wheels help move people and things.

4. Cars, buses, motorcycles, and bicycles have wheels.

5. Wheels can be different sizes.

6. A unicycle is a one-wheeled cycle.

7. Wheels can be made of rubber, plastic, metal, or wood.

8. Wheels can be connected by an axle.

Vocabulary:

1. **wheel**—a form in the shape of a circle.

2. **unicycle**—a vehicle with one wheel.

3. **wheelbarrow**—a vehicle used for moving small loads.

4. **wheelchair**—a chair on wheels.

5. **bicycle**—a two-wheeled vehicle.

6. **pulley**—a wheel that can be connected to a rope to move things.

Bulletin Board

The purpose of this bulletin board is to encourage the development of mathematical concepts. To prepare the bulletin board, draw pictures of a unicycle, bicycle, and tricycle on tagboard. Color, cut out, and post on the bulletin board. Next, construct the numerals 1, 2, and 3 out of tagboard. Hang the numerals on the top of the bulletin board. A corresponding set of dots can be placed below the numeral to assist children in counting. A string can be attached to each numeral by using a stapler. Have the children wind the string around a push pin connected to the vehicle with the corresponding number of wheels.

Parent Letter

Dear Parents,

Wheels! Wheelchairs, wheelbarrows, tricycle wheels, bicycle wheels, and car wheels! Children see wheels almost every day of their lives. We will be studying wheels. Through participating in the activities planned for this unit, the children will discover that wheels can be made from many different materials and that there are many different uses and sizes of wheels.

At School

We have many learning experiences planned for this unit, which include:

* examining tire rubber at the science table.
* painting with toy cars at the art table.
* singing a song called, "The Wheels on the Bus."

At Home

There are many ways that you can incorporate this unit in your own home. Try any of these activities with your child.

* Walk around the neighborhood with your child. To develop observation skills look for different wheels.
* Count the wheels on the different types of transportation. Semi-trucks have several, while a unicycle has only one.
* Recite the following fingerplay with your child to foster language and memory skills. We will be learning it this week.

Wheels

Wheels big.
   (form big circles with fingers)
Wheels small.
   (form little circles with fingers)
Count them one by one.
Turning as they're pedaled
   (make pedaling motion with hands)
In the springtime sun!
1-2-3-4-5
   (count fingers)

Enjoy your child!

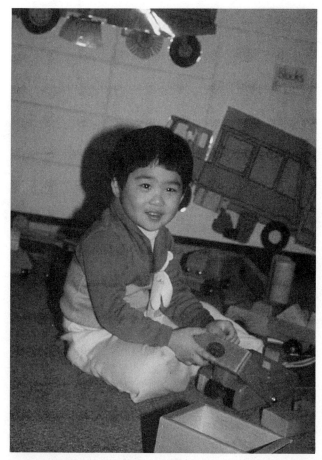

FIGURE 60 Cars and trucks need wheels to get around.

Music:

"The Wheels on the Bus"

The wheels on the bus go round and round,
Round and round, round and round.
The wheels on the bus go round and round
All through the town.

Other verses:
The wipers on the bus go swish, swish, swish.
The doors on the bus go open and shut.
The horn on the bus goes beep, beep, beep.
The driver on the bus says, "Move on back."
The people on the bus go up and down.

Fingerplays:

MY BICYCLE

One wheel, two wheels on the ground.
   (revolve hand in forward circle to form each wheel)

My feet make the pedals go round and round.
   (move feet in pedaling motion)
Handlebars help me steer so straight
   (pretend to steer bicycle)
Down the sidewalk, through the gate.

WHEELS

Wheels big.
   (form big circles with fingers)
Wheels small.
   (form little circles with fingers)
Count them one by one
Turning as they're pedaled
   (make pedaling motion with hands)
In the springtime sun.
1-2-3-4-5
   (count fingers)

Science:

1. **Tire Rubber**

   Cut off several pieces of rubber from old tires. Provide magnifying glasses. Encourage the children to observe similarities and differences.

2. **Pulley**

   Set up a pulley. Provide the children with blocks so they may lift a heavy load with the help of a wheel. Supervision may be necessary for this activity.

3. **Gears**

   Collect gears and place on the science table. The children can experiment, observing how the gears move. When appropriate, discuss their similar and different characteristics.

4. **Wheels and Axles**

   Set out a few wheels and axles. Discuss how they work as a lever to help lift heavy loads. Encourage the children to think about where they might find wheels and axles.

Dramatic Play:

1. **Car Mechanic**

   Outdoors, place various wheels, tires, tools, overalls, and broken trikes. The children can experiment using tools.

2. Floats

Paper, tape, crepe paper, and balloons can be provided to decorate the wheels on the tricycles, wagons, and scooters.

Arts and Crafts:

1. Circle Templates

Cut out various-sized circle templates from tagboard. Provide paper, pencils, and crayons for the children to trace the circles.

2. Car Painting

Provide small plastic cars, tempera paint, and paper. Place the tempera paint in a shallow pan. Car tracks can be created by dipping the car wheels in the tempera paint and rolling them across paper.

3. Wheel Collage

Provide magazines for the children to cut out pictures of wheels. The pictures can be pasted or glued onto sheets of paper.

4. Tracing Wheels

Provide sewing tracing wheels, pizza cutters, pastry wheels, carbon paper, and construction paper. The children can place the carbon paper on the construction paper and run one of the wheels over the carbon paper, making a design on the construction paper.

Sensory:

Sensory Table

Add the following items to the sensory table:

- sand with wheel molds
- rubber from tires
- gravel and small toy cars and trucks

Large Muscle:

1. Wheelbarrow

Place wheelbarrows in the play yard. Provide materials of varying weights for the children to move.

2. Wagons

Place wagons in the playground. Provide objects for the children to move.

Field Trips/Resource People:

1. Cycle Shop

Visit a cycle shop. Observe the different sizes of wheels that are in the shop. Talk about the different materials that wheels can be made of.

2. Machine Shop

Visit a machine parts shop. Look at the different gears, pulleys, and wheels. Discuss their sizes, shapes, and possible uses.

3. Resource People

- cycle specialist
- mechanic
- machinist
- person who uses a wheelchair

Math:

1. Wheel Sequence

Cut out various-sized circles from tagboard to represent wheels. The children can sequence the wheels from largest to smallest.

2. How Many Wheels?

Pictures of a unicycle, bicycle, tricycle, cars, scooters, and trucks of all sizes can be cut from magazines and catalogs. Mount the pictures on tagboard. Laminate. Sort the pictures according to the number of wheels.

Social Studies:

Wheelchair

Borrow wheelchair (child-sized if possible) from a local hospital or pharmacy. During group time discuss how wheelchairs help some people to move. Children can experience moving and pushing a wheelchair.

Group Time (games, language):

Who Took the Wheel?

(Variation of "Who Took the Cookie from the Cookie Jar")

Who took the wheel off the car today?
_____ took the wheel off the car today.
(fill _____ with a child's name)
Chosen child says, "Who me?"
Class responds, "Yes, you!"

Chosen child says, "Couldn't be!"
Class responds, "Well then, who?"

The chant continues as the chosen child picks another child. Continue repeating the chant using the children's names.

Cooking:

1. **Cheese Wheels**

   Cut cheese slices using a cookie cutter into circle shapes to represent wheels. Top the pieces with raisins or serve with crackers.

2. **Pizza Rounds**

   Provide each child with a half an English muffin. Demonstrate how to spread pizza sauce on a muffin. Then lay a few skinny strips of cheese across the top, making the cheese look like wheel spokes. Now let the children prepare their own. Bake in an oven at 350 degrees for 5 to 7 minutes or until the cheese melts. Cool slightly before serving.

Multimedia:

The following resources can be found in educational catalogs:

1. Raffi. "The Wheels on the Bus," *Rise and Shine* [record].

2. Penner, Fred. "Marvelous Toy," *Special Delivery* [record].

3. *The Bear's Bicycle* [video]. Live Oak Media.

Books:

The following books can be used to complement the theme:

1. Kovalski, Maryann. (1987). *The Wheels on the Bus: An Adaptation of the Traditional Song*. Boston: Little, Brown.

2. Crews, Donald. (1991). *Truck*. New York: Morrow.

3. Scioscia, Mary. (1993). *Bicycle Rider*. New York: Harper Collins.

4. Wolcott, Patty. (1991). *Double-Decker Double-Decker Double-Decker Bus*. New York: Random House.

5. Ziefert, Harriet. (1992). *Where's Daddy's Car?* New York: Harper Collins.

6. Ziefert, Harriet. (1992). *Where's Mommy's Truck?* New York: Harper Collins.

7. Pienkowski, Jan. (1992). *Wheels*. New York: Simon and Schuster Trade.

8. Stone, Venice. (1991). *Wheels*. New York: Scholastic Inc.

9. Strickland, Paul, & Flint, Russ. (1990). *Wheels at Work and Play* (6 vols). Milwaukee, WI: Gareth Stevens, Inc.

10. Dodds, Dayle A. (1989). *Wheel Away!* New York: Harper Collins Children's Books.

11. Hughes, Shirley. (1991). *Wheels*. New York: Lothrop, Lee, & Shepard Books.

12. Raffi. (1990). *Wheels on the Bus*. New York: David McKay Co.

13. Zelinsky, Paul O. (1990). *Wheels on the Bus: With Pictures That Move*. New York: Dutton Children's Books.

14. Rosen, Suri. (1992). *Wheels to Go: On the Go*. Los Angeles: Price Stern Sloan, Inc.

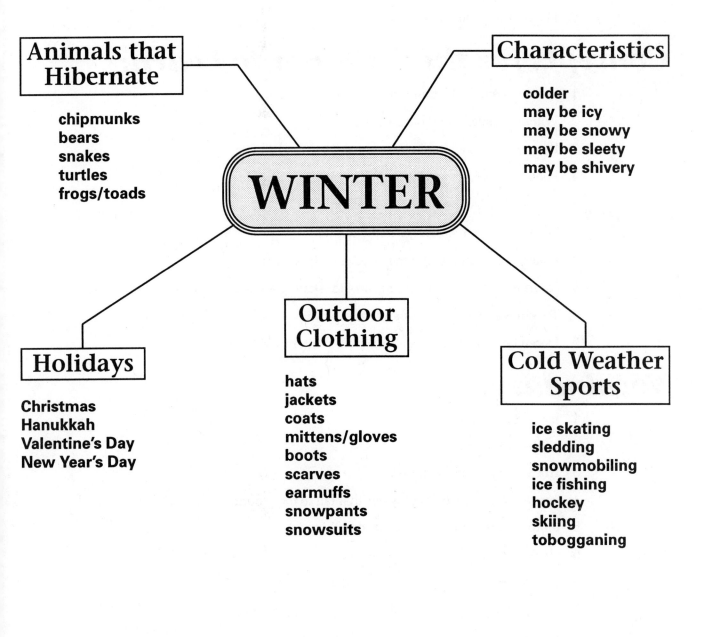

Animals that Hibernate

chipmunks
bears
snakes
turtles
frogs/toads

Characteristics

colder
may be icy
may be snowy
may be sleety
may be shivery

WINTER

Holidays

Christmas
Hanukkah
Valentine's Day
New Year's Day

Outdoor Clothing

hats
jackets
coats
mittens/gloves
boots
scarves
earmuffs
snowpants
snowsuits

Cold Weather Sports

ice skating
sledding
snowmobiling
ice fishing
hockey
skiing
tobogganing

Polaroid
Education
Program

Here's an exciting new way to turn instant photography into an effective teaching tool. Refer to the full-color insert for the activity entitled *Photo Lotto*.

Theme Goals:

Through participating in the experiences provided by this theme, the children may learn:

1. Winter holidays.
2. Characteristics of winter weather.
3. Winter sports.
4. Winter clothing.
5. Hibernating animals.

Concepts for the Children to Learn:

1. Winter is one of the four seasons.
2. Winter is usually the coldest season.
3. It snows in the winter in some areas.
4. People wear warmer clothes in the winter.
5. Some animals hibernate in the winter.
6. Trees may lose their leaves in the winter.
7. Lakes, ponds, and water may freeze in the winter.
8. Sledding, skiing, toboganning, and ice skating are winter sports in colder areas.
9. To remove snow, people shovel and plow.
10. December, January, and February are winter months.

Vocabulary:

1. **ice**—frozen water.
2. **cold**—not warm.
3. **frost**—very small ice pieces.
4. **snow**—frozen particles of water that fall to the ground.
5. **temperature**—how hot or cold something is.
6. **sleet**—mixture of rain and snow.
7. **hibernate**—to sleep during the winter.
8. **snowperson**—snow shaped in the form of a person.
9. **ski**—a runner that moves over snow and ice.
10. **icicle**—a hanging piece of frozen ice.
11. **sled**—transportation for moving over snow and ice.
12. **boots**—clothing worn on feet to keep them dry and warm.
13. **shiver**—to shake from cold or fear.

Bulletin Board

The purpose of this bulletin board is to provide the children with an opportunity to match patterns. Construct several pairs of mittens out of tagboard, each with a different pattern, as illustrated. Laminate them. On the bulletin board, string one of each pair of the mittens through a rope or clothesline (one or two rows). Tie enough clothespins in place by putting the line through the wire spring of the clip clothespins to put up the matching mittens. (Tie the clothespins beside the first mitten.) Children can match the mittens by hanging the second next to the first with a clothespin. This is a good matching exercise for twos, who sometimes need help with the clothespins. It is mainly a small motor exercise for older children, unless you make the mittens fairly similar so that finding the correct pairs is a more difficult task.

Parent Letter

Dear Parents,

We are beginning a unit on winter. The children will be learning about the coldest season by taking a look at winter clothing, changes that occur during this season indoors and outdoors, and winter sports. Throughout the unit, the children will develop an awareness of winter activities.

At School

Some of our learning experiences related to winter include:

- creating cottonball snowpeople.
- sorting mittens by size, shape, and color.
- enjoying stories about winter.
- setting up an ice-skating rink in the dramatic play area.
- experiencing snow and ice in the sensory table.

At Home [Delete this paragraph if snow is unavailable.]

To experience winter at home, try this activity—snow in the bathtub! Bring in some snow from outside and place in your bathtub. Also place some measuring cups, spoons, and scoops in the bathtub and let your child use mittens to play in the snow. In addition, a spray bottle filled with colored water (made with food coloring) will allow your child to make colorful sculptures. This is sure to keep your children busy and will develop an awareness of the senses.

From all of us!

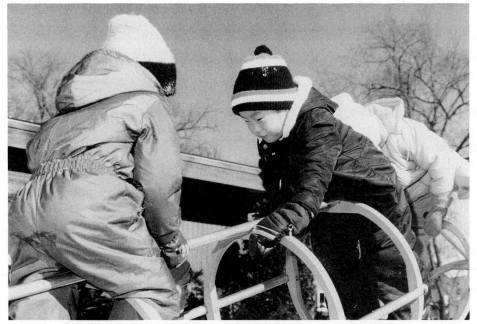

FIGURE 61 Some children live in areas where there is no snow in the winter.

Music:

1. **"Snowperson"**
(Sing to the tune of "Twinkle, Twinkle, Little Star")

Snowperson, snowperson, where did you go?
I built you yesterday out of snow.
I built you high and I built you fat.
I put on eyes and a nose and a hat.
Now you're gone all melted away
But it's sunny outside so I'll go and play.

2. **"Winter Clothes"**
(Sing to the tune of "Did you Ever See a Lassie?")

Children put your coats on, your coats on, your coats on.
Children put your coats on, one, two, and three.

(hats, boots, mittens, etc.)

3. **"Mitten Song"**

Thumbs in the thumb place, fingers all together.
This is the song we sing in mitten weather.

Fingerplays:

FIVE LITTLE SNOWPEOPLE

Five little snowpeople standing in the door.
This one melted and then there were four.
    (hold up all five fingers, put down thumb)
Four little snowpeople underneath a tree.
This one melted and then there were three.
    (put down pointer finger)
Three little snowpeople with hats and mittens too.
This one melted and then there were two.
    (put down middle finger)
Two little snowpeople outside in the sun.
This one melted and then there was one.
    (put down ring finger)
One little snowperson trying hard to run.
He melted too, and then there were none.
    (put down pinky)

Variations:
- Make five little snowpeople finger puppets and remove them one by one.
- Make five stick puppets for children to hold and sit down one by one at appropriate times during fingerplay.

587

MAKING A SNOWPERSON

Roll it, roll it, get a pile of snow.
  (make rolling motions with hands)
Rolling, rolling, rolling, rolling, rolling here we go.
Pat it, pat it, face it to the south.
  (patting motion)
Now my little snowperson's done, eyes and nose and mouth.
  (point to eyes, nose and mouth)

ZIPPERS

Three little zippers on my snowsuit,
  (hold up three fingers)
Fasten up as snug as snug can be
It's a very easy thing as you can see
Just zip, zip, zip!
  (do three zipping motions)
I work the zippers on my snowsuit.
Zippers really do save time for me
I can fasten them myself with one, two, three.
Just zip, zip, zip!
  (do three zipping motions)

THE SNOWPERSON AND THE BUNNY

A chubby little snowperson
  (make a fist)
Had a carrot nose.
  (poke thumb out)
Along came a bunny
And what do you suppose?
  (other hand, make rabbit ears)
That hungry little bunny
Looking for his lunch
  (bunny hops around)
Ate that snowperson's carrot nose.
  (bunny nibbles at thumb)
Crunch, crunch, crunch.

BUILD A SNOWPERSON

First you make a snowball,
  (rolling motion)
Big and fat and round.
  (extend arms in large circle)
Then you roll the snowball,
  (rolling motion)
All along the ground.
Then you build the snowperson

One-two-three!
  (place three pretend balls on top of each other)
Then you have a snowperson,
Don't you see?
  (point to eyes)
Then the sun shines all around and
Melts the snowperson to the ground.
  (drop to the ground in a melting motion)

Science:

1. **Weather Doll**

   Make a felt weather doll. Encourage the children to dress and undress the doll according to the weather.

2. **Make Frost**

   Changes in temperature cause dew. When dew freezes it is called frost. Materials needed are a tin can with no lid, rock salt, and crushed ice. Measure and pour 2 cups of crushed ice and 1/2 cup rock salt in a can. Stir rapidly. Let the mixture sit for 30 minutes. After 30 minutes, the outside of the can will have dew on it. Wait longer and the dew will change to frost. To hasten the process, place in a freezer.

3. **Make Birdfeeders**

   Roll pinecones in peanut butter and then birdseed. Attach a string to the pinecones and hang them outside. Encourage the children to check the birdfeeders frequently.

   A birdfeeder can also be prepared from suet. To do this, wrap suet in a netting. Gather the edges up and tie together with a long string. Another method is to place suet in a net citrus fruit bag.

4. **Snow**

   Bring a large container of snow into the classroom. After it is melted, add colored water and place the container outdoors. When frozen, bring a colored block of ice back into classroom and observe it melt.

5. Examine Snowflakes

Examine snowflakes with a magnifying glass. Each is unique. For classrooms located in warmer climates, make a snow-like substance by crushing ice.

6. Catching Snowflakes

Cover a piece of cardboard with dark felt. Place the cardboard piece in the freezer. Go outside and let snowflakes land on the board. Snowflakes will last longer for examination.

7. Coloring Snow

Provide children with spray bottles containing colored water, preferably red, yellow, and blue. Allow them to spray the snow and mix colors.

8. Thermometers

Experiment with a thermometer. Begin introducing the concept by observing and discussing what happens when the thermometer is placed in a bowl of warm water and a bowl of cold water. Demonstrate to the children and encourage them to experiment under supervision during the self-selected activity period.

9. Signs and Sounds of Winter

On a winter walk in colder climates have the children watch and listen for signs and sounds of winter. The signs of winter are weather: cold, ice, daylight is shorter, darkness is earlier; plants: all but evergreen trees are bare; and people: we wear warmer clothes, we play inside more, we shovel snow, we play in the snow. Some of the sounds of winter are: boots crunching, rain splashing, wind howling, etc. (Adapt this activity to the signs of winter in your climate.)

Dramatic Play:

1. Ice-skating Palace

Make a masking tape border on a carpeted floor. Give child 2 pieces of waxed paper. Show children how to fasten waxed paper to their ankles with rubber bands. Play instrumental music and encourage the children to skate around on the carpeted floor.

2. Dress Up

If available, put outdoor winter clothing such as coats, boots, hats, mittens, scarves, and earmuffs in the dramatic play area of the classroom with a large mirror. The children may enjoy trying on a variety of clothing items.

Arts and Crafts:

1. Whipped Soap Painting

Mix 1 cup Ivory Snow flakes with 1/2 cup warm water in bowl. The children can beat with a hand eggbeater until mixture is fluffy. Apply mixture to dark construction paper with various tools (toothbrushes, rollers, tongue depressors, brushes, etc.). To create variety, food coloring can be added to paint mixture.

2. Cottonball Snowman

Cut a snowperson figure from dark construction paper. Provide the children with cottonballs and glue. They can decorate the snowperson by gluing on cottonballs.

3. Snowflakes

Cut different-sized squares out of white construction paper. Fold the squares in half, and then in half again. Demonstrate and encourage the children to cut and open their own designs. The snowflakes can be hung in the entry or classroom for decoration.

4. Windowpane Frost

On a piece of construction paper, draw an outline of a window. Spread glue around and on the frame and sprinkle with glitter.

5. Winter Mobile

Cut out pictures of winter from magazines or have children create their own winter pictures. Attach several pictures with string or yarn to a branch, hanger (masking taped), or paper plate. Glitter can be added.

6. Ice Cube Art

Place a popsicle stick in each ice compartment of a tray and fill with water. Freeze. Sprinkle dry tempera paint on paper. Then to make their own design, the children can move an ice cube on the paper.

7. **Frosted Pictures**

   Mix 1 part Epsom salts with 1 part boiling water. Let the mixture cool. Encourage the children to make a crayon design on paper. The mixture can be brushed over the picture. Observe how the crystals form as the mixture dries.

8. **Winter Shape Printing**

   Cut sponges into various winter shapes such as boots, snowmen, mittens, snowflakes, fir trees, and stars. The children can use the sponges as a tool to print on different pieces of colored construction paper.

9. **Easel Ideas**

   Feature white paint at the easel for snow pictures on colored paper. Or, cut easel paper into winter shapes: snowmen, hats, mittens, scarves, snowflakes, etc.

10. **Snow Drawings**

    White chalk and dark construction paper can be placed in the art area.

11. **Snow Painting**

    Using old spray bottles filled with colored water, let the children make pictures in the snow outside. This activity is limited to areas where snow is available.

Sensory:

The following items can be placed in the sensory table.

- snow and ice (plain or colored with drops of food coloring)
- cottonballs with measuring/balancing scale
- pinecones
- ice cubes (colored or plain)
- snow and magnifying glasses

Large Muscle:

1. **Freeze**

   Play music and have the children walk around in a circle. When the music stops, the children freeze by standing still in a stooped position. Vary the activity by substituting other actions such as hopping, skipping, galloping, sliding, etc.

2. **Snowperson**

   During outdoor play make a snowperson. Decorate with radish eyes, carrot nose, scarf, hat, and holding a stick. Other novel accessories can be substituted by using the children's ideas.

3. **Snow People**

   After a snowfall, have the children lie down in the snow and move their arms and legs to make shapes.

4. **Snowball Target**

   Since children love throwing snowballs, set up a target outside for children to throw at.

5. **Shovel**

   Provide child-sized shovels for the children to help shovel a walk.

6. **Balance**

   Make various tracks in the snow, such as a straight line, a zig-zag line, a circle, square, triangle, and rectangle.

Field Trips/Resource People:

1. Visit an ice-skating rink. Observe the ice and watch how it is cleaned.

2. Visit a sledding hill. Bring sleds along and go sledding.

3. Invite a snowplow operator to school to talk to the children. After a snowfall, the children can observe the plowing.

4. Take the children to a grocery store and view the freezer area. Also, observe a refrigerated delivery truck.

Math:

1. **Shape Sequence**

   Cut three different-sized white circles from construction paper for each child to make a snowperson. Which is the largest? Smallest? How many do you have? What shape? Then have children sequence the circles from largest to smallest and smallest to largest.

2. **Mitten Match**

   From construction paper or tagboard design and cut several pairs of mittens. On one pair of mittens write a numeral and on the other, the corresponding number of dots. The children can match the dots to the numerals locating the pairs of mittens.

3. **Winter Dominoes**

   Trace and cut 30 squares out of white tagboard. Section each square into four spaces diagonally. In each of the four spaces, draw different winter objects or stick winter stickers on. The children can match the pictures by playing dominoes.

4. **Dot to Dot**

   Make a dot-to-dot snowperson. The children connect the dots in numerical order. You can also make dot-to-dot patterns of other winter objects such as hats, snowflakes, mittens, etc. This activity requires numeral recognition and order, so it is restricted to the school-aged child.

5. **Puzzles**

   Mount winter pictures or posters on tagboard sheets. Cut into pieces. The number of pieces cut will be dependent upon the children's developmental age. Place in the small manipulative area of the classroom for use during self-selected activity periods.

Social Studies:

1. **Travel**

   Discuss ways people travel in winter such as sled, toboggan, snowmobile, snowshoes, skis, etc.

2. **Winter Happenings**

   Display pictures of different winter happenings, sports, clothing, snow, etc., around the room at the children's eye level.

3. **Winter Book**

   Encourage the children to make a book about winter. Do one page a day. The following titles could be used:

   - What I wear in winter.
   - What I like to do outside in winter.
   - What I like to do inside in winter.
   - My favorite food during winter.
   - My favorite thing about winter.
   (This activity may be more appropriate for the school-aged child.)

4. **Winter Clothing Match**

   Draw a large paper figure of a boy and of a girl. Design and cut winter clothing to fit each figure. The children can dress the figures for outdoor play.

Group Time (games, language):

1. **Who Has the Mitten?**

   Ask the children to sit in a circle. One child should sit in the middle. Make a very small mitten out of felt or construction paper. Tell the children to pass the mitten around the circle. All the children should imitate the passing actions even if they do not have the mitten in hand. When the verse starts the child in the middle tries to guess who has the mitten. Chant the following verse while passing a mitten.

   I pass the mitten from me to you to you,
   I pass the mitten and that is what I do.

2. **Hat Chart**

Prepare a hat chart by listing all the types and colors of hats worn by the children in the classroom.

Cooking:

1. **Banana Snowpeople**

   2 cups raisins
   2 bananas
   shredded coconut

   Chop the bananas and raisins in a blender. Then place them in a mixing bowl. Refrigerate until mixture is cool enough to be handled. Roll the mixture into balls and into shredded coconut. Stack three balls and fasten with toothpicks.

2. **Hot Chocolate**

   Add warm water or milk to instant hot chocolate and mix. Heat as needed.

3. **Snow Cones**

   Crush ice and spoon into small paper cups. Pour a fruit juice over the ice. Serve.

4. **Snowballs—China**

   1/4 cup walnuts, ground
   1/4 cup almonds, ground
   1/4 cup sesame seeds, toasted
   1/2 cup sugar
   1 tablespoon shortening
   1 pound glutenous rice flour

   In a bowl, mix nuts, sesame seeds, sugar, and shortening. Form mixture into 1/2-inch balls. Fill a big mixing bowl with 1/2-inch layer of rice flour. Moisten the nut balls by dipping them into water. Place balls individually in floured bowl and shake bowl back and forth, coating the balls with flour. Redip coated balls in water and coat three times. Slip balls into boiling water and gently boil for about 5 minutes until balls float to the surface. Add a cup of cold water and boil for about 3 to 4 minutes. Serve about 4 to each person along with the hot liquid. This activity requires supervision.

Multimedia:

The following records can be found in educational catalogs:

1. Jenkins, Ella. *Seasons for Singing* [record].

2. "Alpine Blizzard," *Environment* [record]. Syntonic Research, Inc.

Books:

The following books can be used to complement the theme:

1. Neitzel, Shirley. (1993). *The Jacket I Wear in the Snow*. New York: Morrow.

2. London, Jonathan. (1993). *The Owl Who Became the Moon*. New York: Dutton.

3. Cowcher, Helen. (1990). *Antarctica*. New York: Farrar, Straus & Giroux.

4. Martin, Bill, Jr. (1991). *Polar Bear, Polar Bear What Do You Hear?* New York: Henry Holt.

5. Sing, Rachel. (1992). *Chinese New Year's Dragon*. Cleveland, OH: Modern Curriculum Press.

6. Tran, Kim-Lan. (1992). *Tết: The New Year*. Cleveland, OH: Modern Curriculum Press.

7. Hoban, Julia. (1993). *Amy Loves the Snow*. New York: Harper Collins.

8. Keown, Elizabeth. (1992). *Emily's Snowball: The World's Biggest*. New York: Macmillan.

9. Tibo, Gilles. (1991). *Simon and the Snowflakes*. Plattsburgh, NY: Tundra Books.

10. Chlad, Dorothy. (1991). *Playing Outdoors in the Winter*. Chicago: Children's Press.

11. Fowler, Allan. (1991). *How Do You Know It's Winter?* Chicago: Children's Press.

12. Good, Elaine W. (1991). *White Wonderful Winter*. Intercourse, PA: Good Books.

13. Hirschi, Ron. (1990). *Winter*. New York: Dutton Children's Books.

14. Moncure, Jane B. (1990). *Step into Winter: A New Season*. Mankato, MN: Child's World, Inc.

15. Adams, Pam. (1990). *On a Cold and Frosty Morning*. New York: Child's Play—International.

16. Blades, Ann. (1990). *Winter*. New York: Lothrop, Lee, & Shepard Books.

17. Ewart, Claire. (1992). *One Cold Night*. New York: Putnam Publishing Group.

18. Erickson, Gina, & Foster, Kelli C. (1991). *The Sled Surprise*. Hauppauge, NY: Barron's Educational Series, Inc.

19. Lewis, Rob. (1990). *Henrietta's First Winter*. New York: Farrar, Straus and Giroux, Inc.

20. Rice, Eve. (1993). *Oh, Lewis!* New York: William Morrow and Co., Inc.

21. Stevenson, James. (1991). *Brrr!* New York: Greenwillow Books.

22. Velthuijs, Max. (1993). *Frog in Winter*. New York: William Morrow and Co., Inc.

23. Sanchez, Isidro, & Peris, Carme. (1992). *Winter Sports*. Hauppauge, NY: Barron's Educational Series, Inc.

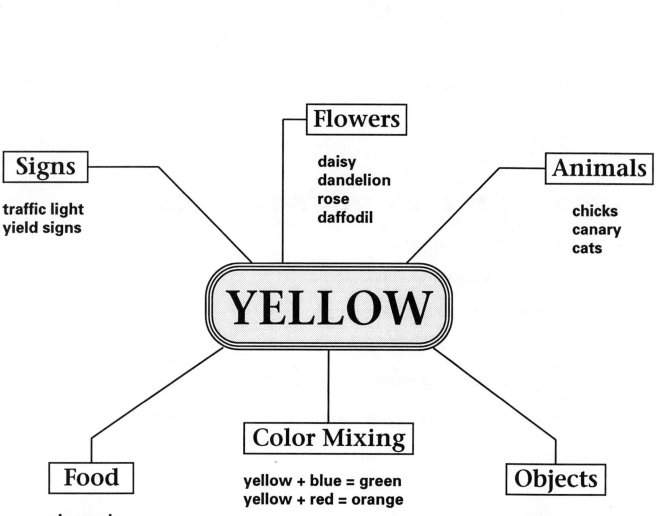

Flowers

daisy
dandelion
rose
daffodil

Signs

traffic light
yield signs

Animals

chicks
canary
cats

YELLOW

Color Mixing

yellow + blue = green
yellow + red = orange

Food

pineapple
banana
lemon
corn
grapefruit
cheese
egg yolk

Objects

sun
paint
cars
bikes
clothes

Polaroid Education Program

Here's an exciting new way to turn instant photography into an effective teaching tool. Refer to the full-color insert for the activity entitled Photo Lotto.

Theme Goals:

Through participating in the experiences provided by this theme, the children may learn:

1. Yellow flowers.

2. Yellow traffic signs.

3. Yellow animals.

4. Yellow-colored foods.

5. Colors formed by adding yellow.

6. Yellow objects.

Concepts for the Children to Learn:

1. Yellow is a primary color.

2. Yellow mixed with blue makes green.

3. Yellow mixed with red makes orange.

4. The sun is a yellow color.

5. The middle color on a traffic light is yellow.

6. Daisies, dandelions, and daffodils are yellow flowers.

7. A canary is a yellow bird.

8. Pineapples, bananas, and corn are yellow foods.

9. Bikes, cars, and cats can be yellow.

Vocabulary:

1. **yellow**—a primary color.

2. **primary colors**—red, blue, and yellow.

Bulletin Board

The purpose of this bulletin board is to have the children match the shapes, providing practice in visual discrimination. To prepare the bulletin board, collect yellow tagboard, a black felt-tip marker, scissors, yellow string, and push pins. Using yellow tagboard, draw sets of different-shaped balloons as illustrated. Outline with a black felt-tip marker and cut out. Take one from each set and attach to the top of the bulletin board. Staple a yellow string to hang from each balloon. Next, attach the remaining balloons on the bottom of the bulletin board. A push pin can be fastened next to each balloon, and the children can match the balloons by shape.

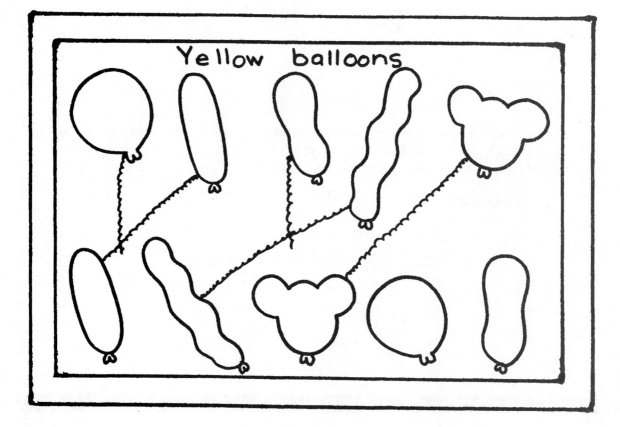

Parent Letter

Dear Parents,

Colors are such a big part of our world. Consequently, our new theme will focus on the color yellow. Throughout this week, the children will become aware of the color in their environment. It should be a bright time discovering the color yellow!

At School

Some learning experiences planned for the unit include:

- making scrambled eggs.
- visiting a paint store.
- learning the fingerplay, "Six Yellow Chickadees."
- making yellow soap crayons.
- playing with corn kernels in the sensory table.

At Home

At school we will be making yellow playdough. The children enjoy helping prepare the playdough and, of course, playing with it! It would be great fun for them to make it at home and they will be exposed to the mathematical concepts of amounts, fractions, and measurements. Here is the recipe.

2 cups flour
1 cup of salt
1 cup of water
2 tablespoons cooking oil
food coloring

Let your child assist in gathering and measuring the ingredients. Then mix all the ingredients together. To encourage play, provide some tools for your child to use: rolling pins, cookie cutters, spatulas, or potato mashers. Have fun!

Enjoy your child!

FIGURE 62 The yolk of an egg is yellow in color.

Fingerplays:

SIX YELLOW CHICKADEES
(Suit the actions to the words.)

Six yellow chickadees sitting by a hive.
One flew away and then there were five.
Five yellow chickadees sitting by the door.
One flew away and then there were four.
Four yellow chickadees sitting in a tree.
One flew away and then there were three.
Three yellow chickadees sitting by my shoe.
One flew away and then there were two.
Two yellow chickadees sitting by my thumb.
One flew away and then there was one.
One yellow chickadee flying around the sun.
He flew away and then there were none.

TEN FLUFFY CHICKENS

Five eggs and five eggs
    (hold up two hands)
That makes ten.

Sitting on top is the mother hen.
    (fold one hand over the other)
Crackle, crackle, crackle
    (clap hands three times)
What do I see?
Ten fluffy chickens
    (hold up ten fingers)
As yellow as can be!

Science:

1. **Paper Towel Dip**

   Fold a paper towel in half several times. Dip the towel into red water and then into yellow water. Open the towel carefully and allow it to dry. Orange designs will appear on the paper towel.

2. **Carnation Coloring**

   Put a carnation into a glass of water that has been dyed yellow with food coloring. Soon the carnation will show yellow streaks. During the summer other white garden flowers can be substituted.

3. **Yellow Soap Crayons**

   Measure one cup of mild powdered laundry soap. Add one tablespoon of food coloring. Add water by the teaspoonful until the soap is in liquid form. Stir well. Pour the soap into ice cube trays. Set in a sunny, dry place until hard. Soap crayons are great for writing in the sink, tub, or sensory table.

Dramatic Play:

Paint Store

Set up a paint store by including paint caps, paintbrushes, pans, rollers, drop cloths, paint clothes, a cash register, and play money.

Arts and Crafts:

1. **Yellow Paint**

   Provide yellow fingerpaint and yellow tempera paint in the art area.

2. **Corncob Painting**

Cover the bottom of a shallow pan with thick yellow tempera paint. Using a corncob as an applicator, apply paint to paper.

3. **Popsicle Stick Prints**

Cover the bottom of a shallow pan with thick yellow tempera paint. Apply the paint to paper using a popsicle stick as an applicator.

4. **Yellow Playdough**

Combine two parts flour, one part salt, one part water, and two tablespoons cooking oil. Add yellow food coloring. Mix well. If prepared dough becomes sticky, add more flour.

5. **Baker's Clay**

Combine 4 cups flour, 1 cup salt, and 1½ cups water. Mix the ingredients. The children can shape forms. Place the forms on a cookie sheet and bake at 350 degrees for about 1 hour. The next day the children can paint the objects yellow.

6. **Yarn and Glue Designs**

Provide yellow yarn, glue, and paper for the children to make their own designs.

7. **Record Player Designs**

Punch a hole in the middle of a paper plate and place on the turntable of a record player. Turn the record player on. As the turntable spins around, the children can apply color by holding a yellow felt-tip marker on the paper plate. Interesting designs can be made.

Sensory:

1. **Shaving Cream Fun**

Spray the contents of one can of shaving cream in the sensory table. Color the shaving cream by adding yellow food coloring.

2. **Corn Kernels**

Place corn kernels in the sensory table.

3. **Yellow Goop**

In the sensory table, mix one cup cornstarch, one cup water, and yellow food coloring. Mix together well.

4. **Water Toys**

Add yellow food coloring to three inches of water in the sensory table. Provide water toys as accessories to encourage play during self-selected play activites.

Field Trips:

1. **Paint Store**

Visit a paint store and observe the different shades of yellow. Collect samples of paint for use in the art area. If possible, also observe the manager mix yellow paint.

2. **Yellow in Our World**

Take a walk and look for yellow objects. When you return to the classroom prepare a language experience chart.

3. **Greenhouse**

Visit a greenhouse and observe the different kinds of yellow flowers.

Math:

Sorting Shapes

Cut circles, triangles, and rectangles out of yellow tagboard. Place on the math table. The children can sort the yellow shapes into groups. For younger children, the objects can be cut from different colors. Then the objects can be sorted by color.

Social Studies:

Tasting Party

Cut a banana, a pineapple, a lemon, and a piece of yellow cheese into small pieces. Let the children sample each during snack time. The concept of color, texture, and taste can all be discussed.

Group Time (games, language):

Guessing Game: What's Missing?

Use any yellow familiar objects or toys that can be easily handled. The number will depend upon developmental appropriateness. For two-year-olds choose only two objects. On the other hand several objects can be used for five-year-olds. Spread them out on the floor and ask children to name each item. Then ask the group to close their eyes. Remove one item. When the group opens their eyes, ask them to tell you which item is missing.

Cooking:

1. **Banana Bobs**

   Cut bananas into chunks and dip into honey. Next roll in wheat germ and use large tooth-picks for serving.

2. **Carribean Banana Salad**

   3 green (unripe) bananas, peeled
   2 cups water
   1 teaspoon salt

   2 medium carrots, shredded
   1 small cucumber, sliced
   1 medium tomato, chopped
   1 avocado, cubed
   1 stalk celery, sliced
   vinaigrette dressing

   Heat bananas, water, and salt to boiling; reduce heat. Cover and simmer until bananas are tender, about 5 minutes. Drain and cool. Cut bananas crosswise into 1/2-inch slices. Toss bananas and remaining ingredients with vinaigrette dressing.

   Source: *Betty Crocker's International Cookbook.* (1980). New York: Random House.

3. **Corn Bread**

   1 cup flour
   1 cup cornmeal
   2 tablespoons sugar
   4 teaspoons baking powder
   1 teaspoon salt
   1 cup milk
   1/4 cup cooking oil or melted shortening
   1 egg, slightly beaten

   Preheat oven to 425 degrees. Grease (not oil) an 8- or 9-inch square pan. In medium mixing bowl, combine the dry ingredients. Stir in the remaining ingredients, beating by hand until just smooth. Pour batter into prepared pan. Bake for 20 to 25 minutes or until toothpick inserted in center comes out clean.

Multimedia:

The following resources can be found in educational catalogs:

1. Palmer, Hap. "Colors," *Learning Basic Skills through Music—Volume 1* [record].

2. Caspell, Jerry. *Color Me a Rainbow* [record].

3. *There's Music in the Colors* [record]. Kimbo Records.

Books:

The following books can be used to complement the theme:

1. Felix, Monique. (1991). *Colors*. New York: Stewart, Tabori, and Chang.

2. Lundell, Margaretta. (1989). *The Land of Colors*. New York: Putnam.

3. Morrison, Blake. (1987). *The Yellow House*. San Diego: Harcourt, Brace, Jovanovich.

4. Cox, Molly. (1988). *Louella & the Yellow Balloon*. New York: Harper Collins.

5. Van Fleet, Matthew. (1992). *One Yellow Lion: Fold-out Fun with Numbers, Colors, Animals*. New York: Dial Books for Young Readers.

6. Rogers, Alan. (1990). *Yellow Hippo*. Milwaukee, WI: Gareth Stevens, Inc.

7. Imershein, Betsy. (1989). *Finding Red Finding Yellow*. San Diego: Harcourt Brace Jovanovich.

8. Woolfitt, Gabrielle. (1992). *Yellow*. Minneapolis: Carolrhoda Books.

9. Bang, Molly. (1991). *Yellow Ball*. New York: Morrow Junior Books.

10. Mazer, Anne. (1990). *Yellow Button*. New York: Alfred A. Knopf Books for Young Readers.

Kinds

elephants
giraffes
monkeys
snakes
lions
bears
zebras
camels

Homes

cages
fences
water
trees

ZOO ANIMALS

Caretakers

zookeeper
veterinarian

Needs

food
water
shelter
air

Here's an exciting new way to turn instant photography into an effective teaching tool. Refer to the full-color insert for the activity entitled Graphing.

Theme Goals:

Through participating in the experiences provided by this theme, the children may learn:

1. Names of zoo animals.

2. Needs of zoo animals.

3. Types of animal homes.

4. The caretaker's role.

Concepts for the Children to Learn:

1. A zoo is a place for animals.

2. Zoo animals are kept in cages, fences, water, or in trees.

3. Elephants, giraffes, monkeys, snakes, lions, zebras, camels, and bears are zoo animals.

4. A zookeeper feeds and takes care of the animals.

5. Zoo animals need food, water, and shelter.

6. Veterinarians are animal doctors.

Vocabulary:

1. **zoo**—a place to look at animals.

2. **cage**—a home for animals.

3. **zookeeper**—a person who feeds the zoo animals.

4. **veterinarian**—an animal doctor.

Bulletin Board

The purpose of this bulletin board is to encourage the children to place the correct number of balls above each seal corresponding to the numeral on the drum. To prepare the bulletin board, construct seals sitting on a drum as illustrated. Place a numeral on each drum with the corresponding number of dots. Construct colored balls from tagboard. Laminate. Staple the seal figures and drums to bulletin board. Place a magnetic strip above each seal. Also adhere a magnetic strip on the back of each ball.

Parent Letter

Dear Parents,

Our new theme is called zoo animals. This is an appropriate theme to introduce to the children because they are fascinated by the zoo and the animals that live there. Through our study of zoo animals, the children will become familiar with the names of many familiar zoo animals. They will also be introduced to new occupations: the zookeeper and the veterinarian.

At School

Some of the experiences planned for the zoo animal unit include:

- looking at peek-a-boo pictures of zoo animals.
- using zoo animal-shaped cookie cutters with playdough at the art table.
- pretending to be caged zoo animals using boxes as cages in the dramatic play area.

Field Trip

Our class will be taking a field trip to the Dunn County Reserve Park on Friday. There we can see some unusual animals. Please let me know by Wednesday if you are interested in accompanying the group. We will be leaving the center at 9:30 a.m. and be returning by 11:30 a.m.

At Home

To develop observation skills, you can show your child pictures of zoo animals from books or magazines. Plan a family trip to a zoo. Many opportunities for learning present themselves at the zoo. Children can actually see different kinds of animals and many times, such as at petting zoos, are able to touch and feed them. What a great way to develop an appreciation for and respect of animal life!

Enjoy your child!

FIGURE 63 Can you roar like a leopard?

Music:

1. **"Zoo Animals"**
   (Sing to the tune of "Muffin Man")

   Do you know the kangaroo
   The kangaroo, the kangaroo?
   Oh, do you know the kangaroo
   That lives in the zoo?

   (Adapt this song and use other zoo animals
   such as the monkey, elephant, giraffe, lion,
   turtle, bear, snake, etc.)

2. **"One Elephant"**

   One elephant went out to play
   On a spider web one day.
   He had such enormous fun
   That he called for another elephant to come.

   (Makes a nice flannel story or choose one child
   to be an "elephant." Add another "elephant"
   with each verse.)

3. **"Animals at the Zoo"**
   (Sing to the tune of "Frere Jacques")

   See the animals, see the animals
   At the zoo, at the zoo.
   Elephants and tigers, lions and seals
   Monkeys too, monkeys too.

Fingerplays:

LION

I knew a little lion who went roar, roar, roar.
   (make sounds)
Who walked around on all fours.
   (walk on both hands and feet)
He had a tail we could see behind the bars
   (point to tail)
And when we visit we should stand back far.
   (move backwards)

ALLIGATOR

The alligator likes to swim.
   (two hands flat on top of the other)
Sometimes his mouth opens wide.
   (hands open and shut)
But when he sees me on the shore,
Down under the water he'll hide.

THE MONKEY

The monkey claps, claps, claps his hands.
   (clap hands)
The monkey claps, claps, claps his hands.
   (clap hands)
Monkey see, monkey do.
The monkey does the same as you.
   (use pointer finger)
   (change actions)

ZOO ANIMALS

This is the way the elephant goes.
   (clasp hands together, extend arms, move
   back and forth)
With a curly trunk instead of a nose.
The buffalo, all shaggy and fat.
Has two sharp horns in place of a hat.
   (point to forehead)
The hippo with his mouth so wide—
Let's see what's inside.
   (hands together and open wide and close
   them)
The wiggly snake upon the ground
Crawls along without a sound.
   (weave hands back and forth)
But monkey see and monkey do is the funniest
animal in the zoo.
   (place thumbs in ears and wiggle fingers)

THE ZOO

The zoo holds many animals inside
   (make a circle with your hands and peer
   inside)
So unlatch the doors and open them wide.
   (open your hands wide)
Elephants, tigers, zebras, and bears
   (hold up one finger for each animal)
Are some of the animals you'll find there.

Science:

1. **Animal Skins**

   Place a piece of snakeskin, a patch of animal
   hide, and animal fur out on the science table.
   The children can look and feel the differences.
   These skins can usually be borrowed from the
   Department of Natural Resources.

2. **Habitat**

   On the science table, place a bowl of water, a
   tray of dirt, and a pile of hay or grass on the
   table. Also, include many small toy zoo
   animals. The children can place the animals in
   their correct habitat.

Dramatic Play:

1. **The Zoo**

   Collect large appliance boxes. Cut slits to
   resemble cages. Old fur coats or blankets can
   be added. The children may use the fur pieces
   pretending to be animals in the zoo.

2. **Pet Store**

   Cages and many small stuffed animals can be
   added to the dramatic play area.

3. **Block Play**

   Set out many blocks and rubber, plastic, or
   wooden models of zoo animals.

Arts and Crafts:

1. **Paper Plate Lions**

   Collect paper plates, sandwich bags, and
   yellow cotton. Color the cottonballs by
   pouring powdered tempera paint into the
   sandwich bag and shaking. The children can
   trim the cut side of the paper plate with the
   yellow cotton to represent a mane. Facial
   features can also be added. This activity is for
   older children.

2. **Cookie Cutters**

   Playdough and zoo animal-shaped cookie
   cutters can be placed on a table in the art area.

Sensory:

Additions to the sensory table include:

- sand and zoo animal models
- seeds and measuring scoops
- corn and scales
- hay
- water

Large Muscle:

1. **Walk Like the Animals**

   "Walk Like the Animals" is played like "Simon Says." Say, "The zookeeper says to walk like a giraffe." The children can walk as they believe that particular zoo animal would walk. Repeat using different animals such as monkeys, elephants, lions, tigers, bears, etc. This activity can also be used for transition.

2. **Zookeeper, May I?**

   Designate one child to be the zookeeper. This child should stand about six feet in front of the remainder of the children. The zookeeper provides directions for the other children. To illustrate, they may say take three elephant steps, one kangaroo hop, two alligator glides, etc. Once the children reach the zookeeper, the zookeeper chooses a child as his successor.

Field Trips:

1. **Zoo**

   Visit a local zoo if available. Observe the animals that are of particular interest to the children such as the elephants, giraffes, bears, and monkeys.

2. **Reserve Park**

   If your community has a reserve park, or an area where wild animals are caged in a natural environment, take the children to visit. Plan a picnic snack to take along.

Math:

1. **Animal Sort**

   Collect pictures of elephants, lions, giraffes, monkeys, and other zoo animals from magazines, calendars, or coloring books. Encourage the children to sort the pictures into labeled baskets. For example, one basket may be for large animals and another for small animals.

2. **Which Is Bigger?**

   Collect many toy models of zoo animals in various sizes. Encourage the children to order from smallest to biggest, etc.

3. **Animal Sets**

   Cut and mount pictures of zoo animals. The children can classify the pictures by sorting. Examples might include birds, four-legged animals, furry animals, etc.

Social Studies:

Helpful Zoo Animals

Discuss how some animals can be useful during large group. Show the children pictures of various helping animals and discuss their uses. Examples include:

- camel (transportation in some countries).
- elephant (often used to pull things).
- dogs (seeing-eye dogs, sled dogs).
- goats (used for milk).

Group Time (games, language):

What Am I?

Give the children verbal clues in which you describe an animal and the children guess which zoo animal you are talking about. An example is, "I am very large, gray-colored, and have a long nose that looks like a hose. What zoo animal am I?"

Cooking:

1. **Animals on Grass**

   Take a graham cracker and spread either peanut butter or green-tinted cream cheese on the top. Stand an animal cracker on the top of the graham cracker.

2. **Peanut Butter Log**

   1/2 cup peanut butter
   1/2 cup raisins
   2 1/2 tablespoons dry milk
   2 tablespoons honey

   Mix together, roll into log 1 inch x 10 inches long. Chill and slice.

Multimedia:

The following resources can be found in educational catalogs.

1. Palmer, Hap. *Animal Antics* [record].

2. *What's New at the Zoo?* [record]. Kimbo Records.

3. *Walk Like the Animals* [record]. Kimbo Records.

4. *Animal Walks* [record]. Kimbo Records.

5. *Ping & Kooky's Cuckoo Zoo* [IBM/Mac software, PK–1]. EA Kids.

6. *Kid's Zoo* [IBM/Mac software, PK+]. Knowledge Adventure.

7. *Alphabet Zoo* [Apple/IBM software, PK–2]. Queue.

Books:

The following books can be used to complement the theme:

1. Hoban, Tara. (1987). *A Children's Zoo.* New York: Morrow.

2. Ata, Te. (1989). *Baby Rattlesnake.* San Francisco: Children's Book Press.

3. Caduto, Michael, & Bruchac, Joseph. (1991). *Keepers of the Animals: Native American Stories & Wildlife Activities for Children.* Golden, CO: Fulcrum Publishing.

4. Arnold, Caroline. (1992). *Cheetah.* New York: Morrow.

5. Arnold, Caroline. (1992). *Hippo.* New York: Morrow.

6. Davis, Kerry. (1993). *The Swetsville Zoo.* Kerry Tales.

7. Douglas-Hamilton, Oria. (1991). *The Elephant Family Book.* Saxonville, MA: Picture Book Studios.

8. Hefer, Angelika. (1991). *The Lion Family Book.* Saxonville, MA: Picture Book Studios.

9. Moerbeek, Kees. (1989). *New at the Zoo.* New York: Random House.

10. Brown, Margaret W. (1993). *Don't Frighten the Lion!* New York: Harper Collins.

11. Baker, Keith. (1991). *Hide & Snake.* San Diego: Harcourt Brace.

12. Ruschak, Lynette. (1992). *Counting Zoo: A Pop-up Number Book.* New York: Macmillan Children's Group.

13. Brennan, John, & Keney, Leonie. (1989). *Zoo Day.* Minneapolis: Carolrhoda Books.

14. Carle, Eric. (1989). *One, Two, Three to the Zoo*. New York: Putnam Publishing Group.

15. Oremerod, Jan. (1991). *When We Went to the Zoo*. New York: Lothrop, Lee, & Shepard Books.

16. Parramon, J. M. (1990). *My First Visit to the Zoo*. Hauppauge, NY: Barron's Educational Series, Inc.

17. Unwin, Pippa. (1990). *Great Zoo Hunt!* New York: Doubleday and Co., Inc.

18. Lunn, Carolyn. (1991). *Bobby's Zoo Big Book*. Chicago: Children's Press.

INTERNATIONAL HOLIDAYS

When planning the curriculum, it is important to note international holidays. The exact date of the holiday may vary from year to year; consequently, it is important to check with parents or a reference librarian at a local library. These international holidays for Christians, Buddhists, Eastern Orthodox, Hindus, Jews, and Muslims are as follows:

Christian

Ash Wednesday
Palm Sunday—the Sunday before Easter, which commemorates the triumphant entry of Jesus in Jerusalem.
Holy Thursday—also known as Maundy Thursday; it is the Thursday of Holy Week.
Good Friday—commemorates the crucifixion of Jesus.
Easter—celebrates the resurrection of Jesus.
Christmas Eve
Christmas Day—commemorates the birth of Jesus.

Buddhist

Nirvana Day (Mahayana Sect)—observes the passing of Sakyamuni into Nirvana. He obtained enlightenment and became a Buddha.
Magna Puja (Theravada Sect)—one of the holiest Buddhist holidays; it marks the occasion when 1,250 of Buddha's disciples gathered spontaneously to hear him speak.
Buddha Day (Mahayana Sect)—this service commemorates the birth of Gautama in Lumbini Garden. Amida, the Buddha of Infinite Wisdom and Compassion, manifested himself among men in the person Gautama.
Versakha Piya (Theravada Sect)—the most sacred of the Buddhist days. It celebrates the birth, death, and enlightenment of Buddha.
Maharram—marks the beginning of Buddhist Lent, it is the anniversary of Buddha's sermon to the first five disciples.
Vassana (Theravada Sect)—the beginning of the three-month period when monks stay in their temple to study and meditate.
Bon (Mahayana Sect)—an occasion for rejoicing in the enlightment offered by the Buddha; often referred to as a "Gathering of Joy." Buddha had saved the life of the mother Moggallana. The day is in remembrance of all those who have passed away.
Pavarana (Theravada Sect)—celebrates Buddha's return to earth after spending one Lent season preaching in heaven.
Bodhi Day (Mahayana Sect)—celebrates the enlightment of Buddha.

Eastern Orthodox

Christmas
First Day of Lent—begins a period of fasting and penitence in preparation for Easter.
Easter Sunday—celebrates the resurrection of Jesus.
Ascension Day—the 40th day after Easter, commemorates the ascension of Jesus to heaven.
Pentecost—commemorates the descent of the Holy Spirit upon the Apostles, 50 days after Easter Sunday. Marks the beginning of the Christian Church.

Hindu

Pongal Sankrandi—a three-day harvest festival.

Vasanta Pachami—celebrated in honor of Saraswati, the charming and sophisticated goddess of scholars.

Shivarari—a solemn festival devoted to the worship of Shiva, the most powerful of deities of the Hindu pantheon.

Holi—celebrates the advent of spring.

Ganguar—celebrated in honor of Parvari, the consort of Lord Shiva.

Ram Navami—birthday of the God Rama.

Hanuman Jayanti—birthday of Monkey God Humumanji.

Meenakshi Kalyanam—the annual commemoration of the marriage of Meenakshi to Lord Shiva.

Teej—celebrates the arrival of the monsoon; Parvari is the presiding deity.

Jewish

Yom Kippur—the most holy day of the Jewish year, it is marked by fasting and prayer as Jews seek forgiveness from God and man.

Sukkot—commemorates the 40-year wandering of Israelites in the desert on the way to the Promised Land; expresses thanksgiving for the fall harvest.

Simchat Torah—celebrates the conclusion of the public reading of the Pentateuch and its beginning anew, thus affirming that the study of God's word is an unending process. Concludes the Sukkot Festival.

Hanukkah—the eight-day festival that celebrates the rededication of the Temple to the service of God. Commemorates the Maccabean victory over Antiochus, who sought to suppress freedom of worship.

Purim—marks the salvation of the Jews of ancient Persia through the intervention of Queen Esther, from Haman's plot to exterminate them.

Passover—an eight-day festival marking ancient Israel's deliverance from Egyptian bondage.

Yom Hashoah—day of remembrance for victims of Nazi Holocaust.

Sahvout—celebrates the covenant established at Sinai between God and Israel and the revelation of the Ten Commandments.

Rosh Hashananh—the first of the High Holy Days marking the beginning of a ten-day period of penitence and spiritual renewal.

Muslim

Isra and Miraj—commemorates the anniversary of the night journey of the Prophet and his ascension to heaven.

Ramadan—the beginning of the month of fasting from sunrise to sunset.

Id al-Fitr—end of the month of fasting from sunrise to sunset; first day of pilgrimage to Mecca.

Hajj—the first day of pilgrimage to Mecca.

Day of Amfat—gathering of the pilgrims.

Id al-adha—commemorates the Feast of the Sacrifice.

Muharram—the Muslim New Year; marks the beginning of the Hedjra Year 1412.

Id al-Mawlid—commemorates the nativity and death of Prophet Muhammad and his flight from Mecca to Medina.

APPENDIX B

EARLY CHILDHOOD COMMERCIAL SUPPLIERS

ABC School Supply, Inc.
6500 Peachtree Industrial Boulevard
P.O. Box 4750
Norcross, Georgia 30091
(404) 447-5000

American Guidance Service
Publisher's Building
Circle Pines, Minnesota 55014

Beckley Cardy
One East First Street
Duluth, Minnesota 55802
1-800-227-1178

Chaselle, Inc.
9645 Gerwig Lane
Columbia, Maryland 21046-1503
1-800-242-7355

Childcraft Educational Corporation
20 Kilmer Road
P.O. Box 3081
Edison, New Jersey 08818-3081
1-800-631-5652

Children's Book and Music Center
2500 Santa Monica Boulevard
Santa Monica, California 90404
1-800-443-1856

Children's Press
5440 North Cumberland Avenue
Chicago, Illinois 60656
1-800-621-1115

Classic School Products
147 Semoran Commerce Place A106
Apopka, Florida 32703
1-800-394-9661

Community Playthings
Route 213
Rifton, New York 12471
(914) 658-3141

Constructive Playthings
1227 East 119th Street
Grandview, Missouri 64030-1117
1-800-832-0224

Cuisenaire Company of America, Inc.
12 Church Street, Box D
New Rochelle, New York 10802
1-800-237-3142

Delmar Publishers Inc
3 Columbia Circle
Box 15-015
Albany, New York 12212-5015

Didax Educational Resources
6 Doulton Place
Peabody, Massachusetts 01960

Education Plus
720 West 6th
Amarillo, Texas 79101
(806) 372-9473

Educational Teaching Aids
199 Carpenter Avenue
Wheeling, Illinois 60090
(312) 520-2500

Environments, Inc.
P.O. Box 1348
Beaufort Industrial Park
Beaufort, South Carolina 29901-1348

Gryphon House, Inc.
3706 Otis Street
Mt. Rainier, Maryland 20712

The Highsmith Co., Inc.
W5527 Highway 106
P.O. Box 800
Fort Atkinson, Wisconsin 53538-0800
1-800-558-2110

J. L. Hammett
P.O. Box 9057
Braintree, Massachusetts 02184-9704
1-800-333-4600

J. R. Educational Supplies, Inc.
1489 Roswell Road
Marietta, Georgia 30062
(404) 565-4889

Judy/Instructo
4325 Hiawatha Avenue
Minneapolis, Minnesota 55406

Kaplan School Supply Corporation
P.O. Box 609
Lewisville, North Carolina 27023-0609
1-800-334-2014

Kentucky School Supply
Dept. 23
P.O. Box 886
Elizabethtown, Kentucky 42702
1-800-626-4405

Kimbo Educational
10 North Third Avenue
Long Branch, New Jersey 07740
1-800-631-2187

Lakeshore Learning Materials
2695 E. Dominguez Street
Carson, California 90749
1-800-421-5354

Latta's School and Office Supplies
2218 Main Street
Cedar Falls, Iowa 50613
(319) 266-3501

Nasco
901 Janesville Avenue
Fort Atkinson, Wisconsin 53538
1-800-558-9595

Play Thinks
201 Old Town Road
P.O. Box 2628
Setauket, New York 11733
(516) 751-2421

Primary Educator
1200 Keystone Avenue
P.O. Box 24155
Lansing, Michigan 48909-4155
1-800-444-1773

Redleaf Press
450 North Syndicate
Suite 5
St. Paul, Minnesota 55104-4125
(612) 641-6629

Scholastic, Inc.
P.O. Box 7502
Jefferson City, Missouri 65102
1-800-392-2179

St. Paul Book and Stationery
1233 West County Road E
St. Paul, Minnesota 55112
1-800-338-SPBS (7727)

Valley School Supply
1000 North Bluemound Drive
P.O. Box 1579
Appleton, Wisconsin 54913
1-800-242-3433

Walter's Child Care Supplies
P.O. Box 14260
Madison, Wisconsin 53714
1-800-433-6252

Warren's Educational Supplies
980 West San Bernardino Road
Covina, California 91722-4196
1-800-523-7767

1. Get Acquainted Game

The children sit in a circle formation. The teacher begins the game by saying, "My name is ——— and I'm going to roll the ball to ———." Continue playing the game until every child has a turn. A variation of the game is have the children stand in a circle and bounce the ball to each other. This game is a fun way for the children to learn each other's names.

2. Hide the Ball

Choose several children and ask them to cover their eyes. Then hide a small ball, or other object, in an observable place. Ask the children to uncover their eyes and try to find the ball. The first child to find the ball hides it again.

3. "Which Ball is Gone?"

In the center of the circle, place six colored balls, cubes, beads, shapes, etc., in a row. Ask a child to close his eyes. Then ask another child to remove one of the objects and hide it behind him. The first child uncovers his eyes and tells which colored object is missing from the row. The game continues until all the selections have been made. When using with older children, two objects may be removed at a time to further challenge their abilities.

4. "What Sound is That?"

The purpose of this game is to promote the development of listening skills. Begin by asking the children to close their eyes. Make a familiar sound. Then ask a child to identify it. Sources of sound may include:

tearing paper	blowing a pitch pipe	raising or lowering
sharpening a pencil	dropping an object	window shades
walking, running,	moving a desk or	leafing through
shuffling feet	chair	book pages
clapping hands	snapping fingers	cutting with
sneezing, coughing	blowing nose	scissors
tapping on glass,	opening or closing	snapping rubber
wood, or metal	drawer	bands
jingling money	stirring paint in	ringing a bell
opening a window	a jar	clicking the tongue
pouring water	clearing the throat	crumpling paper
shuffling cards	splashing water	opening a box
blowing a whistle	rubbing sandpaper	sighing
banging blocks	together	stamping feet
bouncing ball	chattering teeth	rubbing palms
shaking a rattle	sweeping sound,	together
turning the lights on	such as a brush or	rattling keys
knocking on a door	broom	

A variation of this game could be played by having a child make a sound. Then the other children and the teacher close their eyes and attempt to identify the sound. For older children this game can be varied with the production of two sounds. Begin by asking the children if the sounds are the same or different. Then have them identify the sounds.

*Carefully select games for young children. Most games are more appropriate for older four-, five-, six-, and seven-year-old children.

5. "Near or Far?"

The purpose of this game is to locate sound. First, tell the children to close their eyes. Then play a sound recorded on a cassette tape. Ask the children to identify the sound as being near or far away.

6. Descriptions

The purpose of this game is to encourage expressive language skills. Begin by asking each child to describe himself. Included with the description can be the color of his eyes, hair, and clothing. The teacher might prefer to use an imaginative introduction such as: "One by one, you may take turns sitting up here in Alfred's magic chair and describe yourself to Alfred." Another approach may be to say, "Pretend that you must meet somebody at a very crowded airport who has never seen you before. How would you describe yourself so that the person would be sure to know who you are?"

A variation for older children would be to have one of the children describe another child without revealing the name of the person he is describing. To illustrate, the teacher might say, "I'm thinking of someone with shiny red hair, blue eyes, many freckles, etc...." The child being described should stand up.

7. Mirrored Movements

The purpose of this game is to encourage awareness of body parts through mirrored movements. Begin the activity by making movements. Encourage the children to mirror your movements. After the children understand the game, they may individually take the leader role.

8. Little Red Wagon Painted Red

As a prop for the game, cut a red wagon with wheels out of construction paper. Then cut rectangles the same size as the box of the red wagon. Include purple, blue, yellow, green, orange, brown, black, and pink colors.

Sing the song to the tune of **"Skip to My Lou."**

*Little red wagon painted **red.***
*Little red wagon painted **red.***
*Little red wagon painted **red.***
What color would it be?

Give each child a turn to pick and name a color. As the song is sung, let the child change the wagon color.

9. Police Officer Game

Select one child to be the police officer. Ask him to find a lost child. Describe one of the children in the circle. The child who is the police officer will use the description as a clue to find the "missing child."

10. Mother Cat and Baby Kits

Choose one child to be the mother cat. Then ask the mother cat to go to sleep in the center of the circle, covering his eyes. Then choose several children to be kittens. The verse below is chanted as the baby kittens hide in different parts of the classroom. Following this, the mother cat hunts for them. When all of the kittens have been located, another mother cat may be selected. The number of times the game is repeated depends upon the children's interest and attention span.

Mother cat lies fast asleep.

To her side the kittens creep.

But the kittens like to play.

Softly now they creep away.

Mother cat wakes up to see.

No little kittens. Where can they be?

11. Memory Game

Collect common household items, a towel, and tray. Place the items on the tray. Show the tray containing the items. Cover with a towel. Then ask the children to recall the names of the items on the tray. To ensure success, begin the activity with only two or three objects for young children. Additional objects can be added depending upon the developmental maturity of the children.

12. Cobbler, Mend My Shoes

Sit the children in a circle formation. Then select one child to sit in the center. This child gives a shoe to a child in the circle, and then closes his eyes. The children in the circle pass the shoe around behind them while the rhyme is chanted. When the chant is finished, the shoe is no longer passed. The last child with the shoe in his hand holds the shoe behind his back. Then the child sitting in the center tries to guess who has the shoe.

Cobbler, cobbler, mend my shoe

Have it done by half past two

Stitch it up and stitch it down

Now see with whom the shoe is found.

13. Huckle Buckle Beanstalk

Ask the children to sit in a circle. Once seated, tell them to close their eyes. Then hide a small ball in an obvious place. Say, "Ready." Encourage all of the children to hunt for the object. Each child who spots it returns to a place in the circle and says, "Huckle buckle beanstalk." No one must tell where he has seen the ball until all the children have seen it.

14. What's Different?

Sit all of the children in a circle formation. Ask one child to sit in the center. The rest of the children are told to look closely at the child sitting in the center. Then the children are told to cover their eyes while you change some detail on the child in the center. For example, you may place a hat on the child, untie his shoe, remove a shoe, roll up one sleeve, etc. The children sitting in the circle act as detective to determine "what's different?"

15. Cookie Jar

Sit the children in a circle formation on the floor with their legs crossed. Together they repeat a rhythmic chant while using alternating leg-hand clap to emphasize the rhythm. The chant is as follows.

Someone took the cookies from the cookie jar.

Who took the cookies from the cookie jar?

Mary took the cookies from the cookie jar.

Mary took the cookies from the cookie jar?

Who, me? (Mary)

Yes, you. (all children)

Couldn't be. (Mary)

Then who? (all children)

———— *took the cookies from the cookie jar.* (Mary names another child.)

Use each child's name.

16. Hide and Seek Tonal Matching

Sit the children in a circle formation. Ask one child to hide in the room while the other children cover their eyes. The children in the circle sing, "Where is ———— hiding?" The child who is hiding responds by singing back, "Here I am." With their eyes remaining closed, the children point in the direction of the hiding child. All open eyes and the child emerges from his hiding place.

17. Listening and Naming

This game is most successful with a small group of children. The children should take turns shutting their eyes and identifying sounds as you tap with a wooden dowel on an object such as glass, triangle, drum, wooden block, cardboard box, rubber ball, etc.

18. Funny Shapes

Ask each child to choose a partner. One partner must make a large shape with his body. The other partner must follow the directions of movement. Roles reverse for the second set of directions. Provide directions such as:

1. Make a big shape.

go **over**
go **under**
go **through**
go **around**

2. Make a small shape.

go **over**
go **under**
go **through**
go **around**

19. Drop the Handkerchief

Direct the children to stand in a circle formation. Ask one child to run around the outside of the circle, dropping a handkerchief behind another child. The child who has the handkerchief dropped behind him must pick it up and chase the child who dropped it. The first child tries to return to the vacated space by running before he is tagged.

20. "If You Please"

This game is a simple variation of "Simon Says." Ask the children to form a circle around a leader who gives directions, some of which are prefaced with "if you please." The children are to follow only the "if you please" directions, ignoring any that do not begin with "if you please." Directions to be used may include walking forward, hopping on one foot, bending forward, standing tall, etc. This game can be varied by having the children follow the directions when the leader says, "do this," and not when he says, "do that." Play only one version of this game on a single day. Too much variety will confuse the children.

21. Duck Duck Goose

Ask the children to squat in a circle formation. Then ask one child to walk around the outside of circle, lightly touching each child's head and saying "Duck, Duck." When he touches another child and says "Goose," that child chases him around the circle. If the child who was "it" returns to the "goose's" place without being tagged, he remains. When this happens, the tapped child is "it." This game is appropriate for older four-, five-, six-, and seven-year-old children.

22. Fruit Basket Upset

Ask the children to sit in a circle formation on chairs or on carpet squares. Then ask one child to sit in the middle of the circle as the chef. Hand pictures of various fruits to the rest of the children. Then to continue the game, ask the chef to call out the name of a fruit. The children holding that particular fruit exchange places. If the chef calls out, "fruit basket upset," all of the children must exchange places, including the chef. The child who doesn't find a place is the new chef. A variation of this game would be bread basket upset. For this game use pictures of breads, rolls, bagels, muffins, breadsticks, etc. This game is appropriate for older children.

23. Bear Hunt

This is a rhythmic chant which may easily be varied. Start by chanting each line, encouraging the children to repeat the line.

Teacher: *Let's go on a bear hunt.*

Children: *(Repeat. Imitate walk by slapping knees alternately.)*

Teacher:
I see a wheat field.
Can't go over it;
Can't go under it.
Let's go through it.
(arms straight ahead like you're parting wheat)

I see a bridge.
Can't go over it;
Can't go under it.
Let's swim.
(arms in swimming motion)

I see a tree.
Can't go over it;
Can't go under it.
Let's go up it.
(climb and look)

I see a swamp.
Can't go over it;
Can't go under it.
Let's go through it.
(pull hands up and down slowly)

I see a cave.
Can't go over it;
Can't go under it.
Let's go in.
(walking motion)

I see two eyes. I see two ears.
I see a nose. I see a mouth.
It's a BEAR!!!
(Do all in reverse very fast)

24. "Guess Who?"

Individually tape the children's voices. Play the tape during group time, and let the children identify their classmates' voices.

25. Shadow Fun

Hang a bed sheet up in the classroom for use as a projection screen. Then place a light source such as a slide, filmstrip, or overhead projector a few feet behind the screen. Ask two of the children to stand behind the sheet. Then encourage one of the two children to walk in front of the projector light. When this happens, the children are to give the name of the person who is moving.

26. If This Is Red— Nod Your Head

Point to an object in the room and say, "If this is green, shake your hand. If this is yellow, touch your nose." If the object is not the color stated, children should not imitate the requested action.

27. Freeze

Encourage the children to imitate activities such as washing dishes, cleaning house, dancing, etc. Approximately every 10 to 20 seconds, call out "Freeze!" When this occurs, the children are to stop whatever they are doing and remain frozen until you say, "Thaw" or "Move." A variation of this activity would be to use music. When the music stops, the children freeze their movements.

28. Spy the Object

Designate a large area on the floor as home base. Then select an object and show it to the children. Ask the children to cover their eyes while you place the object in an observable place in the room. Then encourage the children to open their eyes and search for the object. As each child spies the object he quietly returns to the home base area without telling. The other children continue searching until all have found the object. After all the children are seated, they may share where the object is placed.

29. Who Is Gone?

This game is played in a circle format. Begin by asking a child to close his eyes. Then point to a child to leave the circle and go to a spot where he can't be seen. The child with his eyes closed opens them at your word, then looks around the circle and identifies the friend who is missing.

30. It's Me

Seat the children in a circle formation, and place a chair in the center. Choose one child to sit on a chair in the circle, closing his eyes. After this, ask another child to walk up softly behind the chair and tap the child on the shoulder. The seated child asks, "Who is tapping?" The other child replies, "It's me." By listening to the response, the seated child identifies the other child.

31. Feeling and Naming

Ask a child to stand with his back to you, placing his hands behind him. Then place an object in the child's hands for identification by feeling it. Nature materials can be used such as leaves, shells, fruit, etc. A ball, doll, block, Lego piece, puzzle piece, crayon, etc., may also be used.

32. Doggy, Doggy, Where's Your Bone?

Sit the children in a circle formation. Then place a chair in the center of the circle. Place a block under the chair. Select one child, the dog, to sit on the chair and close his eyes. Then point to another child. This child must try to get the dog's bone from under the chair without making a noise. After the child returns to his place in the circle, all the children place their hands behind them. Then in unison the children say, "Doggy, Doggy, where's your bone?" During the game, each dog has three guesses as to who has the bone.